Knowledge and Practice in English Medicine, 1550–1680

This is a major synthesis of the knowledge and practice of early modern English medicine in their social and cultural contexts. The book maps out vividly some central areas: remedies (and how they were made credible), notions of disease, advice on preventive medicine and on healthy living, how surgeons worked upon the body and their understanding of what they were doing, and the prevention and treatment of plague.

The structures of practice and knowledge examined in the first part of the book came to be challenged in the later seventeenth century, when the 'new science' began to overturn the foundation of established knowledge. However, as the second part of the book shows, traditional medical practice was so well entrenched in English culture that much of it continued into the eighteenth century. Various changes which set the agenda for later medical treatment did, however, occur, and these are discussed in the final chapter.

ANDREW WEAR is Senior Lecturer in the History of Medicine, University College London and the Wellcome Institute for the History of Medicine. He was editor of *Medicine in Society: Historical Essays* (1992) and joint author of *The Western Medical Tradition* (1995), and a volume of his collected essays has been published under the title *Health and Healing in Early Modern England* (1998).

Knowledge and Practice in English Medicine, 1550–1680

ANDREW WEAR

CAMBRIDGE
UNIVERSITY PRESS

PUBLISHED BY THE PRESS SYNDICATE OF THE UNIVERSITY OF CAMBRIDGE
The Pitt Building, Trumpington Street, Cambridge, United Kingdom

CAMBRIDGE UNIVERSITY PRESS
The Edinburgh Building, Cambridge CB2 2RU, UK   http://www.cup.cam.ac.uk
40 West 20th Street, New York, NY 10011–4211, USA   http://www.cup.org
10 Stamford Road, Oakleigh, Melbourne 3166, Australia
Ruiz de Alarcón 13, 28014 Madrid, Spain

First published 2000

Printed in the United Kingdom at the University Press, Cambridge

Typeset in Baskerville 11/12.5pt   System 3b2   [CE]

A catalogue record for this book is available from the British Library

ISBN 0 521 55226 5 hardback
ISBN 0 521 55827 1 paperback

In memory of my grandfather
Spiridon A. Malaspina
1890–1983

Contents

Acknowledgements

Many people and institutions helped me to write this book, and it is a pleasure to be able to thank them. The Wellcome Trust awarded me a research leave fellowship to carry out the research for the book, and the President and fellows of Wolfson College, Cambridge, by making me one of their visiting scholars, provided a congenial and happy environment to work in. I would like to thank David Allen, Janet Browne, Susan Ferry, David Harley, Natsu Hattori, Peter Jones, Fiona Macdonald, Michael McVaugh, Malcolm Nicolson, Vivian Nutton, Richard Palmer, Roy Porter, Nancy Siraisi and Richard Smith for commenting on drafts of the book and giving their valuable time to it. When a reader is faced with a raw first draft, the skill of balancing criticism with encouragement is especially useful, and I was very fortunate in my readers. Caroline Essex provided invaluable assistance in putting the book together as well as staying calm and cheerful through the hectic process of revision. Marilyn Heasman typed the book from its drafts with amazing patience and accuracy, and was always encouraging and positive about the whole project.

I also have some wider debts. At a time when higher education has become a cut-throat business, I feel privileged to have been taught by Rupert and Marie Hall who inculcated into their students a belief in the freedom of expression and a sense of collegiality. Aberdeen University, where I first taught, also shared these values and I was very fortunate to have experienced early on such an environment. I have also been very lucky to have had parents who have shown a real interest in my work and given great encouragement throughout my academic career. My greatest debt is to Maria, my wife, who has put up with ruined weekends and holidays, has encouraged and pushed me to write this book, and whose love has made it possible.

Introduction

Anthropologists used to spend years immersing themselves in the life of small foreign communities in order to bridge the unbridgeable cultural gulf that existed between themselves and the people they studied. What they did with that transfer of cognition lay usually along a spectrum represented at one end by the persona of the naïve observer who tries to retell to the home audience what the alien society is like, and at the other by the theoretician who draws upon the material he or she has collected to reconstruct social structures. Influencing all the points along the spectrum are the present-day concerns and interests of the anthropologist's own society.

Like the 'naïve' observer I have tried to recreate the knowledge and practice of that foreign culture: early modern medicine.[1] The subject has been strangely neglected whilst the new discipline of the social history of medicine has been redrawing and enriching our understanding of early modern medicine. Old Whiggish notions of concentrating solely upon what appears to be 'rational' and progressive in a modern sense have been abandoned, as has the emphasis on elite professional groups. Instead, demographic studies have uncovered the facts of life and death for the population, the experiences of patients, the poor and women have emerged to the foreground, and the wider cultural and political contexts to medicine have been explored.[2] The achievements of this new history of

---

[1] I make no claims to be an anthropologist, let alone one belonging to any particular school. The reference to anthropology is by way of analogy.

[2] On demography see, for instance: E. A. Wrigley and R. S. Schofield, *The Population History of England 1541–1871* (Cambridge University Press, Cambridge, 1989); M. W. Flinn, *The European Demographic System, 1500–1820* (Harvester Press, Brighton, 1981). On the relationship between geography and demography: Mary Dobson, *Contours of Death and Disease in Early Modern England* (Cambridge University Press, Cambridge, 1997). On patients and medicine: Roy Porter (ed.), *Patients and Practitioners* (Cambridge University Press, Cambridge, 1985); Roy Porter and Dorothy Porter, *In Sickness and in Health: the British Experience 1650–1850* (Fourth Estate, London, 1988), and *Patient's Progress: Sickness, Health and Medical Care in*

medicine have been immense. But it has not perhaps been able to capture so well the central aspects of medical knowledge and practice. In the very process of expanding and reshaping the boundaries of early modern medicine it has neglected what was for many people in the sixteenth and seventeenth centuries central to their experience of medicine: the treatments, explanations and advice that they were given. This is understandable as present-day interests such as the rights of patients or the growth in feminism have shaped the agendas of historians together with a general critical concern about the role of medicine in our societies. Such 'presentist' input has always acted to make historical writing relevant to its age; it has also had the potential to distort the past, as with the Whig history of the nineteenth century which reflected the driving ideologies of newly industrialised nations. Moreover, the social history of medicine has also tried to get closer to general history, partly because of the need within the field for recognition from the wider

England, 1650–1850 (Polity Press, London, 1989); see also Michael MacDonald, *Mystical Bedlam, Madness, Anxiety and Healing in Seventeenth Century England* (Cambridge University Press, Cambridge, 1981); Lucinda McCray Beier, *Sufferers and Healers: The Experience of Illness in Seventeenth Century England* (Routledge, London, 1987); Doreen G. Nagy, *Popular Medicine in Seventeenth Century England* (Bowling Green State University Popular Press, Bowling Green, Ohio, 1988); Matthew Ramsey, *Professional and Popular Medicine in France, 1770–1830: the Social World of Medical Practice* (Cambridge University Press, Cambridge, 1988); Mary Fissell, *Patients, Power and the Poor in Eighteenth Century Bristol* (Cambridge University Press, Cambridge, 1991); for a more anthropological view see François Loux, *Pierre-Martin de la Martiniere, un Médecin au XVIIe Siècle* (Imago, Paris, 1988), and for a later period: (with Phillipe Richard) *Sagesses du Corps* (Maisonneuve et Larose, Paris, 1978), and *Le Jeune Enfant et son Corps dans le Médecine Traditionelle* (Flammarion, Paris, 1978). On the poor see Margaret Pelling, *The Common Lot. Sickness, Medical Occupations and the Urban Poor in Early Modern England* (Longman, London, 1998). On women see: Barbara Duden, *Disembodying Women. Perspectives on Pregnancy and the Unborn*, trans. Lee Hoinacki (Harvard University Press, Cambridge, Mass., 1993), and *The Woman Beneath the Skin: a Doctor's Patients in Eighteenth-Century Germany*, trans. Thomas Dunlop (Harvard University Press, Cambridge, Mass., 1981); Antonia Fraser, *The Weaker Vessel: Woman's Lot in Seventeenth Century England* (Mandarin, London, 1993); I. Maclean, *The Renaissance Notion of Women* (Cambridge University Press, Cambridge, 1980); S. H. Mendelson, *The Mental World of Stuart Women* (Harvester Press, Brighton, 1987); Linda A. Pollock, *With Faith and Physic. The Life of a Tudor Gentlewoman Lady Grace Mildmay 1552–1620* (Collins & Brown, London, 1993); M. E. Wiesner, *Women and Gender in Early Modern Europe* (Cambridge University Press, Cambridge, 1993). More general books influenced by the new social history of medicine include: L. Conrad, M. Neve, V. Nutton, R. Porter and A. Wear, *The Western Medical Tradition 800 BC to AD 1800* (Cambridge University Press, Cambridge, 1995); David Cressy, *Birth, Marriage, and Death. Ritual, Religion, and the Life-Cycle in Tudor and Stuart England* (Oxford University Press, Oxford, 1997); Laurence Brockliss and Colin Jones, *The Medical World of Early Modern France* (Clarendon Press, Oxford, 1997); Gianna Pomata, *Contracting a Cure. Patients, Healers, and the Law in Early Modern Bologna* (Johns Hopkins University Press, Baltimore, 1998); Mary Lindemann, *Health and Healing in Eighteenth-Century Germany* (Johns Hopkins University Press, Baltimore, 1996).

community of historians and partly from the desire to broaden the subject. The enterprise of aligning the social history of medicine with the themes of the 'grand narrative' of history has meant that some significant areas of medicine have been ignored, because the historian's spotlight becomes highly selective in choice of material and interpretation.[3] I believe that there were considerable expanses of medical culture that were largely unaffected by major historical changes. For instance, the political and social transformations associated with the Restoration of Charles II have been used to explain late seventeenth-century medicine,[4] but the continuities within medical practice have often been overlooked. Similarly, histories of controversy have tended to ignore the large areas of agreement that existed between warring groups; in the first half of this book controversies appear but not to the exclusion of all else. Certainly, the findings of the new social history of medicine influence this book. But in writing it I have tried not to follow the by now standard approaches and interpretative tracks of early modern historians of medicine; to have done so would inevitably have resulted in a shift in focus away from the content and meaning of medical knowledge and practice. Instead, I have tried to get as close as possible to the medical mind-sets of early modern medicine as represented in vernacular medical books.

In some ways this book is a mapping of medical beliefs and culture written as post-social history. It is not concerned with the origin of beliefs as in some traditional history. Much of early modern medical knowledge could be found in the Middle Ages and in Greek and Roman times, but this does not lessen its reality for people living in the sixteenth and seventeenth centuries. Just like other aspects of pre-modern material and cognitive culture, the culture of medicine had long roots in time and changed slowly, but for individuals it was part of the lived present, the world of events. Such a view, which

---

[3] For a critique of grand narrative in the history of science see Andrew Pickering, *The Mangle of Practice: Time, Agency and Science* (University of Chicago Press, Chicago, 1995), esp. pp. 179–242; see also Jean-François Lyotard's comment cited at p. 213: 'The grand narrative has lost its credibility' (from *The Postmodern Condition: A Report on Knowledge* (University of Minnesota Press, Minneapolis, 1984), p. 37). Also Pickering, 'Cyborg History and the World War II Regime', *Perspectives on Science*, 3, 1995, 1–48, especially pp. 1–4 for some incisive comments on the master narratives of 'Nature, Reason and Society'. David Harley has informed me that *Social History of Medicine* will be publishing a paper in which he describes what has fallen out of sight in the social history of medicine.

[4] For instance, in the admirable and nuanced study by Harold J. Cook, *The Decline of the Old Medical Regime in Stuart London* (Cornell University Press, Ithaca, 1986).

comes from the French *Annales* school of history, helps to justify my approach in most of the first part of the book, where I look for continuities and find little significant change in medical knowledge and practice from the mid-sixteenth to the mid-seventeenth century. Such an emphasis on continuity allows the focus to remain on how, for instance, diseases or advice on healthy living were envisaged, rather than on searching for the reasons for change, when there was little or no change.

I have decided, as a 'naïve' observer, to ignore the now perhaps faltering interpretative orthodoxy of the history of medicine and science, that of the social constructivists.[5] Social constructivism is not much in evidence in historical writing on the early modern period, but the title of my book might be interpreted as belonging to this school. Such a way of writing history would detract from the work of uncovering how illness was explained and treated, and also, in my view, it is an approach that works well only for particular contexts such as colonial medicine, where power and knowledge are closely intertwined. In relation to this book, a reader can easily work out how some knowledge, for instance, relating to plague – the belief in contagion, the building up of hope for cure – fitted the interests of governments concerned with preserving social order. But much of the medical knowledge of this time was socially constructed only in the weak sense of being produced by human beings, or at most of being a convenient way for a group of practitioners to claim an expertise and hence a monopoly of practice. One also has to ask whether any work on the social construction of medicine has influenced general historians. The answer is likely to be 'no'. This is not surprising since, in a post-modern age, where to interpret is to deconstruct, no system of explanation has explanatory priority over any other. The claims, therefore, of the social sciences to provide normative explanations of knowledge that would replace those of the philosophers are caught within the paradox of post-modernism: infused with the social sciences and yet undermining of their claims and those of all others, including philosophy and history.

The book covers the period between *c.*1550 and *c.*1680. By 1550 the attempt of learned, that is university-educated, physicians to reform English medicine was well under way, as was the printing of vernacular medical books which sought to spread medical knowledge

---

[5] See, for instance, the work of Steven Shapin, Simon Schaffer and Roger Cooter.

widely amongst lay people and practitioners. Although there were ripples of change coming from Paracelsian medicine from the later sixteenth century, it was not until the Helmontian attempt to revolutionise medical knowledge and especially therapeutics that there was a real challenge to orthodox Galenic medicine and its various popularised versions. The book ends in the 1680s, because by then the future shape of eighteenth-century medicine had begun to emerge from a maelstrom of change that involved Helmontians, empirics, the critiques and innovations of Thomas Sydenham, the modernisation of learned medicine by Thomas Willis and others, and institutional and educational transformations. The new medicine was also shaped by the long-term continuities charted in earlier chapters.

The book begins with an overview of the context of early modern medicine for those not familiar with it. Chapters 2 and 3 focus on remedies and diseases, in my view the most important parts of early modern medicine, reflecting the central concerns of patients and practitioners. To help redress the strange neglect of remedies by modern medical historians, I have placed them before diseases. The two chapters also indicate what underpinned medical practice: giving remedies and 'discoursing' with the patient about disease. Chapter 4, on preventive medicine, examines the advice given on diet, lifestyle and what constituted a healthy environment; this catered for the widespread interest in healthy living among the literate classes, and was usually provided by the learned physicians. Chapter 5, on surgery, discusses the third branch of medicine after pharmacy and diet: it attempts to recreate something of surgical theory and practice. It shows that, in contrast to the physicians, the surgeons acted far more extensively upon the patient's body. A major point of continuity shared with medical views of disease is the surgical concern with putrefaction as one of the causes of disease and death. I have been concerned to show how putrefaction and corruption are pivotal to early modern medicine. The two chapters on plague also illustrate this point, as well as showing how medicine, regimen and surgery were all brought into play to counter the disease.

Change, Anglo-American historians will be glad to know, does come into this history. If there are any heroes of this story, they are the Helmontians, who around the 1660s tried but failed to overthrow the therapeutics of the learned physicians derived from Greek

Galenic medicine. The insights of the Helmontians into the nature of learned medicine were sharp and critical. But, as they themselves admitted, the Galenic physicians had been successful in getting a wide spectrum of society to accept their theories and practices (which sixteenth-century Galenists saw as part of their push to reform medicine). Consequently, Helmontians faced opposition from the public to their new type of medicine. The nature of this medicine and the opposition to it from patients are charted in chapters 8 and 9. Finally, the new developments that shaped medicine as it entered the eighteenth century are set out. They ranged from the eclecticism of the empirics and the innovation of Sydenham to the modernising of learned medicine. It is in these last three chapters, which make up the second part of the book, that I switch historiographical gear, bringing the book closer to the history of controversies and grand narrative. But even in the midst of change continuities remained, whether in the picturing of disease in the body, in the need to evacuate putrefaction and disease, or in the relationship of health to diet, lifestyle and the environment. The earlier chapters, which try to capture the more 'placid' and long-lasting aspects of medical knowledge and practice, provide an important background for understanding and assessing continuity and change in later seventeenth-century medicine. Such continuities have too often been missed. Two large topics, midwifery and madness, have not been discussed except in passing, since there is excellent work on them elsewhere.[6] More generally, magic and witchcraft have not been included as they are not central to the literate vernacular medical tradition.

The sources for this history are largely vernacular texts on remedies, diseases, regimen, etc. that range from those designed to be read by lay people to those mainly for practitioners. However, despite such distinctions, literate medicine represents a unified medical culture largely shaped by elite learned medicine from the Middle Ages and especially from the sixteenth century. The texts include many translations of continental European works. Their popularity indicates that

---

[6] See especially Adrian Wilson, *The Making of Man-Midwifery: Childbirth in England, 1660–1770* (Harvard University Press, Cambridge, Mass., 1995) and the forthcoming book on midwifery by Doreen Evenden. On madness see especially MacDonald, *Mystical Bedlam*; R. Porter, *Mind Forg'd Manacles: Madness and Psychiatry in England from Restoration to Regency* (Athlone Press, London, 1987; Penguin, Harmondsworth, 1990); Jonathan Andrews et al., *The History of Bethlem* (Routledge, London, 1997).

much of medical knowledge was crosscultural. The vernacular texts are discussed at greater length in chapter 1. What I have done is to read them and try to capture and interpret the medical culture they transmitted to early modern England.

PART I

CHAPTER I

Setting the scene

INTRODUCTION

This chapter gives the background and context to the rest of the book.[1] It sets out some of the basic findings of historical demographers on mortality and morbidity in early modern England (*c*.1550–*c*.1700). It then sketches in the wide range of medical provision patients could use as described by recent work in the social history of medicine, and discusses how medicine co-existed with the other healing main resource, religion. Finally, the texts that communicated medical knowledge and practice are considered. Most were written in English and this helped to create a literate medical culture that both recognised popular–elite distinctions and accepted that educated lay people and practitioners could share in a common medical culture.

LIFE AND DEATH

Our Clocks of Health seldome go true: those of Death more certaine than beleeved.[2]

Medical writers and practitioners in the early modern period lived in a world where disease and death were ever present, or so it seemed. Death was highlighted in the Christian teaching that emphasised the need to be constantly prepared for death. Illness was 'the messenger of death', and the devout declared that 'every day shall be as my dying day'.[3] However, not all age groups were equally at risk of dying.

---

[1] And it should help those readers not already well acquainted with the recent social history of medicine in early modern England.

[2] Stephen Bradwell, *Helps for Suddain Accidents* (London, 1633), sig. A3^{r}.

[3] Robert Yarrow, *Soveraigne Comforts for a Troubled Conscience* (London, 1634), p. 406; Robert Horne, *Life and Death, Foure Sermons* (London, 1613), cited in A. Wear, 'Puritan Perceptions of Illness in Seventeenth Century England' in R. Porter (ed.), *Patients and Practitioners: Lay*

Death especially dogged the footsteps of the young. Early modern England had higher infant mortality rates than many Third World countries today, although those in continental Europe and Scotland were worse. Of a thousand babies born alive, around a hundred and sixty would be dead by the end of their first year. Life expectancy at birth in the period 1600–49 was 36.4 years; however, if childhood was safely navigated, then a long life was on the cards. Expectation of life for both men and women at age thirty was about another thirty years.[4]

Geography and social status helped determine an individual's chances of life. Towns and cities generally had higher mortality rates than the countryside. For instance, the parish of Hartland in Devon enjoyed the lowest mortality rates so far discovered in early modern England. Its infant mortality was below 100 and life expectancy at birth was more than 55 years; such figures were, as E. A. Wrigley points out, 'attained nationally only about 1920'. Hartland was relatively isolated, bounded on two sides by the sea, and far from major roads, its 1,000–1,500 inhabitants living in widely spaced houses and farms.[5] Cities and towns, on the other hand, had high density populations and housing, and were usually centres for trade and communication routes that also brought in diseases. In urban areas the lack of effective sewage disposal led to more illness than was the case in the less crowded countryside, and clean water supplies were less available in the towns. Morbidity and mortality flourished in such conditions. Small towns suffered worse death rates than their surrounding countryside. The populations of cities such as York, Bristol, Norwich, Newcastle and, most famously, London, were not self-sustaining and only the constant inflow of people from the countryside allowed them to grow.[6] However, some parts of the

---

Perceptions of Medicine in Pre-Industrial Society (Cambridge University Press, Cambridge, 1985), p. 64, and see pp. 61–70 generally.

[4] R. A. Houston, *The Population History of Britain and Ireland 1500–1750* (Macmillan, London, 1992), pp. 50–1; E. A. Wrigley and R. S. Schofield, *The Population History of England 1541–1871* (Edward Arnold, London, 1981), pp. 250–3; Michael Flinn (ed.), *Scottish Population History from the Seventeenth Century to the 1930s* (Cambridge University Press, Cambridge, 1977).

[5] E. A. Wrigley, 'No Death Without Birth: the Implications of English Mortality in the Early Modern Period' in R. Porter and A. Wear (eds.), *Problems and Methods in the History of Medicine* (Croom Helm, London, 1987), pp. 137–8.

[6] Wrigley, 'No Death Without Birth', pp. 136–7; R. A. Finlay, *Population and Metropolis: the Demography of London, 1580–1650* (Cambridge University Press, Cambridge, 1981), pp. 51–69.

countryside were unhealthy, especially the marshy and estuarine areas of the south-east of England where 'agues' or malaria and water-borne diseases flourished and infant mortality was as high as 250–300 per 1,000.[7]

Social differences showed themselves in the mortality statistics. The poor, who almost by definition lived in the unhealthiest parts of towns, fared worse than the rich. In the well-to-do central London parishes life expectancy was 35 years at birth, whilst in the poor densely populated suburban parishes it was almost a third lower and infant mortality was also higher.[8] Of a thousand live births in the period 1580–1650, 631 children survived to the age of fifteen in the wealthy parish of St Peter Cornhill, but only 508 in deprived Allhallows between 1570 and 1636.[9]

Expectation of life was almost identical for both sexes,[10] although women certainly faced the additional dangers of childbirth. If they experienced six or seven full-term pregnancies they ran a 6 or 7 per cent risk of death in childbirth. Maternal mortality caused up to 20 per cent of all female deaths between the ages of 25 and 34, and 11–14 per cent for women aged between 20 and 24 and 35 and 44, but these were the age groups when women's overall mortality, like men's, was relatively low.[11]

DISEASES

Given four hundred years' difference in the diagnosis and classification of disease, the diseases of early modern England are less easily identified and quantified in modern terms. Although the use of modern disease labels often hinders an understanding of how

---

[7] Mary Dobson, 'Mortality Gradients and Disease Exchanges: Comparisons from Old England and Colonial America', *Social History of Medicine*, 2, 1989, 265, and *Contours of Death and Disease in Early Modern Europe* (Cambridge University Press, Cambridge, 1997), pp. 176–7, and pp. 81–220 for mortality in general in south-east England.

[8] Houston, *Population History*, p. 50; Finlay, *Population and Metropolis*, pp. 107–8.

[9] Finlay, *Population and Metropolis*, pp. 171, 168, 107.

[10] Houston, *Population History*, pp. 52–3. There has been, in Houston's view, an inconclusive debate as to whether the female infants born to a family that already had a number of children were neglected and suffered a higher mortality than male.

[11] Houston, ibid., p. 56, points out that a village of 1,000–1,500 population, of which a quarter were women aged 15–49, 'would experience only one maternal death on average every third year', and that higher female mortality should be balanced by higher male mortality in the same years due to occupational risks such as coal-mining in north-east England, etc.; also Adrian Wilson, *The Making of Man-Midwifery: Childbirth in England, 1660–1770* (Harvard University Press, Cambridge, Mass., 1995), pp. 18–19.

diseases were perceived in the past (see chapter 3), they have been frequently employed to draw the demographic map of disease and death in early modern England, an enterprise that is self-consciously based on modern methods and categories. Acute infections undoubtedly accounted for many deaths. Gastro-enteric infections such as dysentery, typhoid, salmonella and 'fluxes' or undifferentiated diarrhoeas were prevalent, as were the respiratory infections of whooping-cough, diphtheria, scarlet fever, influenza, smallpox and typhus. Many of the very young were culled by these diseases, while smallpox was more deadly to children over two.

In addition, periods of very high mortality, or short-term mortality crises (defined as an average yearly mortality at least 10 per cent above the expected trend, or at least a 25 per cent rise in the monthly total above the trend, where often it rose above 100 per cent), produced enormous social, economic, cultural and psychological devastation. Between 1550 and 1750 England suffered thirty-seven periods of crisis mortality.[12] Plague, one of God's three arrows along with war and famine, was a major cause. After the initial pandemic of 1347–1351, when a third of Europe's population died, it continued to visit different areas in a series of epidemics. Death rates in the subsequent epidemics were lower but still high. In sixteenth- and seventeenth-century England at least 10 per cent of an affected population would die in a year in a plague outbreak; around a fifth of London's population died in the plagues of 1563, 1603, 1625 and 1665 (mortality was less in 1578, 1593 and 1638), whilst a third of the population of Norwich died in 1579 and even more in Newcastle in 1636 and in Colchester in 1666.[13] However, given that England was still a rural country and that plague was largely an urban disease, the overall national figures were lower.[14]

Another of God's arrows, famine, was less prevalent than in continental Europe where famine years were frequent up to the mid-eighteenth century. In England, crises of subsistence affected parts of the north and isolated areas of the south in 1596–8 and 1623–4, but after the mid-seventeenth century famine had largely left England. Agricultural innovations, for instance, no longer relying on one grain crop, the spring sowing of oats and barley to supplement

[12] Wrigley and Schofield, *Population History*, p. 333.
[13] Paul Slack, *The Impact of Plague in Tudor and Stuart England* (Routledge & Kegan Paul, London, 1985), pp. 14–16, 145–51; Finlay, *Population and Metropolis*, pp. 17, 112.
[14] Slack, *Impact*, p. 16; Houston, *Population History*, p. 55.

winter sowing, and the establishment of a unitary market for grain, helped eradicate large-scale starvation.[15] However, regular as opposed to extraordinary levels of starvation continued to be suffered by small numbers of the poor even in times of plenty.[16] Nevertheless, the poor suffered disproportionately from infectious diseases. Plague came to be associated with the poor and their living conditions (see chapters 6 and 7).[17] Typhus, which entered Europe at the end of the fifteenth century, was a disease of prisons ('gaol fever'), hospitals and armies, and also spread through the crowded slums of the poor. However, except for the impressions of contemporary observers, there is no precise data differentiating levels of morbidity between the rich and poor.

Apart from plague, it was the 'pox', which probably included modern syphilis, that had the greatest cultural and psychological impact, although its impact on mortality levels was small. Plague had been the great 'new' disease of the Middle Ages; in the Renaissance it was the pox (how it was understood and treated is discussed in chapter 5). Other novel diseases such as the 'English sweat,' which appeared in 1485, left after 1551, and may have been influenza, and a variety of strange fevers added to the uncertainty of a world already overfilled with familiar diseases.[18]

It was only in the period 1850–1950, when England and then the rest of Western Europe went through 'the demographic transition' from high to low infant and childhood mortality, that the major

---

[15] J. Walter, 'The Social Economy Dearth in Early Modern England' in J. Walter and R. Schofield (eds.), *Famine, Disease and the Social Order in Early Modern Society* (Cambridge University Press, Cambridge, 1989), pp. 75–128; Massimo Livi-Bacci, *Population and Nutrition* (Cambridge University Press, Cambridge, 1991), pp. 50–62.

[16] John Graunt, *Natural and Political Observations . . . Upon the Bills of Mortality*, 5th edn (London, 1676), p. 25: 'starved' was one of Graunt's 'accidents of life'; from the bills of mortality, which were compiled from the weekly returns by London's parish clerks of numbers of deaths and their causes, Graunt calculated that in fourteen years 51 people had been certified as dead in London due to starvation.

[17] Slack, *Impact*, p. 153, notes that by the seventeenth century the topography of plague was clearly biased towards the poor areas of London.

[18] Lloyd G. Stevenson, '"New Diseases" in the Seventeenth Century', *Bulletin of the History of Medicine* 39, 1965, 1–21; cf. also Henry Whitmore, *Febris Anomala Or, The New Disease that Now Rageth Throughout England* (London, 1659). There has been a recent debate on what the English sweat really was: A. Dyer, 'The English Sweating Sickness of 1551: an Epidemic Anatomised', *Medical History*, 41, 1997, 362–84; M. Taviner, G. Thwaites and V. Gant, 'The English Sweating Sickness, 1485–1551: a Viral Pulmonary Disease?', *Medical History*, 42, 1998, 96–8. J. R. Carlson and P. W. Hammond, 'The English Sweating Sickness (1485–c.1551): a New Perspective on Disease Aetiology', *Journal of the History of Medicine and Allied Sciences*, 54, January 1999, 23–54.

causes of death shifted from acute infectious diseases to the chronic degenerative diseases of middle and old age, and the expectation grew that only the elderly faced a real threat of death. However, in early modern England chronic illness was also present, though unquantifiable. Cancers, heart disease, arthritis, gout and paralysis could slowly and painfully handicap life, as could psychological conditions such as melancholy, and even conditions such as thrush, which today seem minor, could cause constant trouble for years.[19]

A question that springs to mind from the perspective of the twenty-first century is whether early modern 'medicine' addressed itself to the three great health problems that are apparent from the findings of historical demography: high infant and child mortality, the allied threat of infectious diseases and the higher mortality of the poor.[20] With the exception of plague, and to a lesser extent the pox, English governments did not initiate any action against diseases.

[19] See, for instance, Samuel Jeake of Rye who complained of oral thrush that lasted for many years: 'About this time I began to be troubled with a white pertinacious Thrush in the upper Jaw within side in the Mouth, which gradually slowly encreased, & all means I used proved ineffectuall. I could never be cured of it; but it was without pain, & not very much till 4 or 5 years after': Michael Hunter and Annabel Gregory (eds.), *An Astrological Diary of the Seventeenth Century: Samuel Jeake of Rye 1652–1699* (Clarendon Press, Oxford, 1988), p. 194. On madness see: Michael MacDonald, *Mystical Bedlam, Madness, Anxiety and Healing in Seventeenth Century England* (Cambridge University Press, Cambridge, 1981); R. Porter, *Mind Forg'd Manacles: Madness and Psychiatry in England from Restoration to Regency* (Athlone, London, 1987; Penguin, Harmondsworth, 1990).

[20] To argue that 'medicine' should have addressed itself to the demographic facts of death is also to misunderstand how those facts were changed. The demographic transition phase was largely due to a combination of public health measures rather than better medical treatments: better sanitation, clean water supplies, improved diet and working conditions. It was pushed through by political rather than medical action, though doctors were involved and there were some medical developments such as vaccination and the later discovery of sulpha drugs and antibiotics that were important for reducing smallpox deaths and maternal mortality. Moreover, it was not until the twentieth century that British governments envisaged the provision of universal health care through insurance schemes or from general taxation, which meant that for the first time the health of the different parts of the population came under government scrutiny. I. Loudon, 'On Maternal and Infant Mortality, 1900–1960', *Social History of Medicine*, 4, 1991, 29–73; Loudon, 'Deaths in Childbed from the Eighteenth Century to 1935', *Medical History*, 30, 1986, 1–41; Loudon, 'The Transformation of Maternal Mortality', *British Medical Journal*, 305, 1992, 1557–60; Loudon, *Death in Childbirth: an International Study of Maternal Care and Maternal Mortality, 1800–1950* (Clarendon Press, Oxford, 1992); A. Hardy, *The Epidemic Streets: Infectious Disease and the Rise of Preventive Medicine, 1856–1900* (Clarendon Press, Oxford, 1993); A. Hardy, 'Smallpox in London: Factors in the Decline of the Disease in the Nineteenth Century', *Medical History*, 27, 1983, 111–38; S. R. S. Szreter, 'The Importance of Social Intervention in Britain's Mortality Decline *c.*1850–1914: a Re-interpretation of the Role of Public Health', *Social History of Medicine*, 1, 1988, 1–37 and 'Mortality in England in the Eighteenth and Nineteenth Centuries: a Reply to Sumit Guha', *Social History of Medicine*, 7, 1994, 269–82.

Further, they seem to have been blind to the young as a high-risk group, which is understandable as quantified mortality statistics did not exist, and in any case England appeared healthier than neighbouring France.[21] They could have made existing medical expertise and treatment more widely available, but only during the English revolution was such action envisaged and even then not at government level. Moreover, what action could they have taken? Pouring funds into medical research on infectious diseases? That would have been difficult in 1550 when, it was claimed, the best medical knowledge was to be found in the works of Greek and Roman medical writers, with 'research' lying either in the retrieval of that knowledge in its purest form or in its refinement. In any case, it was not until the later seventeenth century that the state, especially in France, supported medical research. The role of the state was limited to action against the contagious diseases of the plague and the pox where it initiated isolation and public health measures (plague being seen as both a contagious and an environmental disease). 'Research' by individuals searching for curative remedies did take place. However, there was a widespread realisation that in the absence of medical trials (see chapter 8) it was well nigh impossible to know for sure if a remedy was effective:

It is a great Question what does the cure, the Vulgar [the public] will tell you the last thing they took did the cure, as the last thing they did caused the disease; Some Physicians will ascribe it to the rarity and dearnesse, others to the variety and composition [of the remedies], others to the fitnesse and order [of the treatment] etc. others think it is not Physick or Physicians, but Nature being disburthened returns to her functions by degrees . . . And some adde, that it is not Nature but the God of Nature

---

[21] On attitudes to children see: L. Stone, *The Family, Sex and Marriage in England 1500–1800* (Weidenfeld & Nicolson, London, *c.*1977), especially pp. 64–81 on infant mortality; Linda Pollock, *Forgotten Children: Parent–Child Relations from 1500 to 1900* (Cambridge University Press, Cambridge, 1983); Philippe Ariès, *Centuries of Childhood* (Penguin, Harmondsworth, 1979). Medical treatises on infant health include: James Guillemeau, *Childbirth, or the happie deliverie of women. Wherein is set downe the gouernment of women . . . together with the diseases which happen to women. To which is added, a treatise of the diseases of infants, and young children: with the cure of them. Written in French by Iames Guillemeau* (London, 1612); Robert Pemell, *De morbis puerorum, or, a treatise of the diseases of children; with their causes, signs, prognosticks, and cures. For the benefit of such as do not understand Latine tongue, and very useful for all such as are house-keepers, and have children . . .* (London, 1653); Gualtero Harris, *De morbis acutis infantum* (London, 1689); Walter Harris, *A treatise of the acute diseases of infants. To which are added, medical observations on several grievous diseases [and 'Of the venereal disease']. Written originally in Latin by the late learned Walter Harris . . . Translated into English by John Martyn* (London, 1742).

which heals us, and as the Proverb is, God heals, and the Physician hath the thanks.[22]

The diseases that affected the young and the poor were not the subject of any concerted campaign whether by medical practitioners, the government or the public. Medicine, as we shall see, was largely practised by individuals who were paid by individual patients, and their horizons were necessarily foreshortened. Medical institutions, the usual foci of concerted action, did exist but were few in number and membership. Moreover, though there were specialist practitioners for the pox, cutting for kidney and bladder stones, for eye problems and for setting bones, most practitioners were generalists rather than specialists. This is one reason why the question of medical research on the demographic fault lines of early modern England is misconceived though illuminating.

THE SICK POOR

A distinction has to be made between welfare and medical treatment. As part of the parish welfare support the poor sometimes had their treatment paid for them; and the English governing elite did concern itself with the welfare of vulnerable groups. For the young it set up charitable institutions such as Christ's Hospital in London, encouraged parishes to take care of foundlings through to apprenticeship, and took steps to protect apprentices from abusive masters.[23] The poor, especially, were the focus of attention by the English government and by some medical practitioners and writers. Christianity had originally given the poor a special status as chosen of God, the objects for charitable good works. In the early sixteenth century, they came to be differentiated as either undeserving and dangerous or the deserving, respectable, shame-faced poor: 'A faulte maketh necessitie, in this case of begging, in them, whyche might laboure and serve, and wil not for idlenes: and therfor not to be pitied, but rather to be punished. Necessitie maketh a fault in them,

---

[22] Henry Edmundson, *Comes Facundus in Via, The Fellow Traveller* (London, 1658), pp. 111–12; see A. Wear, 'Interfaces: Perceptions of Health and Illness in Early Modern England' in R. Porter and A. Wear (eds.), *Problems and Methods in the History of Medicine* (Croom Helm, London, 1987), pp. 240–3, 248–52 on uncertainty in medicine and on the early modern awareness of demographic facts.

[23] Carol K. Manzione, *Christ's Hospital of London, 1552–1598: 'A Passing Deed of Pity'* (Associated University Presses, London, 1995).

whiche wold labor and serve, but cannot for age, impotency, or sickenes, and therfore to be pitied and relieved.'[24]

Together with a new less positive view of the poor came new ways of funding poor relief. Across Europe, starting early in the sixteenth century in the Low Countries, towns and cities amalgamated charitable funds into single centralised 'common chests' for the poor. Charity became subject to secular regulation; face-to-face charity between individuals continued, though on a decreasing scale. In England, a series of Poor Laws, culminating in that of 1601, uniquely financed poor relief on a national level through rates collected and distributed locally by the parish. Treatment of the sick poor was sometimes contracted out. In Norwich a variety of men and women practitioners and former lazar house keepers (leprosy having declined) were contracted to cure the poor, the aim being to get them back to work. London parishes often paid the poor to look after the sick poor as well as giving them money to pay for treatment and medicines from practitioners in the commercial medical marketplace.[25] However, only when one was completely penniless was any aid given.[26] Moreover, there had to be a perception that a person could not work, usually because of sickness or the infirmities resulting from old age, for relief to be given. Old age did not by itself make a person eligible for poor relief, though many recipients were old. Men and women were expected to work into very old age if they could. John Ward, the vicar of Stratford-upon-Avon between 1662 and 1681, who practised medicine and took a lively interest in the development of the 'new science' and in medicine generally, noted in

---

[24] John Caius, 'A Boke or Counseill Against the Disease Commonly Called the Sweate or Sweating Sicknesse' (1552) in *The Works of John Caius MD*, ed. John Venn (Cambridge University Press, Cambridge, 1912), p. 28. See Paul Slack, *Poverty and Policy in Tudor and Stuart England* (Longman, London, 1988); Robert Jütte, *Poverty and Deviance in Early Modern Europe* (Cambridge University Press, Cambridge, 1994). For a seminal essay on the topic see Natalie Zemon Davis, 'Poor Relief, Humanism, and Heresy' in Natalie Zemon Davis (ed.), *Society and Culture in Early Modern France* (Stanford University Press, Stanford, California, 1975), pp. 17–64. Barbara Harvey traces a negative attitude to sections of the poor back to the second half of the fourteenth century in her *Living and Dying in England 1100–1540: the Monastic Experience* (Clarendon Press, Oxford, 1993), pp. 30–3. I am grateful to Professor Nancy Siraisi for this reference.

[25] Margaret Pelling, 'Healing the Sick Poor: Social Policy and Disability in Norwich, 1550–1640', *Medical History*, 29, 1985, 115–37; Andrew Wear, 'Caring for the Sick Poor in St Bartholomew Exchange: 1580–1676' in W. F. Bynum and R. Porter (eds.), *Living and Dying in London*, *Medical History*, Supplement 11, 1991, 41–60.

[26] The sick poor often pawned their clothes to pay for treatment, and any money they had could be appropriated towards the cost of treatment before a parish released its money; see Wear, 'Caring for the Sick Poor', pp. 48, 50–51.

his diary: 'George Green, of Woodstock, 90 years of age, that will mowe and doe a good days work still', and 'Cripps, of Woodstock, 90 years of age, that works all the yeer as other men doe, hath as much wages; he is wondrous vivacious, and the last two very hard laborers all their time'.[27]

The poor often had to make do with the minimum of medical care. Thomas Fuller, the antiquarian, observed how in Cheshire, 'if any here be sick "they make him a posset [a hot drink of milk, mixed with beer or wine and sugar and spices] and tye a kerchieff on his head; and if that will not mend him, then God be merciful to him"'. But, he added, 'be this understood of the common people, the Gentry having the help (no doubt) of the learned in that profession [medicine]'. The Kent physician Robert Pemell wrote that the poor had to be their own doctors, and he and other practitioners published remedies that the poor could afford.[28] It was up to the individual practitioner whether to charge the poor less, as did 'Dr. Chamberlayne, the man midwife . . . his fee is five pound, yett I heard, if he come to poor people, hee will take lesse'.[29] However, ethical injunctions stressed the need for practitioners to be charitable: young surgeons were urged 'not [to be] to covetous for money, but a good demander, being good unto the poore, let the rich pay therefore'.[30] Nevertheless, organised charitable medical treatment

---

[27] John Ward, *Diary of the Rev. John Ward, A. M., Vicar of Stratford-Upon-Avon . . . 1648 to 1679*, ed. Charles Severn (London, 1839), p. 136. On Ward see Robert G. Frank, 'The John Ward Diaries: Mirror of Seventeenth Century Science and Medicine', *Journal of the History of Medicine* 29, 1974, 147–79. For a general discussion of old age and work see Margaret Pelling, 'Old Age, Poverty and Disability in Early Modern Norwich: Work, Remarriage and Other Expedients' in her book *The Common Lot. Sickness, Medical Occupations and the Urban Poor in Early Modern England* (Longman, London, 1998); at pp. 140–3, she notes that elderly women when no longer looking after children often went back to work.

[28] Thomas Fuller, *The History of the Worthies of England*, 1st edn 1662, 2 vols, (London, 1811), vol. I,, p. 190, quoting William Smith, *Vale Royal*, p. 16. Robert Pemell, ΠΤΩΧΟΦΑΡΜΑΚΟΝ . . . Or Help for the Poor (London, 1650), sig. A3^v. Richard Hawes, *The Poor-Mans Plaster Box* (London, 1634), p. 10, took the material conditions of the poor into account: 'If the man faln or bruised be so poore that he hath no bed to sweat in, then annoynt him with this following [melted butter, parsley, rue or hearbgrace fried in the butter and strained], and set him for to sweat in horse dung up to the chin, and cover his head with hay. . . but it be neither cleanly, nor chargeable [expensive]'.

[29] Ward, *Diary*, p. 107. Not all practitioners were so charitable. In 1659, for instance, the churchwarden of St Bartholomew's Exchange in London noted that in the case of Widow Hall, one of the pensioners of the parish who needed treatment for a fall, a broken arm and injured head, the overseers of the poor 'were also desired to mediate with Mr. Thicknes in her behalf who required £6 for her cure . . . but he would not abate any thing'; quoted in Wear, 'The Sick Poor', p. 51.

[30] William Clowes, *A Briefe and Necessarie Treatise, Touching the Cure of the Disease Called Morbus Gallicus* (London, 1585), fol. 42^r.

for the sick poor was not provided until the end of the seventeenth century when the London College of Physicians set up a charitable dispensary. Despite the Christian ethic of the charitable care of the sick, the learned or university-educated physicians especially were viewed as expensive and uncharitable. Remedies for the poor were not only composed of cheaper ingredients than those for the rich (see chapter 2), but the poor were excluded from expensive medical expertise, as one puritan minister and physician advised in the time of plague: 'Let the rich seeke for the godly, wise and learned Physician . . . And let the poorer sort with good advise and counsell (if they can have any) use Master Phares medicines in his short but learned Treatise of the Pestilence, which hee wrote of purpose for the benefit and comfort of the Poor'.[31] Because of the ethic of charity the poor were provided with some medical help that they would not otherwise have enjoyed, but on the whole they were not the object of concerted medical attention, with the exception of Paracelsian and Helmontian physicians (on this, see chapters 8 and 9).

MEDICAL PRACTITIONERS

It would be a mistake to think of medical provision only in terms of the commercial medical marketplace and its expensive end at that. Many would have agreed that 'All the Nation are already Physitians, If you ayl any thing, every one you meet, whether man or woman will prescribe a medicine for it.'[32] Social historians of medicine in the past fifteen years have confirmed that medical expertise was widespread across society.[33] Lay medical practice was centred on the family. Patients often treated themselves, and the women members

---

[31] Henry Holland, *An Admonition Concerning the Use of Physick* (London, 1603), p. 53. The charitable care of the sick was taught by Christianity as one of the six (later seven) corporal works of mercy based on Matthew 25.35–6: 'For I was an hungred, and ye gave me meat [food]: I was thirsty, and ye gave me drink: I was a stranger and ye took me in: Naked, and ye clothed me: I was sick and ye visited me: I was in prison, and ye came unto me.'

[32] Nicholas Culpeper, *A Physical Directory Or a Translation of the London Dispensary Made by the College of Physicians* (London, 1649), sig. A2ᵛ.

[33] See, for instance, the essays in Roy Porter (ed.), *Patients and Practitioners* (Cambridge University Press, Cambridge 1985); Roy Porter and Dorothy Porter, *In Sickness and in Health: the British Experience 1650–1850* (Fourth Estate, London 1988), and *Patient's Progress: Sickness, Health and Medical Care in England 1650–1850* (Polity Press, London 1989); Margaret Pelling, *The Common Lot: Sickness, Medical Occupations and the Urban Poor in Early Modern England* (Longman, London, 1998), Mary Fissell, *Patients, Power and the Poor in Eighteenth Century Bristol* (Cambridge University Press, Cambridge, 1991).

of the family especially were the sources of medical knowledge and treatment. Relatives, neighbours and friends also acted as medical advisers. Charitable gentlewomen, clergymen and their wives treated the poor and provided an informal medical service, which some of the learned physicians saw as a threat and which medical reformers in the 1640s took as the prototype for utopian schemes of nation-wide medical provision organised around ministers.[34]

Practitioners who offered cures for money ranged from village wise women or white witches, who were 'in every village, which if they be sought unto, will help almost all infirmities of body and mind', to the expensive physicians at the top end of the medical market.[35] In villages and towns, midwives, usually women who had children and had trained with another midwife, provided medical expertise during births. Only in the last third of the seventeenth century did male midwives or surgeons begin to manage first difficult and then normal deliveries; previously, they had been called in only in desperate situations to extract the dead foetus, though the midwife might do that in any case.[36]

Empirics, mountebanks, herbalists, astrologers and uroscopists offered their services either as itinerants or from fixed locations. They advertised themselves as cheaper than the physicians.[37] In the

[34] Charles Webster, *The Great Instauration: Science, Medicine, and Reform, 1626–1660* (Duckworth, London, 1975), pp. 246–323.

[35] Robert Burton, *The Anatomy of Melancholy*, 1st edn (1621), ed. Floyd Dell and P. Jourdan-Smith (Tudor, New York, 1948), p. 382. Alan Macfarlane, *Witchcraft in Tudor and Stuart England* (Routledge & Kegan Paul, London, 1970), p. 120 confirms Burton, stating that in the county of Essex no village was more than ten miles from the services of a white witch.

[36] Doreen Evenden, 'Seventeenth Century London Midwives: Their Training, Licensing and Social Profile' (Ph.D. thesis, McMaster University, 1991); Hilary Marland (ed.), *The Art of Midwifery: Early Modern Midwives in Europe* (Routledge, London, 1993). For the later seventeenth century see Wilson, *The Making of Man-Midwifery.*

[37] It is difficult to provide an accurate assessment of the fees and costs of medical treatment. A physician's visit to a patient usually cost between ten shillings and a pound. Some physicians made fortunes, others died in penury: Harold J. Cook, *The Decline of the Old Medical Regime in Stuart London* (Cornell University Press, Ithaca, 1986), pp. 58–9. Empirics might charge two shillings for a bottle of medicine, but as unlicensed practitioners they also contracted with patients to cure them. For instance in 1607 Elizabeth Googe complained that 'Moore of Knightsbridge had accepted twenty shillings of her to restore her to health but after forty days of an ordinary diet and frequent purging, she felt no relief'. In the same year 'Doughton, a surgeon, was accused by Mr. Flud, an attorney, because he had made an agreement with him to cure his wife for the sum of twenty pounds . . . but he had done nothing to earn the reward . . . for after a month or two she relapsed into that madness from which she formerly suffered'. In 1640 James Trikley was accused of giving 'Mrs Smith a powder against the stone in the bladder for one whole month . . . he took 15 s[hillings] as a fee and was to receive 3 l [pounds] afterwards'. Clearly, charges for a cure varied enormously; often the money was paid before the cure and on its completion. The method

eyes of the university 'learned' physicians the only other legitimate practitioners apart from themselves were the surgeons and the apothecaries. The physicians viewed them as subordinate and believed that they should be forbidden to practise internal medicine, which the physicians claimed as their own. In reality, not only did lay people, empirics and others constitute important medical resources despite vitriolic attacks on them by physicians and surgeons, but the occupational distinctions set up by the physicians were often ignored. Surgeon-physicians and apothecary-physicians, such as the Exeter apothecary William Dove, who in 1580 was licensed to practise medicine and surgery, were common in the provinces well before the set-piece debate in London in the later seventeenth century as to whether apothecaries could practise medicine (see chapter 9). Moreover, the distinction between barbers and surgeons was frequently broken in London and was non-existent elsewhere in the country.[38]

Numbers of practitioners are difficult to estimate. London attracted them, as the city's large and expanding population (70,000 in 1550, 200,000 in 1600, 575,000 in 1700) provided a ready supply of buyers for the remedies of empirics, and its wealthy citizens could afford the fees of the physicians who 'usually flock up to London (for there is the money)'.[39] The increasingly central role of London in the national economy also meant that patients from the provinces came to the capital to consult physicians and surgeons. Pelling and Webster calculated that in 1600 London, with a population of 200,000, was served by 50 members affiliated to the College of Physicians, 100 surgeons and 100 apothecaries, and a further 250

---

of payment indicated that a measure of success was expected. However, few charged 'a featherbed cover' which 'a woman called Pople' did in 1599 for a cure. *Annals of the College of Physicians* in the typescript transcription and translation by the Royal College of Physicians (abbreviated as *Annals*), 2, fol. 193a; 2, fol. 199b; 3, fol. 207a; 2, fol. 140a.

[38] Fundamental are: R. S. Roberts, 'The Personnel and Practice of Medicine in Tudor and Stuart England Part I. The Provinces', *Medical History*, 6, 1962, 363–82, esp. 369, and 'The Personnel and Practice of Medicine in Tudor and Stuart England Part II. London', *Medical History*, 8, 1964, 217–34, which discusses the attempts by London surgeons and apothecaries to practise medicine. See also: Margaret Pelling and Charles Webster, 'Medical Practitioners' in Charles Webster (ed.), *Health, Medicine and Mortality in the Sixteenth Century* (Cambridge University Press, Cambridge, 1979), pp. 165–235; Margaret Pelling, 'Medical Practice in Early Modern England: Trade or Profession?' in Wilfred Prest (ed.), *The Professions in Early Modern England* (Croom Helm, London, 1987), pp. 90–128.

[39] Finlay, *Population and Metropolis*, p. 51; Anon., *Lex Talionis Sive Vindiciae Pharmacoporum: Or a Short Reply to Dr. Merrett's Book; and Others, Written against the Apothecaries . . .* (London, 1670), sig. D4ʳ.

mainly unlicensed practitioners (of whom 60 or slightly fewer were women), not including nurses and midwives. This gives a ratio of one practitioner for every 400 of London's inhabitants, though not every practitioner made a living solely from medicine. In Norwich, which in 1575 had a population of 17,000 at the most, they found a minimum of 73 practitioners, of whom 37 were surgeons or barber-surgeons, many of whom also practised physic or medicine, plus 12 apothecaries, 10 women practitioners, 6 practitioners of physic, 5 university-educated physicians and 3 undetermined, giving a ratio of one practitioner to every 250 or so of the population. Small towns such as Ipswich and King's Lynn had 24 and 15 practitioners respectively in the second half of the sixteenth century.[40] In urban areas at least, England was well provided with medical practitioners. In the countryside, wise women, lay people and the resources of the local town could be drawn upon, whilst a surprising number of licensed medical practitioners and men with medical degrees lived in country areas, though whether they all practised is less clear.[41]

The place where most people were ill was the home. After the Reformation many hospitals were abolished, though a few like St Bartholomew's in London survived or were refounded;[42] but even in the Middle Ages, when hospitals were thick on the ground in England, they did not dominate the medical world as they did in the twentieth century. Hospitals had looked after abandoned children, the poor and vagrants as well as the sick; it was not until the nineteenth century that treatment of the sick became the sole duty of the hospital, and only in the twentieth century did they become the power houses of clinical research and essential to medical careers.

In addition to the patient's house, there were also available small-scale domiciliary facilities for the ill. Sometimes this was an inn near to a practitioner's house. Nursing homes or small informal hospitals were also used for treatment and convalescence. For instance, when Thomas Brockbank caught smallpox in 1691 while a student at Oxford, he was cared for in a nurse's home: 'I sent for my apothecary Hopkins and he told me the smallpox were appearing on

[40] Pelling and Webster, 'Medical Practitioners', pp. 182–8, 225–7; also R. S. Roberts, 'London Apothecaries and Medical Practice in Tudor and Stuart England' (Ph.D. thesis, University of London, 1964).

[41] John H. Raach, *A Directory of English Country Physicians 1603–1643* (Dawsons, London, 1962); see the criticism of Roberts, 'Personnel and Practice . . . Part I', 364–5.

[42] Nicholas Orme and Margaret Webster, *The English Hospital 1070–1570* (Yale University Press, New Haven, 1995), pp. 147–66.

my face. I desir'd him to get a nurse for me which he did, and he accompanied me to her house . . . I grew very ill.' As he recovered, he 'was removed from my old quarters (widow Tipler's in Coach and Horses lane) to Henry Clinches in St. Clements for airing [a change of air was considered beneficial in recovering from illness] where I stayed 1 month at 12/- [shillings] the week. Here I purged and was cleans'd and lay on great expenses.'[43] As well as students far from home care, there were groups like soldiers, sailors, travellers, migrants and those seeking specialised or expert medical care in the metropolis who could not be looked after at home. Nursing homes, embryonic hospitals, catered for their needs. One such was the home of Ellen Wright in the London parish of St Botolph without Aldgate. From at least 1588 to 1599 she took in a variety of sick people and pregnant women, whose presence, either because they were delivered or died there, was recorded by the parish.[44] Surgeons also took patients into their houses or lodged them nearby if they were far from home and needed prolonged treatment (see chapter 5).

The fact that the most serious of illnesses were usually treated at home and the small-scale and specialised nature of semi-institutional care for the sick confirm the individualistic, one-to-one nature of early modern English medicine, centred on transactions between single patients or their families and single practitioners. In such a setting it made sense for medical knowledge to be accessible to lay people as well as practitioners, whereas today institutions like hospitals, the state or professional organisations claim to assess medical expertise and practical skill on behalf of patients.

There were no nation-wide medical institutions. The London College of Physicians, founded in 1518 along the model of the Italian city colleges of physicians, and the London guilds of barbers and surgeons, which were formally united in 1540, were limited to the metropolis. Like other trades, the provincial barber-surgeons,

[43] Thomas Brockbank, *The Diary and Letter Book of the Rev. Thomas Brockbank 1671–1709*, ed. R. Trappes Lomax (Chetham Society, Manchester, 1930), pp. 36–7, 39. On small hospitals or homes for the mad ('mad-houses') see A. Fessler, 'The Management of Lunacy in Seventeenth-Century England: an Investigation of Quarter Sessions Records', *Proceedings of the Royal Society of Medicine*, Section of the History of Medicine, 49, 1956, 901–7; William Parry-Jones, *The Trade in Lunacy. A Study of Private Madhouses in England in the Eighteenth and Nineteenth Centuries* (Routledge & Kegan Paul, London, 1972). A number of Oxford apothecaries seem to have taken the ill into their homes; see T. D. Whittet, 'The Apothecary in Provincial Gilds', *Medical History*, 8, 1964, 245–73, at 258.
[44] For details, see Wear, 'The Sick Poor', 57–8.

who might include physicians, had their own guilds, as in Norwich and York.[45] London apothecaries were members of the Company of Grocers until 1617 when the Society of Apothecaries was established. In the provinces apothecaries either had their own guilds or were part of a composite guild.[46] The training of apothecaries and barbersurgeons was by apprenticeship. Physicians, if they had gone to university in England, would have had to study medicine based on classical sources for seven years after taking their BA and MA degrees. However, after taking an arts degree in England they could go abroad to Italian, French or Dutch universities and acquire an MD degree in less than a year, sometimes in weeks or months on the completion of a brief thesis. Practical medical knowledge was often gained by working with a more experienced physician. Practitioners who had not gone to university or who were not licensed (see below) also often acquired their knowledge by a process of informal apprenticeship. In the latter category, for instance, was Francis Roe alias Vintner. When accused in 1639 of undertaking to cure a woman suffering from 'tympany' (a kind of dropsy or accumulation of water or air in the abdomen), he told the College of Physicians that he had been a student at Cambridge and that 'hee had been instructed in physicke from a boy by his father meaning Mr. Vintner the Emperick'.[47]

Licensing of medical practitioners existed, but was not universal.

---

[45] Pelling and Webster, 'Medical Practitioners'; Margaret Pelling, 'Occupational Diversity: Barbersurgeons and the Trades of Norwich, 1550–1640', *Bulletin of the History of Medicine*, 56, 1982, 484–511; Margaret Barnet, 'The Barber-Surgeons of York', *Medical History*, 12, 1968, 19–30.

[46] Whittet, 'The Apothecary in Provincial Gilds', 245–73: Juanita G. L. Burnby, *A Study of the English Apothecary from 1660–1756, Medical History*, Supplement 3, 1983, 12–13, 15–16, 59–60.

[47] *Annals*, 3, fol. 203b. On unlicensed practitioners and education see Margaret Pelling, 'Knowledge Common and Acquired: the Education of Unlicensed Medical Practitioners in Early Modern London' in V. Nutton and R. Porter (eds.), *The History of Medical Education in Britain* (Rodopi, Amsterdam, 1995), pp. 250–79. On medical education: Cook, *Decline*, pp. 49–52; A. H. T. Robb-Smith, 'Medical Education in Cambridge Before 1600' in A. Rook (ed.), *Cambridge and its Contribution to Medicine* (Wellcome Institute for the History of Medicine, London, 1971), pp. 1–25, and 'Medical Education at Oxford and Cambridge Prior to 1850' in F. N. L. Poynter (ed.), *The Evolution of Medical Education in Britain* (Pitman, London, 1966), pp. 19–52; Robert G. Frank, Jr, 'Science, Medicine and the Universities of Early Modern England: Background and Sources', *History of Science*, 2, 1973, 194–216, 239–69; Gillian Lewis, 'The Faculty of Medicine' in James McConica (ed.), *The Collegiate University*, vol. III of *The History of the University of Oxford* (gen. ed. T. H. Aston) (Clarendon Press, Oxford, 1986), pp. 213–57; Peter Murray Jones, 'Reading Medicine in Tudor Cambridge' in *The History of Medical Education in Britain*, pp. 153–83; also the sections on European medical education by Olaf Pedersen and Laurence Brockliss, in H. De Ridder-Symoens (ed.), *A History of the University in Europe* (Cambridge University Press, Cambridge, 1996), vol. II, pp. 452–5, 609–20.

The London College of Physicians had a membership of fellows, candidates and licentiates who were admitted by examination, whilst the barber-surgeons and apothecaries granted the freedom of their guilds after apprenticeship and examination. From 1511, bishops could license physicians, surgeons and midwives, and although an Act of 1523 gave the College of Physicians the duty of examining all physicians throughout England, the College was unable to enforce the right except in London. Bishops' licences were usually granted on the strength of testimonials from former patients and worthies in the community. Given the lack of a uniform system of licensing, the geographical limits of the licensing bodies, as well as the constant legal challenges which resulted in the authority especially of the College of Physicians to regulate and prosecute unlicensed practitioners draining away in the seventeenth century, it is not surprising that not only were there many practitioners who were unlicensed, but that there was no rigid uniformity in medical knowledge and practice.[48] This also reflects the nature of English law, which had few national enforcement agencies. Although judges from London travelled on assize circuits through the country to dispense national norms of justice, the apprehension of criminals was left to the victims of crime and to local lay officials such as the constables and justices of the peace. Such local and devolved powers are also characteristic of medical regulation. Moreover, English common law, with its piecemeal approach based on precedent, and its hostility to the codifying tendency of the continental Roman law tradition to legislate systematically for all possibilities, was not the instrument to create a uniform legal framework for medical practice. The parts of continental Europe, especially Spain and southern Italy, that regulated a variety of medical practitioners through the tribunal of the Protomedicato, had more uniform and comprehensive systems of medical regulation, even if they were not universally applied.[49]

[48] For the legal basis of the College of Physicians' powers, see G. Clark, *A History of the Royal College of Physicians* (2 vols., Clarendon Press, Oxford, 1964 and 1966). Cook, *Decline*; Cook, ' "Against Common Right and Reason": The College of Physicians versus Dr Thomas Bonham', *American Journal of Legal History*, 29, 1985, 301–22; Cook, 'The Rose Case Reconsidered: Physicians, Apothecaries, and the Law in Augustan England', *Journal of the History of Medicine*, 45, 1990, 527–55. The court and the nobility also often intervened on behalf of empirics and further weakened the College's ability to police medical practice, on which see Clark, *College of Physicians*, vol. I.

[49] J. T. Lanning, *The Royal Protomedicato. The Regulation of the Medical Professions in the Spanish Empire* (Duke University Press, Durham, 1985); D. Gentilcore, *Healers and Healing in Early Modern Italy* (Manchester University Press, Manchester, 1998); Gentilcore, ' "All that

The overall impression of English medicine in the sixteenth and seventeenth centuries is of a large number of different kinds of practitioners. Those who made a living from medicine were often in fierce competition with each other. The College physicians and barber-surgeons had institutional rules that limited competition between members: they were enjoined not to poach patients from each other and advised on how to make a joint consultation without bad-mouthing each other in front of the patient.[50] These were, however, minor obstacles to the flow of free market competition that dominated medicine.

THE MEDICAL MARKETPLACE

Historians have fitted the different kinds of medical practitioners into a model that they have only recently created: the medical marketplace. It has been a very useful virtual space for placing disparate groups of practitioners together on an equal footing. Quacks and empirics were condemned by the learned physicians and it is the latter's hostile writings that largely survive. As a result, the historical evidence creates bias and distorts the reality, which was that empirics provided cheap medicines for many, though how many is impossible to know. Placing in the medical marketplace physicians, surgeons and apothecaries, the three occupational groups which had institutional identities and claimed to be superior to other practitioners, makes it easier to recognise that, like their hated enemies, the empirics, they were also driven by financial competition.

However, a note of caution is necessary. The medical marketplace model was conceived by historians in the mid-1980s at the time of Reagan and Thatcher and reflects these politicians' ruthless free

Pertains to Medicine": "Protomedici" and "Protomedicati" in Early Modern Italy', *Medical History*, 38, 1994, 121–42; Gentilcore, ' "Charlatans, Mountebanks and Other Similar People': the Regulation and Role of Itinerant Practitioners in Early Modern Italy', *Social History London*, 20, 297–314; Gentilcore, 'Il regio Protomedicato nella Napoli spagnola', *Dynamis*, 16, 1996, 219–36. See also Esther Fischer-Homberger, *Medizin vor Gericht. Gerichtsmedizin vor der Renaissance bis zur Aufkärung* (Hans Huber Verlag, Berne, 1983). Ethical-legal writings were absent in early modern England, whilst the Canon and Civilian law traditions of continental Europe encouraged them as, for instance, Pauli Zacchiae, *Quaestiones Medico-Legales*, 3rd edn (Amsterdam, 1651); D. Johannis Bohnii, *De Officio Medici Duplici Clinici nimirum ac Forensis* (Leipzig, 1704). Also A. Wear, 'Medical Ethics in Early Modern England' in A. Wear, J. Geyer-Kordesch and R. K. French (eds.), *Doctors and Ethics: the Earlier Historical Setting of Professional Ethics* (Rodopi, Amsterdam, 1993), pp. 98–130.
50 Clark, *College of Physicians*, I, pp. 284–5, 414–6; A. T. Young, *The Annals of the Barber-Surgeons of London* (Blades, East & Blades, London, 1890), p. 119.

market ideology, which, such is the influence of the present on historical writing, shaped the thinking and behaviour of even the most left-wing of historians.[51] As with modern free market ideology, the medical marketplace model can be overemphasised. It stresses economic imperatives and discounts the cultural forces that shaped medicine, especially religion, the most powerful ideology of the time. A free market attempts to expand to fill all possible niches, and yet dying, as is discussed below, was not medicalised but continued to be managed by religion. Similarly, the members of a free market know no ethical constraints or charitable impulses in the search for profit, but that was not always the case with early modern practitioners, as the concern with the poor and the example of the Helmontians, discussed in chapters 8 and 9, especially demonstrate. The medical market model is also inappropriate for understanding lay medicine, where, if any transactions occurred, they were social rather than economic. Moreover, it tends to take attention away from the cognitive and practical aspects of medicine. How practitioners perceived disease and how they treated it have been downplayed by historians intent on exploring the variety of the medical marketplace, though they have related medical theories and practice to competition for patients.[52] Despite these caveats, the model of the medical marketplace together with the destruction of the Whig view of historical progress has helped to make available for study, groups, topics and sources which had been ignored or condemned as wrong, superstitious or unimportant by historians.[53]

RELIGION

One important topic ignored until recently was the relationship between religion and medicine. Just as free market economics today

---

[51] One of the first historians to use the term (health economists may have anticipated them) was Harold Cook in his admirable *Decline*; Roy Porter used the concept to good effect in his *Health for Sale: Quackery in England 1660–1850* (Manchester University Press, Manchester, 1989).

[52] See the influential paper by the sociologist N. Jewson, 'Medical Knowledge and the Patronage System in Eighteenth-Century England', *Sociology*, 8, 1974, 369–85. Also C. Rosenberg, 'The Therapeutic Revolution: Medicine, Meaning, and Social Change in 19th Century America' in J. Walzer Leavitt and R. L. Numbers (eds.), *Sickness and Health in America: Readings in the History of Medicine and Public Health*, 2nd edn (University of Wisconsin Press, Madison, Wis., 1985), pp. 39–52.

[53] For instance, the patient, the poor, quacks, midwives, religion, witchcraft, diaries and autobiographies.

is the driving ideology of globalisation by multinational corporations and the justification of American economic power, so religion in the sixteenth and seventeenth centuries was the ideology that justified wars between nations and shaped public and private morality. It is not surprising, therefore, that religion should have penetrated also into the area of medicine and illness. It did so in two ways: it took on the role of medicine by explaining why disease occurred and by offering healing through prayer and repentance; and it arrived at a *modus vivendi* with physicians and their remedies and allowed secular medicine to exist without much interference.

Christianity was from its beginning a healing religion. Christ, as a sign of his divinity, had healed the sick in body and mind, and the early Church Fathers and later writers used the image of Christ the Physician, and constantly employed medical metaphors in religious teaching. Christianity was concerned with both spiritual and physical healing. The Latin word *salus* came to mean salvation, but salvation also meant health: 'God's word worketh marvellously unto the health of them that believe. And therefore in the word of God it is called the word of health, or salvation.'[54] God also caused illness; he was a destroyer as well as a healer. The Fall of Adam and Eve brought disease into the world together with death.[55] English Protestants, especially Calvinists, added to the sense of original sin the view that illnesses were also God's punishment for their own present-day sins. Illness became a sign of God's providence, a running commentary on an individual's or, in the case of plague, a community's behaviour. It was a rod or punishment and a warning, or it could also be a trial of one's faith as it was for Job.[56] However,

[54] The early English Protestant writer, Thomas Becon, *Prayers and Other Pieces of Thomas Becon*, ed. F. Ayre for the Parker Society (Cambridge University Press, Cambridge, 1844), p. 490. On early Christianity and medicine see D. Amundsen, 'Medicine and Faith in Early Christianity', *Bulletin of the History of Medicine*, 56, 1982, 326–50; also G. Ferngren, 'Early Christianity as a Religion of Healing', *Bulletin of the History of Medicine*, 66, 1992, 1–15.

[55] On the dual nature of God see, for instance, Samson Price, *Londons Remembrancer for the Staying of the Contagious Sicknes of the Plague* . . . (London, 1626), p. 6; Theodore de Beze, *A Shorte Learned and Pithie Treatize of the Plague* (London, 1580), sig. A4ᵛ: 'Sinne in deede wherewith we are all borne infected, and from which all this dying commeth, by a certayne spiritual infection not without the decree of God, is conveighed and spread into all Adam his posteritie.' Burton, *Anatomy of Melancholy*, p. 114: 'the cause of death and diseases, of all temporal and eternal punishments, was the sin of our first parent Adam, in eating of the forbidden fruit, by the devil's instigation and allurement'.

[56] Andrew Wear, 'Puritan Perceptions of Illness in Seventeenth Century England' in R. Porter (ed.), *Patients and Practitioners: Lay Perceptions of Medicine in Pre-Industrial Society* (Cambridge University Press, Cambridge, 1985), pp. 55–99 and 'Religious Beliefs and Medicine in Early Modern England' in H. Marland and M. Pelling (eds.), *The Task of Healing: Medicine,*

God in his mercy mitigated the punishment of the Fall and gave to humankind the means to alleviate illness. As the Apocrypha puts it, 'The Lord hath created medicines out of the earth', and, in a verse often quoted by physicians, 'honour the physician with that honour that is due unto him for the Lord hath created him'.[57]

From the time of the early Church Fathers Christianity taught that it was permissible to use natural means to cure illness, with the proviso that the patient and the doctor pray to God to give healing power to the remedies being used.[58] The remedies, as the influential Calvinist Puritan divine William Perkins wrote, also had to be 'lawful', not magical or diabolical, such as 'all charmes or spels . . . characters and figures either in paper, wood, or waxe . . . and yet neverthelesse, these unlawfull and absurd meanes are more used and sought for of common people, then good physicke'. And he warned 'all men . . . in no wise to seeke foorth to enchanters, and sorcerers, which indeede are but witches and wizzards, though they are commonly called cunning men and women'.[59]

In a sense, Christianity gave medicine permission to exist; by incorporating it as a work of God, Christian theologians lessened the possibility of conflict between physical and spiritual healing. Clergymen and physicians taught that the Christian had a duty to look after the body, for it housed the immortal soul, and to neglect that duty affected the soul's spiritual health. Not taking care of one's health and not using the resources of medicine also wilfully lessened the lifetime that God had allotted to an individual; such action was tantamount to the sin of self-murder. However, medicines could not be used to prolong life beyond one's allotted span, and they could

Religion and Gender in England and the Netherlands, 1450–1800 (Erasmus Publishing, Rotterdam, 1996), pp. 145–69. On early modern Christianity and medicine, see also the essays in W. J. Sheils (ed.), *Studies in Church History*, vol. XIX, *The Church and Healing* (Basil Blackwell for the Ecclesiastical History Society, Oxford, 1982); O. P. Grell and A. Cunningham (eds.), *Medicine and the Reformation* (Routledge, London, 1993); O. P. Grell and A. Cunningham (eds.), *Religio Medici: Medicine and Religion in Seventeenth-Century England* (Scolar Press, Aldershot, 1996); D. Harley, 'Medical Metaphors in English Moral Theology, 1560–1660', *Journal of the History of Medicine* 48, 1993, 396–435.

57 Ecclesiasticus 38.4, 1.
58 Amundsen, 'Medicine and Faith in Early Christianity'; Wear, 'Puritan Perceptions of Illness', pp. 78–9. The puritan theologian William Perkins wrote, 'by prayer we must intreat the Lord for a blessing upon them [medicines], in restoring of health, if it bee the good will of God. 1. Tim. 4.3': William Perkins, *The Workes* (3 vols., London, 1616–1618), vol. I, *A Salve for a Sicke Man Or, A Treatise Containing the Nature . . . of Death, As Also the Right Manner of Dying Well*, p. 506.
59 Perkins, *Salve*, pp. 505, 506; also Burton, *Anatomy of Melancholy*, pp. 381–4 on 'unlawful cures'.

not, in any case, counter the will of God.[60] The injunction to use medicine and to see disease as natural or as coming from God through natural or secondary causes was emphasised in times of plague when the government and most churchmen argued that a fatalistic do-nothing attitude was sinful; they also feared that behind such a view lay a disbelief in the contagious nature of plague and hence in isolation measures.[61]

Until the 1640s Protestant writers such as Perkins saw learned medicine as the best and most 'lawful' form of medicine. Calvin had praised Galen, who together with Hippocrates was the classical inspiration and source for learned physicians. By emphasising the value of learned medicine, Calvinists could use it as a substitute for the healing sacraments of the Catholic Church which they argued had no power, as well as presenting it as the proper alternative to the 'magical' healing of wise women. Calvin and his followers argued that the age of miracles was past and that the gift of healing had been given to Christ's disciples only for their lifetimes; it ceased with their deaths and had not been passed down to the present-day priests of the Catholic Church. Henry Holland, a Puritan minister and medical practitioner, saw that this gave further legitimacy to medicine and especially to his favoured version of it: 'Now then the gift [of healing] ceasing . . . the learned physician [is] the comfortable and ordinary means which God hath left unto us as long as the World endureth', and he cited the famous verse of Ecclesiasticus on honouring the physician.[62]

Learned medicine gained not only approval from Puritans but also added support in its fight with empirics. For a while it was seen

---

[60] Andrew Boorde, a clergyman and physician, wrote in his *The Breviary of Helthe* (London, 1547), sig. B1ʳ, that the 'patient provyde for his body, and take counsell of some expert physicion . . . at all tymes redy to folowe the wyll mynd and counsell of his phisicion, for who so ever wyll do the contrary saynt Augustine saythe "Seipsum interimit qui precepto medici observare non vult" . . . He doth kyll him selfe that doth nat observe the commaundement of his phisicion'; also sigs. B2ᵛ–B3ʳ; William Bullein, 'The Booke of Compounds' in *Bulleins Bulwarke of Defence Against all Sicknes, Sornes and Woundes* (London, 1562), fol. 2ᵛ; Perkins, *Salve*, pp. 505, 506: 'all sicke persons must bee carefull to preserve health and life till God doe wholly take it away', and 'wee must not thinke that physicke serves to prevent old age or death, it selfe. For that is not possible, because God hath set downe that all men shall die and be changed'.

[61] See, for example, James Mannings, 'minister of the word', *A New Booke Intituled I Am For You All, Complexions Castle: As Well in the Time of the Pestilence As Other Times* (Cambridge, 1604), pp. 1–6, which relates the above arguments to the case of the plague.

[62] Holland, *An Admonition*, pp. 49–50; see Wear, 'Religious Beliefs and Medicine', pp. 155–9.

as God's preferred medicine in contrast to the medicine of the empirics. The dramatist Thomas Dekker echoed such a view:

Is Sickness [the plague] come to thy doore! . . . Make much of thy Physitian: let not an Emperick or Mountibancking Quacksalver peepe in at thy window, but set thy Gates wide open to entertaine thy learned Physitian: Honour him, make much of him. Such a Physitian is Gods second, and in a duell or single fight (of this nature) will stand bravely to thee.[63]

However, physicians attacked ministers alongside empirics and charitable gentlewomen for practising medicine. Despite the occasional prayer and reminder to the physician in medical texts to invoke God's blessing on the medicines, the general impression is that the physicians did not usually reciprocate the interest that religious writers showed in their subject.[64] The basis of the physician's attacks was, ironically, religious: Calvin's insistence that everyone should keep to their calling or occupation. In *The Anatomy of Melancholy* (1621), the definitive compendium of views on madness, medicine and society in English and European culture, Robert Burton, who was a clergyman and Oxford academic, countered by arguing that any physician who objected that 'no cobbler go beyond his last, and find himself grieved that I have intruded into his profession' should look at the number of physicians who had become clergymen, and at the

agreement . . . betwixt these two professions [of medicine and religion]. A good Divine either is or ought to be a good physician, a spiritual physician at least as our Saviour calls himself and was indeed. They differ but in object, the one of the body, the other of the soul, and use divers medicines to cure: one amends the soul through the body, the other the body through the soul.[65]

Nevertheless, from the Middle Ages physicians had often been associated in popular sayings with atheism and uncharitableness.

---

[63] Thomas Dekker, 'London Loocke Back at that Yeare of Yeares 1625, and Looke Forward upon this Yeare 1630', in F. P. Wilson (ed.), *The Plague Pamphlets of Thomas Dekker* (Clarendon Press, Oxford, 1925), p. 188.

[64] John Cotta, *A Short Discoverie of the Unobserved Dangers of Severall Sorts of Ignorant and Unconsiderate Practisers of Physicke in England* (London, 1612), pp. 86–94; James Hart, *The Arraigment of Urines* (London, 1623), sigs. A3^v–A4^r, and *The Anatomie of Urines . . . Or, the Second Part of Our Discourse of Urines* (London, 1625), sigs. A5^v–A6^r, p. 110; Wear, 'Religious Beliefs and Medicine', pp. 155–65; D. Harley, 'James Hart of Northampton and the Calvinist Critique of Priest-Physicians: an Unpublished Polemic of the Early 1620s', *Medical History*, 42, 1998, 362–86.

[65] Burton, *Anatomy of Melancholy*, p. 29.

John Ward noted that the saying 'Ubi tres medici, ibi duo Athei [where there are three physicians, there be two atheists], hath been an old though a false calumnie.' Though he also recorded: 'one told the Bishop of Gloucester not long since, that hee imagined that physitians, of all other men, were the most competent judges of all others in affairs of religion; and his reason was, because they are wholly unconcerned in the matter'.[66]

The new medical movements, Paracelsianism and Helmontianism (discussed below), which challenged Galenic learned medicine, latched on to such associations. Their followers attacked Galenic physicians as atheistic and uncharitable, and presented their own medicine as Christian, their practitioners being chosen of God and especially concerned with charitable medical provision for the poor. Religion thus not only allowed the practice of medicine but was also an integral part of the debate between rival medical systems. It also remained a medical resource in its own right, giving rationales for illness and offering healing through prayer from God, if not from his saints or the sacraments as in Catholic belief. Moreover, it kept medicine away from the death bed. Ministers insisted that the physician leave the bedside if the prognosis was imminent death. The time of dying was seen as a Christian ritual: the passing from this life to the next whilst beset by the temptations of the devil; a time when worldly affairs were settled and spiritual meditation prepared one for death. From the Middle Ages to the eighteenth century the 'art of dying' in its different guises helped to make dying a religious rather than a medical event. Physicians agreed, moreover, that it hurt their reputation to take money for incurable cases.[67] It was not until the later eighteenth century that death became medicalised and physicians managed dying with the use of opiates; as the performance of the art of dying declined in the Enlightenment, so the need for the patient to remain rational lessened.

---

[66] Ward, *Diary*, pp. 119, 100. On a medieval criticism of extortionate physicians see *The Metalogicon of John of Salisbury*, trans. D. D. McGarry (Peter Smith, Gloucester, Mass., 1971), Book 1 ch. 4, p. 18.

[67] M. C. O'Connor, *The Art of Dying Well* (AMS Press, New York, 1966); D. Stannard, *The Puritan Way of Death* (Oxford University Press, New York, 1977); P. Ariès, *The Hour of our Death* (Penguin Books, Harmondsworth, 1983); C. Gittings, *Death, Burial and the Individual in Early Modern England* (Croom Helm, London, 1984); R. Houlbrooke (ed.), *Death, Ritual and Bereavement* (Routledge, London, 1989), and *Death, Religion and the Family in England, 1480–1750* (Clarendon Press, Oxford, 1998); David Cressy, *Birth, Marriage and Death. Ritual, Religion and the Life Cycle in Tudor and Stuart England* (Oxford University Press, Oxford, 1997).

LITERATE MEDICAL KNOWLEDGE

Our knowledge of how early modern English practitioners and readers of medical works understood the nature of remedies, diseases and the healthiness or otherwise of the world around them and how their views changed or remained the same comes largely from medical writings. These were written against the background of the Renaissance recreation of Greek medicine. They express at different levels medical knowledge whose sources in the sixteenth century, as in the Middle Ages, were mainly the Hippocratic treatises (written by various authors mainly between 420 and 350 BC) and the writings of Galen (AD 129–216) who had produced a coherent and all- encompassing medical system from different strands of ancient medicine and philosophy as well as from his own researches. Arabic authors were also referred to, although they were less influential than in the Middle Ages.

In the Renaissance, as part of the humanistic love of classical knowledge, the recreation was attempted of the *prisca medicina*, the pure ancient medicine of the Greeks, and to a lesser extent of the Romans. Despite having retrieved Galenic medicine for western Europe, the Middle Ages were seen as having defiled the ancients with incorrect and 'barbarous' texts and translations. By going back to the pure founts of medical wisdom, medicine, it was believed, would be improved. Just as the reformation of religion involved a return to the original word of God, the Bible, so the reformation of medicine would take place through better knowledge of the words of medicine's founders. A landmark of medical scholarship was the 1525 Venetian Aldine Press edition of the complete works of Galen in Greek; in the same year the Hippocratic Corpus was published in Latin and the next year in Greek. The translation and editing of classical medical texts brought fame to a number of humanist physicians, with Nicolaus Leoniceno (1428–1524) chief amongst them. Italian universities, and then from the 1530s Paris, were at the forefront of retrieving Greek medicine. Between 1500 and 1600 around 590 different editions of Galen were published.[68] In

[68] R. J. Durling, 'A Chronological Census of Renaissance Editions and Translations of Galen', *Journal of the Warburg and Courtauld Institutes*, 24, 1961, 230–305. See especially Michael R. McVaugh, *Medicine before the Plague: Practitioners and their Patients in the Crown of Aragon, 1285–1345* (Cambridge University Press, Cambridge, 1993); Luis García-Ballester, '*Artifex factivus sanitatis*: Health and Medical Care in Medieval Latin Galenism' in Don Bates (ed.),

England, there were a few humanist medical scholars such as
Thomas Linacre (1460? – 1524) and John Caius (1510–1573), but
the medical Renaissance came largely at second-hand through the
dissemination of vernacular medical texts that handed down what
were often diluted versions of Galenic teaching. The one great
exception was the London College of Physicians, which expected its
members to know the Latin texts of Galen and Hippocrates, and
which saw the propagation of Galenic learned medicine as its
mission. The College has tended to have a bad press. Modern
historians have often emphasised its limited membership, its authori-
tarian obscurantism, its persecution of empirics and poor wise
women, its hostility to new ideas, and, of course, its being on the
losing side in the debate between the ancients and the moderns in
the later seventeenth century. With the exception of George Clark
and a few others they have found it difficult to see that the College in
the sixteenth century was part of a general European movement that
aimed to improve medicine and make it safer.

Some of the improvement could also come by making medicine
more 'methodical', by putting medical teaching into a logical order
going from the most general principles to the particular details of a
patient. Often such information was put into tables, or set out in a
text as in a table.[69] Giambatista da Monte (1498–1552), the
professor of the practice of medicine in Padua, the foremost
European university of the sixteenth century, was the most famous
exponent of the methodical teaching of medicine. Influenced by
Linacre's Latin translation of Galen's *Method of Healing* (1519), da
Monte tried to recreate a Galenic practice of medicine which, rather
than merely relating treatment to the causes of disease as with the
medieval *practica* or compendia on practice, also considered the
patient's constitution, lifestyle and environment. On the continent
few medical writers followed da Monte's time-consuming method,
and even fewer did so in England.[70] However, the patient-centred

Knowledge and the Scholarly Medical Traditions (Cambridge University Press, Cambridge, 1995),
pp. 127–50.

[69] Alexander Read, 'A Treatise of the First Part of Chirurgery' in *The Workes of that Famous
Physitian Dr. Alexander Read*, 2nd edn (London, 1650) is self-consciously set out in a
methodical fashion; see p. 14: 'Having described as it were in a table, the divers sorts of
extraneous bodies, to help the memory.'

[70] Two treatises on bloodletting, by Nicholas Gyer, *The English Phlebotomy: Or, Method and Way
of Healing by Letting Blood* (London, 1592) and by Simon Harward, *Harwards Phlebotomy: Or, a
Treatise of Letting of Bloud* . . . (London, 1601), are examples of learned and methodical
vernacular medical works. A. Read, 'Chirurgicall Lectures of Tumors and Ulcers' and 'A

nature of Galenic methodical medicine was retained as part of the
ideological rhetoric used by the learned physicians to distinguish
themselves from their competitors, the empirics, who treated the
disease and not the patient. By the later seventeenth century
'method' was attached to Galenic physicians as a term of abuse,
signifying blind adherence to old-fashioned dogma,[71] but in the
sixteenth century it symbolised the attempt to put into order the
cutting-edge knowledge that was being produced, paradoxically to
the modern mind, by scholars. Before discussing how English
vernacular texts were seen by some as part of the Renaissance push
to improve medicine and by others as inimical to the new learned
medicine, it is worth looking at the medical theory that lay at the
heart of Galenic therapeutics, whether in Latin or in vernacular
texts, and which informs much of the present book.

THE HUMORAL THEORY OF HEALTH AND ILLNESS

Galenic physicians from the Middle Ages followed the humoral
theory as did much of the literate population. Four humours or fluids
– blood, phlegm, yellow bile or choler, and black bile or melancholy
– made up the body and, like the Aristotelian four elements (earth,
water, air and fire) out of which the sublunary world was formed,
they were the products of the combinations of the four qualities of
hot, cold, dry and wet that Aristotle (384–322 BC), the Greek
philosopher, had stated were the primary constituents of the world.
Figure 1 shows how the microcosm or little world of the body had
the same qualitative foundation as the macrocosm, or the world at
large. It also indicates how the humours were linked to the seasons,
so that in spring blood was in greatest quantity and at that time a
routine annual prophylactic bleeding would be carried out. The four
ages of humankind also corresponded to the four humours, so that
in old age phlegm predominated. Every person had an individual

---

Treatise of the First Part of Chirurgery' in *The Workes* set out to teach surgery methodically.
John Caius, *De Medendi methodo libri duo, ex CL Galeni Pergameni, et Jo. Baptistae Montani
Veronensis, principum medicorum, sententia* (Basle, 1544). Andrew Wear, 'Explorations in
Renaissance Writings on the Practice of Medicine' in A. Wear, R. K. French and I. M.
Lonie (eds.), *The Medical Renaissance of the Sixteenth Century* (Cambridge University Press,
Cambridge, 1985), pp. 118–45, 312–17; J. Bylebyl, 'Teaching Methodus Medendi in the
Renaissance' in F. Kudlien and R. J. Durling (eds.), *Galen's Method of Healing* (E. J. Brill,
Leiden, 1991), pp. 157–89.
[71] See, for instance, George Starkey, *Nature's Explication and Helmont's Vindication* (London,
1657), sig. A6ᵛ, pp. 51–3.

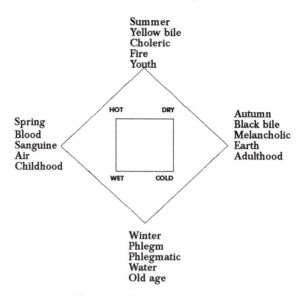

Figure 1 The humoral system

mixture of humours, their constitution, temperament or complexion, in which normally one humour was dominant and shaped their physical and psychological predisposition. They would be phlegmatic, melancholic, choleric or sanguine.

Regimens or rules for healthy living were supposed to take the humoral temperament of the individual into account. So choleric patients should avoid hot and dry foods and eat ones with moist ingredients. Treatment was based on the allopathic principle that opposites cure opposites, so a hot illness was cured by a cold remedy. The assessment of a patient's and a remedy's heat, coldness, etc. was subjective, though it was given a sense of precision by the use of degrees of heat, wetness, etc.[72] However, as is discussed in chapter 3, it was believed not only that illness was the result of an imbalance in the humours or the qualities, but also that it could be caused by a humour taking on a pathological character or by pathological humours being generated within the body, sometimes through

---

[72] Aristotle in *On Generation and Corruption*, 329^b7-330^a29 argued that hot, cold, dry and wet were the primary qualities. Sanctorius Sanctorius (1561–1636), professor of the theory of medicine at Padua and one of Galileo's acquaintances, at the beginning of the seventeenth century invented a thermometer and a hydrometer so that the four qualities could be measured objectively.

contagion by some poison as in plague. The result was that putrid, corrupt or burnt humours were often seen as the cause of disease, and the evacuative procedures of bleeding, purging and vomiting that figure largely in the story of the English and European practice of medicine were the favoured therapies. They were also employed to recreate a balanced humoral mix and to get rid of a *plethora* or excess of a humour.

The humoral theory and Galenic medicine in general were challenged first by Paracelsian and then by Helmontian medicine, both of them based on chemical principles (on salt, sulphur and mercury, and on water respectively). Both saw chemical processes in the body in vitalistic terms, but Helmontianism was less tainted with magical associations, it often repudiated astrology and it was more careful in its experimental methods than Paracelsianism. Helmontians stood half-way between Paracelsianism and the 'new science' of Galileo, Descartes, Boyle and Newton that sought to replace the old qualitative vision of the cosmos and the body. In England, Paracelsianism as a medical philosophy began to make an impact in the late sixteenth century, though it was Paracelsian chemical remedies rather than Paracelsian theory that were popularised by John Hester and others. English surgeons like William Clowes, John Banister, George Baker and John Woodall also espoused Paracelsianism, which is understandable given their routine use of mercury to cure the pox, a remedy of which Paracelsus cautiously approved, but to which Galenic writers were often opposed.[73] In the Civil War period Paracelsian medicine, as Charles Webster has shown, became popular with reformers, both for its medical theory and its Christian ethic. As chapters 8 and 9 indicate,

[73] See William Clowes, *A Right Frutefull and Approoved Treatise for the Artificiall Cure of that Malady Called in Latin Struma, and in English, the Evill, Cured by Kinges and Queenes of England* (London, 1602), sig. A2ᵛ: 'I had heere likewise thought good to have spoken somewhat of Paracelsus, but I must confesse his Doctrine hath a more pregnant sense, then my wit or reach is able to construe: onely this I can say by experience, that I have practised certaine of his inventions Chirurgicall, the which I have found to be singular good and worthy of great commendations.' Surgeons such as Clowes and Woodall did give very brief outlines of Paracelsian theory. A lawyer, Richard Bostocke, wrote the first major English Paracelsian treatise: *The Difference Betwene the Auncient Phisicke . . . and the Latter Phisicke* (London, 1585). C. Webster, 'Alchemical and Paracelsian Medicine' in Webster (ed.), *Health, Medicine and Mortality in the Sixteenth Century* (Cambridge University Press, Cambridge, 1979), pp. 313–34, argues that interest in alchemical medicine was endemic in sixteenth-century England, and against A. Debus, *The English Paracelsians* (Oldbourne Press, London, 1965), citing pp. 49, 80–1, 101–5, 127, that in the last twenty-five years of the sixteenth century Paracelsian ideas became widely known in England.

the medicine of the Flemish nobleman-physician and devout Christian Johannes Baptista van Helmont (1579–1644) and his followers then provided from the mid-seventeenth century a strong alternative to Galenic treatments; that it failed indicates the strength of some of the elements of traditional therapeutics.

THE ENGLISH VERNACULAR MEDICAL TEXTS

Knowledge of medical theories and therapeutic practices was largely communicated to practitioners and to the literate public by vernacular medical texts.[74] The vast majority of the sixteenth- and seventeenth-century medical books published in England were written in English and not in Latin, the international language of scholarship. This created a spectrum from popular to elite medicine, ranging from remedy books, giving lists of medicines and their ingredients for particular diseases, and herbals, to the more complicated, theoretically-based regimens, and textbooks explaining medical theory and practice. There were also works on specific diseases, such as plague treatises, works on medicinal springs and spas, and textbooks on medicine and surgery explicitly written for practitioners. Distinctions between lay and medical readerships were blurred and both groups might read works which were ostensibly for

---

[74] Despite what appears to be an educational revolution between 1558 and the 1640s, the poorest part of the population remained illiterate. Male literacy in higher social groups such as the gentry, yeomen and merchants increased, while husbandmen, poor artisans, labourers and servants continued to have high illiteracy rates. Nevertheless, as Keith Wrightson and Margaret Spufford have pointed out, the need to be literate was felt by the poorest and much of oral culture was in the process of being put into print. Some parishes, especially where there was a school or teacher, had rates of male illiteracy as low as 28 to 40 per cent in the early 1640s, while other parishes had rates as high as 90 per cent. Reading on its own was much more widely practised than reading and writing. Women were often taught only to read. It is impossible to calculate rates of reading, as reading unlike writing leaves behind no record. However, despite the large gains in literacy, half the population (60 per cent women, 40 per cent men) was probably illiterate in 1750 (Peter Laslett, *The World We Have Lost – Further Explored* (Methuen, London, 1983), pp. 232–3), and there were still many whose culture was totally oral, though their numbers were declining. Laurence Stone, 'The Educational Revolution in England 1560–1640', *Past & Present*, 28, 1964, 41–80; David Cressy, *Literacy and the Social Order* (Cambridge University Press, Cambridge, 1980); Margaret Spufford, *Small Books and Pleasant Histories* (Methuen, London, 1981), ch. 2; Keith Wrightson, *English Society 1580–1680* (Hutchinson, London, 1982), pp. 183–99; Laslett, *The World We Have Lost – Further Explored*, pp. 228–37; R. A. Houston, *Literacy in Early Modern England: Culture and Education 1500–1800* (Longman, London, 1988); Peter M. Jones, 'Book Ownership and the Lay Culture of Medicine in Tudor Cambridge' in Marland and Pelling (eds.), *The Task of Healing*, pp. 49–68.

the other.[75] In contrast to the 153 different vernacular medical works that Paul Slack has found were published in England from 1486 up to the end of 1604 (in 392 editions), the number of Latin medical works published in England up to 1640 was paltry. Linacre's and Caius' Latin translations of Galen were published abroad, as was William Harvey's work announcing his discovery of the circulation of the blood (1628). Thomas Mouffet's chemical-medical writings and his 'medical letters' were published in Frankfurt, whilst his treatise on blockage of the mesaraic veins was issued from Basle. A few works were printed in London, such as Thomas Geminus' shortened version of Andreas Vesalius' massive and famous work on anatomy, which was printed there in 1545 and reprinted in 1552, and Thomas Lorkyn's treatise on regimen for students (1562). A treatise on melancholy by André Du Laurens was translated from French into Latin in 1599, as was Brice Bauderon's *Pharmacopea* in 1639; both were published in London.[76] Charles Webster has calculated that between 1640 and 1660 238 medical books were published, of which 207 were in English and 31 in Latin.[77] The figures, however, hide what was probably a large number of Latin medical books imported from the continent.

Publishing Latin medical works abroad ensured they reached the larger pool of continental learned readers, whilst writing in English meant, as Caius put it when explaining why he was determined never to publish again in English, that 'the commoditie of that which is so written, passeth not the compasse of Englande, but remaineth enclosed within the seas'. He was also contemptuous of the 'iudgement of the multitude', and deplored how 'the common settyng furthe and printig of every foolishe thyng in englishe, of phisicke unperfectly . . . diminishe the grace of thynges learned set furth in thesame'.[78] Latin texts marked out, for some, true scholarly medicine; Latin ensured that medical knowledge was limited to the few, and this was justified on the grounds that it discouraged unlearned, and hence unskilled, practitioners and preserved the integrity of

---

[75] Paul Slack, 'Mirrors of Health and Treasures of Poor Men: the Uses of the Vernacular Medical Literature of Tudor England' in C. Webster (ed.), *Health, Medicine and Mortality in the Sixteenth Century* (Cambridge University Press, Cambridge, 1979), pp. 237–73.

[76] J. W. Binns, *Intellectual Culture in Elizabethan and Jacobean England. The Latin Writings of the Age* (Francis Cairns (Publications), c/o University of Leeds, 1990), pp. 266–7, 379–80.

[77] Webster, *The Great Instauration*, p. 267.

[78] Caius, *A Counseil Against the Sweat*, p. 6.

classically based medicine. James Primrose, a staunch Galenist, pointed out that vernacular books simplified and distorted medicine:

> Againe they [women] usually take their remedies out of English bookes, or else make use of such as are communicated to them by others, and then they think they have rare remedies for all diseases. But Galen in his bookes of *Method*, teaches that remedies are to bee altered according to the person, place, part affected and other circumstances.[79]

In general, the more extreme learned physicians aimed for a cadre of physicians fluent in Latin who would take over medical practice; books in English, they believed, at best diluted such learning, and at worse were the means of allowing empirics and others to practise medicine more easily. The Salisbury physician John Securis, who had studied in Paris with the conservative leader of French Galenism, Jacques Dubois, wrote that medicine had to be studied in its philosophical context, which was taught in Latin:

> englishe bookes teacheth nothinge of the trewe foundation of Phisike . . . howe can it be well understanded without logike and naturall philosophie. For Aristotle saith "Ubi desinit Physicus, ibi incipit medicus" [where the philosopher ends, there begins the physician]. A man must first peruse naturall Philosophie, before he entre into phisyke.

This reflected university teaching where the student first took an arts degree before going on to medicine. Money underpinned the intellectual basis of learned medicine. English books devalued the investment of time and money expended on becoming a learned physician by letting anyone practise medicine.[80]

---

[79] James Primrose, *Popular Errours Or the Errours of the People in Physick*, trans. Robert Wittie (London, 1651), p. 20.

[80] John Securis, *A Detection and Querimonie of the Daily Enormities and Abuses Commited in Physick* (London, 1566), sigs. B1^{r-v}. Securis complained at B3^{r-v}: 'doo you thynke to have in youre Englyshe Bookes, all the perfecte knowledge that is required in Physicke . . . If Englyshe Bookes could make men cunnyng Physitions, then pouchemakers, threshers, ploughmen and cobblers mought be Physitions as well as the best yf they can reade. Then wer it a great foly for us to bestow so much labour and study all our lyfe tyme in scholes and universities to break our braines in readynge so many authours . . . yea and the greatest follye of all were, to procede in any degree in the Universities with our great coste and charges, when syr Johne Lacke Latin, a pedler, a weaver and oftentymes a presumptous woman, shall take uppon them (yea and are permytted) to minister Medicine to all menne, in every place, and all tymes.' See also A. Wear, 'Epistemology and Learned Medicine in Early Modern England' in D. Bates (ed.), *Knowledge and the Scholarly Medical Traditions* (Cambridge University Press, Cambridge, 1995), pp. 151–73, esp. pp. 162–72. Other attacks on English books are in Cotta, *A Short Discoverie*, p. 23; Eleazar Dunkan, *The Copy of a Letter Written by E. D. Doctour of Physicke to a Gentleman, by whom it was published. The former part conteineth rules for the preservation of health, and preventing of all diseases untill extreme olde age. Herein is inserted the authors opinion of tobacco. The latter is a discourse of Emperiks or unlearned Physitians,*

However, such voices were few compared with the many that defended the medical books written in English. Classical medicine had been increasingly translated into English from the Middle Ages, and English vocabulary had grown to be able to express Latin medical terminology.[81] Literacy rose between 1558 and the 1640s especially amongst the urban 'middling' and higher classes, though women would often only be taught to read and the poorest sections of the population remained illiterate. Publishers of vernacular books were responding to the demand of increasingly confident groups such as the gentry, yeomen and merchants who saw the possession of useful knowledge as confirmation of their status. Moreover, vernacular books were seen as ways of reducing what was perceived by translators like the lawyer-physician Thomas Phayre as a sea of public ignorance.[82] The widespread dislike of monopoly in all areas

wherein is plainly prooved that the practise of all those which have not been brought up in the Grammar and University, is alwayes confused, commonly dangerous, and often deadly (London, 1606), pp. 35–6.

[81] Juhani Norri, *Names of Sicknesses in English, 1400–1550: an Exploration of the Lexical Field* (Suomalainen Tiedeakatemia, Helsinki, 1992), and *The Names of Body Parts in English, 1400–1550* (SuomalainenTiedeakatemia, Helsinki, 1998); R. W. McConchie, *Lexicography and Physicke. The Record of Sixteenth-Century Medical Terminology* (Clarendon Press, Oxford, 1997); Linda E. Voigts, 'Multitudes of Middle English Medical Manuscripts, or the Englishing of Science and Medicine' in Margaret R. Schleissner (ed.), *Manuscript Sources of Medieval Medicine* (Garland, New York, 1995), and 'What's the Word? Bilingualism in Late-Medieval England', *Speculum*, 71, 1996, 813–26; V. Nutton, 'The Changing Language of Medicine' in O. Weijers (ed.), *Vocabulary of Teaching and Research Between the Middle Ages and Renaissance* (Brepols, Turnhout, 1995), pp. 184–98. William Eamon, *Science and the Secrets of Nature* (Princeton University Press, Princeton, 1994); Luis Cifuentes, 'Vernacularisation as an Intellectual and Social Bridge. The Catalan Translations of Teodocio's *Chirurgia* and of Arnau de Vilanova's *Regimen Sanitatis* and Laurence M. Eldredge, 'The English Vernacular Afterlife of Benvenutus Grassus Ophthalmologist', *Early Science and Medicine*, 14, 127–48 and 149–63 respectively. In the sixteenth century English writers were still finding it difficult to choose or coin the right English words for classical terms. Sir Thomas Elyot, *The Castel of Helthe* (London, 1541), fol. 57ᵛ, wrote that he had not been able to convey everything that was in the classical writers since 'there be dyvers [various] thinges, whereunto we have not yet found any names in englishe'. He also made up new words, fol. 74ᵛ, as 'cruditie' and 'lassitude' 'whyche although they be wordes made of latyne, havynge none apte englyshe worde therefore, yet by the defynytions and more ample declaration of them, they shall be understande suffycyentely, and from henceforthe used for englyshe'. See also Humfrey Lloyd's comment that he has kept many names of medicines in Latin, 'because that many of them be suche that they cannot be well Englyshed': Petrus Hispanus [Pope John XXI], *The Treasuri of Helth*, trans. Humfrey Lloyd (London, *c*.1550), Introduction. Also, more generally, Robert Recorde, *The Castle of Knowledge* (London, 1556), pp. 4, 89.

[82] See Christopher Brooks, 'Professions, Ideology and the Middling Sort in the Late Sixteenth and Early Seventeenth Centuries' in Jonathan Barry and Christopher Brooks (eds.), *The Middling Sort of People. Culture, Society and Politics in England, 1550–1800* (Macmillan, London, 1994), pp. 113–40, esp. pp. 117–23 on the dissemination of learned knowledge amongst professions and the 'middling sort'. A. Wear, 'The Popularization of Medicine in Early

of life also fuelled the justifications in the prefaces, as did the protestation that the author's aim was the good of the commonwealth, sometimes with the added aside that an English book should be used only if a learned physician was not available. The most famous defence of writing about medicine in English was in *The Castel of Helthe* (*c.*1536) by the layman Sir Thomas Elyot, whose status as a humanist scholar and royal diplomat gave his views added weight. He emphasised that he wrote 'without hope of temporall rewarde, onely for the fervent affectyon whiche I have ever borne toward the publike weale of my countray', and he stressed that his enterprise was nationalistic and demotic, to make medical learning as available as it had been in previous ages:

> But if phisitions be angry, that I have wryten phisike in englyshe, let theym remember, that the grekes wrote in greke, the Romanes in latyne, Avicena . . . in Arabike, whiche were their owne propre and maternal tonges. And if they had bene as moche attacked with envy and covaytise, as some nowe seeme to be, they wolde have devysed somme particular language, with a strange syphre [cypher] or fourme off lettres, wherin they wold have written their science, which no man shoulde have knowen that had not professed and practised phisycke: but those, although they were painimes [pagans] and jewes, in this parte of charitye they farre surmounted us Christianes, that they wolde not have soo neccessary a knowledge as phisicke is, to be hyd frome them whyche would be studiouse about it.[83]

The accusation against the learned physicians was that they would 'have the people ignoraunt', sentiments also echoing Protestant anger at how Catholics kept the people in the dark by refusing to translate the Bible into English.[84] The rewriting of religion in the vernacular was a powerful counter-example to the elitism of medical classical humanism. But both enterprises aimed at improvement, and many medical men who wrote in English, like the physician-scholars, also endeavoured to improve medicine, by educating practitioners and lay people in classical medicine. This was clearly the intention of William Bullein (whose work is discussed in later chapters), whilst learned surgeons like Thomas Gale and William

---

Modern England' in R. Porter (ed.), *The Popularization of Medicine 1650–1850* (Routledge, London, 1992), pp. 17–41.

[83] Elyot, *Castel of Helthe*, Preface sigs. A2^r, A4^{r-v}.

[84] Thomas Phayre, 'A Preface to the Reader' in J. Goeurot, *The Regiment of Life* ([London], 1545); Phayre probably remained Catholic to his death. Nicholas Culpeper, *Culpeper's School of Physick* (London, 1659), Preface, n.p.: 'there are not such slaves to the Doctors, as the poor English are; most of them profess themselves Protestants, but their practices have been like those of the Papists, to hide the grounds of Physick from the vulgar'.

Clowes wrote to raise the standards of their colleagues. (However, later, in the second half of the seventeenth century, as we shall see in chapters 8–10, some English medical books explicitly attacked Galenic learned medicine and its spread through the country.)

Could 'Englyshe Bookes . . . make . . . cunnyng Physitions'? Opinions varied on what was required in the first place. Elyot answered the accusation of the learned physicians that he was unlearned with the retort that he had extensively studied the classical and Arabic works, and that going to university was unnecessary.[85] On the other hand, the poet George Herbert wrote that 'it is easy for any Scholar [referring to clergymen] to attaine to such a measure of Phisick as may be of much use to him both for himself and others'; he did this by reading one medical book (by Fernel), owning a herbal and gaining a knowledge of English rather than imported herbs.[86] Admittedly, clergymen might read a Latin medical compendium, and Fernel was not in English, but the perception that medicine was easily mastered was a common one, and was implicit in many of the English medical texts. Moreover, the charitable lay women, discussed in the next chapter, often relied on English books to 'learn up' medicine. In the end, medicine could be as simple or complicated as one wanted to make it; everyone could be a physician by making remedies, diagnosing illnesses and offering advice on regimen. A variety of English medical texts allowed one to do all of this, and in the process they helped to create a medical culture that was based on the transformation of learned medicine into a popularly accessible medicine, whilst still preserving the impression that there was a learned medicine, a higher level of expertise.

---

[85] Elyot, *Castel of Helthe*, sig. A4^r.
[86] George Herbert, *A Priest to the Temple* (London, 1652), c.xxiii, quoted in Clark, *College of Physicians*, vol. I, pp. 248–9.

CHAPTER 2

Remedies

INTRODUCTION AND SUMMARY

Plant, animal and mineral remedies were central to therapeutics in the sixteenth and seventeenth centuries. They were 'the principall part of Physick': they formed a large part of the published medical literature, and they constituted practically the only type of medical information that lay men and women set down on paper.[1] Their numbers were immense: the whole of the natural world seemed to comprise a vast repository of remedies. Scripture gave credence to the Greek and Arabic use of nature for remedies, for as Ecclesiasticus 38.4 put it, 'The Lord hath created medicines of the earth, and hee that is wise, will not abhorre them'.[2] Plants, especially, seemed to have been God-given to cure or alleviate humankind's ills. A sign of this was that herbals were both botanical (in the post-medieval sense) and medical works: they described plants and also their healing virtues, almost all of them being written by medical practitioners.

Historians have shown how remedies constituted a battleground between differing medical groups, notably Galenists with largely herbal remedies[3] and Paracelsians who advocated chemical medicines.[4] They have also seen remedies as crucial components in the medical marketplace, for they were what apothecaries, quacks and

---

[1] James Primrose, *Popular Errours. Or the Errours of the People in Physick*, trans. Robert Wittie (London, 1651), p. 196.

[2] From the Geneva Bible.

[3] But not exclusively herbal, as mineral remedies were used from the time of Dioscorides.

[4] Allen Debus, *The English Paracelsians* (Oldbourne Press, London, 1965), and *The French Paracelsians* (Cambridge University Press, Cambridge, 1991); Bruce Moran, *The Alchemical World of the German Court: Occult Philosophy and Chemical Medicine in the Circle of Moritz of Hessen 1572–1632* (Steiner, Stuttgart, 1991); Walter Pagel, *Paracelsus: an Introduction to Philosophical Medicine in the Era of the Renaissance* (S. Karger, Basle, 1958); Charles Webster, *The Great Instauration, Science, Medicine and Reform 1626–1660* (Duckworth, London, 1975).

empirics advertised, sold and made their money from,[5] whilst physicians with business links to apothecaries had a financial interest in their patients buying the remedies of their apothecary.[6] However, there are large gaps in our understanding of early modern medicines.

The sheer importance of remedies for different aspects of the history of the medicine of this period has often been ignored. The making and giving of remedies, together with the ability to diagnose illness discussed in chapter 3, were skills that lay people shared with medical practitioners, though the latter claimed greater knowledge and expertise in both. This chapter illustrates the multiform significance of remedies in different contexts and ends by discussing how remedies were understood. It begins by locating remedies in the female culture of medicine, which was a major component of the provision of medical care and treatment available in early modern England. The manufacture of remedies was one of the household skills expected of women, and was learned by well-to-do women from medical books as well as by word-of-mouth. The relationship between women as family and neighbourhood physicians and learned medicine was, however, a disputed one. Popular books on remedies were written for lay as well as medical readerships, but some learned medical writers were hostile to women's knowledge and practice of medicine. Also widespread but with little surviving evidence, because it was oral, was the knowledge of remedies of wise

---

[5] On quacks see R. Porter, *Health for Sale: Quackery in England 1650–1850* (Manchester University Press, Manchester, 1989); on apothecaries see Cecil Wall, H. Charles Cameron and E. Ashworth Underwood, *A History of the Worshipful Society of Apothecaries of London, Volume I, 1617–1815* (Oxford University Press, Oxford, 1963); Juanita G. L. Burnby, *A Study of the English Apothecary from 1660–1760, Medical History*, Supplement 3, 1983.

[6] In 1670 Gideon Harvey wrote that most physicians were tied to particular apothecaries and gave their patients very obscure bills or prescriptions so that they were forced to go to their own apothecary to decipher what appeared a 'secret, which onely they have the key to unlock: whereas in effect it's no other than the commonest of Medicines, disguised under an unusual name, on design to direct you to an Apothecary, between whom and the Physician there is a private compact of going snips, out of the most unreasonable rates of the said Medicines'.: Anon [Gideon Harvey], *The Accomplisht Physician, the Honest Apothecary and Skilful Chyrurgeon* (London, 1670), p. 74. Earlier Walter Cary directed his readers to his apothecary 'Maister Graie apothecarie in Fenchurchstreet', who produced Cary's special purgative potion from his prescription, as 'I have made long triall of his honest and faithfull dealing, also of his excellent skill in his profession': Walter Cary, *A Breefe Treatise, Called Caryes Farewel to Physicke* (London, 1587), p. 3. On physician-pharmacist partnerships in Italy see Richard Palmer, 'Pharmacy in the Republic of Venice in the Sixteenth Century' in A. Wear, R. K. French and I. M. Lonie (eds.), *The Medical Renaissance of the Sixteenth Century* (Cambridge University Press, Cambridge, 1985), pp. 100–17.

women and 'old wives'. Learned medicine constructed an image of this knowledge, that of mistaken ignorance, yet, paradoxically, learned medicine itself incorporated some folk knowledge. Medicines, especially simples or herbs, were part of the common or public culture of medicine. Anyone could pick them from the fields or grow them in gardens or pots, and wise women and herb women were recognised as having special herbal knowledge. However, medical writers appropriated such knowledge as exclusive to themselves. They asserted that the expert medical practitioner knew better how to pick, store and process herbs, and that popular knowledge of herbs, whether local or from the Indies and America, the sources of new medicines, could be discounted.

This chapter then focuses more on the significance of remedies within the literate medical tradition, in order to show how remedies had broader cultural, economic and social implications, as well as being of central importance in the story of medicine. The vast numbers of medicines are considered. In the sixteenth century they increased as northern European herbs were added to those rediscovered from southern Europe and Asia Minor that had been used in classical times. Exotic foreign remedies also came into Europe from other continents. Remedies are thus part of the story of the Renaissance retrieval of ancient medicine, coupled with its confident assertion of present-day knowledge that is also found, for instance, in the history of Renaissance anatomy. They also form part of the commercial justification for exploration and settlement, being seen as precious commodities alongside gold and silver. The study of the debate as to whether local or foreign drugs were best shows how it raised large-scale social issues such as the affordability of expensive exotic remedies by the poor. Also at issue were general notions about the environmental relationships between plants and people and diseases, which reflected strong beliefs about the power of a given environment to shape the characteristics of plants and people. In the background lay the question of whether the Galenic medical system, into which foreign drugs had been incorporated, was justified in its claim to universal applicability across different times and continents.

From considering how remedies sparked off wide cultural and social as well as medical responses, the chapter then focuses on issues of credibility. How was it that, despite there being so many remedies, this was not such a problem as it might appear today (if we forget our own multitude of medicines)? Some of the answer lay in the belief that remedies were part of God's bounty to humankind, and more of God's gifts were still to be discovered. In medical writings confusion was avoided by using indexes to facilitate the retrieval of information about remedies. How were remedies shown to be efficacious, to have powers and effects upon the body and disease? Simples (that is, single remedies made from one ingredient as opposed to compound reme-dies made from many) played a central role in the process. They were the gold standard against which all other kinds of remedies were judged. Simples as God-given incorporated notions of primal purity, yet their curative effectiveness depended, paradoxically, on their potential to harm the body. Both Galenic physicians and Helmontians (the latter are discussed at length in chapters 8 and 9) took simples as their starting point, but in their different ways hoped respectively to 'correct' their dangers or to chemically purify them. Different medical schools, therefore, shared with the lay public the belief that herbs were curative, albeit they might assert that their knowledge of them was best or that they could improve them further. Until the late seventeenth century, when Sydenham voiced some scepticism (see chapter 9), it seems that everyone agreed that remedies worked, though which ones was a matter for debate.

DOMESTIC KNOWLEDGE AND EXPERTISE

The knowledge and use of plant remedies was widespread and not confined to medical practitioners and apothecaries. Literate lay people collected recipes for drugs from books and friends just as they collected recipes for cosmetics and foods. Families such as the Blundells of Crosby kept books in which they and their visitors wrote down medical recipes. Families, friends and neighbours benefited from the exchange of medicines as well as of medical information; as John Donne put it, 'some shall wrap pils, and save a friend's life so'.[7]

Women, as the providers of medical care within the family, were especially concerned with the making of medicines. Indeed, before the increase in the commercial provision of services and products which occurred during the 'commercial revolution' of the early

---

[7] T. Ellison Gibson, *A Cavalier's Note-Book* (London, 1880), pp. 244–6; Margaret Blundell (ed.), *Cavalier Letters of William Blundell to his Friends 1620–1698* (Longmans, London, 1933), pp. 56–61; John Donne, 'Upon Mr. Thomas Coryat's Crudities' in *Complete Poetry and Selected Prose*, ed. John Hayward (Nonesuch, London, 1962), p. 141.

eighteenth century and then in the Industrial Revolution,[8] the household produced many of its own goods and services, including medicines. Women were usually in charge of their production. Gervase Markham, who was a prolific writer of 'how-to' books on fishing, fowling, farming and the care of horses, as well as a middling dramatist, set out in his *English Hus-wife* (first edition 1615) the 'inward and outward Vertues which ought to be in a complete Woman'. They included 'her skill in Physick, Surgery', as well as 'Cookery, Extraction of Oyles, Banquetting stuffe, Ordering of Great Feasts, preserving of all sorts of Wines, conceited Seekrets, Distillations, Perfumes, ordering of Wool, Hemp, Flax, making Cloth and Dying, the knowledge of Dayries, Office of Malting of Oates, their excellent uses in a Family, Of Brewing, Baking and all other things belonging to a Household'.[9] The technical and material conditions of life in principle enabled housewives to act as distillers, brewers, cloth-makers, physicians and apothecaries, even though such activities were also carried out commercially. The manufacturing processes and allied skills were not beyond the capacity of many households, at least if they were well-to-do.

Medical knowledge in literate households seems to have been transmitted by word of mouth, by manuscript collections of remedies, by books, and sometimes by all three. Elizabeth Walker (1623–1690), the daughter of a London pharmacist and the pious wife of a clergyman, fulfilled the teaching role expected of the mistress of the house by instructing 'her Maids in Cookery, Brewing, Baking, Dairy, ordering Linen . . . and the like'. Her husband recorded that she also taught her daughters 'Whatever might fit them for all Family-Imployments, in Pastry and Seasoning . . . causing them to transcribe her best Receipts for things which were curious, but especially for Medicines, with Directions how to use them, that if God had spared their Lives, they might have been as usefull in their Generation, as God vouchsafed her the Honour to be

---

[8] On the increase in consumerism and commercialism in the eighteenth century see G. Holmes, *Augustan England: Professions, State and Society 1680–1730* (Allen & Unwin, London, 1982); N. McKendrick, J. Brewer and H. J. Plumb, *The Birth of a Consumer Society: the Commercialization of Eighteenth-Century England* (Europa Publications, London, 1982); John Brewer and Roy Porter (eds.), *Consumption and the World of Goods* (Routledge, London, 1992). On women and medicine see Introduction, n. 2.

[9] From the expanded title page of Gervase Markham's 1653 edition of *The English House-Wife* (London, 1653).

in hers'.[10] Elizabeth Walker's combination of oral and literary methods of teaching mirrored the way she herself had learned medicine and surgery. Her brother-in-law, a member of the London College of Physicians, told her what methods to use for the common diseases and 'wrote her many Receipts'. Her sources of information were of a high level, and 'she was very inquisitive of other Doctors, and had many English Books, *Riverius, Culpepper, Bonettus* etc, which she read'.[11] Mrs Walker clearly liked to learn through oral and literary means, but it is significant that medical receipts or recipes were written down both by her daughters and her brother-in-law. The large numbers of manuscript collections of medical recipes indicate a need to fix them in the certainty of writing rather than trusting to a fallible memory. Yet there is often also a sense of the personal associated with medical receipts, which makes it appear as if word-of-mouth knowledge underlies the writing. Recipes were frequently seen as originating or belonging to a particular person. Mrs Walker's daughters got 'her best Receipts', and William Blundell's servant, Walter Thelwall, recorded how one remedy was passed along from different people, each one sharing ownership and attesting to its efficacy:

The elder Lady Bradshaigh sent my master a bottle containing as we guess, about one ounce of balsam, which in her letter she calls (if we read it alright) balsam of sulphur. Her Ladyship then saith that it is an approved cure for a cough; that she had it from Sir Peter Brooks that it had cured him of a most violent cough, and that the Lady Ossory had sent it to him.[12]

The ascription of ownership in a medical recipe was made in the context of both oral and literary medical cultures. Lady Ranelagh (1614–91), the sister of Robert Boyle who was one of the leading English chemists and natural philosophers of the period, was probably the compiler of a manuscript collection of household recipes written in the late seventeenth century. As well as describing how 'to make Sassages', 'almond butter', 'Lady Essex ['s] a Cream Cheese', the collection also gave prescriptions for serious illnesses. Some are from lay people and presumably given by word of mouth, such as 'Mrs. Rodgers. A Drink for the Ricket's which never yet failed', Mrs Seager's recipes for the stone as well as her instructions on how to make vinegar and orange wine, and Mrs Billingsby's

---

[10] A. W. [Anthony Walker], *The Holy Life of Mrs Elizabeth Walker* (London, 1690), pp. 67, 72.
[11] Ibid., p. 178.
[12] Gibson, *A Cavalier's Note-Book*, p. 244.

'most Excellent Receipt for a Cancer'. Others were probably taken from books such as 'Quercetans [Quercetanus or Du Chesne, a French Paracelsian] Decoction for the jaundice' which came via 'Sir' Richard Wiseman.[13] If one did not have the network of informants and sources, then the printing press could provide a ready-made alternative personalised source, often from an ostensibly noble or royal 'receipt book'.[14]

Medical recipes were thus closely associated with household skills. The link between cooking food and making medicines placed medicine squarely in the realm of the kitchen and women's work (for further connections between medicine and cooking see chapter 4). The 'good housewife' was expected to make provision for her family's health, and an information network consisting of her mother, relatives, neighbours, medical practitioners and books could often be drawn upon.[15] In a literate household, information about medical recipes was both oral and written, and the oral would often be written down as it was communicated. But, as we saw, it often retained a sense of being linked to a particular person, conveying both a sense of familiarity and of authority. Medical recipes were, like recipes for particular dishes, incorporated into the domestic world, so a remedy with a doctor's name attached to it became part of the household economy. The medicine of the learned medical writers could in this way be appropriated and transformed into, if not popular medicine, at least middling lay medicine. Physicians, however, sometimes viewed domestic medicine as being in opposition to their own. John Cotta, a Northampton physician who attacked all types of practitioners who were not learned university-educated physicians, wrote that some women disparaged drugs that came from the 'Apothecaries shops, or from Physitions hands and directions', because they preferred 'their owne private ointments, plaisters, cearecloathes, drinkes, potions, glysters, and diets, because by time and custome they are become familiarly knowne unto them, and now are of their owne domesticall preparation, and therefore

---

[13] Collection of 712 Medical Receipts with some Cooking Recipes, Wellcome MS 1340, Boyle Family, nos. 223, 225, 240, 85, 625, 620, 622, 626, 101.

[14] W. M., *The Queens Closet Opened. Incomparable Secrets in Physick, Chirurgery, Preserving, Candying, and Cookery; As they were presented to the Queen. By the most Experienced Persons of our Times, many whereof were honoured with her owne practice, when she pleased to descend to these more private Recreations. Never before published. Transcribed from the true Copies* . . . (London, 1655).

[15] See, for instance, John Partridge, *The Treasure of Hidden Secrets, commonly called the Good-huswives Closet of provision for the health of her Houshold* (London, 1627).

are by their knowledge, acquaintance, and avouching of them, growne into some credite and reputation with them'.[16] As with cooking, women combined knowledge and practice in the making of remedies. Most relatively well-to-do women would have grown herbs, either in a patch of their garden, the herb garden, or in pots. John Parkinson, the herbalist-apothecary to James I and Charles I and author of two major botanical texts, expected that every woman grew rosemary: 'This common Rosemary is so well knowne through all our Land, being in every womans garden . . . every one can describe it'.[17] They might then dry the herbs, boil them into syrups or distill them.

The recommended medical and surgical equipment for a household was extensive and expensive. A 'Catalogue of such instruments as are requisite in a private house, for those that are desirous to compound [make] medicines themselves' listed:

First a great Morter of marble, and another of brasse
A rowler to rowle lozenges
Spatulaes of all sizes
Copper pannes to make Decoctions
An iron ladle to prepare lead
A grinding stone and mallet
Pulping sieves
Haire sieve covered
Hippocras bags
Little cotton blankets for straining
Scales and weights
Presses
Raspes to raspe hartes horne, quinces etc
A square wooden frame with nailes at each corner to hold the
    strainers
An incision knife
A levatory
Probes
Siringes to make injections
Forceps to drawe teeth
A lancet and cupping-glasses

---

[16] John Cotta, *A Short Discoverie of the Unobserved Dangers of Severall Sorts of Ignorant and Unconsiderate Practisers of Physicke in England* (London, 1612), p. 29.

[17] John Parkinson, *Paradisi in Sole Paradisus Terrestris Or A Garden of All Sorts of Pleasant Flowers* (London, 1629), p. 425.

Gally pots and boxes of all sorts to keep syrups, oiles etc
Glasses for cordiall powers
Cauteries to make issues
Pipes with fenestrells, and needles fit for sutures
Ligatures, bandes, swathes, of woolens and linnen
Powder to stay bloud
Pledgets, compresses, boulters
A bathing chaire
A limbecke and small still with receivers[18]

The last item involved expensive equipment but Markham urged the housewife to 'furnish herself of verie good stils, for the distillation of all kindes of Waters . . . and in them shee shall distill all sorts of waters meete for the health of her Houshold'.[19] Large-scale production of medicines was sometimes carried out in the context of the charitable care of the neighbouring sick poor. The formidable and devout Lady Grace Mildmay (1552–1620) was taught medicine by her governess-cousin, 'Mistress Hamblyn', who had 'good knowledge in phisic and surgery', and who 'set me to read in Dr. Turner's Herball and Bartholomew Vigoe' (Johannes de Vigo's book of surgery translated by Bartholomew Traheron).[20] Her intense interest in medicine and her deep religious sensibility were given combined expression through her charitable treatment of the sick. The inventory of her still-room reveals it to be extensive and well equipped with a great number of bottles and medicinal ingredients. Lady Mildmay produced drugs in large quantities, for instance, aqua vitae and metheglin were made in batches of ten gallons at a time, and to make oil of cinnamon she employed five pounds of cinnamon and five gallons of wine. As Linda Pollock, her biographer, puts it, her still-room appears 'like an apothecary's shop'.[21] The cost of 'a most precious balm' composed of twenty-four different kinds of roots, seventy-three herbs, fourteen seeds, twelve flowers, ten spices, twenty-five gums, six purgatives and five cordials came to ten guineas. This represented an appreciable slice of Lady Mildmay's total annual budget of 130 pounds for running her household.[22]

---

[18] Thomas Brugis, *The Marrow of Physicke* (London, 1640), pp. 86–7.
[19] Gervase Markham, *The English Hus-wife* (London, 1615), p. 79.
[20] Autobiography of Lady Grace Mildmay in Linda Pollock, *With Faith and Physic. The Life of a Tudor Gentlewoman Lady Grace Mildmay 1552–1620* (Collins & Brown, London, 1993), p. 26.
[21] Ibid., p. 102; on the large-scale production of drugs see pp. 102–4.
[22] Ibid., pp. 103, 128–9.

Only the wealthy could manufacture such costly drugs and in such large quantities, but a charitable practice like Lady Mildmay's may not have been completely exceptional in terms of skill and relative expenditure. Further down the social scale Elizabeth Walker went beyond 'what strictly concerned her Family': 'in Physick, Chirurgery, to assist the Neighbours of the Parish, and some Miles about, which she performed Skillfully, Readily, and with great success, as they acknowledge by their grief for her loss, and the Furniture of her Closet still will witness, which she left furnished better than many [apothecaries'] Country Shops'.[23] She possessed an alembic and 'good store of Vomits, Purges, Sudorifics, Cordials, Pectorals, almost all kinds of Syrups, strong and simple distilled Waters, several Quarts of which she left (yea Gallons of them she used most) . . . These cost Money, but more Pains and Labour to prepare them, and as much variety for Chyrurgery, Ointments, Oils, Salves, Searclothes, etc.'.[24]

Clearly, a lay person could manufacture drugs as well as an apothecary. But ingredients were also bought at apothecaries' shops as well as being grown in gardens or picked from the wild. And the apothecaries also sold ready-prepared remedies. The expectation of medical writers was that a household was able to take up any or all of the available options. Knowledge of medicines was, therefore, both a medical and household matter, which meant that medicine became associated with female household skills, and women, the kitchen and the garden were linked to medicine.

THE KNOWLEDGE OF 'OLD WIVES'

Country housewives and especially wise-women and herb women were, according to some written reports, especially expert in the use of locally-grown medicinal herbs. In terms of medical and lay literate culture the figure of the woman wise in herb lore, gained either from experience or as part of God's gift of healing, was used either to link learned elite medicine to the level of ordinary, everyday humble localised and yet fundamental knowledge or to contrast, favourably or unfavourably, with learned medicine. Such little knowledge of the oral herbal tradition as we have largely comes from medical writers. They created particular constructions of what it was like, but this

---

[23] A. W., *Mrs Elizabeth Walker*, pp. 67, 68. [24] Ibid., pp. 89,178.

does not mean it did not exist, or that it is a fiction. Clearly writers such as William Bullein, a Galenic physician who practised in Durham and Northampton, and wrote extensively on many aspects of medicine both didactically and satirically, would not have referred to herbal lore if their readers were ignorant of it. That it did exist should not be surprising; as David Allen has observed, every society has employed the products of nature as remedies, and the problem is that an oral tradition leaves few traces.[25] What is significant from the point of view of this book is that the linkage, however tenuous, between the literate and the oral traditions of herbal remedies gives the former a kind of validation which is different from its association with the world of learning, for it can be seen as having its roots in the countryside, the fount of health and the home of plants, the distant relation of paradisiacal Eden, the place which was untouched by illness. The countryside was where health resided, for country people had the healthiest lifestyles; thus wrote writers on regimen (see chapter 4). It was also where God had placed health-restoring plants, and it formed a link between both the popular and the elite learned medical cultures, as both employed its products. Moreover, learned medicine could be receptive to country knowledge. Galen incorporated country people's experience into his writings and lay people moved easily between the medicine provided by a poor or old woman, by empirics and by learned medicine.

The countryside was viewed as a place either of wisdom or of ignorance. Timothie Bright, who was a moderate Paracelsian and physician to St Bartholomew's hospital in London before becoming a clergyman, was concerned to praise local remedies over foreign ones, and drew a positive picture of familiar gardens, fields and orchards on one's doorstep filled with medicinal plants. 'For what can be more pleasant unto thee, then of the inioying of medicines for cure of thine infirmities out of thy native soyle, and countrie, thy Fielde, thy Orchard, thy Garden?'[26] And yet, while the countryside provided a rich store of remedies, the 'old women' who lived in it and might be thought to have most experience of it were sometimes

---

[25] D. E. Allen, 'Herbs for Herbivores: the Prehistory of Veterinary Medicine' in A. R. Mitchell (ed.), *The Advancement of Veterinary Science*, vol. III, *The History of the Healing Professions* (C.A.B, Wallingford, Oxford, 1993), pp. 31–43. I am grateful to Dr Allen for allowing me to read in manuscript his paper on the oral herbal tradition.

[26] Timothie Bright, *A Treatise: Wherein is Declared the Sufficiencie of English Medicines, for Cure of all Diseases, Cured with Medicines* (London, 1580), p. 7.

perceived as ignorant by medical writers. Although lay people may well have agreed with Burton when he wrote that 'Many an old wife or country woman doth often more good with a few known and common garden herbs than our bombast Physicians with all their prodigious, sumptuous, far-fetched, rare, conjectural medicines',[27] the skills and knowledge of 'old wives' were often denigrated, not only by Galenists but also by Paracelsus, who, when he castigated Greek and Arabic humoral medicine and asserted that a proper German medicine could only be based on German experience, did not always conclude from this that the symbols of popular knowledge, old women, were possessed of such experience. Of modern herbals he wrote:

These patch this and that together but have no knowledge of whether it is true or fictitious . . . If one asks, 'Who told you this?' it turns out to be nuns and old women . . . it is not idle babble [*Schwerzwerk*], not the work of a monk, nor the gossip of old women on which the writers of herbals would place their foundations. But they build their church on sand, and for that reason the illness is stronger than they and their medicines.[28]

The Galenic and Paracelsian branches of the literate medical tradition agreed, as they often did when attacking what they took to be unlearned or unskilled competitors. Although 'herb women' and other country people might be closest to plants, medical writers and practitioners nevertheless often claimed that they knew better. William Bullein, for instance, created an image of the ignorance of folk knowledge, in contrast to the authoritative knowledge of the literary tradition. Of the dandelion, he wrote, 'though this herbe bee commonly knowen, and counted of many as a vile weede, yet it is reported of Dioscorides, to be an excellent herbe', good against hot,

---

[27] Robert Burton, *The Anatomy of Melancholy*, 1st edn (1621), ed. Floyd Dell and P. Jourdan-Smith (Tudor, New York, 1948), p. 563.

[28] Bruce T. Moran (translation and introduction), 'The *Herbarius* of Paracelsus', *Pharmacy in History*, 35, 1993, p. 117. Galenists condemned all types of female practitioners; see, for instance, Cotta, *A Short Discoverie*, who condemned both women and witches practising medicine, pp. 24–34, 49–71; James Hart, *The Arraignment of Urines* (London, 1623), a translation of Pieter van Foreest's *De Incerto ac Fallaci, Urinarum Judicio quo Uromantes, ad Pernicium Multorum Aegrotantium Utuntur* (Leiden, 1589), constantly joins 'women-physicians' with empirics and mountebanks, as on pp. 45–56. Primrose, *Popular Errours*, saw women as especially prone to error. But Paracelsus elsewhere wrote: 'The physician does not learn everything he must know and master at high colleges alone; from time to time he must consult old women, gypsies, magicians, wayfarers, and all manner of peasant folk . . . and learn from them; for these have more knowledge about such things than all the high colleges': Paracelsus, *Selected Writings*, ed. Jolande Jacobi, Bollingen Series 28 (Princeton University Press, Princeton, 1973), p. 57.

smoking vapours in the head, heat in the stomach, and burning agues or 'venerous and fleshely heate'.[29] Moreover, despite a herb's widespread use its real virtues might lie hidden from the common people. Marcellus, the countryman, says in Bullein's dialogue on simples: 'I do know Sage by name, because it doth grow in my garden and is used in my kitchin, but Christ doth know, the vertu thereof is hidden from me',[30] while Hillarius, the learned gardener or herbalist, replies with a display of his classical and botanical knowledge before enumerating the powers of sage:

This noble herbe called *Elesihacon, Salvia,* or Sage, as it shoulde appeare by *Theophrastus* [Greek botanist; Bullein gave the location of the passage in the margin] there bee twoo kindes of Sage, the one of the garden whiche is roughe, longe and broade leaves, whiche sayth *Mathiolus* [major sixteenth-century Italian botanist], I suppose to be the female herbe, the other Sage which is shorter, narower, with twoo small eares in the beginnyng of their leaves, whiche the sayd *Theophrastus* cal Sphacelo, whom *Mathiolus* clepeth [calls] the male herbe, and of this groweth greate plenty in Italy, in the toppes of Mountaines, in the noble countries both of *Apulie* and *Calabrie,* so dooe there almoste in everye Garden in Englande. This herbe is hot and drie saieth *Aetius* [sixth-century Greek medical writer], so saieth Galen . . .[31]

The recitation of classical and modern learned knowledge of names and of descriptive botany was part of the packaging that expressed the superior knowledge of the literate tradition. These precise botanical details also contrasted with the amorphous and imprecise popular knowledge of herbs as it was often presented by medical writers. Yet, the literate medical tradition often incorporated and gave recognition to the same folk knowledge that it depicted as ignorant or inaccurate.

The literate tradition was not free from problems of its own. A herb could be difficult to identify in the ancient sources, especially if it came from northern Europe, which was largely *terra incognita* to Dioscorides and other classical writers on remedies. Terminology also often created confusion. Greek, Latin and the various early modern European languages had different words for the same herb and it was not always certain that one and the same herb was being referred to in the lists of synonyms that herbalists compiled for a

29 William Bullein, 'The Boke of Simples' in *Bulleins Bulwarke of Defence Againste all Sicknes, Sornes and Woundes* (London, 1562), fol. 10ᵛ.
30 Ibid., fol. 5ʳ.   31 Ibid., fol. 5ᵛ.

herb. One of the aims of herbals was to provide accurate identification of herbs in the field, and the elimination of linguistic confusion was designed to increase herbal expertise amongst the learned and those like apothecaries who served the learned tradition in medicine, but the attempt to provide synonyms in different languages for herbs also helped to incorporate the oral into the literate tradition. For instance, the second edition (1633) of *The Herball or Generall Historie of Plantes* by the botanist-surgeon John Gerard, which was enlarged by Thomas Johnson, identified the dandelion as close to succory or endive, as having different forms and as being difficult to locate in ancient sources.[32] Into this learned botanical description of the problems of identifying the dandelion were inserted its different names. They ranged across nations and language registers. The 'proper' and the slang or popular names were listed, as were the apothecary and botanical names. The learned writers of herbals assumed that different types of readers would use their books, including those who would have been familiar with folk knowledge. To this extent the learned herbals recognised and incorporated into themselves popular terminology, but they also clearly labelled it as distinct and separate from classical and 'proper' modern nomenclature:

Divers [several] of the later Physitions do also call it Dens Leonis, or Dandelion: it is called in high Dutch, *Kolkraut*: in low-Dutch, *Papencruit*: in French, *Pissenlit ou couronne de prestre*, or *Dent de lyon*: in English, Dandelion and of divers Pisseabed. The first is also called of some, and in [apothecaries'] shops *Taraxacon, Caput monachi, Rostrum porcinum* and *Urinaria*. The other is *Dens Leonis Monspeliensium* of *Lobell*, and *Cichoreum Constantinopolitanum* of *Mathiolus*.[33]

Despite Bullein's comment that the dandelion was popularly credited with no powers, the dandelion's ability to provoke urine was commonly known, as 'pisseabed' and 'pissenlit' indicate, and in the markets of Normandy 'pissenlit' is still sold today.[34] The herbals thus

---

[32] 'These plants belong to the Succory which *Theophrastus* and *Pliny* call *Aphaca*, or *Aphace Leonardus*. Fuchsius thinketh that Dandelion is *Hedynois Plinii*, of which he writeth in his 20 booke, and eighth chapter, affirming it to be a wilde kinde of broad leafed Succorie, and that Dandelion is *Taraxacon*; but *Taraxacon*, as Avicen teacheth in his 692 chapter, is garden Endive . . .' John Gerard, *The Herball or Generall Historie of Plantes*, enlarged by Thomas Johnson (London, 1633), p. 291.

[33] Ibid., p. 291.

[34] Personal observation, spring 1997 at Pont Audamer, where farmers' wives were selling it on market day. The word is now part of standard French, but still carries its folk connotations.

recognised folk knowledge and brought it into the literary tradition. The apothecary name of 'urinaria' also indicates a common perception of the power of the dandelion that unites folk and literate medicine.

Given the need felt by Bullein and other learned physicians to educate English practitioners and the public in learned medicine, as well as their desire to achieve greater authority and a medical monopoly in practice, it is not surprising that popular herbal medicine was often presented as ignorant and in need of enlightenment by learned medicine. What is interesting is that, at times, popular knowledge is shown to be correct or partially so, and that rather than a stark contrast between ignorance and knowledge there is a sense that the learned tradition was open to the popular tradition. Although he still wants 'instruccion' about the medical properties of beans and peas, Marcellus clearly feels that he has in his ownership the basis of many medicines: 'I am a rurall man of the countrie: and love Pease and Beanes, and as I heare tell, many good medicenes bee made of theim, to helpe in the tyme of sicknesse. I have good plentie of them: more than any other Poticarie [apothecary] stuffe'.[35] Oral knowledge, 'I heare tell', provides the initial spur for the request for further information from learned medicine, but there is a sense here that both popular knowledge and commonly available commodities are seen by Marcellus as constituting worthwhile knowledge and material in their own right.

Although the literate medical tradition sometimes gave space to popular knowledge and often linked itself with it, it usually presented itself as superior and more knowledgeable. Books of popular or vulgar errors were published by such diverse medical writers as Laurent Joubert in France and the Galenist James Primrose in England with the intention of correcting them (they were, in fact, more often than not concerned with learned errors). Particular popular ideas such as the common belief that the mandrake root was shaped in the figure of a man were held up to ridicule as superstitious 'old wives' tales', as was the gullibility of those who bought counterfeit mandrake root made in human shape.[36] Even a 'popular'

---

[35] Gerard, *The Herball*, fol. 29[r].

[36] Bullein, 'Boke of Simples', fols. 43[v] – 44[r]; William Turner, *The Seconde Parte of William Turners Herball*, p. 46[r] wrote: 'The rootes whiche are conterfited and made like litle puppettes and mammettes, which come to be sold in England in boxes, with heir and such forme as a man hath, are nothyng else but folishe feined [feigned] trifles, and not naturall.

writer like Nicholas Culpeper (d. 1654), who supported the poor against the medical establishment and who, unlike Bullein, was strongly influenced by Paracelsian and chemical medicine (see further, chapter 8), shared in the superior attitude of the learned tradition, and like it distinguished between the country person's experience of herbs and the physician's knowledge of their properties.[37]

Sometimes, the need to educate practitioners and public alike in the 'best' medicine, which was an aim of the sixteenth-century Galenic writers, meant that the oral tradition was all but ignored. For instance, William Turner, Dean of Wells Cathedral, who after studying medicine and botany on the continent set about modernising English medical botany, believed in an occupational and intellectual hierarchy of physicians, apothecaries and lay people. He assumed that apothecaries would teach 'the olde wyves that gather herbes', but that the former being ignorant of Latin would not have the knowledge that was available to the physicians; hence the need

For they are so trymmed of crafty theves to mocke the poore people with all, and to rob them of both of theyr wit and theyr money'. Gerard, *Herball*, p. 351, wrote of 'dreames and old wives tales'. However, the Company of Barber-Surgeons in 1627 gave five shillings 'to a poore souldier that showed a Mandrake to this Courte': A. T. Young, *The Annals of the Barber-Surgeons of London* (Blades, East & Blades, London, 1890), p. 397. Jean de Renou (Renodaeus), *A Medicinal Dispensatory, Containing the Whole Body of Physick: Discovering the Natures, Properties, and Vertues of Vegetables, Minerals, and Animals: The Manner of Compounding Medicaments* . . ., trans. Richard Tomlinson (London, 1657), p. 344, wrote that the old wives' tales may have originated from classical authors, thus exemplifying the difficulty of distinguishing between popular and learned knowledge.

[37] In general, Culpeper was critical of popular knowledge of medicines. In *The English Physician* (London, 1652), 'To the Reader' he wrote that knowledge of why herbs worked had been lost from the past and 'some footsteps of which and but a few onely, are now in use with us to this day'. For instance, he warned, 'Of wild Cucumer Roots or Cowcumber as the vulgar call them; they purge flegm, and that with such violence, that I would advise the Country man that knows not how to correct them, to let them alone': Nicholas Culpeper, *Pharmacopaeia Londinensis: or the London Dispensatory* (London, 1653), p. 5. The references to the popular name 'cowcumber' in contrast to its proper name, and to 'the vulgar' with its connotations of mass ignorance, or at the least of imprecise knowledge, prepared the ground for the advice to the country man who knew something of the powers of cucumber roots but not enough of medicine to bring into play the complete, sophisticated, treatment which countered the side-effects of the roots. Medical writers, however radical, were concerned to write with authority and despite their critiques of medical orthodoxy they rarely equated their medicine with folk medicine. Even for Paracelsus and his followers the personal experience of the physician, especially if he was gifted by God in the ability to heal, was more important than the knowledge of the common people, though that knowledge could be sifted to provide valuable medical insights which in the right hands could be put to good use; see Pagel, *Paracelsus*, pp. 56–7 for Paracelsus' use of the Book of Nature theme, and the need for the physician to walk in that book. On Paracelsus' belief that he was gifted by God to heal see Paracelsus, *Selected Writings*, ed. Jacobi, pp. 5, 55–6, 93–5.

for his English herbal. Despite Turner relying on local knowledge when compiling his herbals, there was no sense of the 'olde wyves' informing the apothecaries and physicians. Instead, Turner envisaged only a top-down dissemination of information, which had hitherto been faulty, because the physicians did not share their knowledge. They:

committ not their knowledge of herbes unto the potecaries . . . as the potecaries do to the olde wyves, that gather herbes, and to the grocers . . . Then when as if the potecari for lack of knowledge of the Latin tong, is ignorant in herbes and putteth ether many a good man by ignorance in ieopardy of his life, or marreth good medicines to the great dishonestie both of the Phisician and of Goddes worthy creatures, the herbes and the medicines; whereas by havyng an herball in English all these evelles myght be avoyded.[38]

A century later the herbalist William Coles, who was part of the rising tide of scepticism enveloping the old learning, saw error on all sides of the medical hierarchy. He condemned the ignorance of physicians with regard to herbs and he wrote that they relied upon the apothecaries:

who for the most part are as ignorant as themselves, and rely commonly upon the words of the silly Hearb-women, who many times bring them *Quid* for *Quo*, then which nothing can be more sad. So that by reason of this their ignorance in Simples, their Medicines oft-times sort not their wished, but sometimes contrary effects to the great prejudice of their Patients.[39]

The creation of botanic and physic gardens in the universities and cities of continental Europe in the sixteenth century and in England in the seventeenth[40] enabled physicians and apothecaries to gain practical experience of plants, as did also the field trips which were organised in many places for medical students and apprentice-apothecaries.[41] The London Society of Apothecaries required their apprentices to go 'asimpling' in the fields, and from the early seventeenth century appointed 'simpling days' and organised herbarising expeditions.[42] The herbals, the *hortus siccus* or dry garden

---

[38] William Turner, *A New Herball* (Part 1) (London, 1551), Prologue, sig. A3ᵛ.
[39] William Coles, *The Art of Simpling* (London, 1656), p. 4.
[40] Pisa and Padua, 1544–5; Bologna, 1568; Leiden, 1587; Basle, 1588; Montpellier, 1597; Oxford, 1621; Paris, Jardin du Roi, 1626; Chelsea Physick Garden, 1673.
[41] Karen Reeds, 'Renaissance Humanism and Botany', *Annals of Science*, 33, 1979, 519–42; John Prest, *The Garden of Eden. The Botanic Garden and the Re-Creation of Paradise* (Yale University Press, New Haven, 1981), p. 92.
[42] Wall et al., *The Worshipful Society of Apothecaries Volume I, 1617–1815*, pp. 78, 88–9.

with its specimen stuck on the pages of books (the modern herbarium), botanical gardens and education in the fields all served to recreate herbal knowledge in a learned framework. Just as the wise women and herb women possessed experience of plants so now would the physician and the apothecary, but it would be of a superior kind – more accurate and knowledgeable in the secret virtues of plants. And one of the aims of the enterprise of educating medical men in plants was to assert their pre-eminence over oral, popular knowledge and the unlearned. As Gideon Harvey, a physician who enjoyed hitting out in all directions at medical targets but who was ultimately concerned to retain the traditional medical hierarchy, put it in 1670, the medical student should, whilst at Oxford, 'enter himself Scholar to the Gardener of the Physick Garden, to be acquainted with the foetures [features] of Plants; but particularly with those, that are familiarily prescribed by Practitioners, to praevent being out-witted by the Herb-women in the Markets'.[43]

Some of the English Helmontian physicians, the followers of the Flemish physician van Helmont who developed a medical system based on chemical principles and was strongly against Galenic medicine, did give a degree of credit to the 'accidental experiments of old wives, and good folks, who have found or known much good done by this or that Herb or Simple'. George Starkey, a New England Harvard-educated puritan who came to England in 1650 and was among the first generation of English Helmontians, contrasted such knowledge with the Galenic physicians who 'castrated' the virtue of a herb by including it in compounds. Starkey also pointed out that, in reality, the Galenic physician's receipts were based on experiment rather than on medical theory, but as an interest in the experience and knowledge of simples 'exposeth oft a Doctor to scorn', it was left to 'some well-meaning women' to cure 'a deserted Patient, to the Doctors disgrace'.[44] Starkey's praise of the knowledge of 'old wives' was, however, limited, for their knowledge was accidental, they were simple 'silly' women'.[45] And, when he

[43] Anon. [Gideon Harvey], *The Accomplisht Physician*, p. 18.
[44] George Starkey, *Nature's Explication and Helmont's Vindication* (London, 1657), pp. 30, 31. Starkey was also the writer of alchemical works that were published under the name of 'Eirenaeus Philalethes'. The standard work on Starkey is William R. Newman, *Gehennical Fire. The Lives of George Starkey, an American Alchemist in the Scientific Revolution* (Harvard University Press, Cambridge, Mass., 1994). This important book was drawn to my attention by Professor Nancy Siraisi when the present volume was in press.
[45] Ibid., p. 30.

came to discuss how women actually gathered herbs, Starkey was very negative about their capabilities: 'As for Simples, are they not collected by women, where they can finde them, without distinction of time when, and season in which they are gathered?' and he continued with a long list of mistaken practices such as cutting herbs in rain or in moist air.[46] Clearly, Starkey was ambivalent about the knowledge of 'old wives': it could be useful but also naïve, and 'old wives' could often be mistaken.

It was the Baconian interest in all types of experience and knowledge that in the seventeenth century gave a degree of importance to popular knowledge of remedies. William Coles, despite his disparaging comments about 'silly Hearb-women', had read Francis Bacon's *Natural History* and admitted that he had been influenced by it, and perhaps it was because he had done so that he gathered information about remedies not only from reading books and talking with scholars but also 'sometimes with Countrey people'.[47] Coles gave some credence to popular knowledge and he collected it, almost as a nineteenth-century folklorist. He recounted popular beliefs in a chapter entitled 'Other traditions concerning Plants', which included such items as: 'if a Footman take *Mugwort* and put [it] into his shoos in the Morning, he may goe forty Miles before Noon and not be weary' and 'the Seeds of Docks tyed to the left arme of a Woman, doe helpe Barrennesse'.[48] Marchamont Nedham, a Helmontian physician who tried to get Robert Boyle to support Helmontian medicine, picked up the point made by Boyle, that the knowledge of 'Midwives, Barbers, Old Women, Empericks, and other illiterate Persons' could provide medicine with additional information about the powers of medicines and how to use them, because such people tried out remedies under a very large variety of circumstances.[49] Such factual knowledge gleaned from informal experiments was of interest to the 'new science' that Boyle and others were creating under the umbrella of a Baconian ideology.

---

[46] Ibid., pp. 62–3.

[47] Coles, *The Art of Simpling*, pp. 75, 118 (repaginated), sig. A3ʳ.

[48] Ibid., pp. 68, 71; some of Coles' information of 'other traditions' came from books, and it is not clear which items were communicated orally to him.

[49] M[archamont] [N]edham, *Medela Medicinae. A plea for the free profession, and a renovation of the art of physick, out of the noblest and most authentick writers* (London, 1665), pp. 475–6, citing Boyle's *Some Considerations Touching the Usefulness of Experimental Philosophy* (London, 1663), p. 220. Boyle also believed that the experimental knowledge of 'the Indians and other barbarous Nations' as well as the poor and illiterate of Europe could be useful to medicine.

Helmontians also had a similar interest in such knowledge. But the 'old wyves' were not given credit for possessing practical skills and knowledge which were more than accidental.

PICKING HERBS — TOP-DOWN KNOWLEDGE

The picking of plants was viewed as the first stage in the making, or the manufacture, of remedies. As such it was placed within the area of expertise of the apothecary and of his ostensible supervisor, the learned physician. The efficacy and goodness of the herbs that were used in remedies were a constant source of concern; not only might they be counterfeited (see below) but their powers depended especially on when and how they were gathered. Jean de Renou, whose *Institutionum Pharmaceuticarum* (1608) was translated in 1657 for apothecaries, made it clear that differentiation or 'splitting', so typical of learned medical knowledge, applied also to the picking of herbs. Roots, stalks, leaves, flowers, fruits, seeds and juices were 'effectual and wholesome' at different times.[50] The times of gathering different plants and their parts was knowledge, it can be argued, that needed to be appropriated away from folk or popular knowledge in order to put the final product, a medicine, firmly within the ambit of literate medicine, as a commodity produced by one of its occupational groups. This process of differentiation from popular medicine was made all the more necessary because many of the herbs involved were within the public domain, routinely used by the general public, and knowledge about them was spread by word of mouth.

Timothie Bright's attitude to the picking of foreign herbs by foreigners lends support to this argument. Despite believing that local herbs were best for local diseases, Bright did not give foreign local knowledge of herbs any credit. Locally based knowledge of foreign drugs was absent from his account. Rather, as part of his

---

[50] De Renou, *Medicinal Dispensatory*, p. 40. And within a category such as that of 'roots' there were different optimum times. Some plants could be picked for their roots: 'at any time, to wit, such as are always vegetive and juicy, although the stalks be dry, as the roots of Bugloss, Sorrel, Licorish, Saint *Christophers* herb, Smallage, Butchers broom, Cyperus . . . Others as soon as their leaves are fallen, at which time the virtue of the Plant goes into the root . . . as *Enula campana, Angelica*, Peony, Briony, Bugloss. Others are to be pulled up and gathered ere the virtue of the Plant be diffused into branches, leaves, flowers and seed, as Polypody, Flower-de-luce, Saint *Maries* seal, Gentian, Ragwort. And some are best gathered in Spring and Autumn, as the roots of Mallows and Lillies, Eringes, Galalgal, Sourdock, Radish, and many more which have store of natural juice in them': ibid., p. 41.

polemic against foreign drugs, it is the European merchants who are presented as unlearned and incapable of giving the right directions for the picking and storing of plants.

> The *Coloquintida* growing alone upon the plant, is much suspected of good Physicians, the *Squilla* that hath no fellowes, is thought to favour of a venomous nature . . . now, when these are gathered to ye Merchants hand, who shall tell him how they grewe, or who shal inquire but the Philosopher that knoweth what may come thereby to these simples, neither is the daunger lesse in the manner of laying them up, and keeping them over long: besides the iust time of gathering being either overpassed, or prevented, greatly diminisheth the vertue of the Medicines . . . And as the *Peonie* roote is to be gathered in the wane of the Moone, and the *Crayfish* to be taken after the rising of the Dogge starre, the same entering into *Leo*, so are there many other, which if they misse their due time of gathering, faile greatly in their vertues.[51]

Physicians and philosophers, in Bright's opinion, possessed the required practical knowledge of plants. The products that merchants imported by their 'navigations' were dangerous, because, wrote Bright, merchants 'buy to sell onely, and thereof to reape gaine, and by reason they be unlearned'.[52] The flow of information was one-way: from the learned physicians to the merchants and thence to the pickers. Bright could be describing the cash crops of Europe's colonies which were produced according to the orders of white settlers. What mattered for Bright was the expertise that came from the literate medical tradition which, in his case, was based on both Galen and Paracelsus. De Renou expressed the appropriation and transformation of local materials and knowledge by learned medicine most starkly when he wrote:

> The all-seeing providence of God hath thought good to bless the remotest part of the East (Indies) with better Medicaments than Physicians; Plants of such rare worth, and admirable virtue that Medics of a more polish life and conversation, of greater learning and experience than those rude Barbarians, have to their perpetual renown, demonstrated their virtues and operations, and by long use and observation, have found them fortunately successful in many desperate distempers.[53]

Local traditions, whether in England, continental Europe or further afield, were deemed inferior in the eyes of many medical writers

---

[51] Bright, *Sufficiencie of English Medicines*, p. 13.
[52] Ibid., p. 12.
[53] De Renou, *Medicinal Dispensatory*, p. 270.

whose learning and experience sought to transform and all but obliterate the knowledge of herb women, the 'vulgar' and non-Europeans.

Having shown that remedies formed part of a medical culture that went well beyond that of medical practitioners, it is time to focus on the remedies themselves. This can be difficult for anyone living in a developed country in the twenty-first century who has been brought up on scientific medicine, and for whom the long lists of medicines and their ingredients in many early modern medical books might seem like long lists of nonsense. Yet for early modern patients and practitioners, credibility in the power of remedies was in principle not an issue. Medicines were eagerly sought after, though there was debate about which ones were effective and appropriate to use, especially if they came from foreign and exotic parts.

THE MULTIPLICITY OF REMEDIES: THE NEW AND EXOTIC

The number of remedies increased in the sixteenth century through the acceptance and inclusion of northern European drugs into learned herbals and books of simples, and the rediscovery and identification of the drugs of antiquity, and also through the voyages of discovery at the end of the fifteenth and the beginning of the sixteenth century. Northern and central European writers and illustrators of herbals became aware that the herbal drugs of the ancients, which grew in Greece and Asia Minor, were often not to be found north of the Alps, and that numerous northern and central European medicinal plants had not been known to writers like Galen, or Dioscorides whose *De Materia Medica* written around 60 AD was one of the foundation texts of medical botany.[54] The study of herbs became, like anatomy, part of the enterprise of giving a realistic and independent representation of what was being observed, whilst at the same time retrieving in a pure form the knowledge of the ancients. There was a concerted effort to identify and retrieve the plants and remedies of antiquity. Pier-Andrea Mattioli (1501–77), the imperial physician, acted as a clearing house for new information on the plants of the eastern Mediterranean and

---

[54] On the history of herbals see the classic work by Agnes Arber, *Herbals*, 3rd edn (Cambridge University Press, Cambridge, 1986).

Asia Minor which came mainly from Italian traveller-botanists. In 1544, he translated Dioscorides into Italian and then in the successive editions of his *Commentarii in Libros Sex Pedacii Dioscoridis Anazarbei de Materia Medica* (*Commentaries on the Six Books of Pedacius Dioscorides of Anazarbus on Materia Medica*) (first edition, 1554), Mattioli identified an increasing number of Dioscoridean plants.[55] In the 1548 edition of Dioscorides he noted that true Cretan dictamnus (dittany) and true Dioscoridean rhubarb from the Bosphorus were being imported into Venice – in fact, the search for the 'true' and most efficacious rhubarb which Marco Polo had reported at the end of the thirteenth century as coming from China continued into the nineteenth century.[56] The co-operative, largely informal efforts of physicians, herbalists, apothecaries, travellers and traders to recreate the *materia medica* of the ancients bore fruit, and drugs such as balsam, myrrh and petrosolinum (parsley), which were unknown to western Europe, were rediscovered.

The voyages of discovery transformed the trade and supply of exotic drugs. The Portuguese renewed and augmented European knowledge of Africa, India and the Far East. By 1512–13 they had found in the Pacific the long sought-after and fabled Spice Islands, the Moluccas, from whence exotic spices such as nutmegs, cloves and cinnamon, which were both condiments and medicines, had up to this time travelled to Europe via the 'overland route' through India, the Middle East and the Mediterranean. The new sea route allowed first the Portuguese and then in the seventeenth century the Dutch to challenge Arab and Venetian control of the spice trade. And, as one writer put it, England could now have as ready a supply of drugs as Venice had in the heyday of the overland trade:

---

[55] For instance, theriac, the legendary panacea and antidote to poisons of the ancients, compounded of at least eighty-one plant, animal and mineral ingredients, appeared in the 1540s to be impossible to recreate as many of its ingredients were not identified and more than twenty substitutes had to be used. But by 1566 Francesco Calzolari, the Veronese botanist-pharmacist, claimed that he only needed to use three substitutes, and in 1568 Mattioli declared that the theriac of the present age was as good as that mixed by Galen for the emperors. Richard Palmer, 'Medical Botany in Northern Italy in the Renaissance', *Journal of the Royal Society of Medicine*, 78, 1985, pp. 149–57, and 'Pharmacy in the Republic of Venice in the Sixteenth Century' in A. Wear, R. K. French and I. Lonie (eds.), *The Medical Renaissance of the Sixteenth Century* (Cambridge University Press, Cambridge, 1985), pp. 100–17, 303–12. Sara Ferri (ed.), *Pietro Andrea Mattioli (Sieca 1501–Trento 1578): la Vita, le Opere con l'Identificazione delle Piante* (Ponte San Giovanni, Quattroeme, 1997).

[56] On the search for rhubarb see Clifford Faust, *Rhubarb. The Wonder Drug* (Princeton University Press, Princeton, 1992).

For in these dayes, the spices and other thinges brought from the Indians by navigation to Lishburn [Lisbon], and then to other countreys of Europe, may as soone be transported to us as to Venice. Where in times past such merchandise were caried from the east Indians to Alexandria by land upon Camels that trade is now decayed, and for the most part such drugges are imported by sea, and the ships doe commonly light in some part of Portingal: so that it is easie to see that our Apothecaries in England may with as good conveniency procure them from these places, and in as good perfection as the merchaunts of Venice and Constantinople.[57]

The Spanish sailing to the west discovered a 'new world' in 1492–3. Riches were expected from the new-found lands, not only gold, silver and rare commodities but also new medicines. Aztec remedies were recorded by the Spanish.[58] The Spanish Crown ordered its officials in America to be on the lookout for medicinal plants, as when Philip II, on appointing Francisco Hernandez, in 1570, *protomedico* for New Spain,[59] directed him to collect reports from all the 'physicians, surgeons and herbalists' of all the 'herbs, trees and medicinal plants' that grew there, and to learn how precisely they could be used as medicines.[60]

Remedies were often associated with money, and the more novel and exotic a remedy, the more profitable it was likely to be. The Spanish and the other governments and explorer-entrepreneurs involved in the European enterprise of discovery and colonisation were eager that the medical and commercial benefits of the American and Far East plants should be garnered. For instance, guaiac wood (*Guaiacum officinalis*), the Native American cure for the American disease of the pox, was imported to Europe, along with sarsaparilla (*Smilax aristolochiae-folia*), sassafras (*Sassafras elbidum*) and from the East Indies chinaroot (*Smilax china*). Guaiac, especially,

---

[57] Anon, *A Discourse of the Medicine called Mithridatum* (London, 1585), sig. C7[r–v]. See also T. M. [Thomas Mun], *A Discourse of Trade, From England unto the East Indies* (London, 1621), pp. 8, 9.

[58] The Franciscan College in Santa Cruz, Mexico, produced in 1552 a manuscript description of Aztec medicines with illustrations of hundreds of medicinal plants written by an Aztec, Martin de la Cruz, 'an Indian physician . . . who is not theoretically learned, but is taught by experience'; it was translated into Latin and sent to Europe: Arber, *Herbals*, pp. 109–10. The local rationales for the plants' powers were omitted (personal communication from David Harley).

[59] The post involved the regulation of medical practice and was an extension of the tribunal of the *protomedicato* which, partially at least, controlled medicine in Spain. See John Tate Lanning, *The Royal Protomedicato: the Regulation of the Medical Profession in the Spanish Empire* (Duke University Press, Durham, 1985).

[60] Ibid., pp. 58–9.

brought in large revenues, and the monopoly in its trade was sold by the Spanish Crown to the Fuggers, the wealthiest bankers in Europe. Knowledge of the new plants coming from America was spread across Europe by Nicolas Monardes, a Spanish physician working in Seville who grew and observed many of the plants in his botanical garden. His *Dos Libros, El Uno Que Trata de Todas las Cosas Que Traen de Nuestras Indias Occidentales* (*Two Books. One which Deals with All Things that are Brought from our Western Indies*, in three parts, 1565, 1571 and 1574) praised the therapeutic virtues of the American plants. The eagerness of Europeans to learn about new remedies for their ills is conveyed by the English title of John Frampton's version of the *Dos Libros*: *Joyfull Newes out of the New Founde Worlde* (1577).

The remedies of India were publicised, though not so widely, by Garcia d'Orta, a Portuguese physician living in Goa, who, significantly, was also a ship-owner and trader in precious stones and *materia medica*. His *Colóquios dos Simples, e Drogas he cousas Medicinais da India* (*Dialogues about Simples and Drugs and Medical Matters from India*, 1563), which was printed in Goa, was based on his observations of plants in his gardens in Goa and Bombay, and on reports from Indian, Persian and Chinese traders. Another Portuguese physician, Christovão da Costa, in his *Tractado de las Drogas y Medicinas de las Indias Orientales* (*Treatise of the Drugs and Medicines of the Eastern Indies*, 1578) written in Spanish, expanded on the work of d'Orta. He travelled further to the east, reaching the Straits of Malacca and China, and he added his descriptions and illustrations of the plants that he had observed there. Charles de l'Ecluse translated d'Orta's book into Latin in 1567 and da Costa's in 1582.

The English were relative late-comers to the European voyages of discovery, colonisation and trade, but they were well aware that remedies from new-found lands were valuable commodities. Frampton, who had been a merchant dealing in the Spanish-English trade before he retired and translated Monardes, praised the new remedies for their worth in curing diseases that were previously incurable,[61] and he also placed them amongst world trade items:

And since the afore said Medicines mentioned in the same worke of Doctour Monardes, are now by Marchauntes and others, brought out of the West Indias into Spaine, and from Spain hether into Englande, by

---

[61] Nicolas Monardes, *Ioyfull Newes out of the New Founde Worlde*, trans. John Frampton (London, 1577), Epistle Dedicatory, sig ii^{r-v}.

suche as dooth daiely trafficke thether, and that the excellencie of these Hearbes, Trees, Oyles, Plantes and Stones etc hath been knowen to bee so precious a remedie for all manner of diseases, and hurtes, that maie happe unto Man, Woman or Childe.[62]

The new remedies' 'precious' commercial as well as medical values are also stressed in *A Briefe and True Report of the New Found Land of Virginia* by Thomas Hariot, the mathematician and surveyor who accompanied Sir Walter Ralegh's first colonising venture. It listed the 'marchantable commodities' of Roanoke island, or Virginia as it was then named, and of the nearby mainland, for the benefit of the 'adventurers, favourers, and welwillers of the enterprise for the inhabiting and planting in Virginia'.[63] Although 'golde and silver was not so soone found',[64] he noted commodities such as grass-silk, silk worms, flax, hemp, furs, iron, copper, and also medicinal substances such as 'wapeth' which was 'a kind of earth . . . very like to *Terra sigillata*, and having beene refined, it hath bene found by some of our Phisitions and Chirurgions, to bee of the same kind of vertue, and more effectuall. The inhabitants use it very much for the cure of sores and wounds', and 'sweet gummes of divers kindes, and many other Apothecary drugges'. Hariot also took care to mention the availability of sassafras, which he publicised as a superior alternative to guaiacum.[65]

Although guaiacum was being imported into England by the 1530s, it was probably not until the 1580s that it was joined by two other exotics, chinaroot and sarsaparilla. Apart from suspicion of novelty, the prohibition of direct trade between Spain's possessions and third countries as well as the perennial state of hostility between Spain and England slowed down the entry of new American remedies into England.[66] As Hariot put it, the produce of an English colony in America would 'by way of traffique and exchaunge with our owne nation of England . . . enrich your selves the providers: those that shall deale with you, the enterprises in generall, and greatly profite our owne countreymen, to supplie them with most

[62] Ibid., sigs. ii^v–iii^r.
[63] Thomas Hariot, 'A Briefe and True Report of the New Found Land of Virginia' in Richard Hakluyt, *The Principall Navigations, Voiages and Discoveries of the English Nation* (London, 1589), pp. 749, 750.
[64] Ibid., p. 749.
[65] Ibid., pp. 750–2.
[66] See R. S. Roberts, 'The Early History of the Import of Drugs into Britain' in F. N. L. Poynter (ed.), *The Evolution of Pharmacy in Britain* (Pitman, London, 1965), pp. 168–70.

things which heretofore they have beene faine to provide either of strangers or of our enemies'.[67] Once peace was signed with Spain in 1604, English overseas trade including that concerned with medicinal drugs expanded.[68]

Learned physicians quickly assimilated the new drugs into the traditional humoral medical system[69] and did not hesitate to recommend them; they believed that they could be used in Europe despite coming from different continents. Foreign drugs were costly, however. This added to the existing association of physicians with expense and uncharitableness. Some writers called for the use of cheap local remedies rather than foreign remedies, their medical argument being the localist one that such drugs were alien to the constitution of an English patient as they had not grown in the same land and air. William Harrison, the topographer and historian, recognised the new world of plants brought into England and marvelled to see 'how many strange herbs, plants, and annual fruits are daily brought unto us from the Indies, Americans, Taprobane [Ceylon], Canary Isles, and all parts of the world'. Although they could be 'cherished' for their appearance and smell, he believed that 'in respect of the constitutions of our bodies they do not grow for us, because that God hath bestowed sufficient commodities upon every country for her own neccessity'.[70]

Given Harrison's nationalism and dislike of all things foreign he was naturally suspicious of the new exotic medicines, believing that the powers of home-grown remedies should be better investigated and used. He cited Pliny's attack on the use of luxurious foreign

---

[67] Hariot, 'Briefe Report', p. 750.

[68] In 1588 14 per cent of drugs entering England originated outside Europe, in 1621 the figure had grown to 48 per cent and by 1669 it had risen to 70 per cent, most of which at that time came from India and the East Indies. Roberts, 'The Early History of the Import of Drugs into Britain', p. 170.

[69] See Andrew Wear, 'Medicine in Early Modern Europe, 1500–1700' in L. Conrad, M. Neve, V. Nutton, R. Porter and A. Wear, *The Western Medical Tradition, 800 BC to AD 1800* (Cambridge University Press, Cambridge, 1995), pp. 306–10. See also Wear, 'The Early Modern Debate about Foreign Drugs: Localism versus Universalism in Medicine', *Lancet*, 354, 1999, 149–51.

[70] William Harrison, *The Description of England*, ed. Georges Edelen (Dover Publications, New York, 1994), p. 265; the text is based on Harrison's 1587 edition of his *An Historical Description of the Island of Britain* (London, 1587).

drugs amongst the Romans, and wrote that were it not for the popularity of 'outlandish [foreign] drugs ... the virtues of our simples here at home would have been far better known'. God, he believed, had 'so disposed' matters that the plants that were in most abundance, in other words weeds, would be found to have medical uses.[71]

A providential and nationalistic or localist view of remedies was common amongst critics of learned medicine. Harrison himself did not take an extreme position, believing that the constitutions or qualitative temperaments (the balance of hot, cold, dry and wet qualities in people and plants) of foreign plants could be altered by being grown in the English climate and soil so that they became suitable for the constitutions of English people.[72] But those hoping to replace Galenic medicine contested its claims to universal applicability, and used the issue of local remedies as the means to make their point. The two revolutionaries in the medicine of the sixteenth and early seventeenth centuries, Paracelsus and van Helmont, attacked foreign remedies. Paracelsus wanted to create a German medicine, which would not be influenced by that of Galen and the Arabs, and he wrote, 'Each land, to be sure, gives birth to its own special kind of sickness, its own medicine, and its own physician ... I really have to laugh at those Germans who want to prepare medicines from across the seas while there are better remedies to be found in front of their noses in their own gardens'.[73] Allied with this local and nationalist view, which linked people, places and remedies together, was a widespread fear that foreign drugs were often counterfeited, adulterated, substituted, or rotten. Paracelsus tapped into this fear of impurity when he wrote of 'the deception of merchants, shopkeepers and sellers of medicine, for these bring nothing pure to us from foreign shores'.[74] Van Helmont, Paracelsus' follower and critic, also 'perceived the theevish adulteries of Merchants, wherewith they load, defile, estrange and substitutively dissemble foreign Medicines or Drugs'.[75] The fear of adulteration was widespread and even supporters of learned medicine, such as the German humanist physician Leonhard Fuchs, were worried that foreign remedies

---

[71] Ibid., pp. 267–8.   [72] Ibid., p. 268.
[73] Moran, 'The *Herbarius* of Paracelsus', p. 104.   [74] Ibid., p. 105.
[75] John Baptista van Helmont, 'The Power of Medicines' in *Oriatrike Or, Physick Refined*, trans. J[ohn] C[handler] (1st edn, London, 1662; 2nd impression, 1664), p. 472.

would be used in place of well-tried local ones which were more likely to be pure. Fuchs wrote:

I have been on my guard against exotic and expensive medicaments, and those which are difficult to prepare only because there is a danger of many of these being adulterated, since they are insufficiently known either by those that sell them or by those who buy them . . . Wherefore I am not able to give my approval to the practice of foolish and unlearned physicians who in practising use no medicines except those which they compose from the four parts of the world.[76]

Nationalism, a dislike of foreigners and their commodities, a strong appeal to religious arguments, and the use of Galenic theory against the enlarged Galenic *materia medica* were combined in a powerful argument against foreign remedies. In England Timothie Bright wrote an extended English critique of foreign remedies in his *Treatise Wherein is Declared the Sufficiencie of English Medicines* (1580). From the Bible Bright argued that, as God had provided food and clothing, so also he provided medicines, as the preservation of the creature was part of the goodness of the Creator.[77] He added that it detracted from God's providence to depend on the 'adventures of Merchantes' for health, and 'the disease beeing in the one parte of the worlde, to have the medicine in the other, yea, as farre distant as the East is from the West'.[78] Mixing xenophobia with a Christian-centred view of the world, he also asked whether it was not 'absurde, that the health of so many Christian nations should hang upon the courtesie of those Heathen and barbarous nations, to whome nothing is more odious then the very name of Christianity? And who of malice do withhold from us such medicines as they knowe most for our use . . . ?'[79]

The corruption and counterfeiting of foreign drugs led people, wrote Bright, to use instead those plant remedies amongst which they lived and were most familiar, 'those wee knowe both in the blade, and in the seede, in the roote and in the fruite, and knowe the aire, the hill, the valley, the medowe where they growe'.[80] In addition to this pragmatic argument for the use of home-grown remedies for local diseases, Bright used the Galenic theory of

---

[76] Leonhard Fuchs, *De Medendis Singularum Humani Corporis Partium a Summo Capite ad Imos usque Pedes Passionibus ac Febribus* (Basle, 1539), fol. 3ʳ.

[77] He asserted that such aspects of God's providence had to be incorporated into philosophy for 'being a trueth in Divinitie and Christianitie, can not be false in Philosophie': Bright, *Sufficiencie of English Medicines*, p. 9.

[78] Ibid., p. 11.   [79] Ibid., pp. 11–12.   [80] Ibid., p. 14.

qualitative constitution to establish the point that there was a fit between a place, its inhabitants, its diseases and the remedies that grew there. He concluded that 'if the difference of our bodyes from those of straunge nations be so great, that then the thing which helpeth them, destroyeth us, that cureth them without annoyance, doth vehemently torment us'.[81] Some foreign plants could, he conceded, be grown in English gardens and 'receive, as it were a taming, and are broken unto us by our owne soyle', and 'growe into acquaintance with us', and so lose their poisonous nature to English people.[82] On the other hand, whatever could not grow in England, by that very fact, indicated its hostility to English bodies: 'Such of straunge medicines as will not brooke our climate, thereby declare the evill disposition they have to cure the infirmities of our bodyes'.[83] As we shall see in chapter 4 there was a strong link between particular environments and the creatures and plants that they supported, of which this argument was part.

That there was a debate about home-grown versus foreign remedies illustrates how deeply remedies were embedded in the general culture of early modern England. It also indicates that remedies raised in an acute form the social and Christian issue of how the poor could afford medicines. The cost of medicines was a crucial determinant of who could use them. Foreign remedies were more expensive, they were of 'unmeasurable charge and cost',[84] and the poor would have been excluded from the benefits of a medicine largely based on them. As medicines were from God, this implied that God's bounty was denied to the poor, something that was inconceivable in the religious teaching of the time.[85] Bright protested:

Hath God so dispensed his blessings, that a medicine to cure iawndies [jaundice], or the greene sicknes, or the rheume, or such like, should cost more oftentimes then one quarter of the substance that the patient is worth? and the provision of an whole yere, whereof wife and children and the whole familie shuld with things necessarie be mainteined in health, be wasted upon the curing of a Palsey, or a Cholike, or a swimminge of the braine, or any other disease whatsoever? Is Physicke only made for rich men? and not as wel for the poorer sort?[86]

---

[81] Ibid., p. 18.   [82] Ibid., pp. 18, 19.   [83] Ibid., p. 22.   [84] Ibid., p. 23.
[85] One should perhaps add the 'deserving' poor, as the poor were in the process of being differentiated into deserving and undeserving at this time.
[86] Ibid., p. 23.

The disquiet of Bright and others about foreign remedies represents a mixture of social Christian concerns often united with a wish to overturn the claims of Galenic medicine that it could be applied universally across all ages and in all places. As in the work of Paracelsus, nationalism and social, religious and medical radicalism could be merged to form a series of arguments against foreign, expensive and uncharitable remedies. The link between suspicion of foreign remedies and medical radicalism continued well into the seventeenth century. George Starkey, for instance, wrote in 1657 that foreign remedies were efficacious for English bodies, but were not necessary for 'no medicaments are so proper for our *English* bodies, as those which *England* produceth. And so in other Countreys . . . their native Simples are sufficient'.[87] Starkey's fellow Helmontian, Marchamont Nedham, argued that the universality claimed by Galenic medicine, created as it was in classical times, implied a lack of progress and flexibility to deal with the illnesses of places with different climates and geography from Greece and with new illnesses. He would rather, he wrote, put himself in the hands of 'a prudent Apothecary or any prudent Practiser that is no Scholar' than commit himself to a pedantic practitioner 'that pins himself up to the old Scholastick Learning and Medicins':

because he that is no *formal Doctor* will probably follow his own observation and experience, as he finds things alter'd in the Age and Climate wherein he lives, and so may hit on a cure, because he projects to himself such Means and Method, as seems agreeable to such Alteration; whereas a *Doctor* that is inspired with the Divinity of *Hippocrates* and *Galen*, having heard them boast in their Books, that their Maxims and Remedies are little less than infallible, and will hold so, in all Ages and Countries, to the end of the world.[88]

The medical imperialism of Galenic medicine that Nedham attacked was asserted with approval and enthusiasm by James Primrose, a conservative Galenist and fellow of the London College of Physicians, whose *De Vulgi in Medicina Erroribus* (1638), translated by Robert Wittie in 1651 as *Popular Errours*, was a defence of Galenic medicine and an attack on popular misconceptions and mistaken practices. He wrote that 'it was wisely ordered by the Spaniards and Portugals, that in India where they beare rule, Physick should be practised after the self same manner that it is in

---

[87] Starkey, *Nature's Explication*, p. 60.   [88] Nedham, *Medela Medicinae*, pp. 432–3.

Europe according to the doctrine of Galen and Hippocrates'.[89] This was because medicine was 'of universals, not of particulars' and using those universal principles it could be applied to different places and climates.[90] He also attacked the assumptions of localism by pointing out that a particular place did not produce people all of one constitution, which was what was logically implied by those who believed in local remedies, for 'whatsoever the Climate and Country be, even in the most Northern Climates, there are men of every temper [constitution], hot, cold, cholerick, flegmatick, sanguine, melancholick'.[91] Primrose, instead, argued, as might be expected from a believer in the universal applicability of Galenic medicine, that God's providence was to be seen in global terms. A country could not be self-sufficient in everything, but trade distributed God's providence so that it was widely spread.[92] He disagreed with Pliny's view that foreign remedies were costly and that 'every poore man eates dayly to his supper the right remedies'. Rather, he wrote, no 'Nation' has 'been so happy, that it could be sufficiently furnished with its own remedies, except the Indians'. Moreover, it was 'lawful to fetch them out of those Countryes where the best doe grow, for the vertue of plants doth vary according to the nature of the places'.[93]

As it was, foreign remedies were increasingly imported into continental Europe and England. And, despite the strong arguments put forward for local remedies, it was the trade and the corresponding belief in overseas remedies that prevailed. With the globalisation of trade came a belief in the global efficacy of remedies; remedies that were thought to work only within a localised geographical area were worth less than those that were marketed across geographical, cultural and national boundaries. For patients and practitioners the strength of exotic remedies was their great attraction, especially so in the case of purgative drugs which, as de Renou wrote, 'are for the most part exotical and forreign, conveyed to us dry, from savage and barbarous Regions. Yet some we have growing with us, especially in hot Regions; yet they do not retain the same virtues and qualities that the other have, but come far short; and

---

[89] Primrose, *Popular Errours*, p. 126.   [90] Ibid., pp. 125–6.   [91] Ibid., p. 127.
[92] Ibid., p. 235: 'God would not that every Country should abound with all things, nor alwayes, that humane society might be maintained. For as in every Country, one City supplies necessaries to another, so one Country to another.'
[93] Ibid., p. 234.

therefore it is that they are rejected, and the foreign (which are brought from *India* and *Arabia*) used'.[94]

The controversy surrounding exotic foreign drugs shows that medicines as a whole did not merely consist of lists of ingredients. They had economic, political and cultural connotations which were intertwined within medical discourses. The end result, however, was that the number of remedies, already enormous, was further increased, but without creating scepticism, as in nineteenth-century Paris medicine, when the very multitude of medicines was evidence that they did not work. How credibility in large numbers of medicines was sustained is discussed next.

UNDERSTANDING AND COPING WITH A MULTIPLICITY OF REMEDIES

> O! mickle is the powerful grace that lies
> In herbs, plants, stones, and their true qualities:
> For nought so vile that on the earth doth live,
> But to the earth some special good doth give . . .[95]

Everything in the created world could have a medicinal use. Animals, minerals and especially plants were potential medicines. Their numbers were huge, as were the numbers of objects and organisms that God created. The classical plethora of medicinal substances was given a Christian justification. As Andrew Boorde, a former Carthusian monk and agent for Thomas Cromwell who had learned medicine in continental universities, put it, 'There is no Herbe, nor weede, but God hath gyven vertue to them, to helpe man'.[96] Pierre de la Primaudaye, whose *French Academy* (1618) became an influential compendium of natural theology and morality in England, wrote that from the humblest herbs 'often times trodden underfoote – many are commonly delivered, not onely from great paines and grievous maladies, but even from death it selfe'.[97]

---

[94] De Renou, *Medicinal Dispensatory*, p. 252. Primrose also argued that purgative drugs, such as senna, had to be imported; if they were grown in England they did so 'not without a manifest wasting of their strength, nor in that plenty which may be sufficient for the whole Country': *Popular Errours*, p. 235.

[95] W. Shakespeare, *Romeo and Juliet*, Act II Scene III, lines 15–18.

[96] Andrew Boorde, *A Compendious Regyment or A Dyetary of Helth* (1542) in Boorde, *Introduction and Dyetary*, ed. F. J. Furnivall, Early English Text Society, Extra Series (London, 1870), p. 283.

[97] Pierre de la Primaudaye, *The French Academie* (London, 1618), p. 788; Thomas Mun, in *A Discourse of Trade* (London, 1621), p. 6, advised his readers to read Elyot's *Castle of Health*,

Nowadays, the pharmaceutical companies working within the framework of western scientific medicine expect only some or a few plants to have commercially useful medical properties. But in the accommodation between Christianity and medicine, God's bounty, his legacy of the creation, was taken to be for mankind's use. Such a view is important for the discussion in the next section on why remedies were believed to be powerful, and it also illustrates how the multiplicity of remedies was legitimised by the most powerful ideology of the time, religion.

Although God had placed virtues in all plants, not all plants nor all their virtues were known. A sense of eager discovery linked God's providence with the discoveries of exploration and the research of botanists. As la Primaudaye put it:

if wee will consider of the medicines and remedies which men finde in herbes and plants onely, besides those which they may take from other creatures, who can in truth either declare or write, I will not say of all of them, but onely the thousanth part? For although the most excellent phisitions have alwaies travelled in this part of their art, which is commonly called the knowledge of Symples, yet how farre off are they from the full and perfect theoricke of them? For what a number of herbes and rootes be there which are unknowne, and have yet no name? And how many are there which are taken one for another, and wherein the most skilfull Phisitions and Herbarists are oftentimes deceived?[98]

Although 'there was no Plant whereof Adam understood not the name or vertue before his Fall',[99] the ignorance that followed could only be overcome by long and hard work over time. Burton wrote that medicine was still in the process of being perfected:

Time nourisheth knowledge, and experience teacheth us every day many things which our predecessors knew not of. Nature is not so effete . . . or so lavish to bestow all her gifts upon an age, but hath reserved some for posterity, to shew her power, that she is still the same, and not old or consumed. Birds and beasts can cure themselves by nature, but men must use much labour and industry to find it out.[100]

Dodoens' *Herbal* and the *French Academy* if they wanted detailed justification of the necessity of drugs.
[98] Ibid., p. 787.
[99] Coles, *The Art of Simpling*, p. 10.
[100] Burton, *Anatomy of Melancholy*, p. 572. As William Coles put it, 'every plant' was endowed with 'an inward power and secret virtue', and the virtues of many plants were still to be discovered, 'left by providence for the enquiry of succeeding ages': Coles, *The Art of Simpling*, p. 95.

The number of known medicinal plants was expected to increase with each generation.

The strong sense of geographical location prevalent in the early modern period meant that 'every clime, every country, and more than that every private place hath his proper remedies growing in it'.[101] Such a view also led to the expectation that there would be the same huge variety of curative plants as there was of places. The opposing opinion, that a medicine could be applied universally across many different geographical locations, might in theory have led to a more limiting view of the number of remedies, but the hope that a great number of new exotic drugs from the Indies and America could be used in Europe reinforced the belief that a profusion of remedies was the expected and normal state of affairs. Moreover, localist and universal beliefs could be merged so that a remedy could be taken from its local setting and employed in different parts of the world, just as a disease moved from one area of the world to many others. The most famous example of this process for early modern Europeans was the pox, which was believed to have come from America. One of the remedies for the pox was guaiacum wood which the Native Americans used to treat it or something very like it (perhaps yaws). The justification for introducing guaiacum wood into Europe was that it was a local remedy for a local disease which had become an international disease, and so likewise the local remedy could also span different places and nations. As William Bullein explained:

This wodde was founde by the saylers into the new Ilandes called *Carterali*, *Hispaniola* . . . wheras the people of those landes be often infected with sores, biles, and a sicknesse muche like the Poxe . . . to recover the same: the sicke folkes doo eate of the fruite of *Guiacum*, and are made whole: this fruit will sone rotte, but whereas the fruites can not bee gotten, then they do make a decoction of the wood or barkes of the same which bringeth the like health, the Spaniard perseving the same, did bring this woode into Europe, not only for to heale their owne Pox, but also for Fraunce, Italy, Germany and for England, in whome this woodde taketh no small effecte for the forsaide Pox.[102]

The combination of God's bounty, novelty and the transformation of the local into the universal conveyed the strong sense that guaiacum really cured – creating an optimistic belief in the powers of remedies being the aim of most medical writings.

---

[101] Burton, *Anatomy of Melancholy*, p. 562.   [102] Bullein, 'Boke of Simples', fol. 60ᵛ.

Religion, new geographical and botanical discoveries, and localist and universalist beliefs about remedies justified a multitude of remedies. Also the need to provide alternatives given constraints of cost and availability, patient choice concerning taste, etc., and, perhaps, the sheer interest in collecting information, so prevalent at this time, may have all contributed to the publication of large numbers of recipes for medicines. Yet there was also an awareness that there might be too many. Burton wrote that there was an 'infinite variety of medicines' to be found 'in every Pharmocopeia, every Physician, Herbalist etc' and for melancholy there was 'a vast Chaos of medicines, a confusion of receipts and magistrals [or Sovereign Recipes] amongst writers, appropriated to this disease.'[103] His pragmatic solution was to discuss 'some of the chiefest' of the remedies.[104] Culpeper was reported as also whittling down the numbers of remedies and giving guidance on the best of them:

the practical part of Physick, do swell to no purpose with such infinite variety of medicaments that the practitioners are confounded, as not knowing amongst so many which of them to choose. Mr. *Culpeper* being truly sensible of this their error, made it his business not to puzzle his young students with the multiplicity of Medicines, but onely to select and set down such as are most proper, choice and effectual against the disease.[105]

In reality Culpeper set down in his books and translations a huge number of remedies, but choosing a few of the most effective, a sort of World Health Organization list of the hundred most useful remedies, was a possibility. Country people were presented as using only a small number of herbal medicines.[106] Another way out of the forest of remedies was to use panaceas, whether ancient ones like

---

[103] Perhaps, as Peter Jones has pointed out, compilers of remedy books and manuscripts added 'on the commonplace book principle' remedies under the headings of specific conditions and illnesses as and when they came across ones which they particularly liked, hence the rather haphazard listing of large numbers of remedies for one condition, Peter Jones, 'Harley MS 2558: a Fifteenth-Century Medical Commonplace Book' in Margaret R. Schleissner (ed.), *Manuscript Sources of Medieval Medicine* (Garland, New York, 1995), pp. 35–54, esp. pp. 41, 45.

[104] Burton, *Anatomy of Melancholy*, pp. 562, 586.

[105] Nicholas Culpeper, *Culpeper's School of Physick* (London, 1659), Preface by R. W. [William Ryves], sig. B1^r.

[106] See, for instance, William Bullein, *The Government of Health* (1st edn, 1558; London, 1595), fol. 82^{r-v}: 'We plaine men in the country wel farre from great cities, our wives and children be often sicke and at deaths doore, wee can not tell what shift to make; wee have no acquaintance with the apothecaries, commonly we send for aqua vitae or malmesey whatsoever our disease be, these be our common medicines, or else we send for a box of triacle: and when these medicines faile us, we cause a great posset to be made; and drink up the drink'.

mithridatium or theriac, or new ones like Daffy's elixir or Lockyer's pills created in the later seventeenth century, which would cure all manner of diseases. Sometimes a remedy came to be seen as standard for a particular condition or for producing a specific effect. Senna, for instance, became a common ingredient of purgatives: 'no purgative [is] now more frequent, more usual, more usefull'.[107]

DATA RETRIEVAL

Nevertheless, throughout this period large numbers of remedies and a wide choice of them for any particular condition remained the norm. In a culture that was still largely oral the processing and memorising of many individual bits of information may have been undertaken more easily than in today's paper-based culture. Parkinson listed, named and described over fifty-eight apples and sixty-five pears,[108] and such piecemeal information was common, not only in medicine and agriculture, but also in the trades and the law. However, once the information was on paper a clear attempt was made by some writers to make the mass of data more accessible. In modern terminology we can say that readers were given help in information retrieval. The humble index, which today we take for granted, was a simple but powerful technique that allowed a reader to find information about a remedy and to pick one for a particular disease. The prominence given to indexes and tables of information in some early modern medical books makes it clear that they were deliberately designed as tools for the extraction of data from what could be a confusing mass of material, and were considered important parts of a book.

For instance, William Langham advertised to his reader that his book was user friendly. The simples and plants that were the subject of the *Garden of Health* (1597) were set out in alphabetical order 'that thou mayst without any difficulty finde them by the titles of the pages, and to every Simple is annexed a brief Table of the effects thereof'.[109] He devoted a chapter to each plant, describing its parts and their uses, the different processes such as distillation that could be applied to it, and how the resulting products could be used for particular diseases. To every item of information he added a

---

[107] De Renou, *Medicinal Dispensatory*, p. 257.
[108] Parkinson, *Paradisi in Sole Paradisus Terrestris*, pp. 587–8, 590–3.
[109] William Langham, *The Garden of Health*, 2nd edn (London, 1633), 'To the Reader', sig. 2^{r-v}.

number, and at the end of the chapter there was an index or table of conditions with the numbers that were in the main text. The reader could thus see at a glance that one herb could be used in a wide variety of conditions, and whether a specific illness could be helped by a particular drug. For instance, under fennel, which had one of the longer entries, there were 132 items of information listed in the space of seven pages, ranging from 'Adder biting 83' (i.e. item 83 in the chapter) to 'Yard ache 117'.[110]

Langham also produced 'two generall Tables', one consisting of a page index of the 421 simples discussed in the book. The second table was the converse of the indexes at the end of individual chapters, for rather than showing that one plant could cure many diseases, it indicated that for each ill there were many different plants that could be employed.[111] Forty-eight plants were indexed under consumption and eighty-eight under colic, whilst 'lust to abate' merited twenty, with thirty-five to cause it. The table listed over 10,000 plants that could be used for the more than 1,150 named conditions and functions, and one plant would often be mentioned as useful in a number of different conditions.

Langham was not unusual in offering the reader guidance in retrieving and making sense of a large amount of information. Henry Lyte's translation of Dodoens' herbal, *The New Herball* (in the 1619 edition), had three separate indexes: one for the classical Latin names of plants, one for the names used by apothecaries, the Arabs and modern herbalists, and one for the English names, together with a fourth index, 'wherein is contained the Nature, Vertues and Dangers of all the Herbes, Trees and Plants, of which is spoken in this present Booke, or Herball'.[112] The fourth index was essentially a subject index of what plants could do, such as 'against the *bloudy* flux' (listed alphabetically under 'bloudy') or 'to clense and mundifie old rotten *ulcers*', with page references to the different plants that would be helpful. Gerard's *The Herball Or Generall Historie of Plantes* (second edition, 1633) also had an index of Latin names, of synonymns, of English names, of Welsh names and, as in Dodoens, of the powers of plants beginning with 'causing *Abortment*'.[113]

Books on the practice of medicine also helped their readers to

---

[110] Ibid., pp. 235–41, 242.   [111] Ibid., sig. 2ᵛ.

[112] Rembert Dodoens, *A New Herbal, Or Historie of Plants*, trans. Henry Lyte (London, 1619), sig. Eeeʳ.

[113] Gerard was commissioned to complete an English translation of Dodoens' *Pemptades*

access information about plants. Christopher Wirsung's German medical textbook, translated as *A Generall Practise of Physicke* (1598), which was an influential work in the first half of the seventeenth century, contained a general subject index of ills, and a 'Second Index' listing 'Rootes, Flowers, Fruits, Iuices, Gums, Woods, Stones, Barks, Metals, Minerals and Earths; also all the parts of Beasts and the body of man, that are or may be used in Physicke'.[114] Books on the practice of medicine as well as herbals took note of the confusion created by different names for the same plant and tried to mitigate it. The name of a plant and knowledge about its morphology and virtues usually went together, and if the two were separated then problems of identity arose which were noted in the index:

Our baulme undoubtedly is the right *Mellisophyllum* of the ancient Phisitions, although divers [several] will gainesay it, for both in forme, virtues and operation do they agree. There be also two kinds of this herbe, the one which is common and dayly used, of the which in this place we speake. The other hath long and iagged leaves and browne flours, and it beareth the smell of a strong and odoriferous Limon [i.e. our lemon balm], and is called *Melissa Cretica*, and *Melissa Turcica*, to distinguish it from the other: both kinds are in use.[115]

Problems of identification and the variety of names as well as the large number of different plants and their varieties created the need for indexes such as Wirsung's. Vernacular medical works also had to explain a certain amount of classical and Arabic medical terminology for their readers. They often brought classical terms into a modern language by printing the classical words at the same time as translating or explaining them, and in this way readers were educated in the language of learned medicine. The burden of information was therefore greater for vernacular texts than for Latin ones. Wirsung's 'third and Latin Index' gave an impression of how information

(1583); he did so whilst altering the arrangement from that of Dodoens to that of de l'Obel, and published it as his own. See Arber, *Herbals*, p. 129.

[114] It consisted of forty-seven large (folio) pages divided into two columns, and was essentially a pared down herbal concerned with the different names of plants and sometimes with their properties. Here the multiplicity of names rather than the virtues of plants and other remedies was brought into order by the creation of groupings of similar data. For instance, antimony was given its different names. The classical names were 'Stibi, Stibium, Stimmi, of Galen Gynacium, and of Plinie Platyophthalmon', whilst 'it is called at the Apothecaries by the barbarous name *Antimonium* . . . it is a minerall like to Lead, and knowne to all men'. Baulme (balm), likewise, was given its different names: Greek, Latin, those 'of the herbarists' and 'at the Apothecaries'. Christopher Wirsung, *Praxis Medicinae Universalis; Or a Generall Practise of Physicke*, trans. Iacob Mosan (London, 1598), sig. Eee4ᵛ.

[115] Ibid., sig. Eee4ᵛ.

multiplied once a text was in the vernacular, and also how remedies lay at the heart of the information mountain. The index gave the: 'Latin, Greeke, and other strange names of all Simples, especially of those which are mentioned in this Booke . . . Also all mixed and compounded Medicines . . . with their names, not only as they are called by the auncient Greeke and Latine Physitions, but also as they are now named amongst the common Physitions and Apothecaries.'[116]

The fifty-seven large pages of Wirsung's index, divided into two columns, had around two thousand entries of classical, medieval ('barbaric') and Arabic medical terms, translated into the vernacular. Thus the physician whose classical learning was less than it might be, and surgeons, apothecaries and lay people without Latin could tap into the jargon of learned medicine. Such indexes confirm the enormous amount of information that existed about remedies, whilst helping readers in processing these data. Even household manuscript books of remedies had indexes created by their compilers,[117] which shows that they were not merely publishers' and authors' fancy additions to a book but a response to a real need. If a multitude of remedies was expected, and the data about them were made accessible, the question remains as to how they were made to appear efficacious and powerful.

THE VIRTUES AND POWERS OF REMEDIES

Medicines can be medicines only if they have power, or are perceived as possessing it. Much of the discourse about remedies was concerned with convincing readers that they worked. The evidence from purgative and deadly drugs whose obvious physiological powers had been experienced and agreed upon over the centuries, gave weight to the rhetoric. There was a consensus amongst medical writers that remedies did exist which affected the body and produced cures, though there was often disagreement as to the value of particular types of medicines, as, for instance, between Galenists and chemical physicians. There was no sign of the 'therapeutic nihilism' that prevailed in the Paris and Vienna hospital medicine of the first half of the nineteenth century when the opinion was forming that most of the traditional *materia medica* was ineffective. As we have seen

---

[116] Wirsung, *Practise of Physicke*, sig. L113ᵛ.
[117] See, for instance, the medical recipe books of Mrs Corylon and of Lady Ayscough, Wel. MSS. 213, 1026.

above, one source of the power of medicines was God. The finger of
God, claimed Paracelsus and the Galenists, put virtues into metals
and plants. This was a divine act which could not be analysed in a
natural philosophical way.[118] With power came danger, and, as some
medical writers pointed out, God's remedies could be lethal in
ignorant hands: '. . . remedies are the finger of God, but as a sword
in the hand of a mad man, they are good indeed to him that uses
them aright, but dangerous, being administered by him that neither
knowes well the disease, nor the method of curing'.[119]

The potential danger of remedies contributed to their aura of
power. Medicines balanced uneasily between 'nourishments and
poysons', as Timothie Bright wrote.[120] Medicines were often viewed
as derived from dietetics or from a knowledge of food (see the
Hippocratic treatise *On Ancient Medicine*; also chapter 4 on the
relation between food and medicine), but the Greek word for
medicine, 'pharmakon', also meant poison. As Shakespeare put it:

> Within the infant rind of this weak flower
> Poison hath residence, and medicine power:
> For this, being smelt, with that part cheers each part;
> Being tasted, slays all senses with the heart.
> Two such opposed kings encamp them still
> In man as well as herbs – grace and rude will;
> And where the worser is predominant,
> Full soon the canker death eats up that plant.[121]

As Galen and later writers noted, medicine altered the body and
was, therefore, to some extent inimical to it.[122] 'Medicine', wrote
James VI of Scotland and I of England, 'hath that vertue, that it
never leaveth a man in that state wherein it findeth him: it makes a
sicke man whole, but a whole man sicke'.[123] For a remedy to be a
remedy it had to have the potential to harm the body; for, as James

---

[118] As different places in the Bible emphasised, God's absolute fiat was indicated by the
metaphor of the pointing finger: Paracelsus, *Of the Supreme Mysteries of Nature*, trans.
R. Turner (London, 1656), sig. B2ᵛ; Exodus, 8.19, and 31.18; Luke 11.20.

[119] Primrose, *Popular Errours*, p. 43.

[120] Bright, *Sufficiencie of English Medicines*, pp. 22–3, 34. In 1634 'Mr George Haughton
Apothecarye' was accused of giving 'Lac Sulphuris' (perhaps sublimated sulphur) to
Zachary Fawnes who then died. The College of Physicians found 'nourishmentt itt is not:
and itt is therfore either Phisicke or poyson.' *Annals*, 3, 142a.

[121] Shakespeare, *Romeo and Juliet*, Act II Scene III, lines 23–30.

[122] Anon., *A Defence of Tobacco* (London, 1602), pp. 45–6; Daniel Sennert, N. Culpeper and
Abdiah Cole, *Chymistry Made Easie and Useful Or, the Agreement and Disagreement of the Chymists
and Galenists* (London, 1662), p. 140.

[123] [James VI and I], *A Counterblaste to Tobacco* (London, 1604), sig. C3ʳ⁻ᵛ.

Primrose pointed out, 'all remedies have in them a nature in some measure contrary to our body, because they alter it, otherwise they were not remedies, and so they may also do harm'.[124]

The association of remedies with danger was increased by the way in which medical practitioners accused their opponents of peddling dangerous medicines. Galenists such as Cotta and his fellow Northampton physician Hart linked particular remedies like *aurum potabile* or drinkable gold and those based on mercury with deceit, death, empiricism and Paracelsianism. Paracelsians and Helmontian chemists, on the other hand, argued that chemical processes such as distillation cleaned remedies of their impurities, poisons and danger which since the Fall of Man had adhered to all sublunary substances.[125] Helmontian writers tried to separate the power of their chemical remedies from their association with danger. George Starkey reported that the 'main objection' of the Galenists against chemical remedies was that they were 'dangerous and desperate', and that their 'aim in all is to make the sick believe, that their medicaments only are gentle, safe and agreeable to nature, the other [chemical remedies] forcible, violent and desperate'. In reply, Starkey stated that chemical preparations had the effect of making what was poisonous less so. Marchamont Nedham stated more directly that chemical remedies were becoming popular 'because now adaies Princes, and Nobles generally apprehend the usefulness, gentleness, pleasantness and mighty power of Medicines so prepared', and he noted 'the current of the stream of Practise running every day in other Nations and our own also, toward this new and more safe, as well as delicate way of preparation of Medicins'.[126]

The debate between Galenists and chemists as to the efficacy and safety of remedies is discussed further below, but here it is worth noting that one of the major issues in the polemical medical works was the danger of the opposing side's remedies. And as power or efficacy was linked to dangerous remedies, the debate would have increased belief that remedies worked. Everyone, however, acknowl-

---

[124] Primrose, *Popular Errours*, p. 232.

[125] Cotta, *Short Discoverie*, pp. 37–9, and *Cotta Contra Antonium: Or an Ant-Anthony: Or An Ant-Apology, Manifesting Doctor Antony his Apologie for Aurum Potabile . . . to be False, and Counterfeit* (London, 1623); James Hart, ΚΛΙΝΙΚΗ, or Diet of the Diseased (London, 1633), p. 3; Primrose, *Popular Errours*, pp. 212–13; Sennert et. al., *Chymistry Made Easie*, pp. 2, 8, 140. Nedham, *Medela Medicinae*, p. 444, emphasises how Paracelsian chemistry purified the medical compositions of the Galenists and Arabs.

[126] Starkey, *Nature's Explication*, pp. 82, 95; Nedham, *Medela Medicinae*, pp. 434, 437.

edged that herbal medicines, which formed the basis of any pharmacopeia for both Galenists and medical chemists (on the latter see
below), could be dangerous. Some herbs, like hemlock, were considered to be outright poisons and 'not to be used in physicke';[127]
others could only be given selectively and with caution. For instance,
white hellebore was thought to be a 'strong medicine' which
'procureth vomite mightily'; it 'expelled superfluous slime and
humours' and was therefore useful against epilepsy, dropsies, poisons
and 'against all cold diseases that bee of hard curation, and will not
yeeld to any gentle medicine'. However, it could 'not be given
inwardly unto delicate bodies without great correction' (either by
dilution, mixing with other herbs or with inert materials as in pills),
while country people, who were viewed as intrinsically more healthy
and durable, could be 'more safely given it' as they 'feed grossely,
and have hard, tough and strong bodies'.[128] The existence of
obviously dangerous and powerful herbs, like nightshade, the 'deaths
hearbe',[129] purging plants like senna and cassia (known to the
Greeks), and vomiting ones like white hellebore that produced
violent and visible effects upon the body meant that it was easy to
imagine that all herbs would have some power. Indeed, Galenic
theory itself expressed such a belief, for all plants and other remedies
were assigned a grade or degree of qualitative power. In Galenic
medicine plants were thought to work upon the body and its diseases
because of their qualities, the most important of which were the four
primary ones of heat, coldness, dryness and wetness. The qualities
were graded on a scale of one to three or four, with qualities of the
first degree acting gently and imperceptibly and those of the third
degree violently and vehemently; the fourth degree represented
perfect heat or cold, etc., and would not be found in a body
composed of a mixture of qualities such as a herb.[130] This scheme
meant that all remedies would have some power to act upon the
body and that the appropriate medicine could be used against the
corresponding qualitative intensity of the patient's illness. Galenic
pharmaceutical and therapeutic theory were mutually reinforcing,
as Nedham perceptively noted: 'the Doctrinals, and the Dogmatical
[Galenic] Method, and the common Remedies, have a dependence
upon each other. Indeed if you keep to the Doctrin, you must hold to

[127] Gerard, *Herball*, p. 1063.   [128] Ibid., p. 441.
[129] Wirsung, *Practise of Physicke*, sig. Rrr3ᵛ.
[130] De Renou, *Medicinal Dispensatory*, p. 11.

the Medicins; and if you use the Medicins you must proceed in the Method, according to that Heathenish Galenick Doctrin.'[131]

Belief that remedies could work may have also been increased by their association with the senses. Qualitative intensity was judged by the senses of touch, taste and smell. The senses could also discover a plant's virtue or power. De Renou, for instance, wrote that 'by how much a purging Medicament recedes more from sharp and bitter sapours [tastes], by so much it is less noxious', and he listed various remedies according to their relative degrees of bitterness or sweetness.[132] The senses, moreover, gave an indication of what medical power was possessed by a plant, for they not only placed plants into an order of effectiveness, but they could also help to discover what they were good for. Van Helmont wrote disparagingly that 'the Schools [of the Aristotelians and Galenists] have by sapours or tastes, promised an entrance into the knowledge of Simples'.[133] For most early modern people the senses provided the most vivid, immediate information about the world, so the linking of the senses to remedies ensured that belief about the particular therapeutic power of a remedy would be the stronger because it seemed to be validated by the senses. The strong conviction that bad smells caused plague and good ones protected against it would have also reinforced the association of the linked senses of smell and taste with medicine. In addition, the perceived closeness of medicine to cooking would have made smell and taste appear natural means of judging the virtues and powers of remedies. Of course, the senses were educated to interpret information in particular ways, and it is not surprising that bitter remedies were often linked to violent, purging ones, or that it was apparent that 'Hemlocke doubtlesse is not possessed with any one good facultie [power], as appeareth by his lothsome smell'.[134] But the possibility that the healing function of a plant could be discovered *de novo* from the senses remained one which helped to sustain belief that plants did have healing virtues. So, for

[131] Nedham, *Medela Medicinae*, p. 429.

[132] De Renou, *Medicinal Dispensatory*, pp. 39–40. On the senses in medicine see W. Bynum and R. Porter (eds.), *Medicine and the Five Senses* (Cambridge University Press, Cambridge, 1993).

[133] Van Helmont, *Oriatrike*, p. 459. However, van Helmont did agree with the Galenists that 'most Remedies, do by their odour and savour, as well within as without, help our infirmities', p. 463; but in 'The Power of Medicines' states that if a poison has a pleasing taste it is because there is a 'property issuing forth, yet unperceivable by the tongue, and to be comprehended by the Archeus alone', p. 474. In other words, tastes and smells could not by themselves account for the power of substances.

[134] Gerard, *Herball*, p. 1063.

instance, John Parkinson could write of the 'Crowne Imperiall' or
Fritillaria imperialis that 'For any Physicall [medical] Vertues that are
in it, I know of none, nor have heard that any hath been found out:
notwithstanding the strong sent would perswade it might be applyed
to good purpose.'[135]

The language used to describe how herbs worked was also
important in bolstering confidence in their powers. It evoked images
of the activity of plants within the body that reinforced belief in their
virtues. Moreover, the powers of a plant were expressed in the same
language that was used to describe illnesses and their causes. Belief
in remedies was linked to belief in diseases. Many plants had the
virtue of cleansing and drawing out corruption from different areas
of the body; this reflected the common view of disease as consisting
of impurities, corruption and putrefaction within the body (discussed
in the chapter 3), a view which found expression in the frequent
bleedings, purgings and vomitings which were designed to expel
putrefying and malignant materials and humours from the body.[136]
Dirt and disease were seen to be intimately connected, and a
cleansing virtue was correspondingly common in herbs. The graphic
realism of language used to describe dirt lent the action of the herb a
similar degree of concreteness. For instance, the garden artichoke
healed 'the stinkyng and filth in the bladder or yarde of a mannes
bodie: and maketh the urine swete, and clenseth melancholy or
fleume, whiche doth abaunde'. Columbine (a species of *Aquilegia*), it
was stated, 'doth drie up Scabbes and Fistulaes . . . it helpeth also to
resolve clense and scoure Struma or painefull swellyng in the
throate, called the kinges Evill'.[137] The declaratory certainty with
which the virtues of a herb were set out, together with the graphic
nature of the language used, would have left a reader with little
doubt as to the effectiveness of the herb.

The fear so prevalent amongst medical writers that drugs could be

---

[135] Parkinson, *Paradisi in Sole Paradisus Terrestris*, p. 28; also on p. 396 he wrote of the 'Virginian
Climer', a species of passion fruit: 'What property [healing virtue] that of Virginia hath, is
not knowne to any with us I thinke, more then that the liquor in the greene fruit is pleasant
in taste; but assuredly it cannot be without some speciall properties, if they were knowne.'

[136] Some herbs like filipendula had the power of internally cleaning and drying out the body.
It was, according to Bullein, hot and dry in the third degree, and it 'drieth up windy places
in the guttes and clenseth the raines of the backe [kidneys] and bladder'. Another hot and
dry herb, horehound, was excellent for women, 'to clense their monthly termes' and it
helped 'them which have a moiste Reume falling from the head upon the Lunges'. Bullein,
'Boke of Simples', fols. 6ᵛ, 8ʳ.

[137] Ibid., fols. 33ʳ, 34ʳ.

counterfeited, adulterated or allowed to become rotten was not merely a stick with which physicians could beat apothecaries and exert their authority over them. It indicates a belief that an impure remedy would not work. De Renou devoted a chapter to the detection of counterfeit remedies[138] and writers like Elyot and Bullein fulminated against 'sophisticated' or counterfeit ingredients.[139] Of course, the possibility of counterfeit remedies also provided an excuse for failure, and created a climate of belief in the power of remedies, as long as they were pure and unadulterated.

The ethos of certainty surrounding the powers of herbs was enhanced by the mass of detail that often accompanied descriptions of a plant's virtues. The plant was divided into its parts, and each part had powers to cure different diseases and different parts of the body. Moreover, there was a variety of ways in which a herb could be prepared and made into medicines, and this often meant that, for instance, a syrup was appropriate for one illness and a pill for another. This process of 'splitting' or resolving a remedy into its constituent parts and corresponding powers might, it could be argued, have a connection with the general movement in early modern learned medicine to methodically resolve, analyse or break down a problem into its parts. However, there is little evidence of the move from general principles to specifics which is characteristic of 'methodical' medicine. What seems to have probably been the case was simply a wish to make the fullest possible use of a herb. Medical writers made little distinction between the natural products of a plant – its leaves, stalks, roots and seeds – and medicines such as syrups which involved a greater degree of production. Bullein set out the 'vertue of fenell' in this way. He listed with declaratory certainty its wide range of uses and the variety of ways it could be presented to patients and to the healthy:

It hath powre to warme in the third degree, and drie in the first, and maketh sweet the breath: the seede eaten oftentimes upon an emptie stomache, doth helpe the eye sight. The rootes . . . washed be very holsome in Potage, and is good in Tisanes [teas]. The greene or red tufts, growyng upon the stalkes, sodden in Wine, Potage or Ale, helpeth the bladder,

---

[138] De Renou, *Medicinal Dispensatory*, pp. 157–9.

[139] See, for instance, Thomas Phayre, *The Regiment of Life, whereunto is added a treatise of the pestilence, with the boke of children* (London, 1545), sigs. N7^r, N8^v; Elyot, *Castel of Helthe*, fol. 80^r; Bullein, 'Boke of Simples', fol. 55^r, and *A Dialogue Against the Fever Pestilence*, ed. Mark W. Bullen and A. H. Bullen, Early English Text Society (Trübner, London, 1888), p. 27; based on the edition of 1578.

raignes [kidneys], and breaketh the stone: encreaseth Mylke in Womens breastes, and seede of generacion . . . The Syrup is very good and holsom, it helpeth a Flegmatike stomache. And Fenell, Parsely, and Watercresses, of eche like quantitie stamped together, pouringe white wine to them, and the crums of Barly breade, standing al one night in a stone morter, the next day being strained, clarified and drunke, this will clense the raignes from gravel, stone, and choler, and cause one to make much water that hath the strangurie.[140]

A reader may well have been convinced of fennel's virtues by its being tied into Galenic theory ('warme in the third degree'), by the listing of its virtues in terms of a breakdown or analysis of the plant into its products, and by the very precise and detailed instructions that Bullein gave for making some of its products or medicines. All this carried the implicit message that it was not the virtues of the plant that were the issue but the education of the reader into the minutiae of the plant's powers.

COMPOUND REMEDIES

Compound remedies made not only from plants but also from mineral and animal substances were recommended by learned physicians, compilers of books of 'secrets' and popular medical writers. There is no doubt that recipes for compound remedies were much sought after. Theriac and mithridatium were the most famous of the ancient compound remedies, but there was by the early modern period a multitude of compound preparations, and one of the aims of the authorisation by European cities of official pharma-copeias was to ensure that certain compound remedies were made according to standard sets of ingredients.[141] Compound remedies present a paradox: they were immensely popular, but they were often disparaged, with the result that they generated a great deal of rhetoric that reinforced the primacy of simples.

Compound remedies were criticised for their expense, especially if they had costly foreign ingredients.[142] There were, however, cheap

---

[140] Bullein, 'Boke of Simples', fol. 6[r].

[141] Official pharmacopeias were established in Nuremberg, 1546; Augsburg, 1564; Cologne, 1565; Bergamo, 1581; Rome, 1585; London, 1618 (by the London College of Physicians).

[142] See, for instance, Harrison, *Description of England*, pp. 266–7; Bright, *Sufficiencie of English Medicines*, pp. 28–9, approvingly quoted Martin Ruland (the Elder) writing that native simples cured more easily and safely than 'the long compoundes of the Apothecaries, which are costly, evill gathered without knowledge of the Physician oftentimes unperfectly

compounds which were publicised to the poor. For instance, 'A.T.' in *A Rich Store-House or Treasury for the Diseased* (1596, and often reprinted) provided remedies 'for the poorer sort of people that are not of abilitie to go to the physicians'.[143] A number of writers of plague treatises took care to insert recipes for compound medicines that could be afforded by the poor. Robert Pemell, who practised in Cranbrook in Kent, in his *ΠΤΩΧΟΦΑΡΜΑΚΟΝ . . . Or . . . Help for the Poor* (1653), attacked physicians and surgeons who deserted the poor, and who only gave their 'Soveraigne Medicines' to the rich. In response he set out a large number of cheap compound remedies, often listing a number of them for a particular condition to take into account the availability of ingredients to a poor person at any time and allow a wide choice from which to find a favourite recipe. For boils, for instance, he listed ten recipes, of which one directed: 'Take Rag-wort, Rue and Hysope, of each as much as you can hold in two of your fingers, one clove of Garlick and a little piece of sowre Leaven, a spoonful of Bay Salt, and a piece of rusty Bacon; beat them together and lay it on for twenty four hours space.'[144]

Compound medicines were also suspect in a medical sense, for they literally hid the true virtues of simples. For simplicity they substituted the exotic and the complex, and seemed to represent a move away from what was natural. Burton noted how Pliny, who praised home-produced remedies, 'bitterly taxeth all compound medicines, "Men's knavery, imposture, and captious wits have invented these [apothecaries'] shops in which every man's life is set to sale: and by and by came in those compositions and inexplicable mixtures, far-fetched out of India and Arabia." '[145] Moreover, the need for apothecaries to store the large range of ingredients necessary for compounds meant, as Burton noted, that they were often out of date and corrupt.[146]

However, the main charge against compound medicines was that they were frequently put together without any good reason: 'Many

mixed, and unskilfully confused, and as unskilfully boyled, oftentimes putrified, and by age of force wasted, slovenly and with great negligence confected'.

[143] A.T., *A Rich Store-House Or Treasury for the Diseased* (London, 1596), title page; it has over 300 remedies/treatments – compounds of plants, especially herbs, wine, vinegar and animal products (e.g. 'Boares grease', fol. 5 E^r).

[144] Robert Pemell, *ΠΤΩΧΟΦΑΡΜΑΚΟΝ . . . Or . . . Help for the Poor* (London, 1653), sig. A3, p. 18.

[145] Burton, *Anatomy of Melancholy*, p. 570, citing Pliny, *Natural History*, book 24, ch. 1.

[146] Burton, *Anatomy of Melancholy*, p. 570.

times . . . there is by this means more danger from the medicine than from the disease, when they put together they know not what, or leave it to an illiterate Apothecary to be made, they cause death and horror for health'.[147] The learned physicians constantly declared that medicine that was not based on rational principles was dangerous, yet it was difficult to see how complex compounds could be justified in terms of rational and methodical medicine for, as William Harrison wrote, 'the greater number of simples that go unto any compound medicine, the greater confusion is found therein because the qualities and operations of very few of the particulars are thoroughly known'.[148] Often remedies would conflict with one another in terms of their qualitative powers, and it would be practically impossible to adjust the whole composition so that it was appropriate to the disease and to the patient's circumstances. Burton declared:

Let the best of our rational Physicians demonstrate and give a sufficient reason for those intricate mixtures, why so many simples in Mithridate or Treacle [theriac], why such and such quantity; may they not be reduced to half or a quarter? 'Tis vain to do with much (as the saying is) what can be done with a little; 300 simples in a Julip, Potion, or a little Pil, to what end or purpose? I know not what Alkindus, Capivaccius, Montagna, and Simon Eitover, the best of them all and the most rational have said in this kind; but neither he, they, nor any one of them, gives his reader, to my judgement that satisfaction which he ought; why such, so many simples.[149]

Compound remedies were, nevertheless, immensely popular, and Burton noted how 'the Venetian, Florentine states, have their several receipts and magistrals [sovereign recipes], they of Nuremberg have theirs, and Augustana [Augsburg] Pharmacopoeia, peculiar medicines to the meridian of the City: London hers, every City, Town, almost every private man, hath his own mixtures, compositions, receipts, magistrals'.[150] In his usual even-handed way Burton set out the reasons that justified the use of compound medicines: diseases which were 'mixed', that is caused by a variety of qualities and humours, required mixed remedies; different ingredients were appropriate to the different parts of the body that were affected by a disease, and also served different functions, one to change the quality of an affected part, another to comfort or strengthen it. Moreover, simples could do harm or be unpleasant and had to be

---

[147] Ibid.   [148] Harrison, *Description of England*, p. 266.
[149] Burton, *Anatomy of Melancholy*, p. 571.   [150] Ibid.

'corrected' by the addition of other ingredients, but underlying all the justifications was the simple pragmatic need to create new and better remedies.[151]

Despite their popularity and their use by learned physicians, compound remedies represented a weak point in learned medicine. There was little to distinguish them from the 'secrets', panaceas and other remedies of the empirics and mountebanks, as both were made from a mixture of ingredients. The learned physician would protest that he, unlike the empiric, had rational reasons for the ingredients that made up his compounds. But it was a touchy subject. James Primrose, for instance, felt the need to distinguish the 'Mountibanks Antidote' against poison from 'that ancient, and in all ages well approved Triacle of *Andromachus*, as also the Mithridate of Damocrates, and Matthiolus his Antidote'.[152] Although Primrose wrote that it was 'an easie thing for any Physician that knowes the matter of Physick, and the art of compounding medicaments, presently to prescribe such things',[153] what the art consisted of, and whether it had any rules as opposed to *ad hoc* justifications was doubtful to many opponents of Galenic medicine.

SIMPLES AS HELMONTIAN MEDICINES

Van Helmont, whose views on the nature of medicines were repeated by his followers in England, latched on to the apparently random nature of many compound remedies, and it formed a major part of his plea for a 'modern pharmacapolion [pharmacy] and dispensatory':

I pitty the so many connexions, and confused hotch-potch mixtures in the [apothecaries'] shops, the bewrayers of ignorance, and uncertainty. For the Schooles hope, that if one thing help not, another will help: and so

[151] 'Carden and Brassavola both hold that no simple medicine is without hurt or offence; and, although Hippocrates, Erasistratus, Diocles, of old, in the infancy of this Art, were content with ordinary simples, yet now, saith Aëtius, necessity compelleth to seek for new remedies, and to make compounds of simples, as well to correct their harms if cold, dry, hot, thick, thin, insipid, noisome to smell, to make them savoury to the palate, pleasant to taste and take, and to preserve them for continuance by admixtion of sugar, honey, to make them last months and years for several uses. In such cases compound medicines may be approved, and Arnoldus in his 18th Aphorism doth allow of it. "If simples cannot, neccessity compels us to use compounds."' Ibid., p. 257. For a similar defence of compounds see de Renou, *Medicinal Dispensatory*, pp. 128–30.

[152] Primrose, *Popular Errours*, pp. 24–5.

[153] Ibid., p. 25.

(through the preachment of Herbarists) they joyn many things together with each other . . . the concourse and confounding of crude Simples, do afford a conjectural event.[154]

Simples and not composite medicines were, in van Helmont's opinion, the basis of a 'modern' pharmacy. Like many critics of learned medicine, he drew upon Christianity and beliefs of primal simplicity to attack the corruption and complexity of the practices of his time. Van Helmont agreed with christianised Galenic medicine that herbs were providentially given by God to mankind. But the compounding of complicated remedies, which was typical of much of the pharmacy of learned medicine, constituted in his eyes a blasphemy, for it signified that the divine power of God in the original creation was insufficient and imperfect:

God out of the eternal providence of his goodness and wisdom, hath abundantly provided for future neccessities. He himself hath made and endowed Simples for the appointed ends of all neccessities. Therefore, I believe, that the Simples, in their own simplicitie, are sufficient for the healing of all Diseases . . . And by consequence, that Dispensatories, which will us to compound and joyn most things together, do destroy the whole, and through a hidden blasphemy, do as it were strive to supply divine insufficiency.[155]

As well as praising the curative powers of simples, van Helmont and his followers in England were concerned with two allied issues: how knowledge of the power of simples was to be gained, and how simples could be improved as therapeutic agents. The answer to the first question defined the Helmontians' position on the contested problem of what was certain knowledge and how it was acquired (epistemology). The answer to the second question allowed Helmontians to show that a chemical pharmacopeia represented a development and refinement of simples, and that, therefore, their medicines should not be taken as a rejection of traditional God-given remedies. Chemical remedies lay, as it were, in direct line of descent from the medicine of simples.

[154] Van Helmont, *Oriatrike*, pp. 456, 461.
[155] Ibid., p. 457. Van Helmont saw his attack on compounds as repeating that of Paracelsus: 'Hence *Paracelsus* rightly writeth to Chyrurgions: "To what end to ye over-adde unto Symphytum or the root of greater Comfrey, Vinegar, Bole [a medicinal earth] and such like wan addiments? when as God hath composed this Simple as altogether sufficient against the ruptures of bones? finally, whatsoever thou shalt adde unto it; thou makest, as if thout woudest by thy correction, supply the place of God" . . . In like manner, I also think, that God hath perfectly, and sufficiently composed in Simples, compleat Remedies of any Diseases whatsoever': pp. 457–8.

Van Helmont denied that Galenists had any links with God, in terms both of how knowledge of simples was arrived at, and of how they could be improved. He emphasised that it was only the true chemist who was inspired by God. Galenic physicians, he wrote, based their knowledge of the virtues of herbs upon Dioscorides, 'as if the power of medicine had attained unto its end, in the first Author [i.e. Dioscorides]', and he complained that they were more concerned with identifying and naming herbs than investigating their virtues.[156] Van Helmont perhaps exaggerated the reliance on Dioscorides, though he was immensely influential and much effort was exerted in retrieving Dioscoridean plants lost to early modern Europe. But he was right to note that more effort was put into identifying 'the faces and names' of plants than their virtues, and that knowledge of virtues was derived from books rather than from experience.

What was a pejorative comment would have been taken as a compliment by many medical writers of the sixteenth and early seventeenth centuries. They believed that they used their learning, skill and experience to select from the treasure trove of past knowledge those pieces of information about the virtues of plants that they thought most valuable, in the same way as recipes for compound medicines were chosen by lay compilers of manuscript remedy books and by medical writers from the vast oral and published knowledge of medicines. Such a widespread practice of selection and assimilation indicated the value placed on past and present knowledge and on the personal judgement that was brought to bear upon it. As the sixteenth-century surgeon and writer on the pox William Clowes put it when setting out 'certaine approved remedies, by mee collected' for the pox, 'I have gleaned and gathered these together, like as the poor Bee, which gathereth hir Honnie from everie sweete flower.'[157]

Van Helmont also condemned attempts to discover the virtues of

---

[156] Ibid., p. 457: 'But even unto this day, the more learned part of Physitions do as yet carefully dispute only about the faces and names of Herbs. As if the vertues could not speak before their countenance were known.' See also Paracelsus, '*Herbarius*', p. 105: 'But everyone pays attention only to names. If the medicine has the right name, that's that, everybody is satisfied.'

[157] William Clowes, *A Briefe and Necessarie Treatise, Touching the Cure of the Disease called Morbus Gallicus* (London, 1585), fol. 26ʳ. John Sadler in *The Sick Woman's Private Looking Glasse* (London, 1636), sig. A6ʳ, wrote of the way in which, like a bee, he had gathered knowledge from the Greeks, Latins and the 'experience of my owne practice'.

plants according to the doctrine of signatures (which held that a plant which looks like a part of the body will be able to cure it) and from astrology, which were both associated with Paracelsianism and were popular in mid-seventeenth-century England, being especially prominent in the works of Nicholas Culpeper (see chapter 8). There were those, wrote van Helmont, 'who would observe signatures in Herbs, as it were a Palmestry'.[158] Astrology was also unacceptable as a means of discovering a plant's powers: 'The powers of the Stars, are grown out of date,' declared van Helmont, and he argued 'the whole property of Herbes, is from their Seed, and the seminative power is drawn from the earth, according to the holy Scripture: but not from the faces of the lights of Heaven'.[159] Knowledge of the powers of plants should, instead, come from observation. The belief that observation rather than books was the source of knowledge was a common trope in the medicine of Paracelsus and in the natural philosophy of Galileo, and it had entered learned medicine in the area of observational if not physiological anatomy. Van Helmont reflected this strand of epistemology, which united diverse but innovative groups, when he wrote that 'Neither doth the reading of Books make us to be of the properties [of simples], but by observation.'[160]

However, who was to observe, and how would observation give knowledge? Here, van Helmont showed himself to be a follower of Paracelsus, and he clothed himself and his knowledge, as did his followers, with divine legitimation. This epistemology was intensely personal and visionary, and could not be put into practice by just anybody. This distinguishes it from the philosophies of Bacon and Descartes where the promise is held that a person's relationship to God does not affect whether he or she can acquire true knowledge.

---

[158] Van Helmont, *Oriatrike*, p. 457; van Helmont argued on grounds of religion that it was a matter of faith for him that man was not derived from nature (that is, that he was created by God), and 'likewise that nature is not the Image, likeness or engravement of man'. And he added that he laughed at Paracelsus because he 'erected serious trifles into the principles of healing', one of which was his doctrine of signatures or what van Helmont derisively called 'Palmestrical affinity': pp. 457, 458.

[159] Ibid., p. 458. Van Helmont did not completely reject astrology, and wrote, for instance, of the planetary influences upon metals, in 'The Power of Medicines' in ibid., p. 478. See also for van Helmont's natural philosophy Walter Pagel, *Joan Baptista van Helmont: Reformer of Science and Medicine* (Cambridge University Press, Cambridge, 1982), and 'The Religious and Philosophical Aspects of van Helmont's Science and Medicine', *Supplements to the Bulletin of the History of Medicine*, no. 2 (The Johns Hopkins University Press, Baltimore, 1944).

[160] Van Helmont, *Oriatrike*, p. 459.

Only the physicians chosen by God could, wrote van Helmont, attain knowledge of the secret properties of a herb. It was not 'the Schooles, but Physicians chosen of God, whom the Almighty hath chosen from their Mother's Womb, in time to come, shall know'.[161]

Just as the choice of physician was an act of divinity so the acquisition of knowledge was a gift of God. Observation and the chemist's fire were aids for the physician chosen by God who wanted to discover the hidden virtues of plants, but observation was as much spiritual as physical, for only when the chemical physician had lost the dross of the flesh which blinds the mind's eye could he attain knowledge of the archeus or inner chemist which gave a plant its power:

But the figurative power of the Seeds, lurketh in the Archeus, the Vulcan of herbs and things capable of generation, which cannot subsist with fleshy eyes. It is to be begged only of God, that he may vouchsafe to open the eyes of the mind, who to *Adam*, and who to *Salomon*, demonstrated the properties of things at the first sight. St. *Theresa* having once, mentally seen a Crucifix, perceived it to be the eyes of her soul; the which she thenceforth kept open for her life-time, and the flesh hath shut them up in us, through the corruption of nature . . . But the descriptions of all kinds of Medicines are read, being delivered in the Shops [of apothecaries], with a defect of the knowledge of properties and agreements. For I speak concerning a knowledge of vision, such a one, as the soul hath, being separated from the Body, and such a one, as God bestoweth in this life, on whom he will, and hitherto hath he removed this knowledge from the company of those who ascribe all reverence unto heathenish Books. The *Father of Lights* therefore is to be intreated that he may vouchsafe to give us knowledge.[162]

Galenic physicians clearly were not, in van Helmont's view, chosen by God. Their knowledge was derived from un-Christian sources and they could not, therefore, be gifted the divine vision with which to observe and know the properties of plants. This emphasis on the visionary and the divine distinguishes van Helmont's writings from those English natural philosophers, the 'virtuosi' and chemists like Robert Boyle who were creating 'new science' in the later seventeenth century. Although divine approval and aid in investigating the secrets of nature were not excluded by the proponents of a new science, especially in the case of Newton, knowledge for them was public, repeatable to witnesses, and often laid out according to a philosophical rather than a personal and visionary method (on the context to English Helmontians, see chapter 8).[163]

IMPROVING REMEDIES

The business of being a Helmontian chemical physician was thus permeated by a sense of godly mission. This gave Helmontian remedies divine legitimacy, and may have given patients additional confidence in their powers. Part of the mission, as it was presented by van Helmont, was to improve simples. Both Galenists and Helmontians had similar agendas: both believed that simples were God-given, and both groups tried to improve them. Galenists 'corrected' herbs and their virtues if they were perceived as too strong for a particular type of constitution or as generally dangerous, by drying, boiling, straining, reducing to powder, putting into syrup or pill form or by mixing with counteracting or neutralising substances. They attempted to create more efficacious remedies by compounding herbs together, often with mineral and animal substances. 'Corrections' and compounds were the two main methods used by Galenic physicians and apothecaries to improve upon simples. In the eyes of van Helmont, it was an approach which did not change the nature of the simple itself. The 'corrections' weakened its qualities, but as in van Helmont's view qualities were not part of the essence of a substance, the change was not a real one, whilst for Galenists any change in quality, for instance making a remedy less hot, represented a real transformation.[164] Moreover, van Helmont made play with the notion of Galenic physicians weakening remedies: 'I have hated the preparations of Simples, as oft as washing, boyling, burning or scorching, adjoyning or calcining, makes havock of their faculties [powers]. For Aloes [a purgative] looseth its juice by washing, and the residue remaines a meer Rosin [resin], the which, by its adhering unto the bowels is a stirrer up of wringings, and the piles.'[165] Although he accepted that some corrections worked, for instance, arum or wake-robin boiled in vinegar 'waxeth milde and becomes a healing Medicine against great falls', in general the powers of a plant were diminished by 'corrections',

---

[163] See, for instance, Betty Jo Dobbs, *The Janus Faces of Genius: the Role of Alchemy in Newton's Thought* (Cambridge University Press, Cambridge, 1991).

[164] Van Helmont, 'The Power of Medicines' in *Oriatrike*, pp. 471, 472.

[165] Van Helmont, 'A Modern Pharmacapolion and Dispensatory' in *Oriatrike*, p. 463.

and he wrote that the 'corrections' of the 'Schooles' were ridiculous and gelded and withdrew the faculties or powers from herbs.[166] In the case of compounds, the mixture might produce a remedy with new powers but the simples inside the compound still retained their intrinsic nature. Van Helmont and his followers offered improvements of simples based on chemical processes which would purify them of dangerous powers, whilst retaining their therapeutic power. They might also transform simples into new substances with new powers, for 'Chymistry produceth those things, which else should never be made, or had in Nature.'[167]

Despite acknowledging that simples were God's gift, the charge of blasphemously seeking to improve on God's creation was not one that van Helmont made against himself. Simples, he stated, were God's compounds, made from a mixture of bodies or substances, and chemistry could purify and refine them. For, as van Helmont wrote, it had not been properly taken into account 'that Herbs have much dung, which have never cast forth any out of them, and so they are to be refined with the greater wariness'.[168] Chemistry 'enabled a separation of the pure from the invalid or weak part of a herb' and it also produced 'an unlocking of the shut-up virtue' that resided in a simple.[169] The positions of Galenists and Helmontians were in some respects similar and the language of the 'preparation' of remedies was common to both groups, albeit different processes were involved. This ensured that, despite the praise by Galenists and Helmontians of simples as God-given, natural and simple (and hence it might follow also as pure), medical remedies would continue to be manufactured. Although apothecaries were often blamed by Galenists and Helmontians alike for the quality of their medicines, their commercial and manufacturing existence was confirmed by the philosophies and practices of the two medical sects.

Purity lay at the forefront of van Helmont's plea for a chemical preparation of simples. Simples made pure by chemistry could be less dangerous but still powerful. Remedies up to now were essentially impure: 'all things', he wrote, 'are at length, taken crude, hard, unripe, shutup, poysonsom, impure, bound, and unfit for the communicating of their virtues, and to be the more depraved by co-mingling [become even more impure by being compounded]'.[170]

---

[166] Ibid., p. 465.   [167] Ibid., p. 481.   [168] Ibid., p. 458.
[169] Ibid., p. 462.   [170] Ibid., p. 463.

Purification consisted of the 'whole Art of the fire'. At times, van Helmont saw chemical preparations as additions to the preparations or manufacturing processes that were traditionally carried out in the apothecaries' shops: 'the boylings and bruisings of the shop'.[171] Despite his rejection of the Galenic theory of qualities and humours, van Helmont presented himself as improving upon rather than rejecting the Galenic pharmacopeia by better, chemical, preparations of remedies.

However, chemistry could also create new types of remedies. Hidden virtues could be released by it, for, stated van Helmont, 'there are other things [than plants], which being shut up, are hindered from shewing their good will unto us; as gold, and gems or precious stones'.[172] Moreover, the transmutations made by chemistry were real ones, producing novel remedies. Van Helmont's construction of his 'modern' pharmacy combined a partial acceptance of Galenic methods, in that he saw the need to improve simples, together with a promise of radically new remedies. But what is also significant is that, despite being known as a believer in chemical remedies such as mercury, alkali-based substances and distillations, he took care to appropriate simples into his pharmacological philosophy, and like the Galenists to make them the basis or starting point of his pharmacopeia. Given that they were seen to be of divine origin, that they were very popular and that many were especially appropriate to the poor as they were widely available and cheap, it is difficult to see how van Helmont, who based his medicine on Christianity and charity, could have ignored them.

English Helmontian writers such as George Starkey, Marchamont Nedham and George Thomson followed van Helmont's strategy of praising simples, and making them appear to gain even greater purity through chemical processing, whilst attacking Galenic compounds and 'correctives'. Their medicines were mainly chemical ones, but their rhetoric meant that Helmontian medicine could, at least in the eyes of sympathisers, share in the general cultural approval of the primitive simplicity and purity of God-given herbs.[173]

---

[171] Ibid., p. 460.   [172] Ibid.

[173] George Thomson, *Orthomethodos Iatro-Chymike: Or the Direct Method of Curing Chymically* (London, 1675), pp. 69–73; Starkey, *Nature's Explication*, pp. 59–61, 69–74, 106–10; Nedham, *Medela Medicinae*, pp. 496–7.

CONCLUSION

Early modern English people were provided with good reasons to explain why remedies worked. Whether they gathered herbs, made or bought medicines because they were receptive to such reasons or because they were moved by the blind need to avoid pain, disease and death is difficult to discover. But remedies were made by and for the rich and the poor. They were part of the household economy run by women, and expressive of women's expertise in medicine. Remedies constituted a shared material culture between lay people and medical practitioners, even if the latter tried to appropriate it to themselves. The understanding of how remedies worked, although leading to disagreement between Galenists and Helmontians, by emphasising the primacy of simples as God-given allowed remedies to share in cultural attributes that went beyond the purely medical. The emphasis on simples as the starting point of the *materia medica* also meant that the lay and medical cultures had much in common, as their remedies shared many ingredients. Only when secret remedies became popular amongst Helmontians and empirics in the later seventeenth century (see chapters 9 and 10) did this shared culture break down. From remedies one turns logically to the diseases against which the remedies were used.

CHAPTER 3

Diseases

INTRODUCTION AND SUMMARY

The disease regime of England changed between the early modern period and the present day, from one where acute infectious diseases were predominant to one where the chronic illnesses of middle and old age came to the fore. Also, new diseases have appeared whilst others have disappeared, and, in general, it can be difficult to be sure that diseases can be properly identified from past descriptions. Nevertheless, despite these major caveats we can have a hazy, if not precise, certainty that we still share today many of the ills of sixteenth- and seventeenth-century England. And even if the diseases are different, the pains and disabilities of illness and the outcomes of recovery, chronic suffering or death experienced by the sick are recognisable across the centuries, though the environment of illness has moved from home to hospital and though many of the cultural meanings of illness have changed.

This makes the history of diseases relevant and interesting to the present. Historical demographers have assessed the impact of diseases like plague and smallpox upon populations in the past, whilst in recent years medical historians have explored the world of illnesses from the patient's point of view.[1] However, less is known

---

[1] See E. A. Wrigley and R. S. Schofield, *The Population History of England 1541–1871* (Cambridge University Press, Cambridge, 1989), where despite their doubts about identifying illnesses that caused morbidity, they do consider the short-term mortality of plague and the changing mortality and epidemiological course of smallpox; R. A. Houston, 'The Population History of Britain and Ireland 1500–1750' in Michael Anderson (ed.), *British Population History* (Cambridge University Press, Cambridge, 1996); M. Flinn, *The European Demographic System 1500–1820* (Harvester Press, Brighton, 1981). On patients' views of illness see Roy Porter (ed.), *Patients and Practitioners. Lay Perceptions of Medicine in Pre-Industrial Society* (Cambridge University Press, Cambridge, 1985); Roy Porter and Dorothy Porter, *In Sickness and In Health. The English Experience 1650–1850* (Fourth Estate, London, 1988), and *Patient's Progress: Doctors and Doctoring in Eighteenth Century England* (Blackwell, Oxford, 1989); Michael MacDonald,

about early modern perceptions of the range of ill conditions, illnesses and diseases, of lay people's ability to diagnose illness, and of the way medical writers constructed images of disease within the body using anatomical signposting. There was a large degree of agreement between lay and medical views of disease, especially as patients' subjective symptoms were accepted by medical practitioners as real and objective, with the patient's story of disease being often incorporated into medical accounts of disease. However, medical writers offered more esoteric and more detailed descriptions of disease, opening to view what was happening inside the body and employing specialised terminology which would be unfamiliar to most of the public. The body was viewed as porous and interconnected, with putrefaction especially creating disease within it, hence the use of the evacuative treatments of bleeding and purging. Yet, the broad outlines of disease narratives were in the public domain, which indicates that lay and medical understandings of disease overlapped. First, it is necessary to lay out the extent of knowledge of diseases, for the ability to give a name or to describe it was the first step in treating it.

THE RANGE OF ILLS AND DISEASES IN EARLY MODERN ENGLAND

The number of early modern ills and diseases that could be written or spoken about was enormous. The available lexicon of names and descriptions for illness had a variety of origins, local, national and foreign vernaculars together with Greek, Latin and Arabic, which created a mingling of popular and learned terms. What is striking about the early modern vocabulary of illness is that it ranges, often without the modern distinctions of seriousness, from ill conditions like bruises, aches, pains in the joints or in the eye, for instance, to named diseases such as plague or smallpox and conditions caused by humoral imbalances or by malign or noxious humours. This was partly because what appears minor to us today like a cut could become major and prove fatal through unchecked infection or, in

---

Mystical Bedlam: Madness, Anxiety and Healing in Seventeenth Century England (Cambridge University Press, Cambridge, 1981); Doreen G. Nagy, *Popular Medicine in Seventeenth-Century England* (Bowling Green State University Popular Press, Bowling Green, Ohio, 1988); see also, for Germany, Barbara Duden, *The Woman Beneath the Skin: a Doctor's Patients in Eighteenth-Century Germany*, trans. Thomas Dunlap (Harvard University Press, Cambridge, Mass., 1991).

early modern times, by putrefying. It also reflects the fact that the home was the place for all kinds of illness, whereas today the hospital often takes in, for a time at least, more serious cases and its existence helps to create a spatial differentiation between serious and minor illness.

It is also necessary to discard or modify some of our modern terminology relating to disease, especially our distinction between symptom and disease. For instance, what might appear to us to be a symptom, such as a headache, was often viewed as a disease or ill condition in its own right. The definition of what was a disease was not clear-cut: diseases such as plague could be perceived as entities existing outside the body, with a person's underlying humoral state allowing the disease to enter the body. Moreover, the extent of knowledge about disease was variable. Some humoral conditions, such as being melancholic or suffering from too much phlegm in the lungs or stomach, were commonly known about, but they were also part of the explanation of disease provided by Galenic medicine. The humoral system was often used by the learned Galenic physicians to provide underlying and more esoteric explanations of named conditions. They also developed complex descriptions of the body's disorders centred around graphic imaging of the action of the humours inside it. However, the Galenic humours were also within the public domain, at least the literate part of it, and medical explanations based on the humours can be distinguished from lay ones, if at all, only by the level of complexity and by technical medical terminology, for instance, that drawn from anatomy.

A sense of the range of illnesses that were recognised in early modern England comes from the causes of death listed in the London Bills of Mortality. The cause of death of anyone dying in a London parish was certified by the 'searchers of the dead', usually old women, who were also often long-term pensioners of the parish. The causes of death, therefore, represent lay knowledge of illness. John Graunt, a member of the Royal Society and, unusually for that body, a tradesman, made a study of London's population, its ills and deaths, using the Bills of Mortality,[2] and compiled a 'Table of Casualties' for the period 1629–60 as shown in table 1.

Hindsight is very liable to affect an analysis of the illnesses in

[2] John Graunt, *Natural and Political Observations . . . Upon the Bills of Mortality*, 5th edn (London, 1676).

Table 1 *Causes of death drawn from the London Bills of Mortality, 1629–60*

Abortive and Stil-born	Lethargy
Aged	Leprosie
Ague and Fever	Liver-grown, Spleen and Rickets
Apoplex and Suddenly	Lunatick
Bleach	Meagrom [migraine]
Blasted	Measles
Bleeding	Mother [disorder of the womb], rising
Bloody Flux, Scouring and Flux	of the Lights [lungs]
Burnt and Scalded	Murdered
Calenture [fever]	Overlaid and starved at Nurse
Cancer, Gangrene and Fistula	Palsie [paralysis]
Wolf [ulcerous tumour]	Plague
Canker, Sore-mouth and Thrush	Plague in the Guts
Child-bed	Pleurisie
Chrisoms [a child in its first month]	Poisoned
and Infants	Purples and Spotted Fever
Colick and Wind	Quinsie and Sore-throat
Cold and Cough	Rickets
Consumption and Cough	Rupture
Convultion	Scal'd head
Cramp	Scurvy
Cut of the Stone	Smothered and stifled
Dropsie and Tympany	Sores, ulcers, broken and bruised (Limbs)
Drowned	Shot
Excessive drinking	Spleen
Executed	Shingles
Fainted in a Bath	Starved
Falling-Sickness	Stitch
Pox and small Pox	Stone and Strangury
Found dead in the Streets	Sciatica
French Pox	Stopping of the Stomach
Frighted	Surfet
Gout	Swine-Pox
Grief	Teeth and Worms
Hanged, and made-away themselves	Tissick [concumptive or asthmatic cough]
Head-Ach	Thrush
Jaundice	Vomiting
Jaw-faln	Worms
Impostume [abscess]	Wen [tumour, wart, goitrous swelling]
Itch	Suddenly
Killed by several Accidents	
King's Evil [scrofula]	

Source: John Graunt, *Natural and Political Observations . . . Upon the Bills of Mortality* 5th edn (London, 1676), table following p. 114.

Graunt's list. For instance, we can infer from present-day knowledge that 'Apoplex and Suddenly' would have included a number of cases of stroke and heart attack. 'Child-bed' seems too unspecific given the different conditions that can, in our terms, cause death in childbirth, whilst 'Itch', 'Cramp', 'Canker, Sore-mouth and Thrush' might appear to us to be minor symptoms or symptoms of an underlying illness rather than causes of death. While modern medical knowledge is essential for historical demographers who are concerned with producing the most 'objective' picture of the diseases prevalent in the past, it can often act as a barrier to understanding how illnesses were perceived then. For instance, the modern differentiation between symptoms and the underlying causes of diseases can influence the analysis of past descriptions of disease too much.[3] Yet it is also difficult to avoid, as such differentiation was present to some extent from the time of Galen, and certainly helped to structure the learned medical textbooks of early modern Europe. The distinction has connotations of elite authority; it was after all Aristotle who stated that what set the philosopher apart from the mere artisan is that the philosopher knows the causes of things whilst the artisan only knows how to do something.[4] This sense of superiority associated with a knowledge of causes has persisted into present-day medicine, and is deeply inculcated in the modern educational systems of Europe and the United States.

It is, therefore, easy to dismiss lay notions of disease as 'only' based on obvious subjective symptoms. But for many lay people in the early modern period, and for the books that provided them with remedies, the symptoms were often the disease. Sometimes an underlying cause for their illness was sought by patients and this could range from God and sin (especially as for Christians diseases came into the world with the Fall and remedies were part of God's providence) to aspects of regimen such as food and the internal working of the body. Often, however, the disease was seen as the predominant symptom or symptoms and the latter was what had to be treated. Today, in minor conditions symptoms are taken to be the

---

[3] This is especially the case with attempts to discover in modern terms what diseases like the pox or the pestilence 'really' consisted of. There has been a move away from such research by historians of medicine. See, for instance, the refusal to identify the pox in modern terms by Jon Arrizabalaga, John Henderson and Roger French in *The Great Pox. The French Disease in Renaissance Europe* (Yale University Press, New Haven, 1997).

[4] Aristotle, *Metaphysics*, 981^a–982^b 27; *Ethics*, 1139^b 14–1142^a 31.

equivalent of an illness, as, for instance, in the 'Sore-throat' or 'Cold and Cough'. However, such symptoms could, in the opinion of the searchers of the dead, and most probably of the relatives of the deceased from whom they often obtained their evidence, cause death. The reason for this is partly biological. What appear to us to be minor conditions because they are easily treatable were, in the sixteenth and seventeenth centuries, potential killers, especially in the case of infections or infectious diseases. Or the symptoms might be the visible tip of what in terms of modern medical knowledge are serious underlying diseases. There was also a widespread cultural-philosophical acceptance of the importance and reality of knowledge derived from the senses.[5] This meant that the patient's subjective feelings or symptoms were sufficient in themselves to constitute the illness. Moreover, in a system of medicine where lay participation and expertise were widespread, a symptom-based knowledge of illness made sense, for it allowed the largest possible number of people to join in the practice of medicine and to communicate easily with each other, as symptoms were exoteric rather than esoteric, being open to view, or to discussion in the shared language of pain, aches, etc. Although learned medical texts emphasised the importance of causes of illness, they also accepted the reality of symptoms as experienced by the patient and observed by the physician. It is

---

[5] The Elizabethan lawyer and diarist, John Manningham, wrote, 'The divine, the lawyer, and the physicion must all have these three things, reason, experience, and authority, but each in a severall degree; the divine must begin with the authoritie of scripture, the lawyer rely on reason, and the physicion trust to experience.' He also repeated the saying from philosophy that nothing is in the intellect which was not before in the senses. *Diary of John Manningham*, ed. John Bruce (Camden Society, J. B. Nichols, Westminster, 1868), pp. 92, 64. Lady Brilliana Harley, who supported Puritan preachers and the Parliamentarians, stressed to her son that some truths were discovered 'experimentally' or from experience. *Letters of the Lady Brilliana Harley*, ed. Thomas Taylor Lewis (Camden Society, LVIII, London, 1854). See, for instance, A. Wear, 'Perceptions of Health and New Environments in the Early English Settlement of North America: Ideals and Reality' in Mario Gomes Marques and John Cule (eds.), *The Great Maritime Discoveries and World Health: Proceedings of the First International Congress on the Great Maritime Discoveries and World Health held in Lisbon on 10–13 September, 1990* (Escola Nacional de Saude Publica: Orden dos Médicos: Instituto de Sintra, Lisbon, 1991), pp. 273–8; esp. pp. 274–5: everyone's testimony had equal weight as long as it was experienced and reliable. Claims as to the nature of New England were 'made manifest by experience, the most infallible proof of all assertions': G. Mount (pseudonymous), *An Historicall Discoverie and Relation of the English Plantations of New England* (London, 1627), sig. D2ᵛ. The witch-hunter Matthew Hopkins justified his skill as coming not from books but 'from experience, which though it be meanly esteemed of, yet [is] the surest and safest way to judge by': Matthew Hopkins, *The Discovery of Witches* (London, 1647), p. 1. He also argued that the devil's skill in medicine came from his long experience; ibid., p. 9.

true that the new science and philosophy of the later seventeenth century relegated subjective sensations to the status of 'secondary qualities', so that they no longer constituted reality. Instead, they were taken to be the sensory by-products of the particular size, shape and motion of the invisible particles that made up the world as they impinged upon the body in the new universes of Descartes, Newton and Boyle. In medicine, however, sensations or subjective symptoms were taken seriously until around the beginning of the nineteenth century. Then in 'Paris medicine', the medicine created by revolutionary France, a clear-cut distinction was made between the subjective symptoms of the patient and the objective signs observed by the physician such as pulse, temperature and the sounds heard through the stethoscope. The former were considered to be less trustworthy than the latter. But throughout the early modern period symptoms retained their importance for lay people and learned medical writers. They could be the disease itself or be a part of named diseases like 'Plague', 'Measles', 'French Pox' and 'Kings Evil'. These diseases were often seen as entities in their own right, and were viewed as having a concrete or overall reality, but they also consisted in the eyes of contemporaries of symptoms such as the carbuncles of plague, or the skin lesions and joint pains of the French pox, which had to be treated if the disease was to be cured.

That the diagnosis of illness was a lay as well as a medical skill was legally recognised by the duty laid upon the lay men on inquest juries to certify cause of death, usually in cases of suspected violence. Juries were also empanelled to determine if a person was mad, when control of property was at issue.[6] The quasi-legal institution of the searchers of the dead indicates a recognition by London's local government that even the poorest in society had diagnostic abilities. The elderly women who were given the office of searchers had little choice as to whether they could decline, for refusal of such a duty could mean the cutting-off of poor relief.[7] Their certifications were

---

[6] See T. R. Forbes, 'Crowner's Quest', *Transactions of the American Philosophical Society*, 68, 1, 1978, 1–48; on the Court of Wards and its successor the Court of Chancery which dealt with the estates of lunatics see R. Porter, *Mind Forg'd Manacles: Madness and Psychiatry in England from Restoration to Regency* (Athlone Press, London, 1987), pp. 111–14. For a contrary view see Michael MacDonald, 'Lunatics and the State in Georgian England', *Social History of Medicine*, 2, 1989, 299–313.

[7] In 1581, the Lord Mayor ordered that if the searchers gave the wrong cause of death, or refused to serve, they should be imprisoned; T. R. Forbes, 'The Searchers' in Saul Jarcho

collected by the parish clerks to form the Bills of Mortality from which Graunt took his data.[8] His 'Table', therefore, reproduced to some extent the disease terminology and the medical knowledge of the poor. The searchers may have been instructed on how to do their job, but there is, as far as I know, no evidence of this. Graunt discussed the trustworthiness of their findings. He treated their expertise as autonomous in that they made independent judgements of the cause of death. Graunt added that the searchers did not have to rely totally on their own judgements. Their views were often informed and modified by the medical practitioner and by the lay people who had been attending the patient. This is a further indication of how porous were the boundaries of medical knowledge, and of the danger of assuming that any one group in English society had its own compartmentalised medical knowledge and practice. Graunt, who was clearly influenced by the empirical philosophy of Francis Bacon, concluded that, in any case, the searchers' own senses were sufficient.[9]

Graunt began by asking whether the searchers were reliable and if the Bills of Mortality needed to be modified: 'Now to make these Corrections upon, the perhaps, ignorant and careless *Searchers* Reports, I considered first of what Authority they were of themselves, that is, whether any credit at all were to be given to their Distinguishments [i.e. of the causes of death]'. He concluded that by and large the searchers could be relied upon. Many of their reports, he wrote, were based on the senses rather than on expert medical knowledge, for instance, whether a child was 'abortive' or 'stillborn', or if a man had died '*Aged*, that is to say above sixty years old or thereabouts'. The niceties of learned medical diagnosis could be too uncertain, and Graunt added approvingly that in the case of the aged the searchers did not make 'any curious determination, whether such *Aged* persons died purely of *Age*, as for that the *Innate heat* was quite exhausted, or the Radical moisture quite dried up (for I have heard some Candid *Physicians* complain of the darkness which

(ed.), *Essays on the History of Medicine* (Science History Publications, New York, 1976), pp. 148–9. Also A. Wear, 'Caring for the Sick Poor in St Bartholomew's Exchange: 1580–1676' in W. F. Bynum and R. Porter (eds.), *Living and Dying in London, Medical History*, Supplement 11, 1991, p. 46. Richelle Munkhoff, 'Searchers of the Dead: Authority, Marginality, and the Interpretation of Plague in England', *Gender and History*, 11, 1999, 1–29: the searchers were poor respectable women. My thanks to David Harley for the ref.

[8] For a description of this process see Graunt, *Observations*, pp. 16–17.

[9] See the 'Epistle Dedicatory' to Sir Robert Moray, in ibid., sig. a4ᵛ.

themselves were in hereupon)'.[10] Although Graunt differentiated between the searchers' medical knowledge and that of physicians, he accepted that in a rough and ready way the searchers' reports were valid. 'As for *Consumptions*', he wrote, 'if the *Searchers* do but truly Report (as they may) whether the dead Corps were very lean and worn away, it matters not to many of our purposes, whether the Disease were exactly the same, as *Physicians* define it in their Books.'[11] Graunt conceded that the physicians might be able to give an underlying cause for what appeared to be a fatal symptom, but he thought that symptom-based certification was sufficient: 'I say, it is enough, if we know from the *Searchers* but the most predominant Symptoms; as that one died of the *Headach*, who was sorely tormented with it, though the Physicians were of Opinion that the Disease was in the *Stomach*.'[12] Clearly, the patient's account of his or her symptoms was good evidence for Graunt, despite any contrary claims by physicians. He added that most lay people were able to distinguish the major diseases from each other:

> To conclude, In many of these Cases the *Searchers* are able to report the Opinion of the *Physician*, who was with the Patient, as they receive the same from the Friends of the Defunct: and in very many Cases, such as *Drowning, Scalding, Bleeding, Vomiting, making away themselves, Lunaticks, Sores, Small pox, etc.* their own senses are sufficient and the generality of the World are able pretty well to distinguish the *Gout, Stone, Dropsie, Falling sickness, Palsie, Agues, Pleuresie, Rickets,* one from another.[13]

Graunt's attitude to the searchers' diagnostic ability indicates that he accepted, but only partially, that there was a distinction between popular and elite medical knowledge. He believed that the former was valuable in its own right, he recognised that an interchange took place between the two, but he also observed one united medical culture shared, at least in respect of diagnosis, by the 'generality of the World'. The attitude to disease taken by many writers of vernacular medical books fits this pattern. They often accepted that their lay readers were able to diagnose diseases and wrote books for them which named diseases and provided remedies. A few tried to educate them in diagnosis, and some wrote at a higher level about the intricacies of humoral or chemical medicine for a knowledgeable lay and medical readership.

---

[10] Ibid., p. 19.   [11] Ibid., p. 20.
[12] Ibid., p. 21. Headaches were frequently explained as arising from the stomach; see below.
[13] Ibid., p. 21.

The existence of a common medical culture of diagnosis shows itself more generally by the widespread practice of self-treatment, of family-based treatment and the lay treatment offered by neighbours and charitable women. As the majority of the medical books aimed at this market, the books of remedies, whose roots go back to the medieval vernacular manuscript tradition,[14] were silent about the symptoms and causes of disease, their compilers must have assumed that the readers would know what illnesses they or their patients were suffering from, and were only interested in learning of remedies to cure them. The diagnostic skill of readers was taken for granted.

For instance, Leonard Mascall, the translator of *Prepositas His Practise* (1588) which listed 'most excellent and approved Medicines, Receiptes, and Ointments of great vertues, but also most precious Waters against many infirmities of the body', intended that the book should be read by lay people. He wrote that 'herein maist thou [the reader] readily finde medicines for sundry diseases, and how thy selfe maist make the same, or cause them to be made'.[15] *Prepositas His Practise*, like other remedy books, stressed that what were unknown to the reader were the remedies and their manufacture; they were, wrote Mascall, 'secretes' and 'men or women shall, having read this booke, see and understand how that there are in hearbes, plants, gummes etc such severall vertues, and that of them divers [several] so holesome conserves, confections, sirops, and other like may be made, which they have utterly beene ignorant of untill now'.[16] Knowledge of the diseases that the remedies were to be applied against was not the issue. Despite providing the usual caution that the learned physician should be consulted, Mascall justified offering his readers the means of self-treatment on the grounds that they could diagnose illness and might not be able to consult physicians: 'Onely for some diseases ordinarily knowne, for which some are not able, and some dare not to seeke remedie at the

---

[14] See Paul Slack, 'Mirrors of Health and Treasures of Poor Men: the Uses of the Vernacular Medical Literature of Tudor England' in Charles Webster (ed.), *Health, Medicine and Mortality in the Sixteenth Century* (Cambridge University Press, Cambridge, 1979), pp. 237–71, esp. pp. 250–1.

[15] Nicolaus Praepositus, *Prepositas His Practise, A Worke Very Necessary to be Used for the Better Preservation of the Health of Man* (London, 1588), title page, p. 1, 'To the Reader'. The identity of Nicolaus Praepositus and the provenance of the *Dispensarium* published in the late fifteenth and early sixteenth century under his name are matters of dispute; see *A Catalogue of Printed Books in the Wellcome Historical Medical Library Books Printed Before 1641* (Wellcome Historical Medical Library, London, 1962), p. 278.

[16] Praepositus, *Practise*, p. 2.

phisition, no reason is that such yet should be utterly debarred of that ordinarie helpe which God hath appointed.'[17] For instance, after the instructions for making 'an electuary [a medicinal paste or conserve] of the iuce of roses', its uses were set out: 'This doth purge choler easily, and healeth hote diseases in the ioyntes, the head-ach, the turning sickness [vertigo], the paine of the eyes, and it hath beene proved against the yellow iaundis.'[18] The reader was expected to know these conditions. Some of them would have been obviously perceptible to a reader/patient, such as hot joints, headache, vertigo and pains in the eyes. Others, such as too much choler in the stomach and yellow jaundice, might have required a knowledge of humoral medicine, though the yellow colour of the skin in jaundice was obvious, and the name, jaundice, could stand alone without the reader having to know it was caused by too much yellow bile. Detailed descriptions of an illness were unusual in remedy books and in the manuscript collections of remedies, though occasionally a latinate term was explained. For instance, a lengthy compound recipe built around senna was described as curing 'all diseases of melancholy, and madness . . . quartaines [fevers] and diseases of the spleene', and in addition as being effective against 'cardiaca passion which is a gryping about the stomache'.[19]

Although some books set out to educate the reader in how to interpret the body and its ills according to the humoral system, the books of remedies were 'how to' books concerned with the material and practical side of medicine, with the making and administering of remedies, and in general with adding to readers' stores of remedies. The evidence from medical book publishing indicates that there was thought to be little demand for books which would increase readers' diagnostic abilities.

Lay diagnosis of illness had implications for both lay people and medical practitioners. It meant that patients were often, but not always, less dependent on medical expertise than today, where the fog of uncertainty created in the patient's mind by the onset of serious illness is only lifted by the physician's diagnosis and declaration of what treatment is required. Lay knowledge and diagnosis of illness also allowed patients and/or their relatives and friends to have some control over treatment. As they had an idea of what needed to be treated, they were able to go from one practitioner to

---

[17] Ibid.   [18] Ibid., p. 26.   [19] Ibid., p. 24.

another to obtain a successful cure, or they could try to treat themselves (see chapter 1). This contrasts with the power, which is increasingly challenged, of modern scientific medicine to exclude real patient choice in treatments and in practitioners, which partly stems from the medicalisation of the diagnosis of illness, and partly from the link between diagnosis and the treatment of serious illness having become purely a matter for the medical professional.

Lay diagnosis continued throughout the period 1550–1680. At the end of the seventeenth century the compilers of books of remedies still assumed that their readers knew how to diagnose their illnesses, and the searchers of the dead and inquest juries continued to certify cause of death. However, as is discussed below, private autopsies to ascertain cause of death were increasingly carried out by physicians and surgeons in the seventeenth century, though their numbers were never large and in these instances lay people acknowledged the authority of medical diagnosis. Surgeons began to give expert evidence on cause of death from the middle of the seventeenth century and perhaps from much earlier.[20] But there was no requirement by the state for medical certification of the cause of death, nor, to be anachronistic, was the diagnosis of illness integrated

---

[20] Thomas Forbes identifies as the first documented evidence of expert medical testimony given in an English murder trial the 1678 trial of the Earl of Pembroke, where four surgeons and two physicians were called to testify as to the cause and seriousness of an internal haemorrhage in the victim's stomach. T. R. Forbes, *Surgeons at the Bailey. English Forensic Medicine to 1878* (Yale University Press, New Haven, 1985), pp. 46–7. However, there are no full records for early coroners' court depositions. The College of Physicians was asked to give its opinion to the Crown in May 1632 about the safety of the conviction of 'one Cromwell' for murder by poisoning. The body was autopsied and the suspect material, a bolus (or medicinal clayey earth containing, in this case, mercury), analysed by members of the College. Dr Othowell Meverall also of the College had given evidence at the trial. *Annals*, 3, fols. 120a–123a. In continental Europe medical testimony in court was usual well before that date. An early example is from the records of the small Provençal town of Manosque; see Joseph Shatsmiller, *Médicine et Justice en Provence Médievale Documents de Manosque 1262–1348* (Publications de l'Université de Provence, Aix en Provence, 1989). I am grateful to Professor Nancy Siraisi for this reference. The leading sixteenth-century French surgeon, Ambroise Paré, in his *Traité des Rapports* (Paris, 1575), set out how a surgeon should write reports on different types of wounds and violent deaths; Paulus Zacchias, the personal physician to popes Innocent X and Alexander VII and *Protomedicus* to the Papal States, in his *Questiones Medico-Legales* dealt with a range of forensic issues that came within the scope of Canon Law and medical expertise. In England Paré's treatise was translated by Thomas Johnson in his edition of Paré's *Workes* (London, 1634) and appended to the end of Thomas Brugis, *Vade Mecum: Or, a Companion for a Chyrurgion* (London, 1652), as 'the maner of making reports before a Judge of Assize, of any one that hath come to an untimely end'. Lay jurors were given advice on how to decide on cases of suspected violent death, for instance if someone had naturally drowned or had been put in the water after death, in Richard Hawes, *The Poor-Mans Plaster Box* (London, 1634), pp. 38–41.

into the economic fabric of society as it is today when, as in the case of a sick note for sickness benefit, a disease has to be identified by a doctor.[21]

Four things make a practical physician; first, to have a materia medica in his head; second, pertinently to prescribe; third exactly to judge of the disease; fourth, to have good prognosticks; the last is for his credit chiefly.[22]

The importance of learned medical views about disease would at first sight appear to be slight. The learned physicians were few in number, and, as they themselves admitted, the major part of medical practice was undertaken in the family or by empirics or other practitioners who did not have any formal education in medicine. Yet, the influence of the theories of learned medicine about physiology,[23] regimen, pathology and therapeutics upon literate culture was remarkable. Literate lay people took their knowledge of what happened inside a diseased body largely from learned medicine. This knowledge was then reproduced and often had a life of its own in a lay setting. Unlike the case of diagnosis (and therapeutics), there is less evidence of an oral culture or knowledge of the pathology of disease. But diaries, letters and other literate productions such as plays, poems, travellers' accounts, and political and religious tracts indicate how the influence of learned medicine had spread throughout lay literate culture. In a process that began in the classical period and continued through the Middle Ages and beyond the Renaissance, the teachings of learned medicine on the inner workings of the body in health and disease came to frame the way lay literate culture across Europe constructed its images of what was happening inside the body.

Although bits of medical knowledge about disease abound in lay literate culture, the coherent medical textbook exposition of the nature of diseases took place in the context of a genre of writing

---

[21] Though medical notes were provided to excuse non-appearance as a witness. David Harley, 'The Scope of Legal Medicine in Lancashire and Cheshire, 1660–1760' in Michael Clark and Catharine Crawford (eds.), *Legal Medicine in History* (Cambridge University Press, Cambridge, 1994), pp. 45–63.

[22] John Ward, *Diary of the Rev. John Ward, A. M., Vicar of Stratford-Upon-Avon . . . 1648 to 1679*, ed. Charles Severn (London, 1839), p. 265.

[23] The term 'physiology' was not often used in the modern sense, though Daniel Sennert did employ it.

called the *practica* or compendia on the practice of medicine. These dated from the Middle Ages and usually set out diseases in a head-to-toe order, with separate sections on fevers. Unlike many of the works of empirics and remedy books, the *practica* went beyond naming a disease and giving treatments for it. They also gave its signs and causes. In other words, they identified or constructed diseases by selecting salient signs from the huge variety that would be reported by patients or observed upon their bodies. Many specific diseases or ill states of the body had been isolated in classical times, with Galen's *De Locis Affectis* (*On the Affected Parts*) being especially influential, and it also helped to consolidate the tradition of the head-to-toe order of the *practica*.[24]

The ability to identify a disease with precision, to give its causes and then, hopefully, to relate treatment to the causes was considered by physicians one of the achievements of learned medicine, together with the creation of knowledge about anatomy, the normal working of the body or, to use the modern term, physiology, and regimen. It is sometimes assumed that diseases were only identified as specific entities from the early nineteenth century when the researches of the Paris school of medicine created a localised view of illness which replaced the previous holistic perception of disease as a general imbalance of the humours.[25] However, diseases as localised collections of symptoms caused by localised humoral disorders had been constructed from classical times onwards. For instance, amongst the ills of the head were listed headache or 'cephalagia', epilepsy, vertigo, palsy or paralysis, convulsions, apoplexy, lethargy or the need to sleep continually, catalepsy, phrensy and mania, as well as

---

[24] Luke Demaitre, 'Scholasticism in Compendia of Practical Medicine 1250–1450,' *Manuscripta*, 20, 1976, 81–95; C. H. Talbot, *Medicine in Medieval England* (Oldbourne, London, 1967) has useful accounts of the writers of medieval *practica*; A. Wear, 'Explorations in Renaissance Writings on the Practice of Medicine' in A. Wear, R. K. French and I. M. Lonie (eds.), *The Medical Renaissance of the Sixteenth Century* (Cambridge University Press, Cambridge, 1985), pp. 118–145, 312–17; C. H. Talbot in *Medicine in Medieval England* (Oldbourne, London, 1967), p. 15 gives Pliny's *Natural History* as an early example of the head-to-toe order and L. Mackinney, 'Medieval Medical Dictionaries and Glossaries' in J. L. Cate and E. N. Anderson (eds.), *Medieval and Historiographical Essays in Honour of James Westfall Thompson* (University of Chicago Press, Chicago, 1938), p. 243, gives Scribonius Largus as the originator in the *Compositiones Medicamentorum*. Galen also used the order in *De Locis Affectis*. However, who began the use of the order is unknown: V. Nutton, personal communication.

[25] Erwin H. Ackerknecht, *Medicine at the Paris Hospital, 1794–1848* (John Hopkins University Press, Baltimore, 1967); Michel Foucault, *The Birth of the Clinic. An Archaeology of Medical Perception*, trans. by A. M. Sheridan Smith (Tavistock Publications, London, 1973).

disorders of the organs of the head such as cataract in the eyes. All these conditions had their proper signs and causes so that, for instance, palsy was indicated by paralysis of one side of the body, or of all the parts under the head, or of a particular part. Sometimes in palsy there was a loss of the sensitive faculty in a part of the body but not of the motive faculty or vice versa, or: 'Sometimes it happens, that neither sense or motion is quite taken away but onely waxeth dull and is benum'd.'[26] Palsy, it was taught, was caused by disorders of the brain and especially of the 'marrow of the back bone', which from the time of Galen were believed to be the origins of the nerves. A tumour crushing the marrow, wounds, falls, and breaks to the spinal column could cause paralysis, but often its cause was a 'cold and moist distemper' with 'thin and watrish humors derived from the braine' clogging up the nerves so that the passage of the animal spirits which conveyed sensation and motion through the nerves to all the parts of the body was hindered.[27] The confident precision with which the disorder was identified and explained is character- istic, as is the integration of signs and causes, and the mix of localised and generalised reasoning. These were the building blocks from which diseases were constructed from classical times onwards and they represent the hidden iceberg upon which later medicine, including that of the Paris school, created its clinical descriptions of disease. And although it is unfashionable in the history of medicine nowadays to praise past medical writers, there can be little doubt that the construction of diseases by classical physicians and to some extent by the physicians who followed them, as in the case of 'new diseases' like the pox and the English sweat, represents an immense achievement.

A few very committed Galenists such as Gianbaptista da Monte (1498–1552), the professor of the practice of medicine at Padua who was at the forefront of attempts to bring into medicine the purest, most correct form of Galenic practice, were critical of the *practica* tradition in that they wanted therapy to be related not only to the causes of disease, but also to the indications from each individual patient such as their specific humoral constitution and habitual

---

[26] Gualterus Bruele, *Praxis Medicinae, Or the Physicians Practice Wherein Are Contained All Inward Diseases From the Head to the Foot* (London, 1632), pp. 12–15; this was a translation of the *Praxis Medicinae Theorica et Empirica Familiarissima* (Antwerp, 1579).

[27] 'Animal spirits' were the finest and most tenuous part of the arterial blood. Bruele, *Praxis Medicinae*, pp. 12–15.

lifestyle. In England the rhetoric of individualised treatment was used to give authority to learned medicine and to contrast its practice with that of empirics who, whatever the type of patient, had one treatment for a particular disease. But it was mainly rhetoric. No new textbook in medicine based on da Monte's views, which went back to Galen's *Methodus Medendi (Method of Healing)*, was published in England, though John Caius produced a Latin text of the *Methodus* in 1544.[28] However, the *practica* available in English, such as Christopher Wirsung's influential *General Practise of Physicke* (1598, reprinted in 1617 and 1654) and Gualterus Bruele's *Praxis Medicinae, Or the Physicians Practice* (1632, reprinted 1639), did consider the age, sex and habits of patients even if it was not done as consistently and in such a fine-grained way as Galenists like da Monte would have wished.

The way in which diseases were discussed in the books on the practice of medicine was seen by some literate lay people as a reflection of how a learned physician thought and wrote about disease. When Sir Richard Hawkins wrote about his experience of scurvy whilst on his voyage to South America in 1593, he pleaded that 'some learned man would write of it, for it is the plague of the Sea'. He did, however, and this was not untypical, feel confident enough as an educated lay man to write his own brief 'discourse of the Scurvey' which mirrored the format of the *practica*, beginning with the signs of scurvy, its causes, including faults of regimen, and ending with its treatments. These involved changes in the regimen or lifestyles of the crew and the use of specific treatments such as oranges and lemons, Dr Stevens water and 'oil of vitry' or sulphuric acid.[29]

---

[28] Jerome Bylebyl, 'Teaching Methodus Medendi in the Renaissance' in F. Kudlien and R. J. Durling (eds.), *Galen's Method of Healing* (E. J. Brill, Leiden, 1991), pp. 157–89; see also Andrew Wear, 'Medicine in Early Modern Europe 1500–1700' in L. Conrad, M. Neve, V. Nutton, R. Porter and A. Wear, *The Western Medical Tradition 800 BC to AD 1800* (Cambridge University Press, Cambridge, 1995), pp. 256–60. Da Monte did break with Galen on occasion; see Nancy G. Siraisi, *Avicenna in Renaissance Italy. The Canon and Medical Teaching in Italian Universities after 1500* (Princeton University Press, Princeton, 1987), pp. 248–54, esp. 246–51.

[29] 'The Observations of Sir Richard Hawkins, Knight, in his Voyage into the Southern Sea. An. Dom. 1593' in Samuel Purchas, *Purchas His Pilgrimes* (London, 1625), vol. IV, fols. 1374, 1373 and margin. Oranges and lemons were used to treat scurvy from the sixteenth century, well before their general use in the British navy at the end of the eighteenth century. But there was no consensus about their value, which kept being lost and rediscovered. See Kenneth Carpenter, *The History of Scurvy and Vitamin C* (Cambridge University Press, Cambridge, 1986).

THE SIGNS OF DISEASE

The signs and the causes of illness occupied separate sections in medical textbooks, though, in fact, the two were symbiotically linked, for the signs of a disease were often discussed in terms of its causes and vice versa. The sense of sure confidence in the matter-of-fact truth of the descriptions of disease in the *practica* owed something to the way in which the apparently observational nature of the signs of a disease supported the theoretical accounts of its causes, and to the way in which the signs were made sense of by the causes. In the constructions of disease, signs and causes intermingled, and in the process the construction of the identity of a disease was strengthened and made more believable. Nevertheless, it is worthwhile separating signs and causes, as did medical writers, for historians have not often considered the significance in their own right of symptoms and signs in early modern medicine.

As we shall see, symptoms and signs were often interchangeable in this period. There were, however, some signs that were usually only interpreted by practitioners. 'The business and care of the Physician' was 'to visit the Patient, to feel his Pulse, and consider his Urine, discourse of the state of the Disease, and prescribe proper Remedies for it'.[30] Taking the pulse and uroscopy were two specialised skills which enabled the practitioner (and occasionally a lay person) to assess the state of a patient and make a diagnosis. The different types of pulse – rapid, strong, weak, irregular and so forth – had been set out at great length by Galen, and the ability to interpret the pulse was associated especially with the learned physician.[31] On the other hand, uroscopy, if used as the sole means of diagnosis and in the absence of the patient, was attacked by physicians as the fraudulent practice of empirics.[32] Nevertheless, in the Middle Ages uroscopy had been a skill that had helped learned physicians to get their

---

[30] [Daniel Coxe], *A Discourse, Wherein the Interest of the Patient in Reference to Physick and Physicians is Soberly Debated. Many Abuses of the Apothecaries in the Preparing their Medicines are Detected, And their Unfitness for Practice Discovered, Together with the Reasons and Advantages of Physicians Preparing their own Medicines* (London, 1669), pp. 220, 221.

[31] See V. Nutton, 'Roman Medicine, 250 BC to AD 200' in Conrad et al., *The Western Medical Tradition*, pp. 68–9.

[32] James Hart, *The Arraignment of Urines* (London, 1623) and *The Anatomie of Urines . . . Or, the Second Part of our Discourse of Urines* (London, 1625); Thomas Brian, *The Pisse-Prophet Or, Certain Pisse-Pot Lectures* (London, 1655).

medicine accepted.[33] In the early modern period they continued to inspect their patients' urine and faeces as part of the 'visit' to, and assessment of, the patient.

Uroscopy bears some comparison with modern laboratory tests. The colour, precipitation and smell of the urine gave clues about the patient's illness. As urine was believed to be drawn from all parts of the body it indicated both its general state and the state of its parts. For instance, 'exulceration of the lungs and corruption' were signified by a 'leadish oily palew [pale or light yellow]' urine.[34] As in a laboratory the physician had to be alert to any disturbance to the specimen such as shaking or cold, and the effect of different foods, drinks and medicines upon its colour and consistency. Then the instruments of sight and smell were used to judge the qualities of the urine; there was also taste, 'but that being too base for the Physitian, we leave to speake of it'.[35] Modern laboratory medicine has been interpreted as dehumanising the patient, and uroscopy when practised in the absence of the patient can be seen as an early precursor of this process.[36] This is especially so as many uroscopists came from the ranks of the empirics and apothecaries who, through selling medicines for particular conditions, had a disease-centred view of disease. Their increasing presence in the medical marketplace in the later seventeenth century moved medicine away from being patient-centred (see chapter 10).

However, the learned physicians insisted that uroscopy and pulse-taking were not the only means of diagnosis. Physicians listened to the patient's story of their illness. They also observed the patient. They did not give detailed physical examinations in which the

[33] Michael McVaugh, *Medicine Before the Plague. Practitioners and their Patients in the Crown of Aragon 1285–1345* (Cambridge University Press, Cambridge, 1993), pp. 138–41.

[34] John Fletcher, *The Differences, Causes and Iudgements of Urine* (London, 1641), p. 32. Other texts on uroscopy include [Anon.], *Here Begyneth the Seynge of Urynes* (London, 1562, and other editions); Joannes Vassaeus, *Here Beginnith a Litel Treatise Conteyninge the Judgement of Urines . . . Englished by Humfre Lloyd* (London, 1553); Henry Hamand, *Ourography or Speculations on the Excrements of Urines* (London, 1655); Robert Recorde, *The Urinal of Physick* (London, 1651). Recorde (1510?–58) was aware that uroscopists were liable to be tricked: 'I shall exhort all men, not to moch and jest with any Physitian . . . tempting them with Beasts stale [urine], in stead of mens urine: others bringing to them mens water for womens': sig. B1^r.

[35] Fletcher, *Urine*, p. 5.

[36] N. Jewson, 'The Disappearance of the Sick Man from Medical Cosmology, 1770–1870', *Sociology*, 10, 1976, 225–44. On uroscopy and the medical consultation see also Ronald C. Sawyer, 'Friends or Foes? Doctors and their Patients in Early Modern England' in Yosio Kawakita, Shizu Sakai and Yasuo Otsuka (eds.), *History of the Doctor–Patient Relationship* (Ishiyaku Euro-America, Tokyo, 1995), pp. 31–53.

patient was naked or partly so, though surgical procedures might necessitate this. However, touching and palpating parts of the body were not unusual. The physician was both a listener and an observer. The patient's experience or subjective symptoms and the signs observed by the physician both played a role in the process of diagnosis.

Knowledge of symptoms and signs helped to bolster the physician's authority. Because the signs of a disease as taught in textbooks represented in part the patient's sensations and feelings, the physician could anticipate what they were and discuss them, so allowing him to build a bridge of empathy to the patient. This was not only comforting to patients – as their symptoms were recognised, given a collective name and legitimised as a real illness – but the physician also gained the confidence of patients and hence their trade.[37] But a further reading of the *practica* is that the physician would also have been given a sense of control or power over the patient by being taught differential diagnosis and prognosis and by inculcating into the reader-physician the need to observe as well as to listen to the patient.

Medical textbooks did not assume that the physician would learn on the job, though often a young physician would acquire practical bedside knowledge by working with an established physician. Da Monte appears almost alone in sixteenth-century Europe in describing how he gave his students hospital-based clinical experience in Padua. The textbooks provided the information that allowed the physician to ask the patient the right questions and to make sense of the answers. As Bruele put it when writing about headache, 'This disease is knowne by the patients complaints and answers.'[38] The learned medical textbooks of the sixteenth and seventeenth centuries largely taught well-established knowledge. Then, as now, teaching

---

[37] Despite the small numbers of physicians, patients, though not the state, felt the need for an illness to be legitimated by some medical authority, even if it was within the family. Richard Baxter, the Nonconformist minister, believed that he suffered from large kidney stones, but the physicians 'agreed that my disease was the hypochondriack melancholy', and, he wrote, 'I became the common talk of the city, especially the women; as if I had been a melancholy humorist, that conceited my reins [kidneys] were petrified . . . And so while I lay night and day in pain, my supposed melancholy (which I thank God, all my life hath been extraordinary free from) became for a year, the pity or derision of the town': Richard Baxter, *Reliquae Baxterianae* (London, 1696), part 1, p. 10; part 3, p. 173. On Baxter see A. Wear, 'Puritan Perceptions of Illness in Seventeenth Century England' in R. Porter (ed.), *Patients and Practitioners*, pp. 90–9.

[38] Bruele, *Physicians Practice*, p. 3.

texts were not concerned with instilling in physicians the value of research, and the physician was not expected to learn anything new from the patient, whose answers were to be used for diagnostic purposes, rather than for discovering anything new about diseases. Instead, the physician was expected to be armed with book knowledge, especially as the variety of symptoms within a disease like plague could be so large that 'all these signs seldome or never meet in one and the same body'.[39] The physician had to have learned beforehand of the different possibilities that might present themselves in plague victims.[40]

Differential diagnosis also indicated the superior knowledge of the physician, and carried with it the implication that lay or patient diagnosis could be mistaken when faced with complex diagnostic possibilities. For instance, one particularly difficult diagnostic area, then as now, was the abdominal region. Books on practical medicine taught that pain in the abdomen came from a variety of causes, such as the dreaded iliac passion or pain from the 'ileon' (ileum), the part of the intestine lying between the jejunum and the caecum. It could be caused also by obstruction of the colon, and produce the pain of colic, which was in addition, to confuse matters, a term applied to any intense abdominal pain or pain from kidney stones.[41]

ANATOMICAL SIGNPOSTS

One way of helping the physician's eyes and his mind's eye to organise and sift diagnostic information was to relate it to knowledge of surface and deep anatomy. The impression given by some historical writing on sixteenth- and seventeenth-century anatomy is that from the Middle Ages it was seen as useful to surgeons, and that in the sixteenth century it became a fashionable interest of humanist

---

[39] Ibid., p. 398; on Padua see Jerome Bylebyl, 'The Manifest and the Hidden in the Renaissance Clinic', in W. F. Bynum and Roy Porter (eds.), *Medicine and the Five Senses* (Cambridge University Press, Cambridge, 1993), pp. 40–60.

[40] The need for practical bedside experience was seen as necessary by those who were intent on replacing Galenic medicine and discovering and teaching a new medicine. So both Starkey and Willis made the point that they had not had practical experience of plague; see chapter 7.

[41] Christopher Wirsung, *Praxis Medicinae Universalis; Or a Generall Practise of Physicke*, trans. Iacob Mosan (London, 1598), p. 420, wrote of 'great Collicke and gripings' being produced in the ileon, but he added when describing the obstruction of the colon, 'In this foresaid gut doth the Collicke properly ingender.' See also Bruele, *Physicians Practice*, p. 309 and John Tanner, *The Hidden Treasures of the Art of Physick*, 3rd edn (London, 1672), p. 128.

physicians who viewed it in terms of the 'pure' knowledge of structure and function of the body with connotations of Aristotelian-Galenic and Christian praise of the workmanship of nature and God respectively. Historians have tended not to note to any great extent that anatomy helped to structure the diagnostic and causal/aetiological accounts of diseases in learned medicine.[42] Anatomy pointed to where disease was located in the body, and sited its occurrence; for instance, the blockage of the passage of humours, food or excrements from one part to another was seen as a frequent cause of internal disorder in the body.

Wirsung began his account of the ills that afflicted each part of the body by setting out its anatomy. 'Of the Bowls or Guts' and, in particular, of the ileum and the colon, he wrote:

beneathe the stomack the Bowels have their beginning, which are parted [divided] in six parts. The three first and uppermost are very subtile and thin; for which cause they bee called in Latine *Gracilia intestina* . . . The other three sorts of the bowels be the undermost, which are more thicker and fleshier then the three uppermost . . . The Third is by the Grecians called *Ileon* and by the Latinists *Volvulus* which is the winding gut; not onely for that by its length it twisteth and windeth about but also for this cause (as the learned write) because there be ingendred in this gut great Collicke and gripings, which doe drawe hither and thitherwards through their great paines, as now in one, and then in another place they must be violently perceived . . . The fifth is Colon, and by the Latinistes called *Crassum Intestinum*. This gut is fleshier than any of all of the rest; also of a reasonable length, a crookedness, in the which and especially in the end of it, the meat [food] is converted into dung.[43]

Anatomical information helped to differentiate between iliac and colon pains. In the section 'Of the difference of these paines in the

---

[42] Andrew Cunningham, *The Anatomical Renaissance: the Resurrection of the Anatomical Projects of the Ancients* (Scolar, Aldershot, c.1997); Wear, 'Medicine in Early Modern Europe', pp. 264–92; also in a similar vein Robert Burton, *The Anatomy of Melancholy*, 1st edn (1621) ed. Floyd Dell and P. Jordan-Smith (Tudor, New York, 1948), pp. 127–8, wrote that he provided his 'Digression of Anatomy' so that his account of melancholy would be easier to follow, and also that 'it may peradventure give occasion to some men, to examine more accurately, search farther into this most excellent subject, and thereupon . . . to praise God (for a man is fearfully and wonderfully made, and curiously wrought) . . . and what can be more ignominious and filthy (as Melancthon well inveighs) "than for a man not to know the structure and composition of his own body, especially since the knowledge of it tends so much to the preservation of his health and the information of his manners"?'. A notable exception is Nancy Siraisi, *The Clock and the Mirror. Girolamo Cardano and Renaissance Medicine* (Princeton University Press, Princeton, 1997), pp. 113–18, who discusses the significance of anatomy in disease narratives drawn from autopsy.

[43] Wirsung, *Practise of Physicke*, p. 420.

Guts', Wirsung pointed out that iliac pain was located higher up, from the navel and above, it was migratory because the ileum was itself winding, and because the ileum was more sensitive than the colon the pain was much greater: 'in the paine of the uppermost guts, the extremitie [of pain] is much greater, and it can kil a bodie much sooner; for that this uppermost, tender and small guts, are much more sensible than the neathermost great guts'.[44]

Anatomical knowledge was one part of the framework that structured the diagnosis and description of a disease. It was knowledge that was seen as belonging to the experts, its terminology consisting, as Burton acknowledged, of 'many hard words . . . as *myrach, hypochondries, hemrods etc, imagination, reason, humours, spirits, vital, natural, animal, nerves, veins, arteries, chylus, pituita*; which of the vulgar will not so easily be perceived, what they are, how sited, and to what end they serve'.[45] Medical theory and accounts of what a patient might experience also figured prominently, and were often merged with anatomical signposting. John Ward noted, 'A woman, Goodie Southerne, in great paine in her hips and thighs by a fitt of the stone and vomitted much', and he expertly explained that 'the reason of the vomiting in the stone is by reason of the connexion of the reins [kidneys] with the stomach, by the common membrane borrowed from the peritoneum, and likewise by a nerve of the sixth conjugation, two branches whereof are brought from the stomach, and inserted into the inner tunick of the kidneys'.[46] The observation (perhaps from long-forgotten patients) that the pain of the iliac passion was greater than that of the colic was given an anatomical-physiological cause: the greater thinness and hence greater susceptibility to pain of the ileum. As Bruele put it, 'but in the *Iliaca passio*, the paine is more vehement, because the thin gut wherein this disease doth lurk, is tenderer and hath a quicker sense of pain, then the gut colon'.[47]

The account of what the typical patient was likely to experience grounded the description of signs, causes and prognosis in the empirical world of 'real' illness, albeit the construction or description of a disease also contained a good deal of theory as well as information, such as that drawn from anatomy not commonly available to lay people. As such it signified that here was a body of knowledge which, however esoteric and learned, dealt with the

[44] Ibid., p. 421. [45] Burton, *Anatomy of Melancholy*, p. 127.
[46] Ward, *Diary*, p. 249. [47] Bruele, *Physicians Practice*, p. 309.

actual world of illness but – and this was the other part of the package – it did so with further knowledge unavailable to those who had not been educated in medicine. As when giving advice on regimen and lifestyle (see chapter 4), learned medicine always appeared to retain its links with the lived lives and experiences of its patients, but accompanied with the gloss of expertise.

The signs of a disease, which included the 'typical' patient's experience, functioned as an aid to expert diagnosis, as in Wirsung's description of the iliac passion:

Ileos or *Iliaca Passio*, are gripings or stitches in the uppermost small guts, which be caused of some obstruction or swellings of the guts, whereby the congested filthe or corruption cannot fall downe in to the great guts. Whereby such great intolerable pain, sicknes, and gryping do ensue, that the guts seeme to be bored thorow with a bodkin, and that commonly with continuall vomiting and parbraking: yet not in all patients.[48]

Wirsung wrote, 'Concerning the signes, they may be demaunded of the sicke persons or standers by,'[49] but the diagnosis of the learned physician was clearly a matter of expert judgement. He, and not the patient, or lay bystanders, would know how to relate the patient's signs to a particular disease, for the signs, which themselves were often interpretations of sensations, had meanings in terms of the diseases constructed by the learned medical tradition. The way in which the diagnosis, aetiology and therapy of a disease were taught emphasised how a natural process was understood rationally by learned medicine in contrast to the 'ignorance' of ordinary people, as Wirsung wrote: 'The common people which have no understanding of natural things which pertain to mans body, do call this *Iliaca* the mother in men, like as the common people in Italy doe call it *Paron*, which is father, whereas not withstanding men have no mother within them.'

SIGNS AND PATIENTS

As noted above, the description of the signs and symptoms of illness in the books on the practice of medicine empathically linked physician-readers to the feelings experienced by their patients, but also created a sense of distance and alienation between patient and doctor. For instance, in the iliac passion a metaphor brought to life

---

[48] Wirsung, *Practise of Physicke*, p. 421.   [49] Ibid., p. 422.

the type of pain experienced by the patient: 'the guts seeme to be bored through with a bodkin';[50] whilst in the colic: 'the pain is like the boaring of an Auger . . . is greater after [food]', and discomfort is produced because 'the Belly (for the most part) is bound that the Patient cannot so much as break Wind; when he voideth Excrements, they are windy, like Cow dung with Water on the top'.[51] However, descriptions of the patient's subjective symptoms or feelings, the patient's story as it were, were also made part of the description of the disease, a description that was designed to express the knowledge and authority of learned medicine. As well as what the physician observed, such as the patient's windy excrements like cow dung with water on top, the patient's own experiences of the disease, consisting of what many medical practitioners might now term in a rather derogatory way 'merely' subjective symptoms, were made to appear as 'objective' signs observed in the patient by the physician. This is how it appears from a modern perspective, where the difference between subjective symptoms and objective signs is taken to be clear cut, and the latter are closely linked to the professional authority of the physician.

However, writers like Wirsung were not aware of the difference, and they impressed medical authority on to both what the patient felt and what the physician observed. The patient's subjective symptoms or feelings about his or her body that led to diagnosis were also part of the expert, objective discourse of medicine, so that what the patient may have experienced appeared to be observed by the physician, whilst the *persona* of the patient could be reduced to a collection of bodily parts. For instance, in the description of the 'Dropsie Ascites', a type of abdominal swelling caused by an accumulation of fluid, Wirsung wrote:

the belly doth swell and the legs, and contrarily, the upper parts of the bodie do dry away . . . Of all other signes this sickness is a great trouble in the belly, when one clappeth or swoundeth upon it, he doth heare a rumbling or a noyse of water, which is forcibly stirred about, the which also hapneth if the sick person do turne himselfe from one side to the other: the bodie is not so swollen throughout like as in the foresaid Dropsie [discussed previously], neither do there remaine therein any dents or pits if one presse therein with the finger. The Navell doth not stand so puffed up as in the *Tympanie* [a form of dropsy], the pulse is feeble, swift and small.[52]

[50] Ibid., p. 421.   [51] Tanner, *Hidden Treasures*, p. 128.
[52] Wirsung, *Practise of Physicke*, p. 402.

One reason why Wirsung did not distinguish between the symptoms that the patient experienced and the signs that the physician observed is because at the heart of Galenic medicine, and of the Aristotelian philosophy that underpinned it, was the belief that subjective perceptions such as hot, cold, etc. or, as in this case, a patient's symptoms, constituted 'objective' reality. What the patient felt and what the physician observed from the body of the patient were epistemologically identical; they were both objective signs. This meant that learned medicine did not condemn lay notions of disease as 'merely' based on subjective symptoms as is the case today, and, as discussed earlier, the whole of western European culture agreed (until the later seventeenth century) that what was subjective was the very basis of reality. However, it is clear from Wirsung's discourse that the learned physician itemised particular aspects of the patient's experience of illness into signs which, like the observations of the physician upon the patient's body, created a localised, segmented, view of the patient. This to some extent 'objectified' the patient, in the modern sense of the personality of the patient being lost. Yet the voice or report of the patient was noted by Wirsung. This is less paradoxical than it seems, for not only were the personal and subjective considered to be part of the reality of the world, and could, therefore, be made into a medical 'fact', but the nature of medical practice in the early modern period, in which the practitioner had to compete for the custom of the individual patient, ensured that learned medicine taught its practitioners to pay attention to the patient's account of symptoms and not silence him or her.

The sense of expertise and authority was increased by the description of the causes of the disease (discussed further below), which took the discourse into areas of the body hidden from the patient, in this case the liver, and provided an account of its internal working in the general context of the four qualities of Galenic medicine:

The cause of this Dropsie is feebleness of the Lyver which hath not a sanguification or conction [i.e. cannot make blood as it should], and altereth all her moysture into water.

This infection of the Lyver may be caused as well of heate as of cold: also of the water which is ingendred in the Lyver that falleth downe afterwards into the lower parts and hollownes of the belly.[53]

---

[53] Ibid.

The prognosis was bad, declared Wirsung, and the knowledge that treatment was hopeless added to the power bestowed upon the reader-physician (who could in practice be a lay person as well) by Wirsung's text. It appeared to reduce the patient's autonomy, for, by, as it were, revealing why in terms of Galenic theory there was no possibility of cure, it blocked off the patient's freedom of action, especially his or her recourse to the promised cures for all conditions proffered by the remedy books. But, because in practice there was nothing to stop the patient from trying them out, or going to another practitioner, the learned physician was advised to offer something to the patient:

If this Dropsie do come through hote causes, after any paine of the Lyver, after an Ague, by swelling up the belly beneath the Navell even to the very hip; also if one turne the sick person about, one heareth the water, hath an intollerable thirst, avoydeth but little urine, which is fierie red with some clots as it were with small stones: then is there great danger, and but small hope of life to be had. For if so be that one give the patient medicines which do coole the heate, then is the Lyver enfeebled, the water and wind augmented: if that warme and drying things be used for it, then both the heate and excessive thirst increase.

But not to leave this sick person utterly comfortless and to please his friends, you may use for the lengthening of his life moderate cold and warme things, like as is this syrup following.[54]

In this case the conclusion that treatment was hopeless appears from a rational assessment of the implications of applying the Galenic principle of cure by contrary (see chapter 1). Appropriating the symptoms of the patient and making them signs observed by the physician, giving causes and glimpses of what was happening inside the body, and assessing treatment on rational grounds were all part of the package of humoral medicine that provided the learned physician with the opportunity to display expert, esoteric knowledge and terminology.[55] This package also protected the physician's reputation by giving him warning that the prognosis for a particular condition was hopeless and supplying him with reasons, if needed, to convince onlookers why this was so. Although the books of remedies

[54] Ibid.
[55] Such knowledge marked out for the College of Physicians the learned from the ignorant. For instance, in 1630 Richard Powell was accused by Elizabeth Sherburne of 'undertaking to cure a woman suffering with tympanites' and the woman died. 'He confessed that he had given this dropsical woman a medicament to drink (he was examined as to what was dropsy but he did not know what was dropsy or tympanites).' Powell was fined. *Annals*, 3, fol. 99b.

(though not learned textbooks on the practice of medicine) give the impression that all diseases were curable, it is clear that relatives and bystanders round the sick bed could also conclude that the patient's case was hopeless. In such a situation medical success probably enhanced a physician's reputation more than any display of learned acquaintance with the significance of a patient's symptoms. For instance, John Hall, Shakespeare's physician son-in-law, attended Joan Lynes who suffered from a tympany, another form of localised dropsy or swelling around the abdominal region where the abdomen, rather than being filled with water, 'was stretched beyond measure' with wind, and 'a noyse, like unto a taber, is heard, if the belly is somewhat beaten upon'.[56] Hall reported in his case notes that he successfully treated her despite her friends having given her up as past cure: 'Lynes of Stratford, aged 53, in 1630, was troubled with a Timpany, her Belly being much swelled, so that she could scarce go, with hoarsness of her Voice, and loathing of Meat [food], insomuch that she was left by her Friends as hopeless, yet by Gods blessing she was cured as followeth . . .'[57]

Although for lay people a cure may have been the best indicator of medical competence, the ability to explain why a disease occurred and what was happening inside the body was what marked out the educated physician, at least in physicians' eyes, and was important in creating a sense of group identity amongst physicians. They counted themselves amongst those who knew the reason why, like the philosophers, and unlike their competitors the empirics.

THE CAUSES AND IMAGES OF DISEASE

In their rhetoric the learned physicians emphasised that they offered their patients a type of medicine that combined reason and experience, whilst empirics and quacks gave no reasons for therapy and failed to relate it to the causes of disease. The education of physicians, which unlike that of other groups of medical practitioners was based on university study, inculcated a belief in the importance

---

[56] Bruele, *Physicians Practice*, pp. 319, 321.
[57] John Hall, *Select Observations on English Bodies of Eminent Persons in Desperate Diseases* (London, 1679), p. 115. I have used the facsimile included in Joan Lane, *John Hall and his Patients* (Shakespeare Birthplace Trust, Stratford-upon-Avon, 1996), pp. 230–3. Lane, and Melvin Earles who provided the medical commentary, have produced a valuable context to the *Observations*.

of rationality. In the arts faculty, which provided the first tier of university courses, they were taught something of Aristotle's logic and natural philosophy, and when they progressed to the study of medicine they would have read Galen's medical works. Galen, who famously believed that 'the best physician is also a philosopher',[58] reinforced the Aristotelian message that the best type of knowledge was rational, and that an understanding of causes marked out the true philosopher. At the same time, Galen's writings also taught that medicine was a 'techne' or art which had in mind the practical aims of preserving and restoring health and required experience as well as reason.

An example of this approach to medicine was set out by Christopher Langton, a fellow of the College of Physicians, who, like other mid-sixteenth-century physicians, was concerned with reforming English medicine and making learned medicine available in the vernacular, though he cannot have been in complete agreement with the College as he was expelled from it in 1558 for being quarrelsome, vainglorious and immoral.[59] Langton set out the characteristics of the learned physician in *An Introduction Into Phisyke* (1545–50?). Using the standard tropes of medical reformers of the decay of medicine and the rise of murdering practitioners, Langton had the goddess 'Physycke' complain of the state she has come to: 'For where as before I was authour of health, to every man sekyng for me: now I am not onelye a commune murtherer, and a commune thefe, but also a mayntayner of Paricides, moche more vyle than ye stynkynge whore of Babylon.'[60] The remedy for medicine's decline was learning. Practical experience was not enough: 'For what soever he be that hath not exactly learned naturall Philosophye, be he never so well practised, he never knewe me [i.e. "Physicke"].' From a tender age the prospective physician had to study dialectic and mathematics 'settynge his mynde on nothyng but only on learnynge'. Langton's point was that medicine had become murderous and avaricious because men went straight into therapeutic practice based on simples without the background of university learning, and, more specifically, without the knowledge of Galenic medical theory to

---

[58] Galen, 'Quod Optimus Medicus sit quoque Philosophus' in C. G. Kühn (ed.), *Claudii Galeni Opera Omnia* (20 vols., Leipzig, 1821), vol. I, p. 61.

[59] G. Clark, *A History of the Royal College of Physicians* (2 vols., Clarendon Press, Oxford, 1964 and 1966), vol. I, pp. 108–9.

[60] Christopher Langton, *An Introduction Into Physycke* (London, 1545–50?), fol. v[r].

inform their practice. Instead, the true physician 'muste take an
ordre in hys studyes, not begynnyng as the moost parte of you do,
wyth the symples, and practyse at the fyrst, overleapinge the
elementes, the temperatures [humoral constitutions], the section
[anatomy] of the body, with all the faculties of the same'.[61]

With the rejection of a medical practice based simply on naming a
disease and treating it, which, as Langton wrote, characterised much
of the medicine of his time, came an emphasis on words, arguments,
theory and the 'exercise' or practised use in the learning of
Hippocrates, Aristotle, Galen and other ancient authorities.[62] Much
of university teaching was based around 'exercitationes' or exercises
in argument which enabled the student to acquire a facility in the
dialectic of argument, and in manipulating or using ancient philosophical theories and pieces of learning. Part of the identity of being
a learned physician at the bedside was clearly linked to the discursive
knowledge of diseases which filled the gap between naming a disease
and treating it: '[the] discourse of the state of the Disease'.[63] Such
'discourse', and the ability to understand it and to literally 'speak' it
at the bedside, was also used by physicians to distinguish their
learned medicine from empirical practice, good medicine from bad
medicine, that is philosophically based and morally worthy medicine, and hence safe medicine from what they took to be ignorant
and dangerous practice.

In the mid-sixteenth century it was the physicians educated in
Galenic medicine who, through their writings, spread to the rest of
literate culture the humoral view of the internal disorders of the
body. But by the later seventeenth century, as discussed in chapters 8
to 10, their Helmontian intellectual and commercial rivals offered
different accounts of disease. At the same time the chemical
corpuscular view of nature, which had some connections with
Helmontian views and was held in a variety of forms by such leading
physicians as Thomas Willis and natural philosophers as Robert
Boyle, was used to construct a body that worked according to
chemical principles, and whose disorders were chemical ones, at
least at first sight. Like the Galenists, the new groups which were
forming in the intellectual and social maelstrom of the later seven-

---

[61] Ibid., fols. v1[r], v1[v].
[62] Langton advised that, whoever wanted to become a physician, 'let hym be exercysed, even
from hys tendre age in dialect, arithmaticke and mathematicke': ibid., fol. v1[r].
[63] See footnote 30.

teenth century associated their claims to medical authority with the truth of their medical systems which informed their speech at the bedside, and also like Galenists they were concerned to construct rational accounts of what happened in the diseased body. Moreover, as we shall see in chapter 10, at a fundamental level, despite sharp and real theoretical differences about the nature of the body and disease, there were underlying continuities between the older Galenic accounts and images of how the body became diseased and the newer medical philosophies which indicate a degree of consensus about disease.

The diseased body and the causes of disease

The physicians created and mapped a cosmos of diseases within the body. They told stories of how an illness started and how the different parts of the body were affected, and often they provided a number of different possible narratives to account for a disease. Damage to the body and to its functions lay at the heart of all descriptions of disease. As Burton put it, 'What a disease is, almost every Physician defines, Fernelius calleth it "an affection of the body contrary to nature"; Fuchsius and Crato, "an hindrance, hurt or alteration of any action of the body of part of it".'[64] The learned physicians perceived the hurts to the body in specific as well as general terms. General causes such as bad diet and lifestyle and imbalances of the humours had specific, localised effects inside the body, and the humours themselves could change to become putrid, venomous or corroding, and thus transformed were viewed as specific agents that harmed a part of the body and thus began a disease process.

Such a process had a beginning, middle and end or outcome. In other words, diseases lent themselves to being put into narrative formats.[65] Perhaps most influential in this was the patient's experience, in which illness becomes an additional story superimposed upon the usual strands of one's life, sometimes to the exclusion of all

---

[64] Burton, *Anatomy of Melancholy*, p. 119.

[65] An alternative view (David Harley, personal communication) is the nominalist one that diseases *are* narratives, structuring the experience of patients into symptoms/signs. It may be that functionally, as with the debate on nominalism in medieval philosophy, there is little essential difference between the two positions, although philosophically there might be a good deal.

else. The medical practitioner's therapeutic interventions, often paralleling the different episodes of the illness as experienced by the patient, amplified the sense of narrative. Diseases, like stories, were bounded in time, and both patients and doctors shared a wish to discover when illness occurred (especially because it might give a clue as to its cause), to understand what was happening inside the body as it progressed and to assess what the end result would be. Analogous to this popular view of disease was the Aristotelian conception of causality that dominated universities, and which was centred around notions of agency and of consequent effects occurring over time. So, physicians, whilst giving narrative accounts of illness, which may have fulfilled their patients' needs for an explanation of what was happening to them, were also, in their view, providing rational understanding of disease which fitted the educational framework that underpinned their occupation. The Hippocratic tradition of case reports that detailed the changes in patients over time also helped to frame narrative or historical ways of describing a disease.

The physicians were concerned with credibility, and in the early modern period stories were still appropriate for conveying the truth, even if the truth was not fully visible. Narrative description could create matters of fact as if they had been seen. The revealed truth of the biblical stories and the genre of fabulous stories from other parts of the world reinforced the potential of the early modern narrative to be authoritative and creative of the belief that something had been seen, even if the circumstances, such as being far in the past, far away or deep in the body, made for scepticism.

The narrative of disease was facilitated by the medical vision of the body as an interconnected whole. The different parts were connected to each other by veins, arteries, nerves, guts, porosities such as lungs, and canals like the bile duct. Solids, such as food and faeces, liquids such as the humours (including blood), chyle, pus, and more tenuous matter such as air, vapours, smokes and the vital and animal spirits all travelled through the body bringing life, health and disease. Damage to or ill functioning in one part could literally have a knock-on effect on a distant organ. In other words, disease travelled distances across the body and often seemed to develop in stages or episodes across place and time, as in a story. For instance, hypochondrial or windy melancholy, which caused strange fancies, and is close to hypochondria in the modern sense, was seen as a disturbance of the faculty or power of the imagination, which was located physically inside the ventricles of the brain. The disorder, however, originated far from the brain and was caused by 'sharpe and smoky vapours, proceeding from the lower parts: for it so happens, that the temperature [complexion] of the braine is altered by darke and foggy vapours arising from the stomack, liver, mesentary, or from some other adjacent part neere unto them: whereby the imagination is hurt, memory and cogitation remaining perfect'. The account proceeds in stages: an obstruction occurs, which then causes blood in the veins of a part of the body to be burnt; the blood then changes to black (burning) juice which then affects the mesentery and other parts; then there results a heat in the bowels; then from the bowels vapours rise to the brain, which then produces symptoms.[66]

The account or story gains credibility because it is in the logical form of 'because something happened then something else occurred'. The fit between cause and symptom also creates belief: the imagination is clouded and full of irrational fancies because of smoky vapours. As in most causal accounts of disease in this period, there was a strong analogy between causes and symptoms; the physical nature of the causes made sense in terms of the symptoms. This was inevitable given that many causes represented invisible processes, rather than identifiable entities such as the bacteria that we know of today or testable and measurable constituents of the body like white blood cells. Although the humours could be seen (with the possible exception of black bile), what happened to them in the body was a matter of inference, perhaps from uroscopy, from the faeces, from the state of blood when a patient was bled or from the phlegm coughed up. For instance, when Ralph Josselin, the minister at Earls Colne in Essex, became unwell he pictured his body as filled with the ill humours of learned medicine. On 10 December 1648 he noted in his diary that his cold was better, that it had cleansed his chest so that he no longer wheezed at night, but his urine indicated that inside his body trouble still lurked: 'yett by . . . my water, and

---

[66] Bruele, *Physicians Practice*, pp. 34, 36: 'Sometimes it doth happen, that the blood, which is in the veines of the stomack, mesentery, Spleen, bowels, guts and adjacent parts, is burnt up by too much heate, caused by some obstruction, or some other cause; and then the blood doth degenerate into black juyce which runnes over the mesentery, spleene and other parts thereto adjoyning, whereof followeth a great heate of the bowels, and from thence vapours are conveyed to the braine, from whence these Symptomes breake out.'

the fulnes thereof of white crewde phlegme, I conceive my body is
not yett setled, but full of cold waterish humours'.[67] Although
Hippocratic and Galenic medicine had been open to popular
knowledge, and although the four humours were derived from
commonly observable fluids or material in the body,[68] by the
sixteenth century it had become a canonical truth that there were
only four humours. Other bodily fluids or materials could not be
perceived as additional humours, instead being interpreted as states
of the four established humours. As is the case usually in science and
medicine, except perhaps in times of revolutions, Galenic medicine
was a closed rather than an open system, with observations of bodily
processes being expressed in terms of its pre-existing framework or
by analogy to it. In other words, the four humours structured
people's thinking, so that Josselin read his urine as containing 'white
crewde phlegme', and this then made him confident in conceiving
that his body was 'full of cold waterish humours', phlegm according
to Galenic doctrine being made up of cold and wet qualities.

PUTREFACTION

They would but stink and putrefy the air . . .[69]

A crucial component in most accounts of disease was putrefaction.
The corruption and putrefaction of the humours, of parts of the body
and of food in the body were especially potent and widespread
images of physical disorder and disease. Early modern society's
experience of the putrefying dead bodies of animals and of people,
and also of food, was far greater than is the case in modern developed
countries where corrupting flesh and other rotten material are usually
hidden away and/or 'sanitised', or, as in putrefaction inside or
outside living bodies, has become uncommon since the advent of
antibiotics. From the Middle Ages through to the seventeenth century
the experience of putrefaction was strong enough, and unpleasant
enough, for it to come to be seen as one of the causes of the most
destructive of illnesses. External putrefaction, it was believed, could,

---

[67] R. Josselin, *The Diary of Ralph Josselin 1616–1683*, ed. Alan Macfarlane (Oxford University Press for the British Academy, Oxford, 1976; paperback 1991), p. 149.

[68] In the later Hippocratic treatises, black bile or melancholy replaced water as one of the humours. It is a moot point whether it was observable. A. Wear, 'The Spleen in Renaissance Anatomy', *Medical History*, 21, 1977, 43–60.

[69] W. Shakespeare, *Henry VI*, Act IV Scene VII, line 90.

in the case of plague, create by contagion a devastating internal putrefaction in the body. Bad smells were a sign of putrefaction and of an infected deadly air, for it was thought that 'the heart of man [cannot] abide with impure smells, or live long in infected air'.[70] The deaths of prisoners and judges at assizes were often blamed on 'the Nastiness and Stench of the Prisoners',[71] which were communicated to the rest of the court. In many diseases, as, for instance, in smallpox, the humours inside the body were also imagined, or rather stated to be, for medical writers believed that they were describing reality, in differing states of malignant corruption. The confidence with which this was done probably owed a good deal not only to the prevalence of putrid wounds and sores in patients but also to the daily experience of the rotting and evil-smelling detritus of open sewers, cesspits, dungheaps, the mix of animal and human faeces on streets and pavements, and the heaps of decaying offal and blood outside butchers' shops. A town or village in its entirety might well be a rotting rubbish dump, but despite being habituated to putrefaction, there is little evidence that early modern people of whatever class accepted the corruption around them as normal or agreeable, any more than they accepted that a festering body was normal.[72] The attempts at cleansing towns, villages and people's bodies, though only partially successful, indicate a deep distrust of putrefaction.

Food was another aspect of everyday experience that was seen as especially liable to corruption; the rotting of food was viewed as an analogue to the digestive ills that were thought to cause many diseases, and if rotten food was eaten it created disorder in the body. When Josselin ate too many oysters he pictured them as lying together with phlegm in his stomach and corrupting.[73] He cleared out the corruption by drinking beer and by not eating, for food or humours staying too long in the stomach was believed to be

---

[70] Ward, *Diary*, p. 255.

[71] A. W. [Anthony Walker], *The Holy Life of Mrs Elizabeth Walker*, (london, 1690), pp. 29–30.

[72] Keith Thomas, 'Cleanliness and Godliness in Early Modern England' in A. Fletcher and P. Roberts (eds.), *Religion, Culture and Society in Early Modern Britain: Essays in Honour of Patrick Collinson* (Cambridge University Press, Cambridge, 1994), pp. 56–83. Also Mark Jenner, '"Another Epocha"? Hartlib, John Lanyon and the Improvement of London in the 1650s' in M. Greengrass, M. Leslie and T. Raylor (eds.), *Samuel Hartlib and Universal Reformation* (Cambridge University Press, Cambridge, 1994).

[73] Josselin, *Diary*, p. 566: 'there was a surfeit with oysters, which though they did not nauseat my stomacke, mett with so much phlegme in my stomacke, and being bound. they lay corrupting in my stomacke': 27 November 1672.

pathological; this could be cured by getting the food or the humours in motion by a variety of means, such as dissolving or thinning remedies, or expulsive procedures such as bleeding, purging or vomiting.

The extensive use of the metaphor of putrefaction and corruption in non-medical contexts also probably helped to reinforce medical assertions that putrefaction was a key pathological process in contagious ills, digestive disorders and dying. Today, the metaphor of corruption when used in political debate has largely lost its link to physical corruption. But in the early modern period the metaphor was closely associated with the pathological processes of corruption and with medicine and surgery, as demonstrated in one Civil War tract: 'It seemes our peace was so corrupt, that it was held requisite it must be lanced with the Sword. I pray Heaven our Chirurgions cut not so farre, that instead of letting out Putrifaction; they let not out our very Vitals, by too deep, too wide a wound.'[74]

Even more important than the widespread currency of the metaphor for creating a climate of opinion in which the medical use of putrefaction would be unquestioned was the key role that the physical process of putrefaction also played in Christianity. Death, it was taught, was the corruption of the body, but in the second coming of Christ each person's body would be reunited in an incorruptible state. Bodily corruption was thus an essential part of the human experience, as was its subsequent negation when the divine promise was fulfilled and completed the career of a Christian. Moreover, Christ's death and burial gave hope to all that, from that time, instead of the stench of death, sweet smells and perfumes filled the grave of Christians.[75] Some clergymen such as Henry King,

---

[74] [T. Povey?], *The Moderator. Expecting Sudden Peace or Certaine Ruine* (London, 1642), p. 3.

[75] W. Perkins, 'An Exposition of the Symbole or Creed of the Apostles' in *The Workes of . . . Mr William Perkins*, (3 vols., Cambridge, 1616–18), vol. I pp. 230–1. Perkins replied to the objection that Christ as a dead man was no man by writing that 'a dead man in his kinde is as true a man as a living man: for though body and soule be not united by the bond of life, yet are they united by a relation which the one hath to the other in the councell and good pleasure of God . . . And by vertue of this relation every soule in the day of iudgement shal be reunited to his owne body, and every bodie to his own soule. But there is yet a more streight bond between the body and soul of Christ in his death and buriall . . . when he was dead his very Godhead was a meane or middle bond to unite the body and the soule.' Perkins added, 'the buriall of Christ serves as a sweete perfume of all our graves and burials: for the grave in it selfe is the house of perdition, but Christ by his buriall hath as it were consecrated and perfumed all our graves, and in stead of houses of perdition hath made them chambers of rest and sleepe, yea beds of downe: and therefore howsoever to the eye of man the beholding of a funeral is terrible, yet if we could then remember the

Bishop of Chichester, considered Christ's body whilst in the tomb to be incorruptible. King readily used Galenic digestive theory when he stated that the earth could not digest Christ's body:

> His incorruptible body lay indeed like a dangerous surfet in the stomacke of Earth, which was unable to digest it or by assimilation to turne it into its substance, as by that common chyle of putrefaction ordinary courses convert into Earth; and therefore it must needs cast Him up againe, or perish by that distemper.
> And cast Him up it did.[76]

The close link in Christian teaching between putrefaction and dying, expressive as it was of the facts of everyday life and of revealed truth, must, in a Christian society, have made the medical accounts or stories of the putrefactive processes taking place in the body even more believable. The Greek philosophical tradition also located putrefaction as a key process in the cycle of birth and decay. Aristotle's treatise on the subject was entitled in Latin *De Generatione et Corruptione* (though it did not contain much graphic description of corruption) and according to Aristotle out of putrefaction some living creatures such as maggots were born; or, as John Ward put it in the seventeenth century, 'putrefaction cannot long bee without the generation of a new matter'.[77] Philosophy as well as religion seemed to echo the popular view that putrefaction was inextricably linked with death and disease, but they also associated putrefaction with renewal.

At a prosaic level the common therapeutic procedures of bleeding and purging, which were widespread through the population, were also routinely prescribed by learned practitioners as well as by empirics and served to confirm the validity of the pathological narratives of disease.[78] There was intense interest surrounding

---

buriall of Christ and consider how he therby hath changed the nature of the grave, even then it would make us rejoice'.

[76] Mary Hobbs (ed.), *The Sermons of Henry King (1592–1669), Bishop of Chichester* (Associated University Presses, Cranbury, NJ, 1992), p. 102.

[77] Ward, *Diary*, p. 259, referring to Kircher in Rome observing with a microscope 'little small animals' in the putrid blood of plague victims.

[78] Unlicensed practitioners, both men and women, were constantly being accused at the College of Physicians of giving purgatives and endangering patients. For example, in 1635 a Mrs Hansom complained that one of her lodgers when ill had 'sent his water [urine] to Mr Frear a minister whoe sent him a medcyne which wrought upwards and downewarde'. Other medicines were given which also 'wrought with him upward and downewards', and after nine days he died. *Annals*, 3, fol. 155b. The frequency with which evacuative medicines were involved in complaints about practitioners heard at the College makes it clear that they were almost automatic stand-bys in treating most illnesses.

bleeding and purging. The diarist Samuel Pepys, who noted down the ills of his body as conscientiously as everything else that happened to him, grew frantic when he could not produce any stool, the body's most visible putrid matter, or any 'farts', calling on his surgeons and his friends to provide advice. He noted on 17 May 1664: 'to the office, finding myself better than I was and making a little water, but not yet breaking any great stir of wind; which I wonder at, for I cannot be well till I do do it'. Two days later he was even happier: 'So home to supper and to bed – finding myself pretty well. A pretty good stool, which I impute to my whey today – and break wind also.'[79] Health consisted in clearing and cleansing the body, whilst blockages caused a build-up of putrid matter and consequent illness.

Such therapeutics were predicated on the movement of fluids and other substances through a permeable interconnected body. By employing bleeding, purging and other evacuative procedures such as sweating, cupping, vomiting and blistering, patients shared in the general framework of thought about the body and illness which shaped the learned accounts of illness. For instance Sir Charles Lyttelton reported to Lord Hatton in 1682 that Prince Rupert had died because he had failed to clear out an excess of blood: 'he had a pleurisy withal upon him which he concealed, because he would not be let blood, till it was too late and when his blood was all corrupted. He died in great paine.'[80] On the other hand, Archbishop Laud noted in his diary that James I had died because medicines had moved the disease in the wrong direction in the body. The disease had appeared to be an ague: 'But I fear', wrote Laud, 'it was the gout, which, by the wrong application of medicines, was driven from his feet to his inward vital parts.'[81] The learned physicians' accounts of putrid blockages, of foetid vapours and of the movement of diseases around the body were the counterpart to lay and medical

[79] Samuel Pepys, *The Diary of Samuel Pepys*, ed. Robert Latham and William Matthews, (11 vols., Bell and Hyman, London, 1970–83), vol. 5, pp. 152, 153. The Yorkshire yeoman, Adam Eyre, carefully noted in his diary when he, his wife and his horses had been prophylactically bled. Adam Eyre, *A Dyurnall . . . from the 1st of January 1646[7]*, ed. H. J. Morehouse in Charles Jackson (ed.), *Yorkshire Diaries and Autobiographies in the Seventeenth and Eighteenth Centuries* (Surtees Society LXV, Durham, 1875), pp. 31, 39, 59.

[80] Edward Maunde Thompson (ed.), *Correspondence of the Family of Hatton* (2 vols., Camden Society, New Series XXIII, 1878), vol. II, p. 21.

[81] *The Autobiography of Dr. William Laud . . . collected from his Remains* (A compilation from Archbishop Laud's Diary, his History of his Chancellorship of Oxford, and his History of his Troubles and Trial) (J. H. Parker, Oxford, 1839), p. 34.

therapeutic procedures that sought to move disease out of the body. Therapy often consisted of the search for the right means of doing this. As Carew Ralegh, the son of Walter Ralegh, wrote to Lord Conway in 1652: 'but you will let us know . . . whether you have found . . . a cure for Mrs Ramsdells green sickness [anaemic-type symptoms, often believed to be caused by sexual frustration] that it may fall no more into her legges but fynd an upper vent'.[82]

Putrefaction and womens' disease

Putrefaction knew no boundaries: the rich and the poor, men, women and children were all threatened by it, women perhaps most of all.[83] Their bodies were perceived as more moist than men's, which was confirmed by the frequency with which they suffered from 'whites' or vaginal discharges, and especially by their superabundance of blood, necessary in pregnancy to feed the foetus, but superfluous otherwise – hence nature's monthly bleeding.

Menstruation reinforced the belief that health consisted in the free flow of fluids through the body. It gave women an advantage over men: nature bled them regularly, kept their fluids flowing and evacuated noxious products. So, for instance, it was believed that women were not so liable to gout, 'especially if they have their Courses regularly, by means of which Evacuation they are freed from many Distempers'. Conversely, irregularity in menstruation was viewed with suspicion; 'but the stopping of that Evacuation, or any too great Discharges that way, is the only cause of many Distempers attending that Sex'.[84] Lack of menstruation, especially,

---

[82] Marjorie Hope Nicolson (ed.), *Conway Letters. The Correspondence of Anne, Viscountess Conway, Henry More, and their Friends 1642–1684* (Humphrey Milford for Oxford University Press, London, 1930), pp. 19–20.

[83] See Barbara Duden, *The Woman Beneath the Skin: a Doctor's Patients in Eighteenth-Century Germany*, trans. Thomas Dunlop (Harvard University Press, Cambridge, Mass., 1981).

[84] John Colbatch, *A Treatise of the Gout* in *A Collection of Tracts, Chirurgical and Medical* (London, 1699), p. 268. Menstruation was readily latched on to as a cause of physical and mental disorder from ancient times to the nineteenth century. See for instance, Heinrich von Staden, 'Inefficacy, Error and Failure: Galen on δόκιμα φάρμακα ἄπρακτα', in A. Debru (ed.), *Galen on Pharmacology* (Brill, Leiden, 1997), p. 62. See also Helen King, *Hippocrates' Woman: Reading the Female Body in Ancient Greece* (Routledge, London, 1998); Janice Delany, Mary Jane Lupton and Emily Toth, *The Curse: a Cultural History of Menstruation* (Dutton, New York, 1976); Etienne van der Walle, 'Flowers and Fruits: Two Thousand Years of Menstrual Regulation', *Journal of Interdisciplinary History*, 28, Autumn 1997, 183–203; Alexandra Lord, '"The Great 'Arcana' of the Deity": Menstruation and Menstrual Disorders in Eighteenth-Century British Medical Thought', *Bulletin of the History of Medicine*, 73, Spring 1999, 38–63.

was made into a disorder which in turn was a cause of illness. As the body was seen as an interconnected whole, the effects of suppression of menstruation were felt not only in the area of the womb, but in distant parts: 'A young Maiden, by overmuch toyling above her strength, taking cold, fell into a Feverish Distemper, which stopping the course of Nature, strange pains flew all over her Body, and into her head especially.'[85]

Suppressed menstruation, by clogging up the body with putrefying menstrual blood, provided another ready explanation for illness and an excuse for medical failure.[86] Its most dramatic impact, however, was upon the womb itself. It was one of the causes of 'the mother', the female illness above all others, in which the womb is suffocated or choked. Under pressure of the vapours inside it the womb moves up or sideways to crush the organs around it, hence the long-held view of the 'wandering womb'. Physical and mental illness, fits of unconsciousness or of hysteria were likely to follow.[87] The account of 'the mother', like the ill effects of menstruation, was told using the standard building blocks of disease narratives: obstruction, putrefaction and consequent systemic damage to the rest of the body. Bruele, for example, wrote that:

The cause of the Mother is menstrous blood corrupted, and an evill vapor breaking out from the womb, or else some impostume [abscess] in the womb. For the most part it is caused by the [woman's] seed that is sent to the wombe, and therein detayned and corrupted. Sometimes it is caused by corrupt humors which remain there, for when these do putrefy in the womb, they do breed a noysome, and venemous quality. And it happens that from whence life ariseth, from thence also the deadliest bane of venome springs, and then it is an easy matter for venemous matter to be carried not only by veins and arteries, but also by secret breathing holes into the upper parts, and so disturbe their functions.[88]

---

85 W[illiam] W[alwyn], *Physick for Families* (London, 1669), p. 63.

86 The pre-eminent English surgeon of the later seventeenth century, Richard Wiseman, explained how 'the Menstrua being still obstructed, the Ulcer became again distemper'd, and rendred all my endeavours fruitless': Richard Wiseman, *Eight Chirurgicall Treatises*, 4th edn (London, 1705), p. 187.

87 Bruele, *Physicians Practice*, p. 372: 'The stopping or choaking of the womb or Mother, is a running back of the womb, or of malign vapors bred in the wombe, unto the higher parts, whereby the bowels, midriffe, and stomacke, are sometimes so crushed, that they cannot be widened by breathing: for it seems in this disease, that the wombe is lifted up so high, that it drives the other members [parts] above it unto the higher part . . .'. See also King, *Hippocrates' Woman*, pp. 36, 38, 206, 222–4, 244; Mark Adair, 'Plato's View of the "Wandering Uterus"', *Classical Journal*, 91, 1996, 153–63; Lana Thompson, *The Wandering Womb: a Cultural History of Outrageous Beliefs about Women* (Prometheus Books, Amherst, 1999).

88 Bruele, *Physicians Practice*, p. 374.

The way in which the story of 'the mother' was constructed shows the powerful attraction of putrefaction as a prime cause of disease, and the existence of such disease narratives served to confirm in the minds of contemporaries its potent presence as a maker of disease.

Stories that carried conviction

The learned physicians' causal stories of disease moved sure-footedly and with certainty from one happening to the next. Even when, as was often the case, multiple chains of possible events were given to explain why a particular condition occurred, each possibility was endowed with a concrete reality, which was not lessened by its being only one of several possibilities. For instance, a variety of causes was given for consumption or phthisis, which was a sickness or ulceration of the lungs or 'lights' that consumed and weakened the whole body with symptoms of coughing and some fever:

First, this Consumption can proceede of many causes, as of a sore Cough, whereby any vaine doth breake in the Lights [lungs], or of any eager brackish rheume that falleth upon the Lights, and there through his eagerness doth arrode [erode] some vaine of the Lights, as a drop of water thorough continuall falling pearceth a hole in a hard stone.

Secondly this can also be caused through an impostume [abscess] of the throte; the which breaking falleth into the breast and there annoyeth the same.

Thirdly if any impostume in the breast which after the Pleurisie, inflammation of the Lights or spetting of bloud is not well clensed and taken away. . .

Fourthly, such can also be caused through some obstruction of any accustomed course of womens flowers, or course of the Hemorhoides, which being closed up, by their vapors do damage the Lights.

Fifthly, it commeth through extreame outward heate, or colde rawe windes, and especially in the falling of the leafe [autumn]. Also straines, wounds, pestilent aire, through long use of many hot spices, Oinions, Garlicke, and other things moe, which doe ingender much and subtile blood, whereby a vaine quickly commeth to breake, wherby afterwards the blood putrifieth there, and turneth into an impostume.

These sicknesses can also be well provoked through long conversing in quicksilver, the vapor whereof harmeth and putrifieth the Lights.[89]

---

[89] Wirsung, *Practise of Physicke*, pp. 250–1. For an excellent introduction and discussion of the Renaissance medical narrative see Siraisi, *The Clock and the Mirror*, pp. 195–213.

The disease was multicausal. Today, we have come to expect that diseases will have single causes, just as there will be a single 'magic bullet' that will cure a disease, despite the counter-examples of heart disease and cancers, where the model of explanation is pluralistic, involving diet, exercise, stress, environmental and genetic factors. However, in the early modern period it was normal to consider a disease as having many different causes. Again, the modern distinction between a disease as an entity, the ontological view of disease, and as a collection of symptoms is not helpful. Disease was a definable, often localised disorder of the body that showed itself in a number of distinct symptoms. Its name gave it an identity and a nature, and hence it had a being, as Wirsung wrote:

This *Phthisis* (the which by reason of her nature, is called the Consumption and of the Latinists *Tabes*) is an ulcer of the Lights . . . wherewith is alwaies a Cough or a small ague, wherby that the whole body consumeth away, and waxeth impotent. Or *Phthisis* is an exsiccation and weakning of the body, whereby the whole body will be consumed, even as the Greeke name sheweth.[90]

Although a disease was named and definable, yet it could also appear to be composed of a collection of symptoms, so that if each of the symptoms were treated separately the disease would disappear. At first sight this seems to be the case from Wirsung's advice on how to treat consumption. The reader is referred to previous chapters on how to get rid of the cough, the spitting of blood, the ague, and rheum of consumption. Such symptoms were viewed as components of consumption, but also as conditions in their own right, or as components of other diseases as well as of consumption; so, for instance, Wirsung wrote, 'care is to be had to lengthen the sicke bodies breath; for this, looke into the 12 [chapter] of *Astma*'.[91] Even today, in the heyday of the belief in the ontological theory of disease, doctors often pragmatically treat the symptoms of a disease, frequently using the same therapeutic techniques for a symptom that appears in a variety of diseases.

However, Wirsung also set out remedies and a regimen that were specific against consumption, 'this sicknes', as he put it.[92] A disease was not just an empty shell in which symptoms were housed. There was usually a pathological core to it, a disease process, which was unique to a particular disease. In the case of consumption, it was

---

[90] Ibid., p. 250.   [91] Ibid., p. 251.   [92] Ibid.

damage to the lungs resulting in a wasting away of the body. Although there could be many causes of a disease and many therapies, some of the latter being used for a variety of symptoms that were common to a number of diseases, the pathological stories of what happened inside the body ensured that each disease had a meaning of its own. Wirsung's causes of consumption were all possible ways of explaining the central issue of consumption: how it came about that the lungs became damaged, ulcerated, corroded or abscessed. The image of damaged lungs deep inside the body is held with certainty, and is the end point of all the causal stories such as Wirsung's fifth possibility where extreme heat, cold winds or foods such as onions can produce too much blood, with the result that a vein breaks, the blood putrifies and this forms an abscess in the lung.

The authority of the physician in defining the nature and causes of a disease came partly from his education, the authority of past writers, and in general from the self-fashioned status of physic. But it was also derived from the physician's ability to 'see' and describe the deep pathological processes that were the identifying markers of certain diseases. This ability, which to us today appears illusory or imaginative, was embedded within a culture where the boundaries between the visible and invisible worlds were permeable, and was perhaps analogous to the power of the priest or witch-finder to make the hidden visible. This, of course, is only an analogy: the physicians and surgeons who saw deep into the body did so, as discussed earlier, by using natural, anatomical and humoral terms and signposts.

The physician's ability to see into the diseased body and to tell its story created a sense of rationality, of being able to answer the question 'why?', which was the hallmark of rational, learned physic. For instance, Wirsung provided a rational explanation for 'an olde saying that the old and ripe consumption is not to be cured'. He did so in the persona of a learned physician by using the language of the philosophers with its stress on causes, which he integrated with his knowledge of what was happening inside the body:

The cause is, that all such ulcers of the breast doe corrode too deepe. Secondly, because the Lights [lungs] must be in continuall motion, where notwithstanding all cures must have neede of quietnes. Thirdly, through continuall motion doth race and eate in the deeper. Fourthly, for that the disease lyeth so deepe in the bodie, that Phisicke can hardly or slowly come to it. Fiftly, if hot remedies be to be used for it then increaseth the Ague: if colde remedies, then have they but small force to pearce to the place infected: Or if there be drying medicines used thereto, then doe the same oppresse and putrifie there.[93]

Of course, much of what appears to be observed by the medical writer was already in the medical domain. Yet most medical writers, even when they were reflecting the consensus of opinion, by a sleight of hand managed to create an impression of fresh personal observation and thought. For instance, John Tanner, an astrological physician strongly influenced by Galenic medicine, 'collected out of the Works of most of the Antient and Modern Physicians' his 'Compendium or Abridgment of Physick, much of which I have sealed and confirmed by the *Probatum est* of my own Experience, as Providence hath given me occasion'.[94] The mix of authority and apparent experience, together with the model or vision of the body as a porous interconnected whole, allowed Tanner to explain why an ulcer in the lungs caused the whole body to wither away. He declared, with the authority of medical consensus and with the descriptive liveliness of personal observation, what was the case: 'An ulcer in the Lungs, by reason of its nearness to the heart, afflicts it with putrid vapours; the heart disperseth it into all parts: hence commeth a Feaver hectick joyned with a putrid [fever], and by its unnatural heat, does hinder the well concocting of nourishment, hence the whole Body decayeth.'[95]

Autopsies and pathological stories

Tanner's mix of anatomical knowledge and signposting (nearness of lungs to the heart), the technical terms (putrid vapours, 'feavers hectick' and putrid, 'concocting of nourishment') and the vision of active pathological processes (the dispersal of putrid vapours through the body, the development of fever, and the stopping of digestion with consequent consumption of the whole body) together created an impressive unfolding of expert, esoteric knowledge. It may well have impressed patients. There was certainly a demand for information about what had caused a disease. One such source was the autopsy. That performed on Henry, Prince of Wales, in 1612 probably made autopsy fashionable and acceptable amongst the

---

[93] Ibid.   [94] Tanner, *Hidden Treasures*, sig. A4ᵛ.   [95] Ibid., p. 104.

nobility and gentry in England.[96] An autopsy also involved an account or story of illness, but as some of the main characters, the organs and fluids of the body, were open to view, the findings of autopsy seemed to be less speculative and more certain. For instance, John Evelyn, diarist and supporter of the 'new science', blamed 'the woman and maide that tended' his sick five-year-old son Richard for his death: 'in my opinion he was suffocated' by them as they 'covered him too hott with blankets as he lay in a Cradle, neere an excessive hot fire in a close roome'. However, he had his son 'open'd' and there was 'found a membranous substance growing to the cavous [hollow] part of the <u>liver</u>, being neere the edge of it for the compasse of 3 Inches, which ought not to be'. In the end, he substituted the results of the autopsy, which were that death had occurred from an enlarged liver and spleen, for his own opinion.[97] Sometimes, as John Ward noted, despite opening a body to view, an autopsy could not determine cause of death:

I saw Mr. Gwinne, of our house, dissected, but could perceive nothing in him that might cause his death; his spleen was somewhat flaccid, so was his heart, and one of his kidneys; but his lungs had some kind of schirrhus in them, and in those schirrhi, a sabulous kind of matter, but that could not kill him. They pretended hee had a contusion of the liver, in regard that the concavitie of itt was a little stained; but possibly itt was nothing but the settling of the blood when death came. There was a membrane coming from his side to his lungs, which some ignorant people would have interpreted a growing of the lungs to the side; but Mr. Boghill said hee had seen itt severall times in sound men that were opened. His heart was exceeding large, allmost as large as the heart of an ox, but not perisht att all.[98]

Such sceptical agnosticism was rare; medical practitioners did not usually hesitate to pronounce on the cause of illnesses whether fatal or otherwise. The interpretation of autopsy findings often relied on the same pathological narratives that were used to make sense of

---

[96] See David Harley, 'Political Post-Mortems and Morbid Anatomy in Seventeenth-century England', *Social History of Medicine*, 7, 1994, 1–28. The earlier autopsy on Henri IV by Paré, it could be argued, was even more influential in making autopsies fashionable throughout Northern Europe. In northern Italy autopsies were performed in the late thirteenth century and were increasingly frequent in the fourteenth; see Katherine Park, 'The Criminal and the Saintly Body: Autopsy and Dissection in Renaissance Italy', *Renaissance Quarterly*, 47, 1994, 1–33.

[97] John Evelyn, *The Diary of John Evelyn*, ed. E. S. de Beer (6 vols., Clarendon Press, Oxford, 1955), vol. III, pp. 209–10.

[98] Ward, *Diary*, p. 261.

illness in the living body. When Theodore Turquet de Mayerne, the royal physician, reported on the autopsy of Henry, Prince of Wales, he noted the black colour of the lungs, 'stuffed full of over heated blood', and that the ventricles of the brain were full of a clear fluid. He concluded that 'some of these conditions were the result of the fever, which was malignant only because of the putrefaction of various humours long accumulated in the body'.[99] Disembowelling the corpse, where the organs were cut out of the body, also provided an opportunity to inspect the organs for the cause of death. This was carried out sometimes so that the rest of the body could be transported elsewhere to be buried, and took place prior to embalming the body. For instance, when Alice Thornton's father, Christopher Wandesford, Lord Deputy of Ireland, died in Dublin in 1640:

His bodie beeing imbowelled was afterwards imballmed, and all the noble parts was very sound and perfect, saving the heart, which was decaied on one side. It was thought this proceeded from much study and bussinesse which his weighty and great imployments called him to, great watch-fulnesse and paines in the faithfull discharge of his offices.[100]

Lay people in allowing the autopsy of their relatives gave to physicians and surgeons the right to pronounce on the cause of the fatal illness.[101] Autopsies can be used as evidence of a lay wish to defer to the apparent objectivity and expertise of the medical autopsy, as regards the cause of death. The interpretative findings of autopsies, because they are similar to the accounts of illness while the patient was alive, can be used to argue that there was a demand for the medical stories of a patient's illness. But autopsies were very limited in number in seventeenth-century England, and were by no means a normal occurrence.

---

[99] Thomas Gibson, 'Doctor Theodore Turquet de Mayerne's Account of the Illness, Death and Post-Mortem Examination of the Body of His Royal Highness, Prince Henry of Wales', *Annals of Medical History*, 2nd series, 10, 1938, 550–60, 557.

[100] Alice Thornton, *The Autobiography of Mrs. Alice Thornton of East Newton, Co. York*, ed. Charles Jackson, Publication of the Surtees Society, vol. 62, 1875, p. 25.

[101] Surgeons were more likely to embalm the body, and by the end of the seventeenth century physicians were leaving autopsies to surgeons, the former being perhaps less interested in performing such activities as they did not fit their new aspirations to gentility. On directions to surgeons on embalming see Paré, *Workes* and Brugis, *Vade Mecum*. On physicians and gentility see Harley, 'Political Post-Mortems' pp. 21–2, though surgeons like William Hunter also aspired to gentility.

Patients and disease narratives

The diaries, letters and biographies of lay people do not provide much direct evidence of an eagerness for a lengthy unfolding of what was happening in the patient's body. Alice Thornton, who was fascinated by her own and other people's illnesses and had an extensive knowledge of medicine, let the physicians explain how an illness had come about, as in 1659 when her mother, Alice Wandesford, lay dying:

> But then she was seized with a more dangerous simnttome, of a hard lumpe contracted in her stomacke, that laid on her heart, with great paine and riseing up in her throat, almost stopeing her breath, when she either swallowed any thing or laied to sleepe. Which lumpe was conceaved to be contracted of winde and phlegme in the stomacke for lacke of voydance.[102]

The brief, almost shorthand summary of what had happened inside the body was typical of lay reports of medical opinion. The patient and the onlookers at the bedside were even more concerned about diagnosis than about the cause of the disease, and often in lay reports cause and diagnosis were rolled up into one. However, it is likely that at the bedside physicians did use parts of their narrative accounts of illness to explain to the patient what was happening, but often this would be as part of diagnosis, and it was diagnosis that was usually selected by lay people as the most significant aspect of a consultation that may have ranged from a few minutes to hours or days. When John Atkinson, chaplain and steward to Lord Lisle, wrote to Lady Lisle in the summer of 1536 that he had been sick since Easter and that his physicians 'sheweth' him it was consumption, he may have been told something of what was happening inside his lungs as well as being informed about the significance of his symptoms.[103] As medical learning often shaped literate medical knowledge (and perhaps oral knowledge), patients could also appropriate parts of the medical accounts of disease when framing their own images of what was happening to them. This was especially so when they were anxiously wondering if they had a disease like consumption which was notoriously difficult to diagnose and which

---

[102] Thornton, *Autobiography*, p. 107.
[103] Muriel St. Clare Byrne (ed.), *The Lisle Letters* (6 vols., University of Chicago Press, Chicago and London, 1981), vol. III, p. 94. Atkinson added 'which hath made me sore afraid of myself'.

was feared for its lingering course and fatal outcome. Thomas Nashe wrote that it was worse than death and

it is as a man should be roasted to death and melt away little by little, whiles physicians like cooks stand stuffing him out with herbs and basting him with this oil and that syrup . . . to be famished to death is far better, for his pain in seven or eight days is at an end, whereas he that is in a consumption continues languishing many years ere death have mercy upon him.[104]

In March 1703 the Reverend Thomas Brockbank wrote to Betty Whittingham, his future wife, of his fear of consumption which he did not dare to make explicit: 'In mine [last letter] I told you I had not been very well, and I dare not say I am perfectly recovered I am tormented frequently with a corroding pain at my breast, and spit more than usually and what this may be the forerunner of I know not but fear the worst.'[105] Clearly, Brockbank was framing his symptoms into medical accounts of consumption, imagining his lungs corroding away, whilst his spitting also became significant as a symptom of the disease. As his pain had lasted from Christmas up to Easter, he decided to consult a physician: 'I therefore acquainted Dr Tarleton with my Case and begg'd his Advice, which he freely gave me: It was to remove to Leverp. [Liverpool] for a few nights, that he might make the better Observations concerning me: I did so and came to town on wednesday the 31 of March, and lodged in Red cross street . . .'[106] From Liverpool he wrote to Betty that 'the Dr. encourages me', but he still feared the worst: 'If my Distemper proves a Consumption, You know the rest, 'twill be a stop to my wishes.' His doctor tried to provide reassurance and perhaps a counter-story to that of consumption. In a letter to his father, Brockbank wrote: 'I have been 3 dayes in the Town, my business to consult about my health. I have been blouded and purged since I came, and I think I must take physick when I return to Sephton. The pain at my breast was encreased by to[o] much exercising my Lungs at and before Easter, but the Dr gives hope of Recovery.'[107]

    What lay behind this exchange between patient and doctor

[104] Thomas Nashe, 'The Terrors of the Night' in *The Unfortunate Traveller and Other Works*, ed. J. B. Steane (Penguin, Harmondsworth, 1985), pp. 236–7.
[105] Richard Trappes-Lomax (ed.), *The Diary and Letter Book of the Rev. Thomas Brockbank 1671–1709* (Chetham Society, Manchester, 1930), p. 245.
[106] Ibid. On Tarleton see David Harley, ' "Bred Up in the Study of that Faculty": Licensed Physicians in North-West England, 1660–1760', *Medical History*, 38, 1994, p. 417.
[107] Ibid., p. 246.

remains hidden. If Brockbank's physician had feared consumption, then the increase of pain with exercise of the lungs would have formed part of the story of the disease. On the other hand, Dr Tarleton could have reassured Brockbank by telling him that exercise was the cause of his lung trouble and not consumption, whilst in his own mind seeing it as possible consumption. Brockbank's advice to himself and that provided by his physician indicate that the fear of consumption, which began with the sensation and image of the 'corroding', ulcerating pain in his chest described in medical textbooks, was not lessened by the consultation, although he did concede that 'the Drs [Doctor's Prescriptions] (I believe) have done me good'. To his future wife he wrote that:

Sephton is pleasant enough in Summer, but exceeding wet and dirty in Winter, the Air thick and moist, and as such not very agreeable to my constitution. Among other things the Doctor has advised me to take Tobacco to carry off ill humours and I am begun very moderately to follow his directions at bedtime. Perhaps it may do me good, and I am considering 'tis better to have breath stinking of Tobacco than no breath at all.[108]

The references to carrying off ill humours, to exercise and the lungs, and to corroding pain were part of the hidden (from us) discourse of patient and doctor that centred around the disease. The story of what happened in the lungs in a consumption was probably referred to many times, and would have been touched upon in discussions of diagnosis, treatment and outcome. But it was these three topics, rather than extensive causal accounts of disease, which were most important for Brockbank and for most patients, unless they were especially immersed in medicine or viewed their illnesses as providentially caused by God. Certainly, in a disease that could mean a death sentence, diagnosis was seen as highly significant and worth recording. The Reverend John Ward, who practised medicine and was troubled by a chronic cough for many years, took care to note that 'Sweating in a consumption is a mortall signe', and he wrote down the cautionary story of

A scholar att Oxford applying himself to an elderly physitian of that universitie, to know whether hee was in a consumption or not, hee askt the scholar whether hee spitt blood or not? hee answered negatively; then said hee [the physician] 'tis but a ptysick cough, and I will warrant you from a

---

[108] Ibid., pp. 248–9.

consumption [guarantee that it is not a consumption]'; but three months after, his bodie went to the wormes.[109]

Although usually only small sections of the physicians' pathological stories are repeated in lay people's diaries and letters, it is likely that they were used at the bedside to tell the patient what was happening inside his or her body. They 'showed' the disease to the patient, and perhaps helped to confirm and reconcile him or her in the role of a sufferer of a particular disease. The stories, based as they were on the movements and blockages of fluids, vapours, poisons, putrefactions and dirt in the body, were of the same kind as the literate lay view of disease, and they also tied in with common notions of the therapeutics of clearing and cleansing away. The physician's story of illness was familiar to the patient, but novel in its detail. The medical textbooks gave the physician the materials to be a great talker at the bedside. That such talk was caricatured is a sign both of its prominence and of its being different from the ordinary illness discourse of lay people. In *Tamburlaine* a physician diagnoses death using the physiological jargon of vital heat and moisture:

> Your veins are full of accidental heat,
> Whereby the moisture of your blood is dried.
> The humidum and calor [heat] . . .
> Is almost clean extinguished and spent;
> Which, being the cause of life, imports your death.
> . . . Your artiers, which alongst the veins convey
> The lively spirits which the heart engenders,
> Are parch'd and void of spirit, that the soul,
> Wanting those organons by which it moves,
> Cannot endure, by argument of art [i.e. medicine][110]

The stories of the hidden happenings inside the body and the technical terminology that accompanied them were part of the self-fashioning of physicians, and as we shall see also of surgeons. They were the esoteric treasury of knowledge that belonged to learned medicine, hence the anxiety of the examiners of the London College of Physicians that prospective candidates shared in the language and the stories. In a sense, they were, as the caricaturists would have it, part of the professional 'cant' of medicine, a secret language little

---

[109] Ward, *Diary*, pp. 276, 274.
[110] Christopher Marlowe, *Tamburlaine*, Part II, Act V Scene III, lines 82–97. I am grateful to Dr Natsu Hattori for this passage.

understood by the general public. As Peniboy the Canter in Jonson's
The Staple of News, put it:

> The *Doctor* here, I will proceed with the *learned*.
> When he discourseth of *dissection*,
> Or any point of *Anatomy*: that hee tells you,
> Of *Vena cava*, and of *vena porta*, . . .
> What does hee else but *cant*?
> . . . Who here does understand him?[111]

Yet only some of the language was cant. Much of it was understood
by the public, whether at the bedside, in the theatre or in the
church. The causal accounts of illness were part of the occupational
repertoire of physicians, conferring expertise and signifying university learning, but the framework into which they were put and many
of their pieces were also known to the literate public.

---

[111] Ben Jonson, *The Staple of News*, Act IV Scene IV, lines 37–47, cited from Natsu Hattori,
' "Business at Bedsides": Doctors and Healing on the English Stage *c*.1590–1640' (MPhil.
dissertation, Oxford University, 1991), p. 25.

CHAPTER 4

Preventive medicine: healthy lifestyles and healthy environments

SUMMARY

Advice on how to live healthily and prolong life aroused great interest amongst the literate public, if the numbers of books devoted to the subject are anything to go by. They were addressed to the middling and upper sections of society, and did not claim, as did works on therapeutics, to be necessary for everyone. Moreover, despite the interest in prevention, it was widely acknowledged that few took up the advice, a paradox that is still present today. Preventive medicine was therefore limited in its ostensible scope; it was, in a sense, the luxury end of medicine. It provided for a choice of diet and lifestyles for those who had the means to make choices that were not so available to the poor; for instance, whether to eat meat and vegetables. But it was also an important part of medical and surgical treatment, for rules on diet, exercise, etc. were relevant for the ill as well as the healthy. It was also one of the primary means whereby the principles and ethos of learned medicine were spread to the literate part of the population, thus helping to create a unified medical culture, with lay writers in turn also taking part in this process. Medical knowledge about health was transferred to readers who were expected then to apply it to themselves. It is also the case that, as with much of the medicine from the classical period to the later seventeenth century, there was an input to learned medicine from the popular tradition which is difficult to trace.

As well as laying out for the reader some of the content of the health advice literature, this chapter demonstrates the central importance ascribed to diet. It also shows how a strong moralising element was associated with health advice, as is also the case today. This was probably welcomed by the readers of the advice books, just as the admonitions in sermons included in religious texts were

154

eagerly read. The sense of moral imperative associated with health advice lends support to the argument that the very specific and detailed advice given on diet and on healthy places in which to live was a form of medicalisation – that the physicians were trying to bring ways of living, and, indeed, the whole world, under medical scrutiny and control, and were demonstrating that learned medicine had a much wider remit than merely providing cures. Though this process had limited success, it seems, paradoxically, that a medical view of the environment and of diet was shared across literate culture, even if the knowledge was not always acted upon.

The chapter comes close to providing an example of *l'histoire immobile*. There was a great deal of consensus about health advice, with no controversies or significant new arguments across the sixteenth and seventeenth centuries, with the exception of some Helmontian attacks on the whole enterprise of giving health advice (discussed in chapter 9). No doubt the slow change in the material and geographical conditions that shaped people's lifestyles made for continuity in the health advice literature. Also, as is discussed at the end of the chapter, the healthiness of places, foods and peoples was underpinned by a set of long-lasting general assumptions that involved, for example, the healthiness of movement and unhealthiness of stagnation. This reflected the values of a literate world that, despite being pre-industrial, was increasingly urban, yet whose beliefs about health continued to be framed by its preconceived image of the ideal, healthy and pure countryside, which modern historical demographers have confirmed was, indeed, on the whole healthier.

INTRODUCTION

Hygiene (in its original sense of the art of conserving health, from the Greek 'hygeia' or health) and therapeutics have been the two basic parts of learned medicine.[1] Although therapeutics has undergone vast changes since the time of the ancient Greeks, preventive medicine has changed much less. Many of the topics around which the advice has been organised, such as food, exercise and emotional well-being, have remained the same, as have some of the assump-

---

[1] See Galen, *A Translation of Galen's Hygiene (De Sanitate Tuenda)*, trans. Robert Montraville Green (C. C. Thomas, Springfield, Ill., 1951), p. 5.

tions behind the advice. These include the existence of a relationship between people and the food they eat and the environment they live in, and the need for both food and environment to be clean, uncorrupted and 'natural'.

Health advice today is often highly detailed so that every aspect of daily life appears to be under review. For instance, diet is covered in minute detail – how much fat to eat, how many vegetables and fruit, how much salt, etc. In the early modern period keeping healthy was also a matter of paying detailed attention to how one lived. Books on regimen, on the regulation of health, advised on how to lead a healthy and long life, and appeared to cover most aspects of life. They were usually organised according to the 'six non-naturals', which some time after Galen came to provide the canonical categories around which advice on the preservation of health was based. These were (1) air, (2) food and drink, (3) sleep and waking, (4) movement and rest, (5) retention and evacuation including sexual activity, and (6) the passions of the soul or the emotions. Galen set them out in his *Ars Medica* (*The Medical Art*), and he explained why they were necessary for the health of the individual (though he did not in that work coin the mysterious term 'non-naturals', which means the necessary aspects of life over which choices can be made).[2] In the seventeenth century Robert Burton echoed Galen when he wrote that physicians would tell us that the 'six non natural things . . . are the causes of our infirmities', and that they are necessary 'because we cannot avoid them, but they will alter us, as they are used or abused'.[3] And he made it clear that transgressing the rules of health involved blame and morality as well as medicine, for 'offending in some of those six non natural things' caused not only infirmities but also 'our surfeiting [overeating], and drunkeness, our immoderate insatiable lust, and prodigious riot'.[4] The requirement for moderation meant that appetites had to be reined in, and

[2] These categories were not fixed in the Hippocratic writings, and a slightly different list was given in Galen's *De Sanitate Tuenda*; see L. J. Rather, 'The "Six Things Non-Natural": a Note on the Origins and (fate of) a Doctrine and a Phrase', *Clio Medica*, 3, 1968, 337–47; Saul Jarcho, 'Galen's Six Non-Naturals: a Bibliographic Note and Translation', *Bulletin of the History of Medicine*, 44, 1970, 372–7.
[3] Robert Burton, *The Anatomy of Melancholy*, 1st edn (1621), ed. Floyd Dell and P. Jordan-Smith (Tudor, New York, 1948), pp. 118, 189, cited by Rather, ' "The Six Things Non-Natural" ', p. 337.
[4] Burton, *Anatomy of Melancholy*, p. 118.

health advice in the early modern period, as today, had a strong admonitory and moral tone.

The regimens or health advice books were largely, though not exclusively, products of the learned tradition in medicine. Advice on health helped to distinguish learned medicine from its competitors and learned physicians boasted that unlike empirics they were concerned with prevention as well as cure. The advice was aimed at the literate and the reasonably well-to-do. Although the Hippocratic *Regimen in Health* addressed itself to the 'non-professional' person (ἰδιώτης), and *Regimen* 'to the great mass of mankind who of necessity live a haphazard life and since they neglect everything else, cannot [be expected to] take care of their health',[5] Galen had wealthier readers in mind. In the *De Sanitate Tuenda* (*On the Preservation of Health*), he wrote for the leisured, who could set aside everything for the pursuit of health. He accepted that slaves, the poor and even business people could have their health damaged by their work, but he and his followers did not use the banner of health to urge a change in working and living conditions. For, as Galen put it, 'the life of many men is involved in the business of their occupation, and it is inevitable that they should be harmed by what they do and that it should be impossible to change it'.[6] In the Middle Ages and Renaissance regimens continued to be addressed to well-to-do individuals.[7] However, the *Regimen Sanitatis Salernitanum* (*The Regimen of Health of Salerno*), which circulated in manuscript from the thirteenth century and was widely available in book form in the sixteenth century, was exceptional in achieving great popular appeal. It was attributed to the medical school of Salerno, one of the first in medieval Europe. The verses of the *Regimen* were added to over time; they were often witty, easy to understand and remember, and were translated into many European languages. Advice on health constituted one part of the *Regimen*, and the six non-naturals were

---

[5] Hippocrates, 'Regimen in Health', in *Works*, trans. by W. H. S. Jones (8 vols., William Heinemann, London, and Harvard University Press, Cambridge, Mass., 1931), vol. IV, pp. 44–5, and 'Regimen' in *Works*, vol. IV, book 3, ch. 69, p. 381; modified translation.

[6] Galen, *Hygiene*, p. 51.

[7] For an excellent overview see Richard Palmer, 'Health, Hygiene and Longevity in Medieval and Renaissance Europe' in Yosio Kawakita, Shizu Sakai and Yasuo Otsuka (eds.), *History of Hygiene* (Ishiyaku Euro America, Tokyo, 1991), pp. 75–98; Andrew Wear, 'The History of Personal Hygiene' in W. F. Bynum and Roy Porter (eds.) *Companion Encyclopedia of the History of Medicine* (Routledge, London, 1993), vol. II, pp. 1283–308. See also Heikki Mikkeli, *Hygiene in the Early Modern Medical Tradition* (Academia Scientiarum Fennica, Helsinki, 1999), which came to my attention after this book was written.

mentioned together with materia medica, anatomy, physiology and therapies for particular fevers and diseases. The *Regimen* was an *omnium gatherum* of medical information. Its wide scope was rarely copied, but it indicates that the boundaries of health advice were very flexible, and its popular format is a sign that health advice could lie between the spheres of the learned and the popular.

THE ENGLISH HEALTH ADVICE BOOKS

There was a good market for books on regimen: for instance, the highly influential *Castel of Helthe*, written by a layman, Sir Thomas Elyot, was reprinted sixteen times between *c.* 1536 and 1595 and sold for sixpence, which was far cheaper than surgical works or herbals.[8] Yet the authors of books on regimen complained, as do modern advocates of preventive medicine and health education, that living according to rules of health was not popular – understandably

---

[8] Paul Slack, 'Mirrors of Health and Treasures of Poor Men: the Uses of the Vernacular Medical Literature of Tudor England' in Charles Webster (ed.), *Health, Medicine and Mortality in the Sixteenth Century* (Cambridge University Press, Cambridge, 1979), pp. 247–8; Slack, p. 247, writes that Vigo's surgical works cost four shillings and Dodoens' herbal six shillings. Other works on regimen in English included a translation by Thomas Paynell of the *Regimen Sanitatis Salernitanum* (London, 1528), the famous version of the *Regimen* by Sir John Harington, Plutarch's treatise on good health which was translated in 1530 as *The Governance of Good Helthe*, Andrew Boorde's *A Compendyous Regyment or a Dyetary of Helth* (London, 1542), Thomas Phayre's *The Regiment of Life* (London, 1545) (based on a work by Jehan Goeurot, but substantially altered by the inclusion of a large number of remedies), William Bullein's *The Government of Health* (London, 1558), Guglielmo Gratarolo's work translated into English in 1574 as *A Direction for the Health of Magistrates and Studentes*, and Thomas Cogan's *The Haven of Health* (1st edn, 1584; London, 1612). As with Elyot's treatise there were plenty of buyers for such books. Paynell's was reprinted seven times between 1528 and 1597 and Phayre's nine times between 1545 and 1596; Slack, *Mirrors of Health*, p. 248. In the seventeenth century the demand for regimens continued and works by William Vaughan, Tobias Venner, James Hart, Humfrey Brooke and Thomas Mouffet went to press, whilst the Italian treatises by Luigi Cornaro and by his follower Leonard Lessius on how to live to an extreme old age by means of temperance and a very meagre, precisely measured diet, which were popular in continental Europe, were published in English in 1634. Indeed, in 1650 Brooke reported of these last that 'both . . . are almost at every Booksellers to be had in English': Humfrey Brooke, *ΥΓΙΕΙΝΗ, Or a Conservatory of Health* (London, 1650), p. 13. William Vaughan, *Approved Directions for Health, Both Naturall and Artificiall* (London, 1600); Tobias Venner, *Via Recta ad Vitam Longam: or, a Plaine Philosophicall Demonstration of the Nature, Faculties and Effects of all such Things as . . . Make for the Preservation of Health* (1st edn, 1620; London, 1628); James Hart, *ΚΛΙΝΙΚΗ, or the Diet of the Diseased* (London, 1633); Leonardus Lessius, *Hygiasticon: or the Right Course of Preserving Life and Health unto Extreme Old Age . . . now done into English [by T. S.] with A Treatise of Temperance and Sobrietie by Lud. Cornarus*, trans. George Herbert (Cambridge, 1634); Thomas Mouffet, *Healths Improvement: Or, Rules Comprizing and Discovering the Nature, Method, and Manner of Preparing all sorts of Food used in this Nation: Corrected and Enlarged by Christopher Bennett* (London, 1655).

so, because it involved self-discipline – then as now. Thomas Cogan, a fellow of Oriel College, Oxford and subsequently a physician and schoolmaster in Manchester, reported, as did other writers, that 'it is a common saying: "He that liveth by Physicke, liveth miserably". And [that it is] a great punishment . . . for a man to refraine his appetite.' Moreover, physicians complained that people hardly ever went to them to get advice on how to stay well, but only sought medical help when they were ill.[9] On the other hand, physicians were aware of a group of people who were obsessively anxious about their health, to the extent that they became slaves to it. Leonard Lessius, a Jesuit from the Low Countries who supported Luigi Cornaro's sparse and simple diet plan (see below), wrote that there were too many rules about health 'as they bring men into a Labyrinth of care in the observation, and unto perfect slaverie in the endevouring to perform what they [the authors on regimen] do in this matter enjoyn'.[10] Such people were likely to have been eager buyers of the health advice books, even if many others ignored them.

The social and geographical horizons of the regimens

Early modern regimens were intended for the literate and the well-to-do, and in this they continued in the tradition of later antiquity and the Middle Ages, extending their advice from individual princes and nobles to a print audience. More specifically they catered for the studious,[11] and for the sedentary, especially those in towns and cities. As it was these types who were likely to be interested in their health and to buy regimens, it probably made sense to write that they were most in need of them. Poor digestion and worry were believed to be

---

[9] Cogan, *Haven of Health*, Epistle Dedicatory, fols. 2^v–3^r; Lessius, *Hygiasticon*, pp. 3–4; George Cheyne in the eighteenth century repeated the saying, 'he who lives *physically* [by the rules of physic] must live miserably': G. Cheyne, *An Essay of Health and Long Life* (London, 1724), p. 4; Brooke, *ΥΓΙΕΙΝΗ*, p. 4, and p. 2 where he wrote, 'there are few or none that come to the Physitian to keep themselves wel but only when they are forc't thither by the importunity of Sickness'.

[10] Lessius, *Hygiasticon*, pp. 1–2; Brooke, *ΥΓΙΕΙΝΗ*, p. 10, made a similar point: 'These are affrighted with the variety and multiplicity of Rules and Cautions, which they say Physicians have purposely invented, to make their very Healths Tributary unto them; that scrupulosity in Diet and Order keeps the Mind too intent thereupon, and hinders the enjoyment of Health by the fears of Sickness, unto which the very imagination enclines us upon every Default and omission of what is prescribed.'

[11] Marsilio Ficino's *De Triplici Vita* (Basle, 1489) dealt with the health of students, and in England Thomas Cogan devoted his *Haven of Health* to the same topic; Burton's *Anatomy of Melancholy* gave much advice to the melancholic student on staying healthy.

especially common amongst sedentary, idle city dwellers and students 'where the stomache is feeble' and care had to be taken that the quality and quantity of food were appropriate to nature's digestive power.[12] Bad digestion as a chief prognostic sign of impending ill health helped to justify the large amount of space given over to different foods and their properties. City life was seen as especially deleterious to health, its lack of physical labour producing impaired digestion and illness. Labourers in the countryside, by contrast, had iron digestions and consequent health and were not considered in need of any health advice. Although diet was only one of the six non-naturals, it was sometimes equated with health; for instance, *Health's Improvement* by Thomas Mouffet (1553–1604), a leading early English Paracelsian and humanist who was also a not very active fellow of the College of Physicians, was largely devoted to discussing diet and different foods, as was indicated by its subtitle *Or, Rules Comprizing and Discovering the Nature, Method, and Manner of Preparing all Sorts of Food*.[13] (The early modern sense of diet was advice on what to eat; sometimes one of the modern meanings of diet, to reduce weight, was conveyed by phrases such as spare, reducing or 'inch' diet.)

The social and geographical distinctions marked by lack of exercise and poor digestion were also a prolegomenon to the condemnation of idleness and gluttony. Country people, who worked hard, digested well; in Bullein's opinion they 'digest grosse meats [foods], eating them with much pleasure, and sleeping soundly after them'. On the other hand, he condemned:

the idle multitudes in Cities, and noble mens houses, great numbers for lacke of exercise doe abhorre meates [foods] of light digestion and daintie dishes, Marie in deede they may bee verie profitable to Phisitions. But if travaile [labour] be one of the best preservers of health, so is idlenesse the destroyer of life.[14]

Where manual labour was lacking, it could be substituted for by exercise. The choice of recommended exercises – tennis, dancing and horse-riding – indicates that the readership of the regimens would have been, or saw themselves as, among the middling to

---

[12] Sir Thomas Elyot, *The Castel of Helthe* (London, 1541), fol. 45^r, citing Celsus, *De Medicina*, book I, chs. 1–2.

[13] On Mouffet see C. Webster, 'Alchemical and Paracelsian Medicine' in Webster (ed.), *Health, Medicine and Mortality*, pp. 306, 328–30.

[14] Bullein, *Government of Health*, fol. 32^v. See also Andrew Wear, 'Making Sense of Health and the Environment in Early Modern England' in Andrew Wear (ed.), *Medicine in Society. Historical Essays* (Cambridge University Press, Cambridge, 1992), pp. 126–47.

upper ranks of society. Some exercises mentioned, such as running, climbing and dancing, were familiar to all sections of society, whilst 'footeballe play' was usually between villages, but the overall impression is that exercise was an artificial type of physical work suitable for those who did not labour. Like labour, it helped digestion by making the body hotter and therefore better able to alter food; it also cleansed it by opening its pores and so expelling 'crudities', the products of poor digestion.[15]

The writers on regimen were not concerned in their treatises with improving the living conditions of the poor, whether in the countryside or in the cities, though they recognised that city living was unhealthy. In the nineteenth and twentieth centuries medicine and politics combined to campaign for improvement in the conditions of the labouring classes, and references to their bad health were a potent weapon in that fight. Physicians in the sixteenth and seventeenth centuries were certainly aware of different social groups and were not only focused upon the individual client or reader. However, it was not until Ramazzini's *De Morbis Artificium* (1700; translated in 1705 as *A Treatise of the Diseases of Tradesmen*) that there was a comprehensive medical study of occupational illnesses. Tradition taught the regimen writers that the countryside was the healthiest place to live and that country labourers were the healthiest people. As they were the benchmark for health, therefore, it was natural that their conditions of life should not come under medical scrutiny. Cogan wrote that 'husbandmen and craftsmen, for the more part doe live longer and in better health, than Gentlemen and learned men, and such as live in bodily rest'. Ancient authority in the form of Galen, wrote Cogan, supported this view, and he added that Galen himself had indulged in 'rusticall labours' such as chopping wood.[16] Along with tradition and the social make-up of their readership, the slant of the regimen writers also reflected the social policy of English governments which held that there was no need to ameliorate the health and living conditions of the poor, although relief could be given under the Poor Laws to the sick poor.[17] The

---

[15] Elyot, *Castel of Helthe*, fols. 46^v, 48^r–49^v; Bullein, *Government of Health*, fols. 32^v; Cogan, *Haven of Health*, pp. 2–12; Venner, *Via Recta*, pp. 211–19.

[16] Cogan, *Haven of Health*, p. 3.

[17] See Paul Slack, *Poverty and Policy in Tudor and Stuart England* (Longman, London, 1988) for an analysis of the underlying attitudes of English governments to the poor, and for Europe in general see Robert Jütte, *Poverty and Deviance in Early Modern Europe* (Cambridge University Press, Cambridge, 1994).

social division inherent in the regimens comes across most clearly in the casual references to readers and their servants. Elyot advised his readers to get 'their servant' to rub their backs and shoulders as part of the 'fricasies or rubbynges' which prepared the body for exercise.[18] Bullein captured the sense of 'them and us' when he had the layman, John, ask the physician, Humfrey, why it was that 'I have found verie much disquietnes in my body, when my servants and labouring familie have found ease, and yet wee are partakers of one aire.'[19]

However, although the physicians' self-interest in focusing their books upon their readers' lifestyles and sharing in their praise of the countryside (see below) can account for the sense of social and geographical division in the regimens, there is also demographic evidence to support the view that the countryside was healthier than towns and cities. The expectation of life in the countryside could be much higher than in urban areas (see chapter 1). More particularly, the example of London supported such a view, and the first sustained analysis of why London was unhealthy, which was made by John Graunt in 1662, drew upon ideas which were current in the regimens, and in society at large.

The population of London, which had grown from 120,000 in 1550 to 490,000 by 1700, would have suffered a decrease over this period had it not been for the continuous influx of people from the countryside that more than made up for the drain on the city's population caused by its high mortality.[20] This point was made early on by Graunt in his *Naturall and Political Observations . . . upon the Bills of Mortality* (1662).[21] He analysed the weekly bills of mortality, compiled by London parish clerks, which gave the numbers and

---

[18] Elyot, *Castel of Helthe*, fols. 47^r–^{v}.

[19] Bullein, *Government of Health*, fol. 31^v. Not all references to country labourers were positive. Sometimes a note of contempt was present. Cogan, for instance, wrote of bread from peas: 'I leave it to Rustics, who have stomaches like Ostriges, that can digest hard iron.' He added that his student readers could have more choice food: 'And for studentes I allow no bread but that which is made of wheat as before is mentioned': Cogan, *Haven of Health*, p. 31.

[20] See R. Finlay, *Population and Metropolis: the Demography of London 1580–1650* (Cambridge University Press, Cambridge, 1981); and Roger Finlay and Beatrice Shearer, 'Population Growth and Suburban Expansion' in L. Beier and Roger Finlay (eds.), *London 1500–1700: the Making of the Metropolis* (Longman, London, 1986), pp. 37–60.

[21] Seen in hindsight, it appears to be the first study of population demography, but it was part of the late seventeenth-century enterprise of creating natural and civic histories or descriptions of societies, to form the basis for taxonomic schemes such as those found in botany.

causes of death. Graunt's numerate approach was in keeping with the 'new science' of the Royal Society, but his views on the environmental factors causing illness and death can be called neither traditional nor novel, for they were views that were current from the sixteenth through to the eighteenth century. Graunt discussed the reasons why the population of London was not self-sustaining or self-increasing. Like medical writers, he believed that London was less healthy than the country, though people whose bodies were 'seasoned' or adapted over time to London could live long. Graunt drew upon some of the standard beliefs and complaints that related health and illness to the environment, which have continued across the centuries to the present. London was notorious for bad air, and a change of air was often advised for convalescence:

As for unhealthiness, it may well be supposed, that although seasoned Bodies may, and do live as near as long in *London*, as elsewhere, yet new-comers and Children do not: for the *Smoaks*, *Stinks* and close *Air*, are less healthful than that of the Country; otherwise why do sickly Persons remove into the Country-Air? And why are there more old men in Countries than in London, per rata?[22]

As is discussed below, crowded environments as well as bad air were condemned in the health advice books, and Graunt believed that both helped to make London unhealthy:

I considered whether a City, as it becomes more populous, doth not, for that very cause, become more unhealthful . . . London now is more unhealthful than heretofore; partly for that it is more populous, but chiefly because I have heard, that sixty years ago few Sea Coals were burnt in London, which are now universally used. For I have heard that Newcastle is more unhealthful than other places, and that many People cannot at all endure the smoak of London, not only for its unpleasantness but for the suffocation which it causes.[23]

Another possibility was that London's air led to infertility in the same way as it produced more deaths and disease than in the countryside. Graunt thought not, but, like medical writers, he made the connection between the body and the mind, and wrote that city life, which for some put a premium on brain rather than manual labour, created barriers to natural activities: 'The minds of men in

---

[22] John Graunt, *Naturall and Political Observations . . . upon the Bills of Mortality* (1st edn, London, 1662; 5th edn, 1676), p. 62. Graunt also wrote that the number of women of child-bearing age was fewer in London than in the countryside.

[23] Ibid., pp. 94–5.

London are more thoughtful of business than in the country, where their work is corporal Labour and Exercises; All of which promote Breeding, whereas Anxieties of the mind hinder it.'[24]

In the regimens the health of women was largely overlooked. At first sight this seems surprising, since much of the material of the regimens, the qualities of different foods and herbs, how they were to be eaten, whether raw, baked or boiled, and how administered as medicines, would have been the concern of women who were responsible for the preparation of food and medicines in the home. Yet the regimens were rarely explicitly addressed directly to them. Humfrey Brooke, a radical London physician – the only Leveller member of the College of Physicians – did write that, especially with women who mostly led a sedentary life, too much rest led to unhappiness and illness. He recommended that charitable gentle-women (see chapters 1 and 2), who were of the same social status as the intended male readers of the regimens, should learn physic, surgery and 'simpling' (gathering simples).[25] Specific advice relevant to women's physiology was given sporadically, for instance, that lettuce 'increaseth mylke in a womans breastes' whilst peony roots helped to ease the suffocation of the mother (womb) and the stopping of menstruation, and caused a woman to deliver more easily.[26] The implicit assumption of the regimen writers was that their books were intended for a male readership, although there were occasional exceptions, such as Edmund Gayton's *The Art of Longevity, or a Diaeteticall Institution* (1659), which was addressed to the 'Candid Lady-Reader'.[27] This bias towards male readers may to some extent be accounted for by the lack of women medical writers, the male control of the purse-strings, a long line of male medical authorities and the general belief present in society that man was the archetype of humanity. It may also be that physicians believed that the lives of men were more valuable than those of women.[28] A major influence, however, seems to be the long

[24] Ibid., p. 64.   [25] Brooke, *ΥΓΙΕΙΝΗ*, pp. 144–8.

[26] Elyot, *Castel of Helthe*, fol. 28^r; Vaughan, *Directions for Health*, pp. 191–2.

[27] Edmund Gayton, *The Art of Longevity, or a Diaeteticall Institution* (London, 1659), sig. a^r. Also Elyot's reference to 'men and women redinge this worke' at the end of the *Castel of Helthe*, fol. 94^v.

[28] The long education of physicians in the male-only universities and their late marriages may also have been significant: see Margaret Pelling, 'Compromised by Gender: the Role of the Male Medical Practitioner in Early Modern England' in Hilary Marland and Margaret Pelling (eds.), *The Task of Healing: Medicine, Religion and Gender in England and the Netherlands, 1450–1800* (Erasmus Publishing, Rotterdam, 1996), pp. 101–33.

tradition since antiquity of health advice books addressed to men, interrupted only by the richly illustrated medieval *Tacuinum Sanitatis* (handbooks of health) addressed to wealthy male and female readers.

The regimens were thus aimed at a relatively narrow section of society, large enough to provide buyers but small enough to give them a sense of being special, both socially and medically. The regimens are another pointer to the fact that classical Greek medical tradition and early modern learned medicine hoped for well-off, socially respectable clients, and were not concerned with the health of the whole population. Despite expressing their hopes 'to doe the common-wealth most service and to benefite the publike', the regimen writers did not intend to educate all of society in healthy living, as is the aim of health educationalists today, but only a small part of it.[29] Whether there was a 'trickle down' of this knowledge to the population at large, and, conversely, to what extent popular non-literate knowledge influenced medical beliefs, is almost impossible to tell.

HEALTH AND ILLNESS IN THE REGIMENS OF HEALTH

The writers on regimen made a clear distinction between the preservation of health and the treatment of illness. 'The first', as Humfrey Brooke wrote to his readers, is 'properly thy own work, the last is the Physicians.'[30] James Hart, who forcibly put forward the case for learned medicine, was willing to give advice in English on regimen for ill people, but he was adamant that he would not publicise therapeutics. The public, he wrote, could never have the skill and knowledge which the physicians possessed to fit remedies to the particular constitutions and circumstances of individual patients, and he condemned 'the error and ignorance of such as divulge abroad in the vulgar tongue, their [i.e. the empirics'] rare secrets (as they call them) against any disease whatsoever'.[31] The learned physicians claimed therapy as their own, and anyone making it

---

[29] Hart, *KΛINIKH*, Introduction, pp. 24, 27.
[30] Brooke, *ΥΓΙΕΙΝΗ*, To the Reader, A4ʳ.
[31] Hart, *KΛINIKH*, Introduction, p. 26. 'The intent of my labour was that men and women redinge this warke, and observinge the counsayles therin, shulde adapte thereby their bodies, to receyve more sure remedy by the medicines prepared by good phisitions in dangerous sycknesses, they kepynge good dyet': Elyot, *Castel of Helthe*, fols., 94ʳ⁻ᵛ.

public in the vernacular was breaking ranks. Elyot, when defending himself against the possible charge that he as a layman was trespassing upon the learned physicians' province, disingenuously wrote that he was merely educating people how best to prepare their bodies to receive the medicines of the physicians. However, he realised that by educating lay people in health matters he was teaching them the language of learned medicine, for his readers would be able after reading his book to inform 'diligently the same phisitions, of the maner of their affectes, passions and sensible tokens [symptoms]'.[32] In other words, the distinction between the preservation of health and therapeutics was not clearcut.

In reality, despite the rhetoric of learned physicians, there was much in common between the preservation of health or the prevention of illness and therapeutics. They shared the same theoretical basis of elements, qualities and humours, and the same medical procedures such as bleeding and purging which could be used equally to keep the body in health or to cure it.[33] And advice on regimen (what to eat, what types of air to live in, how much exercise to take) based on the six non-naturals was provided for those who were ill as well as those who were healthy. Moreover, despite their ostensible focus on health, the regimens listed large numbers of remedies, which brought them close to the vernacular books of 'every man his own doctor' and to the published collections of remedies.

As well as commercial considerations there were also conceptual reasons derived from the theories of classical medicine for the porous boundaries between hygiene (the preservation of health) and therapeutics. The regimens were written as educational handbooks, and when they set out the theoretical foundations of hygiene they also included those of therapeutics. Elyot, influenced by the most recent developments in the continental resurgence of Galenic medicine (see chapter 1), set out methodically, in tabular form, the fundamentals of health, which could also be the causes of illness. The 'three sortes of thynges' to be considered when conserving health were, following Galenic tradition, 'Thynges Naturall' 'Thynges not naturall', and 'Thynges against nature'. Thynges Naturall,' Elyot explains, are 'vii in number':

---

[32] Elyot, *Castel of Helthe*, fol. 94ᵛ.
[33] Bleeding and purging were discussed in the regimens in the section on 'evacuations', one of the six non-naturals.

Elementes	Powers
Complexions	Operations
Humours	Spirites
Members [parts of the body]	

Things 'not naturall' are six:

Ayre	Emptinesse and repletion
Meate [food] and drinke	
Slepe and watche [waking]	Affections of the mynde
Movinge and rest	

Finally, 'Thynges against Nature' were:

Sycknesse

Cause of sycknesse

Accident, which followeth sicknes[34]

Anything in the first two tables could be a cause of health and also of illness (the third table related only to illness but was included in the regimen). For instance, in the 'things natural' table a balanced complexion or humoral constitution indicated health, but an overly melancholic, phlegmatic, sanguine or choleric one led to ill health. Or, to take an example from the non-naturals table, a good air kept the body healthy, but an ill air, perhaps from fens or marshes, could cause illness.

It can also be argued that, whilst making the distinction between health and illness, the health advice books contrived to undermine it, for medical theory held that hardly anyone was in perfect health. As discussed in chapter 1, Galenic theory stated that each person had a natural constitution, temperament, complexion or humoral balance, and that illness resulted from too much of all or one of the humours or from a humour becoming vitiated. However, the body, even in its natural state, was always liable to disease, for to be sanguine, phlegmatic, choleric or melancholic meant that one humour predominated. The ideal was the golden mean, the perfect balance between the four humours. But, Phayre pointed out, 'this complexion is temperate, never to hote nor to colde, nor to moyste, nor to drye, whych yet is a thyng very seldome sene amonge men'.[35] As Donne wrote:

> There is no health; Physitians say that wee
> At best, enjoy but a neutralitie.
> And can there bee worse sicknesse, than to know

---

[34] Elyot, *Castel of Helthe*, fol. 1ʳ.   [35] Phayre, *Regiment*, fol. 1ᵛ.

That we are never well, nor can be so?
Wee are borne ruinous . . .[36]

Moreover, the natural process of ageing led irreversibly towards death. Biblical authority concurred with the medical view that everything went downhill from the time of birth: 'Man that is borne of a woman, liveth but a while, and is full of miseries, he commeth forth like a floure, and is withered, and passeth away as a shadow, and never abideth in one state.'[37] The ages of mankind had their own humoral tendencies which influenced an individual's particular constitution as they aged. For instance, childhood was hot and moist, whilst old age was cold and dry.[38] Ageing produced the qualitative change from hot and moist to cold and dry, as the radical heat and moisture of the body were used up. Here the domains of physiology and pathology overlapped, for death, even if arrived at through the normal process of ageing, is the opposite of health.

The image of life as the flame of an oil lamp helped medical writers bring home to their readers the point that, although regimen aided the light to remain lit for as long as possible, in the end it must be extinguished:

we may see that a man beginneth to die as soone as he is borne into this world, for that the radicall moisture which is the roote of life, can never be restored and made up againe, so good as it was at our nativitie, but continually by little and little decayeth untill the last end of our life. Yet by that moisture which commeth of nourishment, through meate and drinke, it is preserved and prolonged, so that it is not so soone wasted and consumed as otherwise it would be. Like as a lampe by pouring oyle moderately, the light long kept burning, yet it goeth out at the last.[39]

Natural death occurred when the body could no longer convert food into its own substance. The body's ability to do this declined with age, as its powers gradually became weaker. Ageing was thus a paradoxical process, being both natural but also like an illness.[40] This process, Cogan wrote, 'is called naturall death', which, he

---

[36] John Donne, 'An Anatomie of the World' in *Complete Poetry and Selected Prose*, ed. John Hayward (Nonesuch, London, 1962), p. 199.

[37] Cogan, *Haven of Health*, p. 191, citing Job, 14.1–2.

[38] Elyot, *Castel of Helthe*, fol. 13ʳ; Cogan, *Haven of Health*, pp. 191–3. Paradoxically, phlegm predominated in old age, but this was not the natural moisture of the body.

[39] Cogan, *Haven of Health*, p. 191; see also Elyot, *Castel of Helthe*, fol. 39ᵛ; Bullein, *Government of Health*, fol. 24ᵛ; Lessius, *Hygiasticon*, pp. 138–41; Mouffet, *Healths Improvement*, p. 9; Vaughan, *Directions for Health*, p. 2.

[40] Cogan, *Haven of Health*, pp. 191–2.

added, 'few attaine unto; but are prevented by death casuall, when by sicknesse or otherwise the saide *naturall moysture* is overwhelmed and suffocate'.[41]

Despite the often sharp distinction drawn by writers on regimen between preserving health and treating illness, a variety of reasons ensured that illness had a high profile in their books. Descriptions of remedies sold books, regimen and therapeutics shared a common theoretical basis, and the injunctions on healthy living were given significance by references to the pathological consequences of an ill regimen and by warnings as to the health dangers present in particular foods or ways of life. Even the very rare case of a life without disease involved a pathological decline, which regimen could slow down but never arrest, for death was inevitable. An ordinary life, with sickness and other misfortunes, was perceived as one long illness. Moreover, it made sense for the regimen writers to stress that illness was just round the corner, as this attracted readers' attention. People who thought they were well were likely to take no preventive precautions to preserve their health (nor perhaps were they likely to read regimen books), but regimen writers implied that they were deluded, 'imagining all to be well with them, as long as they feel nothing plainly to the contrarie'.[42] And of course, the convergence between apparent health and illness also allowed for a great deal of moralising.

WE ARE WHAT WE EAT: DIGESTION, HEALTH AND ILLNESS

Central to the conservation of health was food and drink. This was understandable for food was an area where well-to-do readers more than other sections of the population could exercise choice and control, and it was perceived to be the cause of many diseases. Particular foods could be nourishing or unwholesome, they could treat disease or bring it on. Food in general had a dual significance in medicine. It was part of everyday life, but it was also the basis from which knowledge about medicines was developed. Herbs such as thyme, hyssop and sage were used both for culinary purposes and as medicines. The Hippocratic treatise *On Ancient Medicine* had argued that medicine was a specialised form of dietetics, discovered through trial and error. Thomas Mouffet cited *On Ancient Medicine*

---

[41] Ibid., p. 192.   [42] Lessius, *Hygiasticon*, p. 5.

when he wrote that no one had written better on the origins of diet than Hippocrates himself:

avouching that Necessity was the mother, and Reason the father of Diet. For when sickness crept into the world, and men gave the same meats [foods] to sick folks which they did to the healthful, they perceived them to be so far from recovery, that they rather wax'd worse and worse. Hereupon being enforced to alter either the kind or preparation, or the quantity, or the quality and order of nourishments: they knew by diligent observation what was fittest for every disease, for every sexe, age, and complexion, and accordingly committed them to memory, or set them down in writing.[43]

Mouffet, like other Paracelsians, gave prominence to Hippocrates as the founder of medicine,[44] but Galenic writers also shared in the belief that there was a close connection between foods and medicines, health and disease.

Cooking and medicine, the worlds of health and illness, and hence of lay and expert medical cultures, were thus perceived as closely connected. Cogan wrote that almond milk made by skilful cooks was good for hot diseases, whilst almond butter was 'good for a stuffed breast', and, he added, 'the making of which things, I referre to cunning Cookes, or to the learned Physitian, who is or ought to be a perfect Cooke in many points'.[45] And, as Boorde put it, 'a good coke is halfe a physycyon. For the chefe physycke (the counseyll of a physycyon excepte) doth come from the kytchyn.'[46] If physicians had to know cookery, lay people were expected to have knowledge of the therapeutic properties of foods. 'Every kitchin maid knoweth', wrote Cogan, that the small type of setwall called valerian 'is a good pot-herbe, and beside that is very good to heale a cut'.[47] The lay practice of picking herbs in the wild or growing them in herb or kitchen gardens, and the common preparation of remedies at home (see chapter 2) brought medicine within the ambit of the household

[43] Mouffet, *Healths Improvement*, pp. 1–2. For an informative discussion of notions of diet in the Renaissance, see Nancy Siraisi, *The Clock and the Mirror. Girolano Cardano and Renaissance Medicine* (Princeton University Press, Princeton, 1997), pp. 70–90.

[44] Mouffet, however, unlike many Paracelsians, was not especially hostile to Galen; he also argued for the divine origin of dietetics, and wrote that we should 'fetch the invention of Diet from a more worthy teacher, yea from the worthiest of all other, God himself', who would have taught our 'forefathers (having sinned)' not only how to clothe their bodies but also how to feed themselves. Ibid., p. 3.

[45] Cogan, *Haven of Health*, p. 98.

[46] Boorde, *A Compendyous Regyment*, ed. F. J. Furnivall, Early English Text Society, Extra Series, 10 (London, 1870), p. 277; from the edn of 1547.

[47] Cogan, *Haven of Health*, p. 73.

economy. Herbs, vegetables, cereals, fruits, fish, fowl and meats were perceived as food (i.e. good in taste, satisfying appetite, etc.) and also as having the ability to preserve or damage health, and to act as remedies. Lay and medical knowledge and perceptions of food thus appear to converge: in large numbers of manuscripts written by lay people, especially women, food recipes and medical recipes are to be found side by side or inside the same covers.

Food was also central to Galenic physiology, for food was what made the body. It is worth briefly setting out the way in which food was integral to Galen's view of the functioning of the body, as this will provide a context for what follows. Food was concocted in the stomach by the stomach's heat and by that of the surrounding organs, and was changed into chyle, a milky fluid, sometimes called 'juice' in English treatises. According to Galen, as each part of the body had the power to attract nourishment to itself and then change it to its own substance, the chyle was attracted to the mesenteric veins where it became partly blood-like, but when it came to the liver, it was properly changed into venous blood. The liver, the major blood-making organ, was held by Galen to have a substance like that of congealed blood, and the chyle was altered in the ramifications of the liver into the liver's substance, blood. From the liver the venous blood was attracted to different parts of the body as and when they required it. When it came to the heart it was changed to lively, lighter-coloured arterial blood by being mixed with air in the left ventricle of the heart and also by being heated by the heart. The arterial blood or vital, spirituous blood travelled through the arteries to the rest of the body bringing life to it. When the vital blood came to a structure at the base of the brain called the *rete mirabile*, or marvellous network of vessels, which Galen found in Barbary apes and took to exist in man, it stayed in its convolutions and was changed into animal spirits, a highly tenuous material flowing through the ventricles of the brain and the nerves, conveying sensation and motion throughout the body. Food was, therefore, the origin of a tripartite system of bodily functions: growth and nutrition centred on the liver and venous blood, life and motion originating from the heart and arterial blood, and sensation and motion which the animal spirits communicated between the brain and the body.[48]

---

[48] On Galenic physiology see Galen, *On the Usefulness of the Parts of the Body*, trans. M. T. May (Cornell University Press, Ithaca, 1968), in which May's Introduction is especially useful; Galen, *On the Natural Faculties*, trans. A. J. Brock (William Heinemann, London, 1963). On

Underlying the relationship between food and the body was the general view that human beings shared with plants, animals and the rest of the world the same constitutions or mixtures of qualities. The four complexions, stated Bullein, were 'Not onely in man, but in beastes, fish, foule, serpents, trees, herbes, mettals and everie thing sensible and insensible'.[49] This was what allowed food to become part of the body.

Food thus intimately shaped a person, for, although each one was born with a specific humoral constitution, particular foods and the way they were digested produced chyle and blood which could be suitable for or analogous in quality (hot, cold, moist, dry) to it or hostile to it. If the latter was the case, a disordered constitution resulted, which was out of balance either because one or more humours predominated, or because a humour became abnormal and pathological through being burnt or putrefied.[50] The English regimens followed the Galenic tradition in emphasising the connection between food and the body. Cogan argued that, despite opinions to the contrary, food and drink did affect health, as those who had aching heads found after drinking strong drink or those who had a hot stomach or inflammation of the liver discovered after partaking of hot wines and spices. He concluded: 'What meaneth this, but that meats [foods] and drinkes do alter our bodies, and either temper them, or distemper them greatly? And no marvell, seeing that such as the food is, such is the bloud: and such as the bloud is, such is the flesh.'[51] Such coherences and interconnections were further developed. Not only the flesh but also the mind was affected by the type of food that was eaten. In classical and early modern medicine there was a close connection between the body and the mind, the humoral constitution (sanguine, melancholic, etc.) denoting a psychological as well as physical state. William Vaughan, a lawyer, poet, unsuccessful colonizer of Newfoundland and a lay writer on health matters, reported that:

Physitians hold, that men be diversly affected, according to the dyet which they use, as Venison, Conies and Hares-flesh, make men melancholicke,

---

the Renaissance anatomical history of the *rete mirabile* and the debate about whether it existed in man see Andrew Wear, 'Galen in the Renaissance' in V. Nutton (ed.) *Galen: Problems and Prospects* (The Wellcome Institute, London, 1981), pp. 229–62, esp. pp. 233–7.

[49] Bullein, *Government of Health*, fol. 12ᵛ.

[50] See Elyot, *Castel of Helthe* fol. 51ᵛ.

[51] Cogan, *Haven of Health*, Epistle Dedicatory, A3ᵛ–A4ʳ.

and consequently envious and froward: those meates which engender good blood, make men of a sanguine complexion and free-hearted. Excesse of meate make men riotous and drunkards . . . [for] such as the bloud is, such are the [animal] spirits (for they issue from the bloud it selfe) and such as the spirits are, such is the temper or distemper of the braine and heart.[52]

Conversely, digestion could be influenced by the mind, so amongst the list of 'meates [foods] and drinkes' which 'maketh good iuyce, and good bloudde' were 'Mirthe and gladnesse'.[53] The body and the mind were perceived to affect each other reciprocally, and 'the affections of the mind' took their place together with diet as part of the six non-naturals that had to be considered in the conservation of health.

On the whole, regimens did not prohibit particular types of food, though there were debates for and against vegetarianism.[54] The Bible provided guidance, as often happened when the issue at stake pertained to what was permitted or forbidden. It was acknowledged that before the time of Noah meat eating had been unknown, but that after the Flood the human digestive system favoured meat, and found fruits more difficult to cope with. In Genesis 1.29 God tells Adam: 'Behold, I have given you every herb bearing seed, which is upon the face of all the earth, and every tree, in the which is the fruit of a tree yielding seed; to you it shall be for meat.' At the time of the Flood God tells Noah (Genesis 9.2–3): 'And the fear of you and the dread of you shall be upon every beast of the earth and upon every fowl of the air, upon all that moveth upon the earth and upon all the fishes of the sea; into your hand are they delivered. Every moving thing that liveth shall be meat for you; even as the green herb have I given you all things.' Before the Flood, as the regimens told the story, the soil was more fertile, vegetables were more nutritious and people had greater knowledge of diet; afterwards, the human constitution became weaker and less able to digest vegetables and fruits, and in the process life spans shortened. The earlier Golden Age had meant a limited range of food and only water to drink.[55] With variety of foods and drinks came gluttony and drunkenness.[56] But Mouffet, despite being aware of cruelty to animals and of how 'mens hands'

[52] Vaughan, *Directions for Health*, 5th edn (London, 1617), p. 254.
[53] Elyot, *Castel of Helthe*, fols. 14ᵛ–15ʳ.
[54] See Keith Thomas, *Man and the Natural World. Changing Attitudes in England 1500–1800* (Penguin, Harmondsworth, 1984).
[55] Cogan, *Haven of Health*, p. 203.
[56] See also Vaughan, *Directions for Health*, pp. 215–16.

in the 'more healthful ages' before the Flood 'were neither polluted, with the blood of Beasts, nor smelt of the most unwholesome sent of fish', saw meat-eating as a gift of God without which diseases would have increased and lives would have become even shorter. He, therefore, argued against the refusal of 'Adamites' to eat meat.[57] Indeed, in the typically ebullient manner of English nationalism he celebrated England's wealth in meat: 'But now our complexions waxing weaker, and weaker through abundance of sin and riot, and our climate being unapt for wholesome and much nourishing fruits, let us give God thanks for storing us with flesh above all other Nations, making our Shambles [abbattoirs] the wonder of Europe, yea verily of the whole world.'[58] Thomas Tryon at the end of the seventeenth century tried to turn back the clock, arguing for vegetarianism, but most writers on health accepted the whole spectrum of available foods, although, as they were the products of this later more corrupt age, they posed potential health and moral dangers.

Poor digestion produced by too much food or by food unsuitable to an individual's constitution was understood to be the origin of many diseases and humoral disorders. 'The coruption of digestion is the mother of all diseases, and the beginner of all infirmities,' stated Bullein, and all writers on regimen took care to provide rules and advice on how to avoid bad digestion.[59] The advice was complicated because, as well as humoral constitution, the age, sex, strength, health or sickness of the patient, and time of year might be taken into account. As in therapeutics, the consideration of the different circumstances of the patient was a mark of the learned physician, distinguishing him from other practitioners (in reality, the different factors were haphazardly brought into play and the full 'method' rarely employed).

The most important consideration was the constitution (or the humoral complexion, temperament, temperature or temper) of a food and of the person eating it. The two had to be appropriate to each other, and for this to happen, argued John Archer in the later seventeenth century, people had to look at themselves and their food through medical spectacles, to live, in a sense, 'physically' or medically, and earlier writers held the same view:

---

[57] Mouffet, *Healths Improvement*, pp. 194, 31.   [58] Ibid., p. 50.
[59] Bullein, *Government of Health*, fol. 29^r, citing Avicenna 13. fen. 3 tract. 3 cap. 1.

And because I know that People of all Qualities do commonly Feed upon what comes to Table, be it what it will, without considering the Nature or Qualities of any thing, or agreement or disagreement to their Constitutions, so it do but please the Pallat; by which means divers [several] have and do dig their Graves with their Teeth, to prevent which I think very necessary that every one should understand the Nature and Property of his daily Food, as well as his own Constitution, and so by doing himself right, he is truly become his own Doctor.[60]

In theory the different temperaments of foods, and of people, together with factors such as age, season of the year, etc., meant that a very large number of possibilities had to be considered when judging the best diet for someone. This led Luigi Cornaro (*c.* 1463–*c.* 1566), a Venetian landowner famous for his longevity, whose *Trattato de Vita Sobria* (1st edn, 1558) or *Treatise of Temperance and Sobriety* (1634) was immensely influential across Europe, to conclude that the individual was his own best physician. He argued that, by long experience, the individual knew the qualities of his own constitution and what food and drink agreed with it, and that this could not easily be known by others, 'since there is greater diversitie of tempers [temperaments], then of faces'.[61] Despite this recognition of difference, Cornaro and his follower, Lessius, wanted to cut through the myriad rules and different regimens for different people and instead have one very precisely measured and spare diet for everyone (twelve ounces of solid food, fourteen ounces of wine daily) which was tied in with a call for temperate living. The condemnation of gluttony appealed to religious readers such as Ralph Josselin, but he disliked the diet's uniformity:

I read over Lessius and the treatises with it [Cornaro's], and though I am not satisfied concerning a constant measure of provision, yett I concurre with him, that a full diet is not best, plus necat gula quam gladius [gluttony kills more than the sword], a slender and hard diett and exercise is very much conducing to our health, and to mine in particular, and therefore my thoughts are to bee more moderate in my diett, then formerly.[62]

---

[60] John Archer, *Every Man his own Doctor* (1st edn, 1671; 2nd edn, London, 1673), p. 18.

[61] L. Cornaro, 'A Treatise of Temperance and Sobrietie', trans. George Herbert, in Lessius, *Hygiasticon*, p. 24; see also Francis Bacon, 'Of Regiments of Health' in *Essays Civil and Moral* (George Newnes, London, 1902), p. 83, who wrote: 'There is a wisdom in this beyond the rules of physic: a man's own observation, what he finds good of, and what he finds hurt of, is the best physic to preserve health'; also Boorde, *Dyetary of Helth*, p. 300: 'There is no man nor woman the which have any respect to them selfe, that can be a better Phecycion for theyr owne savegarde, than theyr owne selfe can be, to consider what thynges the whiche doth them good, And to refrayne from such thynges that doth them hurter or harme.'

[62] R. Josselin, *The Diary of Ralph Josselin 1616–1683*, ed. Alan Macfarlane (Oxford University Press, for the British Academy, Oxford, 1976; paperback, 1991), p. 154 (Jan. 1649).

The appearance of tailoring advice to the individual was a selling point of the regimens. They gave the impression of being all-encompassing and at the same time focused on the individual. Everyone in the target readership of the regimens was included in their scope by the humoral/qualitative theory. Reading a regimen, a person would find his or her own constitution and feel that what they read was directly relevant to themselves. The four-fold division of humours and qualities was convenient for writers in that it allowed their readership to be divided into four groups, and it was convenient for readers as it made it easy to decide what their temperament was, and to look for it in the regimens. Although degrees of heat, moistness, etc., and fine distinctions within humoral constitutions were sometimes made, they were often bypassed.[63] A sense of precision and individualised attention was also conveyed by the references to age, sex, the seasons, and the strength and health of the reader.

Often, however, especially in the discussion of particular foods, simple, uncomplicated recommendations sufficed, with little theoretical justification. For instance, Boorde's advice about apples appears almost as aphoristic, declaratory knowledge, perhaps a piece of folk wisdom:

Apples be good, after a frost have taken them, or when they be olde, especyally red apples and they the whiche be of good odor and melow; they shuld be eaten with sugar or comfettes or with fenell-sede, or anys-sede, bycause of theyr ventosyte [windiness]; they doth comforte than [then] the

---

[63] Elyot set out the basic principles for matching the qualities or temperaments of foods and people with each other. They expressed the need to take into account the individual, as was usual with learned medicine, and they illustrated the fact that, although blanket prohibitions applicable to everyone were made, often one man's poison was another man's meat: 'To kepe the body in good temper, to theym whose naturall complexion is moyst, ought to be gyven meates [foods], that be moyste in vertue or power. Contrarywise to theym, whose naturalle complexion is drye, ought to be gyven meates drye in vertue or power. [To] the bodyes untemperate, suche meates or drynkes are to be gyven which be in power contrary to the distemperance, but the degrees [of hot, moist, etc., ranging from one to four] are always to be considered [often they were not], as welle of the temperaunce of the bodye, as of the meates. For where the meates doo moche excede in degree the temperature of the bodye, they annoye the body in causyng distemperaunce. As hot wynes, pepper, garlycke, onyons and salte, be noyfull [injurious] to theym, whyche be choleryke, bycause they be in the highest degree of heate and drythe [dryness], above the iuste temperaunce of mannes body in that complexion. And yet be they oftentymes holsome to them whiche be fleumatike': Elyot, *Castel of Helthe*, fol. 17ᵛ. John Donne, *Devotions upon Emergent Occasions*, ed. John Raspa (Oxford University Press, Oxford, 1987), p. 119, wrote: 'and yet a man may have such a knowledge of his own constitution, and bodily inclination to diseases, as that he may prevent his danger in a great part'.

stomacke, and doth make good dygestyon, specyally yf they be rostyd or baken.

The latter was what Pepys was advised by his surgeon, Thomas Hollier or Holyard, to eat at night for his colic.[64] Whether theoretical reasons were given or not, anyone who wondered whether to eat apples or other types of food was given clear advice that they could act upon, which was related to everyday activities such as baking.

The language of the regimens made the processes of digestion accessible to their readers by the use of lively, down to earth and familiar images. Events taking place within the stomach were graphically evoked by a mix of metaphorical and realistic language typical of medical accounts of the happenings inside the body. The stomach was pictured at times as a cooking pot, again bringing medicine and cookery together. For instance, butter which was

unctious, That is to say, butteryshe,-oyle, gresse or fat, doth swymme above in the brynkes of the stomacke as the fatnes doth swymme about in a boylynge potte, the excesse of such nawtacyon or superfyce wyll ascende to the oryse [orifice] of the stomacke and doth make eructuasyous wherfore, eatynge of moche butter at one refection [meal] is not commendable.[65]

Boorde moved easily between the metaphor of the cooking pot and the anatomy of the stomach, his language heightened also by the vividness of his description of butter. The language was largely popular and non-specialised, and the explicit connection between medicine and cooking was a sign of this. However, a greater sense of medical expertise and authority was apparent when food was related to diseases. So butter 'is not good for theym the which be in any ague or fever for the unctuosyte of it dothe . . . augment the heate of the lyver'.[66] The words themselves were not specialised as such, but taken together they have the ring of expertise. The regimen writers, however concerned they may have been to make their advice popular and acceptable, saw themselves as more knowledgeable than their readers, and they let their opinion show.

Although one can analyse how the health advice in the regimens was tailored and made accessible to individuals, it is important not

---

[64] Boorde, *Dyetary of Helth*, p. 284. Lying behind such advice was, as Cogan put it, 'a generall rule in Galen, for meates [foods] that be windy, "whatsoever windinesse there is in meates, it is corrected by things that heate and extenuate"': *Haven of Health*, p. 30 in the section on peas. Samuel Pepys, *The Diary of Samuel Pepys*, ed. Robert Latham and William Matthews (11 vols., Bell & Hyman, London, 1970–83), vol. IV, p. 385.

[65] Boorde, *Dyetary of Helth*, p. 265.   [66] Ibid., pp. 265–6.

to lose sight of a simple fact: the primary aim of regimens was to provide information and advice on a long list of different types of food. Like herbals, they listed individual items and gave their properties, and like encyclopaedias they included in their descriptions information from ancient and recent authorities, from the author's experience and from knowledge common to society at large. The lists of vegetables, fruits, herbs, fish, fowl and meats were lengthy, and their very number must have given that sense of being useful and all inclusive that was one of the aims of the regimens.

The highly detailed advice was part of what might be called the culture of medical detail, by means of which the minutiae of a patient's life are medicalised. If the regimens are viewed as attempts to bring patients' everyday lives and the environments in which they live under medical scrutiny and control, then the emphasis on detail becomes understandable, especially as it might also reflect the obsessional need of some readers for very precise and detailed medical counsel. A healthy life was achieved by avoiding unhealthy possibilities. For instance, in the sections on sleep the different positions of the body whilst asleep were assessed and graded as to their healthiness, with all authors agreeing that lying flat on one's back was absolutely forbidden. The regimens were full of references to the pathological potential of particular foods or environments. Cream, for example, 'used as a delicate dish in the Summer season, either with sugar or with strawberries', could also be dangerous, 'By reason of the fatnesse thereof, beside that it looseth the stomacke, and swimmeth above all the other meate [food] . . . and maketh grosse bloud', which is why going 'from Oxford to Botley, or from London to Islington to eate Creame, [is to] make but a sleevelesse [futile] errand'.[67]

Medicine, intemperance and morality

Advice about diet was not simply descriptive, but was also full of admonitions and warnings about what people should and should not do. In other words, it was easy for moralising to be joined with medicine, for, as the writers on regimen acknowledged, people often preferred to enjoy themselves rather than to look after their health, especially when they believed that regimen or diet was of no effect.

---

[67] Cogan, *Haven of Health*, p. 155.

Mouffet complained: 'So now in our daies the name of Diet seems but a scarecrow to the unwiser sort, who think it best diet, to keep no diet at all, saying (as Will. Somers said to Sir John Rainsford) drink Wine and have the gout, drink no Wine and have it too.'[68] Mouffet immediately equated such pleasure-seeking and disbelief in medical advice with the moral vices of disorder, gluttony and drunkenness: 'Which in effect what is it else, then with the *Sicilians* to erect a Temple to riot: or with the *Barbarians* to praise surfeiting [eating and drinking too much]? or with *Ulisses* drunken companions to open Aeolus his bottle all at once?'[69] The disregard of health advice led to vice, whilst the acknowledged existence of gluttony and drunkenness gave implicit support to the medical case for moderation, temperance and restraint.

The argument that appetites should be restrained was made in a variety of ways. Greek philosophical and medical tradition praised moderation and the golden mean, which was the basis for a healthy humoral temperament. All excess was dangerous, especially of food and drink: it was itself a physical disease. Elyot wrote of 'he that is sicke of abundance' and advised 'eate withoute gourmandyse, or leave [the table] with somme appetite'.[70] Bullein, likewise, wrote of repletion (an overfull stomach): 'And of this I give you warning, for it hath slaine as manie by aboundance as hunger hath killed through scarcitie.'[71] The major cause and the standard cure of disease, putrefaction and evacuation respectively, were strongly in evidence, for not only did excess unbalance and corrupt the humours, it also produced undigested crudities and plethoras which led to disease, unless expelled by purging, bleeding or perspiring following exercise. Lessius wrote that nearly all diseases came from repletion, as 'crudities are the Nurserie of all diseases wherewith men are ordinarily vexed and that almost all might be cured by evacuation'.[72] However, preventive medicine's message of doom was also in evidence: those who ate excessively stored up trouble for themselves in the future, for not all diseases were so cured, and the excesses of

---

[68] Mouffet, *Healths Improvement*, pp. 4–5.
[69] Ibid., p. 5; see also Bullein, *Government of Health*, fol. 1[r–v]; Cogan, *Haven of Health*, A3[v]–A4[r], Epistle Dedicatory; Brooke, *ΥΓΙΕΙΝΗ*, pp. 3–8.
[70] Elyot, *Castel of Helthe*, fols. 76[r], 16[r].
[71] Bullein, *Government of Health*, fol. 29[v].
[72] Lessius, *Hygiasticon*, pp. 101–4.

youth might manifest themselves in diseases that came in old age or an early death.[73]

There was also a strong religious condemnation of excessive eating and drinking. The health advice books have some features in common with the books on practical divinity which sought to order all aspects of people's lives according to religion. Clergymen used metaphors from regimens to make religious points.[74] Temperance, especially, denoted the overlap between medicine and religion and morality. Like salvation (see chapter 1), it had religious and medical meanings – sobriety and restraint and the right humoral balance (achieved by restraint) – and represents another example of a bridge between religion and medicine. Boorde, who was both a cleric and a physician, included a mainly moral definition of temperance and intemperance in his medical work *The Breviary of Helthe* (1547). Temperance, he wrote, 'is a moral vertue' which 'doth set all vertues in a dewe order', whilst intemperance 'doth set everything out of order, and where there is no order there is horror'. Just as in the health advice books, self-knowledge of one's body and appetites was seen as necessary for a temperate and healthy body, so in the wider attempt to subdue 'al the kindes of sensualitie' there had to be 'the recognition and knowlege of a mannes selfe what he is, of him selfe, and what god is'. However, perhaps Boorde's attempts to subdue his own sensuality did not make him the best advocate for morality, as towards the end of his life he was reported to the magistrates as having kept 'three harlots . . . in his chamber at Winchester'.[75] Lessius, a Jesuit, wrote of 'Holy Sobrietie', conflating its moral and medical connotations,[76] and the collection of

---

[73] Bullein, *Government of Health*, fols. 2^v, 12^r. Donne captured the patient's point of view when he wrote of physicians who recommended 'rules for my dyet' after he got ill: 'It were rather a vexation, then a reliefe, to tell a condemnd prisoner, you might have liv'd if you had done this': *Devotions*, p. 47.

[74] See John Morgan, *Godly Learning: Puritan Attitudes towards Reason, Learning and Education, 1560–1640* (Cambridge University Press, Cambridge, 1986); the London preacher Thomas Taylor, in *The Progresse of Saints to Full Holinesse* (London, 1631), pp. 20–1, wrote: 'The health of the body is preserved by exercise, so is the health of the soule by the exercise of grace . . . so suffer wee our graces to decay. . . the case being with the soule as with the body, which is in continuall decay, and needs daily repast, or else it dies. If a man forbeare his ordinary meales, the naturall heate will decay, and vigour, and health and life, and all: so will the Christian if hee neglect the word, the Sacraments, meditation, prayer, watchfulnesse, and the like.'

[75] Andrew Boorde, *The Breviary of Helthe* (London, 1547), fol. 86^r. Sir Leslie Stephen and Sir Sidney Lee (eds.), *Dictionary of National Biography* (Oxford University Press, Oxford, repr. 1959–60).

[76] Lessius, *Hygiasticon*, A2^r–A3^r. On Christianity, temperance and Cornaro see Wear, 'History of Personal Hygiene', pp. 1292–4.

sayings on temperance in *The Countrey-mans New Commonwealth* (1646), which was aimed at a popular readership, indicates how these meanings intermingled:

Temperance calleth a man backe from grosse effects and carnall appetites, letting him not exceed in foolish rejoycing nor ungodly sorrow. Solon.

A young man untemperate and full of carnall affections, quickly turneth the body into age and feeblenesse. Anaxagoras.

Men must eat to live and not live to eate.

Temperance is rich in most losses, confident in all perills, prudent in all faults and happy in it selfe.[77]

More specifically, Cornaro's *Treatise of Temperance and Sobriety* emphasised how the sin of intemperance, of gluttony, led to ill health and to premature old age. The autobiographical content of the *Treatise*, with its story of a conversion at the age of forty, when Cornaro was at death's door, appealed to both Catholics and Protestants. Its use of the language of vice and virtue to unite religion with diet and health brought to the attention of continental European and English readers the linking of temperance with religion and medicine.

The association of morality with the medical condemnation of gluttony is unmistakable. In the *Government of Health*, 'John', the layman, asked whether it was not right that a man should 'make merrie, seeing we have but a time to live' and he complained that 'Abstinence and fasting, is a mightie enemie and nothing pleasant to mee, and bee used of very fewe that love themselves, but onely of beggars, and covetous sparers, which doe spare much, and spend little.' The reply of Humfrey, the physician, was uncompromising: 'you make your bellie your god, and boast of it. You see that all lustie revellers, and continual banket [banquet] makers, come to great estimation . . . but you have an infinite number of your conversation [there are an infinite number of people who hold the same ideas as you do] in these dayes, the more pitie.'[78]

A particular case of gluttony and drunkenness was that of English feasting, which was generally recognised as excessive.[79] The regimens were typical medical publications of their time in that they were both universal and localised in their scope, often illustrating, modifying or contrasting the classical tradition or continental

---

[77] Anon., *The Countrey-mans New Commonwealth* (London, 1646), p. 17.

[78] Bullein, *Government of Health*, fol. 1ʳ⁻ᵛ.

[79] William Harrison, *The Description of England*, ed. Georges Edelen (Dover Publications, New York, 1994), pp. 124–31, 140–1, is more ambivalent.

writings with English experience.[80] English banquets were seen as examples of gross over-eating and over-drinking. Elyot lamented:

> what abuse is here in this realme in the continual gourmandise, and dayly fedinge on sundry meats [foods] at one meale, the spirite of gluttony, triumphynge amonge us in his glorious chariotte . . . dryvynge us afore hym, as his prisoners, into his dungeon of surfet, where we are tourmented with catarres, fevers, goutes, pluresies, frettinge of the guttes; and many other sycknesses, and fynally cruelly put to dethe by them.

As befitted a statesman-like writer, Elyot wished that the laws against 'vayne and sumptuous expenses of the meane people' could also be applied to the nobility, as this would cut down 'superflous expenses in sundry dishes' and increase the health of their bodies as well as their wealth.[81] Boorde complained that 'England hath an evyll use in syttynge longe at dyner and supper', and that the English ate many foods of different operations or qualitative characteristics together at one meal, and left the most nutritious food to be eaten by servants.[82] Perhaps in the condemnation there was also an element of pride, for in such banquets lay evidence of England's prosperity.[83] In general, however, to the early modern medical writer, health and long life were associated with the simple life, especially that of the countryside, and a life that was naturally abstemious and religious.

Religion reinforced the medical message. Ecclesiasticus, especially, was cited in support of the condemnation of gluttony. The book of 'the wisdom of Iesus the son of Sirach' was especially popular with physicians as it enjoined that they should be praised (see chapter 1), and it also provided some telling verses against gluttony in chapter 37 that combined moral and medical admonitions. Gluttony, the Apocrypha confirmed, had serious medical consequences:

---

[80] Elyot wrote, on the times of meals, that he would not refer to authors who had no English experience, and also stated that he would not write of the ointments used in Greek and Roman times as they were never used here in England: *Castel of Helthe*, fols. 41^r, 47^v–48^r.

[81] Elyot, *Castel of Helthe*, fol. 43^{r-v}. He makes the point that 'bodily helth' was not the chief reason why the laws had been enacted.

[82] Boorde, *Dyetary of Helth*, p. 252.

[83] See Harrison, *Description of England*, pp. 125–6, 131 where the feasts of the nobility, of artificers and of husbandmen are celebrated (and at times nationalistically) and yet cautioned against. Of the artificers in cities and towns, he wrote: 'some of them do suffer their jaws to go oft before their claws, and divers of them by making good cheer, do hinder themselves and other men, yet the wiser sort can handle the matter well enough in these junketings and therefore their frugality deserveth commendation. To conclude, both the artificer and husbandman are sufficiently liberal and very friendly at their tables; and when they meet they are so merry without malice and plain without inward Italian or French craft or subtlety, that it would do a man good to be in company among them': p. 131.

28 Be not greedy in all delights, and be not too hastie upon all
     meates [foods]:
29 For excesse of meates bringeth sicknesse, and gluttonie
     commeth [develops] into cholericke diseases
30 By surfet have many perished: but he that dieteth himselfe,
     prolongeth his life[84]

Elyot, Boorde and Cogan referred to these verses to justify their
strictures against excess.[85]

Elyot also cited chapter 31 verses 16–31, which dealt with the
table manners that were conducive to temperance:

16 Eate modestly that which is set before thee, and devoure not,
     lest thou be hated.
17 Leave thou off for nurtures sake, and be not insatiable least
     thou offend
18 When thou sittest among many, reach not thine hand out first
     of all
19 Howe little is sufficient for a man well taught; and therby he
     belcheth not in his chamber (nor feeleth any paine)
20 A wholesome sleepe commeth of a temperate belly: he riseth
     up in the morning, and is well at ease in himselfe: but pain in
     watching [wakefulness] and cholericke diseases are with an
     unsatiable man?

Other verses praised wine, whilst warning against drunkenness.
Verse 21 in particular seemed to provide a way of avoiding the
consequences of excessive eating, one which has been familiar from
Roman times to the present:

21 If thou has bene forced to eate, arise, goe foorth, vomite, and
     then take thy rest: (so thou shalt bring no sicknesse unto thy
     body).

The Puritan editors of the Geneva Bible felt that they had to insert a
strongly worded marginal note that this was no excuse for excess and
intemperance: 'This counsel only concerning the health of the body,
is here alleaged, rather for a remedie to help digestion unto a weake
stomacke, then for an instruction to tolerate intemperancie: for
surfetting is forbidden us, Luk[e] 21.34.' However, despite the
regimen writers' blanket condemnation of gluttony and drunkenness,

---

[84] From the Geneva Bible (1st edn, 1560; 'London', 1599, but probably an imported edition
from the Netherlands of a few years later); the marginal note reads 'Of temperancie'.
[85] Elyot, *Castel of Helthe*, fol. 16ᵛ; Boorde, *Dyetary of Helth*; Cogan, *Haven of Health*, A2ᵛ, Epistle
Dedicatory.

they did suggest remedies for them. For instance, coleworts, quinces, the lungs of goats, almonds and saffron protected against drunkenness, whilst mint helped to allay the effects of repletion,[86] and Bullein did not hesitate to recommend the medical procedure of vomiting as a cure for eating too much.[87]

The consistent message of the regimen books from the first half of the sixteenth century to the later seventeenth century was that gluttony, drunkenness and all excess were medically and morally damaging. Thomas Cocke in his *Kitchin-Physick* (1676) used the same mix of morality and medicine as had earlier treatises to paint a lurid, almost Hogarthian, picture of the effects of a bad diet. Men who are 'addicted to variety, extravagancy and excess . . . become obnoxious to various and great troubles, and frequently commit Rapines, Cheats, violating Justice, Faith and Friendship, and many times precipitate themselves into grievous Diseases, losses and disparagements; which by Frugality, Temperance and Sobriety they might have avoided'.[88] In a more specifically medical sense, Cocke added: 'How many by high drinks and dyet, riot and luxurious compotations have dyed on their Close-stools, expired in privies, and took their leaves of this base world over a Chamber-pot, or at least, only out-liv'd the conflict, with Gout, Palsies, Catarrhs, Surfeits and many other ignominious Diseases.'[89]

HEALTH AND THE ENVIRONMENT

Medical and lay perceptions

The health advice books were concerned not only with the healthiness of food but also with that of the environment in general. There was widespread recognition in the literate culture of early modern England, and probably in oral culture, of a relationship between health and the environment. Such a recognition helped to create a shared lay and 'professional' medical culture. Both medical and non-medical writers believed that some places, airs and climates were healthier than others. The classical medical tradition included a

---

[86] Elyot, *Castel of Helthe*, fol. 28^r; Bullein, *Government of Health*, fols. 59^r, 64^v, 78^v, 82^r; Vaughan, *Directions for Health*, pp. 46–7.
[87] Bullein, *Government of Health*, fol. 29^r.
[88] Thomas Cocke, *Kitchin Physick: Or, Advice to the Poor* (London, 1676), pp. 76–7.
[89] Ibid., p. 78.

sense of medical topography, that is, the relationship between places
and health and illness. The Hippocratic treatise *Airs, Waters, Places*
set out the prevalent illnesses of different locations and, in addition,
described how the effects of geography and climate formed the
psychological as well as physical characteristics of different populations.[90] In the regimens, air was one of the six non-naturals, and was
nearly always defined in terms of its geographical location, so that
airs and places were discussed together.

Non-medical writers also linked places with health, and an
understanding of medical topography was clearly part of lay literate
culture, especially amongst travellers. Travel, exploration and settlement involved assessing the nature of a new place more self-
consciously and explicitly than that of one's own town or village. In
the early modern period, the large number of "itineraries" and
descriptions of England, parts of Europe and lands further afield,
such as America, routinely mentioned the healthiness of the places
that they were describing, and provide evidence of lay beliefs about
the relationship between places and health. Travellers' impressions
of a place visited included health as one of its defining characteristics, almost as a matter of course. For instance, Francis Mortoft, in
the book of his travels to France and Italy in 1658–9, wrote of
Narbonne, 'The Aire of this Citty is not very health full in regard it
is seated very low and has many Ponds about it'; on the other hand,
he noted that Amboise on the Loire 'is a Citty very well seated in a
healthful ground, which was the cause that the kings of France in
former tymes nourished [brought up] their Children in this place'.[91]
Health also figured as one of the items in the reports of a country's
wealth and commodities. The explorations and settlements of the
New World led to judgements being made regarding whether
English people could live on the new continent. Optimistic and
positive reports of the healthiness of a colony, together with reports
of fertile soils, rich minerals and other valuable resources, were used
as part of the prospectus to entice investors and settlers. People who
were being transplanted needed to be reassured that they, like their

[90] G. E. R. Lloyd (ed.), *Hippocratic Writings* (Penguin, Harmondsworth, 1978), pp. 159–61,
168. See also the Hippocratic *Epidemics*. Clarence J. Glacken, *Traces on the Rhodian Shore.
Nature and Culture in Western Thought from Ancient Times to the End of the Eighteenth Century*
(University of California Press, Berkeley, 1967), traces the history of environmental thinking
in the West.

[91] Malcolm Letts (ed.), *Francis Mortoft: His Book. Being his travels through France and Italy,
1658–1659* (Hakluyt Society, 2nd Series, LVII London, 1925), pp. 23, 9.

plants, could survive in a new environment. Some reports gave the appearance of being constructed from simple experience. Thomas Hariot wrote that the plantation in 'Virginia' or Roanoke Island provided more fertile soil than that found in England, and he took care to write that English corn, barley, oats and peas grew well, and that strawberries, mulberries and crab-apples 'as we have in England' could be found there. He also noted the 'holsomnesse' of the place, for, despite a lack of food, clothes and often having to sleep on the open ground in winter, only four people among 108 died in that year [1587], and they had been sick before they had come to Virginia, so he concluded the air there was 'temperate and holsome'.[92]

As with food and bodies, and with medicines and diseases (on the latter, see chapter 2), there was a relationship between air ('the very food of life')[93] and place and the humoral constitution of a nation. The place where one was born and lived was the healthiest, for it shaped an individual's and a nation's humoral constitution, forming the natural link between people and their mother country. To break this link by living in foreign countries was to risk ill health. Such ideas were widely held. William Vaughan, who was a promoter of the Newfoundland colony, asked in his *Directions for Health*, 'What is the best Ayre?'. He replied, 'That which is a mans usuall soyle and Countries ayre is best. This by the Philosophers is approved in this principle: "Every mans naturall place preserveth him which is placed in it". And by the Poet confirmed: "Sweet is the smell of Countries soyle".'[94]

Foreign travel or settlement was therefore dangerous, unless the temperament of the place was the same as that of one's country of origin, or the body became 'seasoned' or acclimatised over time to it and developed a constitution that corresponded to the new environment and climate. Some writers presented the new colonies as being better than the mother country. Underlying all accounts, however, was the view that health and place were intimately connected. *The Planter's Plea* (1630), a tract which publicised the development of the

[92] Thomas Hariot, 'A Briefe and True Report of the New Found Land of Virginia' in Richard Hakluyt, *The Principall Navigations, Voiages and Discoveries of the English Nation* (London, 1589), pp. 754, 756, 763.

[93] Richard Whitbourne, 'A Discourse and Discovery of New-Found-Land' (London, 1622) in Gillian T. Cell (ed.) *Newfoundland Discovered* (Hakluyt Society, London, 1982), p. 165.

[94] Vaughan, *Directions for Health*, p. 4, cited by Karen Kupperman, 'Fear of Hot Climates in the Anglo-American Experience', *William and Mary Quarterly*, 41, 1984, 213–40.

New England settlement, praised the air of the colony as being better suited to English constitutions and even more health-giving than that of England:

> No country yeelds a more propitious ayre for our temper [the humoral constitution of the English], then New-England, as experience hath made manifest, by all relations: manie of our people that have found themselves alway weeke and sickly at home, have become strong and healthy there: perhaps by the drynesse of the ayre and constant temper of it, which seldome varies suddenly from cold to heate as it doth with us: So that Rhewmes are very rare among our English there'.[95]

Such arguments clearly drew upon Galenic medical theories that were in the public domain. Also commonplace was the type of reasoning found in the Hippocratic treatise *Airs, Waters, Places* that related the character of a people to the type of country they lived in, and also stated that some places were more or less healthy than others and led to people suffering from particular diseases. Whether medical or lay culture created such knowledge is a moot question and has a touch of the chicken or the egg about it. Climate was the major factor that determined the character of a nation. At a time of intense nationalism, when national identity was being defined in terms of the new geography of the world, English writers such as William Harrison in *The Description of England* (1577) and the historian and topographer William Camden in his *Britannia* (Latin first edition, 1586) agreed that their country was situated in the most temperate climate in the world, being neither too hot nor too cold.[96] As Camden put it, 'Britaine is seated as well for aire as soile, in a right fruitful and most milde place.'[97] Britain, and especially England, was the measure against which all other places and nations were judged and found wanting. Harrison praised its human products: 'Such as are bred in this island are men for the most part of a good

---

[95] John White, *The Planter's Plea* (1630) in Peter Force (ed.) *Tracts and Other Papers Relating Principally to the Origin, Settlement and Progress of the Colonies of North America* (4 vols., New York, 1836–47; reprinted New York, 1947), vol. II, tract 3, p. 13. In contrast, Thomas Dudley, the deputy governor of the New England colony, wrote home concerning the prevalence of sickness and starvation in the colony: 'And I do the more willingly use this open and plain dealing, lest, other men should fall short of their expectations when they come hither, as we to our great prejudice did, by means of letters sent us from hence into England, wherein honest men out of a desire to draw over others to them wrote somewhat hyperbolically of many things here.' Everett Emerson (ed.), *Letters from New England. The Massachusetts Bay Colony, 1629–1638* (University of Massachusetts Press, Amherst, 1976), p. 75.

[96] Harrison, *Description of England*, pp. 428–9; William Camden, *Britannia, or a Chorographicall description of . . . England, Scotland and Ireland*, trans. Philemon Holland (London, 1637), p. 2.

[97] Camden, *Britannia*, p. 2.

complexion [bodily constitution], tall of stature, strong in body, white of color and thereto of great boldness and courage in the wars.'[98] This was because the 'Britons' are a 'people inhabiting near the North and far from the equinoctial line, where the soil is not so fruitful and the people not so feeble'; in other words, they have to work harder, and the tougher colder environment also produced a tougher people. There was an absolute standard: the feebler lived closer to the equator, the stronger nearer the pole. Harrison continued, and made it clear which nation did best out of geographical determinism:

whereas contrariwise such as dwell toward the course of the sun are less of stature, weaker of body, more nice, delicate, fearful by nature, blacker in color, and some so black indeed as any crow or raven . . . Howbeit, as those which are bred in sundry places of the main do come behind us in constitution of body, so I grant that in pregnancy of wit, nimbleness of limbs, and politic inventions they generally exceed us.

But as a good Englishman and Protestant he added, with an eye on the 'craftiness' of the French and Italians, 'these gifts of theirs do often degenerate into mere subtlety, instability, unfaithfulness and cruelty', and he was able to conclude that the characteristic of northern phlegmatic nations that was courtesy coupled with the 'strength of body and sincerity of behavior' outweighed the 'craft and subleties' of the hotter countries.[99] The relationship between places and a nation's constitution produced an ethnocentrism that went beyond the health and character of individuals to the health and character of a nation. It also indicates the relational and holistic thinking that permeated the medical and lay vision of the world, in this case centred around the pivotal role of climate.

There was another aspect to the relationship between health and the environment, which was simply that some places were perceived as being unhealthy for everyone. Travellers, especially, blamed their illnesses on the places that they visited. In his report of his travels to Mexico, John Chilton described how in 1572 in the town of Panuco (in the Veracruz region of Mexico) he fell sick for forty-one days and was 'in a very weake state, by reason of the unholsomnes of the place'.[100] A place could be contagious and transmit disease. John

---

[98] Harrison, *Description of England*, pp. 444–5.   [99] Ibid., pp. 445–8.
[100] John Chilton, 'A Notable Discourse of Master Iohn Chilton, Touching the People, Manners, Mynes, Cities, Riches Forces and other Memorable Things of the West Indias' in Hakluyt, *Principall Navigations*, p. 592.

Hawkins wrote that Sierra Leone, which he visited with four ships in 1564–5, was responsible for 'the death, and sickenes of our men, which came by the contageousness of the place, which made us haste away'.[101] Nowadays, in developed countries places seem to have lost their links with health and disease. At home, state health regulation over food, water and the environment makes all places healthy (despite worries over pollution, etc.). Tourists going abroad will find sanitised enclaves of western hygiene provided for them, and if they venture beyond them there is available a battery of inoculations and prophylactic pills and injections that help to render their bodies immune to external threats. Associated with the technological and pharmacological umbrella provided for tourists and travellers have been changes in medical theory. It is no longer the case that places, climates and airs are in themselves unhealthy, but rather that in them are various micro-organisms such as bacteria and viruses which cause disease. But until the late nineteenth century, it was believed that places and their associated airs and climates were disease-making. The west coast of Africa was 'the white man's grave' for Victorian explorers, and even into the twentieth century the air of mountain resorts was seen as health-giving, especially for tuberculosis patients.

The association between places and health was clearly one that was widely present in early modern society. Some specific associations were long standing and part of popular belief, and not only the product of travellers' suspicions of new lands. The low-lying parts of Essex were notorious for ill health. Camden described the Thames in Essex as hastening 'through a ground lying very flat and low, and in most places otherwhiles overflowne (whereby are occassioned strong and unwholesome vapours exceeding hurtfull to the health of the neighbour Inhabitants) to Tilbury'.[102] John Aubrey reported what must have been a popular perception when he recounted how John Pell was given as a benefice 'the scurvy Parsonage of Lanedon cum Basseldon in the infamous and unhealthy (aguesh) Hundreds of Essex (they call it kill-priest sarcastically)'. Often, especially in malarial areas, the numbers of those dying shaped perceptions of an area's health and further confirmed

---

[101] John Hawkins, 'The voyage made by the worshipful M. Iohn Hawkins . . . to the Coast of Guinea, and the Indies of Nova Spania, being in Africa and America begunne in An. Dom. 1564' in Hakluyt, *Principall Navigations*, p. 528.

[102] William Camden, *Britannia* (London, 1610), p. 440.

them.[103] Pell was also given the parsonage at Fobbing, four miles away, and Aubrey described how there 'seven curates dyed within the first ten years; in sixteen yeares, six of those that had been his [Pell's] Curates at Laidon [=Lanedon] are dead; besides those that went away from both places; and the death of his Wife, servants and grandchildren'. Not unnaturally, Pell complained to the Archbishop of Canterbury, Gilbert Sheldon, after he had been made one of his chaplains at Cambridge, 'of the unhealthinesse of his Benefice . . . sayd my Lord, I doe not intend that you shall live there. No, sayd Pell, but your Grace does intend that I shall die there.'[104]

Healthy and ill environments

In medical theory air, like food, was essential to life. Its purity determined the body's health: 'For the aire so corrupted, being drawn into our bodies, must of neccessity corrupt our bodies also.'[105] As with food, air formed a link between the body and the outside world. Air could also nourish the body (especially its spirits in the arterial blood and the 'animal spirits' in the brain and nerves), make it ill or act as a medicine. Mouffet wrote that, although the heart of man 'cannot abide impure airs or live long in health with infected airs', yet 'pure aire is to the heart, as balm to the sinews, yea it is both meat [food], drink, exercise, and Physick to the whole body'.[106]

The sources of bad air were topological, biological and man-made. Within one country, it was agreed throughout the early modern period, there were a variety of healthy and unhealthy habitats. Even in England, some places were, as Bullein acknowledged, unhealthy for English people:

to thy self, being a naturall English man of birth and education: this land is very temperat. Howbeit, our dwellinges in this land, be variable as fennes, marishes, woods, heithes, valleis, and rockie places, and near the sea side . . . marish grounds and places where hempe and flax is rotten and dead

---

[103] On malarial mortality see Mary Dobson, ' "Marsh Fever": a Geography of Malaria in England', *Journal of Historical Geography*, 6, 1980, 359–89; Dobson, 'The Last Hiccup of the Old Demographic Regime: Population Stagnation and Decline in Late Seventeenth and Early Eighteenth-Century England', *Continuity and Change*, 4, 1989, 395–428. Also Dobson, *Contours of Death and Disease in Early Modern England* (Cambridge University Press, Cambridge, 1997).

[104] *Aubrey's Brief Lives*, ed. Oliver Lawson Dick (London, 1975), p. 231.

[105] Cogan, *Haven of Health*, p. 7.   [106] Mouffet, *Healths Improvement*, pp. 13, 15.

carrions be cast, or multitudes of people dwelling together, or houses environed with standing waters, whereinto iakes [jakes, privies] or sinks, have issues, or wallowing of swine, or carion unburied or foule houses, or such like places be dangerous, corrupteth the bloud . . .[107]

The filth of towns and cities made them unhealthy, the air there being 'infected with corrupt and filthy vapours, evaporating or breathing out of standing pooles, channels, or other impure places, which in most Townes and Cities, through the neglect of the Magistrate, is very frequent and too offensive'.[108] Their unhealthiness was further attested to by the fact that plague, believed to be the product of such 'filthy vapours', appeared to hit urban areas hardest so that people fled into the countryside for safety. The demographic facts of life and death, as discussed earlier, also indicated that the countryside was healthier than the city. However, even within the countryside there were healthy and unhealthy places.

There was a general consensus that high ground, where the air was clear because it was purified by being blown about by the winds, was healthiest. There the inhabitants could, as Tobias Venner, a Bath physician, put it, live 'to extreme old age' and 'enjoy very good and perfect health'. Marshy, low-lying or enclosed land with foggy, thick, damp and stagnant air was considered dangerous. Its air filled the body with 'excrementall humors', and was 'the very roote of all diseases of the braine and sinewes, as Crampes, Palsies etc. with paines in the ioynts; and to speake all in a word, a general torpidity of both minde and body'.[109] The relativity implicit in the humoral system of medicine (that some food/air etc. is suitable for some constitutions but not for others) was overshadowed in this case by the belief that high ground and low ground produced airs which were respectively healthy and unhealthy for everyone. The realisation that the death rate was high in marshy areas, where 'agues' (in our terms, fevers that would include malarial fever) were endemic, gave support to such a view. The belief that plague was caused by a poisonous air resulting from stagnant, stinking and putrifying air coming from marshes, enclosed valleys, dunghills, crowded rooms

---

[107] Bullein, *Government of Health*, fol. 30[r]. In 1576 William Lambarde had commented in his *Perambulation of Kent* that Romney Marsh was sparsely populated because 'most men be yet still of Porcius Cato his minde, who held them starke madde, that would dwell in an unwholsome Aire': William Lambarde, *A Perambulation of Kent* (London, 1576), p. 159.
[108] Venner, *Via Recta*, pp. 1–2.   [109] Ibid., pp. 8, 3.

and other natural and man-made sources also contributed to the suspicion of low-lying places.

By means of very simple analogical reasoning, human beings were shown to be similar physically and mentally to the places in which they lived. Given the close connection between the mind and the body and the susceptibility of both to external influences in classical and Renaissance medicine, it was natural that the whole person should be shaped by his or her environment. Just as England shaped English constitutions, so different places within it created different types of bodies and characters. The briskness or sluggishness of the air affected people's characters and constitutions. Thus those living on 'the tops of hills (where every wind blows from under the Sun) are for the most part sound, strong, nimble, long-lived and fit for labour', whilst 'the valley people (so seated that no wind blows upon them) are ever heavy spirited, dull and sickly'.[110] The holistic analogy between places and people meant that 'in low and marish places', the inhabitants, because of 'the evilnesse of the Ayre, have grosse and earthy spirits'. ('Holistic' is used without the connotations of 'alternative' medicine that it has today; holistic beliefs were often seen as orthodox until the mid-seventeenth century.) Perhaps Venner had some place in mind when he transposed the evilness of the air onto the people who breathed it in, when he added, 'they are for the most part men . . . dull, sluggish, sordid, sensuall, plainly irreligious, or perhaps some of them, which is a little worse, religious in shew, externall honest men, deceitfull, malicious, distainefull'.[111]

In some ways medical topography can be seen as a useless exercise. Even fewer would act upon medical beliefs about the unhealthiness of a place than would take advice to change their diet, although such beliefs did shape behaviour at a time of plague. What medical topography did was to knit people, places and climates together, to give people an idea of how they were related to the world in which they lived. It also represents an example of the intense interest in typology in early modern culture. Just as publications such as *Aristotle's Masterpiece* catered for the almost prurient interest in the physiological and psychological types (physiognomy) to be found amongst men and women, so medical topography

---

[110] Mouffet, *Healths Improvement*, p. 18.

[111] In a marginal note Venner qualified his invective by pointing out that 'some have their natures rectified by education': Venner, *Via Recta*, p. 9.

answered the need for a full typology of the health of places and people.

Health and illness were, therefore, also shaped by geographical location. The healthiness or otherwise of its inhabitants served to indicate the salubrity of a place. Venner looked for 'an acute wit, a sound and lively colour, a stable integritie of the head, quicke sight, perfect hearing, sound smelling, cleare voyce, and no difficultie of breathing, or unlustinesse of the limnes . . . by these signes the wholesomnesse of the Air is approved, and by the contrary the offensive and noisome breath thereof is detected'.[112] From his stance of environmental determinism, Venner advised in conclusion that 'all such as are ingenious, generous, and desirous of perfection, both in minde and body, that they endeavour by all means to live in a pure and healthy Ayre'.[113] It is, however, unclear how many had the means or the opportunity to do so.

Precision and practicality

The regimen writers produced a picture of a highly differentiated environment, of whose healthy and unhealthy qualities they had precise knowledge. They also provided detailed information on the diseases that could be encountered. The seasons, for instance, had their proper qualities (spring, warm and moist; summer, hot and dry; autumn, cool and dry; winter, cold and moist); unseasonable weather could bring on particular diseases. So if the winter was cold and dry, 'which naturally should be cold and moist, long agues, humoral aches, coughs and plurisies are to be expected, unless the next Spring be of a moist disposition'. Different situations also produced different diseases and ills. Thus 'Cities, Countries or houses situated . . . towards the North-west, North, and North-East, and defended from all Southern gusts and blasts', despite having people who were 'strong and dry, yet are they subject through suppression of excrements unto headaches, sharp plurisies, coughs, exulceration of the lungs, phlegmatick collections, rupture of inward veins, and red eyes'.[114] Once it was accepted that the environment and the body were related, conviction in one's ability to understand and manipulate the relationship came from detailed knowledge. The precise geographical references and the details of specific diseases

---

[112] Ibid., p. 4.   [113] Ibid., p. 9.   [114] Mouffet, *Healths Improvement*, p. 16.

were counterparts to the very precise and detailed instructions given by regimens on how to live, which gave them such an air of confident certainty.

The siting of a house was also discussed with confident precision, and raises the issue of who could actually act on such advice. Just as some Chinese today site their houses in the most beneficial way possible using a *feng shui* expert, so also was the positioning of a house in the early modern period crucial for those seeking to live in a healthy environment. Such information also came within the remit of the expert adviser, albeit one that spoke from the covers of a book.[115] Gervase Markham, in *The English Husbandman* (1635), which was addressed to a newly prosperous group in English society, advised: 'let not your house be too neere great Rivers or Brookes, they may smile in Summer, but they will be angrie in Winter, and it is better to have them wash your Grounds than wet your house. Besides they oft vomit forth ill ayres, and are in their owne natures Aguish and unwholesome.'[116] Burton pointed out that, because air was changeable and could alter from healthy to ill, detailed adjustments had to be made in the structures of a house as well as in a person's lifestyle: 'A clear air cheers up the spirits, exhilarates the mind; a thick, black, misty, tempestous, contracts, overthrows. Great heed is therefore to be taken at what times we walk, how we place our windows, lights and houses, how we let in or exclude this ambient air.'[117]

How many people could follow such advice? It seems that only the rich could build the ideal healthy house. The poor were not able to afford the large sites with extensive prospects or views, or with such perquisites as integral parkland, woods and water. For pleasure and for the health of his body, wrote Boorde, a man 'must dwell at elbowe-rome, havyng water and woode anexed to his place or house', and he added that there had to be a prospect or view.[118] Failure to provide the latter did not merely displease; it led to ill health because the mind and the body were related:

I had rather not to buyld a mansyon or a house, than to buylde one without a good respecte [prospect] in it, to it and from it. For and the eye be not

[115] Fiona Macdonald noted to me that in *feng shui* the air as in early-modern plague 'is also cleansed by bells and clapping and there is clearly an older common pool of folk practice'.
[116] Gervase Markham, *The English Husbandman* (London, 1635), p. 22.
[117] Burton, *Anatomy of Melancholy*, p. 435.
[118] Boorde, *Dyetary of Helth*, p. 233.

satysfyed, the mynde can not be contented. And the mynde can not be contented, the herte can not be pleased: yf the herte and mynde be not pleased, nature doth abhorre. And yf nature do abhorre, mortyfycacyon of the vytall, and anymall, and spyrytuall powers, do consequently folowe.[119]

Boorde added that a garden with sweet herbs, a fish pond and parkland for deer were necessary and pleasant to have around a house. Indeed, 'a great man' would also need a bowling alley. Clearly, such mansions and estates were beyond the reach of most people. But the readers of the regimen books from the 'middling' part of society may have been flattered to think that such instructions were addressed to them, that they were 'great men' in thought if not in deed. They could also be selective in the advice that they followed. After recommending that water and woods should be annexed to a house, William Vaughan gave practical instructions on how to tell if the air was good, where to build the foundations of the house and how to align its windows, advice which the prospective builder of a small house with some leeway as to its site could have found useful:

Next, you must marke, whether the Ayre which compasseth the situation of your house, be of a pure substance, and that shortly after the Sunne is up groweth warme; and contrarily groweth cold after the Sunne is set. Thirdly you must make your foundation upon a gravell ground mixt with clay, upon a hill, or a hils side. Fourthly, looke that your windowes be Northward or Eastward.[120]

Such practical advice formed the basis of the health advice books. The 'middling sort' would find it realistic, and the references to the gluttonous banquets of the rich and to their large houses served to give them a sense that they too were, or could be, part of the upper sections of society. The choices for the poor regarding where to live were limited, as they tended to inhabit crowded rooms and tenements. Significantly, when account was taken of the needs of the poor in relation to the environment, it took the form of advice on affordable remedies that would rectify or modify unhealthy air.[121] This emphasis on the 'medical fix', rather than on changing the living conditions that produced such air, again indicates that preventive medicine was not concerned with social reforms.

---

[119] Ibid., pp. 234–5.
[120] Vaughan, *Directions for Health*, p. 18.
[121] See, for instance, Mouffet, *Healths Improvement*, pp. 23–4, where he gives receipts for 'the poorer sort' to make perfumed 'cakes' which can be burned in a room to keep its air healthy.

It is not clear how far anyone acted on the medical advice concerning healthy and unhealthy places. When the mortality in Jamestown, Virginia, became too great, plans were made to move the settlement to high ground away from the marshy air that was blamed for the deaths. Such action at this time was rare. Romney Marsh, despite its reputation, was not deserted. Lambarde noted that it was 'famous throughout the Realme, as well for the fertilitie and quantitie of the soile', and that 'it offered Wealth without healthe'.[122] If a place was economically attractive, its reputation for ill health was ignored. This was certainly the case with London, the most populous place in England. The authorities were aware of the dangers of overcrowding. A royal proclamation of 1580 tried to limit new buildings in the city and to prevent more than one family living in a house (like others of its kind it was unsuccessful). It justified the policy on medical grounds:

Where there are such great multitudes of people brought to inhabit in small houses, whereof a great part are seen very poor, and they heaped up together, and in a sort smothered with many families of children and servants in one house or small tenement, it must needs follow (if any plague or popular sickness should by God's permission enter amongst those multitudes) that the same would . . . spread itself and invade the whole city and confines, as great mortality should ensue to the same.[123]

Despite the fear of plague, despite the acknowledged higher risk of disease and death, people still flocked to London from the healthy countryside and the city continued to grow. As today, knowledge about health risks did not easily change people's behaviour when faced with the economic opportunity or the social magnet of the city.

---

[122] Lambarde, *A Perambulation of Kent*, p. 158, also note 107. In William Strachy's account of the healthiness of Jamestown in 1610, the need to settle on a hill and the analogy with England illustrates the wide extent of knowledge about the environment: 'True it is, I may not excuse this our Fort, or James Towne, as yet seated in some what an unwholesome and sickly ayre, by reason it is in a marish ground, low, flat to the River, and hath no fresh water Springs serving the Towne, but what wee drew from a Well six or seven fathom deepe, fed by the brackish River owzing into it, from whence I verily beleeve, the chiefe causes have proceeded of many diseases and sicknesses which have happened to our people, who are indeede strangely afflicted with Fluxes and Agues; and every particular season (by the relation of the old inhabitants) hath his particular infirmity too, all which (if it had bin our fortunes, to have seated upon some hill, accommodated with fresh Springs and cleere ayre, as doe the Natives of the Country) we might have, I beleeve, well escaped': William Strachy, 'A true Reportorie of the Wreck and Redemption of Sir Thomas Gates, Knight; upon and from the ilands of the Bermudas: his comming to Virginia and the Estate of that colonie then . . . July 15. 1610', in Samuel Purchas, *Hakluytus Postumus or Purchas His Pilgrimes*, (20 vols., 1625; reprinted Glasgow, 1905), vol. XIX, pp. 58–9.

[123] Cited in Lawrence Manley, *London in the Age of Shakespeare* (London, 1986), pp. 184–5.

Correcting the air

Those who could not move to live in a healthier air had the alternative of 'rectifying', 'correcting' or purging the air. This is what was recommended for those who stayed behind in a plague time, and the general descriptions of correcting the air in the regimens are often indistinguishable from those in plague trea- tises.[124] Rectifying pestilential air was a common practice (see chapter 7), indicating that the recommendations in the health advice books reflected actual practice.

There was tremendous confidence that air could be made heal- thier. Mouffet wrote that, 'at home', the air could always be tempered (that is, made equable and/or appropriate to an indivi- dual's constitution) 'and purified from all infection'. Sweet-smelling herbs, wood and fires achieved this: 'Is it [the air] too cold and moist? amend it by fires of clear and dry wood; and strew the room and windows with herbs of a strong smell as mints, penniroyal cammomil, balm, nep [catmint], rue, rosemary and sage.'[125] Vaughan advised that, if flight from corrupt air was impossible, a man 'must artificially rectifie it, by perfuming his Chamber with Cypresse, Spruce or Firre with Iuniper, Rosemary, Bay tree, or with wood of Aloes'.[126] Bullein listed 'fevers, palsies, fransies, falling sicknesses, leprosies . . . mortal pestilence, horrible fevers, and sicknes, and of late, a generall fever that this land is often greatly plagued withall', which he believed were caused by 'certaine stars called infortunates' that acted as 'God's instruments to punish the earth'. Their influence upon the air could be countered by purifying it: 'one must make a fire in everie chimney within the house, and burne sweete perfumes to purge this foule air'.[127]

Air, like food and the other non-naturals, was essential but also alterable and so controllable. The regimens conveyed a confident sense that air could be made healthy – this was in keeping with the general approach of the regimens to all aspects of life. Burton reflected this medical self-assurance regarding the ability to make

---

124 Some of the regimens, such as those by Boorde, Bullein and Cogan, had specific regimens for plague.
125 Mouffet, *Healths Improvement*, p. 21.
126 Vaughan, *Directions for Health*, p. 14.
127 Bullein, *Government of Health*, fol. 30ᵛ.

the natural world healthy when he wrote that 'many excellent means are invented to correct nature by art', and he extolled:

artificial air, which howsoever is profitable and good, still to be made hot and moist, and to be seasoned with sweet perfumes, pleasant and lightsome as may be: to have Roses, Violets, and sweet smelling flowers ever in their windows, Posies in their hand . . . the smoke of Juniper to [for] melancholy persons, which is in great request with us at Oxford, to sweeten our chambers.[128]

The absolute necessity for pure clean air was not universally accepted. Humfrey Brooke presented the example of 'two sickly bodies who heretofore were hardly out Physick', but who, since they had lived in Lambeth Marsh, 'a place that no-one would choose for the pureness and Clarity of the Aire', had 'enjoyed a sound and uninterrupted Health'. Brooke believed that healthy bodies did not need to live in healthy places, but those whose healths were deranged had to choose 'such Aires as are opposite to their Distempers'.[129] The search for healthy airs and the fear of unhealthy ones, he wrote, led people to 'opinionate themselves into Sickness. Such Imaginations keep the mind in continuall doubts and perplexities, and make us sickly, out of a fear of being sick.'[130]

A moderate degree of scepticism about the use of sweet perfumes came from Mouffet, whose cultural norms modified his medical perceptions. He was scathing about the needless use of perfumes. He quoted Cicero, stating that women 'smell best which smell of nothing', and castigated the men of Plutarch's time who perfumed their clothes and bodies with 'sweet ointments made of most costly spices' as indulging in 'an idle, a needless, a womanly pleasure: nay verily an unnatural and more than bruitish'.[131] Nevertheless, Mouffet conceded that a perfumed air was appropriate for those who were ill, or who needed to expel 'a loathsome stinck' or 'to rouse up dull and sleepy senses'. And he added, despite his moral disapproval, that sweet smells could be medicines: 'I am of *Aristotles* opinion, that sweet smels were appointed to be in flowers, fruits, barks, roots, fields and meddowes, not onely for delight, but also for medicin.'[132] Mouffet's further discussion of the power of smells is significant because it indicates how, until the late seventeenth century, sensory impressions were believed to have a real existence

---

[128] Burton, *Anatomy of Melancholy*, p. 436.   [129] Brooke, *ΥΓΙΕΙΝΗ*, pp. 57–8.
[130] Ibid., pp. 66–7.   [131] Mouffet, *Healths Improvement*, p. 19.   [132] Ibid., p. 19.

and real effects. The world of sensations, whether of sight, touch, hearing or smell, was the world also upon which judgements had to be exercised, for instance when the purity of water or air was being assessed. It followed therefore that the body and the environment could be cured by the sensory medicines of sounds and smells:

the very noise of bells, guns, and Trumpets, breaketh the clouds, and cleanseth the aire [a common practice during plague]: yea Musick itself, cureth the brain of madness, and the heart of melancholy . . . Much more then may it [the air] be tempered, and altered to the good or hurt of our inward parts by smells and perfumes, whereby not onely a meer aire (as in Sounds) is carried to the inward parts, but also invisible seeds and substances qualified [carrying qualities] with variety of divers things. For who knoweth not that the smell of Opium bringeth on sleep, drowsiness, and sinking of the spirits?[133]

What is striking is how confident medical writers were that the means were available to master the ills that the environment could bring. This was partly because their writings were echoed, and in a sense reinforced, by popular practices and beliefs, such as correcting pestilential air with fires and sweet smells, or taking a change of air when convalescing.[134] Their confidence may also be attributed to the fact that the learned medical tradition could come near to consensus on the value of certain therapies, such as those based on smells and on music, the latter of which Marsilio Ficino had famously espoused in his *De Triplici Vita* (1489). But credibility was also conveyed by the sense of detailed practical knowledge and expertise created by the regimen writers.

UNDERSTANDING KNOWLEDGE ABOUT THE ENVIRONMENT[135]

Medical theories came and went in the early modern period – Galenic humoralism, alchemy, iatrochemistry, chemistry, iatrome-chanism. The changes are easy to discern. Tobias Venner rationalised in a traditional Galenic manner that marshy air was bad, 'for impure, grosse and intemperate ayre doth corrupt the spirits and humours'.[136]

---

[133] Ibid., pp. 22–3.   [134] Ibid., p. 27.

[135] The following sections are closely based on my 'Making Sense of Health and the Environment in Early Modern England' in A. Wear (ed.), *Medicine in Society: Historical Essays* (Cambridge University Press, Cambridge, 1992), pp. 119–47. The reader should also consult Mary Dobson, *Contours of Death and Disease in Early Modern England* (Cambridge University Press, Cambridge, 1997).

[136] Venner, *Via Recta*, p. 8.

A hundred years or so later Thomas Short urged parents living in towns or cities to place their children in the countryside, if they could, and justified his argument by using the mechanical and chemical language of his time which had replaced that of the humours. The town's or city's

[a]tmosphere is loaded, and has its Spring lessened by sulphurous, and other Steams, so as it cannot duly inflate and distend the Lungs, nor compress the sanguinous Vessels, cool the Blood, nor communicate fresh Fewel to it, for the City Air is full of perspired Matter, discharged from both dead and living animal bodies, and other noxious Matter; Matter as well from diseased as healthy Bodies, and many insensibly convey the Seeds of several Distempers with the unhealthy State of those Juices they exhaled from.[137]

There were, however, other ways of understanding the relationships between health and the environment apart from the learned theories of medicine, chemistry and natural philosophy. How did early modern society judge whether an environment (or food and drink) was bad? People used their senses: smell, for instance, was very important.[138] Not only could smell indicate that something was healthy or unhealthy, but, as we have seen, smells were employed in an active manner to maintain health and to keep out disease. John Evelyn in his *Fumifugium* (1661) outlined a grandiose scheme to counteract London's foul air, which he believed came from the burning of sea coal and from the stench of churchyards, charnel houses, chandlers and butchers.[139] A mass of sweet-smelling trees, bushes and plants would be planted to surround and vivify London.[140] Evelyn argued that London's air 'carries away multitudes by languishing and deep Consumptions, as the Bills of Mortality do weekly inform us', and that 'almost half of them who perish in London, dye of phthisical and pulmonic distempers; That the inhabitants are never free from Coughs and importunate

---

[137] Thomas Short, *New Observations on City, Town and Country Bills of Mortality*, repr. of 1750 edn, ed. Richard Wall (London, 1973), p. 63.

[138] For a slightly later period see Alain Corbin, *The Foul and the Fragrant: Odor and French Social Imagination* (Berg, Leamington Spa, 1986); also Georges Vigarello, *Concepts of Cleanliness* (Cambridge University Press, Cambridge, 1988), and Richard Palmer, 'In Bad Odour: Smell and its Significance in Medicine from Antiquity to the Seventeenth Century' in W. F. Bynum and Roy Porter (eds.), *Medicine and the Five Senses* (Cambridge University Press, Cambridge, 1993), pp. 61–8.

[139] John Evelyn, *Fumifugium or the Inconvenience of the Aer and Smoak of London Dissipated* (London, 1661), pp. 56, 21.

[140] Ibid., pp. 24–5.

Rheumatisms, spitting of Impostumated and corrupt matter, for remedy whereof, there is none so infallible, as that in time, the Patient change his Aer, and remove into the Country'.[141]

The Dedication to Charles II of the *Fumifugium* was perhaps hyperbolic and other worldly even for its own time, but this was still an age of strange new worlds (just as the Restoration promised to be a new world). Evelyn explained that he wrote:

to render not only Your Majesties Palace, but the whole City likewise of the sweetest and most delicious Habitations in the World; and this with little or no expense; but by improving those Plantations which Your Majesty so laudably affects in the moyst, depressed and Marshy grounds about the Town . . . upon every gentle emmission through the Aer, should so perfume the adjacent places with their breath, as if by a certain charm, or innocent Magick, they were transferred to that part of Arabia, which is therefore styl'd the Happy, because it is amongst the Gums and precious spices.[142]

This language of sweet sensation should not be dismissed merely as the effusions of a keen gardener (Evelyn was the gentleman-gardener of Sayes Court, to which he had retreated during the Interregnum, and was to write treatises on forest and fruit trees). The enterprise of bringing the country into the city (*rus in urbe*) is still with us in the shape of public parks and gardens and in the ethos of the suburban garden. Moreover, Evelyn rightly used as evidence of a longing for the countryside and its health the common practice of the ill and convalescent of travelling into the countryside for a change of air and to escape the diseases of the city.

Behind the idea of *rus in urbe* lay, I think, the Garden of Eden.[143] In a sense, paradise was the absolute measure against which all other environments were measured. The power of Christianity in this period made the Garden of Eden a potent symbol. Paradise represented perfection in a society that lacked today's instruments and scales, which give us our measure of objective degrees of purity and impurity (as for chemicals or bacteria in water). It was also the place where illness and death did not exist, and the smells of plants were most fragrant.

---

[141] Ibid., pp. 12–13. [142] Ibid., sig. A3^{r}.

[143] For a much wider cultural context to the perception of the environment, gardens, paradise and the treatment of animals see Keith Thomas, *Man and the Natural World. Changing Attitudes in England 1500–1800* (Penguin, Harmondsworth, 1984), which is the standard work on the subject. Also Raymond Williams, *The Country and the City* (Hogarth, London, 1985).

The ideal perfection of paradise was not attainable on earth by human art. As John Parkinson phrased it on the title page of his botanical work the *Paradisi in Sole Paradisus Terrestris* (1629), 'who wishes to compare art with nature and our parks with Eden, without wisdom measures the stride of the elephant by the stride of the mite and the flight of the eagle by that of the midge'. Nevertheless, the physician Thomas Short, whose demographic studies ranged across England, was still noting in the eighteenth century that the 'rural life' still bore 'some small image or Resemblance of the Primeval State'. Perfection did not now exist, but we could still glimpse in the countryside what it had been like. There were different opinions on whether the pale images of paradise to be found on earth were creations of nature or of man. Virgin America was often likened to paradise, and the noble savage, the Native American, enjoyed the good health appropriate to such a place.[144]

On the other hand, nature could be seen as hostile. The cartographer John Norden, in his *Surveiors Dialogue* (1610), discussed the different types of agricultural land in England. He felt that, if left to nature, even 'the fairest pastures, and greenest meadows, would become in short time, over-grown with bushes, woods, weeds and things unprofitable, as they were before they were rid and cleansed of the same by the industry of man, who was inioyened that use and travaile to manure the earth, which for his disobedience should bring forth these things'.[145]

In a sense, the Fall ensured that the environment, like man and woman, would always be tainted and unhealthy to some degree. After the Fall there could be no natural paradise, though it could be hoped and worked for. In the *Dialogue* the 'Surveyor' speaks of 'Tandeane' in Somerset as 'the paradise of England', which is a product of its natural fruitfulness but also of its people doing 'their best by art and industry' and the fact that 'they take extraordinarie paines in soyling, plowing and dressing their lands'.[146] The story of

---

[144] Short, *New Observations*, pp. 1–2. See H. C. Porter, *The Inconstant Savage, England and the North American Indian 1500–1660* (Duckworth, London, 1979); C. Glacken, *Traces on the Rhodian Shore* (University of California Press, Berkeley, 1976); Peter Hulme, *Colonial Encounters. Europe and the Native Caribbean 1492–1797* (Methuen, London, 1986). This perception held until epidemics, famine and the need to shape the land, and to take the Native Americans' lands, changed the perception of both land and Native Americans to hostile and unpleasant entities.

[145] John Norden, *The Surveiors Dialogue* (London, 1610), p. 184.

[146] Ibid., pp. 191–2.

the Fall gave a Biblical origin for curative medicine. The means to ameliorate the consequences of the Fall, disease and death, were given by God to man but they could not restore the original situation.

Environment, food and drink

Just as a healthy environment made healthy people, so too a healthy environment was thought to produce healthy plants and animals and pure water, and hence health-giving food and drink. Although the allusion to paradise was a benchmark for judging the health of the environment and its products, it was of little use in the practical daily business of deciding which products one should select to eat and drink. Instead, ideas of cleanliness and dirt, of the natural and unnatural, of light and darkness, of movement and sluggishness underlay many of the descriptions of healthy and unhealthy food and drink that are prominent in the health advice books. Effective official inspection of food and analysis of water were developed in the nineteenth and twentieth centuries. Consumers in the early modern period had to judge for themselves, with help from the regimen writers, for, as we have seen, medicine was closely connected to cooking.

Animals were judged to be healthy (and hence to be healthy food) in the same way as humans. As the husbandman working in the fields was thought to be healthier and longer lived than the city merchant or student, so animals and fish coming from the wild were equated with health and cleanliness. Eating fish could produce 'much grosse, slimie superflous flegme', which in turn could cause gout, bladder stone, leprosy, scurvy and other skin diseases. Therefore, the healthiest fish had to be selected to avoid such consequences. There was consensus as to what conditions produced the healthiest fish: 'Wherefore of sea-fish, that is best which swimmeth in a pure sea, and is tossed and hoysed with winds and surges: for by reason of continuall agitation, it becometh of a purer, and less slimie substance, and consequently of easier concoction [digestion], and of a purer iuyce.'[147] Similarly the best freshwater fish would be that 'which is bred in pure, stonie or gravelly rivers, running swiftly. For that which is taken in muddie waters in standing pooles, in fennes,

---

[147] Venner, *Via Recta*, p. 69; see also Cogan, *Haven of Health*, p. 161.

mores and ditches, by reason of the impuritie of the place, and water, is unwholesome . . .'[148]

Just as fish could be polluted, so could water. The best water was that which came from rain water or from fountains or springs, and flowed swiftly. William Vaughan indicated that good water was known 'By the clearnesse of it. That water is best which is light, transparent, agreeable to the sight, Christalline, and which runneth from an higher to a lower ground.' (He also added that 'some use to try [test] water by putting a clean Napkin in it and if any spots appear upon the same they suspect the goodnesse of the water'.)[149] Venner wrote that it was up to the inhabitants of towns to find and to select wholesome river water which 'runneth with a full streame upon gravell, Pebble-stones, Rockes, or pure earth: for that water, by reason of the purity of the place, motion, and radiant splendor of the Sun is thinner, sweeter and therefore more pure and wholesome'.[150]

There are some common factors underlying these types of explanation. As there was throughout the regimens, a holistic approach is evident in the relationship of the environment and its products. (Again, it is worth stressing that this did not have the modern association with alternative culture.) Not only did the environment affect living things and substances such as water, but the explanations used to make sense of the environment and plants and animals were often the same. As we have seen above, motion was a common key to the healthiness of fish and of water. Cogan expressed this in explicit terms: 'For the flowing water doth not lightly corrupt, but that which standeth still: Even so bodies exercised, are for the most part more healthfull, and such as bee idle more subject to sicknesse.'[151] This finds its counterpart in medical explanations about

---

[148] Venner, *Via Recta*, p. 70. Sir Thomas Elyot, *The Castel of Helth*, pp. 22^v–23^r had written: 'The best fish after the opinion of Galen, is that, whiche swymmeth in the pure sea and is tossed and lyfte up with wynds and sourges. The more calme that the water is, the warse is the fishe, they whiche are in muddy water, doo make much fleume and ordure, taken in fennes and dyckes by [be] warste.'

[149] Vaughan, *Directions for Health*, pp. 25–6. Burton, *Anatomy of Melancholy*, p. 397, described the sensory qualities of good water: 'Pure, thin, light water by all means use, of good smell and taste, like to the air in sight, such as is soon hot, soon cold . . .' Bad water was found in standing pools and marshy ground; river water could also be of poor quality, if, as Venner wrote, 'it be polluted by the mixture of other things, as it commeth to passe in Rivers, that run thorow marish places, or neere unto populous Townes and Cities: for then, by reason of all manner of filth running, or cast into them, they become very corrupt and unwholesome': Venner, *Via Recta*, p. 10.

[150] Venner, *Via Recta*, p. 11.

[151] Cogan, *Haven of Health*, p. 2. Lack of exercise was often thought to lead to disease. Sir

disease where stagnant humours within the body produce putrefaction.

More general and unifying types of explanation were also used. The earth itself could be seen anthropomorphically, as needing to be cared for in the same way as people. John Norden described the land in terms of hot, dry, cold and moist, the four qualities that made up both the world and the body,[152] and he advised the farmer to give the best care to his land: 'For land is like the body, if it bee not nourished with noutriture and comforted and adorned with the most expedient commodities, it will pine away, and become forlorne, as is the minde that hath, no rest nor recreation waxe the lumpish and heavy.'[153]

Farmers also treated the illnesses and hurts of their animals in ways that mirrored human medical practice. Henry Best, a farmer from Elmswell in Yorkshire, wrote about the health of sheep in his manuscript Farming Book (1641). One entry has:

It is usuall with sheepe, and especially with hogges and lambs, to fall blind by reason of an humour that falleth out of the head into the eyes, whereby groweth (as it weare) a scumme over the stine [the cornea] of the eye. Many Shepheards will undertake to cure this by bloodinge them in the wykes of the eyes with a penne-knife, but the only way is to take ground-Ivy-leaves and to chewe them in your mouth, and to take the leafe with your finger after yow have sucked the Juice from it. This Juice you are to spurte into the eye morninge and eveninge, or if you will, thrice a day.[154]

The use of the same types of theories and practices for animals as for people helped to produce a sense of interrelatedness, a sense that, for the link between humans and the environment, was

Richard Hawkins gave as one of the causes of scurvy 'the want of exercise also either in persons or elements, as in calmes. And were it not for the moving of the Sea by the force of windes, tydes and current, it would corrupt all the world.' He advised 'to keepe the company occupied in some bodily exercise of worke, of agilitie, of pastimes, of dancing, of use of Armes; these helpe much to banish this infirmitie': 'The Observations of Sir Richard Hawkins, knight, in this Voyage into the South Sea, An. Dom. 1593' in Purchas, *Hakluytus Postumus*, vol. XVII, pp. 76–7.

152 Norden, *Surveiors Dialogue*, p. 196.
153 Ibid., p. 76. That the analogy between the earth and the body was a believable one in early modern culture is also evident from Donne's extended comparison of the earth and its ills to those of the body: *Devotions*, p. 116, Meditation 22.
154 David Woodward (ed.), *The Farming and Memorandum Books of Henry Best of Elmswell, 1642* (British Academy Records of Social and Economic History, New Series VIII, London, 1982). In the sixteenth century William Turner argued that medicinal baths should be made in Bath for animals in addition to those for humans: William Turner, 'The Rare Treasor of the English Bathes' in Thomas Vicary, *The Englishmen's Treasure* (London, 1586), p. 108.

formally expressed in the quasi-philosophical belief that the micro-cosm (the body of man) was a miniature version of the macrocosm (the greater world of the universe), and that events in the latter affected the former.[155] Moreover the unity between the environment and living organisms such as plants, animals and humans was expressed in the food cycle. As we have seen, animals were what they ate, and we in turn were what we ate of them.

Given the view that there was a close union between all the parts of the organic and inorganic worlds, it is not surprising that specific beliefs such as the healthiness of motion were applied to a wide range of objects and creatures. At the level of these specific beliefs there was a perceived dichotomy between town and country, short life and long life, the unhealthy and the healthy, the stultifying and the fresh, the stagnant and the moving, dark and light, crowded and uncrowded, the tame and the wild ('unhealthy places in the country-side' could be substituted for town or city in the first pair of opposites). These were not merely opposing pairs of ideas, as towns, for instance, could be associated with one part of each pair: with tameness, bad stagnant air or water, and with darkness and smoke, overcrowding, bad health, etc. The more man tamed Nature, the more unhealthy were the results. That such contrasts really were current is clear from the example of the pig.

Swine's flesh was looked on with some suspicion, but it was believed to be healthy if the pig had been allowed to roam in the wild and to eat natural foodstuffs. Cogan wrote:

brawne, which is of a bore long fed in a stie can in no wise be wholesome meat, although it be young. For beside that it is hard of digestion (as common experience proveth) it must needs breed ill iuce in the body, considering the want of motion and grosse feeding thereof for which course we use commonly to drinke strong wine with brawne to help digestion.[156]

Thomas Fuller, in his *History of the Worthies of England* (1662), praised 'Hampshire Hoggs' as producing the best bacon because 'Here the swine feed in the Forrest on plenty of Acorns (mens meat in the Golden, Hog's food in this Iron Age); which going out lean, return

---

[155] A small illustration of this occurs in Henry Whitmore, *Febris Anomala Or, The New Disease that Now Rageth Throughout England* (London, 1659), at p. 126 where the author notes that the new disease 'begun to visibly abade and slacken; which if I mistake not was about the latter end of November, when the cold weather begun to break forth, which on a sudden growing sharp made in the microcosm, the body of man a change as well as in the macrocosm'.

[156] Cogan, *Haven of Health*, p. 133.

home fat, without either care or cost of their owners . . . they lodge at liberty (not pent up, as in other places to stacks of Pease), which some assign the reason of the fineness of their flesh.'[157] Thomas Mouffet agreed that the pig was especially nourishing 'if he feed abroad upon sweet grass, good mast and roots; for that which is penn'd up and fed at home with taps droppings, kitchin offal, soure grains and all manner of drosse cannot be wholsom'.[158] And Thomas Tryon, at the end of the century, held a similar view: 'That Bacon and Pork, which is fed with Corn and Acorns have their liberty to run, is much sweeter and wholsomer, easier of digestion and breeds better blood than that which is shut up in the Hogg-Sties, such Bacon for want of motion becomes more of a gross phlegmatic Nature.'[159]

The idea that fresh air, fresh food and freedom to move were good for pigs (and for men and women) remained the same despite changes in theoretical perspectives, and these ideas can also be found today amongst the 'green' or environmental movements as well as amongst many other groups. A characteristic of such 'natural' ideas is that they were generalised enough to be applicable to many different types of situation. Thomas Mouffet, for instance, united the view that lack of exercise produced unhealthy food with another basic concept (already referred to) that there is a close connection between the qualities (psychological as well as physical) of the bodies that we eat and our own, when he asked:

Whether this penning up of birds, and want of exercise, and depriving them of light, and cramming them so often with strange meat, makes not their flesh as unwholesome to us as well as fat? To which I answer that to cramb Capons, or any bird and to deprive them of all light, is ill for them and us too: for though their body be puffed up, yet their flesh is not natural and wholesom; witness their small discoloured and rotten livers; whereas Hens and Capons feeding themselves in an open and clean place with good corn have large, ruddy and firm livers . . .[do not feed them] in a coope or close roome, for then the aire and themselves will smell of their own dung, but in a cleane house spacious enough for their little exercise; not in a dark place, or stitching up their eyes, for that will cause them to be timerous, or ever sleepy; both which are enemies to their bodies, and consequently ours.[160]

[157] Thomas Fuller, *The History of the Worthies of England* (2 vols., London, 1811), vol. I, p. 400.
[158] Mouffet, *Healths Improvement*, p. 68.
[159] Thomas Tryon, *The Way to Health, Long Life and Happiness* (London, 1683), p. 67.
[160] Mouffet, *Healths Improvement*, pp. 43–4. Thomas, *Man and the Natural World*, p. 189 cites this in part when discussing the perceived cruelty of poultry farming.

CONCLUSION

Despite the great changes that have taken place in medical ideas, many views about the healthiness of the environment and its products have remained largely the same. In a sense, they express the aspirations of certain parts of society; condemnation of present-day developments and a yearning for a natural world whose attributes – cleanliness, light, space to roam, lack of crowds etc. – are still viewed today, unquestioningly, as good and positive character-istics. Perhaps an anthropologist would use such attributes, and the pairs of opposites listed earlier, as evidence from which to construct a picture of the type of society that created them. A historian of medicine, after caveats about our limited knowledge of the currency of such ideas in the population, can note that early modern England possessed a well-articulated body of knowledge about the health of the environment that was largely shaped by medical writers and was also in the public domain, at least the literate part. At a time when cities and towns were growing in size and in unhealthiness, a set of values was present in the health advice literature and elsewhere which acted as a counter weight, and to which some of the literate classes, at least, could refer even if they did not always act on them.[161] That physicians and lay writers constructed such a view of the world attests not only to a common medical culture, but also to their development of an overview of preventive medicine in which the world and everything in it was seen through medical spectacles as an organic whole. The fact that such a vision existed gave added weight to learned medicine's claims to expertise in other areas of medicine, such as therapeutics, which were related to preventive medicine.

Like food, drink and lifestyle, the environment remained subject to medical assessment through the eighteenth century, though not in the active and investigative sense of the nineteenth-century public health movement. When faith in the humoral system declined after the mid-seventeenth century, writers such as Nathaniel Henshaw and George Cheyne, who supported the new chemical and mechanical

---

[161] Though, as Philip Curtin has shown in his study of mortality in the tropics, the mortality of European armies declined when some of these ideas, such as siting camps on hill stations, good ventilation and clear water, were put into practice in the nineteenth century. Philip Curtin, *Death by Migration. Europe's Encounter with the Tropical World in the Nineteenth Century* (Cambridge University Press, Cambridge, 1989).

natural philosophies, repeated many of the beliefs in the regimens. Even George Thomson, one of the most committed of English Helmontians, whose work is discussed in chapters 8 and 9, could not free himself from using the traditional structure of the six non-naturals, despite their Galenic associations, though Helmontians on the whole viewed health advice with some suspicion (see chapter 9).[162] It is commonly thought that medicalisation is a recent phenomenon, but the partial medicalisation of the world had already taken place in the early modern period. This should not be all that surprising given the enduring belief that from the world and a person's relationship to it come health and illness.

---

[162] Nathaniel Henshaw, *Aero-chalinos: Or, A Register for the Air* (London, 1664); George Cheyne, *An Essay of Health and Long Life* (London, 1724). George Thomson, Ορθο-μέθοδος ιατρο-Χυμικὴ *[Orthomethodos Iatro-chimike]: Or the Direct Method of Curing Chymically* (London, 1675), pp. 22–50; see, for instance, his praise of clear air and his warning as to the dangers to health of misty foggy air 'stuffed full of foul corpuscles': p. 41.

CHAPTER 5

Surgery: the hand work of medicine

INTRODUCTION AND SUMMARY

Much early modern surgery dealt with cutting out disease by excision or amputation or with mechanical repairs such as setting bones or putting dislocations back in place. It possessed methods such as dressing, bandaging and stitching which helped to heal the effects of accidents, war and surgery.[1] Surgeons were in constant demand. The damage caused by disease, by a variety of accidents at home or at work, as in farms or the fulling and tanning mills, and by falls from horses, the standard mode of transport, all provided a steady stream of clients. Surgeons also treated burns, which were especially frequent amongst young children and the elderly, who often fell into unguarded fires in their homes. Since Hippocratic times, war had been thought to provide excellent training for surgeons, and they did not hesitate to boast of their battlefield experience.[2] Knife wounds and contusions from blunt instruments were repaired by surgeons, as was the new type of wound from gunshot, which resulted from the fact that 'Man in every age doth devise new instruments of death . . . we have in our age, *Gun-shot*, the imitation of God his thunder; but the example is more fierce, and sendeth more souls to the devil, than the pattern.'[3]

The body's outer covering also lay within the province of the surgeon, who applied topical medicines, cauteries of burning iron or corrosives, or the knife to the growths and blemishes that appeared

---

[1] On accidents see Craig Spence, ' "Accidentally Killed by a Cart": Workplace, Hazard, and Risk in Late Seventeenth Century London', *Revue Européene d'Histoire*, 3, 1996, 9–26.

[2] Thomas Gale, 'An Institution of a Chirurgian' in *Certaine Workes of Chirurgerie* (London, 1563), fol. 9[r–v].

[3] Alexander Read, 'A Treatise of the First Part of Chirurgery' in *The Workes of that Famous Physitian Dr. Alexander Read*, 2nd edn (London, 1650), p. 20.

on the skin, such as ulcers, tumours, swellings, spots and discolourations. The new disease of the pox was classified partly as a disease of the skin and was usually treated by surgeons. In cases of plague, either the surgeon or the physician could be called in, but the surgeon was seen as responsible for lancing or extirpating plague buboes (glandular swellings). The surgeons had one final duty, in which from the Middle Ages they had the monopoly, that of embalming the dead. This gave them some limited experience of the internal organs.[4]

Our understanding of how surgeons acted upon the body and how they interpreted their actions comes largely from surgical treatises, which were usually concerned with creating a learned surgery. Surgeons' case records are few. In England one cache of material comes from the seventeenth-century practice of the London surgeon, Joseph Binns, which has been admirably analysed by Lucinda Beier.[5] Cases are also mentioned in surgical treatises, but they usually illustrate the theoretical and practical guidelines of the treatise rather than giving an idea of daily surgical practice. Much of this chapter is, therefore, based on prescriptive material, telling surgeons what to do and how to think. This, of course, is largely also the case with physic or medicine (for this chapter, I use the term physic rather than medicine in order to retain the contrast that was made at the time between it and surgery). However, much of Galenic physic spread into the public domain, and we can have some confidence that its theories and practices were widely known and imitated by many more people than the small group of learned physicians. But, with the exception of some topical remedies, salves and wound dressings, surgery was not popularised; it was rarely set out in domestic manuscript or popular books on medicine, and it was highly unusual for a lay gentlewoman to practise surgery, though Lady Margaret Hoby was one exception.[6] Some surgeons

---

[4] See Carole Rawcliffe, *Medicine and Society in Later Medieval England* (Alan Sutton, Stroud, 1995), pp. 127–9, citing as a principal source: C. A. Bradford, *Heart Burial* (London, 1933).

[5] Lucinda McCray Beier, *Sufferers and Healers. The Experience of Illness in Seventeenth-Century England* (Routledge & Kegan Paul, London, 1987), pp. 51–96, and 'Seventeenth-Century English Surgery: the Casebook of Joseph Binns' in C. Lawrence (ed.), *Medical Theory, Surgical Practice* (Routledge, London, 1992), pp. 48–84.

[6] Philip K. Wilson, 'Acquiring Surgical Know-How. Occupational and Lay Instruction in Early Eighteenth-Century London' in R. Porter (ed.), *The Popularization of Medicine 1650–1850* (Routledge, London, 1992), pp. 42–71, esp. 45–9. Lady Margaret Hoby, *Diary of Lady Margaret Hoby, 1599–1605*, ed. Dorothy M. Meads (Routledge, London, 1930).

specialised in one or two operations, but they have left little or no evidence of their work, and they do not fit the picture of the general surgeon competent in all areas for whom the learned surgical treatises were written. In other words, the limitations and biases of the source material may present surgery in a distorted light. This is especially so in its tendency to portray the surgeon as someone who theorises about the body, rather than just repairing it. On the other hand, surgical treatises also provided much practical information, and there can be little doubt that their writers, who were often experienced practical surgeons, believed in the theory and learning that they wrote about.

In this chapter the differences and similarities between surgery and physic are explored. The push to make surgery learned meant that the learned surgeons shared with physicians the same theoretical perspectives, yet the physicians wished to prevent surgeons practising physic. On the other hand, surgeons stressed the unity of medicine, whilst pointing out that surgery was distinct because it was based on manual skill. By studying how surgeons operated, or at least how they described operations, it becomes clear that surgery was, indeed, *sui generis* in being a work of the hand, and that it also shared much with physic, as in the use of medicines and diet, and the expectation that treatment could be a prolonged affair. Moreover, surgeons viewed the body and its parts in much the same way as did physicians. They emphasised its humoral characteristics and the danger of putrefaction, which could travel through the connections of the body, and their treatment of choice in addition to surgery was often evacuation. There were constraints upon surgery that physicians did not have to face. The failure of an operation was much more obvious than the failure of physic and induced a sense of caution. Patients were put off by the prospect of pain, and surgeons had to balance their patients' wishes against what they took to be the requirements of treatment. Moreover, in the case of the pox, patients faced destructive treatment with mercury, which often led them to empirics who offered mercury-free alternatives. The pox, however, confirms the finding that the surgeons' view of disease and treatment centered on putrefaction and evacuation had much in common with that of physicians, and that there was a shared medical culture amongst the physicians and surgeons who wrote on medicine.

SURGERY AND PHYSIC

At first sight, the work of the surgeon was very different from that of the physician. 'Chirurgery', the word used in early modern English, came from two Greek words meaning hand and work.[7] The surgeon actively worked upon the body with hands and instruments. Surgery, as one standard definition put it, was concerned to cure the body 'by manual *Operation*. Its parts are four. *First*, to unite parts disjoynt. *Secondly*, To separate such unnaturally joyn'd. *Thirdly*, To remove things superfluous. *Fourthly*, To supply things wanting.'[8]

The surgeon's job was to repair the body's fabric or make it as perfect as possible. Most of the body's faults were obvious rather than being hidden from view, as with some of the illnesses that were treated by physicians. Alexander Read, when lecturing to the Barber-Surgeons Company in the early 1630s, gave some examples to illustrate the scope of surgery. The first part of surgery treated wounds, ulcers, fractures, dislocations and also tumours, for 'although the parts seeme to eye united; yet reason teacheth us, that there is a divulsion of them'. The second part comprised separating parts of the body for either cosmetic or functional reasons, such as, for instance, those who 'have been brought into the world with the *anus* and *vulva* quite shut up', and dealt with problems with the hymen, 'tongue-tyed children' and wry neck when 'the head is drawn towards the claves [collar-bone] more than on the other: whereby . . . the face groweth awry and distorted: and so the beauty of the countenance is much impaired'. The third part of surgery removed what was superfluous to the body, such as a dead child in the womb, ruptures or hernias, limbs that had mortified, and parts of the body such as a breast that had become cancerous; also 'things by their owne nature superfluous', such as wens, cataracts and 'stones in sundry parts of the body'. The fourth part made good 'the defects of the body', for instance 'restoring of the Nose lost or curing of the haire-lip' using parts of the body, or artifically 'repairing . . . the losses in other parts, as the eye, the eare, arme and legge'.[9]

[7] On the etymology and its use to define surgery as 'a hand working', see Thomas Vicary, *The Anatomie of the Bodie of Man*, ed. F. J. Furnivall and P. Furnivall, Early English Text Society (Trübner, London, 1888), part 1, p. 12. The main body of the text is that of the edition of 1548, the dedication and the epistle to the reader being from the edition of 1577 which was issued by the surgeons of St Bartholomew's hospital where Vicary had been a surgeon.
[8] James Cooke, *Mellificium Chirurgiae* (London, 1662), pp. 1–2.
[9] Alexander Read, 'Chirurgicall Lectures of Tumors and Ulcers' in *Workes*, pp. 8–10.

The operations and instruments that enabled the surgeon to repair the body represented techniques and technologies that, if the separation between the branches of medicine were adhered to, were unknown to the physician. In practice, some physicians were skilled in the use of the dissecting, if not of the surgical, knife, and in London members of the College of Physicians lectured to the Barber-Surgeons Company on anatomy and surgery. However, instruments were not an essential part of a physician's equipment, nor were they symbolic of their job. Surgeons, on the other hand, like other craftsmen, took pride in them. In their wills they specifically mentioned the silver instruments that they gifted to their servants or apprentices. Thomas Vicary, royal surgeon to Henry VIII, Master of the Barber-Surgeons Company and governor of St Bartholomew's hospital, in 1561 willed to a fellow surgeon 'my best plaister box, garnisshed with silver, my salvitory [small box] of silver, and a sering [syringe] of silver, with all other instruments of silver'. Another Sergeant-Surgeon to the Crown, Robert Balthrop, bequeathed to John Deighton, his servant,

my newe and last made Chirurgery chest . . . with all that is therein except golde and silver. Also I bequeath to him my plaster box of leather . . . and all the silver instruments therein. Also I give to him my rownde silver salvatory and one catheter of silver and annother of leade . . . Also I give unto him a case with silver Instruments therein that ys to saye a silver splatter a chockbarr of silver for the uvula a silver Syringe parcell gilted. Also I give him my silver precipitate [mercury] box all which things are in the aforesaid chest.

Other servants who practised surgery were also willed a variety of instruments and surgical books.[10] The quality of instruments reflected upon the surgeon's public reputation, hence the advice, for instance, that 'the stitching quill . . . ought for the credit of the Chirurgeon to be of silver'.[11] Surgery and surgical instruments were inseparable. The Barber-Surgeons Company not only examined sea surgeons as to their proficiency, but also inspected their surgical chests before each voyage, as without their instruments they could not practise their craft.[12] Surgeons were linked by their instruments to other crafts. They depended on the instrument makers. In one

---

[10] A. T. Young, *The Annals of the Barber-Surgeons of London* (Blades, East & Blades, London, 1890), pp. 522–3, 530–2.
[11] Read, 'The First Part of Chirurgery', p. 43.
[12] Young, *Annals*, pp. 131, 330–1.

case recorded by Richard Wiseman, the Sergeant-Chirurgeon or royal surgeon to Charles II, whose *Eight Chirurgicall Treatises* (1676) became a standard surgical text, the instrument maker was an integral member of the team that operated on a cancer of the mouth. Wiseman 'gave directions for the making actual Cauteries of various sorts, some Bolt like, others like Chisels, others of other Fashions. There were Instruments also made to defend his [the patient's] Tongue and Lips . . . we met again, and had the Instrument-maker attending to heat the Cauteries, and mend or alter them as occasion should offer. One of the Assistants held his [the patient's] Head.'[13] Instruments were the visible signs that surgery was a craft which depended on the surgeon's handiwork.

Surgeons and physicians also differed in that the success or failure of a surgeon's handiwork was easier to judge than that of a physician who healed using internal medicines and evacuations. Ambroise Paré (1517–90), the French royal surgeon whose writings had a Europe-wide influence, and whose works were read by the London Barber-Surgeons in manuscript translation before they were first printed in 1634,[14] pointed out how difficult it was to be sure whether the physician had actually been responsible for a cure:

For seeing that Fortune is very powerful in Diseases, and the same Meats [foods] and Medicines are often good and often vain, truly it is hard to say, whether the health is recovered by the benefit of Diet and Pharmacy, or by the strength of the body. Moreover in those cases in which we most prevail in with Medicines, although the profit be most manifest, yet it is evident that health is often sought in vain even by these things, and often recovered without them. As it may be perceived by some troubled with sore eyes, and others with Quartan Fevers [fevers recurring every fourth day], who having been long troubled by Physicians are healed without them.

On the other hand, what the surgeon did was much more obvious, so that 'the effect of Chirurgery as it is very neccessary, so it is the

---

[13] Richard Wiseman, *Eight Chirurgicall Treatises*, 4th edn (London, 1705), p. 112.

[14] Robert Balthrop had bequeathed in 1591 'unto the companie of the Barbors and Chirurgeons of the Cittie of London the Chirurgery of that most excellent writer John Tagaultius the lattin booke and also the English translation that I have made thereof. And also the Chirurgerie of the expert and perfect practitioner Ambrose Parey both which workes I have written into Englishe for the love that I owe my brethren practisinge Chirurgerie and not understandinge the latin Tounge and given them into the Hall for theire Dayly use and Readinge both in lattin and Englishe and Desiringe that they may be kept faire and clean for my sake': Young, *Annals*, p. 531, also Margaret Pelling and Charles Webster, 'Medical Practitioners' in C. Webster (ed.), *Health, Medicine and Mortality in the Sixteenth Century* (Cambridge University Press, Cambridge, 1979), p. 177. Some barber-surgeons may have been able to read Paré in French if not in Latin.

most evident amongst all the parts of Physick. For who without Chirurgery can hope to cure Broken or Luxated parts, who Wounds and Ulcers, who the Falling of the Matrix [womb], the Stone in the Bladder, a Member infested with a Gangrene or Sphacele?'[15]

Not only were the physical actions of the surgeon upon the body, such as lancing, cutting, binding and stitching, foreign to the physician, but the patient's reaction to surgical procedures was likely to be much more extreme than to anything that the physician did, with the possible exception of the administration of violent poisons. As Paré noted, pain and surgery were intimately bound together, for 'in performing those things with the hands, we cannot but cause paine: (for who can without paine cut off an arm or a leg, or divide and tear asunder the neck of bladder, restore bones put out of their places, open ulcers, bind up wounds and apply cauteries and such like?)'.[16] The ideal surgeon, therefore, as presented by Paré and others, who followed the characterisation of the surgeon by the Roman writer Celsus, had to be strong and, to a greater or lesser degree, merciless. This was very different from the image of the scholarly Christian physician whose aim was to minister to the needs of the sick, though as we shall see the surgeon was urged by some to take on learning and Christian charity:

For my part, I very well like that saying of *Celsus*: A Chirurgeon must have a strong, stable and intrepide hand, and a minde resolute and merciless; so that to heale him he taketh in hand, he be not moved to make more haste than the thing requires; or to cut lesse than is needfull; but which doth all things as if he were nothing affected with their cries; nor giving heed to the judgement of the vaine common people, who speake ill of Chirurgeons because of their ignorance.[17]

Surgeons also differed from physicians not only in their actions and idealised character, but also in their education and status. The

---

[15] Ambroise Paré, *The Workes*, trans. T. Johnson (London, 1634), Preface, sig. A^r. The belief that the principles of surgery were 'more certain' than those of physic continued into the eighteenth century; see R. Campbell, *The London Tradesman* (London, 1747), p. 47: 'The Physician in the Discharge of his Profession, is frequently obliged to grope in the dark, to act by Guess and bare Conjecture, and depends (in many Cases) more upon Chance and the Strengths of the Patient's Constitution than upon any infallible Rules in his Art; but the Surgeon for the most part has the Evidence of his Senses, as well as his Judgement, to guide him in his Operations; his Method of Cure depends upon the known Mechanism of the Human System, and the Medicines he uses act by known Laws, established by a long Course of Experience'.

[16] Paré, *Workes*, pp. 4–5.

[17] Ibid., p. 5.

apprentice-based training of barber-surgeons was organised within the guild structure of the trades in contrast to the university-based education of the physicians. In the eyes of the latter, this provided physicians with a better rational knowledge and greater social status, and served to justify their attempts to regulate the other two branches of medicine: surgery and pharmacy.[18] As it turned out, the College of Physicians, despite several attempts, failed to exert control over the barber-surgeons, especially on the question of their claim to have the right to supervise the work of surgeons.[19] However, in London the physicians did hold on to their formal legal right to be the only occupational group able to prescribe internal remedies. The surgeons were legally limited to external medicines, despite their repeated attempts to overturn this limitation.[20] Although co-operation also occurred – physicians were chosen by the Company to give anatomy lectures to its members – there was clearly hostility between the two groups. Such institutional and educational differences seem to mirror differences in practice, the physicians being learned, the surgeons practical, as well as reflecting the need to lessen competition and protect livelihoods.

Yet, while the differences were real ones, from other perspectives they appeared to be less so. A strong argument was being made in the sixteenth and seventeenth centuries that physic and surgery had much in common. The enterprise of making surgery learned and rational, that is, based on Greek and Arabic surgical writings and medical theory, so that the learned surgeon gave reasons for what he was doing, had begun in the Middle Ages. In that time physic and surgery (as well as pharmacy) became further separated, although

---

[18] On the Barber-Surgeons Company see Young, *Annals*, which is still essential; Jessie Dobson and R. Milnes Walker, *Barbers and Barber-Surgeons of London* (Blackwell Scientific Publications, Oxford, 1979).

[19] On such unsuccessful attempts see Young, *Annals*, pp. 126–7, 411; G. Clark, *A History of the Royal College of Physicians* (2 vols., Clarendon Press, Oxford), vol. I, pp. 154–5, 207, 239–40, 264, 274; Harold J. Cook, *The Decline of the Old Medical Regime in Stuart London* (Cornell University Press, Ithaca, 1986), pp. 101–40.

[20] For instance, in 1572 the Court of High Commission rejected James Versalius' claim to be able to prescribe internal medicines for sciatica, syphilis, ulcers or wounds. In 1604 the Barber-Surgeons Company failed to acquire a new charter which would have allowed them to give internal remedies and would have stopped physicians practising surgery and pharmacy. In 1641, when the College of Physicians petitioned the House of Lords for a bill to strengthen its rights, the Barber-Surgeons Company counter-petitioned for the right to prescribe internal remedies. See Clark, *College of Physicians*, vol. I, pp. 121, 207, 273–4; Cook, *Decline*, p. 101.

they shared a common foundation in Greek medical knowledge.[21] Institutionally, the separation was expressed most strongly in England and other parts of northern Europe, where surgery was established as a craft within the guild system whilst physic was studied in the universities.[22] In the Renaissance there was renewed emphasis on making surgery learned; not only were ancient Hippocratic and Galenic surgical texts published, but also vernacular surgical texts which distilled the surgical knowledge of the past and present and made it available to the many surgeons who could not read Latin.[23]

Learned physicians welcomed the push to create surgeons educated in classical learning, seeing this as part of the reformation of medicine and the war on empirics, but they still wished to retain the separation between physic and surgery. The London College of Physicians continued to assert the superiority of physic over surgery and pharmacy. The Salisbury physician, John Securis (fl.1566), who reflected the conservatism and learning of his Paris teacher, Jacques Dubois, deplored the existence of unlearned surgeons just as he had that of unlearned physicians and empirics. 'There be', he wrote, 'many surgions in this oure time, that practise surgerie, more by blynde experience, then by any science who . . . knowe almost the vertue and operation of nothinge that they do use. For howe shoulde they knowe it, when they are altogether unlearned? Yea and many of them there are that know never a letter in the book.' As a learned physician, Securis hoped that surgeons would be 'well learned in philosophie and phisicke', but he also wanted to retain the medical hierarchy that had been established in the minds of physicians by the tripartite branching of medicine. A surgeon could not give inward remedies 'without the Physitions counsayle', and he 'should undertake no hard or dangerous cure, without the phisitions advyse'.[24]

---

[21] For an excellent account of the development of medieval learned surgery see Nancy G. Siraisi, *Medieval and Early Renaissance Medicine* (University of Chicago Press, Chicago, 1990), pp. 162–86. Surgeons such as Bruno Longoburgo and Teodorico Borgognoni in the thirteenth century and Henri de Mondeville and Guy de Chauliac in the fourteenth century had created a distinctive book-based type of surgery.

[22] Ibid., p. 179; for an illuminating discussion of medieval English surgery see also Rawcliffe, *Medicine and Society in Later Medieval England*, pp. 125–47.

[23] For a detailed account of the humanist retrieval of classical surgery and of its dissemination throughout Europe in the vernacular see V. Nutton, 'Humanist Surgery' in A. Wear, R. K. French and I. M. Lonie (eds.), *The Medical Renaissance of the Sixteenth Century* (Cambridge University Press, Cambridge, 1985), pp. 75–99.

[24] John Securis, *A Detection and Querimonie of the Daily Enormities and Abuses Committed in Physick* (London, 1566), sigs. E3^v, E5^r.

Securis acknowledged that in the past medicine had been united, and this gave the physician the right to be also 'a poticarie, and have a poticaries shop . . . in his owne hous or maye be a Surgeon, and heale woundes and sores, or let bloud him selfe: *Sed non e diverso* [but not vice versa]. A Poticarie or Surgeon beyng onely of that arte may not be a physition.' Securis wanted to have his cake and to eat it. He acknowledged 'that in the olde time, the phisitions were wonte to exercise surgerie themselves', but 'it hath bene nowe of a longe time, that the Surgions do onely exercise this part of phisicke'.[25] The surgeon in the view of the learned physician was a paradoxical creature, someone who had taken over part of the physician's job, who should be educated, yet limited in what he could do, and under the physician's orders. In response to the argument that, as only one in a hundred physicians knew anything of surgery, surgeons should not take advice from physicians, Securis pointed out that 'the moste parte of the authors of phisicke intreateth of surgerie in their woorkes, and although we meddle litle or nothinge with outward diseases: yet doo we knowe what belongeth to them and how they ought to be cured'. In particular, surgery had need of what the physicians possessed: learning, 'or a reasonable waye of proceeding which is called in Latin *Rationalis methodus*, the whiche the moste part of Surgions have not'. The example that Securis gave makes it clear that he believed that the logical division and ordering of medical knowledge would provide greater precision in treatment: the general treatment for inflammation was 'to repel and drive backe the fluxion of humours', but in the particular cases of inflammation in the sweat glands or in a plague victim, such a treatment would be dangerous.[26]

Securis, whilst wishing to keep the hierarchical distinction between physician and surgeon, recognised that surgeons, when they became educated, would be tempted to encroach upon the physician's territory of inward diseases and remedies. This was partly because the learned surgical texts read by surgeons were concerned to provide complete treatments, rather than be limited to external remedies, and they routinely gave advice on internal medicines and on diet. When Securis listed the authors who would help the surgeon to master the 'speculative' or theoretical part of his subject, he cautioned anyone reading the works of the Italian surgeon Johannes

---

[25] Ibid., sigs. D4^v, E6^v–E7^r.   [26] Ibid., sigs. E8^r–F2^v.

de Vigo (fl. 1500), 'whom the Surgions of our daies doo now most follow', not only for 'the obscuritie and doubtes yea and errours that be in him' but even more, one suspects, because 'He bringeth in manye thinges in his boke, which belongeth rather to the phisition to knowe and practise, then to the Surgion: as Electuaries [medicinal pastes mixed with honey or syrups], potions, purgations and manye other inward medicines.' Securis conceded that 'if the Surgion have knowledge in Phisicke, I meane that he know the complexions, the nature of simples, and the effect and operation of compositions: he may use them, els not'.[27] Although Securis may have believed that there was little chance of that being the case, this was what the new learned surgeons hoped that they could create: a surgeon who would be manually skilled but who could think like a physician as well as a surgeon. Unlike the learned medieval surgeons, they wanted to reunite medicine. It was almost inevitable, once medieval surgical writers had established learned surgery, that their sixteenth-century successors should seek to share in the knowledge and status bestowed upon physicians by their learning.

LEARNED SURGERY AND THE UNITY OF PHYSIC AND SURGERY

The English reformers of surgery, men like Thomas Gale, Thomas Vicary, John Banister, John Hall and William Clowes, used the same rhetoric as their physician counterparts in making their case. Like them, they especially attacked empirics, and the lack of learning.[28] However, they were not concerned with the distinction between physicians and surgeons. Rather, they stressed with great unanimity that both groups had much in common in terms of medical theory and practice, and that this was why surgery and physic should be united as they had been in the past. (The army or naval surgical experience of Gale, Vicary, Banister and Clowes also contributed to their belief in the unity of medicine).[29] For instance, Thomas Gale,

---

[27] Ibid., sig. E7ᵛ.

[28] See, for example, Gale, 'Institution', fols. 4ᵛ, 9ʳ, 10ʳ; and John Hall, 'An Historiall Expostulation against the Beastlye Abusers, bothe of Chyrurgerie and Physyke' in *A Most Excellent and Learned Woorke of Chirurgerie, Called Chirurgia Parva Lanfranci* (London, 1565), where Hall attacks empirics in surgery and physic alike.

[29] Two other leading English surgical writers, Woodall and Wiseman, were also naval surgeons.

who as a Master of the Barber-Surgeons Company and a royal surgeon represented the elite of the craft of surgery, in *An Institution of a Chirurgian* (which was set out in dialogue form, the different speakers being surgeons), wrote that, although the surgeon cured by the hand:

JOHN FEILDE . . . yet Chirurgerie hath nede both of that parte which curith by dyet, and that whiche helpeth by medicyne. As is moost evident and clare in great inflammations, and also in those bodyes in whiche Cacochimia (that is to say yll Juce) is found, where the humours are defilyd and corrupted.

Expertise about diet marked out the physician, as did knowledge of medicines and of corrupt humours, but Gale saw such expertise as also lying within the surgeon's ambit, and he therefore concluded:

IOHN YATES Then it shold seme that Chirurgery is so ioyned to the other two partes [physic and pharmacy], that it can not be well seperatyd from them: although they be now two distincte artes.
THO. GALE Truth it is, and in the begynnynge, phisicke and Chirurgery were both one: and one man exercised both, for so did the princes of phisicke Hippocrates and Galene.
IOHN YATES Then I perceyve that Chirurgerie is not so base, as it is taken for.[30]

Reading the prefaces and dedications of sixteenth-century surgical works, it is clear that there was a concerted attempt to raise the status of surgery. In a very typical Renaissance manner, Gale and his colleagues, when tying in surgery with physic, stressed, following

---

[30] Gale, 'Institution', fol. 3ᵛ. See also Vicary, *Anatomie*, p. 14: the surgeon 'ought to be learned, and that he knowe his principles, not onely in Chirurgerie, but also in Phisicke, that he may the better defend his Surgery'. Hall, 'Expostulation', sigs. Eee1ᵛ–2ʳ: 'Chirurgerie . . . is the most aunciente, ye the most sure and excellente parte of the arte of medicyne . . . And Chirurgery is not an arte properlye of it selfe withoute Phisike, or separated from the same as some doe thinke; neyther can Phisike be an whole or perfecte arte wythout Chirurgery, as some woulde imagin.' John Banister, in *A Needefull, New and Necessarie Treatise of Chyrurgerie* (London, 1575), sigs. vᵛ–viʳ, wrote, 'some of late more precise then wise have fondly affirmed that the Chyrurgian hath not to deale in Physicke . . . it is mad dotage, to parte that which can not be separated. How can Phisicke be praised and Chirurgerie discommended? can any man despise Chyrurgerie, and not defame Physike? . . . For although they be at this time made twoo distincte Artes . . . yet sure, the one can not woorke without some aide of the other nor the other practise without the helpe of both. For further assuraunce whereof learne of Hyppocrates, who practised both together, and in reading Galenes bookes, you shall clearely see how they embrace one another with firme frendshippe and inseparable amitie.' See also Paré, *Workes*, sig. A6ʳ⁻ᵛ, where he argues for the pre-eminence and antiquity of surgery and for its ties with physic and pharmacy.

Celsus, its antiquity and listed the 'noble persons' who had practised and improved surgery.[31]

However, more significant from the perspective of this book is how the links with physic were made and how they affected the theory and practice of surgery. Practitioners trained in surgery and knowledgeable in physic, either by formal education or self-taught, facilitated the interchanges between the two subjects. John Banister, the author of surgical treatises and of an anatomical book for surgeons, practised surgery and physic in Nottingham, and had combined the two as a ship's surgeon. After he settled in London in 1587, he was supported by Elizabeth I in his attempt to persuade the College of Physicians to allow him to practise as a physician.[32] The influence of physic can be clearly seen in his surgical works, as it can, later, in those of Alexander Read, who, after taking his Arts degree at Aberdeen University, first trained as a surgeon in France, and became a member of the Barber-Surgeons Company and then of the College of Physicians. His appointment in 1632 to read the weekly surgical lectures to the Company indicates at the institutional level both the antagonism between surgery and physic and their close relations. After the death of Dr Matthew Gwinne (or Gwyn) in 1627, the Company had decided that the surgeons should in turn read the lectures rather than a physician. In 1632, however, Charles I ordered that a physician, Dr Andrews, should deliver them, and when he declined, the surgeon-physician Read was chosen. Read recognised that a physician had been imposed upon the surgeons, 'But seeing (as I understand) the highest power of this Realm, from which there is no appealle, hath decreed that this exercise shall be performed by a Doctor of Physick, and that the worshipfull Company hath for the present made choice of me, who profess my self to be a Member of the Company; I shall labour by diligence . . .'[33] The Company was, however, keen to learn of physic. For instance, in 1566 it had financially supported Thomas

---

[31] Gale, 'Institution', fols. 4^{r-v}; such *encomia* of a discipline tended to be repeated by different authors intent on the same aim. For a discussion of how anatomy was similarly raised rhetorically in status by anatomy writers, which also involved the unity of medicine and the antiquity and dignity of the subject, see A. Wear, 'Medicine in Early Modern Europe, 1500–1700' in L. Conrad et al., *The Western Medical Tradition* (Cambridge University Press, Cambridge, 1995), pp. 285–90.

[32] Clark, *College of Physicians*, I, p. 154. On the title page of *The Historie of Man* (London, 1578), written in Nottingham, Banister called himself 'Master in Chirurgerie and Practitioner in Phisicke'.

[33] Read, 'Chirurgicall Lectures', p. 2; Young, *Annals*, pp. 334–5, 365–6.

Hall with an exhibition worth forty shillings annually 'towards hys studye in the unyvercytie for Surgery anexynge physycke therunto, and thereby hereafter to prophet [profit] his other brethren . . . Readynge lectures unto them in the Common Hall . . .'. Hall kept to his part of the bargain and was appointed examiner in surgery and lecturer in anatomy for ten years.[34]

Physic, which included natural philosophy and whose practitioners would have first studied the arts curriculum at university, provided surgery with its theory, whilst unlearned surgery was seen as concerned with practice alone. Hall's namesake, John, wrote that:

nether can Chirurgerye be perfectlye learned withoute theorike, nor Phisike wythoute Practise . . . Yet some there be that thinke onlye to Phisike belongeth Theorike, or Speculation, and that to Chirurgery belongeth onlye practise; but howe farre their judgements differ from the truthe, let everye wyse man judge. What knowledge is there in Phisike that is not requisyte in Chirurgerye? whether it be Gramer, Philosophy, Astrononomye, Anatomye, or anye other; ye, the very judiciall of urine and the pulse . . . the knowledge of Chirurgerye consisteth in ii thinges, namelye, speculation and practise, and therfore it is not only a workinge, but an excellente knowledge and understandynge howe to worke well and perfectly.[35]

Given such a view it made sense for learned surgical writers to educate their surgical readers in the theory of physic. Paré set out at great length the foundations of physic: the elements, temperaments and humours, together with the faculties, actions and spirits of nature in the body, the six non-naturals, the causes of disease, and definitions of a disease, a symptom and an indication. He also gave a detailed anatomical description of the body, which was of increasing interest to physicians, and knowledge of which had been seen from the Middle Ages onwards as necessary for the learned and practical surgeon.[36] A grasp of the temperaments, humours, etc. enabled the surgeon to integrate physic with surgery, and allowed him when faced with a particular case to decide on a specific course of action. Such knowledge provided a rational framework for assessing a patient and his or her treatment. As Paré put it: 'That the Chirurgeon may rightly and according to Art, performe the foresaid

[34] Young, *Annals*, p. 183; cited in Pelling and Webster, 'Medical Practitioners', p. 176. Young, *Annals*, p. 187.
[35] Hall, 'Expostulation', sig. Eee2ʳ.
[36] Paré, *Workes*, pp. 5–248.

[surgical] workes, he must set before his eyes certaine Indications of working: Otherwise he is like to become an Empericke, whom no Art, no certaine reason, but onely a blind temerity of fortune moves to boldnesse and action.'[37]

Like the learned physician, the surgeon, if he would not be an empiric, took into account the humoral temperament and lifestyle of his patient. In addition, the part of the body that was being operated upon had, like the body as a whole, to be considered as possessing its own individual character. 'The condition of the part affected' had to be assessed by the surgeon when deciding on a particular treatment. He methodically checked out its

substance, consistence, softnesse, hardnesse, quicke or dull sense, forme, figure, magnitude, site, connexion, principallity, service, function and use. From all these, as from notes the skilfull Chirurgion will draw Indications according to the time and part affected: for the same things are not fit for sore eyes, which were convenient for the eares; neither doth a Phlegmon in the jawes and throat admit the same forme of cure, as it doth in other parts of the body.[38]

Paré, like other learned surgeons, was integrating surgery into physic, and he set up the same enemy of the physicians, the empirics, the better to move his colleagues to his point of view.

Surgery was thus being drawn into the Renaissance Galenic ideology of individualised treatment and of methodical teaching and practice. Read, who hoped to impress upon his audience that he was using the most up to date and learned approach to teaching, told them that he would lecture by going 'through all the points of Chirurgery methodically' and thereby 'help the memory'.[39] As well as being pedagogically effective, rational medicine based on what Securis called *rationalis methodus* was meant to be put into practice. At a general level it provided a means of gaining the confidence of patients. Read wrote that the surgeons of the Company, who had taken it in turn to lecture on the theory of surgery before his appointment, had increased their theoretical knowledge. This 'had made them able to give greater contentment to their Patients by their rationall discourses and more emboldened them in particular operations', and it also justified their practice against the bad mouthing of empirics.[40] As well as being confidence-boosting for

---

[37] Ibid., p. 5.   [38] Ibid., p. 43.
[39] Read, 'Chirurgicall Lectures', p. 3.   [40] Ibid., pp. 1–2.

patient and practitioner, methodical and rational medicine was seen as maximising effectiveness and safety. The medical method (as discussed in chapters 1 and 3) was supposed both to be brief and compendiously to cover all possibilities. It was centred around the indications from the patient, his or her lifestyle, the disease and the environment. For Paré, the knowledge of indications not only made the surgeon a rational rather than an empirical practitioner, it also represented 'a certaine safe and short way, which leades the Physician, as by the hand, to the attainement of his purposed end, of preserving the sound, or curing the sicke. For *Galen* doth define an Indication to be a certaine insinuation of what is to be done, or a quick and judicious apprehension of that which may profit or hurt.' Paré also tried to make the use of indications acceptable to surgeons by incorporating the concept of indication into the domain of secret craft knowledge:

And as Faulconers, Mariners, Plowmen, Soldiers, and all manner of Artizans, have their peculiar termes and words, which are neither knowne, nor used by the vulgar [the public]; so this word Indication is proper and peculiar to Phisitions and Chirurgeons, as a Terme of Arte not vulgar; by consideration of which, as by some signe, or secret token, they are admonished what is to be done to restore health, or repell an imminent danger.[41]

Diet

Surgeons believed that they had to use diet and pharmacy, and that those who were successful without them succeeded by chance; in other words, they were dangerous empirics and 'for some one happy chance, a thousand dangerous errors happen afterwards'.[42] Surgeons wanted to share in the two areas of practice that lay at the centre of physic: diet, which symbolised the individualised treatment of learned physic, and rational pharmacy, based on the cure by contrary quality, as opposed to empirical experience. Or, put more simply, without the self-justifying rhetoric of learned medicine, the surgeons wanted to offer advice on diet and to prescribe medicines, as the physicians were doing.

Surgical treatises often included diet and the six non-naturals as

---

[41] Paré, *Workes*, pp. 42, 43. [42] Ibid., p. 3.

one aspect of the patient's treatment that had to be borne in mind.[43] John Banister produced an extensive set of recommendations on regimen for ulcer sufferers organised around the six non-naturals. Banister, as a surgeon and physician who believed in the unity of medicine, emphasised that ulcers were, according to Galen, curable by 'Diet, aide of medicines, and operations of hand', and that since 'diet [regimen] is the moste noble, and excellent instrument among the rest (as Galene supposeth) I have . . . set foorth the onely order of diet, to bee used in curation of Ulcers'. As with descriptions of the humours, temperaments, etc., a great deal of the advice on regimen was presented unchanged, so that surgeons were given the same information as physicians. The move to unite surgery and physic had as part of its agenda the project of encouraging surgeons to think more like physicians. So Banister repeated the standard advice to eat fish that live in 'harde stonie and gravelie waters' and 'whiche swimme in the pure and cleane sea', but he also tried to relate the advice to the cure of ulcers; for instance, as the disease was cold and moist, hot and dry air would cure it, but it should not be so hot that 'the putrefaction be thereby burned, and the disease made more sharpe and fearce'. Given the moist nature of ulcers, it was easy to show that the general prohibition against low fenny places and marshes made sense for patients suffering with them, especially as 'that ayre is corrupt, and encreaseth superfluous moisture, whereby the Ulcers are nourished and mainteined'.[44]

Read, who was conscious of his status as a physician, saw such advice as belonging properly to the province of the physician, though as a surgeon he clearly believed that surgeons should be taught it. He told his audience of barber-surgeons that, in a case of a wound in the throat, if 'a learned Physitian cannot be had, you must see that he use a convenient diet'.[45] He showed his expertise in

---

[43] Johannes de Vigo, *The Most Excellent Workes of Chirurgery* (London, 1543), fol. 16ʳ, wrote that the first intention or part of the cure of phlegmon (an inflamed tumour, boil or carbuncle that came from an antecedent cause) was 'to ordre the lyfe or dyete'.

[44] Banister, *Treatise of Chyrurgerie*, fols. 81ʳ, 86ʳ, 81ᵛ–82ᵛ; for Banister's belief in the unity of medicine see footnote 30.

[45] Read, 'The First part of Chirurgery', p. 161; Thomas Gale in 'An Excellent Treatise of Wounds Made with Gonneshotte' in *Workes*, fol. 13ʳ, clearly wanted the surgeon to prescribe regimen though he recognised the physician's greater expertise. Gale gave concise advice on diet (chicken broths) and drink for head wounds and how they should be altered over the days of convalescence after an operation, and he added 'other thinges required for the order of 6. *rerum non nat.* [the six non-naturals] Let the Chirurgian lerne of the skilful Phisition'.

'kitchin physic', as the enemies of learned medicine termed it (see chapter 9), by drawing up a lengthy list of recommendations:

His [the patient's] diet then must be slender, cooling, glutinous, and somewhat astringent, that no great store of blood be engendered, that it may be cooled, made thick, and so lesse apt to flow; wherefore flesh, egges, and strong drinkes are to bee shunned. The party may eat Lettice, Purslaine, Endive, Spinach, Sorrell, Barly-creame . . . As for fruit, he may eat Quinces, Medlars, Pomgranes, Prunes, Peares baked or stewed, Slowes stewed. As for flesh, he may eat calves and sheepes feet stewed, calves and sheeps head boyled . . . Let the drinke be spring-water, wherein steel hath been quenched . . . vinegar and water, the juyce of Pomgranets, Barly-water . . . If the party be weake, let him, or her, feed upon mountain birds, poched egges, Partridges . . . If the party sleepe not well, it is to be procured by art . . .[46]

The rationale for the diet was surgical: to slow down and thicken the blood, so helping in the healing of the wound. However, the structure of the advice, consisting of a list of recommended foods and drinks, would have been familiar to a learned physician. Advice on diet and regimen was clearly imported from physic, and helped to make surgery learned. However, learning and status were not the only issues; there is no doubt that those who wanted to create a learned surgery believed that this was the way to improve the therapeutic results of surgery. Read's reason for bringing in the learned advice on diet and so on was that 'these wounds are extreme dangerous, you cannot be too circumspect in curing of them'. In other words, knowledge from physic produced a more complete and effective surgical outcome.

Medicines

Medicines, the other part of physic, were more central to surgery than regimen. Because surgeons and physicians held to the same images of the diseased body and its parts and told similar stories (discussed below) with corrupt humours playing leading roles, it made sense that surgeons should employ the same therapies.[47] They used the same rhetoric as physicians when praising God's or Nature's mercy in creating for mankind's benefit medicines of herbs and of

---

[46] Read, 'The First Part of Chirurgery', p. 161.
[47] Gale, 'Institution', fol. 3ᵛ.

the animal and mineral products of the earth.[48] Like physicians, they set out in their treatises the remedies and their ingredients to be used for particular conditions, and they also compiled lists of simple and compound medicines, and *antidotaria* of ointments, plasters, oils, pills and other specifically surgical remedies. They were usually for local, topical use on wounds, ulcers, growths, etc., though more general remedies for internal use were also noted. Sea surgeons, who had to be surgeon, physician and apothecary in one, were not affected by the occupational barrier erected against surgeons giving internal remedies, so John Woodall, surgeon-general of the East India Company, set out the ingredients of 'medicines Physicall and Chirurgicall' as well as listing as necessary not only unguents (ointments), emplasters (medicated plasters) and electuaries, but also simples, spices, gums, laxative pills, syrups, opiates and distilled waters, as well as chemical oils and minerals, which reflected Woodall's interest in Paracelsian remedies. The occupational barrier was often ignored, sometimes with the standard excuse when medical boundaries were transgressed of isolation from the usual medical resources.[49] The space devoted to medicines was large: Vigo's 1543 English version had 73 pages devoted to simples and to *antidotaria*, Gale's *Antidotarie* (1563) was 183 pages long, whilst the 1579 version of *Guydos Questions* had 186 pages detailing the ingredients of remedies collected from Greek, Arabic, medieval and sixteenth-century sources. Even when they produced no *antidotaria*, surgeons such as Clowes and Wiseman filled their pages with the details of the ointments, plasters, powders, etc. constantly alluded to. Medicines, in other words, were almost as important to surgeons as they were to physicians, and as we shall see later, there was a constant interplay between surgical operations and procedures and the use of topical, and sometimes systemic, remedies.

---

[48] See, for instance, Paré, *Workes*, Preface sig. A2ʳ; Read, 'The First Part of Chirurgery', pp. 28–9.

[49] John Woodall, *The Surgions Mate*, facsimile of 1617 London edn with Introduction by John Kirkup (Kingsmead Press, Bath, 1978), pp. 39, sigs. A1ᵛ–A3ᵛ; Vigo, *Workes*, fol. 212ᵛ: 'Here foloweth a table of medicines compounde and symple, wherwyth Chirurgiens ought to be furnyshed that dwell in villages and townes, where no potycaries be, and also such as go to the see.'

THE IMPACT OF LEARNED MEDICINE

It is difficult to assess the impact that the push to make surgery learned had upon the practice of surgery. Although 'methodical' or compendious teaching is clearly evident in surgical textbooks, it is unlikely that it was put into practice to any great extent, as the mental effort to take into account the myriad possible indications when treating a patient would be too great for most. Like physicians, surgeons probably mainly concentrated on the condition and, if they were conscientious, they took into account the different aspects or kinds of condition as, for instance, the variety of ulcers, and they might also consider the age, sex, strength and temperament of a patient when devising a treatment. There were other types of knowledge conveyed by learned surgical texts. One, which is discussed below, shaped the surgeon's interpretation of pathological processes and was centred around the corruption and putrefaction of parts of the body. This knowledge was shared or borrowed from physic, and as it was spread widely at a popular level, albeit in a generalised form, surgeons would not have had much difficulty in assimilating it.

Anatomical knowledge also figured in the surgical treatises of the Middle Ages and Renaissance. It was seen as far more essential for a skilled and safe surgeon than the ability to think through a case methodically, and its possession helped to make a surgeon learned. Guy de Chauliac, the fourteenth-century French surgeon, argued for the necessity of anatomy for surgeons (in *Guydos Questions* (1579)), and cited Henri de Mondeville's view that a surgeon without anatomy is like a blind man sawing a log and that a workman has to know what he is working on. Surgeons who studied anatomy were reminded of its theological and physiological meanings, which were significant to the learned physicians when, during the course of the sixteenth century, anatomy increasingly held the latter's interest (see chapter 3). De Chauliac wrote that anatomy had other uses, the greatest being 'for the mervayle of the great power of God the creator of men, that so hath made them to his lykeness and forme', and for the knowledge it gave of the parts of the body, their 'dispositions' or temperaments.[50] More brutally, it was pointed out that a surgeon ignorant of anatomy created the 'daunger of homicide

---

[50] Guy de Chauliac, *Guydos Questions* (London, 1579), fol. 5^{r-v}.

or manslaughter'.[51] The Crown, by granting in 1540 the Company of Barber-Surgeons the right to dissect four executed criminals a year and to use their bodies as material for anatomy lectures, had created an institutional framework for the anatomical education of surgeons, and had given official recognition to the belief that 'better knowledge, instruction, insight, learning in the said science or faculty of surgery' would come from the study of anatomy. The Company required its surgical apprentices and members to attend the lectures. Apprentices, it was decided in 1556, were to be examined on 'what ys Surgery and also what an Anatomye ys and how many perts it ys, of what the four Elements and the 12 signes [of the zodiac] be'. Anatomical knowledge was also emphasised in the formal letter or diploma confirming that a successful apprentice, who had been made free of the Company and had subsequently shown evidence of his skill, was 'a master of Surgery and of Anathomye', the examiners being 'assured by the experyence we have of the man that he is not onely substancyally well exercysed the curing of infyrmities belonging to Surgery of the parts of mans bodye commonly called the Anathomye . . .'[52] Whether all surgeons attended the anatomy lectures is a moot point. In 1563 Thomas Gale, who had been an examiner in surgery and anatomy for the Company, was complaining of 'some, who beynge Chirurgians in name, doe not onlye neglecte thys knowledge of Anotomye: but also Invieth those that doe therein travayle'.[53]

It is difficult to assess the numbers of those willing and able to become learned surgeons or who wished to be knowledgeable in anatomy. It is likely, given the encouragement of the learned surgeons by the London Company, that they were largely located in that city. But we hardly know who was a barber and who was a surgeon, nor the numbers of those who, despite the Company's rules, practised both crafts.[54] Literacy was essential for anyone

---

[51] Vigo, *Workes*, fol. 1ʳ; the surgeons of St Bartholomew's who reissued Vicary's *Anatomie* wrote of 'ignoraunt Practitioners, not knowing the Anatomie, commonly doth ensue death and separation of soule and body': Vicary, *Anatomie*, 'To the Reader', p. 9.

[52] Act of 1540 uniting the Barber-Surgeons and Surgeons Companies in J. W. Willcock, *The Laws Relating to the Medical Profession* (J. & W. T. Clarke, London, 1830), p. clxxiv; Young, *Annals*, pp. 310–13.

[53] Gale, 'Institution', fol. 7ʳ.

[54] Pelling and Webster, 'Medical Practitioners', p. 174, believe that it is reasonable to suppose that half of the 185 freemen of the Company in 1537 would be involved in surgery, and that towards the end of the sixteenth century the Company had between 70 and 100 surgeons. However, as Doreen Evenden has noted, it is extremely difficult to distinguish from the

wishing to become a learned surgeon. In 1556, as part of the Company's push to create a new learned surgery, it was ordered that a barber-surgeon could not take on an apprentice who did not know Latin and 'cannot wryte and reade suffycientlye'. However, the next year this regulation was rescinded, so that one could be apprenticed although 'not lerned in the Latin Tonge'. The Company seems, with the rest of Europe, to have concluded that a surgeon could acquire learning through vernacular texts. In practice, even under the 1556 regulations, it was recognised that some apprentices did not fulfil the more basic requirement of reading and writing, and they were required to give reports on their progress.[55] Although we have no figures, it appears that some surgeons were not able to read or write easily, and certainly would not fulfil the long-standing hope of learned surgeons that a surgeon should be 'lettered and learned', which Gale took to mean 'that he can wright, red and understande the mynde of latyne authour'.[56] It may be that literacy had improved amongst the surgical freemen of the Company by 1604, when Edward Caldwell presented them with 500 copies of Horatius Morus' *Tables of Surgery* (1585), which had been translated by his father or uncle, Richard. Certainly, the book conveyed the essence of learned surgery. It was methodical, in that it distilled Jean Tagault's surgical work into tabular form, and it was published, very unusually, with both the original Latin text and the English translation in close proximity to each other. Perhaps Edward Caldwell hoped that those surgeons who had no Latin would become familiar with Latin terminology by comparing the two texts.

Many who specialised in particular operations or in particular parts of the body and were licensed in London to practise only in their area of expertise were probably not learned surgeons. Literacy may have been a bar, as would have been their narrow focus on particular parts of the body. For instance, in 1602 'Edward Stutfeyld a practicioner in bone setting . . . was lycensed to practize in bone settyng onely'. In 1608 'Mathias Jenkinson was examyned concerninge his skyll in the arte of Surgery. And was lycensed to cut for the

Company's records who was a barber or a surgeon: 'Gender Differences in the Licensing and Practice of Female and Male Surgeons in Early Modern England', *Medical History*, 42, 1998, p. 196. The matter will hopefully be decided in Margaret Pelling's forthcoming major study of the barber-surgeons.
55 Young, *Annals*, pp. 309–12.
56 De Chauliac, *Guydos Questions*, fol. 4ᵛ; Gale, 'Institution', fol. 11ʳ; Gale was explicitly expounding on 'Guido' (de Chauliac) who was following Galen.

hernia or Rupture to couch the Catrac to cut for the wry neck and the hare lip'. This was on condition that the Masters of the Company or their appointed assistants were present at 'every such cure'. Jenkinson had his licence revoked a year later for not following its conditions. James Blackborne, on the other hand, may have shown evidence of surgical learning, despite being given a limited licence; his examiners were promised a dinner when in 1611 he applied to practise, which made the occasion more formal and celebratory. It is also likely that a knowledge of gynaecology and midwifery amongst surgeons would have involved book learning: 'James Blackborne was examined touchinge his skill in the generatyve parts of women; and bringing of women to bedd in their dangerous and difficult Labors: And he the said Blackborne was found fitt and allowed to practize (in that Chirurgicall parte of Surgery touching the generatyve parts and bringinge them to bedd in their dangerous and difficult Labours).'[57]

The many operators who were not incorporated even in a limited way into the Company probably had very little knowledge of the learned surgery that was available through books and the weekly lectures. On the other hand, the self-taught practitioner of physic armed with a few books was not unusual amongst lay people, and there is no reason why a specialist operator or unlicensed surgeon should not also become learned in the same way. However, the comparison does not stand close scrutiny. Lay people left diaries and letters that describe how they acquired medical knowledge from books; this is not the case with unlicensed surgeons. Moreover, what surgeons learned from practical experience, whether as an apprentice in a Company or less formally, is also hidden from us.

A re-creation of surgical practice and knowledge that relies heavily on surgical treatises can lead to distortion. The integration of surgery with physic and natural philosophy as expressed in the treatises may have been largely absent in practical teaching. However, the pathological processes that the surgical writers warned the surgeon to take note of in the patient were probably also pointed out in practical teaching. Abscesses, inflammation and the different effects of infection leading to purulent discharges and ultimately to gangrene are obvious, as is the need to respond to them. Moreover,

[57] Young, *Annals*, pp. 325, 327, 330–1.

the surgical treatises were not merely concerned with theory; they also provided good evidence of operations and operative techniques.

LEARNING AND PRACTICE

Although most learned surgical treatises imported the theory of physic into surgery without their authors being too concerned about setting it into a craft tradition, they explicitly recognised and emphasised the practical side of surgery. They made it clear that the surgeon had 'to learne, and then worke and use experience . . . the onely readinge in bookes is not sufficient, as manye a one at this day (to the great hurte of muche people) thinketh'.[58] Books, learning and the theory of physic were necessary but not to the extent of supplanting practical experience. John Hall wrote that in surgery 'practise and experience is the chiefest learnyng', but to reach perfection in surgery the learning of books was required. He stressed that such learning had not only to be understood but also to be experienced through practice:

And for this dothe learninge (in bookes conteined) chieflye serve, to teache men to knowe the workes of learned masters of old tyme. But assure thy selfe (what so ever suche masters have wrytten), thou shalt never perfectlye digest to thine owne use, anye thinge in them: except thou be able to ioyne by comparison that which thou haste sene in other mennes workes before thine eies, and in the practise of thine owne handes, wyth that which thou findest wrytten in olde authors: for lyttle profit, swetenesse, or under-standinge shall one gette of authores, except he see the same also put in practise. Therfore when thou haste sene proved by cunning masters the whych thou haste red, thou arte truelye learned in thine arte, and therfore apte to worke and use experience thy selfe.[59]

Thomas Johnson, the translator of Paré's works, put it more succinctly when he warned his readers that 'No man becomes a Workmane by Bookes.'[60] The Dutch surgeon Paul Barbette (d. before 1675), who had the reputation of being a 'modern surgeon', innovative in operative techniques and up to date in taking on board the circulation of the blood and chemical ideas, also

---

[58] Hall, 'Expostulation', sig. Eee2[v].

[59] Ibid.; Hall also emphasised in the manner of Renaissance anatomists that Galen had 'admonished us, that we ought not (if we will be perfectlye cunninge) to trust onlye to doctrine wrytten in bokes, but rather oure propre eyes: which are to be trusted above all other authores, ye before Hippocrates and Galen': sig. Eee3[r].

[60] Paré, *Workes*, 'To the Reader', n.p.

emphasised that some techniques could not be learnt by reading. When discussing fractures he wrote, 'The manner of extending I describe not, because that it is better learnt by the frequent view of Practice than by Reading.'[61]

Practical, technical skill was recognised even if bereft of learning. Clowes, when attacking surgical empirics, nevertheless acknowledged that there was a group of practitioners standing between the empirics and the learned surgeons whose skill he admired:

for my selfe doe know divers verie honest men, both English and strangers [foreigners], that daily use to cutte for the stone and ruptures. And I have beene oftentimes in presence when they did cut for the same. And in truth it cannot be denied, but that they have performed their workes which they tooke upon them to do, both honestly, carefully, painfully and skilfully, to their great praise, and to the comfort and health of their patients . . .[62]

An empiric's surgical technique was also of interest, particularly if the observer was not too concerned with medical status. John Ward recorded in considerable detail the operative technique of 'the mountebank that cutt wry necks'. From Ward's account it is clear that the 'mountebank' had anatomical and surgical skills, provided some after care, and also saw the patient's post-operative condition in humoral terms like a learned surgeon, which raises the question of how real were the distinctions between surgeons.[63]

Despite their warning that books did not make surgeons, writers on surgery were intent through their treatises on making expert as well as rational and learned surgeons, with ideally both qualities being merged together. Expertise came from experience, from having 'seene other masters worke', but this medieval definition was expanded by a surgeon such as Gale, concerned to create a new type of educated surgeon. The surgeon, he wrote, 'must be experte, that

---

[61] Paul Barbette, *The Chirurgical and Anatomical Works* (London, 1672), p. 4. Barbette also acknowledged the value of the experience of 'expert Masters', who did not need porringers or bowls marked in ounces as they had learnt to calculate the weight of blood by sight, despite the fact that 'Blood is really weightier than it outwardly seems': p. 42.

[62] William Clowes, *A Briefe and Necessarie Treatise, Touching the Cure of the Disease Called Morbus Gallicus* (London, 1585) (hereafter *Treatise* (1585)), fol. 10^r. Sir Thomas Browne commented that in Norwich 'hath been a mountebanck these 2 months, who cuts for wrye necks, coucheth cataracts, cures hare lipps, etc wherin no chirurgeon of this place being versed hee hath a great deal of employment, to the shame of our Chirurgeons'. Letter to his son, Edward, Sir Thomas Browne, *Sir Thomas Browne's Works*, ed. S. Wilkin (4 vols., London, 1836) vol. I, p. 245.

[63] John Ward, *Diary of the Rev. John Ward, A. M., Vicar of Stratford-Upon-Avon . . . 1648 to 1679*, ed. Charles Severn (London, 1839), pp. 273–4.

is he muste be garnished wyth muche and longe experience, which is excogitated be [by] firme and certayne reasons, and by them also confirmed, otherwise he is to be accompted rude, and an Empericke, if he hath not reason annexed and ioyned to his experience'.[64] Expertise also consisted in knowing medicines. William Bullein, who also wished to reform medicine through learning, not only stressed the importance of theory for surgery, but also wanted its practice to consist of a high level of skill and knowledge, as in the case of remedies:

Also . . . *Practica*, I meane not as the common people doe terme every trifeler, or light doer, to be a practicioner. But rather he is a practicioner, that is able to separate the qualities of ointementes, and to deserne perfectly of Herbes, Gummes, stones, trees, fruites etc. And to compounde simples togither, through knowlege, iudgement, and quicke invencion. For compounded ointmentes maketh plasters, and aleith Cerotes [hard wax or lard mixed with medicinal ingredients] and then the practitioner must minister, and the medicen must take its effect, with nature and God to give the health, through his good instrument, whom the auncient learned men doe terme, the artificiall *Chyrurgian*, to whom greate reverence was given, and wer in great estimacion somtyme, but now not very moche.[65]

The most important aspect of skilful practice was technical manual expertise. Paré, whose reputation as a skilled operator was recognised by the French Crown, was able to express that skill in words. Clowes wrote of 'that famous Chyrurgian maister Ambrose Parry' who published 'in French that learned worke of Chyrurgerie, who as it is thought, hath small understanding in the Latine tongue, howsoever it is knowen that he is not unskilfull in anie part of this art of Chyrurgerie'.[66] Much more than was the case in physic, fame as a skilled surgeon enhanced the value of one's writings. As Richard Wiseman put it in his *Eight Chirurgicall Treatises* (1676), there was an interplay between his readers' practical experience acquired on the job and the practical instructions in his surgical treatises. The more that was acquired of the former, the more the latter became understandable. Wiseman added that he had been concise rather than academically verbose, and that he had the greater credibility because he himself had done what he described:

[64] De Chauliac, *Guydos Questions*, fol. 4[r]; Gale, 'Institution', fol. 11[v].
[65] W. Bullein, *A Little Dialogue Betwene Twoo Men, the One Called Sorenes, and the Other Chyrurgerie* in *Bulleins Bulwarke of Defence* (London, 1562), fol. 5[v].
[66] Clowes, *Treatise* (1585), fol. 44[v].

I doubt not but the farther he goeth on in Practice, the more of Clearness and Plainness he will find; and the whole so much better perform'd than a meer Academick could have done it without being a Practioner himself, as a Traveller can describe a Country to one that is taking a Journey into it, more sensibly and usefully than one that hath only read it, and seen it in Maps.[67]

In addition, the invention, use and publication of novel techniques increased a surgeon's reputation. Surgical treatises, therefore, provide insights into the practice as well as into the theory of surgery. They acted as a means of practical instruction, even though their limitations in comparison with experience were emphasised, and they helped communicate descriptions of old and new operative techniques. Before discussing how surgeons treated their patients by a combination of manual expertise and of therapeutics that drew upon a pathological vision similar to that of the physicians, we must first consider the constraints upon undertaking surgery in the first place.

THE PRACTICE OF SURGERY: DANGEROUS AND INCURABLE CONDITIONS

Like Galenic physicians, who believed that some conditions were incurable, the learned surgeons listed a number of conditions on which the surgeon should not operate. Wounds to the heart, penetrating wounds to the brain, large-scale damage to the lungs, and wounds to the diaphragm, mouth of the stomach, mesentery and small intestines were considered to be usually fatal, whilst amputations, the cure of some cancers and the treatment of complications such as gangrene were uncertain.[68] Gale advised that the surgeon 'maketh no warrantyse of suche sicknes, as are incurable, as to cure a Cancer not ulcerate, or elephantiasis confirmyd: but circumspectlye to consider what the effect is, and promyse no more then arte can performe'.[69] The context of such advice was ostensibly ethical. Vicary, in the manner of the writer of the Hippocratic Oath, enjoined surgeons to keep their patients' secrets, to do their best for the poor as well as the rich, and not to covet any

---

[67] Richard Wiseman, *Eight Chirurgicall Treatises*, 4th edn (London, 1705), 'Epistle to the Reader', 2nd page.

[68] Read, 'The First Part of Chirurgery', pp. 5–7; Wiseman, *Treatises*, pp. 97–101; for the diseases deemed incurable by physicians see chapter 7.

[69] Gale, 'Institution', fols. 46ᵛ–47ʳ.

woman in a patient's house or be a drunkard, as well as forbidding them 'for covetousnes of money, [to] take in hande those cures that be uncurable, nor never set any certaine day of the sickemans health, for it lyeth not in their power'.[70] But mixed with morality came practical advice, such as not taking on any 'person, except he wyl be obedient unto their preceptes; for he can not be called a pacient, unlesse he be a sufferer'.[71] And behind the advice not to treat incurable cases lay the realisation that a surgeon's ability to attract and keep patients depended on his reputation. The obedience of patients could be temporary, and potential patients would be put off by a high death rate, the result of failed cures; as John Hall wrote, 'See . . . ye take no thing in hande, whiche incurable for to be . . . For if thou doe it will thy fame In utter shame confounde.'[72] The London Barber-Surgeons Company tried to give surgeons and patients some protection; whilst not condoning treating an incurable case, it laid down that, in all cases where there was danger of death or of maiming, the surgeon had to consult with senior surgeons of the Company and the patient should be 'presented' or examined by them.[73] Such presentations offered a measure of shelter from blame. John Hall more generally recommended consultation when the cure was 'to greate and ponderous for thee':

> Gette one or two of experte men,
> To helpe thee in that nede
> And make them partakers wyth thee
> In that worke to procede . . .
>
> And if it happe to frame amisse,
> Suspicyon can be none:
> Sythe thou haste soughte all meanes of healthe
> And wouldste not be alone.[74]

---

[70] Vicary, *Anatomie*, pp. 15–16. Clowes had such advice in mind when the friends of a clothier from the north of England who had seriously damaged his knee asked Clowes when he would be cured, as 'he is a man of great trade, and doth daily keepe many people at worke' and could not be absent; they also wanted a guarantee 'to cure him without a maime, or any imperfection to his travelling'. Clowes replied 'to these their unreasonable demands . . . I would make no warrant [guarantee] at all, neither could I set any certaine day or time when he should be made Whole': William Clowes, *A Profitable and Necessarie Booke of Observations, for All Those That Are Burned with the Flame of Gun-Powder* (London, 1596), p. 86.

[71] Vicary, *Anatomie*, p. 16.

[72] Hall, 'Expostulation', sig. Eee4^{r-v}.

[73] In ordinances of 1530, repeated in those of 1606: Young, *Annals*, pp. 584, 119.

[74] Hall, 'Expostulation', sig. Dddl^{r-v}; Hall added that joint practice checked errors and allowed the surgeon to improve on his work.

The Company fined or imprisoned those who disobeyed, such as John Frende, who on the 13th July 1568 was 'comytted to warde for a pacient dyeing under his hands and not presented', and who in 1573 offended and was fined fifteen shillings 'for not presentinge Mr. Watson of the Towne which dyed of Gangrena in his fote'.[75] In 1605, in another case, 'Pascall Lane a practioner in the art of Surgery was by our Masters order commited the Compter [a prison] for cuttinge of one Thomas Thorntons child for the stone who died presently under his hands by his neckligence and ignoraunce where he is to continue till he hath payed the fine of 40 s[hillings] for not making presentacion to the Masters of the case according to the ordere of the Company.' In addition, Pascall Lane had to pay forty shillings to the father, either as damages or for not fulfilling his contract, and it seems that 'presentations' served to protect surgeons in relation to the bargain or contract that was deemed to be made between the two parties before a cure.[76] Contracts to cure would have induced a sense of caution in some surgeons as the patient was able to sue for the money back. In 1589 the court of the Barber-Surgeons Company adjudicated on the complaint of

the wyfe of Richard Selbye of London Ironmonger plantyf against William Wyse, for that he cured not her housbonds leg as he promysed he wolde have don, and yt is ordered that William Wyse shall repaye againe of the money which he received in parte of the bargayne made betwene them and then was in the presence of this Courte payde unto Agnes the wyf of the above said Richard Selby six shillings and eight pence.[77]

The patient had to be told if a dangerous operation was proposed. Surgeons offered a type of treatment which by its nature was painful and unpleasant and, as surgeons such as William Clowes and Richard Wiseman often complained, there were plenty of empirics and other competitors who took away their customers by promising easier cures. The temptation was not to tell the patient what was in

---

[75] Ibid., pp. 316–7.
[76] Young, *Annals*, p. 327; on contracts see Margaret Pelling, *The Common Lot. Sickness, Medical Occupations and the Urban Poor in Early Modern England* (Longman, London, 1998), pp. 87–91, 224. For the eighteenth century and beyond, see Anne Digby, *Making a Medical Living: Doctors and their Patients in the English Market for Medicine, 1720–1911* (Cambridge University Press, Cambridge, 1994). For Italy, see Gianna Pamata, *Contracting a Cure. Patients, Healers and the Law in Early Modern Bologna* (The Johns Hopkins University Press, Baltimore, 1998).
[77] Young, *Annals*, p. 316; in another case when the patient, a girl, died, the father got back the gown he had put in pawn to pay the surgeon but had to pay the surgeon's boat hire of five shillings for the journey to Putney: *Annals*, p. 319.

prospect. Indeed, Vicary advised that surgeons 'shall never discomfort their pacient, and shall commaunde all that be about him that they doo the same: but to his friendes, speake truthe, as the case standeth'.[78] But in cases such as amputation, whose result was certain maiming and possible death, the patient had to give fully informed consent. The cultural and religious prohibition on medical practitioners treating the dying is here, in a sense, broken with the surgeon bringing death close to the patient, hence the need for him or her to know the possible outcome and to prepare for death. John Woodall wrote that as 'amputation . . . is the most lamentable part of chirurgery', everything else should be tried first, but since 'necessitie hath no law', the surgeon's 'Dismembring saw [should] be alwaies in a readinesse, well filed, and cleane kept in oyly clouts [cloths] to save it from rust' and:

If you be constrained to use your Saw, let first your Patient be well informed of the eminent danger of death by the use therof; proscribe him no certainety of life, and let the worke bee done with his owne free will and request; and not otherwise. Let him prepare his soule as a ready sacrifice to the Lord by earnest praiers, craving mercie and helpe unfainedly: and forget thou not also thy dutie in that kind, to crave mercie and help from the Almighty, and that heartily.[79]

Given the emphasis on the need for full disclosure of risk to the patient in serious cases, it is likely that in less serious cases many surgeons were less than frank and were tempted to be so also when a dangerous operation was in the offing. However, the protection of one's reputation against criticism was a powerful incentive either not to perform such operations or to take precautions to avoid blame. Clowes described the dilemma surgeons faced when deciding whether to treat a dangerous or apparently incurable case. He described how he cured 'a certaine traveller' who had a sword thrust through his chest and out of his back. When Clowes first saw the patient his initial reaction was to shun the case and avoid blame; he 'tolde those that were in presence, that I doubted much there was no cure in him, but that death would very shortly follow, and I was unwilling to dresse him, supposing he would die under my hand'. However, the patient begged him to 'dresse him, and take him in

[78] Vicary, *Anatomie*, p. 16.
[79] Woodall, *The Surgions Mate*, pp. 171–2, though when the patient was prepared for the operation Woodall recommended (p. 173) that 'the sharpe instruments being as neere as you can hidden from the eyes of the patient'.

cure: for (said he) my hart is good, although my wound be great'. Clowes rehearsed the two positions available to the surgeon: one was: 'the learned counsell of *Celsus*, who willed us in no wise to meddle with him that cannot be preserved . . . yet to countervaile this, I read in other good authors, that we ought in conscience to attempt all that may be possible be done, either by arte or reason for the safetie of the patient . . . for . . . many by a woonderfull and miraculous maner do escape death and are cured'. Clowes faced the choice between the imperative of the Christian duty of care, for 'if we shall leave the wounded man destitute of all aide and helpe, and so he die, we shall woorthily be called esteemed wicked, and without all charitie and humanitie', and the fear of loss of fame, good name and business, as

often times it so falleth out, that many worthy and skilful Artists are most fearfull, and very unwilling to enterprise any such great and dangerous cures, partly by reason of the slanders of backbiters and others of the like rude sort of evill speakers: for if it so fall out at any time, that some one disordered or unfortunate patient die, or chaunce to die uncured, by reason of the greatnes of the griefe or disease, then a man shall be condemned without mercie, notwithstanding all honest endevours truly performed.

As Clowes put it, the surgeon's skill could be overridden by 'Gods divine providence': it was impossible 'to foretell, know and understand, whether it be his good will and pleasure, to grant health and recoverie unto the sicke or wounded patient or not'. What Clowes, who was a pessimist about human nature, did 'know assuredly' was that a surgeon got 'more discredit and infamous reports by such bad patients, than ever they got credit by all the famous cures they have done all the daies of their lives'.[80] The London Company's regulations against its members bad-mouthing the work of fellow barber-surgeons and taking away each other's patients is an indication that Clowes was not only thinking of patients and their friends.[81]

The limitations upon what a surgeon could do were flexible; in

---

[80] Clowes, *Observations*, pp. 79–80. See also Read, 'The First Part of Chirurgery', p. 109, on taking cases where 'the wounded party be like to die' and how 'to avoid scandall to the profession, and free your selves from discredit, by acquainting his friends, or whom it most concerneth, with the danger wherein he lieth'.

[81] Young, *Annals*, pp. 119–20; on '30th April 1605 This daye Mr. Ffenton complayned of Robert Morrey for supplantinge him of divers cures. And for slanderinge him in his profession. And also for his evill practize. And was for his said abuses fyned at five pounds which hee is to bringe in at the next Court orels to be committed to the Compter': *Annals*, p. 326.

the end they were up to the surgeon and patient. But moral injunctions, guild regulations, contractual obligations to patients and concern for their reputations and for their business, constrained surgeons from attempting dangerous operations or difficult or impossible cures. Such factors not only helped to decide what operations were carried out; they were also a form of quality control, which was probably more effective in surgery than physic, 'seeing the operation of a Chirurgion is more subject to the eye and other senses, than the exhibition of medicaments is, it behoveth every one to be well verst in that which he taketh in hand, seeing his practice is more subject to censure'.[82]

PAIN, THE SURGEON AND THE PATIENT

In an era before anaesthesia and antibiotics, it is easy to assume that the world of the surgeon was filled with pain and that surgeons had to ignore it. The assumption is true but only up to a point. Pain was one of the great barriers in surgery. Pain and shock can kill, and early modern surgeons were not unaware of this. They were also very conscious that the prospect of pain could put patients off and lose them as customers. Although surgeons respected Celsus' recommendation that the surgeon be impervious to the patient's cries, for, as Bullein put it, 'softe Chyrurgians maketh fowle sores', nevertheless, Bullein added, the surgeon should not be hard-hearted nor be needlessly cruel: 'he maie not plaie the partes of a Butcher to cutte, rende or teare, the bodie of manne kynde'.[83] The other qualities of a surgeon served to mitigate pain: nimble fingers, a steady hand that did not tremble, sharp sight, quick wit, boldness and sobriety (on the last Hall wrote that it was reported of too many surgeons, 'he is a good chirurgyen in the forenone [morning]').[84] They helped to ensure that the surgeon could fulfil his occupational and ethical obligations to the patient of speed and safety and 'so lytle payne' as possible.[85]

[82] Read, 'Chirurgicall Lectures', p. 7.
[83] Bullein, *A Little Dialogue*, fol. 8[r]; Paré, on the other hand, believed that, as surgery and pain were inseparable, no one had any right to accuse a surgeon of cruelty, and he sympathised with Archagathus 'the butcher' who had been the first Greek doctor in Rome and had subsequently been driven from the city because of his cruelty: *Workes*, p. 5.
[84] Bullein, *A Little Dialogue*, fol. 8[r]; Gale, 'Institution', fol. 7[v]–8[r]; Hall, 'Expostulation', sig. Eee3[v].
[85] Gale, 'Institution', fol. 46[v], and 'A Treatise of Gonneshotte', in *Workes* fol. 13[r], where a surgeon using the trepan in gunshot wounds to the head was advised to 'worke safly, spedely, and wyth so little pains to the pacient as possible you may'.

Clearly it paid a surgeon to be as quick, safe and painless as possible, even if the advice of Celsus was not to hurry. His reputation and the numbers of his patients would increase. The fear of pain was a crucial factor in patient–doctor relations. It often determined whether patients or their relatives would agree to an operation. Bleeding, purging, cupping, etc., which were prescribed by both physicians and surgeons, were tolerated and indeed expected by patients (see chapter 8), but the knife, the saw, the trepan and the cautery were feared.

Not telling the patient what was going to happen was one strategy. Paul Barbette, for instance, discussed whether to use the lancet or the potential cautery in treating an abscess (the 'actual cautery' was the application of a red hot iron, the 'potential cautery' was the use of corrosive acids to burn away a growth or putrefaction, and was considered gentler). The potential cautery, he wrote, had 'this advantage that it does not terrifie timorous Patients, nor is painful to the Tender'; this was especially the case as his cautery of lime mixed with Holland soap 'worketh deep enough into the flesh, but yet much gentlier than the Corrosive of *Ambr. Paraeus*' (Paré had popularised the use of the potential cautery over the actual cautery). However, the disadvantage of the potential cautery was that 'it eats deeper than needs', sometimes 'through the skin and Muscles to the very cavity of the Belly' or through the peritoneum so that death ensued; it also spread out more widely than was needed with consequent needless damage. The lancet, on the other hand, allowed the surgeon to be more precise. Against the medical advantages of the lancet was 'this trouble, that many people are affrighted at it, and that it's painful'. Barbette's solution, which may have been a widespread practice, was a degree of deception: 'But the fear may be prevented by silence, and the pain is little considerable.'[86] Fear lessened the body's natural heat and its powers of recuperation; it limited the use of the cautery to cases of great necessity 'because it is horrible to the sight and apprehension; for it doth in a manner exanimate cowardly persons'.[87] Gale advised that,

---

[86] Barbette, *Works*, pp. 44–5; Henry E Sigerist, *A History of Medicine* (Oxford University Press, New York, 1961), vol. II, p. 308 cites the Hippocratic advice: 'Perform all these things quietly, skilfully, and conceal from the patient most of what you are doing. Give necessary orders cheerfully and with serenity, turn his attention away from what is being done to him; sometimes you have to reprimand him sharply and severely, and sometimes you must comfort him with attention and solicitude.'

[87] Read, 'First Part of Chirurgery', p. 12.

when the trepan was to be used, the patient should have cotton or wool put into his or her ears 'and commaunde a man to compresse wyth hys handes the Pacientes eares, lesse the noyse [of the trepan drilling through the head] make hym to muche affrayed and faynte hearted'.[88] However, given the contractual nature of patient–doctor transactions, it was expected that a patient would be informed of the proposed treatment. The wishes of the patient could override what from purely surgical considerations was the preferred procedure. Barbette wrote of the technique of burning that 'Those Diseases that can neither be Cured by Medicine, nor by the knife, require the Fire, whether they be in the soft or hard parts.' Patient choice determined how the burning was effected: 'That Burning is certainest which is made by an actual Cautrey, viz a Red hot Iron, than that which is performed by a Potential, that is by Corrosive Medicines: yet for the most part, the Patients fearfulness makes choice of this.'[89]

Sometimes relatives had to decide on a patient's behalf whether to go ahead with a surgical procedure. In one case reported by Wiseman, an eleven-year-old girl had her surgical fate decided for her by negotiation between mother and surgeon. The girl was of a noble family living in the country. She had on her cheek a 'noli me tangere', a 'tubercle' or growth which when touched became painful and hot (hence its Latin name: 'do not touch me'). Her parents wanted it to be treated for cosmetic reasons, so that she could bear to put a patch over it. As was usual, she was brought to London for expert care. Wiseman, who made a point of working in consultation with physicians, described how she was first purged and given a mercurial medicine by Dr Stanly whilst he applied topical ointments to the girl's cheek. Wiseman clearly had a policy in this type of case of first trying out gentle treatments, but here they failed. The mother, in the meanwhile, was getting impatient and 'had some thoughts of going with her Daughter into *Gloucestershire* to a Man who pretends to the Cure of Cancers'. The possible loss of a client led Wiseman to decide on extreme measures, but he needed first to get the mother's consent, though not the daughter's:

Which coming to my knowledge, I made an offer to Dr. *Stanly* (the physician in the case) to undertake the Cure by extirpating that Tubercle

---

[88] Gale, 'A Treatise of Gonneshotte', fol. 12^r.
[89] Barbette, *Works*, pp. 69–70.

by the actual Cautery. But he replying, that the very mention of it would fright them out of Town; I then proposed it by Caustick to the Lady-mother: which she accepted upon a promise not to do it while she was in Town nor then till I heard from her in the Country.

The mother sent her friends and relatives to witness the burning out of the growth, which Wiseman recorded was performed to their satisfaction – he took care to demonstrate to them that the caustic had not spread beyond the area of the growth.[90]

As with most reports of surgical cases, the patient's reaction to pain was not described in any detail. Once the operation was agreed upon by the patient and it had begun, even adult patients were unlikely to renegotiate the transaction, or back out of it. Tying down the patient and/or holding down, the methods which are described for particular operations in the surgical treatises, were physical signs that the patient no longer had much freedom of choice. However, surgeons did at times respond to a patient's plea to stop, especially in cases where the operation was a matter of cutting or burning more or less, rather than an all-or-nothing procedure such as cutting off a leg. Wiseman described his attempt to extirpate a cancer that had spread from an original 'small Excrescence' under the tongue. The patient, an army captain, had delayed consulting Wiseman, and by the time he did, it was 'encreasing and spreading, much infected the internal salivary Glandules on both sides the Tongue, all the lower *Maxilla*, and parts of the right. 'Twas fixing upon the lower Lip, the Teeth all loose, and some of them fallen out: there were also some Glands without [outside] under the Jaws.' Wiseman informed the patient's friends that it was incurable, the only hope being to burn it out, and he made it clear that the patient's consent was not gained because of any promise of cure 'but at his own desire'. The operation, which involved burning much of the mouth with different shaped pieces of red hot iron, was done over three days, giving the patient some respite and the possibility of telling the surgeon when to stop:

The next day he sent for us to meet at his Chamber in order to [proceed] the extirpation . . . we placed the Patient in a clear light, then pulled out the Teeth that lay loose, and as it were buried in the *Fungus*. Then having his Head held firm, and his lower Lip defended, I passed in a plain Chisel-cautery under the *Fungus*, as low as I could, to avoid scorching of the Lip, and thrust it forward towards the Tongue, by which I brought off that

---

[90] Wiseman, *Treatises*, pp. 117–8.

Fungus and the rotten *Alveoli* . . . then with Bolt-cauteries dried the *basis* to a crust. After with a Scoop-cautery I made a thrust at the *Fungus* over-spreading the left Jaw, and made separation of, and what was rotten of the Alveoli: then with Olive and Bolt-Cauteries, I dried [burned] that as well as he would permit and left the rest for the next day's work.[91]

After a 'good night's rest', the patient, who had clearly been less than enthusiastic, 'was chearfull, and resolved for the work'. Over the next two days Wiseman burned out the rest of the cancer that was visible, he cauterised the salivary glands from inside the mouth, and he also burned the glands under the jaw from the outside. Later, however, the cancer spread, 'the Patient not permitting me to keep down the *Fungus* [the cancer] afterwards as it arose, it quickly over-run all his Mouth, and those Glands swelled again and Apostemated [abscessed], and afterwards indurated amongst the internal Muscles of the *Larynx* and hastned his Death. Yet long before that he admitted me to use the actual Cautery, but so sparingly as it signified nothing.'[92]

Patients were driven by pain to surgeons as well as being put off from going to them. As Read put it when describing the extraction of weapons, 'if the pain be intollerable, the weapon is presently [immediately] to be taken out, although we must add pain to pain, for this being done, all pain will cease'.[93] Another of Wiseman's patients, who was suffering from an enormous cancerous mouth ulcer, when informed that the operation was always unsuccessful and extremely painful, replied: 'I had rather die than live thus.' Wiseman also commented on why he had operated on cases which he knew were likely to be unsuccessful, although such operations were considered unethical. He wrote that 'These unsuccessful Attempts may render us extream cruel to those who feel not the Misery of those poor Creatures suffer with Cancers in their Mouths.' It was the patients' response to their pain, produced by 'Cancers over spreading the Mouth eating and gnawing the Flesh, Nerves, and Bones', which rendered them unable to swallow and to eat and drink, and 'Death is their only desire', that drove them 'to try a doubtful Remedy though painful'. And, Wiseman added, to absolve himself from blame: 'What I have attempted of this kind hath been at the earnest request of the Patients and their Friends, and

[91] Ibid., pp. 114–5.   [92] Ibid., p. 115.
[93] Read, 'First Part of Chirurgery', p. 18.

by the authority of a Consultation of eminent Physicians and Chirurgeons.'[94]

The patient's ability to bear pain not only helped to determine whether he or she would agree to be operated upon; it was also a physiological sign of the patient's state. At its most basic it indicated to the surgeon how far he could proceed. Extreme stoicism allowed the surgeon to do the best that was possible. John Ward described an operation for cancer of the breast on Mrs Townsend of Alverston, where her ability to put up with intense pain led to the continued use of the knife, which was considered the optimum method, rather than of a caustic. After the initial operation her wound was opened daily:

> Every time they dress itt, they cutt of something of the cancer that was left behind; the chyrurgions were for applying a caustick, but Dr. Needham said no, not till the last [not till the end], since shee could endure the knife . . .One of the chyrurgeons told her afterwards, that shee had endured soe much, that hee would have lost his life, ere hee would have suffered the like; and the Dr. said hee had read that women could endure more than men, but did not beleeve it till now.[95]

Surgeons were taught to notice a patient's pain and to react to it, this being part of the scrutiny of the patient's condition even if not often recorded. Vigo constantly emphasised that pain was a cardinal sign. It could be a diagnostic sign; for instance, when a 'byting' medicine produced little pain it indicated 'good fleshe', but 'evyl [corrupt, ulcerated] fleshe is ever paynful, therfore byting medicines by the reason of sensibilitie of the evyll fleshe, necessarilye cause greater payne in evyl ulcers'.[96] Pain also produced pathological effects: it not only 'weakeneth the hole body' and the affected parts, but it also drew ill humours to wounds and to ulcers and created abscesses.[97] The avoidance of pain was, therefore, integrated into surgical pathology and therapeutics. For instance, in ulcers the treatment of choice was the application of drying remedies, but if the ulcer was very painful, then mollifying, pain-relieving remedies were recommended even though they tended to be moist, otherwise 'the humours [would] arryve to the ulcered place in great abundans,

[94] Wiseman, *Treatises*, p. 116.
[95] Ward, *Diary*, pp. 244–6; partly quoted in R. Porter and D. Porter, *In Sickness and In Health. The British Experience 1650–1850* (Fourth Estate, London, 1988), p. 110. See also ibid., pp. 97–132 for a wide-ranging discussion of pain and illness.
[96] Vigo, *Workes*, fol. 119[r].
[97] Ibid., fol. 104[r]; Read, 'First Part of Chirurgery', p. 25. This was a Hippocratic and Galenic view.

whyche hindreth the cure'.[98] Similarly, wakefulness was recommended for wounds as it had a drying effect upon the body, whilst sleep was contraindicated as it moistened it; but when the patient was in great pain, then he or she was to sleep, with the help of medicines if necessary.[99]

The positive avoidance and relief of pain before, during and after an operation was constantly emphasised by surgical writers. Methods of bandaging and stitching were described from the point of view of minimising pain, whilst certain topical medicines were considered too painful for some patients.[100] Large numbers of anodyne and narcotic preparations were published, some of which may have worked to a lesser or greater degree, but in the absence of any modern trials we have to be largely content with the early modern belief in their powers, though clearly some opiates worked. Read described anodyne medicines, which heat and 'gently open the pores of the body; by the subtilnesse of substance they enter into the pores, and make all the humours uniforme, they soften and loosen the part, and so it becommeth lesse apt to receive paine'. Narcotic medicines, on the other hand, 'neither take away the cause of pain, neither asswage the pain, but stupifie the part, that it cannot feel that which is painful'. Anodyne oils and cataplasms (poultices or plasters) could be made, according to Read, from camomile, dill, mallow, the roots and flowers of lilies, linseed, barley, oil of sweet almonds, 'Mans grease, Capons grease, Swines grease, Goose-grease, Butter without salte, Marrowes, creame and sweet milke,' etc. Narcotic topical remedies were made from water lilies, henbane, hemlock, deadly nightshade, mandrake, black poppy and opium.[101] In their practice, surgeons made pain-killing after an operation a matter of routine. The young girl who had her 'noli me tangere' cauterised with a caustic was given some relief when Wiseman 'washed out the Salts of the Caustic with Wine warmed, then divided the Eschar [a black slough caused by burning or corrosion],

---

[98] Vigo, *Workes*, fols. 120ᵛ, 122ᵛ.

[99] Read, 'First Part of Chirurgery', p. 26; see p. 20 on the need for dryness.

[100] See, for instance, Read, 'First Part of Chirurgery', p. 44: 'Let the stitches be distant by the distance of the breadth of the fore-finger, or the least finger at the least: for if they be too thick [too close together] they will cause the more pain.' Also, Vigo, *Workes*, fol. 124ʳ, recommending his powder of mercury rather than 'unguentum Egyptiacum' (made from verdegris or copper acetate, vinegar, alum, arsenic and honey, fol. 206ᵛ) which 'causeth great payne and inflammation . . . and therefore make the ulceres, sometyme to resiste curation'.

[101] Read, 'First Part of Chirurgery', pp. 35–6.

and washed it again with Milk, till I had freed the Eschar and the Part from pain',[102] and in many of the other cases described by Wiseman pain relief is prominent.

However, pain clearly remained a major concern to patients and surgeons. The constant association by surgeons of their work with pain is evidence that pain relief was not very successful. Pain was not only an essential part of the negotiation on whether an operation should take place or continue; it was also deeply integrated into the thinking and practice of surgeons, unlike the situation today where an anaesthetic enables the surgeon to ignore pain except as a post-operative issue, and allows the prospective patient to focus more on questions of possible danger, loss of function and cosmetic damage. Pain helped to determine the surgeon's assessment of the patient, it influenced the treatment and led the surgeon to the management of pain. Having explored the constraints placed on surgeons and patients, we should now focus on the surgeon's hand work and then on how he interpreted or visualised the body's pathological processes and the effects of his interventions.

SURGICAL TECHNIQUE AND CRAFT PROGRESS

Operative techniques have been discussed in some detail in histories of surgery. What should be emphasised is that, unlike the theoretical perspectives of surgery, from classical times through to the end of the early modern period, new surgical methods were not only being invented and old ones improved, but if made public were subject to assessment and criticism from the point of view of practical experience and patient approval.[103] For instance, Wiseman cautioned against the use of a new type of hollow needle and procedure for paracentesis, or 'tapping' out the water from the stomach of patients with ascites, publicised by Paul Barbette: 'Several Experiments I have made of that Instrument, and one lately, rather to satisfie the

---

[102] Wiseman, *Treatises*, p. 118.

[103] Such techniques are detailed in general histories of surgery such as Daniel de Moulin, *A History of Surgery* (Martinus Nijhoff, Dordrecht, 1988) and Owen Harding Wangensteen and Sarah Wangensteen, *The Rise of Surgery: From Empiric Craft to Scientific Discipline* (Dawson, Folkestone, 1978). Michael McVaugh has discussed in detail one example of such a process: 'Treatment of Hernia in the Later Middle Ages: Surgical Correction and Social Construction' in Roger French, Jan Arrizabalaga, Andrew Cunningham and Luis Garcia-Ballester (eds.), *Medicine from the Black Death to the French Disease* (Ashgate, Aldershot, 1998), pp. 131–55.

Patient and his Relations that the Swelling was an *Ascites*, than that we could propose any Cure by it.' Wiseman removed a pint of water, partly by the use of the old standby of a cannula, and, as two gallons were left 'in Opening the dead body', he felt that the needle was not practical as it would have to be inserted in many different places to evacuate the water. Moreover, patients would not stand for it: the patient 'as he was at first for the Operation, chose rather to die with the Water in his Belly, then suffer a second Apertion'.[104] In other words, surgical techniques, though they might be believed in with great passion, were not like the knowledge of learned medicine which remained essentially unchanged, even though the learning of scholars brought to light some of the operative techniques of the ancients.[105]

The craft emphasis on practicality, dexterity and the value of experience, together with the need to attract customers, meant that surgical innovation and possible (though not inevitable) improvement occurred regularly throughout the period. Material rewards in the form of increased numbers of patients helped to fuel the process; Hall advised a young surgeon who was far from any experts and faced with a bragging competitor who sought 'his infamy and dishonour', 'to be ingenious . . . to devise new remedies for new diseases'.[106] Surgical ingenuity also brought fame and praise from colleagues. English surgeons in this period were not prominent in discovering new techniques, but they were aware of new developments such as Gaspare Tagliacozzi's restoration of a nose by grafting. They took positions on Paré's conservative method of treating gunshot wounds, which replaced Vigo's use of boiling oil to burn the wound of the poison that was believed to be in the gunpowder and/ or the bullets – a belief that Paré argued was false.[107] However,

---

[104] Wiseman, *Treatises*, p. 121; Barbette, *Works*, pp. 50–3, where he writes of 'the industry' of their posterity improving upon the ancients.

[105] Such inventiveness could come from closed family operators such as the Sicilian Branca family which first invented the technique of rhinoplasty, or reconstruction of the nose by grafting, which Tagliacozzi developed and publicised in 1597, or the Chamberlens in England who brought from France the forceps for delivering babies and kept them secret throughout the seventeenth century. Once the technique was made public it was subject to critical appraisal, or, as we might now say, peer review.

[106] Hall, 'Expostulation', sig. Eee^v. The Renaissance praise of ingenuity in the arts is well known; Hall here was, as an advocate of learning, limiting it to diseases unknown to the ancients. Improvement did not necessarily follow, however, although contemporaries might think it did; see McVaugh, 'Treatment of Hernia'.

[107] For instance, Read, 'Chirurgicall Lectures', pp. 5–6 (on rhinoplasty), and 'First Part of Chirurgery', p. 157, and pp. 88–95, where he states that gunshot wounds were not

operations and surgical techniques were not carried out in isolation. Surgeons integrated their hand work with extensive and extended medical treatment of the part of the body on which they had operated and of the patient as a whole.

Time and healing

Days, weeks or months might be needed to coax an operative or a bullet wound, an amputated limb or a fracture to heal. Moreover, the usually lengthy cure of ulcers, tumours, burns and venereal diseases lay within the remit of surgery and helped to accustom surgeons to treating their patients over long periods of time by responding to the changes taking place in the operative area and in the body. Repeated consultations were normal, although, as with those of physicians, there was a popular perception that they were often unnecessarily drawn out to acquire more of the patient's money.[108] Of 600 patients that Joseph Binns treated in mid-seventeenth-century London, he saw 184 for a week or less, 211 for up to a month, 164 for between one and six months, 28 for between six months and one year and 13 for a year or more.[109]

Surgeons such as Binns provided extended care by visiting patients in their homes, or patients took lodgings near their surgeon's house or lodged in it. Many of Richard Wiseman's patients came to London from the country and took lodgings close by, such as the woman with the nodes of the pox who 'importuned me to put her in a Course of Salivation by Unction, and took a Lodging near me' (the procedure entailed rubbing the body with a mercury ointment, usually in a hot room, to produce copious salivation). In such cases as the pox, which required lengthy treatment (see below), the lodgings were transformed, as we might now say, into a hospital

poisoned *per se*, but only if poison has been added to the molten metal from which the bullets were made. Paré had argued that the smelting process would destroy any poison: Paré, *Workes*, pp. 412–13. Read, like Paré, did not recommend the use of boiling oil or caustics. Gale, who made no mention of Paré's 1552 work on gunshot wounds, argued from the authority of Galen, Dioscorides and Aetius that sulphur and nitre, the ingredients from which gunpowder was normally made, were not poisonous and so gunpowder was not normally poisonous, despite the opinion of surgeons like Vigo and Hieronymus Brunschwig: Gale, 'A Treatise of Gonneshotte', fols. 1^r–6^v.

108 Clowes wrote that in one case he was 'loth to prolong and abuse the time, as that vilde slander goeth unto Surgeons generally, but chiefly of the Surgeons of London undeserved'; *Observations*, p. 17.

109 Beier, 'Casebook of Joseph Binns', p. 52.

room adapted to the requirements of the treatment. Wiseman advised:

Your Patient ought to lodge near your house in a close warm Chamber; if the Season be cold the windows must be covered with Blankets, and the bed near the fire, and incompassed with a Screen if the Chamber be large. You ought also to have a strong healthy Nurse, such as hath been accustomed to the imployment, that she may in the absence of the Chirurgeon know how to wash the Patients mouth, and direct and encourage him in such Rules as may be neccessary in the time of Salivating.[110]

It is clear from the prohibition in the 1540 Act on surgeons doing barbering and barbers practising surgery, that surgeons lodged patients in their houses.[111] More rarely, a surgeon set up a small accommodation unit or hospital, such as that of Josias Nicholes, a surgeon of Deal in Kent, whose 'hospitall for sick and wounded seamen' with twenty-three beds was set apart from his house.[112]

Extended treatment over time meant that surgeons, like physicians, were concerned with the course of pathological events and their interpretation. But, unlike physicians, who fused together a localised and holistic vision of the body, surgeons had a strongly developed sense of localisation to which they added the physician's concern for the whole body. The drama of an operation as well as the work required to learn how to perform it was central to the surgeon's focus on the parts of the body.

The operative moment

An operation was not an isolated act; the patient had to be prepared beforehand and treated after it, but the discussion that follows should not make us lose sight of the operation itself. This was when the manual, craft training of the surgeon came into its own, and the operating table or chair was the place where the differences between surgery and physic were displayed most clearly. Precision, dexterity

---

[110] Wiseman, *Treatises*, pp. 510, 475.

[111] 'And forasmuch as such persons using the mystery or faculty of surgery, oftentimes meddle and take into their cures and houses such sick and diseased persons as have been infected with pestilence, great pox and such other contagious infirmities, do use or exercise barbery, as washing or shaving . . . which is very perilous for infecting the kings liege people': Willcock, *The Laws*, p. clxxiv.

[112] Kent Archives Office, Canterbury Consistory Court, Probate inventories PRC/27/33/160. I am grateful to Dr Richard Palmer, Librarian of Lambeth Palace, for the information.

with instruments and coolness under pressure defined the good surgeon, but not the physician. Moreover, in major operations such as amputation, the patient–doctor relationship as it applied to physic was suspended. The patient lost his or her power to refuse or change treatment or practitioner; this rarely occurred in physic unless the patient was unconscious, in delirium or considered mad.[113] Gale recommended that, in amputation, the patient should be told 'that the feare is much more than the payne', and then his eyes should be covered, and suitable persons should 'holde hys bodye and hys armes that he let [hinder] not your operation, and other apte personnes to holde the member that you wil take away'.[114] In contrast to Wiseman's cases of mouth cancer, in amputations the skill of the surgeon was exercised without interference from the patient, who, at least in surgical texts, was reduced to the leg or arm that was being cut off.

The patient having been prepared, the surgeon was in Woodall's words instructed to:

then take your dismembring knife and with a steddy hand and good speed, cut off flesh, sinewes and all, to the bone around the member, which done, take a smaller incision knife and divide the panicle called the *periosteon*, from the bone, it is a tough thin skinne, covering all the bones of the body, also thrust your said incision knife betwixt your fossels or bones, cutting away whatsoever is to be found there with like expedition . . .[115]

This reads like the instructions for cutting a joint of meat (and it is not wise to read even modern descriptions of how to amputate after having eaten a big juicy steak). But the sense that the leg was connected to the rest of the body and to a person was nearly always restored after the technical description of amputation or bone-setting. Woodall brought the reader's attention to the systems that kept the body alive when he stressed that the person holding the leg should hold 'the upper part . . . with all his strength, griping the member to keepe in the spirits and bloud'. As the surgeon's vision constantly moved to and fro between the specific part and whole body, so Woodall switched back to a localised perspective to impart a trick of the trade: 'it were also very good that the saide party holding

---

[113] See Thomas O'Dowde, *The Poor Man's Physician*, 3rd edn (London, 1665), p. 87 on the case of Mary Biggs, 'very Lunatick and a dying person . . . to whom I prescribed one Medicine, and by force got very little into her Stomach'.

[114] Thomas Gale, 'An Enchiridion of Chirurgerie' in *Workes*, fol. 54ʳ.

[115] Woodall, *Surgions Mate*, pp. 173–4.

the member, the flesh and sinewes being cut asunder, should immediately draw or strip upward the flesh so much as he could, keeping his hold, that thereby the Sawe may come so much the neerer, which would occasion a quicker and better healing, the flesh being thereby made longer than the end of the bone'.[116]

Anatomical knowledge also helped to guide the surgeon, and reminded him of the connection of the leg to the body's vascular systems. Woodall advised, if the leg was taken off above the knee, 'great care [is] to be had to the great veine and artery'. Dealing with them was a localised problem that the inexperienced surgeon might find difficult to manage: 'take them up and pierce them through, and make a strong ligature about them which must be speedily done, if thou canst do it: but at first thou wilt misse, yet be not discouraged, not stand too long to seeke them, but goe on with like hope'.[117] Wiseman suggested the 'ancient' technique of a ligature instead of 'a Gripe, which Gripe is commonly made by some assistant who hath the strength to do it . . . in Amputations it seems to me to be very inconvenient: For I never yet saw any man so gripe, but that still the Artery bled with a greater force then was allowable; yea [even] when Mr. *Woodall* griped, who was so applauded and made for the work. It being so, in what a huddle [hurried confusion] is the Stump then dressed.'[118]

The localised and more general visions of the body can be interpreted as representing the surgeon's manual skill and learned knowledge respectively. The latter consisted of an awareness of anatomy, and also of the humoral pathology which, as is discussed below, was often central to the lengthy therapeutic care provided by surgeons. Surgical discourse was not limited to describing operations, though some surgeons such as Wiseman could go into great technical detail. Throughout accounts of operations there was a concern with both the immediate and longer-term viability of the part being operated on and of the body as a whole. A rough way of putting it is that the surgeon spent some time preparing the patient, operated and secured the patient's immediate safety, and then with serious operations spent a great deal of time and effort in after-care, having laid the groundwork for it at the time of the operation.

[116] Ibid., p. 174.   [117] Ibid., pp. 175–6.
[118] Wiseman, *Treatises*, p. 427. The ligature, by preventing the stump from bleeding, avoided the panicky search amongst the operators to find the blood vessels to ligate or cauterise; it also numbed the leg and allowed it to be held steady more easily.

Before an amputation Woodall, like most surgeons, used bleeding, the standard preliminary to any medical procedure or treatment.[119] He advised it especially in gangrene to get rid of the poison in the blood. Although he stressed that, if the patient 'had a weak spent body', the surgeon should 'preserve his bloud and spirit, as carefully as if they were thine owne', Woodall added, 'and yet remembring this one rule, which all the London Hospitall [St Bartholomew's] Surgeons holde, there is more hope in a weake spent body, then in a full body'.[120] After the leg was cut through, the immediate aim was to secure the operative wound: ligating and cauterising the blood vessels, then stitching the skin together with needle and thread, and drawing the 'threds so close as you thinke convenient, the better to stop and choake the great Veynes and Arteries, then tye them fast'.[121] Then 'restrictive plegents' or medicated lint compresses were pressed close over the stump together with linen cloth, and long 'rowlers' or bandages were bound tightly round the compresses and the stump, the aim being to stop any further bleeding.

These procedures depended upon manual dexterity and technical skill learnt by example and practice; as Woodall put it, 'your rowling must be very Artificiall [technically proficient] in such a case, or all will not serve, for it exceedeth all medicines'.[122] Added to this was knowledge of medicines and diet. The compresses were dipped into medical preparations such as oil of turpentine mixed with egg yolk or other ointments designed as 'defensatives' to prevent inflammation, into 'digestives' to allow new sound flesh to grow, and into 'restrictives' to prevent bleeding. At each dressing of the wound, which could take place daily or after a few days, new and sometimes different preparations were applied to it, just as they were with lesions such as ulcers where healing and the growth of new flesh were the aim. The surgeon assessed how the wound was progressing and adjusted his medications accordingly, just as the physician did during the course of treating a patient.[123] Diet was also part of the after-care of the patient, usually consisting at first of a very 'slender diet' of broths with no meat and everything in a small amount. Surgeons, such as Wiseman, appeared to defer to physicians'

---

[119] See also Vigo, *Workes*, fol. 161ᵛ for the relationship between local and systemic measures: 'local medicines are not be applyed, accordynge to the rules of chirurgerie before purgations of the bodye'.

[120] Woodall, *Surgions Mate*, p. 175.   [121] Ibid., p. 171.

[122] Ibid., p. 174.   [123] Ibid., pp. 174, 176–7.

knowledge on matters of diet, but still advised on it.[124] Clearly, surgeons expected that they would provide complete after-care of the patient, either by themselves or together with physicians.

SURGEONS AND THE PATHOLOGY OF PUTREFACTION

The pathological vision of surgeons was based on humours and corruption. They shared with physicians the same stories of disease, albeit at times more localised. But to this has to be added the recognition that, in an era before antibiotics, infection leading to inflamed, putrefying and gangrenous flesh and finally to death was common. Surgeons easily made the link between stinking, discharging, corrupt wounds and death. As we have seen, similar associations were also made in relation to the environment and food, and characterised how physicians pictured disease within the body. Surgeons would have been influenced by the widespread cultural and medical significance of stenches and corruption, and by their own experience that confirmed what the theory of physic was teaching them. Indeed, surgical experience probably played a major role during the classical period in establishing the pathological role of putrefaction, for it is in surface wounds and lesions that the effects of putrefaction, what we now translate as infection, are most evident.

Surgeons treated the part of the body on which they were operating as if in certain respects it was a body in its own right, a microcosm, yet linked by skin, bones, nerves, blood vessels and the humours to the real body. Each part had its own humoral temperament, whilst a wound or ulcer had its excrements or discharges that indicated its state of health. The surgeon, like the physician, had to observe and smell their different types.[125] Humours, especially

---

[124] Woodall, *Surgions Mate*, p. 175; Wiseman, *Treatises*, pp. 119–20; Clowes, *Observations*, p. 102: 'I speake . . . of diet and purging which the patient wounded for the most part ought to follow . . . especially where the learned Physitions are not to be had at the seas, in great and long voiages.'

[125] Read, 'First Part of Chirurgery', p. 30. The discharges from a wound might be benign as in 'ichor', which was odourless, thin and waterish, and in 'laudable pus' of a 'white smooth and . . . uniform' consistency, 'without any ill smell'. Other 'excrements' such as 'sanies' or 'virus' were corrupt, stinking forms of ichor, which, 'if it flow from a part possessed with a cancer it is wonderfully maligne and stinking: if it issue out of a part . . . mortified by reason of a *sphacelus*, it is cadaverous [stinks and looks like dead flesh]'. 'Sordes' was another kind of foul excrement, 'compact and viscous, so cleaving to the wounded parte, that it will not be removed without the use of a firm instrument: for lint upon a probe will not bring it away': pp. 30–1.

putrid ones, could move by 'fluxion' towards a wound or ulcer, keeping it from drying and making it putrefy, or the humours in the area of the lesion could become corrupt; in both cases, inflammation, corruption and at worse gangrene resulted in the wound or affected part. Foul humours were also believed to collect and produce localised tumours and abscesses.[126] The therapeutic response was to systemically evacuate the body of corrupt humours by bleeding and purging, and locally by bleeding the area, and/or drying it with medical preparations, and by 'defending' it from foul humours by repelling medicines.[127] In Clowes' description of a gunshot wound to the shoulder, he constructed a metaphorical image of malign humours that merged with the rotting flesh and pain of the patient. The shoulder had over time become 'overgrown with corrupt and spongious flesh: the humors also were continually fleeting, corrupt and of a stinking savor, the whole ioint was marvellously swolne and sore oppressed with very great paine: by reason of the humors that were gathered about the ioint, being heated, and full of rancour and malice'. Clowes was concerned to extract the pieces of bone from the shoulder, which he did by enlarging and probing the wound and by using caustic, 'biting' medicines, but he also had to deal with the threat posed by the humours: 'I did forthwith fortifie, strengthen and defend the weake parts by applying about the ioint repelling medicines, to the intent to staie the streame, and interupt the flux of humors that was stirred up, by often searching [the wound], and also by sharpe and biting medicines'.[128]

The procedures used by surgeons reflected their views of pathology. Wounds were often kept open to prevent discharges from collecting together and corrupting. Like physicians who purged the body, so surgeons helped wounds to purge and clean themselves. Clowes, when sewing a wound, took care to leave 'a decent place for

[126] Wiseman, *Treatises*, pp. 3–6; Peter Lowe, *A Discourse of the Whole Art of Chirurgerie*, 3rd edn (London, 1634), p. 67, defined fluxion as 'a motion of the humor of the body, to some certaine part, the which either by quantitie or qualitie, or both together, may not be received by the part without offence'.

[127] See, for instance, Read, 'First Part of Chirurgery', p. 24: 'First in great wounds, from whence small store of blood hath issued, and when weak parts are wounded . . . whither superfluous humours may be turned, phlebotomy is necessary . . . If the wound hath bled but little, the part not being sufficiently dried, fluxion and inflammation may be caused.' On drying medicines see pp. 27, 53–4.

[128] Clowes, *Observations*, pp. 16–18.

the wound to purge at'.[129] Tents, made from absorbent material or hollow cylinders of silver or gold, were used to keep wounds open, and sometimes an artificial ulcer was created by caustics and prevented from healing by the insertion of a pea or thread, again with the aim of allowing the wound to purge itself of discharges. As with the environment, so also with the body: cleanliness and the elimination of filth were the surgeon's aim. Gale explained why tents were used:

First we use tentes to enlarge . . . a wounde, or mundify [cleanse] the same, and wheras matter and sanies [see footnote 125] is to be taken out of deape woundes. Secondly . . . in profounde and deape woundes, whiche of necessitye requyre a newe regendrynge of fleshe. Thirdlye in woundes whyche through the ayre are altered, and therefore are made fylthy and sanious.[130]

One of the most feared complications of surgery, apart from gangrene, was that a wound would become apostematous, that is, that an abscess would form and fill with corrupt matter. 'Apostemes' in the form of phlegmons or hot, painful boils and carbuncles could also spontaneously erupt. So important to surgery did Vigo believe them to be that, after dealing with anatomy, he began his book with the different kinds of 'aposteme' and how to cure them. The body had, he wrote, the ability to dissolve or mature them, and the surgeon could apply maturative plasters to bring them to a point and, if need be, incise them out. When this did not happen, they 'comme to putrefaction'. Again, the emphasis was on dirty, poisonous corruption: 'and [if] the coloure to waxe grene, or blacke, ye maye saye that, that Aposteme inclineth to corruption and cankerdness . . . Thys corruption . . . commeth oftentymes thorough venemous malignitie of humours, whych nature canne not amende nor moderate, nor bringe to maturation or suppuration nor to a true resolution.'[131] The surgeon had to use the systemic vision and methods of the physician to ensure that such abscesses did not recur: 'yf the bodye be fylled wyth humours, the naughtye mattyer muste be purged before medicines ben minystred upon the Aposteme. For els when resolutyon shulde be made always newe matter wolde comme.' If the body as a whole was not full of humours but 'cleane',

---

[129] Ibid., p. 86.
[130] Gale, 'Institution', fols. 49ᵛ–50ʳ; see fol. 50ᵛ for the different types of tents.
[131] Vigo, *Workes*, fol. 12ᵛ.

then only local mollifying (or softening), resolutive and digestive remedies that dealt with the local corruption were needed.[132]

There were also many medicines used by surgeons to help healing that had nothing to do with fighting corrupt humours. Agglutinative preparations that congealed blood and staunched bleeding, and cicatrizing medicines that helped the skin to grow back were listed in surgical texts in large numbers. However, the immense number of medicinal preparations as well as the pathological interpretations of surgeons confirmed the unity of medicine, for both were conspicuous in physic. This was not surprising as the learned surgical texts were designed to achieve precisely such a sense of unity.

The books on birth written by surgeons, physicians and midwives for lay women and midwives also expressed the unity of surgery and medicine. They contained diets for pregnant women and large lists of medicines to bring on the birth, alleviate pain and, if necessary, to start up menstruation again, as well as giving instructions on how to manually reposition the foetus inside the womb and help its entry into the world.[133] They also provided advice to the midwife or surgeon on dismembering a dead foetus in the womb.[134] Moreover,

---

[132] Ibid., fols. 13[r–v].

[133] See, for instance, Eucharius Roesslin, *The Byrth of Mankynde, Newly Translated out of Latin into Englysshe* [by Richard Jones](London, 1540), and *The Birth of Mankinde, Otherwise Named the Womans Boke Set Foorth in English by Thomas Raynalde Phisition* (London, 1552), my edition of 1598 is a very much changed version of the previous with many additions; Jacques Guillemeau, *Child-Birth Or, The Happy Deliverie of Women* (London, 1612); Paré, *Workes*, pp. 885–960; Iames [Jacobus] Rueff (1500–58), *The Expert Midwife* (London, 1637); Nicholas Fontanus, *The Womans Doctour* (London, 1652); Nicholas Culpeper, *A Directory of Mid-Wives: Or, A Guide for Women* (London, 1651; Edinburgh, 1668); Jane Sharp, *The Midwives Book. Or the Whole Art of Midwifery Discovered* (London, 1671); François Mauriceau, *The Diseases of Women with Child, And in Child-bed* (London, 1696); William Giffard, *Cases in Midwifry Written by the Late Mr William Giffard Surgeon and Man-midwife* (London, 1734); Sarah Stone, *A Complete Practice of Midwifery* (London, 1737). Also Percival Willughby (1596–1685), *Observations in Midwifery*, ed. Henry Blenkinsop with new introduction by John Thornton; this was first published in 1863 and reissued by S. R. Publishers, Wakefield, 1972. Rueff, Paré, Guillemeau, Mauriceau and Giffard were surgeons; Raynalde, Fontanus and Culpeper were physicians, the last two did not include much surgical content; Roesslin was an apothecary and physician; Sharp and Stone were midwives; and Willughby was a surgeon-physician.

[134] Although the standard view is that surgeons dismembered or cut up the dead foetus inside the womb, Roesslin advised midwives on how to use surgical instruments like hooks and knives on the dead foetus: *Byrth of Mankynde* (1540), fols 51[r]–52[v], and *Birth of Mankinde* (1598), pp. 144–6. The retention of the midwife as surgeon in the later edition is significant, as it was very much an English production, though sections such as this remained largely the same. Rueff, *The Expert Midwife*, pp. 106–9 similarly saw the midwife as a surgeon. Some surgeons, such as Paré, saw it as the surgeon's business rather than the midwife's: *Workes*, pp. 914–17. Jane Sharp did not mention cutting up and extracting the dead foetus, presumably because she saw it as the surgeon's job, but Sarah Stone, who

these treatises mirrored physic and surgery in creating narratives of what was happening inside the body, which were signposted by anatomical structures that were clearly described to lay readers.[135] Putrefaction and evacuation also played an important role in explaining the pathological complications of birth. As we saw in chapter 3, women, even more than men, fitted into medicine's paradigm of putrefaction and evacuation (being moist and having the natural evacuation of menstruation), and birth increased the sense of fit. By giving birth, women naturally evacuated their child, but failure to expel either the child or the afterbirth led to internal localised putrefaction and to systemic symptoms in such far-off regions of the body as the brain, heart and stomach.[136] Such accounts of pathological events created common ground between surgery and physic.

Moreover, the careers of individual surgeons, such as Banister or James Yonge (1647–1721), a sea and army surgeon, who towards the end of his career in 1702 was made a licentiate of the College of Physicians as well as a fellow of the Royal Society, and of the many barber-surgeons and apothecaries who also practised physic in the provinces and at sea, indicate that the unity of medicine was not merely a literary fiction. However, how specialist operators and others who worked on the body thought about their work remains largely hidden from us.[137]

Any discussion of surgery would be incomplete without including

delighted in attacking surgeons turned men-midwives, stressed that she had surgically extracted a dead foetus: *Practice of Midwifery*, pp. 36–9. See Audrey Eccles, *Obstetrics and Gynaecology in Tudor and Stuart England* (Croom Helm, London, 1982), pp. 109–15 for a well-informed discussion of the issue.

[135] The description of the anatomy of female, and often male, genital organs was often advertised in the contents of books on conception, birth and women's diseases, and no doubt helped to sell them. Such books provided a form of sex education and information about one's body at a time when explicit references to sex, though greater than our post-Victorian sensibilities might lead us to believe, were still scanty. They were also a source for prurient jokes for, as Thomas Raynalde's opponents pointed out, his book could lead men 'in their communications to iest and bourde of womens privities, not wont to be knowne of them': Roesslin, *Birth of Mankinde*, p. 9.

[136] For instance, Roesslin, *Byrth of Mankynde*, fol. 29ʳ: 'the seconde byrth retayned and kept within, wyll sone putrifye and rot: whereof wyll ensue yll noysom and pestiferous vapours, ascendynge to the harte, the braynes, and the mydryffe . . . the woman . . . many tymes is planly suffocated, strangled and dead of it'. See also Paré, *Workes*, p. 914, who wrote of the infant's body corrupting in the womb with vapours rising from it, travelling to the brain and heart, making the woman's face 'livid and ghastly', her breasts 'hang loose and lank', and 'her belly will be more hard and swollen then it was before'.

[137] James Yonge, *The Journal of James Yonge Plymouth Surgeon*, ed. F. N. L. Poynter (Longmans, London, 1963), pp. 214–16.

the pox, the new disease that brought the surgeon face to face with sex, sin and shame. Surgeons developed a new evacuative treatment and with it came customers and profits. The pox gave surgery even more self-confidence.

THE POX

This yere [1498] shalbe many syknesses as fevers contynuall and tercyans pestylence bledynge at nose paynes of the heed the eyes the bely and many bytwene the skynne and fleshe carbuncles pockes scabbes and such, but ther shall not many men deye thereof . . . As for the pockes and the cure of theym who lust to rede, lete theym see the latyn boke of this yere and the last and there he shall fynde that may contente his mynde.[138]

Three years before this prognostication the pox had struck the French army at the siege of Naples and forced it to disperse, thus spreading the 'French' disease throughout Europe. This became, by the end of the sixteenth century, the canonical account, with Columbus' sailors bringing it in the first place to Europe from America.[139]

The impact of the pox was immense. The mortality initially arising from it seems to have been great, though by the later sixteenth century it had lessened. It was believed that 'the disease [was] daylie dying'. It had lost its youthful vigour and had grown old and weaker, either because of the medicines used against it, or because of better personal and civic cleanliness.[140] There was frequent confusion between what we would call syphilis and gonorrhea, 'pox' and 'clap' often being used for both.[141] But the sense that the pox was a new and distinct disease was not lost, despite debates as to whether it was known to the ancients and the lumping together of what to us are different conditions under its umbrella. As with

---

[138] Anon [Prognostication for 1498] [Wynkyn de Worde, 1497], n.p.
[139] On the debate regarding whether the pox came to Europe from America, either in its venereal form or in a non-venereal form which mutated, or whether the pox was an Old World disease, see Jon Arrizabalaga, John Henderson and Roger French, *The Great Pox. The French Disease in Renaissance Europe* (Yale University Press, New Haven, 1997) pp. 4–19. See also C. F. Quétel, *A History of Syphilis* (Blackwell, Oxford, 1990); Johannes Fabricius, *Syphilis in Shakespeare's England* (Jessica Kingsley, London, 1994).
[140] Additions by John Read to his translation of Arcaeus, *A Most Excellent and Compendious Method of Curing Woundes in the Head, and in Other Partes* (London, 1588), fol. 59ᵛ, cited in Fabricius, *Syphilis in Shakespeare's England*, p. 24. Arrizabalaga et al., *Great Pox*, pp. 266–9.
[141] Arrizabalaga et al., p. 18. See Fabricius, *Syphilis*, pp. 255–68, on the confusion between syphilis and gonorrhea.

plague, the pox was seen as contagious, perhaps, as Girolamo Fracastoro conjectured in his poem *Syphilis* (1531), carried through the air by seeds of disease which corrupted it, or, as others believed, by a poisonous putrefaction transmitted by intercourse. Whatever its mode of diffusion, the effect in the body was that of putrefaction.[142]

The pox was not an ordinary disease. Its sexual transmission elicited strong moral responses. The stigma of a diagnosis of the pox was avoided wherever possible. Sufferers would be shunned by neighbours, which is why in 1577 the Barber-Surgeons Company heard

a complainte made by one Mrs Riche against Robt. Bewsy for that he had her husbonde to cure who died and the said Bewsye said and reported that she was an evell liver and that he died of a botch called Bubo veneria [i.e. of the pox] and taken of her, which he denied, but being proved she put the matter wholie to this worshipfull howse who did award that he sholde in the presence of her nighbors who were here present in the parlor upon his knees ask her forgevenes, which he did and so the matter was finally ended.[143]

---

[142] Vivian Nutton, 'The Seeds of Disease: an Explanation of Contagion and Infection from the Greeks to the Renaissance', *Medical History*, 27, 1983, pp. 1–34, and 'The Reception of Fracastoro's Theory of Contagion: the Seed that Fell Among Thorns?', *Osiris*, 6, 2nd series pp. 196–234; Wear, 'Medicine in Early Modern Europe', p. 219; Arrizabalaga et al., *Great Pox*, p. 35; Clowes, 'Treatise' (1585), fol. 4ʳ, wrote of evil and corrupt humours corrupting the liver and so poisoning the whole body; Wiseman, *Treatises*, p. 469, called the agent of the disease 'a downright venom'.

[143] Young, *Annals*, p. 319; see also the complaint in 1578 against John Gerard, the barber-surgeon herbalist: 'Here was complainte against Jo[hn] Jerrard for saying that Richard James his wief had the ffrenche pocks, and he made answere and said he wolde justifie the same, and he was dismist to the Comon Lawe' (the case was left to the ordinary courts): ibid., p. 541. See also *Annals* (College of Physicians), 3, fols. 95a–b, 1629, when Frederick Porter accused Henry Dickman, an apothecary, of diagnosing him as suffering from the French pox, telling him that the doctors would desert him and prescribing pills which ulcerated his mouth. His landlord, who had been at school with him, said that if he had known that Porter had the pox he would not have let him into the house. The landlord himself also diagnosed that it was pox, and held to it despite being 'warned by the doctors that he could not correctly diagnose that'. His maid 'moreover confessed that after she had lain in that [Porter's] bed and not knowing what ill might follow from it, had for that reason bought a potion for herself from Henry Dickman'. The College in fact diagnosed a bad case of scurf and scabies. See also Winfried Schleiner, 'Moral Attitudes toward Syphilis and its Prevention in the Renaissance', *Bulletin of the History of Medicine*, 68, 1994, 389–410, and 'Infection and Cure through Women: Renaissance Constructions of Syphilis', *Journal of Medieval and Renaissance Studies*, 24, 1994, 499–517; Anna Foa, 'The New and the Old: the Spread of Syphilis (1494–1530)' in E. Muir and G. Ruggiero (eds.), *Sex and Gender in Historical Perspective* (The Johns Hopkins University Press, Baltimore, 1990); R. Davenport-Hines, *Sex, Death and Punishment, Attitudes to Sex and Sexuality in Britain Since the Renaissance* (London, 1990); M. Healey, 'Fictions of Disease: Representations of Bodily Disorder in Early Modern Writings' (Ph.D. thesis, University of London, 1995).

A new slander came with a new disease. It joined the long list of insults that men and women, then as now, had at their disposal, as Robert Doughty, a justice of the peace, heard when in 1665 he issued 'a general warrant against Frances Riches of Bickling upon complaint of Richard Smith of the same, malster, who[m] she hath abused by words and saying he had the French pox'.[144] Samuel Pepys was desperate to avoid having his brother, Tom, labelled with the pox. In March 1664 he heard the news 'that my brother is deadly ill', and 'which is worse, that the disease is the pox'. The shame of it meant that 'if he lives, he will not be able to show his head – which will be a very great shame to me'. The diagnosis and the consequent shame were legitimised by medical authority, but it could be contested by another practitioner, which is what Pepys' cousin 'Madam [Jane] Turner' engineered: 'at noon comes Madam Turner . . . her chief errand to tell me that she had got Dr. Wiverly her Doctor to search my brother's mouth, where Mr. Powell [the original practitioner] says there is an Ulcer; from whence he concludes that he hath the pox. But the Doctor swears there is not nor ever was any.' Tom Pepys also denied to the doctor 'that ever he had that disease or that ever he said to Powell that he had it – all which did put me into great comfort as to that reproach which was spread against him'. Such was Pepys' relief that, while his brother, whom, admittedly, he disliked, lay dying, he 'sent for a barrel of oysters . . . and we were very merry'. In the evening of the same day Pepys needed more reassurance, so while his brother lay in delirium he and Doctor Wiverly 'by ourselves searched my brother again at his privities; where he was as clear as ever he was born, and in the Doctor's opinion had ever been so'. Tom Pepys died during the night and Pepys was happy to have the imputation of the pox rejected by other witnesses who would spread the word: 'I stayed till he was almost cold, while Mrs. Croxton, Holden and the rest did strip and lay him out – they observing his corps, as they told me afterwards, to be as clear as any they ever saw.'[145]

Surgeons faced real problems of diagnosis, especially in differentiating between venereal and non-venereal ulcers and pustules.[146]

[144] James Rosenheim (ed.), *The Notebook of Robert Doughty*, Norfolk Record Society, 54, 1989, p. 53.

[145] Samuel Pepys, *The Diary of Samuel Pepys*, ed. Robert Latham and William Matthews (11 vols., Bell & Hyman, London, 1970–88), vol. V, pp. 81, 85–6.

[146] Wiseman, *Treatises*, p. 469: 'I would not have any man rash in judging all Ulcers to be

Moreover, patients often refused to reveal the full facts that would allow a diagnosis to be made. In one of Wiseman's cases, the patient denied the 'visible symptoms of the *Lues* . . . but he did not acknowledge it till some few days after, and then he shewed me some corrosive Ulcers on the *penis* . . . yet denied that it was an infection of a late date [i.e. that he had had intercourse recently]'. In another case, a thirty-year-old woman from the country who came to be treated for the king's evil had an inflamed palate which aroused Wiseman's suspicions that 'her Disease was Venereal; but she denying it, I prescribed . . .' In fact, Wiseman, as we would expect from such medical case histories, recorded that he was right. Clearly, the patients' information on their sexual history and intimate symptoms was shrouded in shame and deception. In trying to draw it out surgeons might lose their patients. Wiseman, though, did not hesitate to use bullying tactics; one patient with inflamed and ulcerated eyes was questioned as to whether he ever had 'a *Gonorrhea* [a purulent discharge that Wiseman believed occurred soon after intercourse in someone infected with the pox and which was one of the first signs of the pox], he denied it faintly. I urged him farther, and looked upon his *penis* and saw a hard *callus*, the remains of a Chancre.' However, patients could refuse completely to accept a diagnosis, as with a patient who came to London with 'an inflammation on his belly . . . pretending he had overheated his body by disorder in drinking'; when told he had the pox 'he grew passionate and denied it to be Venereal . . . and to avoid the Discovery of his Disease, he dismist me and entertained another Chirurgeon'.[147]

John Graunt in his study of London's population famously commented that the stigma of the pox was avoided even in death, even though 'by the ordinary discourse of the World it seems a great part of men, have at one time or other, had some *species* of this Disease, I wondering why so few died of it, especially because I could not take that to be so harmless, whereof so many complained very fiercely'. He discovered that deaths from the pox in the London

---

Venereal that do resemble them for I have seen Nurses with chapt Nipples, and serpiginous Ulcers on the Breasts and Maids likewise in the same condition, who have been cured without any respect to the *Lues*. I have seen also many Infants broken out about the Lips, Face, Head and Body, with many suspicious *pustulae* and Ulcers that were born of chast Parents. In our public healings [the king "touching" for the king's evil] we present many such; if there be any diseased glandules found about the *musculus mastoideus*, I supposing them rather to be strumous.'

[147] Ibid., pp. 490–1, 505, 499, 489.

hospitals were certified as 'ulcers and sores', and that only the parish clerks of St Giles and St Martin's in the Fields, where 'most of the vilest and most miserable Houses of Uncleanness were', recorded the cause of death as the French pox. 'From whence', he concluded, 'that only *hated* persons, and such, whose very *Noses* were eaten off, were reported by the *Searchers* to have died of this too frequent Malady.'[148]

The pox fitted well with or was fitted into the surgeons' vision of disease. It was given a localised origin, usually the genital region, from which it spread and communicated itself to the whole body. It thus conformed to the local–general perspective of surgical pathology. Its symptoms were visible rather than internal, and lay within the surgeon's remit of skin disorders, though in the latter stages of the disease the bones were affected. The pox was also constructed or explained to fit into the prevailing aetiology of disease with which surgeons and physicians normally worked. Both sufferers and patients emphasised its putrid, corrupting nature.[149]

William Clowes, whose treatise on the pox in three different editions dominates English surgical writings on the subject in the last three decades of the sixteenth century, described the signs of the pox:

paines or aches, ulcers, nodes and foule scabbes, with corruption of the bones . . . venemous pustules, scabbes upon the forehead, browes, face and beard, and . . . about the secret partes, or in the corners of the lippes, and especially in Infants, soreness in the throat and mouth, and paines in the head, ache in the ioyntes . . . the botch about the shave bone [groin], called *Bubo Venerea.* Many times nodes and filthie abcessions or Apostumes . . . The pustules or moist scabbes differ in coolour and disposition, according to the humour which most ruleth in them . . .[150]

---

[148] John Graunt, *Natural and Political Observations . . . Upon the Bills of Mortality,* 5th edn (London, 1676), pp. 33–4. Nancy Siraisi (pers. com.) points out that there is a large question mark over how many died of the pox and whether deaths occurred in significant numbers.

[149] Ulrich von Hutten (1488–1523) gave one of the first descriptions of the early fulminant form of the disease, when the physicians 'cared not even to behold it, much less to touch the infected; for truly when it first began it was so horrible to behold . . . They had *Boils* that stood out like Acorns from whence issued such filthy stinking Matter, that whosoever came within the Scent, believed himself infected. The Colour of these was dark Green, and the very Aspect as shocking as the Pain itself, which was as if the Sick had lain upon a Fire.' As the 'Disease abated' and 'became not so filthy', the sores were smaller, 'though there is often a broad creeping Scab, under which the Poison lurketh': Ulrich von Hutten, *A Treatise of the French Disease,* rev. version by Daniel Turner of 1533, trans. T. Paynel (London, 1730), pp. 3–4.

[150] Clowes, 'Treatise' (1585), fol. 4ᵛ; a revised and enlarged version of *A Short and Profitable Treatise Touching the Cure of the Disease Called Morbus Gallicus by Unctions* (London, 1579); also

Filth, 'apostumes' or abscesses, sores and ulcers were the very stuff of surgeons' dreams, if we are to believe the surgical texts. The pox was made into the surgical disease *par excellence*. Like putrefying wounds, ulcers and cancers, it began in the 'outwarde partes', and they 'being once infected, the disease immediatly entreth into the bloud, and crepeth on lyke a Canker, from parte to parte, untill it commeth to the Lyver, where being once entred, it corrupteth the fountaines of bloud, and from thence sendeth forth the infection by the vaines, into everye parte of the bodie . . . and poisoneth the whole bodie'.[151] Nevertheless, given the learned physicians' and surgeons' shared view of pathology, it is not surprising that physicians also wrote on the pox and treated patients. Clowes recommended that the patient should be treated by evacuation, diet and 'the use of Unctions' or ointments. The advice of 'the learned Physicion or Chirurgion' was to be sought on purging. Clowes' rationale for its uses, with images of blocked passages and unripe humours, would have been familiar to both: 'it is verie expedient to purge the digested humor, and in no wyse to move the unconcocted and rawe matter. Therefore that which is thick, is to be thinned, and that which is clammie must be obsterged, and the obstructed passages must be opened, by convenient syrups and waters . . . And the humors being thus riped, are afterwards to be purged.'[152] However, when it came to diet Clowes was confident enough not to mention physicians, despite its being central to the physicians' area of expertise and Clowes' usual care in disclaiming any unnecessary intrusion into it.

The confidence came from the knowledge that 'the perfection of the whole cure', the 'use of unctions or ointments' was indisputably the surgeons' business. Surgeons and not physicians worked upon the patient's body. The cure by unctions involved placing the patient in a hot room, giving him or her a caudle or a spiced alcoholic drink, 'a good meane to procure sweat the sooner', and then next to a

---

'A Briefe and Necessarie Treatise, Touching the Cure of the Disease Now Usually Called Lues Venerea . . .' (hereafter 'Treatise' (1596)) in Clowes, *Observations*.

[151] Clowes, 'Treatise' (1585), fol. 4^r. Many of the authors that Clowes alluded to were physicians, such as Nicholas Massa and Giambatista da Monte, as well as surgeons such as Vigo. Clowes published medical remedies from both physicians and surgeons. His account of the progress of the pox in the body was unexceptionable, see for instance Bruele (one of whose remedies Clowes used), *The Physitians Practice*, pp. 389–90: from small beginnings the pox ends up by affecting the liver, natural functions and the temperature (humoral constitution) and substance of the whole body. Its cause was 'a malign and filthy quality'.

[152] Clowes, 'Treatise' (1585), fol. 5^v.

'good fire of coles' the patient would be anointed over most of the
body, except for the head, belly and 'principal' parts like the heart.
Clowes advised that patients should rub in the mercury-based
ointment 'with their owne hands if it be possible', so that the
surgeon avoided mercurial poisoning and perhaps because of the
patient's modesty. The aim after the patient was anointed was to get
him or her to sweat and salivate as much as possible and so bring out
the disease. Clowes described how the patient was put into bed with
'as many clothes as he is well able to beare', and if need be 'verie hot
brickes well wrapped in warme double clothes' or hot water bottles
were to be placed all round the patient (sometimes the patient was
encased in a hot box). After sweating for two, three or more hours,
the patient was gradually allowed to cool. After this treatment was
repeated for up to four days, salivation – 'the fluxe of flegmatike
matter' – began, which was the signal to stop anointing the patient,
'for otherwise it is verie daungerous'.[153] In addition, as with most
surgical procedures, the surgeon had to remedy the iatrogenic results
or side-effects of his work on the patient. Exposure to mercury
routinely produced ulceration, swelling and pain in the gums,
cheeks, tongue and throat. Clowes recommended medicated
gargles.[154] Like most of his contemporaries, he was also aware that
the use of mercury could produce effects almost as bad as the
disease, and that these made patients hesitate before seeking
treatment.

Constraints upon surgeons

Not only was the pox made into a disease that fitted well into the
theoretical and practical frameworks with which surgeons were
familiar, it was also a disease that brought them patients and profits.
A large number of Joseph Binns' clients were patients with the pox,
and James Yonge was able to sum up his business for 1679 as having
been 'the best practice – especially for the pox – that ever I had. By
that one disease I got this year above £120.'[155] It was also a disease
in which the surgeons' mercurial treatment became the standard
against which others were judged or to which they were advertised

---

[153] Ibid., fol. 16ʳ–17ʳ.

[154] Ibid., 17ʳ⁻ᵛ; if they did not work, which often was the case, he advised that a 'good
Mercury water', or a caustic such as Egyptian ointment, be placed on the ulceration.

[155] Beier, 'Casebook of Joseph Binns', pp. 48–84. Yonge, *Journal*, p. 162.

as more effective alternatives. Decoctions of guaiac wood were seen for a while as an alternative to mercury, but by the later sixteenth century mercury had regained its place as the primary treatment for the pox. This was less, I suspect, because guaiac was judged as unsuccessful in the modern sense of cure, and more because the evacuative effects of mercury were dramatic and visible, with patient and practitioner convincing themselves that, with the sweat and saliva, there also exited the putrefactive matter that produced the pox. In addition, mercury had traditionally been used for skin diseases. Certainly, Clowes believed that the cure for the pox had been found, and he cautioned his 'country men . . . speedily to amend their lyves, least the Lorde God, in his iuste wrath, doe one daye make the disease to be incurable'.[156] In practice, Clowes was not always successful in the eyes of contemporaries. In 1575 there 'came' to the Barber-Surgeons court 'one William Goodnep and complayned of William Clowes for not curing hies wief de morbo-gallico [the French disease, the pox] and yt was awarded that the saide Clowes sholde either geve the saide Goodnep 20 s[hillings] orells cure his saide wief'. Clowes was not so confident that he could do so: 'which Clowes agreed to pay the 20 s[hillings] and so they were agreed and eche of them made acquittance to other'.[157]

However, surgeons did not have it all their own way. Large numbers of practitioners offered cures; as Bullein put it, 'Purgations venerous there be so many practitioners thereof, that I neede to write no rules but this, that affection, lust, and fantasie have banished chastitie, temperance and honestie.'[158] Some clearly were barbers despite the prohibitions on their treating patients with the pox.[159] Others were empirics, some of whom offered to satisfy the special needs of poxed patients. Secrecy, an escape route from moral condemnation, and pain-free treatment were promised. The need for secrecy was often prominent in sufferers' and practitioners' minds. Pepys heard of his brother being diagnosed with the pox through 'a secret told his [Tom's] father Fenner by the Doctor

---

[156] Clowes, 'Treatise' (1585), fol. 2^r; see also fol. 5^r, let 'no man looke for helpe therby, but such as fully purpose to live honestly: for that God otherwise will bring a curse upon the verie medicines, and take away the benefit of healing, by that meanes'.

[157] Young, *Annals*, p. 427; for a complaint against another surgeon for failing to cure a patient with the pox see p. 426.

[158] William Bullein, *The Government of Health* (1st edn, 1558; London, 1595), fol. 23^{r-v}.

[159] See the Act of 1540, footnote 111; Young, *Annals* p. 320, on prohibition by the Lord Mayor in 1583.

[Powell]'. Clowes wrote that some 'for shame dare not to be-wraye it' or disclose it and seek help.[160]

Moral condemnation for sexual immorality came together with the pox. As we have seen already, medical moralising about lifestyles was not unusual (see chapter 4). If the patients were poor, such as the inmates of St Bartholomew's, half of whom according to Clowes suffered from the pox, then the same vitriolic condemnations used against masterless men and vagabonds, who were seen as posing a threat to Tudor social order, were applied to them. They were, wrote Clowes, filthy like the disease. The 'huge multitudes', which were infected, 'staine . . . the whole nation'. The causes of the epidemic were the 'beastly disorder of a great number of rogues and vaga-bonds, the filthy lyfe of many leude and idle persons, both men and women about the Citie of London, and the great number of leude Ale-houses, which are the very nestes and harbours of such filthy creatures'. And he hoped 'that the magistrates seeke correction and punishment of that filthie vice'.[161] One feels sorry for Clowes' hospital patients, many of whom had been coerced into becoming inmates. Clowes was not beholden to them or to their fees, and he could afford to condemn them. But all patients of whatever social standing seemed to be stigmatised, since the pox 'is said first to be ingendred by the unlawful copulation and accompanying with uncleane women, or common harlots'.[162]

However, there was a way out for the respectable. Sexual inter-course was, according to Clowes, not the only means of catching the pox: 'this sicknesse is many times bred in the mouth by eating and drincking with infected persons, sometimes in other parts of the bodie, some time lying in the bed with them [this often happened, with no implication that intercourse would occur], or by lying in the sheetes after them. Sometime . . . by sitting on the same stoole of easement [toilet], where some infected person frequenteth [a lay view that has persisted to the present day] . . .'[163] A strong piece of empirical support was the fact that wet nurses and babies caught the pox from each other. Clowes had also seen victims of the pox

---

[160] Clowes, 'Treatise' (1585).   [161] Ibid., fols. 2ʳ, 1ᵛ.

[162] Clowes, 'Treatise' (1596), p. 150.

[163] Clowes, 'Treatise' (1585), fol. 3ᵛ, cited in Margaret Pelling's admirable discussion of Clowes in her 'Appearance and Reality: Barber-Surgeons, the Body and Disease' in A. L. Beier and R. Finlay (eds.), *The Making of the Metropolis: London 1500–1700* (Longman, London, 1986), pp. 99–100.

without any marks of the disease on their genitalia.[164] On the other hand, although Wiseman agreed that children could be infected by their parents and that wet nurses and children could infect each other, he did not believe that infection could occur by 'other secundary means', such as sitting on the same toilet seat as an infected person or using the same clothes. He realised, however, that this was what patients wanted to hear: 'These are all such convenient excuses for the more shie and coy Patients who will not otherwise be brought to confess their distempers, that it is a pity to discountenance them.'[165] Perhaps, in the light of this, he modified his views along gender lines. Most people of sound constitution, and especially men, he wrote, only caught pox by intercourse, and some bodies would be resistant to it whilst others caught it, for, Wiseman explained, 'in the generality of Patients, we find the disease not so active as to conveigh it self from the subject to another without actual coition'. But some people, he conceded, 'may be infected with the tenth part of what another would escape from', either through prior illness or, especially if they were women, because 'the softness and tenderness of [their] Sex renders them liable to very quick impressions'.[166]

Not only did patients want to avoid the stigma of the disease, they often hoped to escape its standard treatment. Mercury was dreaded; its normal side-effects as noted above by Clowes were bad enough, but when used in excess or repeatedly they could be disastrous. Ulrich von Hutten (1488–1523), an itinerant German scholar and doctor and a sufferer from the pox himself, who wrote one of the first descriptions of the disease, also described how patients who were anointed with mercury and then heated suffered: 'their Throats, their Lungs, with the Roofs of their Mouths were full of Sores, their Jaws did swell, their Teeth loosen'd and a stinking Matter continually was voided these places'.[167] Mercury, which was known to the Arabs as an ingredient in topical ointments, was used instead of the initial method of burning the lesions of the pox. It was

---

[164] Clowes, 'Treatise' (1585), fols. 2ᵛ–3ᵛ; also 'Treatise' (1596), p. 151: 'three good and honest Midwives' who caught the disease from 'bringing abed three infected women, of three infected childred, which infection was chiefly fixed upon the Midwives fingers and hands': Pelling, 'Appearance and Reality', p. 100.

[165] Wiseman, *Treatises*, p. 468.

[166] Ibid., pp. 468–9.   [167] Von Hutten, *Treatise*, p. 9.

essentially a surgical remedy.[168] Physicians often opposed its use, especially when it came to be associated with Paracelsianism.[169] Surgeons acknowledged that mercury was believed to lead to very serious side-effects, such as 'putrified' bones. John Banister noted that the healthy suffered when exposed to it:

which thing I have observed in Barbours, and my servants, which used to annoint these pacients, being ignorant of the effect of the medicine, whome straight way feared themselves to be catcht with the same disease, bicause they were urged [impressed upon] with the lyke accidents, as those pacients whome they had annoynted, that is to say with flux of the belly, or mouth, eating of the gummes, stinking breath, inflammation, ulcers etc.[170]

Surgeons protected themselves by wearing gloves or getting the patient to rub in the mercury.[171] Whilst they accepted that it produced dangerous side-effects for the patient, they swore by it. In the surgeons' eyes the powers of mercury were extraordinary: it 'driveth back al things that it meeteth, and enlargeth the wayes, and expelleth whatsoever humour it findeth, and this moving ceaseth not, until the thick burnt, and flegmatick humor be repulsed by the force thereof'.[172] Or, as Wiseman wrote in the language of the new science, 'we find not yet any other medicine Mineral, Vegetable or Animal that can imitate it'; it had the power of 'Salivation, by vertue of which it melts down the serum of the blood, and with it all the acid venom contracted in it by this disease, bringing it away by the mouth'.[173] Mercury was attractive because it appeared to be the supreme evacuative medicine, and also because it healed ulcers and sores (though it was also recognised that it could cause them).[174] It

---

[168] Ibid., p. 8; Fabricius, *Syphilis*, p. 33; Vigo, *Workes*, fols. 160[r]–164[r] does not, as far as I can see, recommend actual cautery, despite Fabricius' assertion at p. 69, *Syphilis*. For a discussion of the dangers of the available treatments for the pox see ibid., pp. 33–56.

[169] Before the influence of Paracelsianism, Vigo stated, 'I knowe not why the phisicions shulde condempne medicines made wyth quycksylver': *Workes*, fol. 162[r]. John Banister, *An Epilog* in Clowes, 'Treatise' (1585), fol 50[v]: 'the moste sorte [of physicians] doe detest Quick silver'.

[170] Banister, *Epilog*, fols. 50[v], 53[r]; he explained that quicksilver was not a poison *per se*, but produced a movement in the humours which, in the healthy, by collecting in parts of the body in too large an amount and staying too long, became putrid: fol. 53[r]. Cited also in a different context in Pelling, 'Appearance and Reality', p. 101.

[171] Clowes, 'Treatise' (1585), fol. 16[r]; Wiseman, *Treatises*, p. 475.

[172] Banister, *Epilog*, fol. 51[r].   [173] Wiseman, *Treatises*, p. 480.

[174] Woodall, *Surgions Mate*, p. 194: 'repelling and cooling hot humors . . . it is so extreame subtill and penetrative . . . and being in the body, so volatill and busie, so causticke and corrosive, so extreame Laxative, so diaphoreticke, so diauereticke, so mundificative, so incarnative and so sigillative or siccatrizing, as the like medicine by the art or wit of man was never found out'.

was 'the Surgeons friend, his worke thou canst begin and end', but Woodall added:

> But mend thy faults . . .
> For many a guiltles man thou has lam'd
> and many a modest wight [man] defam'd.[175]

Surgeons mitigated the dangers of mercury by a variety of strategies. Other, unskilful people, 'horse-leeches and bauds', 'fooles', wrote Woodall, caused the greatest damage, whilst knowledgeable surgeons curbed mercury's effects; learning, as in other areas of medical practice, provided safety.[176] The medicine could be weakened or, as Clowes put it, 'its mallice and force . . . may be killed sufficientlie to be used', by being prepared in different ways and mixed with other ingredients. New preparations, such as mercurius dulcis (calomel, mercurous chloride), noted by Woodall, promised greater safety, and Wiseman in the later seventeenth century advocated a graduated use of mercury, beginning with weaker preparations taken by mouth and only 'when the *Lues Venerea* is grown inveterate . . . and the habit of the body debilitated and vitiated by the frequent exhibition [use] of Mercury, it then requireth a more powerful Remedy, *viz.* Salivation by Unction'.[177]

However, patients faced with rotting bones and ulcerated mouths with 'their Uvula or roofe of their mouth eaten away, whereby they have lost their speeches and voices . . . their teeth . . .' may well have wished to avoid treatment with mercury, and might have disagreed with Clowes that 'extreme remedies are to be used against extreme diseases'.[178] Empirics offered non-mercurial treatment. When Wiseman gave up on one of his unco-operative patients, 'the next news I heard of him, was, that one pretending to Chirurgery had undertaken the Cure of it by bathing it with a Decoction of *Broom*'.[179] As well as avoiding 'the dangerous use of *Mercury*', empirics also offered secrecy and an escape from shame, as the advertisement in figure 1 illustrates. Taking a medicine brought by a messenger, as advised in the advertisement, also avoided the need to

---

[175] Ibid., pp. 302, 305.   [176] Ibid., pp. 300, 305.
[177] Clowes, 'Treatise' (1585), fol. 24ᵛ; Woodall, *Surgions Mate*, pp. 300–1; Wiseman, *Treatises*, p. 475.
[178] Clowes, 'Treatise' (1585), fols. 18ʳ, 25ʳ.
[179] Wiseman, *Treatises*, p. 501; Wiseman, p. 472 wrote of the 'wickedness of many Pretenders, who will in this Cure declaim against the use of Mercury'.

Figure 1 'Three Infallible Cures . . .': an advertisement for a cure for the pox. (from the British Library collection of medical advertisements, c. 112.f.9. By permission of the British Library.)

visit and be interrogated and examined by someone like Wiseman. Modesty was also preserved. Although physicians probably did not undertake extensive physical examinations, surgeons by the nature of their job were more likely to. Wiseman was aware that a surgeon might be constrained in touching a patient – 'anointing of the Legs and Arms (or Thighs, if modesty prevent you not)' – but he regularly carried out examinations of the genital areas of both men and women, not only in relation to the pox but also for discharges and for cancers.[180] However, modesty and the fear of mercury, as well as the desire to avoid shame and publicity, were, no doubt, powerful disincentives to going to a surgeon. The conjunction between mercury treatment, loss of modesty and death was evident in a case at Rochester Assizes in February 1601:

One Tristram Lyde, a surgeon, admitted to practise by the archbishops letters, was arraigned for killing divers women by annoyntinge them with quicksylver etc. Evidence given that he would have caused the women to have stript themselves naked in his presence, and himselfe would have annoynted them; that he tooke upon him the cure, and departed because they would not give him more than their first agreement [the money they first agreed on, or first instalment]. He pleaded theire diseases were such as required that kinde of medicine, that it was there owne negligence by takinge cold, by going abroade sooner than he prescribed, soe he was acquited.[181]

Despite the disadvantages that they faced, and the general fear of their treatment among the public, surgeons succeeded in creating belief in the value of their work. The pox was made into a surgeon's disease, and its cure, centred on mercury's evacuative powers, appealed to the deepest therapeutic instincts of the age. For surgeons the pox was a success story. Taken as a whole, surgery provided a counterbalance to the theoretical side of physic. Yet, as we have seen, it also shared with physic its view of the interconnected body, liable to putrefaction and cured by evacuation. This was despite the fact that surgery was quite different from physic. Clearly, not only did literate lay people and physicians share a common medical culture but so did surgeons.

Plague, the subject of the next chapter, was different from the pox. Unlike the pox which, after its initial virulence, killed its victims only

---

[180] Wiseman, *Treatises*, pp. 475–6, 487, 100. See also Pepys, *Diary*, vol. I, pp. 213, 216, 279, and vol. IV, pp. 347, 383–5. Pepys' wife, Elizabeth, had a 'pain in the lip of her *chose*' and when it recurred Pepys and his surgeon, Thomas Hollier or Holyard, who often worked with Wiseman, 'went about our great work to look upon my wife's malady in her secrets'. The episode is discussed in A. Wear, 'Interfaces: Perceptions of Health and Illness in Early Modern England' in R. Porter and A. Wear (eds.) *Problems and Methods in the History of Medicine* (Croom Helm, London, 1987), pp. 233–5.

[181] Robert Parker Sorlein (ed.), *The Diary of John Manningham of the Middle Temple, 1602–1603* (University Press of New England, Hanover, New Haven, 1976), pp. 23–4; the strength in the belief in the danger of cold is notable.

after many years, the plague did so in a few days and in vast numbers. Against the plague all the forces of medicine as regards knowledge and practice were deployed, as were those available to the state and religion, such was the threat posed by the disease to society.

CHAPTER 6

Plague and medical knowledge

SUMMARY

The next two chapters are about plague, the most multifaceted of early modern diseases. Its fatal impact upon the population has aroused the interest of demographers, whilst social, religious and medical historians have examined the complex and often interrelated responses that it elicited. The medical understanding of the cause and spread of plague and of how to prevent and treat it was disseminated to the literate part of the population by numerous plague treatises, and by the advice of the College of Physicians appended to the Plague Orders (first issued in 1578 and unchanged until 1666), together with the Orders themselves and other national and local regulations which justified measures on medical grounds. After discussing the people whom medical writers believed were most liable to contract plague, I will consider a central issue: whether it was thought possible that plague could be treated. This basic question has been generally ignored by historians. As the answer was a qualified yes, the accounts about how the plague entered the body and where it came from were not put forward in the context of fatalistic despair. In chapter 7, the focus will be on the practical advice given on preventing plague and on the instructions on how to treat it.

Both chapters show that traditional medical knowledge from the regimen genre and from well-established theories of disease causation is prominent in the medical understanding of the plague. Most historical accounts of the medical construction of plague have treated it as isolated and free standing in relation to the rest of medicine. There were also breaks with and partial repudiations of the past, coming, as so often was the case, in the second half of the seventeenth century. Medicine, as is discussed at length in chapter 8, was affected by the development at that time of a new natural philosophy or science which replaced Greek, and especially Aristotelian, natural philosophy. This meant that the theoretical foundations of Galenic learned medicine were undermined. The plague poison and its transmission were re-interpreted by the language of the 'new science' in chemical, corpuscular terms, and its source was seen as universal rather than localised. The logical consequence was to make plague less amenable to preventive measures such as the cleansing of cesspits, but plague disappeared from England around this time, so it is impossible to know whether preventive policies would have been changed. Despite such breaks, continuities abound, such as the central role played by putrefaction both in the identification of sources of plague and in explanations of how plague destroys the body. The one novelty, the early recognition that plague was contagious, was easily integrated with the putrefactive theory of disease.

What I have also tried to capture is how medical writers, although they recognised and helped to spread abroad the fear and horror that the public had of plague, at the same time offered hope to the same public that plague could be cured and provided them with advice on avoiding plague whilst living in the midst of it. Here it seems as if medical knowledge, consciously or unconsciously, was tailored to the needs of preserving social order; or, maybe, rather than social interests being at play, it was more a matter of humanity: of providing some hope at a time of intense fear.

INTRODUCTION

Together with war and famine, plague was one of the three arrows of God. Thomas Dekker, the great literary commentator on plague, expanded on the martial image and wrote of a plague outbreak as a great battle fought by God against the sinful nations of mankind. During the plague of 1625, when 'None thrive but Apothecaries, Butchers, Cookes and Coffin-makers', he warned that:

Wee are now in a set Battaile; the Field is *Great Britain*, the Vantguard (which first stands the brunt of the Fight) is *London* . . . the king of Heaven and Earth is the Generall of the Army; reuenging Angels, his Officers; his Indignation, the Trumpet summoning and sounding the Alarum; our innumerable sinnes, his enemies; and our Nation, the Legions which he threatens to smite with Correction.[1]

---

[1] Thomas Dekker, 'A Rod for Run-awayes. Gods Tokens of his Feareful Iudgements' (1625) in

In the battle, mortality was immense and immediate. Huge numbers died within a few days of 'being struck down' and some were reported as dying suddenly, without warning, in the streets. Not surprisingly plague, more than any other disease, elicited religious, social and political responses. In times of plague, matters of illness and death were on everyone's lips, and became of concern to local and central government as they rarely did otherwise. Clergymen also reacted to plague in a more intense and sustained way than any other illness, seeing it as one of the greatest manifestations of God's power. By the sixteenth century English governments felt they had to act to control the spread of plague and provide some help for its victims.[2] Moreover, medical practitioners faced a supreme test of their art, their knowledge, procedures and remedies; plague posed the ultimate challenge. Its spread and its mortality seemed to argue for its immunity to preventive measures and to medical intervention. Indeed, for the few who publicly stated that plague was sent directly by God rather than by God acting through secondary or natural means, plague could not be cured by natural means; only prayer and repentance might avert his anger. If modern historical demographers have detected a decline in the number of plague outbreaks and in their mortality from the sixteenth to the seventeenth century, contemporary writers appear to have been unaware of it. For them the visitation of God was as punishing as ever. Indeed, it was two seventeenth-century plagues, those of 1603 and 1665, that were successively called 'the great plague' following the 'great plague' of

---

F. P. Wilson (ed.), *The Plague Pamphlets of Thomas Dekker* (Clarendon Press, Oxford, 1925), pp. 139–40.

[2] The standard, and magisterial, account of such measures, and for plague generally, is Paul Slack, *The Impact of Plague in Tudor and Stuart England* (Routledge & Kegan Paul, London, 1985). On cultural perceptions of plague see also M. Healy, 'Fictions of Disease: Representations of Bodily Disorder in Early Modern Writings' (Ph.D. thesis, University of London, 1995) and 'Discourses of the Plague in Early Modern London' in J. A. I. Champion (ed.), *Epidemic Disease in London* (Centre for Metropolitan History, Institute for Historical Research, London, 1993), pp. 19–34; Colin Jones, 'Plague and its Metaphors in Early Modern France', *Representations*, 53, 1996, 97–127; A. Wear, 'Popularised Ideas of Health and Illness in Seventeenth Century France', *Seventeenth Century French Studies*, 8, 1986, 229–42. The older works by Walter Bell, *The Great Plague of London*, (1st edn, 1924; Bracken Books, London, 1994) and F. P. Wilson, *The Plague in Shakespeare's London* (Clarendon Press, Oxford, 1927) are still very useful. See also J. F. D. Shrewsbury, *A History of Bubonic Plague in the British Isles* (Cambridge University Press, Cambridge, 1970) which has much useful information and focuses on the biological-epidemiological aspects. For a detailed demographic-social analysis of London and the 1665 plague see J. A. I. Champion, *London Dreaded Visitation. The Social Geography of the Great Plague in 1665*, Historical Geography Research Series 31, 1995.

1563.[3] However, despite the immense destruction of plague and its close association with the wrath of God, medical writers exuded quiet (or sometimes clamorous) optimism that plague could be prevented and cured, as they drew upon the knowledge and practices of medicine, surgery and pharmacy, and of regimen and environmental health. Against plague all the resources of medicine were brought into play.

Moreover, medical practitioners faced moral dilemmas. Their most important decision was whether to flee or stay with the plague victims. There was also debate on the moral and medical justifications of the policy of 'shutting up', whereby when someone was diagnosed as having the plague they and the healthy members of the household were shut up together in the house for forty-two days. And plague, as no other disease, brought into close proximity religious and natural explanations of illness and death. Generally, there was little open conflict between the two, but some religious and medical writings indicate implicit tensions and in a few cases religion and medicine clashed.

THE HORROR OF PLAGUE

Anyone reading one of the numerous plague treatises, which were usually brief – around twenty to seventy pages long – might initially have felt their heart sink. The horrors of plague were conveyed by medical writers in religious as well as medical rhetoric. It was not until 1665 that the religious element, which is most conspicuous in the prefaces and introductions of the plague treatises, declined. Medical writers began, like their religious counterparts, by stressing that plague exceeded all other diseases in its destructiveness. In their evocations they mixed together medicine and religion, illness and sin: their opening pages echoed the language of the pulpit and the religious treatises on plague. For instance, Thomas Phayre wrote in his *A Goodly Bryfe Treatyse of the Pestylence* (1545) that after the Fall of Adam 'synne had entered in to the world, and by synne deathe'. But since that time,

our corrupte lyvynges have made us more corrupte, so that nowe the lyfe whych we leade here is not very pleasaunt unto the mooste of men . . . it is excedyng grevous, sorowfull, and tedyous, subject to diseases, infortunes,

---

[3] Slack, *Impact of Plague*, p. 54.

and calamities innumerable, which for the moost part done encrease dayly, ever the iust vengeaunce of God fallyng upon us for our greate abhominations, and without doubt wil ever more endure, unlesse we do repent, and lyve in hys commaundements.[4]

Just as plague poison, the physical cause of plague, was widespread and caused a 'public' disease, so public sins, the spiritual causes or contagion of plague produced also a public, communal, judgement of God, a plague epidemic. 'Consider', declared William Gouge, a prominent London Puritan minister, 'how farre the contagion of these publique sinnes spreadeth it self. For when the infection of a sinne is diffused all abroad, farre and neare, the lord is forced to send some publique judgements, thereby as it were with a fire to purge the aire. "All Israel have transgressed (saith Daniel) therefore the curse is powred upon us".'[5] The physical corruption of plague was mirrored in the spiritual corruption of sin. Diseases were part of the world of calamities and misfortunes; they were created by God to punish mankind, and consisted, wrote Phayre, of 'the hole swarme of so manye, bothe olde and newe diseases, wherewythe the bodye of man (alas for our synnes) is continuallye tourmented and vexed'.[6] Above all the rest stood plague, which elicited a European-wide rhetoric of horror that stretched back to Boccaccio's description of the coming of the Black Death to Florence in 1348, and beyond that to Thucydides' account of what contemporaries identified as the plague of Athens in 430–27 BC. Plague, the 'scurge of God', surpassed all other diseases: 'What disease is there in the worlde, so venomous in infectynge, so full of paine in suffrynge, so hastye in devourynge, and so dificile in curynge, as the plage is?' Medical writers relied on religious as well as medical reasoning to justify their belief that plague could be prevented and cured. As with other illnesses sent by God, repentance and the medicines provided by God mentioned in Ecclesiasticus could turn aside his wrath: 'to them that doo repente, and put theyr onelye truste in hym . . . that even in the myddest of all the sayde afflictions, provydeth them of remedyes, lest they shulde dispayre, cureth and amendeth all their grevous sores, languours and diseases, he created medicines even out

[4] Thomas Phayre, 'A Goodly Bryfe Treatyse of the Pestylence' in *The Regiment of Life* (London, 1545), sigs. Li^v–Liii^r (properly Lii^r); the 'Treatyse'; is based on the *Regime Singulier Contre la Peste* (*c.* 1530) of Jehan Goeurot.

[5] William Gouge, *God's Three Arrowes: Plague, Famine, Sword, in Three Treatises* (London, 1631) p. 7. The reference to fires purging the air refers to a common practice (see chapter 7).

[6] Phayre, 'Treatyse of the Pestylence', fol. L3^r.

of the earth, and of the wyse man it shal not be despysed'.[7] God's punishment was directed at individuals and groups. Medical writers, like their religious counterparts, analysed who was most at risk and why. Their answers exhibit a mix of medical and moral reasoning.

THE PLAGUE, GROUPS AND INDIVIDUALS

Plague forced English medical writers to acknowledge that society mattered. The apparently contagious nature of plague brought groups and communities and not just individuals into medical view. Plague was both a public and a private disease. It hit whole communities, as well as being an illness that killed individuals. The discourses of the plague treatises, in contrast to the patient-centred focus of most medical writing, addressed themselves to a population, 'the City', 'England', etc. and, often using a distinctly different voice, to the individual man and woman. Explanations for the plague to some extent mirrored this duality. Large populations suffered from plague because of God's providence, which showed itself by a contagious plague poison that came from particular localities and from plague victims or from a source such as the centre of the earth from where it permeated the whole world. Certain individuals were believed to be predisposed to catching plague, which was often explained in terms of their humoral make-up. People of humid and hot constitutions were especially in danger as their pores were most open, so letting the plague poison enter more easily.[8] In other words, it was something very personal, the constitution of one's body, that made one liable to the plague. This allowed learned medicine's personalised treatment to continue to be used in a disease that, by the sixteenth century, was generally recognised to be contagious. It also spoke to the intense sense of vulnerability felt by individuals during a plague epidemic. In addition, other factors such as age or pregnancy, moral characteristics or aspects of lifestyle with moral connotations like over-eating and drinking, were all considered as predisposing causes. In general, contagion was used as a basis for explanation at the community-wide level, while a mix of contagion and humoral reasoning was employed to explain the onset of plague in the individual.

---

[7] Ibid., sigs. L3^r–L4^r.

[8] For instance, Thomas Cogan, *The Haven of Health* (1st edn, 1584; London, 1612), p. 255, wrote that plague was common to people of all complexions, but some complexions were more apt to receive it. See Slack, *Impact of Plague*, pp. 28–9

THE MEDICAL VISION OF PLAGUE AND THE POOR

The public/individual distinction made by medical writers, although widespread, was not always clearcut and it hid a range of continuities and connections between the two. Not only individuals but groups within the population were viewed as being at higher risk. One group, the poor, was so large that it was seen as part of the 'public' or population-wide aspect of plague. Of all groups the poor were perceived as suffering disproportionately to the extent that by the seventeenth century plague was often taken as a disease of the poor.[9] This was a perception shared by medical writers, religious writers, governments and the literate public, and is a reflection of how medical attitudes to the social and moral implications of plague were shaped by the wider beliefs and prejudices that surrounded the disease.

The vulnerability of the poor to plague was recognised across time:[10] in William Bullein's *Dialogue Against the Fever Pestilence* (first edn 1564), *Civis* says that if the plague continues unabated, 'It will not onely take awaie a number of poore people, but many wealthie and lustie Marchauntes also.'[11] The association of the poor with plague continued until the last great plague in England, of which Nathaniel Hodges, a Fellow of the College of Physicians who stayed on in London to treat plague victims wrote, in his *Loimologia: Or, An Historical Account of the Plague in London in 1665* (English translation, 1720) that 'it is incredible to think how the Plague raged amongst the common People, insomuch that it came by some to be called the *Poors Plague*'.[12]

In London especially, the poor and plague were associated through geography. Plague was recognised as spreading from the

---

[9] Slack, *Impact of Plague*, pp. 194–5.
[10] The connection between the plague and the poor was made by the administrators of late fifteenth-century Florence; see Ann G. Carmichael, *Plague and the Poor in Renaissance Florence* Cambridge University Press, Cambridge, 1986), pp. 1, 103–7, 123–6.
[11] William Bullein, *A Dialogue Against the Fever Pestilence*, ed. Mark W. Bullen and A. H. Bullen, Early English Text Society (Trübner, London, 1888), p. 9; based on the edition of 1578.
[12] Nathaniel Hodges, *Loimologia: Or, An Historical Account of the Plague in London in 1665* (London, 1720), p. 15. Cook sees Hodges as a College of Physicians conservative who engaged in polemical controversies on behalf of Galenism: Harold J. Cook, *The Decline of the Old Medical Regime in Stuart London* (Cornell University Press, Ithaca, 1986), pp. 150–2, 159. Hodges was also aware of modern trends and could be called a 'modern' Galenist. His translator, John Quincy, saw him as old-fashioned in medical theory in 1720 terms, but the passages quoted in this book have not been 'modernised' by Quincy from the Latin original.

overcrowded poor suburbs into the rich City parishes, and it was also well known that the poor could not afford to flee. These facts tied in well with one view of the poor, which saw them as suffering without resources and being in need of charitable help from their richer neighbours and of the services of ministers and physicians. However, the environment in which the poor lived and their ways of life could also be seen as causes of plague. In *A Treatise of the Plague* (1603),[13] the playwright and poet Thomas Lodge reflected the widespread suspicion of the poor and saw them as sources of danger, whilst the respectable and well-off were less likely to be contagious. He advised the 'Lord Mayor and Sherifs' in a city to bar entry to those who came from infected places, 'except they be men of note, of whose prudence and securitie they may be assured'. Not all inhabitants of a city visited by plague were infected, 'especially when they are men of respect, who have the meanes, and observe the methode to preserve themselves'. There were in Lodge's treatise two clear categories: the well-to-do people of repute and the disreputable poor. The latter were not to be let in.[14] In fact, the government Plague Orders never distinguished between rich and poor in relation to quarantine, but legislation did see the poor and their housing as sources of plague.

Medical writers at times referred to the poor as an undifferentiated whole, for whose benefit some recorded cheap remedies (see chapter 2). Plague, however, caused them to examine the state of the poor more closely. The situation of the poor left without help was a central issue in the moral question of flight, whilst their conditions of life seemed conducive to generating and spreading plague. Just as the poor (as we saw in chapter 1) were viewed by governments and the well-to-do with a combination of benevolence and hostility, as objects of charity and danger, so also did medical writers have mixed views regarding them. Francis Herring, a long-serving Fellow of the College of Physicians, included in his *Certaine Rules, Directions, Or Advertisements for this Time of Pestilentiall Contagion* (1603, 1625) 'Certaine directions for the use of the poorer sort of people that shall be visited by the Pestilence'. In them he set out some of the classic

---

[13] A partly unacknowledged translation of a French treatise by François Valleriola; Lodge wrote that it was based on 'certaine notes which I received from Valenolaes sonne now Doctour of Phisique in Arles': Thomas Lodge, *A Treatise of the Plague* (London, 1603), sig. A3ᵛ.

[14] Ibid., fol. F1ᵛ. Slack, *Impact of Plague*, p. 45. Healy, 'Fictions', p. 70.

definitions of the poor, first, as objects of charity: 'God . . . hath disposed, that there should be poore among us, that the richer sort might have fit obiects whereupon to exercise, their Mercy and compassion . . .' While those in power should take care to provide food and physic for 'the true and honest poore miserable people', 'bone of their bone, and flesh of their flesh', they should, however, 'restraine' those 'idle Vagabonds, by whose wandring up and downe, the infection may well be spread and increased'.[15] In the case of plague, given that the poor, whether deserving or undeserving, suffered most from it, they were seen both as in need of succour and also as dangerous sources of infection.

Medical writers sought reasons why the poor died more from plague, apart from the mere fact that more of them remained in a plague-stricken place. They found the answer in the body of medical knowledge that linked health, environment and lifestyle, with corruption and putrefaction, as so often in early modern medicine, providing the thread that bound the different factors together. The environment and the lifestyle of the poor appeared to contribute to their greater susceptibility to plague. Bullein, for instance, condemned, in a moral as well as medical sense, those who were dirty and who undertook heavy physical work. To the question, 'to what personnes . . . doeth the Pestilence come?', Medicus replies: 'Moste chiefly to theim under the place infected, then to sluttishe, beastly people, that keepe their houses and lodynges uncleane, their meate, drinke, and clothyng, moste noysome, their laboure and travaile immoderate . . . and whereas [where] many people doe dwell on heapes together.'[16]

In plague times, orders were issued to prevent building and overcrowding in London and to stop the rental of rooms which were often packed with people.[17] However, the emphasis was on advising people to avoid crowds and crowded buildings, rather than on ameliorating living conditions as such. Thus theatres and fairs were closed as well as crowded lodgings. Although there were clear religious and secular imperatives that the poor, especially in a time of plague, should be given charitable relief, neither charity nor the perceived danger of the poor as sources of infection, nor the fear of

[15] Francis Herring, *Certaine Rules, Directions, Or Advertisements for this Time of Pestilentiall Contagion* (1st edn, 1603; London, 1625), fol. C1^r.

[16] Bullein, *Dialogue*, p. 37. Partly cited also in Healy, 'Fictions', p. 188.

[17] Bell, *The Great Plague*, pp. 25, 84; Wilson, *Plague in Shakespeare's London*, pp. 24–6.

economic and social breakdown consequent upon plague changed the situation noted in chapter 4. There was no wholesale reform of the living conditions of the poor. This happened in the nineteenth century, when the need for a healthy workforce was frequently put forward as a justification for public health measures. In the sixteenth and seventeenth centuries, the *status quo* was generally accepted by medical writers, as by many others, even in the context of plague, though they might show sympathy for the plight of the poor. The comments of Stephen Bradwell, the grandson of surgeon John Banister, on the plague and the poor were typical of medical thinking. Bradwell was an unlicensed London practitioner, who, despite having no medical education, had been to university; he was well-read in the subject and generally displayed orthodox medical views in his writings.[18] He used the paradigm of putrefaction to make sense of why the poor suffered most from plague. Although Bradwell sympathised with their plight, he was, like most medical writers, interested more in the medical than in the underlying social reasons for their vulnerability, yet he was aware of the latter. He wrote that the constitutions of the poor were corrupted and weakened by their living conditions and so were more susceptible to plague (an already corrupt, putrid constitution would be more easily attacked by the plague poison which putrified its victims' bodies):

Poore People (by reason of their great want) living sluttishly, feeding nastily on offals, or the worst and unholsomest meates; and many times too long lacking food altogether; have both their bodies much corrupted, and their Spirits exceedingly weakened: whereby they become (of all others) most subiect to this Sicknesse. And therefore we see the *Plague* sweeps up such people in greatest heapes.[19]

Given that plague was thought to originate in stinking, dirty, putrid places (in the literal early modern sense of being places where putrefaction took place), and that the bodies of the poor shared those qualities, it is no surprise that the poor were often thought to be sources of contagion (especially as they comprised the greater number of plague victims, and the plague spread from poor localities). They were at once most dangerous, and in most danger. Respectable people were advised to avoid 'all publick meetings . . .

[18] On Bradwell see Norman Gevitz, ' "Helps for Suddain Accidents": Stephen Bradwell and the Origin of the First Aid Guide', *Bulletin of the History of Medicine*, 67, 1993, 51–73.

[19] Stephen Bradwell, *A Watch-Man for the Pest* (London, 1625), pp. 46–7.

and peoples steams and breaths especially of nasty folks, as beggars, and others: whence those houses happen to be soonest infected, that are crouded with multiplicity of lodgers and nasty families'.[20] However, despite the danger posed by the poor, the ethics of charitable care ensured that medical writers, like religious writers, did not countenance their abandonment.[21] The policy of 'shutting up' meant that, in theory at least, a modicum of food and care was provided by the parish authorities and for some this excused the need for neighbourly charity.[22]

Richard Kephale, a dissenting minister, recounted one example of a lack of charity, which also showed the poor as especially liable to plague, their living conditions and the nature of the disease seeming to be symbiotically connected. His *Medela Pestilentiae* (1665) was both a theological and medical treatise, providing answers to such questions as whether it was lawful to flee, and whether 'true Believers may die of the plague'.[23] It also supplied receipts (recipes) for plague remedies and reprinted much of Bradwell's 1636 plague treatise (see footnote 25). Kephale's account of a poor family dying alone was, therefore, sensitive to the medical and religious aspects of the case, though there was nothing unusual in ministers being knowledgeable about medicine:

At this present, most of those houses which are infected are the habitations of poverty, in some obscure close place in the Suburbs; as towards *St. Giles* etc. One house I know more especially by *Cursitors-Alley*, where the Man, his Wife and Childe liv'd in a Room that look'd more like, for bigness, a great Chest than any thing else: They had not space enough (according to the vulgar saying) to swing a Cat in; so hot by reason of the closeness, and so nastily kept besides, that it took away a mans breath to put his head but within the doors. In this house, all this little family died lately, in two dayes. The childe dying suddenly, the neighbours were afraid to come near them. The man having languished a long time, for want of Air, as well as money, and he not able to stir out, and none coming to his relief, dyed quickly after. The woman being as big with child as she could tumble, seeing her

---

[20] Gideon Harvey, *A Discourse of the Plague* (London, 1665), pp. 15–16.

[21] Though, as was frequently pointed out, many ministers and physicians fled from their duties.

[22] Richard Kephale, *Medela Pestilentiae, Wherein is Contained Several Theological Queries Concerning the Plague* (London, 1665), pp. 31–2, wrote that 'publick persons' such as magistrates and ministers did not have to visit the sick and could substitute others to take their place, but he also approved of the 'martyrdom' of ministers visiting the sick and so dying.

[23] He believed that God often spares them, a view that was held less and less; see Slack, *Impact of Plague*, p. 247.

child dead on the one side and her husband in his cloaths on the other, and forsaken by all, fell in labour and dyed too, instantly. A very true and sad accident, which doubtless was occasioned by their loathsom living, but perfected by the cruelty of those that lived near them.[24]

The medical view of the plague poor reflected such general notions about the poor, but it was also constructed from the same specific and rather limited theoretical framework that, as we saw, was used for preventive medicine, and which linked lifestyle, environmental living conditions and morality together. Most prominent of all was the linking of the poor and plague to corruption and putrefaction, which, with the humours, was the overarching theory of medicine.

SUSCEPTIBILITY AND MORAL BLAME IN OTHER GROUPS

Some groups liable to plague, such as pregnant women (who were moist and hot), young children (who had moist bodies), costive and fasting people (who had, respectively, pent-up humours and empty bodies ready to be filled with plague air), as well as others with moist and hot constitutions, were seen in neutral terms, and were not the subject of derogatory or moralising comments.[25] As victims they were not to be blamed. However, other groups as well as the poor were blamed. There was a general consensus among medical and religious writers that revelry, licentious living and heavy drinking led to plague. Morally speaking, impurity such as sinful living angered God and, medically, excessive habits weakened the body and made it susceptible to plague. Medical writers, as in the regimens, habitually mixed medicine and morality.

Drunkards were informed that they were deluded to think that they could keep out the plague poison with drink:

On the other side *Gluttons* and *Drunkards* (let them argue what they will for the filling of the veynes, as they use to say, to keepe out the evill ayre) can never be free from crudities and distemper'd bloud; which easily takes infection: As *Hippocrates* testifies, when he sayes: 'Corpora impura quo magis aluntur; eo magis laduntur'. Impure bodyes the more they are nourished the more they are endangered.[26]

[24] Kephale, *Medela Pestilentiae*, pp. 57–8.
[25] Stephen Bradwell, *Physick for the Sicknesse, Commonly Called the Plague* (London, 1636), pp. 9–10; also William Boghurst, *Loimographia: An Account of the Great Plague of London In the Year 1665*, ed. J. F. Payne (Shaw & Sons for the Epidemiological Society of London, London, 1894), pp. 24–6.
[26] Bradwell, *Physick for the Sicknesse*, p. 10.

Moreover, too much wine 'in contagious seasons' could inflame the blood, leading to putrefaction of the humours 'which will easily turne to the Pestilence'.[27] This drew upon the general belief that in a plague time all other diseases or ill states of health were changed into plague.[28] There were thus plenty of medical reasons available to support moral condemnation of a lack of sobriety during plague. In the manner of the regimen writers, Bradwell openly combined moral and medical indignations when he discussed the 'disease of Surfeiting' or eating and drinking too much, whose 'Remedy must be Sobriety':

In this *Disorder of Quantitie*, I cannot but admire at my Countrey men . . . It was wont to be said, *The Drunken-Dutchman*: but the Dutch have played the God-fathers, and have too kindly, bestowd their names upon *our men*, such names I meane as *Diotemus* of *Athens* had; who was intituled the Tunnell, for his filthy delight in drinking and drinking in a *Tunnell* . . . These riotous abuses of Gods good gifts, are a maine cause why the Lord at this time striketh this Land with *Sicknesse* [i.e. plague], and threatneth it with the *Famine*.[29]

The mere fact of greater susceptibility was not sufficient to bring into play moral condemnation, although the religious cause of plague, sin, made it likely that it would be present in some way. Some people were seen as susceptible but without any moral stigma. Conversely, others might be at less risk of catching plague, but were not viewed as morally superior. These included those with discharges from ulcers or from 'issues'[30] which evacuated 'the hurtful humors', or '*Old folkes*, whose bodyes are cold and dry'.[31] Indeed, it was sometimes believed that catching the pox, which was often morally stigmatised, could confer immunity to plague or, at least, make plague less deadly. Such groups who survived the plague, as the 'common prostitutes of Lukener's Lane and Dog Yard', who, as the apothecary William Boghurst observed in his lively and often iconoclastic account of the plague of 1665 (in his *Loimographia* which remained in manuscript until the nineteenth century), were 'full of old sores, itch, scabs, running sores, pox . . .', won no particular approval.[32] Generally,

---

[27] Bradwell, *A Watch-Man for the Pest*, p. 30.
[28] See Boghurst, *Loimographia*, p. 26: a belief going back to Thucydides.
[29] Bradwell, *A Watch-Man for the Pest*, p. 31.
[30] Surgically created openings which drained away pus, or which, by creating irritation, produced a flow of serous material.
[31] Bradwell, *Physick for the Sicknesse*, p. 11.
[32] Boghurst, *Loimographia*, pp. 25, 66; but Hodges, *Loimologia*, pp. 77–80 was strongly sceptical,

while the greater chances of dying and of surviving did not automatically bring with them moral censure and approbation respectively, there was a tendency to consider the ways of life of some groups, notably the poor and those of low moral standing such as drunkards, as being, in part at least, responsible for their deaths. Blaming some victims for a disease that threatened the whole of society allowed those doing the blaming to create a sense of control and social order at a time of potential chaos. Medical writers, given the tradition of moralising about lifestyles in the regimens, were well able to add their quota of blame.

THE BELIEF IN MEDICAL SUCCESS

One measure was seen as the best means of avoiding plague. Flight, and not medicine, was the traditional and preferred option when plague drew near. But many, and they were mostly the poor, could not flee as they had nowhere else to go. In 1665 some of the well-to-do such as Samuel Pepys remained, and some Nonconformist ministers and medical practitioners stayed on out of a sense of duty, but generally whoever could, fled. The advice to flee indicates the limits of medicine, and also, logically, that the plague treatises were most useful for those practitioners and their poor patients who stayed behind. Treatises such as Thomas Moulton's *This is the Myrrour or Glasse of Helth* (*c.* 1539, written by a fifteenth-century friar but presented as contemporary) were written for 'compassion that I have of the poore people, that was and is betrayed every day therby for defaute of helpe'.[33] The extent of literacy would have set a limit on the readership, and perhaps some of the treatises were in reality addressed to those who would help the poor, though some of the poor might be able to read if not write. In any case, the advisability of flight meant that medical optimism about prevention and cure was concerned with the second best courses of action, and was often

writing that 'many were hereby encouraged to seek the most lascivious and filthy Prostitutions, on purpose to be secur'd by one previous Infection against another', but all it did, wrote Hodges, was to attract plague more strongly to the 'rash Adventurer': p. 77.

[33] Thomas Moulton, *This is the Myrrour or Glasse of Helth* (London, *c.* 1539), fol. A7^r. On Moulton see Faye Getz, 'Medical Practitioners in Medieval England, *Social History of Medicine*, 3, 1990, 279. Francis Herring, in his *Certaine Rules*, addressed part of his treatise to the needs of the poor and wrote that 'I purpose to set downe certaine curative directions, for the poorer sort, with such parable and cheape Medicins as may come within the compasse of their short and meane abilitie': C1^r.

aimed at a group of people for whom the best natural remedy, flight, was not available.[34]

Despite the vast numbers of the dead and the desertion of many physicians into the countryside, the writers of the plague treatises believed that medicine could offer effective, practical advice on preventing and curing plague, though the latter might be more difficult. The issue of therapeutics was on one level simple. Many writers advised on medical procedures such as bleeding and sweating and detailed the ingredients of a variety of remedies with the implicit or explicit promise of success. However, the gravity of the illness, in the eyes of contemporaries the most devastating of all illnesses, clearly raised doubts about medicine's ability to fight it. In *Newes from Graves-end* (1604) Dekker first praised 'Phisicke . . . borne in heaven . . . Equall friend to rich and poore' and '(Mens *Demigods*) Phisitions', but then despaired of its impotence in the face of plague:

> But (ô griefe) why do we accite
> The charmes of Phisick? Whose numbd sprite
> Now quakes, and nothing dare or can,
> Checkt by a more dread Magition?
> Sick is Phisicks selfe to see
> Her Aphorismes prov'de a mockery.[35]

But even Dekker was not consistently pessimistic about medicine's usefulness during the plague[36] and the reports of the increased trade

---

[34] Phayre wrote: 'And for bycause the other souerayne remedy preseruatyve is to flye the corrupte ayre. Accordyng to the prouerbe, *Longe, cito, tarde*. Flye be tymes, flye farre, and come slowelye agayne. Yet for so muche as everye man can not, nor is of abilitye so for to do, it is good for them to loke upon thys lytle regiment, wherin wyth the ayde of almyghtye god, the hye [high] Phisition, yf the venyme be not to outragyouse, he shall fynde howe to preserve hym selfe well ynough from it': 'Treatyse of the Pestylence', fol. M4^{r-v}. On literacy see chapter 1 footnote 74.

[35] Wilson, *Plague Pamphlets*, pp. 80, 81.

[36] In the Dedication to the surgeon Thomas Gilham in 'A Rod for Run-awayes', Dekker wrote, 'To whom, in an Epidemiall confusion of Wounds, should a man flye, but to Physicke and Chirurgery': p. 137; in *London Looke Backe at that Yeare of Yeares 1625. And Looke Forward upon this Year, 1630* (1630), Dekker wrote that medical books and physicians were of good use and religious medicine was even better: 'Is Sicknesse come to thy doore! Hath it knock't there? And is it entred? There are many good Bookes set forth, to drive back Infection . . . Make much of thy Physician . . . Such a Physitian is Gods second, and in a duell or single fight (of this nature) will stand bravely to thee . . .': p. 188; Wilson, *Plague Pamphlets*. For a different view see V. B., *The Run-awayaes Answer* ([London?], 1625), p. 5: 'Was it not hie time to take our heeles and be gon, when the Doctors themselves played the Runne-awayes? . . . into your *City* a crew of prating Emperickes, cozzing Mountibanckes, and cheating *Quacksalvers*, who if they cure one, kill twenty . . . *Phisick* and *Chirurgery* (those two divine Sisters sent from Heaven) are both of them puzzled in their Readings and driven to a stand[still] in their own Practise. This sicknes turnes knowledge into Ignorance, for

for mountebanks' remedies, and also the publication by government authority of the College of Physicians' remedies, indicate that there was some belief, even if it was a desperate belief, in the power of medicine. Medical practitioners were aware of popular doubts; the surgeon Thomas Thayre in his *Treatise of the Pestilence* (1603) wrote of 'manie other blinded with a foolish opinion, that phisicke can doe them no good',[37] and Boghurst reported how those at death's door seemed to smile (the Hippocratic *risus sardonicus*, or death smile):

soe in this disease, about a minute or two before they dye they will look in your face and give a smile or two when they have least reason for it, and if there were any in the room from whom they expected most help, as a Physitian, Apothecary, or Chyrurgeon, to bee sure they fixed their eyes on them, deriding in a kind of contempt their vain help and the world's deceitfulness'.[38]

However, when Boghurst wrote of curing plague, his doubts were not about whether it could be done but as to precisely how it could be effected: what types of regimen and what kinds of remedies and procedures such as sweating and vomiting should best be used.[39] There was a basis for medical optimism. Some plague victims survived. As the identification of medieval and early modern plague with modern plague is contested, it is best not to impose modern understanding of plague, which involves three different variations of the disease with different fatality rates, on to the disease of the past. However, two types of plague were known early on. The medieval French surgeon Guy de Chauliac recognised two kinds, one of three days' duration, the other of five, and at least one English writer, Stephen Bradwell, also observed two sorts of plague, one of which, he wrote, God sent directly without using natural means and was therefore inevitably fatal.[40] The fact that recovery occurred in some

experimented Salves and Medicines forfet their wonted Vertues to astonishment and admiration.'

[37] Thomas Thayre, *A Treatise of the Pestilence* (London, 1603), p. 34; Charles Creighton, *A History of Epidemics in Britain* (Cambridge University Press, Cambridge, 1891), p. 489, wrote that Thayre's treatise was a 'mystification' or 'very close reproduction' of Phayre's treatise. In my view the two treatises differ significantly.

[38] Boghurst, *Loimographia*, p. 40.

[39] Ibid., pp. 74–80.

[40] See the comments by L. Brockliss in his review of A. Lynn Martin, *Plague? Jesuit Accounts of Epidemic Disease in Sixteenth Century*, American Historical Review, 103, 1579–80. Ann G. Carmichael, *Plague and the Poor in Renaissance Florence* (Cambridge University Press, Cambridge, 1986), pp. 1–26 identifies Renaissance plague as bubonic plague, but argues that it was difficult to differentiate it from other 'plagues'. Philip Ziegler, *The Black Death* (Penguin, Harmondsworth, 1982), p. 19.

cases meant that medical writers could present plague as a devastating but not hopeless illness.

The question of success against the plague was not a purely medical matter, especially before 1665. Paul Slack has pointed out that from 1665 there were fewer religious treatises on plague than there were medical treatises, in contrast to the early part of the century,[41] and he takes this as a sign of a lessening in the religious significance of plague. Within medical treatises there is a similar decrease in religious sentiment. Hodges drew a clear line between medicine and religion, stating that the purposes of God 'are Secrets too awful for Mortals to pry into', and making a distinction between the areas of competence of physicians and clergymen: 'it is sufficient to the Purpose of a Physician, to assign natural and obvious causes; and where such are discoverable, it is unworthy of him and the divine Art he professes, as well as an Affront to good Sense, to have Recourse to any other'.[42] This early Enlightenment approach to the separation of medicine from religion was echoed by Boghurst who wrote that, although the plague was unusual, God brought plague to earth by natural means. It was not created after the Creation 'de novo and immediately from God'; it was not, therefore, a special act of God which lay outside the scope of natural explanations. In a manner reminiscent of nineteenth-century geological debates, when 'special creations' by God were being put forward and then rejected as explanations for new species and for large-scale geological events, Boghurst argued that, if plague was a new creation, 'then . . . I see wee shal make noe end of multiplying new Creations and miraculous productions of things every day'. Instead there was something of the Hippocratic divine, 'Tὸ Θεῖον', in all illnesses.[43] He concluded: 'Now as God brings warr and Famine not by any new-created Agents, but by the ministry of known and second Causes [i.e. natural causes], making them the Executioners of his Decree upon Mankind, soe wee cannot with reason suppose hee doth otherwise in the Pestilence.'[44]

This reasoning, with its rejection of the supernatural and of special acts of God, had been the standard position of most Protestants from the sixteenth century, but it was here reiterated

---

[41] Slack, *Impact of Plague*, pp. 228–47, charts the changing balance between religious and medical explanations of plague. I am grateful to David Harley for pointing out that the churches were full and plague sermons continued to be published.
[42] Hodges, *Loimologia*, p. 31.   [43] Boghurst, *Loimographia*, p. 15.   [44] Ibid., p. 16.

with a view to drawing lines of demarcation between the domains of religion and medicine. This was in keeping with establishment thought newly evolving after the Restoration, and allowed medical writers to concentrate solely on the natural causation and cure of plague. Before this time the boundaries between medicine and religion had been more permeable, and medical success in preventing and curing plague was often seen as involving religion. For instance, Thomas Phayre wrote that regimen based upon the six non-naturals might 'easelye' prevent and cure plague, but spiritual medicine would also help. He took care to 'Councell everye christen man . . . to cure fyrst the fever pestilentiall in his soule . . . And this done undoubtedlye the syckenesse of the bodye shall be the easyer to be cured.'[45] Both religious and medical writers were optimistic that plague could be cured and prevented. They did not advocate what they perceived as Muslim fatalism in the face of plague.[46] The act of Christian repentance, for instance, might avert plague, and the injunction against self-murder legitimated such measures as flight and the use of medicine.[47] The language of religious writers combined terror and retribution with hope. Medical writers also echoed the tropes of horror and optimism, giving the impression that the discourses of medicine and religion not only shared metaphors such as Phayre's 'cure fyrst the fever pestilentiall in his soule', but also held a similar view of the possible outcomes of plague for human beings. Nevertheless, as we shall see below, it is also possible to interpret some of the religious injunctions placed at the end of medical instructions as perfunctory or, at least, as not infringing upon the autonomy of medicine.

How was a sense of optimism created? Medicines and God were efficacious; only rarely did medical writers doubt the former and never the latter – and it is worth reminding ourselves how the state instilled into the population the belief that God was efficacious (in the case of plague, with set days of prayer and humiliation across the country), as did many of the written media. However, there were conditions to medical success, which made failure very easy to explain. But even so medical failure could still be retrieved by God's help. The message from medicine was the politically acceptable one of 'don't give up hope'. Despair only added to the social chaos

---

[45] Phayre, 'Treatyse of the Pestylence', sigs. M3^v, M4^r.
[46] Boghurst, *Loimographia*, p. 58.
[47] See also Slack, *Impact of Plague*, pp. 49–50.

caused by plague. But behind the message of hope lay also the recognition of possible failure and death. It was stressed that medicines had to be given at the onset of infection. If delay occurred, then death was almost inevitable unless God intervened. Immediate treatment was necessary so that the medicine 'maye descende into the hert afore the venyme, have the upperhande of nature. For yf it [the venom] be ones settled at the hert, I affirme playnely, there is no hope at al.'[48] If delay was unavoidable, medicine taken in the name of God might work. Phayre, in the following quotation, moved between two types of reader, the physician and patient ('take or gyve your medicine and yf ye cannot brooke it'), and the religious (and medical) exhortation was perhaps easier to convey because he addressed the patient directly and personally after advising the physician. Given the unstructured and open nature of much of English medicine at the time, in which lay and self-treatment were commonplace, it is not surprising to find authors, especially those using the vernacular, addressing both practitioners and lay people in the same treatise:

Notwithstandynge yf the case so be that ye be not called, or can gette no remedye afore the sayde tyme, caste not your selfe into dispayre, or put not the pacient in discomfort, take or gyve your medicine in the name of God, and yf ye can not brooke it, take as muche agayne and do so many tymes tyll ye maye retayne it, then laye ye downe to sweate, and lyft up your hert to God, callynge upon him, without whome there is no helth, and by the grace of Jesu, ye nede not to be fearefull of deathe, for that which is impossyble to man, is easye ynoughe with God, yea many times nature worketh it selfe, above all natural expectation.[49]

This also suggests, as with all sicknesses, a kind of religio-medical spectrum for action or cure, ranging from the purely physical at one end to the spiritual at the other; in the latter, divine intervention was most operative and the presence of medicine was almost nominal, or was merely the vehicle for the divine. But one can find in the medical treatises on plague, even those with a strong religious element, sections where medicine or the natural cure appears as isolated from divine power, even when the two were placed in close proximity. Thomas Thayre described his order of cure and the medicines whereby with 'Gods leave and his holy assistance to performe . . . not one in six persons shall die'.[50] However, failure

---

[48] Phayre, 'Treatyse of the Pestylence', fol. P1[r].
[49] Ibid., fol. P1[v].   [50] Thayre, *Treatise*, p. 44.

was not due to God, but because the patients were in ill health before they caught plague. The secular nature of the reasoning is unmistakable: it was the same reasoning used by early settlers to North America such as Thomas Hariot, who argued that the new land was healthy, any illnesses having been contracted before the voyage. Despite Thayre's injunction to heed God, it was the 'order and direction' of his treatment, based on natural remedies and procedures, that appear to be responsible for the cure of the patient. In other words, medicine was often given a measure of autonomy,[51] although, as God was deemed to work through secondary means, medicine was never fully isolated from religion.

Other writers alluded to medical success without reference to religion. Bullein, for instance, in his highly moralistic and Christian *A Dialogue Against the Fever Pestilence*, created a clear space for medical cure. 'Antonius' summarised the views of 'Medicus' to the effect that plague 'is almost past cure of any phisicion' when the pestilential venom in the air is drawn to the heart and putrefactive symptoms appear, such as the carbuncles and the buboes (the latter were intensely painful swellings usually under the armpits, groin and neck).[52] However, delay in treatment might not be inevitably fatal, as the course of plague varied in different people. Rather than hoping for the intervention of God, 'Medicus' points out that there are circumstances when nature and medicine could still effect a cure, for 'the feareful sore [a carbuncle]' is incurable if it is black in colour, but 'when nature is so stronge to caste it forthe with a redde colour, palishe or yellowishe, the cure is not then verie harde'.[53]

Medical success in preventing and curing plague depended not only on God, medicine and nature, but also on the patient. As is discussed in the next chapter, the patient's state of mind, especially the need to avoid fear that made one vulnerable to plague, was seen as crucial. Medical outcomes were also affected by the fallibilities of patients: delay, trusting in their own strength, or in weak medicines,

---

[51] Ibid., pp. 43–4; Thomas Hariot, 'Briefe and True Report of the New Found Land of Virginia' in Richard Hakluyt, *The Principall Navigations, Voiages and Discoveries of the English Nation* (London, 1589), p. 763.

[52] Bullein, *Dialogue*, pp. 38–9.

[53] Ibid., pp. 41, 44–5. However, in the *Goverment of Health*, Bullein was more pessimistic, writing that a patient has to take medicines within twelve hours of the onset of symptoms 'or it wil be his death', and within twenty-four of being infected, if no medicines are given or blood-letting undertaken, 'then miracle helpeth him, but truly no medicine hath vertue to doe it': fols. 86ʳ, 19ʳ.

or believing that medicine could not help.[54] Patients were also fooled by the deceptive nature of plague, for its signs were not always 'manifest, for somtymes it is sene, that one hath had the pestilence and felt nothyng at all'; at other times the plague venom was strongly opposed by nature at the beginning, so the patient felt that he or she was getting better, but at the second assault nature was not strong enough.[55] Moreover, the common belief that in times of plague many other diseases ceased (or were converted into plague) led to the advice that any slight feeling of ill health should be taken to be plague.[56] In a sense, medicine saw only plague in times of plague – all other illnesses seemed to diminish or disappear (on this see below): this is understandable when one looks at the bills of mortality with their huge preponderance of plague deaths (the general bill for the year ending 19th December 1665 gave 68,596 plague deaths among 97,306 burials).

Failure to cure the plague was not put down solely to the failings of patients. The disease, as we have seen, had a strong social element: it was contagious, it was largely a disease of the poor (the rich having fled), and living conditions and the environment seemed to be especially implicated in its pathology and spread. Moreover, the nurses who looked after plague patients were frequently demonised as ignorant, cruel and thieving. Theophilus Garencières, a French physician working in London during 1665, boasted of curing nineteen out of twenty plague patients if they came to him within four hours of the onset of the disease.[57] He expected success but his long list of reasons for failure acknowledged that most patients, in fact, died.

The cause why so few escape are these. The scarcity of able Physicians

[54] Thayre, *Treatise*, p. 34.
[55] Phayre, 'Treatyse of the Pestylence', fols. O7^v–O8^r.
[56] Ibid., fols. O8^{r-v}. This was a long-lasting belief; see, for instance, Thomas Willis, 'Of Fevers', in *Dr Willis's Practice of Physick*, trans. S. Pordage (London, 1684), p. 107: 'whilst the Pestilence reigns, other Diseases in any one, leave their proper Nature, and change into it'. Also John Ward, *Diary of the Rev. John Ward, A. M., Vicar of Stratford-Upon-Avon . . . 1648 to 1679*, ed. Charles Severn (London, 1839), p. 241: 'Dr. Wharton said all people that died in the plague, dyed of the plague.'
[57] Theophilus Garencières, *A Mite Cast into the Treasury of the Famous City of London*, 3rd edn (London, 1666), p. 2; Boghurst, *Loimographia*, treated this claim with scepticism, p. 70. For new light on nurses see Eric Gruber von Arni, 'Who Cared? A Study of Nursing Care and Welfare Provision for Soldiers and their Families during the Civil War and Interregnum 1642–1660' (Ph.D. thesis, Portmouth University, 1999). Garencières (1610–80) graduated MD at Caen 1636, in 1657 incorporated MD at Oxford and practised at Clerkenwell in London. K. Dewhurst, *Willis's Oxford Lectures* (Sandford Publications, Oxford, 1980), p. 64.

willing to attend that disease, the inefficacy of common Remedies, the want of accommodation as Cloaths, Fire, Room, Dyet, Attendants, the wilfulness of the Patient, his Poverty, his neglecting the first Invasion and trifling away the time till it be too late; a vapouring Chymist with his drops, an ignorant Apothecary with his Blistering Plaisters, a willful Surgeon with his untimely Lancing, an impudent Mountebanke, an intruding Gossip, and a carelesse Nurse.[58]

All the different factors, both medical and social, that accounted for failure were avoidable. Even the lack of efficient remedies was made good by Garencières' own remedy for the plague that he offered for sale. That there were many different ways of explaining the failures and successes of medicine in plague times is an indication that medical success was questionable, but it also shows that medical writers generally did not give up hope when faced with plague. Their discussions of and allusions to success and failure were not simplistic or monocausal. They took into account plague's status as a special disease and its social elements, but many of the factors upon which success or failure turned in preventing or curing it remained the same as in other diseases: God, practitioners and their advice and remedies, and fallible patients as well as the nature of the illness. Despite the horror evoked by religious and medical rhetoric, by the evidence of the bills of mortality and by the flight of many medical practitioners, medical writers (and governments) spread a message of hope by paradoxically 'normalising' plague and seeing it as a disease like any other, amenable to preventive and therapeutic measures, even whilst the same treatise or Plague Order was setting out the horrific and extraordinary nature of plague. It could be argued that medicine, like religion, helped in the near impossible business of keeping social order by giving some of the population the belief that the means were available for exercising control over the plague.

However, the experience of plague led Stephen Bradwell to see no hope of a cure for plague, but this was only in relation to one kind of plague, that sent directly by God. This was the 'simple plague' that struck its victims suddenly, with death occurring almost instantaneously, and he identified it with some of the plagues of God mentioned by the Bible, which were sent directly by God through his

---

[58] Garencières, *A Mite*, pp. 2–3. Why nurses were portrayed in this way is still unclear, but being poor and uneducated they shared in the general stigmatisation of the poor. See Margaret Pelling, 'Nurses and Nursekeepers: Problems of Identification in the Early Modern Period' in *The Common Lot, Sickness, Medical Occupations and the Urban Poor in Early Modern England* (Longman, London, 1398), pp. 179–202.

angels. Treatable plague was the 'putrid plague or the Sicknesse', caused by the plague poison. It was sent by God working through indirect, natural means and could be countered by natural means. He was also hesitant to enter the therapeutic arena, whatever the type of plague. In *A Watch-Man for the Pest* (1625), Bradwell stated that he wrote only of preservation from the plague and not of its cure. Clearly he believed that it would damage his reputation to claim or to appear to be attempting any cures: 'I may not take upon me to cure the Sicke, because I meddle not with the Sicknesse (for to practise on the *Plague* now, would prove a plague to my Practise hereafter) but I must labour to preserve the sound because by profession I am a Physicion.'[59]

By 1636 Bradwell was more optimistic about advertising his ability to cure plague. He wrote in *Physick for the Sicknesse, Commonly Called the Plague* that the putrid or contagious plague 'is by *Art curable* in as many as it pleaseth God to send and sanctifie the right means unto', and that 'it pleased God to blesse my labours and counsailes, and to let a very small number faile under my advice'.[60] He did not go into detail. The nearest he came to doing so was in the final two pages which advertised his preservative medicines, such as his 'Powder of Life', and, for 'the more Ordinary sort of People', his 'Liquor of Life' which if the doses were doubled could be used to cure plague. As he wished to avoid the accusation of being a mountebank, he promised that 'I will not brag what they [the remedies] did, nor court mens beliefe like a *Mountebanck*'. Yet the boundaries between the learned physician and the mountebank were imprecise. By stating that the remedies would be 'fit for all Constitutions', Bradwell seems to join the empirics and mounte-banks who have one remedy for one or more disease, regardless of an individual's constitution. And, like mountebanks, he boasted of the provenance of his remedies which, he wrote, were 'the Inventions of my Grand-father Mr. John Banister that famous both *Physitian* and *Chyrurgion* in this Citie', and again like the mountebanks he adver-tised the price of the remedies and where he lived: 'in *Golden Lane*, over against the signe of the Golden *Flower de Luce*'.[61] But this may be to do Bradwell an injustice. There are few advertisements for his remedies in his treatises, his claims to cure are muted, and the

[59] Bradwell, *A Watch-Man for the Pest*, To the Reader, A2^{r-v}, and *Physick for the Sicknesse*, pp. 2–6.
[60] Bradwell, *Physick for the Sicknesse*, pp. 5, 42–3.   [61] Ibid., pp. 52–3.

learned physicians also publicised remedies that took little account of patients' constitutions. Moreover, classical medicine had always allowed that specific diseases as well as individual constitutions needed to be cured. And the vast mortality of the plague probably encouraged even learned physicians to pay less attention to the individual's constitution and to concentrate on treatments.[62]

Bradwell's initial doubts serve to highlight how success in fighting plague was hardly ever despaired of in the plague literature. Medicine and religion, alone or in combination, could effect a cure. Death was to be expected, but it might be avoided, it was believed, given a sensible patient and the right treatment at the right time. Despite the very strong sense that plague, more than any other disease, was God-sent, secular medicine was able to claim that it could prevent and cure plague by itself. There was no direct opposition between medicine and religion, indeed cures were often seen as due to a combination of prayer to God and medicines, but space existed in the minds of medical writers for medical solutions to plague. Even in the case of the most catastrophic of illnesses medical success was possible.

THE MEDICAL CAUSES OF PLAGUE

Discussion of the causes of plague brought together two strands of medical thinking: the environmental and the narratives of patho-logical happenings inside the body. Medical writers described how a plague poison came from outside into the body and the havoc it wreaked once inside. They also tackled the question of how the plague poison was transmitted, how it was contagious. At this point, it is worth saying that environmental and person-to-person con-tagion were not seen as opposites, but as part of contagion in general: the plague poison spread from both people and places through the air and was breathed in.

Plague's special nature did, however, help to change views of disease. Plague was the disease of diseases, 'the sickness'; it was representative of other diseases, but it was also special and set apart from them. Like the pox and the 'sweat', it was a 'public' or 'popular' disease.[63] What made it a 'popular' or epidemic disease, as

---

[62] Ibid., pp. 8–9; Hodges, *Loimologia*, pp. 61–4.

[63] On the sickness, see Bradwell, *Physick for the Sicknesse*, p. 5 and p. 1 for plague as a 'popular' disease. Hodges, *Loimologia*, p. 29.

nearly all medical writers from the sixteenth century onwards agreed, was that it was contagious. It seems that the brutal reality of a plague epidemic forced Galenic medicine to accept that a disease could be an entity in its own right, and that something from outside, something contagious that was transmitted through the air, caused plague. Galenic physicians, therefore, though retaining their emphasis on individuals' constitutions, went some way to accepting the view of empirics, their hated competitors, that it was diseases that were important, and this view of plague was significant for Sydenham's development of his ideas on the constitution of diseases. The air could in certain years take on a plague constitution, which was the logical development of the popular notion of plague years.[64] Sydenham generalised this to particular years having specific disease constitutions (on this see further in chapter 10).

The medical narratives of plague were worthy of a dramatic disease. They brought together the heart, the vital organ of the body, and a deadly environment. The heart, it was generally believed, was attacked by a plague venom carried in the life-giving air.[65] The venom might come from anywhere, though stinking, evil-smelling places such as sewers and cesspits as well as infected people were especially suspect. Corruption and poison, two keystones of early modern medical pathology, were thus highly prominent in accounts of plague. The *Litil Boke . . . for the Pestilence* (1485?) of 'Canutius' or Knutsson, a Danish bishop, which was the earliest English printed plague treatise, held that plague was caused by the stars or by the bodies beneath them corrupting the air. For instance, a privy could corrupt the substance and quality of the air as could dead carrion, standing waters or ditches 'and other corrupt places'. Knutsson concluded in general that 'the ayer inspired sometime is venomous and corrupt, hurtyng the herte that nature many wayes ys greeved'.[66]

Corrupt, stinking and therefore venomous air, or something corrupt and poisonous suspended in the air,[67] entered the heart,

---

[64] See, for instance, Garencières, *A Mite*, p. 5: 'in a Pestilential constitution of the air'.

[65] Hodges, *Loimologia*, p. 73, was sceptical and doubted that there was a 'specifick Quality in the Poison of a Plague' to affect the heart more than any other part of the body and so 'attack the Principles of Life at once'.

[66] Bengt Knutsson, *A Litil Boke the whiche Traytied and Reherced Many Gode Thinges Necessaries for the . . . Pestilence* ([London], 1485?), fol. 2^{r-v}. This is closely based on a treatise by Jean Jacmé; see Rosemary Horrox, *The Black Death* (Manchester University Press, Manchester, 1994), p. 173.

[67] The air *per se* was thought by some to be in itself always pure.

extinguishing the life-giving spirits that had their origin there. From the time of Aristotle, western literate culture had seen the heart as the source of life, and had bestowed on it praise drawn from metaphors of government as well as from the medical and natural philosophical senses of its primacy.[68] English writers followed in this tradition. John Hall wrote in his *Anatomie* (1565) that the heart,

because he is the pryncipall member, of all other members, and the beginning of life, is thus sette in the myddest of the breaste, as Lorde and Kinge of all the rest: of whome he is obeyed and served as a prince of hys subiectes. And the hearte hathe bloude in hys owne substance, wheras all other members have it but in arteries and veines: and in the hearte is the nutrityve bloude [venous blood] made livelye spirite [i.e. the vital spirits in arterial blood], and caried forth in the arteries.[69]

The catastrophic power of plague was thus expressed by its attack upon this principal and central organ. The attack placed everyone in danger; it was 'common to every man by the corruption of the ayre'.[70] Corruption and putrefaction were spread wide across the environment, and 'commyng sodainly by the impression of aire, creepyng to the harte, corruptying the spirites, this is a dispersed Pestilence by the inspiration of the ayre'.[71] From corrupted airs and waters, from 'putrified vapours' and putrefying material came the plague venom to the heart; from the poisoning of the heart and its spirits came the symptoms of plague, the plague poison spreading to the rest of the body, so that:

they do swone and vomite yellow cholour, swelled in the stomache with muche paine, breaking foorth with stinking sweate; the extreme partes very cold, but the internall partes boiling with heate and burning; no rest; blood

---

[68] Plato and Galen gave the brain the most important role of all the parts of the body. For Plato it was the seat of the immortal soul and for Galen the origin of thought, sensation and motion, but both agreed that the heart conveyed vitality to the rest of the body.

[69] John Hall, 'A Compendious Worke of Anatomie' in *A Most Excellent and Learned Woorke of Chirurgerie, called Chirurgia Parva Lanfranci* (London, 1565), pp. 67–8; see also the famous passage on the centrality of the heart for life in William Harvey, *Exercitatio Anatomica de Motu Cordis et Sanguinis in Animalibus* (Frankfurt, 1628), chapter 8.

[70] Bullein, *Dialogue*, p. 36.

[71] Ibid., pp. 36–7. Vaughan, *Approved Directions for Health, both Naturall and Artificiall* (London, 1600), p. 12 described how the plague poison 'is presently conveighed by ones breath into the lungs and from thence into the heart, which is the center of the body, or fountaine of life, and from thence, as from the Metropolitane Citie of mans little world, this pestilent scent is sent and dispersed by the veines and arteries, into all the parts of the body'. See also John Donne, *Devotions Upon Emergent Occasions*, ed. with commentary by Anthony Raspa (Oxford University Press, Oxford, 1987), pp. 56–7 on the heart, 'this king of man', and its vulnerability, with the opening lines 'They use Cordials to keep the venim and Malignitie of the disease from the Heart.'

distillyng from the nose . . . corrupted mouthe, with blacknesse, quick pulse . . . losse of memorie, sometyme with ragyng in strong people. These and such like are the manifest signes howe the harte hath drawne the venome to it by attraction of the ayre, by the inspiration of the arters [arteries] to the hart, and so confirming it to be the perilous fever pestilentiall.

And the most feared and the most characteristic symptoms of the plague, buboes and carbuncles, seemed to give the clearest signs of the corruption of the heart and the body.[72] The medical narrative of the entry of plague into the body was very accessible: at least until the 1660s (see below), it had very little technical vocabulary and its dramatic language is another example of how medical treatises on plague shared in the heightened intensity of language associated with any type of writing on the subject. However, they also continually drew upon familiar medical tropes and frameworks when trying to make sense of the disease.

Medical writers, given their familiarity with the medical topology of the regimens, had no problems in pinpointing the environmental sources of plague. Although in sensory terms the type of environment that generated plague tended to be uniform – dirty, stinking and putrid, if the stars were excepted – the geography of plague sources was extensive and varied, and included specific localities in both towns and countryside, although, in practice, town and city dwellers fled to the countryside for safety. They were the same sources of ill air that the regimens had warned against: 'For noysome vapours arising from filthy sincks, stincking sewers, channells, gutters, privies, sluttish corners, dunghils and uncast ditches; as also the mists and fogs that commonly arise out of fens, moores, mines and standing lakes; doe greatly corrupt the Aire; and in like manner the lying of dead rotting carrions in channels, ditches, and dunghills; cause a *contagious* Aire.'[73] Such dispersed, external causes were appropriate causes for a 'public' or universal disease. Plague could also come more diffusely, from faraway countries, not only through the transport of people and goods, but invisibly through the air. The plague of 1665, for instance, was thought to have been brought through the 'Vehicle of Air from *Africa*, or Asia, to *Holland* and thence into *Britain*'.[74] Changes in the weather might also bring

---

[72] Bullein, *Dialogue*, p. 38: 'This is most true, of this [the plague venom] commeth foule *bubo*, *antaxis* and *Carbuncles*, sores through putrifaction as *Galen* saith . . .'

[73] Bradwell, *A Watch-Man for the Pest*, p. 4.

[74] Hodges, *Loimologia*, p. 64.

plague, and as the weather was everywhere and unavoidable, this gave another dimension to the special threat of plague.[75]

The sources of plague, all agreed, were geographically extensive both inside and outside of a country, and the plague poison that came from them corrupted the life-giving air and so was unavoidable unless specifically excluded or countered. The medical account of such widespread environmental pollution reinforced the strong popular sense that plague was a universal disease from which it was difficult to escape, and it also articulated and probably created intense anxiety about the sources of contagion – an anxiety that physicians saw as dangerous to health (on the latter see next chapter):

> Hence we may see the misery of man, that (be the *Aire* never so corrupt) he must draw it with his breath continually, for without it we cannot live a moment: for as *meate* [food] and *drinke* are the nourishments of our *bodies*, so is the Aire the nourishment of our Spirits: As therefore by *corrupt meats* our *bodies* are corrupted and diseased; so by *corrupt Aire* our Spirits are easily infected, and some extinguished. Therefore we have great cause to take heed that the *Aire* we draw be pure and wholesome. And this may be effected two wayes: either by flying into a good [air], or by purifying the evill Aire.[76]

(The next chapter discusses what steps were taken to purify the air.) The combination in the medical narratives of dangerous environments, people and air as sources of plague was expressive of the universal and contagious nature of plague, and helped to justify the policy of European governments of isolating plague victims.[77] The transmission from these sources of a plague poison that putrefied the heart and the rest of the body brought the narrative down to the level of the individual, and reflected the quick and catastrophically fatal course of the disease which was often accompanied with intense pain from the carbuncles and buboes that were interpreted as

[75] Bradwell, *A Watch-Man for the Pest*, p. 5: 'And wee cannot forget what a hot and dry parching Summer we had this last yeare; most fit to be the unfortunate forerunner of this yeares pestilence: which now being seconded with such abundance of moyst weather all this Spring and Summer hitherto; we may well doubt that a deluge of destruction is coming upon us.'

[76] Bradwell, *A Watch-Man for the Pest*, pp. 5–6.

[77] Although medical writers used complexion theory to explain who might be more liable to plague, the authorities did not act against those whose complexions made them most susceptible to plague and therefore potential sources of plague. Though it may be straining the point, this indicates the limitations of complexion theory at a time of plague. Some medical writers were aware of them: see Phayre, 'Treatyse of the Pestylence', fols. O8ᵛ–P1ʳ, where he warns people not to trust to their complexions to avoid plague.

collections of putrefied matter. I now turn to the nature of the plague poison. It fascinated writers on plague, and by describing it well enough they would create an image of the essence of plague.

THE NATURE OF THE PLAGUE POISON

Before the plague of 1665, the plague poison was often seen as an occult or hidden quality, very thin, subtle and penetrating. By 1665, the new mechanical and corpuscular explanations of the world were replacing those of Aristotle and Galen. The mechanical philosophy saw the world as composed of particles in motion and the related corpuscular philosophy understood chemical substances in terms of the arrangement of particles. Plague was envisaged by some as composed of particles or corpuscles: again very thin or tiny, subtle and penetrating. Both the old and the new medical philosophies constructed the plague poison in such a way that it could spread widely, silently, powerfully and penetrate through into the body. Both ancient and modern learning also agreed that the poison was contagious and produced rapid and catastrophic putrefaction within the body.

Contagion needed a medium and a way of making contact from an object to a person or from person to person. Bradwell, who represents the old learning, defined contagion as 'That which infecteth another with his owne qualitie by touching it, whether the medium of the touch be Corporeall or Spirituall, or an Airie Breath.' He was interested in different modes of contagion such as '*Itch* and *Scabinesse*, *Warts*, *Measles*, *small Pox*, the *Veneriall Pox*': these conditions were spread 'by rubbing, and corporeall touches', whilst sore eyes infected other eyes 'by their *Spirituous beames*' and 'the *Pthisick* or putrified Lungs . . . by their corrupt breath infect the lungs of others'. Plague combined both 'corporeall touches' and 'Spirituous beames'. In so doing, it seemed to surpass the normal explanatory framework of Aristotelian – Galenic natural philosophy and medicine. There was something extraordinary in the transmission of plague. This was centred on the nature of the plague poison which consisted of 'a *Seminarie Tincture* full of *a venemous quality*'. Its fine, very thin nature made it suitable for being airborne, for piercing the body, and for mingling with the humours and spirits of the body.[78]

---

[78] Bradwell, *Physick for the Sicknesse*, pp. 6, 7. Cited in Slack, *Impact of Plague*, pp. 27–8.

This language has strong similarities with that of explanations of disease based on 'occult qualities' or the powers of the 'total substance' (*tota substantia*), which had been alluded to by Galen, and was a matter of controversy amongst Galenic physicians in the sixteenth century. Occult qualities and the powers of the total substance were used to explain diseases and remedies whose effects could not be understood using the manifest qualities of hot, cold, dry and wet. A hidden quality in, or the total substance of, a remedy could explain a powerful immediate effect that could not be put down to the remedy's manifest qualities. In such a way were the mysterious effects of a poison or the shock of the torpedo fish explained. Thus, when qualitative–humoral theory could not satisfactorily account for an illness or a remedy, the learned physicians had a fall-back position. However, occult qualities and the powers of the total substance seemed to lie outside Galenic rational medicine, and Galen himself had written that they were not amenable to methodical treatment.[79] They appeared uncomfortably close to the empiricists' view of specific disease entities. Nevertheless, plague was out of the ordinary, and seemed to call for extraordinary explanations.

The quality of the plague poison was not hot, cold, dry or wet; rather it was 'venemous', 'very thin and spirituous'. The linking of plague with poison (often associated with the secret, treacherous and stealthy destruction of rulers and hence of order) pointed to its unusual nature. Its description conveys the strong sense of a specific malign external agent, reinforced by the use of anthropomorphic language:

Now by *Venom* or *Poyson*, we commonly understand some thing that has in it some dangerous subtle quality that is able to corrupt the substance of a living body to the destruction or hazard of the life thereof. This working is apparent in this *Sicknesse*, by his secret and insensible insinuation of himself into the *Vitall spirits* . . . offering with suddaine violence to extinguish them. His subtle entrance, his slye crueltie, his swift destroying; the unfaithfulnesse of his *Crisis*, and the other *Prognostick signes*; and the vehemencie, grievousnesse and ill behaviour of his *Symptomes*, all being manifest proofes of his *venemous quality*.[80]

---

[79] On 'total substance' see Linda Deer Richardson, 'The Generation of Disease: Occult Causes and Diseases of the Total Substance' in A. Wear, R. K. French and I. M. Lonie (eds.), *The Medical Renaissance of the Sixteenth Century* (Cambridge University Press, Cambridge, 1985), pp. 175–94; and A. Wear, 'Explorations in Renaissance Writings on the Practice of Medicine' in ibid., pp. 118–45, esp. 140–4.

[80] Bradwell, *Physick for the Sicknesse*, p. 6.

Not only did plague act like a poison, entering by stealth and secrecy, but its effects were so destructive that they could not be comprehended within a normal framework of explanation. The putrefaction that it created was extraordinary; the symptoms of plague defined its nature:

in this Disease the *Seidge*, *Urine*, and *sweat* have an abhominable savour, the breath is vile and noysome; Ill coloured *Spots*, *Pustles*, *Blisters*, *swellings*, and *ulcers*, full of filthy matter arise in the outward parts of the Body: Such as no superfluitie or sharpnesse of Humors, nor any putrifaction of matter (without a *venemous qualitie* joyned with it) can possibly produce.[81]

EARLY ENLIGHTENMENT SCEPTICISM AND CONTINUITY

By the time of the plague of 1665, medicine, like science, was undergoing fundamental changes (discussed in chapter 8), but it had by no means been transformed and there were still many continuities with the past. In relation to plague, the 'ancients', the upholders of classical medicine, and the 'moderns', the supporters of the new chemical and mechanical philosophies that underpinned 'the new science', equally believed in a plague poison, in an environmental origin for the poison and in the destructive role of putrefaction. However, there was some doubt as to the traditional localised sources of plague, and the plague poison was described in the chemical language of the new science. The result was that the main medical story-line remained intact, but the change in the details made plague appear less controllable, because its sources now became less specific and less identifiable as a part of people's familiar world, whether it was a dunghill or a stagnant marsh.

The scepticism of the early Enlightenment threw a question mark over some of the localised sources for plague. William Boghurst best exemplified such scepticism, writing at a time when learned humoral medicine was under attack; he believed in the chemical, corpuscular philosophy, and theorised that plague originated from the very bowels of the earth itself. When the earth farted, plague came to the world, for

the Plague may be generated thus, that in some compasse of yeares or tyme the Foeces of the Earth come to a mature fermentation, which by some

---

[81] Ibid.

accident arriving towards its surface, as by dry weather and south winds, and soe the pores being something extraordinarily opened on its close body, and relaxed . . . its malign effluvia or fume or vapour is drawne forth into the Aire, and drives hither and thither into what place the great Guider of them and all things pleaseth.[82]

The 'foeces' came to the surface and sent their pestiferous vapours into the air in the form of 'corpuscles of plague'. For Boghurst the geography of plague comprised both the earth and the air. He dismissed the previous sources as 'a catalogue of . . . many little Peccadilloes which hitherto by most people and Physitians in the world have beene reckoned for absolute causes of the plague, which the most of them at least can bee but only furthering occassions, not originall causes'.[83] These included:

thickness of inhabitants; those living as many familyes in a house; living in cellars . . . good dyett, washing, want of good conveyances of filth; standing and stinking waters; dunghills, excrements, dead bodies lying unburied and putrifying . . . unseasonable weather, south and west winds, much dry weather coming together, over watching the body, overcharging the body with nourishments, hott and moyst constitutions, overheating the body with too much venery, increase of vermin as Frogs, Toades, Spiders, Mice, wormes . . . want of scouring ditches and pooles, vaults, Fens, and Marshes; hempe, flax, asphaltum, and sweet herbes steeped long in standing waters, expiring out of putrifyed lakes . . . venemous herbes, putrifying above the ground, fumes of metalls and mineralls, Arsenick, quicksilver . . . feeding on rotten meate, mouldy bread; malevolent aspects and mixture of the Planets, Eclipses of the Luminaries [Sun and Moon], corruption of humors, transportation of infected goods from place to place, breaking up tombes and graves, wherein dead bodyes have beene long buryed and crowded together . . .[84]

These traditional causes of the plague were deeply embedded in English society. They reflected the views of a medical culture which in this instance was united. 'Most people and Physitians' as well as governments had believed in many of the particular causes that Boghurst listed, and continued to do so. However, the scepticism of the new reason that was taking shape in the later seventeenth

---

[82] Boghurst, *Loimographia*, p. 18. The view that fumes came from the earth during earthquakes bringing disease is found in a fourteenth-century German plague treatise: Horrox, *Black Death*, p. 181. See also Shakespeare, *Henry IV*, Part 1, Act III, Scene I, lines 25–6: 'Diseased nature oftentimes breaks forth/In strange eruptions'; I am grateful to Dr Carole Rawcliffe for this quotation. By the 1660s this was a common view; see, for instance, Harvey, *A Discourse of the Plague*, p. 5.

[83] Boghurst, *Loimographia*, p. 17.   [84] Ibid., pp. 17–18.

century began the closure of traditional popular beliefs, and the opponents of the old learned medicine equated its beliefs with those of 'superstitious' or ignorant popular culture (a strategy also used by the Helmontians, discussed in chapter 9, who equated learned medicine and popular beliefs). All beliefs were to be interrogated, though much, in fact, remained unchanged. Boghurst pointed out that the breaking open of tombs was unlikely to cause plague, for when the charnel house in St Paul's was demolished 'there was a thousand cartloads of dead men's bones carried away to Finsbury, yet noe plague followed it'. More generally, he took a cynical view of the multitude of causes that had been given by writers on plague: 'in this', he wrote, 'they have only done as a man that would bee sure of the true Religion, therefore would bee of all. Soe because they would bee sure to hitt the nayle, they have named all the likely occasions they could think of.' Boghurst correctly saw that most of the causes given referred to dirt and stench. Such reasoning was part of the consensus between learned medicine and popular belief about the nature of healthy and of unhealthy places. However, he did not agree with the majority 'and all their conjectures tending to nastynes stinking and putrefaction: whereas good aires and sweet and cleanly places were noe more exempt from the disease than stinking places, and healthfull, wholesome bodyes fell under the disease as much as pocky corrupt bodyes, and more too'.[85] But underlying continuities with the past remained. Although he substituted a single universal cause of plague for the many given before, Boghurst, nevertheless, retained the images of venomous, corrupt vapours polluting the air, and his vision of plague issuing from the bowels of the earth reiterated the sense of faecal dirt associated with many of the sources of plague that had been adduced previously:

my opinion falls in wholly with those who make the earth the seminary and seedplott of these venomous vapours and pestiferous effluvia, which vitiate and corrupt the Aire, and consequently induce the pestilence; and that there are such vapors destructive to the principles of life included in the cavities of the earth may be evident to any one that shall but reflect upon those damps frequent in mines and colepitts, which in a moment suffocate the spirits of those that are employed about that work, and extinguish the Lampe of Life.

How many poysoned mineralls are there in the Bowells of the Earth![86]

---

[85] Ibid., p. 18.   [86] Ibid., p. 13.

The belief that a plague venom or poison caused plague also crossed over from learned humoral medicine to the medicine influenced by chemistry and the 'new science' of the later seventeenth century. Boghurst, who praised 'that illustrious Virtuoso Mr Boyle' and echoed many of his views, reviewed in 1666 the different theories about plague whilst keeping in mind his belief that a plague poison corrupted the body's corpuscles. He wrote that 'among all diseases the nature of none is soe mysterious as that of the Pestilence, and therefore it is called by the psalmist the pestilence that walketh in darkness, *quia causae ejus latent* [because its causes are hidden]'. The sense of biblical mystery led Boghurst on to medicine's hidden causes. He wrote that 'the first question' asked by 'Moderne Physitians' was whether plague was a disease of the 'total substance' or a '*Morbus intemperiei* [a disease of an ill temperament or constitution], a disease which proceedes from the excess of some manifest quality, as heat, moisture'.[87] However, occult qualities (and *tota substantia*) face two ways in the history of science and medicine. For Renaissance writers such as Fernel who stood at the boundaries of Galenic orthodoxy, they indicated that certain phenomena could not be satisfactorily explained by the Aristotelian–Galenic synthesis of qualities, elements and humours. Occult qualities implied a willingness to innovate within the ranks of learned medicine, and they probed the adequacy of classical qualitative theory. However, the new science especially condemned recourse to occult qualities, and writers such as Boyle saw them as characterising the empty speculation and ignorance of the old learning (though Newton in his alchemical interests was concerned with occult powers). For Boghurst the corpuscular philosophy meant that, instead of referring to 'hidden' or occult qualities, he could in principle describe the concrete, though minute and invisible bodies, of the plague poison: 'That this venome is a body or concretion of many little bodyes, though very subtle and invisible, can be noe doubt for those that have outgrown Aristotle and are acquainted with the Epicurean or corpuscular philosophy.' Although Boghurst was sure that 'the pestiferous particles' existed, he did not, he confessed, actually know their precise shapes and figures:

But for the shape and figure of these Atomes or small bodyes, which is the foundation of their activity and of that power whereby they corrupt the

---

[87] Ibid., pp. 11, 8, 9.

texture, alter and change the motion of these corpuscles or particles which compose the spirits and blood, wee can say nothing to satisfaction; they fall not under the eyes' perception, though assisted with the best inventions in perspective [microscopes] wherein this last age hath furnished us with, or any other sense, and therefore wee may conclude with the words of Fernelius (*de abditis rerum causis*, libr. 2, cap 12), 'The seedes of the Pestilence are soe hidden and removed from sense that wee see them better in their effects than we can in themselves'.[88]

Others were more confident than Boghurst that they could identify the particles that made up the plague poison. Nathaniel Hodges, using as a 'modern' Galenist the language of the new corpuscular philosophy, wrote that the plague poison was composed of nitro-aerial particles which had become corrupted (nitro-aerial particles accounted for many different effects in the minds of proponents of the new science). Their origin was universal and not localised. It was 'the central nitrous Spirit' which 'does every where transpire and exhale towards the Surface'. It was the source of plant, animal and human life 'straining [in more than one sense?] through the Bowels of the Earth', mixing with life-giving sunlight 'through the whole Region of Air'. The nitrous spirit could be vitiated by too much humidity and rain; or within its womb, the inside of the earth, it could take on 'corrupt and poysonous Vapours from arsenical or other Minerals, and loaded therewith break out into the open Air'. Hodges was confident of his facts. He wrote that the interaction 'between the Sun's Rays, and these saline Exhalations, by a kind of Magnetism between them, is too obvious in a Multitude of Instances to want any comment'.[89] Part of his confidence may have come from the way he, like others, integrated old certainties with new ones. He kept to the old view that plague was caused by a contagious poison, and added the modern opinion that it consisted of corrupted nitrous spirit. Hodges asserted almost as an observational fact that:

The Pestilence is a Disease arising from an *Aura* that is poisonous, very subtle, deadly and contagious, affecting many Persons at the same Time together in one country, chiefly arising from a Corruption of the nitrous Spirit in the Air, attended with a Fever, and other very grievous Symptoms.
Every one of these Particulars are as clear as the Light at Noon-day.[90]

Hodges was aware that the older explanations might still have to be used, and that (see chapter 10) a case could be made, especially by modern Galenists like himself, for the equivalence between the

---

[88] Ibid., p. 10.   [89] Hodges, *Loimologia*, pp. 39, 37, 40–1, 38.   [90] Ibid., p. 32.

humoral theory of the ancients and the mechanical-corpuscular theory of the moderns. He recognised that corruption or putrefaction was for both ancients and moderns the agent that caused pathological change in cases of plague:

It comes down to us for the Opinion of some of them [the ancients], that a Putrefaction of Choler in an humane Body gives Rise to a Pestilence; and of others, that Fire may be so corrupted, as to occassion the same; what therefore the former conceived of Choler, and the latter of Fire, we may judge more justly ascribed here to a vitiated saline Spirit.[91]

Part of the reason why putrefaction was retained by Hodges and by even more whole-hearted supporters of the new science and also by Helmontians[92] may have been that there was no other way available to describe the process whereby the saline spirit became 'vitiated'. The idea of things 'going off', as in food, corpses, stagnant water, etc., was a powerful and long-lasting one, and it was as attractive to the followers of the corpuscular philosophy as it had been to those of traditional Galenic medicine. Putrefaction, as we have seen, had the connotations of disease, dissolution and death. It was perhaps no accident that the most dreaded of diseases was so strongly and enduringly linked to putrefaction, and that putrefaction acted upon the bodies, such as the poor, cesspits or corpuscles, that caused plague. These bodies became putrified or vitiated and they carried putrefaction to other bodies. The symmetry is apparent, for both the causes and the symptoms of plague were expressive of putrefaction.

The corpuscular philosophy, it could be argued, made the sources

---

[91] Ibid., pp. 42–3. Hodges wrote that the nitrous spirit was commonly believed to be incorruptible, and he tried to avoid the association of corruption with humidity, one of the four qualities in the Aristotelian–Galenic system of qualities, elements and humours. Nevertheless, something akin to corruption, he wrote, had to occur to the nitrous spirit: 'Corruption here is not in that Sense strictly as when it is the Produce of Humidity, but somewhat more congruous to the peculiar Nature of nitrous Spirit; which although it cannot, like some other Bodies, putrifie, yet if it can be changed from its Nature and Figure, so as not to be reducible into them again, it does not seem improperly said that such a Change is equivalent to Corruption, its Vitality or Essence being destroyed, and a new Texture being obtained.'

[92] Willis, 'Of Fevers', p. 104, wrote that pestiferous atoms and bodies by 'a long putrefaction' acquired their poisonous powers of creating putrefaction in the bodies of plague victims. Helmontians, such as George Thomson, ΛΟΙΜΟΤΟΜΙΑ, *Or, the Pest Anatomised* (London, 1666), pp. 8–9, 14, kept to the view that it was a 'venemous Gas, or subtle Poyson, fracedious noisom Exhalations' originating 'from putrid bodies' that initiated plague though the body's imagination, and its archeus or internal chemist generated the disease within the body (see chapter 8, for a discussion of Helmontian theories of disease).

and causes of plague more remote from ordinary life, and therefore less easily controlled, but many of the characteristics of the poison remained the same. Like earlier writers, Hodges agreed that it was more deadly than other poisons, and that it was fine and penetrating. The invisibility of the nitro-aerial particles and their fineness echoed and reinforced the older picture of the plague poison. The 'aura' or the collection of corrupted nitro-aerial particles 'is so rare, subtle, volatile, and fine, that it insinuates into, and resides in the very Interstices, or Pores of the aerial Particles'. Thus the language of the new corpuscular philosophy continued to convey the deadliness and terror of the plague poison. The aura of plague was similar to that of a poison, but 'the deadly Quality of a Pestilence vastly exceeds either the arsenical Minerals, the most poisonous Animals or Insects, or the killing Vegetables; nay, the Pestilence seems to be a Composition of all the other Poisons together'. The subtlety of the poisonous aura made it more volatile than any meteor and 'more active than Lightning, and in the Twinkling of an Eye carries to a Distance Putrefaction, Mortification, and Death'.[93] It was not only swift but unexpected; 'its approaches are generally so secret, that Persons seized with it seem to be fallen into an Ambuscade, or a Snare, of which there was no Manner of Suspicion'. Although earlier writers wrote of the secrecy and suddenness of plague, they gave hope that it could be controlled by seeking out and avoiding, modifying or destroying the sources of stenches and evil smells. Like Boghurst, however, Hodges wrote that, on the whole, the plague poison could not be detected by smell. The corpuscular philosophy, with its invisible, fine, particles, seemed to undercut the ability of the senses to distinguish a pathological environment in the case of plague. This was understandable, as underlying the 'new science' in all its forms was the denial of the reality and primacy of sensory qualities such as those of touch or smell in making up the world (they were reduced in John Locke's terminology to 'secondary qualities').

A universal, single source of plague spreading through the world in the air began in the 1660s to replace the huge variety of different sources. Its origin in the bowels of the earth would have logically meant that little could be done about it, whereas the crowded houses, stinking cesspits and rotting bodies that traditionally were thought to give off the plague poison were eminently amenable to

---

[93] Hodges, *Loimologia*, pp. 32–3, 34.

preventive action. What we have here is the partial replacement of one construction of plague with another, the earlier appearing more rooted in everyday life, perhaps more localised and domestic, the later seeming, from a twenty-first century perspective, to be more abstract and distanced from everyday experience and more elitist; however, whether this was seen to be the case in the later seventeenth-century, and by whom, are difficult questions to resolve. Both early and late seventeenth century physicians wrote of the ignorance of the public in relation to the issue of contagion and the sources of plague.[94] The paradigm of the single universal source of plague may have made the disease even more terrifying because it was not located in specific, familiar places, nor was it accessible to the senses. These 'personal instruments', the counterparts of the instruments used by scientists and institutions today to detect dangers in the environment, were useless against the plague:

They are therefore not to be credited or regarded, who affirm the Progress of a Pestilence to be sensible, even to the Smell and Sight, and report (though who will may believe them for me) the Infection to resemble the Fragrancy of Flowers in *May*, or any other sweet Savour; or, on the contrary, to strike the Nose like the Stench of a rotten Carcase; nay, some pretend to be so sharp-sighted, as to discern Clouds in the Atmosphere big with pestilential Poysons, and other such Conceits of a distempered Imagination, that are chiefly the Products of Fear, which construes every Thing for the worst.[95]

Older views such as the importance of smell may represent a powerful traditional practice concerning the recognition of plague, and more generally the continuing role of the senses in the material conditions of most people's lives. There was no general change in the technology governing everyday life, neither were there any alternative instruments to the senses such as an effective microscope. Nor, as we have seen in chapter 4, were there the institutions and agencies, such as laboratories or public health bureaucracies, to act on behalf of the public with the cognitive authority so to do derived

---

[94] For instance, Bradwell, *Physick for the Sicknesse*, p. 6: 'though it may thus by the Learned be acknowledged to be *Venemous*, yet it is, by many of the *Ignorant* sort conceited not to be Infectious'.

[95] Hodges, *Loimologia*, pp. 34–5. He did elsewhere compromise. The subtle plague aura could be 'mixed or loaded with gross and sulphureous Particles, as to be perceptible to the Senses', and some people may have first sensed plague 'upon taking in ungrateful and filthy Smells; for the pestilential *Seminium* . . . when it incorporates with other Bodies that are gross, fat and visciol, may strike the Organs of Sensation very manifestly at its first Entrance': pp. 35, 89.

from political, legal and social processes as is the case today. It therefore appears from hindsight that there was a disjunction between the small group of highly influential intellectuals who believed in the mechanical philosophy and in its downgrading of sensory impressions (a paradoxical downgrading, given the emphasis in the philosophy of Francis Bacon, the father-figure of the new science in England, of the importance of observation), and the vast majority of the population for whom the qualities that they sensed reflected reality, and provided them with a sense of control over the plague. As the plague left England at this time, the effects of this disjunction, in relation to plague at least, were not significant. We do not know if the new, less personal and less localised view of the plague would have trickled down through society and changed the practical measures that had traditionally been employed to prevent its spread, which were based on the belief that the sources of plague were localised and often detected by the senses.

CONCLUSION

Medical writers amplified the horror of plague yet offered hope of cure. They made plague a special disease spread by an invisible poison, but they also made it familiar by describing it in terms of well-known causes of disease, such as putrefaction and environmental and lifestyle factors that were standard in the regimens. The sense of familiarity may have given medical writers and their readers confidence that plague could be prevented and cured. However, the partial redefinition of plague in the language of the new science lessened the sense of control over plague by taking its source away from the everyday public world of sewers and dunghills. In the next chapter these sources of plague assume critical importance. Having established in this chapter how medical writers created a credible body of knowledge, in early modern terms, about the origins, transmission and nature of plague so that medical action against plague was generally considered feasible, the next considers how the prevention and cure of the disease were envisaged.

CHAPTER 7

The prevention and cure of the plague

MEDICINE AND PREVENTION OF PLAGUE

Medical writers did not hesitate to give advice on measures to prevent plague. As discussed in the previous chapter, this was on two levels: one was related to the community, the other to the individual and to the private space around a person, whether inside their house or out of doors. Both types of advice drew upon the principle that foul smells and dirt had to be expelled, counteracted or avoided. The belief that foul airs and places were pathological was well integrated into learned medicine and popular belief, and as we have seen in chapter 4 it formed a central part of regimen, medical topography and preventive medicine in general.[1]

The advice on measures with community-wide application differed from that addressed to the individual in that it was concerned with the government or ordering of society, and was sometimes specifically directed at magistrates and others in authority. Medical writers were not telling them anything new, for the latter were often well aware of the perceived association between stinking air, foul places and diseases such as plague. The dramatic, community-wide measures of quarantine, the shutting up of infected houses, the closing of lodging houses, inns and theatres, and the banning of fairs were ordered not by physicians but by governments and local authorities. In the Italian states of Venice, Florence, Genoa and Milan, which led Europe in public health measures from the time of the Black Death (1347–50) onwards, it was civic authorities rather than physicians who had initiated large-scale responses to plague, though physicians did give advice.[2]

---

[1] Moreover, medical writers often organised the preventive sections of their plague treatises according to the six non-naturals, so that they gave advice on air, diet, sleep and waking, etc.

[2] Cipolla argues that public health first appeared in Italy at the time of the Black Death

When England in the sixteenth century began to put into place measures designed to limit contagion, the physicians, as in Italy, provided advice but had no legal standing to initiate measures. Nor, as became the case in the nineteenth and twentieth centuries, did they work together in government departments with civil servants to govern the health of the public. The magistracies of health (so called because they had judicial powers to enforce health regulations, including by means of imprisonment and execution) in the Italian states came close, but no such departments existed in England. Even the recommendation of a renowned individual such as Charles I's physician Sir Theodore Turquet de Mayerne for an Italian-style magistracy of health for London went unheeded. The advice of the London College of Physicians was sought by the Privy Council, but it was advice from a body that remained outside government.[3] The College's greatest impact on government health policy was probably in the list of remedies for the use of the public which was appended to the Plague Orders published from 1578 onwards. However, the existence of government policy on plague did not deter medical and lay writers from publishing advice for individuals and the community.

Lodge, for instance, who apparently saw no barriers of cultural interchange in publishing a French medical treatise on plague as if it was an English production, proffered advice as if it was novel, setting out 'The order and policy that ought to be held in a City during the Plague time.'[4] He wrote that the magistrates should 'have an especiall care, that their city be kept cleane and neate from al filth, dunghils and stinking rubbige that may breed infection, because the

onwards and not in nineteenth-century England as English historians have argued: Carlo M. Cipolla, *Miasmas and Disease: Public Health and the Environment in the Pre-Industrial Age* (Yale University Press, London, 1992). For the role of physicians see Carlo M. Cipolla, *Public Health and the Medical Profession in the Renaissance* (Cambridge University Press, Cambridge, 1976); for the most penetrating account of how civic authorities rather than physicians led the way in accepting plague as a contagious disease and in preventive measures see R. Palmer, 'The Control of Plague in Venice and Northern Italy, 1348–1600' (Ph.D. thesis, University of Kent at Canterbury, 1978). On medical views of contagion see Margaret Pelling, 'Contagion/Germ Theory/Specificity' in W. F. Bynum and R. Porter (eds.), *Companion Encyclopedia of the History of Medicine* (2 vols., Routledge, London, 1993), vol. I, pp. 309–34.

[3] Paul Slack, *The Impact of Plague in Tudor and Stuart England* (Routledge & Kegan Paul, London, 1985), pp. 218–19. The College's recommendation in 1631 for 'a commission or office of health' such as had been 'found useful in Spain, Italy and other places' along the lines of Mayerne's board of health was not taken up.

[4] Thomas Lodge, *A Treatise of the Plague* (London, 1603), fol. F1[r].

steame of such uncleane heapes and places being drawne up into the aire do for the most part infect and contaminate the same'. A vigorous clean-up of the city was recommended. Across Europe the call went out during plague for spiritual and physical cleanliness and order, and magistrates in London were urged to:

give charge, that in every place the streets should be kept cleane, and daily purged, forbidding every one under a penalty to cast out any uncleanesse or filth out of their dores. They ought also to take order, that the slaughter houses (for the provision of the citty) be not continued and used within the citty, but placed in some remote and convenient place neere unto the river of the Thames, to the end that the bloud and garbige of the beasts that are killed may be washed away with the tide.[5]

The need for cleanliness and the fear of dirt, despite the 'norm' of endemically dirty living environments, had long informed government rhetoric, if not practical action. It was a rhetoric that was as much about order as about medicine, and it echoed the concerns of medical writers. From the Middle Ages, English governments and civic authorities related dirt to disease and reiterated the need for the disposal of dirt. In 1388 the Parliament held in Cambridge passed an Act that stated:

For that so much Dung and Filth of the Garbage and Intrails as well of Beasts killed as of other Corruptions be cast and put in Ditches, Rivers and other Waters, and also many other Places within . . . divers [several] Cities, Boroughs and Towns of the Realm, and the Suburbs of them, that the Air there is greatly corrupt and infect, and many Maladies and other intolerable Diseases do daily happen . . . that all they which do cast and lay all such Annoyances, Dung, Garbages, Intrails and other Ordure in Ditches, Rivers, Waters and other places shall cause them to be removed, avoided and carried away. . .[6]

In early modern England those concerned with the ordering of cities, towns and villages were aware that dirt was unpleasant and dangerous and should be avoided or expelled. In the sixteenth century scavengers were appointed on a regular basis in towns such as London, Ipswich and Exeter, to supervise the sweeping of pavements and to get rid of 'nuisances' such as dunghills and the animal remains from slaughter-houses.[7] In London the scavengers,

---

[5] Ibid., fol. F2r.

[6] Charles Creighton, *A History of Epidemics in Britain* (Cambridge University Press, Cambridge, 1891), p. 324.

[7] Ibid., p. 327.

who were reputable householders appointed for a year (they could not refuse the office), oversaw the rakers who did the actual cleaning and who were paid from parish rates. The scavengers swore to 'diligently oversee . . . that the Ways, Streets and Lanes, be cleansed of Dung, and all manner of Filth, for the honesty of this City'.[8] A rudimentary localised structure existed that recognised the problem of dirt and tried to deal with it. London householders were also drawn into the process of disposing of dirt. During plague they were ordered to draw bucketfuls of water from any well or pump that they owned to flush the channels running through the middle of the streets which were usually full of foul refuse. In 1541 it was twelve bucketfuls three times a week; by 1583 it had risen to at least twenty bucketfuls each morning before six and another twenty after eight o' clock every evening.[9] Even a small community like the Wiltshire village of Castle Combe was influenced by a need for the regulatory control of dirt. In 1590 the villagers were put under the following restraints:

And that the inhabitants of the West Strete doe remove the donge or fylth at John Davis house ende . . . under pain of 3 shillings and four pence.

And that none shall lay any duste or any other fylth in the wey or pitte belowe Christopher Besas house, under pain for each offence of twelve pence.

And that none shall soyle [dirty] in the church yerde nor in any of our stretes, for every default to lose twelve pence.

And that the glover shall not washe any skynes, nor cast any other fylth or soyle in the water runninge by his house, under pain of ten shillings.[10]

Despite an awareness of the need for cleanliness and a degree of regulation and organisation, sanitation in England was often haphazard, characterised by periods of neglect and inactivity punctuated by the issuing forth of exhortations and regulations.[11] It is important to note that England was not a hygienic country in the sixteenth and seventeenth centuries. Today, given the interaction between the state

---

[8] F. P. Wilson, *The Plague in Shakespeare's London* (Clarendon Press, Oxford, 1927), pp. 26–7. See Mark Jenner, 'Early Modern English Conceptions of "Cleanliness" and "Dirt", As Reflected in the Environmental Regulation of London *c.* 1530–*c.* 1700' (D.Phil. thesis, University of Oxford, 1991). The most concerted attempt at eradicating foci of putrefaction and miasmas before plague occurred was undertaken by the Florentine state in the seventeenth century: Cipolla, *Miasmas and Disease.*

[9] Wilson, *Plague in Shakespeare's London*, pp. 28–9.

[10] Creighton, *A History of Epidemics in Britain*, p. 328.

[11] For example, ditches and rivers were constantly clogging up with filth over long periods and having to be specially cleaned: Wilson, *Plague in Shakespeare's London*, pp. 31–4.

and scientific medicine, hygiene is the expected norm, whether in food, water, air or in living and working environments. In western developed countries it is taken for granted that people's everyday world is relatively hygienic. Vast resources are expended to achieve this, largely unquestioningly. In a sense, hygiene is now one of the hidden programmes that shapes the developed world. It is only when the programme goes wrong, when hygienic regulation fails, that there is a sense of shock.[12]

In contrast, in the early modern period instances of dirty foul airs and places were perceived as parts of the normal environment that were also sources of danger needing to be cleaned up. Plague, with the associated belief in local 'hot spots' of contagion, gave added force to such an interpretation of dirt. For instance, in 1574 the Vice-Chancellor of Cambridge University wrote that plague had come to the town through God's secondary causes or means, 'partlie by the apparell of one that cam from London to Midsomer fayer', and 'the other cause as I conjecture, is the corruption of the King's dytch the which goeth through Cambridge, and especially in those places where there is most infection the which I will procure, so sone as we shall have any hard frost, to be clensed'.[13]

The community-wide preventive measures suggested by medical writers were often already being carried out and were likely to have been familiar to their readers. This was in keeping with one aspect of English medicine, namely the common medical culture shared by lay people and medical practitioners. It also indicates, perhaps, that by recommending measures that were being used in towns and cities during plague, medical writers were reinforcing them and giving them added legitimacy. For instance, the London regulations of 1583, which ordered householders to draw bucketfuls of water to flush the channels in the streets, also directed that they had to clean the channel and sweep the street facing their houses and, more particularly, that the water used to flush the channel should not go onto the street, and only a sprinkling of water could be put on the street itself to settle the dust.[14] Bradwell clearly drew upon existing

---

[12] As when, to the great horror of the British public, it was disclosed in 1988 that eggs produced under intensive battery farming conditions were infected with salmonella.

[13] In Laurence and Helen Fowler (eds.), *Cambridge Commemorated, An Anthology of University Life* (Cambridge University Press, Cambridge, 1984), p. 27, extracted from Charles Henry Cooper, *Annals of Cambridge* (Cambridge, 1842–1908).

[14] Wilson, *Plague in Shakespeare's London*, p. 29.

practice when he recommended that people should 'Every morning and evening *sweep cleane the streets* before every mans doore: *Wash downe the channells* to keepe them sweet. But I like not that slabbering of the pavement before the house, which I see many use in moyst wether; for it increaseth the dampishnesse of the Aire: except it be before the stalls of Butchers and Cookes.'[15]

The language of some of the medical advice on preventing plague seems at first sight to reflect the fact that much of the advice was already in the public domain. It appears uncomplicated and devoid of esoteric medical terminology. The criteria for cleanliness were based on the senses, especially of smell and sight, and recognition of stinking smells and of sweet smells was open to anyone. Cleaning of streets and ditches was based on simple manual labour, so the knowledge of sources of plague poison and the means of their elimination were open to all, and did not depend on specialised medical expertise or technology. This demotic quality in plague prevention was very strong. When medical writers described what had to be done to avoid foul airs and places, they used simple language, conjuring up an image of a city intimately linked to people and their senses. Foul smells were portrayed as almost alive, adding force to the contagion:

> that al the streetes, lanes and allies be kept cleane and sweete, as possible may bee, not suffering the filth and sweepings to lie in heapes, as it dooth, especially in the suburbes, but to be caried alwaie more speedily: for the uncleane keeping of the streets, yeilding as it dooth noisome and unsavory smelles, is a meanes to increase the corruption of the aire, and giveth great strength unto the pestilence.[16]

Despite the strong strand of ordinary, non-esoteric language that was used by medical writers, prevention was also brought within a more specifically medical discourse. Bad smells were pathological, corrupting life-giving air, and, when breathed in, they damaged the inside of the body. As Christopher Wirsung's *The General Practise of Physicke* put it, 'it is generally concluded by all learned men, that . . . the heart requireth a sweete, cleane, and healthy ayre, like as the body requireth meate and drinke: also that nothing is more venimous, noysome, nor hurtfull for the same than a foule stinking ayre', so that they 'sooner hurt the heart and inner parts, and by

---

[15] Stephen Bradwell, *A Watch-Man for the Pest* (London, 1625), p. 11.
[16] Thomas Thayre, *A Treatise of the Pestilence* (London, 1603), p. 8: 'al the pondes, pooles, and ditches about the City' were also to be cleansed.

their contagion disease the whole body, and lastly bereave man of his vitall breath'.[17] The foul smells recognised by the public were placed into a medical and anatomical context. Although smells, dirt and cleanliness were known to most people, the allusion to 'learned men' signified that there were some matters which were known only to a few.

Purging the air

The measures to be taken against dirt and foul air were medicalised. Like a diseased body, the air was to be purged, purified, altered and corrected.[18] Fires cleaned the air of the plague poison. Herring urged that juniper, the great stand-by that was used for correcting the air with sweet smells, should be added to the fires: 'Let the air be purged and corrected, especially in evenings which are somewhat cold, and in places low and neare the River (as Thames streete and the Allyes there about) by making fires of Oken or Ash-wood, with some fewe bundles of Iuniper cast into them.'[19] Unlike the cleaning of dirt from the streets, the fires purged a pathological aspect of the natural world – the air of damp evenings and 'the vapoures of the nyghte'.[20] Plague was embedded both in the artificial, man-made world, and in nature. Both had to be cleaned: 'as running water like a broome cleanseth the earth', wrote Mouffet, 'so fire like a Lion eateth up the pollutions of the aire'. Ancient medical authority gave added legitimacy to the lighting of fires. Hippocrates, it was pointed out, had 'freed the Citie of Cranon . . . and Athens also (as Galen testifieth . . .) by making great bonfires, and burning sweet odours and costly oyntments in them'.[21]

Medical advice in this case mirrored actual practice, though often

---

[17] Christopher Wirsung, *Praxis Medicinae Universalis; Or a Generall Practise of Physicke*, trans. Iacob Mosan (London, 1598), p. 654.

[18] Thayre, *Treatise*, p. 7, Bradwell, *A Watch-Man for the Pest*, p. 11; Andrew Wear, 'Making Sense of Health and the Environment in Early Modern England' in Andrew Wear (ed.), *Medicine in Society. Historical Essays* (Cambridge University Press, Cambridge, 1992), pp. 137–8.

[19] Francis Herring, *Certaine Rules, Directions, or Advertisements for this Time of Pestilentiall Contagion* (1st edn 1603; London, 1625), fol. A4ʳ.

[20] Thomas Phayre, 'A Goodly Bryfe Treatyse of the Pestylence' in *The Regiment of Life* (London, 1545), fol. M5ʳ.

[21] Thomas Mouffet, *Healths Improvement: Or, Rules Comprizing and Discovering the Nature, Method, and Manner of Preparing all sorts of Food used in this Nation: Corrected and Enlarged by Christopher Bennett* (London, 1655), p. 24. Stephen Bradwell, *Physick for the Sycknesse, Commonly Called the Plague* (London, 1636), p. 11.

in the medicine of this period it was the reverse. Fires were lit in the streets of London in 1563 thrice weekly at 7 p.m., and in 1603 pitch bonfires were lit twice weekly at night. In 1625 the parish of St Christopher's bought earthen pans, charcoals, stone pitch, frankincense and incense for the fires.[22] Pepys recorded on 6th September 1665, during the height of the plague, that 'I looked into the street and saw Fires burning in the street, as it is through the whole City by the Lord Mayors order.'[23] This was one of the more systematic responses to plague. The purging of the air was a concerted effort. Within the length of a street a fire was lit between every six houses for three nights beginning on 5th September.[24] The College of Physicians, in its official recommendations for the plague published by the Privy Council in 1665, reiterated this well-known remedy: 'Fires made in the Streets often, and good Fires kept in and about the houses of such as are visited, and their Neighbours, may correct the infectious Airs; as also frequent discharging of Guns.'[25]

Fires were expensive for the parishes that had to bear their cost, especially when coal and aromatics like juniper and rosemary became scarce and expensive.[26] Shooting guns into the air was cheaper, wrote Bradwell. It is worth quoting him at length to show how he brought two existing civic practices within medical discourse, mixing medical reasoning, previous authorities and a dash of religion:

Now for *my opinion* what way is best to purge the *Generall Aire of the Region*. I must needs say that of *Hippocrates . . . is the best*, but too costly to be received of our Citizens. Therefore I would advise that *Muskets and such like peeces* might be discharged in every street, lane, and corner of the Cittie every morning and every evening. This way (in hot weather) doth not enflame so much as bonfiers doe by their continued heat, but purifie as much, or rather more. For by the blow, the Aire is first forcibly moved, shaken,

[22] Wilson, *Plague in Shakespeare's London*, p. 31.

[23] Samuel Pepys, *The Diary of Samuel Pepys*, ed. Robert Latham and William Matthews (11 vols., Bell & Hyman, London, 1970–83), vol. VI, p. 213.

[24] Walter Bell, *The Great Plague of London* (1st edn, 1924; Bracken Books, London, 1994), p. 237.

[25] College of Physicians, *Certain Necessary Directions, as well for the Cure of the Plague, as for preventing the Infection: With many easie Medicines of small Charge . . . By the Kings Maiesties special Command* (London, 1665), p. 7; the 1636 *Directions* make the same recommendations.

[26] Bell, *The Great Plague of London*, p. 237; Wilson, *Plague in Shakespeare's London*, p. 31. Thomas Dekker in *The Wonderfull Yeare* (1603) commented that 'the price of flowers, hearbes and garlands, rose wonderfully, in so much that Rosemary which had wont to be solde for 12 pence an armefull, went now for six shillings a handfull': F. P. Wilson, *The Plague Pamphlets of Thomas Dekker* (Clarendon Press, Oxford, 1925), pp. 34–5.

devided and attenuated, and so prepared for purification; and then immediatly (by the heat of the fire) purified: and that kinde of fire purgeth it better then others, for (by reason of the *Sulphur* and *Saultpeeter*) it is exceeding drying; and very wholsome. And that this opinion is not any conceit of mine owne; let those that will, Read *Levinius Lemnius de Occultis Naturae Miraculis* [book 2, chapter 10] or *Crato* [Crato von Crafftheim] *in Consilio* 275. Or *Raymundus Mindererus li*[ber] *de Pestilentia cap. 20.* The Heathens could be at great cost in contagious times; . . . Why may not *Wee* be at a lesser cost, for the safety of a greater Cittie. GOD is nearer to us, then he was to them; we have his promises 'to keepe us in all our wayes'; and to 'prosper our handy workes'; they had no such comforts to rest upon; Yet they endevoured and obtained: we obtaine not, onely because we endevour not.[27]

Each outbreak of plague was an occasion when the question of what measures to take had to be answered afresh. The lack of any permanent board or magistracy of health as in the Italian states would have contributed to the lack of continuity. Also, the recommendation of existing measures not only reinforced what was known, familiarly granting them legitimacy, but it may also have reflected a view that, even if they were known about, they needed to be put more generally into practice. This is the impression that is given by the *Directions* of the College of Physicians. More generally, medical discourse or instructions, especially about regimen, often involved a listing of imperatives which appear innovative in view of the assumption that the patient, or in this case the city, has not in the past carried out the required action. Physicians, and also religious writers, by using the imperative or instructional mode could 'refresh' traditional knowledge and avoid a stale presentation of old knowledge and practices. Bradwell, for instance, like many other physicians, brought off the trick of recommending what seem to be innovations but which were in fact existing practices. Hippocrates supported the use of fires; other, more modern, authorities believed in discharging guns; Bradwell brought life and relevance into his discussion by making it appear that these ideas had not previously been put into practice.

The burning of fires and the firing of guns into the air might seem dramatic and symbolic, and tempt us to interpret such practices. Were they in reality ways of frightening off the disease, as evil spirits might be scared away, or shooting and killing the disease, or was the

---

[27] Bradwell, *A Watch-Man for the Pest*, pp. 12–13.

making of loud noises and the burning of fires in some way analogous to the celebrations bringing in the New Year and the renewal of life? We are the sceptical children of the Enlightenment, ready when some practice does not work to re-interpret it in nineteenth-century terms as superstition, or as having underlying twenty-first-century social, psychological or symbolic functions. Bradwell placed the practices of burning fires and shooting off guns into the rational and normal discourses of his time and justified them as a matter of course by contemporary medical reasoning (purging), from past authorities and religion.

However, the Enlightenment was only just around the corner. Forty years later fires and shots were being sceptically rejected. Hodges recorded that physicians counselled against the fires as the air itself, not being infected, could not be purged. Also, he pointed out that they did not work, for during the three nights that the fires burned 'the most fatal Night ensued, wherein more than four Thousand expired'.[28] Boghurst thought that little effect could be produced by fires and other means of correcting the air, perhaps because he believed in a universal poisoning of the air from fumes rising from the earth's bowels, rather than in localised sources of contagious poison. He wrote concerning air, 'little can be done . . . because all that wee can do will work but little alteration in it, the effect of all that bee done, being so flitting and transitory'. Correction of the air was more feasible if a localised view was taken of contagion. A general poisoning of the air and the existence of a 'pestilent constitution'[29] was, as we have seen in the previous chapter, beyond local correction. And Boghurst also pointed out that another localist belief, that high places, which in traditional medical topography were perceived as healthy, would offer protection during plague, was erroneous.[30] Established medical and popular views

---

[28] Nathaniel Hodges, *Loimologia: Or, An Historical Account of the Plague in London in 1665* (London, 1720), p. 20. Others in 1665 believed that the fires worked, as the deaths for the week in which the fires were lit fell by 444: Bell, *The Great Plague of London*, p. 237.

[29] William Boghurst, *Loimographia: An Account of the Great Plague of London In the Year 1665*, ed. J. F. Payne (Shaw & Sons for the Epidemiological Society of London, 1894), pp. 61, 63.

[30] Ibid., p. 55; also on p. 57 he recommended that 'High grounds, or hills' should be avoided, 'especially bleak windy places to live in. At Hampstead died two hundred, three score and odd, out of about a hundred houses, yet at the West End a little village soe called a quarter of a mile off, at the bottom of the Hill, there dyed none, though there are about thirty or forty houses there; contrary to the doctrine of many authors, who have said that scarce any who live upon hills in cleere air ever have the plague.'

coincided in Boghurst's opinion, and by equating the two he again (see previous chapter) cast doubt on the former as the beliefs of 'the people' were often seen as false:

> Yet a great bustle hath beene made among Authors and the people about correcting the aire . . . I have not spent two farthings this yeare about correcting the aire in my house, yet I think I had as wholesome aire blowing in my house as my neighbours, many of which filled their houses every day to fumigate and correct the aire, yet I had noe body sick or dyed in my house all this year, nor in my life.[31]

Boghurst doubted whether the public city-wide measures of making fires or discharging guns did any good. His tone was dismissive: correcting the air was founded on 'that old story of Hypocrates'.[32] Traditional medical advice, which was also public policy, was equated with a popular custom, shown by personal experience, the new touchstone of truth of the new science, to be ineffective. Yet Boghurst felt, despite his own disbelief, that he had to spell out what types of wood, herbs and spices were best to burn: 'because some people have great conceits about correcting the aire, I will set down all the devises I can think of which may do any good'. Not only did popular demand lead him to list old 'devises', but he seems despite his doubts to have had a lingering belief in them. Nevertheless, the new sense that they are part of popular, folk customs rather than belonging to medicine emerges through his lists: 'Besides these things', he wrote, 'oft flashing of gunpowder is much in esteem with some, and wildfire squibbs, fire balls and other, serpents, crackers and gymnacks which are commonly used on the 5th of November.'[33] Boghurst, like other writers influenced by the new science, balanced between scepticism and acceptance of past practices.

Although Boghurst linked advice of 'Authors and the people' and doubted both, one strand of Baconian thought advocated the recording of traditional practices, some of which might contain useful information (see chapter 2).[34] Moreover, Thomas Willis, who was a major player in the early stages of integrating medicine and

---

[31] Ibid., p. 61.   [32] Ibid., p. 62.   [33] Ibid., pp. 61, 63.

[34] Roy Porter, 'The Early Royal Society and the Spread of Medical Knowledge' in Roger French and Andrew Wear (eds.), *The Medical Revolution of the Seventeenth Century* (Cambridge University Press, Cambridge, 1989), pp. 272–93. Much 'useful' medical information was sent to Henry Oldenburg, *The Correspondence of Henry Oldenburg*, ed. and trans. A. Rupert Hall and Marie Boas Hall (13 vols, University of Wisconsin Press, Madison, 1965–1986).

new science,[35] was happy to combine the old with the new. He believed that plagues could be predicted from earthquakes, and the 'openings of Caverns and secret Vaults, by the gaping of the Ground, by reason of the Eruptions of malignant and empoysoned Airs'. But his was not a monocausal view: excessive heat, cold, dryness or wetness, or the occurrence of famine could foretell plague, and, he wrote, a plague could be of universal extent or localised. Also, he had no problems in accepting the traditional package of public measures for preventing plague, including in them the very traditional advice of avoiding fruit, removing 'Nests of Putrefaction' and correcting the air.[36]

It may be that Boghurst's personal experience of the plague and the failure of preventive measures, together with the availability of a new theory about the plague, allowed him to reject many past practices. Willis, on the other hand, had no personal experience of plague, because, as he explained, the gaps between outbreaks and the practice of physicians deserting patients during plague times meant that some physicians had little first-hand knowledge of plague.[37] Such lack of personal experience may have made it easier to accept long-established preventive measures. In any case, what is clear is that, until the last great outbreak of plague in England, medical writers and public authorities believed in the same largely unchanging set of measures, centred around those pervasive medical concerns: putrefaction, filth and poisonous stenches, whether from the environment or from plague victims.

Private space and the prevention of plague

Contagion was about space. How far or near one was to a source of contagion could determine, it was believed, the chances of catching plague. Certain spaces, such as those around the plague sick or dead

---

[35] Boghurst, *Loimographia*, p. 11, called him 'that great Ornament of the University of Oxon [Oxford]'.

[36] Thomas Willis, 'Of Fevers' in *Dr Willis's Practice of Physick*, trans. S. Pordage (London, 1684), pp. 106, 108.

[37] Ibid., p. 111: 'Concerning the Plague, we cannot so readily write Examples and Histories of sick persons, with exact Diaries of the Symptomes; because these kind of Sicknesses came not every year, neither when they spread, is it lawful for every Physician that takes care of his own health, frequently to visit the sick, or stay long with them, whereby he may denote all Accidents, and diligently consider the reasons of them'. See also George Starkey, *Nature's Explication and Helmont's Vindication* (London, 1657), p. 254, who stated that as he had no experience of plague he would not write about it.

and their houses, crowds, enclosed lanes, dunghills, etc., could all be deadly. People were advised against 'passing close, dirty, stinking and infected places, as Alleys, dark Lanes, Church-yards, Chandlers shops, common Alehouses, Shambles [slaughter-houses], Poultries . . .'[38] Direct contact by touch with plague victims, their clothes, bedclothes or their letters was considered even more dangerous. Both public authorities and individuals were expected by medical writers to lessen such dangers, or at least the exposure to them.

The public–private distinction was clearly recognised by plague writers. Willis wrote that 'Preventive Cautions either respect the Republick, and belong to the Magistrate, or private persons, to whom it should be taught, what is to be done by all men, when the Plague is feared.'[39] There was an awareness also of separate public and private spaces which magistrates and individuals respectively had to manage in the most healthy way. Bradwell wrote

I must distinguish Aire unto two kindes, viz. *Generall* and *Speciall*. By *Aire generall* I meane the whole open *Aire* of the *Region*.[40] By *Speciall*, I intend, either that which is *inclosed in houses*; or that which is *immediately next the person of every one, for the space of some yards compasse round about the Body, whether within doores or without, wheresoever it goeth or abideth*.[41]

All around danger lurked, whether in the privacy of one's house or out of doors in the special personal space that surrounded a person's body. Together with the sense of danger conveyed by medical writers (no doubt reflecting the general public perception) came very detailed instructions on how the individual could protect him- or herself. Avoidance of contagious spaces and airs was the most favoured action advised, whether by fleeing far away to a fresh air[42] or by taking more limited steps to stay away from sources of contagion such as the sick, crowds and dirty contagious places. However, many could not flee and often had to expose themselves to contact with possible sources of danger. For those who stayed, their domestic space, their house or room, had to be made safe, for going outside was a voluntary act, but one's home was a necessary haven. Just like streets, houses were made plague-free, by being kept clean,

---

[38] Gideon Harvey, *A Discourse of the Plague* (London, 1665), p. 16.

[39] Willis, 'Of Fevers', p. 108.

[40] It was to be purged, he wrote, by cleaning the streets, lanes, ditches etc. of a town, as well as using fires or shots to correct the surrounding air, in other words, it was coterminous with geographical structures such as streets.

[41] Bradwell, *A Watch-Man for the Pest*, pp. 10–11, Bradwell's emphasis.

[42] Gideon Harvey, *A Discourse of the Plague*, p. 16.

with no 'sluttish corners'; indoor fires in pans purged and 'aired' the house, and the air could also be perfumed by burning sweet-smelling juniper, bay leaves, etc.[43] A house, if medical advice was followed, became a fortress, its air made free of pestilence. One medical textbook advised:

> But if you may not flie for urgent businesse and just causes, then let your first care be, that the house in which you must tarrie, be without all kinde of stinke, and kept cleane from all filthinesse and sluttishnesse. Let the windowes of it be close shut, specially in cloudy and rainie dayes, that the pestilent aire enter not in. But if you will open them, see that they open upon the East or North quarter [all medical writers agreed that the south was most dangerous and advised that south-facing windows were always kept shut], and do it when the Sunne is risen above the earth some houres.[44]

What is striking from a present-day point of view is the detail of some of the advice that was offered. This was in keeping with the practice of providing highly detailed advice on remedies and regimen, but the fear surrounding plague gave it an almost obsessional air. For instance, the items to be cleaned inside a house were meticulously spelled out: 'Cleanse all your vessels often; wash those roomes that are in continuall use (both floors and wainscoting) *every morning; and (those which are able), wash the Windowes, Tables, Cupboards, Stooles, Benches, and all* wainscotings, *in summer with rose water, and vinegar: and in winter with the Decoction of Rew,* Worme wood, *Balme etc.'*[45] The detail was there because, as the families of victims confirmed, danger lurked everywhere, and it had to be expelled from every possible source, however commonplace.[46] As the advice

---

[43] Bradwell, *A Watch-Man for the Pest*, pp. 14–15.

[44] Philip Barrough, *The Method of Phisick*, 7th edn (London, 1634), p. 250.

[45] Bradwell, *A Watch-Man for the Pest*, p. 14.

[46] In [Anon], *The Shutting Up Infected Houses . . . Soberly Debated* (London, 1665), pp. 12–14, the families of victims and infected persons were reported as being questioned on what they thought had brought on plague. Seventy-five reasons were given, many involving the London environment: an infected hackney coach and sedan, an infected cushion, infected linen, 'a House of Office near a Man's Window', 'By close Chambers nastily kept, and looking southward'. Many reasons involved food (twenty-seven), such as a dish of eels, 'a rotten Shoulder of Mutton', 'By an immoderate eating of Caveare and Anchoves'. A few were medical; one only was 'By neglecting to let blood at the usual time', one only also was 'neglecting to purge at the usual times', and one only was 'the stopping of the monthly courses'. Food and drink were most under suspicion, which gives point to the books on regimen, and then places, things and people such as rakers and rag-women. Some of the reasons are idiosyncratic and detailed enough to make it pretty certain that the list was not made up: 'By Tame Pigeons that flew up and down in an Alley', 'By eating the Fat near the Rump of a Loyne of Mutton, and drinking cold beer immediately upon it', 'By money taken for Physick administred'. See also Slack, *Impact of Plague*, p. 251.

was organised along the lines of the six non-naturals (air, diet, exercise, etc.), it was easy to give specific advice relating to the details of people's lives. Thus, exercise had to be in moderation, not enough to make one sweat, which opened the pores of the body and let in the plague poison; for the same reason, hot baths were not recommended.[47]

But perhaps the advice that would have been most eagerly read was on what to do when leaving the familiar, and hopefully sanitised, environment of one's home. The world outside was not as easily controlled as the inside of a house. In this case, protective measures were advised. The pestilential air could be either kept at bay or purified by holding sweet-smelling herbs near the face, while at the same time cloves, angelica root, citron pills or garlic could be sucked. Such measures were commonly put into practice, as Bradwell made it clear when he criticised the use of wormwood, which, he stated, inflamed the brain: 'And it is a strange thing to see how all sorts of people play the fooles with their own noses, all carrying *Worm-wood* and thus thrusting it up into their nostrills. Wherein ten doe themselves iniurie, for one that doth good.'[48] Even before stepping out of doors precautions were to be taken. Departure had to take place at the right time, as Herring wrote, not 'early in the morning before the Sunne have purified the ayre, or late in the night after Sunne-setting. In rainie, darke and cloudie weather keepe your house as much as you can.' Before going out into danger, 'forth of your house into the ayre', a person should first have breakfast, or, if not accustomed to it, should take a nutmeg sized 'cordiall Electuarie prescribed by the learned Physitian', and then 'As you walke in the streets or talke with any, hold in your mouth a clove, a peece of a Zedoarie, Angelica, or Enula campana roote'. Additionally, 'cordiall and stomachicall pilles' should be taken regularly as a precaution 'to fortifie the heart and stomache against all corruption, and to cleanse your body from such humours as may dispose you to the sicknesse'. Business was also involved here, for at the end of the 1625 printing of Herring's treatise the reader was told that the 'Preservatives men-tioned in this booke, may be had from Mr. James the Apothecarie, at his house in Alderman-bury, neere to the signe of the axe . . .'[49]

---

[47] Cf. Herring, *Certaine Rules*, fol. B1ʳ; Barrough, *Method of Physick*, p. 251; Bradwell, *A Watch-Man for the Pest*, p. 37.

[48] Bradwell, *A Watch-Man for the Pest*, p. 16.

[49] Herring, *Certaine Rules*, fols. B1ᵛ–B2ʳ, C3ᵛ.

People's everyday material world was also put under the spotlight by the fear of plague. Clothes as well as smells could be dangerous, or could provide protection. Woollen clothes were thought to retain the infection for a long time, as also were feathers, leather and furs, and hence these were best avoided.[50] Dekker wrote (deriding the excesses of this fear):

I could tell you . . . how those were held especially very dangerous and perilous Trades that had any woolen about them, for the infection being for the most part a Londoner, loved to be kept warme, and therefore was saide to skip into woolen cloathes, and lie smothring in a shag-hayrde Rugge, or an old fashionde Coverlid: to confirme which, I have hard [heard] of some this last Sommer that would not venture into an Upholsters shoppe amongst dangerous Rugges and Feather-bed-tikes, no, although they had bene sure to have bene made Aldermen when they came out againe: such was their infectious conceyte a harmelesse Coverlid, and would stop their foolish Noses, when they past through *Watling street* by a Ranke of Woolen Drapers.[51]

Bradwell recommended the wearing of linens,[52] silks and satins, and the 'watering of stuffes [clothing materials] through their gumminesse, doth best exclude the Aire from entring or taking up any loging in the stuffs so dressed'. More specifically, he envisaged clothes as barring the pestilential air from the body, and wrote that:

Women usually have Whale-bone bodies which are as good armour as any other. Let the greatest care be to guard the vitall parts: But withall there must be some care of all the body: which to guard the better, it is good to weare *long* Cloakes of such watered stuffes as I have mentioned; which being outermost, excludeth well the outward Aire while one is abroad; and when one is come home, they may be layd by, till they have been aired.[53]

What lay behind such meticulous attention to detail? It conveys the sense that both public and private spaces had to be ordered, brought under control by cleanliness and by obstructing entry of the plague poison, and thus all aspects of the environment were under scrutiny, just as public and private sins and consciences were searched out and cleansed in a time of plague. Perhaps more pressing was the fear that attached to public and personal spaces.

---

[50] Bradwell, *A Watch-Man for the Pest*, p. 18; Harvey, *Discourse of the Plague*, p. 16, wrote: 'nothing breeds or retains Pestilent Atoms more than woolen, and feathers'.

[51] Thomas Dekker, *The Meeting of Gallants at an Ordinarie* (1604) in Wilson, *Plague Pamphlets*, p. 117.

[52] Though other writers such as Boghurst warned against them: *Loimographia*, p. 57.

[53] Bradwell, *A Watch-Man for the Pest*, pp. 18–19.

The detailed listing of many aspects of life, much more than has been described here, was a recognition and naming of people's fears and a way of giving them some sense of control over them. Fear was not only a distressing emotion for an individual to have to experience, it was also socially disruptive of the established norms of behaviour. It led to un-Christian acts such as deserting one's family or acting uncharitably to the poor or to the sick, and to the breakdown of social order. Giving detailed instructions on how to live prophylactically might lessen fear, and bring under some control the dangerous world around the reader. Physicians, moreover, all specifically cautioned against fear, which they believed lowered the body's defences and allowed plague to enter. The remedy was to be 'of a merry heart', to hear sweet music or drink some sack, or to seek the help of a clergyman, the physician of the soul.[54]

Fear was endemic during plague. Boghurst wrote of

the vanity and cruelty of people's unreasonable fear in all places, Cityes, Townes, Villages, single houses . . . They have been wormed in the ears with soe many lying storyes and horrible relations, and having heard some hideous terms and frightning aphorismes: as terrible Plague, noysome pestilence, burning pestilence, and that common speech soe often used in pulpits: 'Fly from sin as from a plague', and many such like expressions, which make many people believe the plague is like a Basiliske, or Salamander, which kills all they see or touch.[55]

People's fears produced 'vain and ridiculous courses'. Letters would be sifted in a sieve or washed in water and dried by a fire; others would 'air them at the top of a house, or an hedge, or a pole, two or three days before they opened them'. Money would be washed, clothes from London were shunned, and some people 'stopped the key-holes of their doors, and avoided the occassions of action and communication with all people and creatures'.[56] Such fears about

---

[54] See A. Wear, 'Fear, Anxiety and the Plague in Early Modern England' in J. R. Hinnells and R. Porter (eds.), *Religion, Health and Suffering* (Kegan Paul, London, 1999), pp. 339–63. More generally, Jean Delumeau, *La Peur en Occident XIV*ᵉ*–XVIII*ᵉ* Siècles* (Fayard, Paris, 1978), and *La Péché et La Peur* (Fayard, Paris, 1978). If the precautions were too obsessional they could be counterproductive. Boghurst, *Loimologia*, p. 29 noted: 'those who took most precautions fared the worst'. Order and the sense of control during plague are discussed in A. Wear, 'Popularised Ideas of Health and Illness in Seventeenth-Century France', *Seventeenth Century French Studies*, 8, 1986, 229–42, esp. 238–41. This paper has been seminal for much in the present book.

[55] Boghurst, *Loimographia*, p. 53.

[56] Ibid., pp. 53–4. See John Allin's plaintive complaint that his letters could be thought to be infectious: W. D. Cooper, 'Notices of the Last Great Plague, 1665–6, from the Letters of John Allin to Philip Fryth and Samuel Jeake', *Archaelogia*, 38, 1857, 1–22, at p. 8.

the minutiae of life were, in a sense, analogous to the advice to the private individual on how to prevent plague. For, although medical writers may have provided reassurance by giving detailed instructions on how to live, they must have also increased the sense of suspicious fear about every aspect of the environment by seeing everywhere (including in the air itself) sources of plague. Nevertheless, their cautions against fear and their categorisation of some reactions as unreasonable (though it is difficult to say what was the difference logically between fearing contagion from a body and from a letter) indicate that they were concerned to provide a basis for stable behaviour in the face of plague.

VISITING THE SICK

. . . the infectiousnes of the disease deterrs them who should assist from comming; Even the *Phisician* dares scarse come, *Solitude* is a torment, which is not threatned in *hell* it selfe.[57]

The time of greatest danger was when visiting the sick, when the imperative of Christian duty came into conflict with fear. Medical writers emphasised that any physical contact could be fatal, yet could be survived, thus echoing their general message that the environment was not impossibly dangerous: 'And as touchynge them that are continually amongst the sycke of this dysease, they must take hede . . . [not] to eate and drynke with them, nor in their vesseles, nor to lye in their couches, nor weare any of theyr apparell, except they be well ysonned [sunned], or weathered in ye cleane ayer.'[58] Contact with the sick was possible, but various physical barriers had to be used to avoid the patient's breath, etc. infecting the visitor, and sweet smells and prophylactic plague pills also acted to bar contagion. The instructions were detailed and conveyed a sense of danger, which may well have discouraged the visiting and care of the sick. Wirsung, for instance, advised that 'the patient be laid upon a high couch or bed, that the venimous damps and stenches [of the patient] may rest above, and be the lesse hurtfull to the standers by'. He further cautioned that 'when one commeth neare or toucheth the patient, then must his mouth be kept close shut, and draw his

---

[57] John Donne, *Devotions Upon Emergent Occasions*, ed. John Raspa (Oxford University Press, Oxford, 1987), pp. 24–5.
[58] Phayre, 'Treatyse of the Pestylence', fol. M7ᵛ.

breath onely at his nose. He shall annoint his nostrils with wine wherewith fine Treacle [Theriac] is tempered.'[59]

Forethought and preparation were the first requirements when visiting the sick, as they were when thinking of going out into the street, but the sense of a present looming danger was greater. Medical writers did not recommend that anyone should visit the sick as a matter of course; rather it should be undertaken only if one was bound to do so by reason of a religious or medical calling, or by ties of blood.[60] The deliberation and the need for minute care in the preparation before, during and after the visit, were both a response to the danger of the occasion and also a means of gaining control over it. Herring's list of precautions was also a dramatic description of an entry into and out of danger, and is worth quoting in full:

If any man be bound by Religion, consanguinitie, office, or any such respect to visite the sicke parties; let him first provide that the chamber be well perfumed with odoriferous trochiskes [medicinal ingredients shaped into little cakes] or such like, the windowes layd with the herbes aforenamed, the floore cleane swept, and sprinkled with rose-water and vineger: that there be a fire of sweet wood burning in the chimney, the windowes being shut for an houre, then open the casements towards the North. Then let him wash his face and hands with rose-water and rose vineger, and enter into the chamber with a waxe candle in the one hand, and a sponge with rose-vineger and wormewood, or some other Pomander, to smell unto. Let him hold in his mouth a peece of Mastic, Cinamon, Zedoarie, or Citron pill, or a Clove. Let him desire his sicke friend to speake with his face turned from him.

When he goeth forth, let him wash his hands and face with rose vineger and water as before, especially if he have taken his friend by the hand as the manner is: and going presently to his owne house, let him change his garments, and lay those wherein he visited his friend, apart for a good time before hee resume them againe.[61]

The right mental attitude was also protective. Those who visited the sick were urged by Lodge, in the manner of the regimens, not only to be sober in their diet but also 'merry and lightsome', 'for those that are fittest to be imployed in this matter, are such as have a good courage, and are merry, pleasant, and well complexioned and

[59] Wirsung, *General Practise of Physicke*, p. 680.
[60] Herring, *Certaine Rules*, fol. B2ʳ; Bradwell, *A Watch-Man for the Pest*, p. 9.
[61] Herring, *Certaine Rules*, B2ʳ⁻ᵛ. Quoted also in Wilson, *Plague in Shakespeare's London*, p. 10.

despite the danger of death, and are ready to doe service to their parents and frends, wives and children'. Moreover, as heroic Christians they gained some protection from God; they were 'in these times in least danger, and whom God (foreseeing their good zeale) protects by his mercy, preserving them from so great danger'. Yet nearly all writers urged the utmost caution when approaching the sick. Foolhardy courage could not conquer 'the secret venome of the plague . . . and except a man be wary and prudent, it wil then seaze him when he least suspecteth'. Only if duty required someone to expose themselves to the plague, Lodge argued, should they do so. But in such case, 'neyther on the contrary side should they be too fearefull, and so cowardly, as to forsake their fathers, mothers, wives and children for feare of death, but those by the commaundement of God, and law of nature, they ought to imploy all their power, yea to adventure life and bloud, to preserve those, who next under God gave them life, being, and living'.[62]

The sense of deliberation and the ritualistic instructions on how to act in the presence of the sick were a reflection of the grave danger of visiting them. Yet, despite modern sociological interpretations, to enter the sick room of a plague victim was no piece of acting, however detailed the play texts of the medical treatises might have been. It required courage of a high order and willingness to sacrifice one's life. But ritual and courage often go together. Such courage was recognised as real rather than feigned by Londoners who praised the dissenting ministers who stayed behind to look after their congregations.[63]

Boghurst, as in much else, was the exception when it came to visiting the sick. Perhaps because he did not believe over much in contagion, his behaviour at the bedside broke all the rules. 'I rendered', he wrote, 'myselfe very familiar with the disease, knowing that the meanes to doe any good it must not bee nice and fearfull.' He dressed forty sores a day and came in direct contact with patients, their breath and sweat, and stayed on through their dying:

I . . . held their pulse [while they were] sweating in the bed half a quarter of an hour together to give judgement and informe my selfe in the various tricks of it. I lett one blood, gave glisters, though but to few, held them up in

---

[62] Lodge, *A Treatise of the Plague*, fol. Ll^v.
[63] Bell, *Great Plague of London*, pp. 148–9, 223–6. Wilson, *Plague in Shapespeare's London*, p.10 noted the ritual aspect.

their bedds to keepe them from strangling and choking half an houre together, commonly suffered their breathing in my face severall tymes when they were dying, eate and dranke with them, especially those that had soares, sate down by their bedd sides and upon their bedds discoursing with them an houre together if I had tyme, and stayd by them to see the manner of their death, and closed up their mouth and eyes (for they dyed with their mouth and eyes very much open and stareing); then if people had noe body to helpe them (for helpe was scarce at such a tyme and place) I helpt to lay them forth out of the bedd and afterwards into the coffin, and last of all accompanying them to the grave.[64]

This was a different discourse, about communicating easily and willingly with the sick. Boghurst was clearly proud of his courage in staying on during the plague whilst others left,[65] but he also was arguing that, in order to make observations about the plague, direct and close contact with patients was necessary. Boghurst, who set out large numbers of prognostic signs and gave meticulous details of treatments based on his experience, was carrying out one aspect of the Baconian programme of the new science: the collection of a large amount of data, personally experienced if possible. When the great Sydenham, the 'English Hippocrates', who had left London at the onset of plague, having seen a few cases (and some more on his return), apologised for basing his theories on only those few observed cases, he generously praised those 'who, throughout all the stages of that scourging calamity, with danger all around them and with the thousand shapes of death before their eyes, had heart and soul to stand at their posts'. But he regretted that they had 'shown no intention of laying before the world those observations upon the nature of this disease which their greater practice may have supplied them with'.[66] If Boghurst had published his manuscript, Sydenham might have been satisfied.

But those who, like Bradwell, Boghurst, Hodges and Thomson, could write from personal experience of plague were few. Many physicians notoriously fled at the approach of plague, like the rest of the population, seeing flight as the best preservative. Bradwell

---

[64] Boghurst, *Loimographia*, pp. 30–1. Making sure that someone did not die alone had greater cultural significance than it does now. The 'good death' involved dying before witnesses and with the help of people around the bedside.

[65] Ibid., pp. 59–60.

[66] Thomas Sydenham, *The Works of Thomas Sydenham M.D*, trans. R.G. Latham (2 vols., Sydenham Society, London, 1848), vol. I, pp. 114, 106.

believed that physicians, surgeons, apothecaries and midwives had no obligation to stay and help the sick in the case of plague, although they did for all other 'griefs'.[67] Hodges excused the physicians by referring to their contracted obligations; they retired, he declared, 'not so much for their own Preservation as the Service of those whom they attend'.[68] Willis stated that case histories of plague were hard to come by, as it was not 'lawful for every Physician that takes care of his own health, frequently to visit the sick or to stay long with them'.[69] Boghurst had no truck with any such excuses. He wrote that all could flee who were not required by their callings to stay, but that magistrates, ministers, physicians, apothecaries, surgeons and midwives were obliged to remain and do their duty. 'Apothecaries', he wrote, 'are bound by their undertakings to stay and help as in other diseases. Every man that undertakes to bee of a profession [occupation] or takes upon him any office must take all parts of it, the good and evill, the pleasure and the pain, the profit and the inconvenience altogether, and not pick and chuse; for ministers must preach, Captains must fight, Physicians attend upon the sick.'[70]

Visiting the sick was a matter of morality and obligation. The natural hesitation to have contact with the sick was recognised by religious writers, who allowed for flight, in the dispensation in the Church of England Canons of 1604 which permitted ministers to neglect their duty of visiting the sick in cases of plague,[71] and by the cautions of medical writers on visiting, and their recommendation of flight as the best preservative. Yet plague raised awareness of ethical issues in medicine, especially of the duties of physicians to patients at a time when there were no agreed upon standards. Moreover, by giving advice on how the sick could be visited, medical writers recognised and facilitated moral obligations.

---

[67] Bradwell, *A Watch-Man for the Pest*, p. 9.   [68] Hodges, *Loimologia*, p. 23.
[69] Willis, 'Of Fevers', p. 111.   [70] Boghurst, *Loimographia*, pp. 59–60.
[71] Ole Peter Grell, 'The Protestant imperative of Christian Care and Neighbourly Love' in Ole Peter Grell and Andrew Cunningham (eds.), *Health Care and Poor Relief in Protestant Europe, 1500–1700* (Routledge, London, 1997), pp. 43–65, and 'Conflicting Duties: Plague and the Obligations of Early Modern Physicians Towards Patients and Commonwealth in England and the Netherlands' in Andrew Wear, Johanna Geyer-Kordesch and Roger French (eds.), *Doctors and Ethics: the Earlier Historical Setting of Professional Ethics* (Rodopi, Amsterdam, 1993), pp. 131–52, esp. 138.

REMEDIES FOR PLAGUE

Plague brought with it a desperate search for remedies and cures. Broadsheets went up everywhere advertising pills, potions, plasters and pomanders that preserved against the plague or cured it. Many of the learned physicians having left,[72] the conditions were right for empirics and quacks, who had either a single cure for the plague, or a battery of remedies. The imminent threat of death made people seek for preservatives against the plague, and when they became ill the most many could expect, especially if they were poor, would be a nostrum or two from an empiric. The quick course of the illness, often less than a week from onset to death and sometimes only two or three days, the fear of approaching the sick, and the policy of 'shutting up' meant that medical care would often be lacking or very infrequent. Often nurses, usually old women paid by a parish, would provide the only care for those 'shut up'. The elaborate courses of physical and surgical cures suggested by plague treatises were unlikely to be put into practice. Willis acknowledged this when he wrote,

now next we should speak of the Method of cure, *viz.* What first and then what next should be done in order: But that Disease hath so precipitous a course, that there is neither place for deliberation, nor is there frequently any Physitian to be gotten, for fear of the Contagion; wherefore, there is no need here of many prescripts, or a long series of Indications; this business is to be quickly performed, and may be comprehended in a few things . . . presently [immediately] Remedies are to be flown to.[73]

In any case the difference between the empirics and the more learned writers in relation to plague, as more generally in medicine, was not always great. An empiric's bill[74] could set out the gist of the standard causes of plague and of preventive advice, and the physical (medical) and surgical cures and procedures that the plague treatise provided, whilst plague treatises which appeared learned were also the means of advertising remedies and preservatives.[75] Many of the

---

[72] Sometimes shamefacedly like George Castle, who confessed that in 1665 'the Plague . . . coming to the Town where I liv'd forc'd me from my House and Studies, having not (I confesse) courage enough, to expose myself and Family to the mercy of so dismall a Disease, against which, flight is the onely infallible preservative': George Castle, *The Chymical Galenist* (London, 1667), Epistle Dedicatory, A3ᵛ.

[73] Willis, 'Of Fevers', p. 110.

[74] In Wilson, *Plague in Shakespeare's London*, pp. 104–5.

[75] Herring, *Certaine Rules*, fol. C3ᵛ; Bradwell, *Physick for the Sicknesse*, pp. 52–3; Richard

poor would not have been able to afford even the cheapest medicines and were recommended garlic, the poor man's medicine, which was sold everywhere for the plague, or their own urine.[76]

The state also searched urgently for effective remedies and was willing to look at the claims of empirics. In 1665 James Angier from France, who claimed to have turned back the plague in a number of French cities including Paris by a process of fumigation, received the support of the Privy Council. It put his remedy to the test, and had it advertised across London as being available for sale at six places.[77] When this failed, the Privy Council asked the College of Physicians to revise the College's *Directions* with the list of remedies that had been published with the Plague Orders. The College also provided some free medicines for a few weeks at William Johnson's apothecary's shop, until Johnson died from plague. The College nominated some of its own practitioners (as it had in previous plagues), who volunteered to stay on in London.[78] These were few. Only ten or eleven College physicians remained in 1665 of fifty-nine fellows and candidate fellows. They practised in the London parishes under the aegis of the Court of Aldermen. Hodges, who was one of them, complained of the 'Practice of Chymists and Quacks, and of whose Audacity and Ignorance it is impossible to be altogether silent; they were indefatigable in spreading their Antidotes; and although equal Strangers to all Learning as well as Physick, they thrust into every Hand some Trash or other under the disguise of a pompous Title'. But he had to admit that at a time of plague, a monopoly of medical practice could be questioned, 'In the same Manner as in a Fire all Hands are required, even of the Croud as well as Workmen, to extinguish it'.[79]

Kephale, *Medela Pestilentiae, Wherein is Contained Several Theological Queries Concerning the Plague* (London, 1665), p. 88.

[76] Phayre, 'Treatyse of the Pestylence', fol. M7ʳ; Bullein, *Dialogue*, p. 43: Bullein cautioned against the use of garlic. Herring, *Certaine Rules*, fol. C2ᵛ; George Thomson, Ορθο-μέθοδος ίατρο-Χυμική [*Orthomethodos Iatro-chimike*]: *Or the Direct Method of Curing Chymically* (London, 1675), p. 122, integrated the popular practice into Helmontian therapeutics: 'To drink of his own Urine preserveth from the Image of the Pest.'

[77] Bell, *Great Plague*, pp. 35–6.

[78] Figures are from Slack, *Impact of Plague*, p. 246. See also Clark, *College of Physicians*, vol. I, pp. 138–9, 191, 321–2; Bell, *Great Plague*, pp. 86–8; the College had nominated physicians to stay previously, possibly in 1583, probably in 1609. The *Annals* list eight physicians chosen on 12 June 1665 to provide medical services to plague victims. The number of fellows was temporarily increased in 1664 to forty-seven instead of the normal forty. Not included are the licentiates and extra-licentiates.

[79] Hodges, *Loimologia*, pp. 21, 23–24.

Plague probably gave empirics their greatest opportunity to make money in a short space of time. Boghurst, like Hodges, remained in London and he also complained of the host of quacks, but unlike Hodges he despaired of the 'official' medical care that was made available. It was the poor especially who suffered:

But two or three of the yongest are appointed in a plague tyme to looke to 30 or 40 thousand sick people, when four or five hundred is too few, and at another tyme, when there dyes but two or three hundred a week, you should have four or five hundred hanging after them if they bee well lined with white Metall [gold]. 'Tis the Rich whose persons are guarded with Angels [a physician's fee was often an angel, a coin worth ten shillings]. These are the carcasses whose stomachs shall bee cloyed with as much phisick for the cure of the Toothache, as the cost would cure half the diseases of the Town if honestly ordered. But if four or five Physitians bee enough in such a plague as this was, surely one is enough for common diseases at other times.[80]

There was probably more organised 'learned' medical help in London in 1665 than in previous epidemics,[81] and chemical physicians such as George Thomson, George Starkey and Thomas O'Dowde (the last two died of plague) provided further aid, as did Boghurst, who believed in the corpuscular philosophy. The expectation, however, was that in a plague time customers for medicines would run to the thousands and that few learned physicians would make themselves available.

Plague gave the opponents of orthodox medicine, such as the Helmontians, the opportunity to criticise its very open failure and to establish themselves on the moral high ground by remaining.[82] Yet the underlying reality was that few people enjoyed any continuous care outside their families. Probably the most attentive of the paid carers were the nurses who, despite being often condemned as ignorant and cruel in their attention to the sick, and as unscrupulous and thieving, did at least visit and stay with them.[83]

---

[80] Boghurst, *Loimographia*, p. 60.

[81] See footnote 78. Slack, *Impact of Plague*, p. 246, states that there were only two volunteers from the College in London in the plague of 1625.

[82] For instance, Thomas O'Dowde, *The Poor Man's Physician, Or the True Art of Medicine*, 3rd edn (London, 1665), p. 89: 'I shall not doubt, by that method which God hath been pleased to communicate to me, to preserve thousands from the grave, and in that confidence, to administer freely and publickly to all that shall desire it, not excepting those persons or places, where other Physicians of the dull road [the Galenists] would be afraid to show themselves.'

[83] J.V., in *Golgotha* (London, 1665) which argued against the policy of shutting up, wrote (p. 10)

THE TREATMENT OF PLAGUE IN THE PLAGUE TREATISES

If in actuality time was short, danger great, learned practitioners, of whatever theoretical persuasion, thin on the ground, and treatment, where available, hurried and piecemeal, a different impression of what was possible emerges from the plague treatises. In these, ideal modes of treatment were set out, but, as we have seen, there was also a sense of urgency in that treatment had to be initiated as soon as possible, and writers such as Herring, Bradwell, Boghurst and Hodges made it clear that conditions were such that the sick could not get the best possible care.

In theory, all the curative parts of medicine were brought into play. Physic and surgery together with pharmacy and regimen might, it was believed, effect a cure.[84] Physic could strengthen the body against a poison which worked inwards and destroyed the heart and the vital spirits and heat, or it could provide the means to expel it. Surgery, which included in its general remit tumours and skin conditions, dealt with the outward eruptions of the plague such as buboes, carbuncles and the plague 'tokens', the discolouration of various hues – red, yellow, blue, black – that in many eyes betokened death. Pharmacy threw into the fight preservatives, cordials, plague pills, electuaries, poultices, blistering plasters, digesting and ripening ointments (for buboes), etc. Regimen provided advice on the best diet and living conditions to help the patient recover. The general aim, with some exceptions, was to help nature. Her course of action was to bring the plague poison to the surface, hence the skin eruptions, and anything which kept the flow of putrid matter coming out through the skin by issues and ulcers was to be encouraged.[85]

---

of how those who were shut had 'with them an old woman, or some poor ignorant creature (a stranger to them, as is usual) for their Nurse'.

84 Willis, 'Of Fevers', p. 109: 'we speak of the Cure of the Plague. The Doctrine of which, is either general, and comprehends Remedies, which for this end, are taken from Diet, Chirurgery, and Medicine; or special, which delivers the use and Cautions to be exhibited about those Remedies . . . Diet comprehends the use of the six Non-naturals, but the chief care, and medical Cautions are to be given about Eating?'.

85 Thomas Moulton, *This is the Myrrour or Glasse of Helth* (London, *c.* 1539), fol. C3^r–C4^r, graphically described how the plague poison circulated in the body. It went first to the heart, which expelled it 'to his clensyng place to the arme hole', but if the poison could not have exited, it went to the next principal part of the body, the liver. This expelled it to its proper 'clensying place betwynne the thyghe and the body', and if that was stopped up the poison would go to the brain and then to its cleansing place under the ears. That could also be closed to the 'thyckness of the fowle and corrupt blode', so the plague poison would move around the body, infecting its chief parts. See also Bradwell, *Physick for the Sicknesse,*

The powers of nature, however, could fail to bring the poison to the surface and deaths without sores or tokens were often reported. Bullein wrote that 'often tymes the Plague sore will not appere; the very cause is this: Nature is to[o] weake, and the poyson of the infection to[o] strong that it can not be expelled, and this is most perilous of all, when such a cruell conquerour doth raigne within the harte, the principall part of life, nowe possessed with death'.[86]

The description of the putrid plague poison inside the body that needed to be let out for a cure to be effected, fitted the therapeutic mind set of classical and early modern medicine. As we have seen, many medical and surgical procedures such as purging, vomiting, sweating, blistering, cupping and bleeding were designed to expel noxious humours or a plethora of humours from the body. Although the causation of plague was the non-humoral process of contagion, what happened inside the body was often seen as analogous to the damage done by corrupt humours, and the procedures available for humoral disorders were ready to be used to free the body from the plague. Which procedures to use, and when, was a matter of debate.

Some, such as Bullein, opted for the standard measures. He recommended bleeding 'in the beginnyng of the sicknesse' for the sanguine and the choleric (who would tend to have too much blood), and purging for the phlegmatic and melancholic (who had too much of other humours). The aim was to cleanse the body: as the environment was made clean from a putrifying poison through fumigation, bleeding and purging achieved this for the body: 'like as a pot is clensed of the scumme or fome in the beginning when it plaieth on the fire, and thereby the liquor is cleansed within the potte, even so blood lettyng and [purging] pilles doe helpe and cleanse the Pestilence when it beginneth firste to boile within the

---

p. 44. The movement of the plague poison in the body, going from major organ to major organ as their cleansing places ('emunctories') were blocked, had a long history and can be found in the plague treatise of John of Burgundy (1365): see Rosemary Horrox, *The Black Death* (Manchester University Press, Manchester, 1994), p. 188. Sir Thomas Browne, writing as a physician to John Hobart, who was living in London during the plague of 1665–6, as well as advising fumigations of the house, recommended issues or blisters kept open for two months: Sir Thomas Browne, *Sir Thomas Browne's Works*, ed. S. Wilkin (4 vols., London, 1836), vol. I, pp. 372–3.

86 William Bullein, *A Dialogue Against the Fever Pestilence*, ed. Mark W. Bullen and A. H. Bullen, Early English Text Society (Trübner, London, 1888), p. 40. Bradwell, *Physick for the Sicknesse*, p. 47, wrote that sometimes the tokens did not appear until after death.

bodie'.[87] However, when the poison had fixed on the heart and the patient was weak, then bleeding was counterindicated. To test whether the heart was affected, Phayre wrote, the patient was to be given a drink of 'bolearmeny' (bole armeniac, a type of clayey earth) made in powder mixed with white wine and water of roses. If he retained the drink in his stomach, 'it is a good sygne that the venyme was not at the hert afore he toke the medicyne, and therefore he maye be let blood well ynough. But yf the pacyent can not broke the said drynke, but cast it up and vomyte, then ye may by sure, that the venymme hath ben at the hert afore the medicine.' The drink should be given repeatedly six or seven times to see if the patient could hold it down; only after that should bleeding be carried out. But, Phayre cautioned, if the patient was infected twenty-four hours before he was given the drink, then 'never let him blood, for that can nothing helpe hym, but rather make hym feble'.[88] Nature and human agency had the same aim of expelling the plague poison, and the physician's role was to help rather than hinder nature. What the practitioner did seemed 'natural', and the only limitation to the use of medical procedures such as bleeding and purging was the danger of so weakening the patient that nature was no longer able to exert her usual powers of expulsion. This rationale for evacuation continued to be used despite changes in the theories of medicine. All that changed was that the caution with regard to bleeding that was already present increased. Following the publication in English in 1666 of the work on plague of the Dutch physician Isbrandus de Diemerbroeck who was credited with successful cures, sentiment amongst physicians in England swung against bleeding and towards sweating.[89] Bleeding was seen as stopping nature, as physician, from moving the disease from the centre to the circumference and so out of the body, as well as weakening her powers of expulsion. Both Garencières and Boghurst used the ancient analogies of nature as a physician and the physician as nature's helper. Orthodox practices such as bleeding in plague, which had been justified using the analogy with nature, could be shown as mistaken if they did not fit

[87] Bullein, *Dialogue*, p. 41.
[88] Phayre, 'Treatyse of the Pestylence', fols. P2ᵛ–P3ʳ.
[89] Isbrandus de Diemerbroeck was a non-Helmontian physician who criticised the practice of phlebotomy in cases of plague because bleeding weakened the vital spirits: Slack, *Impact of Plague*, p. 249. His treatise was translated as *Several Choice Histories of the Medicines, Manner and Method Used in the Cure of the Plague* (London, 1666), see especially pp. 8, 32.

in with a redefinition of nature's actions.[90] This was a gambit that was often used when an innovation in medicine was being proposed.

In contrast, Willis, whom Boghurst had read, appeared to break the link between nature and the physician. His reasons for doing so were pragmatic: the disease was acute and its treatment too urgent to be left in the gentle hands of nature:

> Concerning the curing of very many sicknesses, the business is chiefly committed to Nature to whose necessity, Physick is the Midwife . . . but the Plague hath this peculiar, that its Cure is not at all to be left to Nature, but that it is to be endeavoured any way, by Remedies gathered from Art. Nor are we to be solicitous of a more opportune, or as it were a gentler time, but Medecines are most quickly to be prepared and we must not stay for them some hours, no nor minutes.[91]

However, Willis remained traditional in his therapeutic rationale. The grand vision of expelling the disease remained as in the past, but the corpuscular philosophy allowed for differential expulsion. Certain chemical remedies could leave the blood and vital heat untouched, and be untouched by them, so that, by attaching themselves only to 'extraneous or hostile things' and expelling them, the problem was solved of how to get rid of the plague poison without weakening the body. Medicines were either 'Evacuators or Poyson resisters'. Their action was explained in the new chemical–corpuscular language, so that purging and sweating medicines should have particles 'agreeable to the empoysoned infection, rather than to our Blood or Spirits; for such a Medicine will pass through the various windings of our body, with its whole forces and unmixt, and by reason of the similitude of either, more certainly takes hold of the virulent Matter of the Disease, and carries it forth of doors with it self'. The best medicines, therefore, were those made from 'Mercury, Antimony, Gold, Sulphur, Vitriol, Arsenick, and the like', which could not be 'subjugated' by the body and so retained their

[90] Theophilus Garencières, *A Mite Cast into the Treasury of the Famous City of London*, 3rd edn (London, 1666), pp. 9–10. Boghurst, *Loimographia*, pp. 74, 78–9 also wrote that 'rude and ignorant people had recourse to purging, vomiting and bleeding' and that these procedures were useless against the plague because it came from outside and was not a humoral disorder. But in the end the hold of the evacuative paradigm was too great, and Boghurst, like others, continued to see nature evacuating plague so he cautiously recommended sweating.

[91] Willis, 'Of Fevers', p. 108.

integrity and brought with them through the body's passages the particles of the plague poison.[92]

Thomas Sydenham (discussed further in chapter 10) doubted that nature had any clear and unequivocal ways of expelling plague. If she did, it was through the cleansing places of the body at the groin and armpits, etc., yet buboes which contained the poisonous particles of blood might disappear, only to be replaced by the deadly tokens. 'From all this', he wrote, 'it clearly follows that the physician who, in the cure of other diseases is bound carefully and closely to follow the path and conduct of Nature, must here renounce her guidance . . . We have, then, here a disease, in the extermination whereof it is unsafe to follow the path of Nature.' Although Willis like many other writers did not recommend bleeding,[93] Sydenham, who believed plague to be an inflammatory fever, favoured copious bleeding together with sweating. Bleeding in cases of plague, Sydenham admitted, was 'generally held in horror'. But, he replied, it was too little bleeding that was the problem, for it disturbed nature whilst she was trying to expel the plague by developing a bubo, without substituting a more effective means of evacuation, which was what his method of copious bleeding did. Because he had left London during the plague, Sydenham admitted that he was building his notions 'as a superstructure to a limited number of my own individual observations', but he was honestly sure of his practice.[94]

However, all claims to cures for plague were controversial, noted Sydenham, and the bystanders and the friends of the patient sometimes objected to the means used. The people around the bedside of a plague victim exerted lay authority. They believed in the traditional method of taking neither too much nor too little blood.

In this practice of taking blood freely . . . I found a great drawback to my endeavours in the prejudices of the bystanders. Taken up with their vain conceits, they would not allow me to draw the proper quantity of blood; hence I missed my usual success in several cases. All this was bad for the patient. The whole gist of the treatment lay in taking either no blood at all, or else a sufficient quantity.[95]

---

[92] Ibid., p. 110; Willis did not only consider chemical remedies. For 'poison resisters' he looked for substances which were not so akin to the body that they would be digested, or so alien that they would be expelled; and he recommended rue, scordium (water-germander) and especially the traditional compound remedies of treacle and mithridatium.
[93] Ibid., p. 109.
[94] Sydenham, *Works*, vol. I, pp. 109, 106, 119.   [95] Ibid., p. 115.

Because of the opposition which 'met me so often', Sydenham compromised whilst trying to find an equally good method of cure. He kept drawing blood, but now according to the strength of the patient (i.e. more moderately), and he combined it with copious sweating lasting twenty-four hours.[96] In this way a strong evacuating process was initiated, greater and more definite than nature's.[97]

Evacuation procedures, together with medicines, lay at the heart of plague therapy. Although, as we shall see in the next chapters, Helmontians opposed bleeding and other evacuative measures in medicine, plague confirms that even in the most exceptional of diseases the pattern of evacuating putrefaction was followed by the majority of traditional and 'modern' medical writers.

SURGERY

When the buboes appeared, even Sydenham was afraid of bleeding. Two periods during the course of plague demarcated the formal bounds of physic and surgery: before the appearance of eruptions on the skin, when physic (including bleeding – though often performed by a surgeon) was dominant, and afterwards, when recourse was had to surgery. However, as we have seen, in practice many surgeons may have acted as physicians and surgical treatises discussed medical as well as surgical treatments, including those for plague.[98] Surgery was, nevertheless, especially associated with the most serious and deadly phase of the disease, for although in theory nature expelled the plague poison through the buboes, they were considered to be ill omens: they were sure indicators of the plague and foreshadowed the deadly carbuncles and the plague tokens, the latter being popularly acknowledged as the signs of death, as God's tokens.[99]

---

[96] Ibid., pp. 116–18.

[97] Gideon Harvey also recommended a combined treatment of bleeding and sweating: *Discourse of the Plague*, pp. 27–8.

[98] Johannes de Vigo, *The Most Excellent Workes of Chirurgery* (London, 1543), fols. 28ᵛ–33ʳ; Ambroise Paré, *Workes*, trans. T. Johnson (London, 1634), pp. 817–68; Richard Wiseman, *Eight Chirurgicall Treatises*, 4th edn (London, 1705), pp. 51–4 typically distinguished between the roles of surgeon and physician whilst acting in both; James Cooke, *Mellificium Chirurgiae* (London, 1662; 1700 edn) pp. 533–41. Surgical treatises did pay special attention to buboes and carbuncles.

[99] Bradwell, *Physick for the Sicknesse*, p. 41 wrote that 'the most faithfull' of signs 'are the *Soares and Spots* . . . called *God's Tokens*'. Boghurst wrote that 'They are Tokens of Death approaching' and 'of God's wrath for sin'; some, he observed, died without tokens, whilst

When the plague affected the skin, then the surgeon appeared on the scene. The patient or physician might themselves try to bring the buboes to 'maturation' with plasters, but they were urged to go to an expert: 'let him take ye counsell of a lerned surgeon, or any other of good experience'. Whether surgeons were available and for whom was debatable. Phayre begged the surgeons 'to have some pytye of the poore that be diseased and not to favoure them that have ynough, but rather take so moch of the rych that they may the better have wherewyth to helpe the nedye' – their help, like that of physicians, was not available to all.[100] Herring also associated the appearance of skin symptoms with that of the surgeon, and with the question of his availability and cost:

If in the first, second, or third day, the Botches or Carbuncles appeare, the best and safest way both for poore and rich, is to commit themselves to be ordred and dressed by a skilfull Chirurgion. There will be (no doubt) assigned and mayntayned for the meaner and poorer sort, *Chirurgions ex commune aerario*, out of the common Purse, especially in *London*. Let those that are wealthy, make choice of their owne Chyrurgion, and pay well for their care. For a little health is worth a great deale of gold, which a *Chyrurgion* in that case, must fetch out of the fire, and hazard his owne life every day.[101]

Herring as a College physician was being optimistic about the availability of surgeons for the poor, especially at the height of plague when thousands were dying weekly. Boghurst recorded how he asked a nurse to do a surgeon's job: 'I saw one man at our pest-house with a blain upon his leg almost as big as a stoole ball, as blew as a razor, and as full of matter as the skin would hold, and a great feaver with it; I bid the nurse open it with a penknife, and gave her a playster to lay to it afterwards.'[102] Bradwell wrote that many died for lack of surgical skill.[103]

Surgeons worked on the surface of the body, using digestive plasters to bring the buboes to a bursting point or maturation and then lancing them. They also attempted to excise or to lance

there were others with tokens who lived if they survived for more than eight days; generally they were deadly signs: pp. 47–9. Buboes, carbuncles and the tokens, although distinct, were often confused.

100 Phayre, 'Treatyse of the Pestylence', fols. Q6^v–Q7^r.
101 Herring, *Certaine Rules* fol. C2^v; Bullein, *Dialogue*, p. 46 made the same point that the surgeon should be richly rewarded as he puts his life into danger.
102 Boghurst, *Loimographia*, p. 45.
103 Bradwell, *Physick for the Sicknesse*, pp. 41–2.

carbuncles, and they might try to extirpate the different coloured spots and patches on the skin denoting the tokens. Surgeons were, however, brought in at a late stage and they had to deal with the acknowledged forerunners of death. The language that described the skin symptoms reflected their gravity as well as the pain associated with them. Bullein wrote that 'carbuncle' came from 'Carbo a Cole', and like coal it was hot. It was produced from 'moste sharpe hotte and grosse blood, which nature doeth cast forthe through the skinne to one particular part with extreme paine and perille to the bodie'.[104]

Not only did the surgeon come when the fight to save the patient was nearly lost, but his procedures must have been dreaded. Physicians advised procedures such as sweating the patient or keeping him or her from sleep so that the vital spirits did not withdraw back to the heart which caused discomfort,[105] but the lancing of carbuncles by surgeons and their use of blistering plasters and cauteries would have produced intense pain. Boghurst described how

some upstarts here in Towne used much to lance Carbuncles, others to cutt them round about, and then poure into the greene wound vinegar and salt, but to what purpose I know not, unless they delighted to torment people, for it put them to as much paine as if they had been on a wrack worse than Death itselfe. A Frenchman which I have heard of used to cutt them round, and pluck them out with his Pincers before they were ripe, and put them to much paine.[106]

Hodges advised extreme measures. If despite cataplasms (poultices, plasters) the 'eschar' of the carbuncle did not fall off and if the carbuncle spread, then, Hodges argued, 'it will be neccessary to have Recourse to more effectual Means; in which Case neither the Tenderness of Sex or Age is to be regarded'. Incision was one 'effectual' remedy, as was burning with a red hot iron, 'actual cautery', deep into the carbuncle. Burning had the additional advantage in Hodges' eyes of rarefying the subtle miasma of the

---

[104] Bullein, *Dialogue*, p. 45.
[105] Vigo, *Workes*, fol. 31ᵛ acknowledged that if the plague was not treated early, 'the cure for the moost parte is vayne, and lost . . . it is of so great activitie, that without regard of medicines it ravysheth hys pray', yet by treating the carbuncle, a late symptom, he still hoped for a cure. Bullein, *Dialogue*, p. 43; Thayre, *Treatise*, p. 50; Herring, *Certaine Rules*, C1ᵛ.
[106] Boghurst, *Loimographia*, p. 89.

plague poison and drying it up.[107] Why were carbuncles treated when they were known to be associated with a fatal prognosis?[108] Apart from the obvious reason, 'while there is life there is hope', the buboes and carbuncles were in themselves intensely painful, and further pain from surgical procedures might appear worthwhile if it resulted in the departure of the original pain. Victims and practitioners may also have identified them as the disease itself and so have been desperate to extirpate and to destroy them. In any case, a carbuncle appeared to cause great damage and had to be extirpated: 'burning like a fire-coale . . . is so full of burning poison, that it consumes the flesh and will in a short time (if it be not well looked to) eate so deepe and large a hole, as if the flesh were hollowed with a hot iron'.[109]

Popular remedies for the buboes and carbuncles avoided some of the pain of surgical procedures. Boghurst set out a 'playster or Mixture' of egg, wheat flour, turpentine, honey and oil of lilies, which 'the poor people used all over the Town'. He also wrote that some believed that 'venemous creatures' such as frogs, serpents, scorpions and crabs, placed on the buboes 'draw out all the venom', whilst others held that 'the Rumps of Henns, Chickens, Pigeons and other Fowles applyed to the sores till they dye, holding their bills and putting salt on their Tails will draw out all the venome . . . Some apply living creatures, either Fowles or Beasts still alive.' Although it appears as though Boghurst was distancing himself from such remedies, his own advice for when the patient was faltering was that 'you may cutt up a puppy dog alive and apply him warm to the brest'.[110] In early modern medicine the distinction between popular and elite medicine was porous, and this was even more the case in time of plague when all were on the lookout for remedies whatever their source. In this case the application of live animals for plague was well established in literate medicine. Phayre commended the practice, as did Hodges more than a century later.[111]

[107] Hodges, *Loimologia*, pp. 200, 202.

[108] Boghurst, *Loimographia*, p. 86, wrote: 'Almost all the other evill signes, about 30 in number, will hardly admit of any Cure, wherefore I think it needless to write anything concerning them, for what Cure can bee made upon Tokens, Buboes fallen flat, bad pulses, cold sweats, bad urine, white soft Buboes, Carbuncles, Blaines[?]'.

[109] Bradwell, *Physick for the Sicknesse*, p. 46.

[110] Boghurst, *Loimographia*, pp. 88, 86.

[111] Phayre, 'Treatyse of the Pestylence', Q5ᵛ; Hodges, *Loimologia*, p. 201. Phayre's description almost corresponded with that of Boghurst: 'take a cocke and pull his fethers of, about hys foundament and put a litle salt in it, and set his foundament upon the sayde botche,

CONCLUSION

Surgery was never completely separate from physic, for both applied medicines, the one to the surface of the body, the other internally.[112] Indeed, as we have seen in chapter 5, it would be misleading to overemphasise physic and surgery as separate enterprises. What united and, in a sense, overwhelmed them in the plague treatises was the huge number of receipts for medicines that preserved from infection, comforted the heart, resisted the plague before it settled in the heart, cured the plague if taken within twelve to eighteen hours after infection, expelled the 'venemous infection', purged the infection, purged once the sore began to run, provided plasters to 'suppurate, draw forth and ripen the sore or botch', and receipts especially designed for the rich and the poor.[113] Specific antidotes were sought even though they were associated in the minds of the learned with quackery and danger. Sydenham, who was learned despite his rejection of the learned medicine of the Galenists, wrote scathingly of 'pestifuges and antidotes, of which we may find our fill in the hands of empirics'.[114] Boghurst fulminated against empirics and their antidotes and purging pills, but he also sold his own antidote, which he believed to be effective, 'to many both in ye parish and other places'.[115]

Although all the armamentarium of medicine was employed to counter plague, it was in the end remedies that were most sought after. As Boghurst put it, 'wee have Cartloads of receipts yet few of any great certainty', and he advised his readers to 'pick and chuse which you like best'.[116] It was hardly ever admitted that the disease was in itself incurable, only that it was fatal if allowed to progress to its later stages. Traditional views as to its causes, prevention and treatment were very long-lasting. Where changes occurred they were due more to radical alterations in the foundations of medicine, which also affected views about other diseases, but even those were

kepyng hym on a good whyle, stoppyng many tymes hys byll, that his breth may be reteyned, and let hym blowe againe . . .'
[112] Hodges thanked 'those skilful and faithful Surgeons . . . whose Task in this raging Calamity was very hard and dangerous, how they had the Care of all pestilential Tumours and Ulcers etc': *Loimologia*, p. 204.
[113] Thayre, *Treatise*, pp. 25, 30, 33, 35, 51, 61, 9, 36.
[114] Sydenham, *Works*, vol. I, p. 106.
[115] Boghurst, *Loimographia*, pp. 75, 91, 71.
[116] Ibid., pp. 75, 90–91.

only partial changes. A few modifications were made in the light of experience: bleeding, for instance, was practised more cautiously. But the only apparent promise of innovation came from empirics offering new pills and treatments, and such offerings had long been part of the traditional structure of medicine.

PART II

CHAPTER 8

Conflict and revolution in medicine – the Helmontians

SUMMARY

As the Introduction indicated, this is the point in the book where a historiographical switch occurs, with more attention being paid to the history of controversies and to the need to be aware of the themes of the 'grand narrative' of history. Nevertheless, the topics of the previous chapters, which were examined in terms of more continuous and 'placid' history, are also extremely important for understanding the focus of the next two chapters: the Helmontian enterprise to establish a revolution in therapeutics in England and its failure.

After leading the reader into the 1660s, the height of Helmontian influence, I discuss how the changes in natural philosophy were seen as affecting medicine, it being generally agreed that the former underpinned the latter. In their programme for reforming medicine Helmontians argued that, as the foundations of medicine had been destroyed, so the theories of disease and therapeutics that had been built upon them (especially the cure by contrary quality) should be pulled down and new ones erected on a surer base. The Helmontians also used less intellectual and more emotive and vituperative arguments, for instance, Galenic medicine's therapeutic failure, and its cruelty and lack of Christian charity. In particular, the evacuative procedures of bleeding, purging, etc., which were essential parts of Galenic therapeutics, were attacked as cruel, un-Christian and harmful. They should be replaced, argued the Helmontians, by their own powerful yet safe remedies. In fact, from the case study of William Walwyn, Leveller turned chemist-physician, which ends the chapter, it is possible to see him as arguing that his medicines could replace not only Galenic therapeutics but also the whole panoply of medicine, including doctors' visits. Walwyn thus placed enormous emphasis on the powers of his medicines. He made them appear patient-friendly: pleasant and yet powerful. Helmontian medicines were commercial products to be advertised and sold as well as symbols of a new medicine. Why this medical revolution failed is discussed in the next chapter.

GENERAL INTRODUCTION TO THE LATER SEVENTEENTH CENTURY

Change initially came slowly to English medicine; then in the 1660s its pace quickened and threatened to overturn old truths and institutions. As indicated in chapter 1, Paracelsianism was well known in England in the later sixteenth century, but was only put into limited practice at that time in medicine and surgery.[1] Chemical remedies were included in the first official London *Pharmacopeia* of 1618 published by the London College of Physicians, and were placed at the end as 'auxiliaries' to rational or Galenic medicine.[2] Theodore Turquet de Mayerne, a Huguenot and a royal physician to Henri IV, who in 1610 became royal physician to James I and then to Charles I, brought Paracelsian medicine to the court, and as a fellow of the College helped to produce its *Pharmacopeia*. But his presence at the court did not lead to the overthrow of Galenic medicine at the College, perhaps because his energies were directed more at organisational rather than doctrinal change.[3] In the Civil War and Commonwealth period, as Charles Webster has convincingly shown, Paracelsian and then Helmontian medicine became popular amongst reformers.[4] Both medical systems were attractive because of their stress on divine enlightenment and Christian charity. The Paracelsian and Helmontian physician believed himself to be directly illuminated by God with medical knowledge; this echoed the claims of many religious sects during the Civil War that their members were specially singled out by divine illumination. Such claims became suspect after the Restoration, when 'enthusiasm' was politically unacceptable to the government, though it

[1] See chapter 1, footnote 73.
[2] A. Debus, *The English Paracelsians* (Oldbourne Press, London, 1965), p. 152.
[3] Ibid., pp. 151–2; Harold J. Cook, *The Decline of the Old Medical Regime in Stuart London* (Cornell University Press, Ithaca, 1986), pp. 95–8. Mayerne helped to establish the Society of Apothecaries and proposed a health board on the Italian model.
[4] Charles Webster, *The Great Instauration: Science, Medicine and Reform, 1626–1660* (Duckworth, London, 1975), pp. 246–323.

continued to find favour amongst religious dissenters. The Paracelsian and Helmontian emphasis on Christian charity to the poor also appealed to Puritan reformers. As we saw in chapter 1, the learned physicians in the sixteenth century had been encouraged to be charitable to the poor, but nevertheless since the Middle Ages greed and the learned physicians had been joined together. In the Civil War and Commonwealth period, Christian charity gained even more importance and was incorporated into the ethos of political reform. In particular, various projects for reforming medicine were set out in the 1640s and 1650s centred around a medical service that would encompass all the country, or at least provide medical treatment for the poor, though parishes had for some time before been paying for the medical treatment of the poor through charitable donations, through local rates and through Poor Law rates.[5] A sense of Christian charity underpinned these proposals and this was reflected by Gabriel Plattes' choice, in his utopian *Macaria* (1641), of ministers as the providers of such medical care, because he believed they would be motivated by charity rather than profit.[6]

Anger at the uncharitable refusal of physicians to treat the poor helped to fuel the call for a new type of medicine that would replace Galenic medicine. The image of the uncharitable physician became a constant trope in the revolutionary period and in the two decades that followed. For instance, Nicholas Culpeper, a political and medical radical, used the strategy of simultaneously condemning the lack of charity by learned physicians and denigrating their medicine. Culpeper had fought in the Civil War on Parliament's side and, although not a Helmontian (he died in 1654 just as Helmontianism was becoming well known in England), he was sympathetic to chemical remedies and medicine. Culpeper styled himself 'student in physick and astrology', and astrology provided the bedrock for his medical theories. As the foremost populariser and translator of medical texts of the late 1640s and the 1650s (his name was also included in the titles of various translations of continental texts after his death, as well as in posthumous collections and a huge number of

[5] Webster, *The Great Instauration*, pp. 246–64; on the parish care of the sick poor see Margaret Pelling, 'Healing the Sick Poor: Social Policy and Disability in Norwich 1550–1645', *Medical History*, 29, 1985, 115–37; Andrew Wear, 'Caring for the Sick Poor in St Bartholomew Exchange: 1580–1676' in W. F. Bynum and Roy Porter (eds.), *Living and Dying in London*, *Medical History* Supplement 11 (1991), 41–60; see also David Harley, 'Pious Physic for the Poor: the Lost Durham County Medical Scheme of 1665', *Medical History*, 37, 1993, 148–66.
[6] Webster, *The Great Instauration*, p. 259.

reprints), Culpeper's brand of medical radicalism had a wide reader-ship.[7] In his unauthorised translation into English of the College of Physicians' *Pharmacopoeia* in 1649, he expounded upon the medical and moral failure of traditional learned medicine:

> Would it not pity a man to see whol estates wasted in Physick ('all a man hath spent upon Physicians') both body and soul consumed upon out-landish rubbish? . . . Is it handsom and wel beseeming a Common-wealth to see a doctor ride in State, in Plush with a footcloath, and not a grain of Wit [knowledge], but what was in print before he was born? Send for them into a Visited House [with plague], they will answer, they dare not come. How many honest poor souls have been so cast away, will be known when the Lord shall come to make Inquisition for Blood. Send for them to a poor mans house who is not able to give them their Fee, then they will not come, and the poor Creature for whom Christ died must forfeit his life for want of money.[8]

None of the utopian schemes for the reform of medicine was put into practice. Nevertheless, chemical medicine was becoming more popular and influential. The College of Physicians responded by building in 1648 a chemical laboratory and appointing William Johnson as its chemist. But it was not until the 1660s that there was a clear threat to Galenic medicine. In a general sense it came from the development of the 'new science' which repudiated the learning of the ancients, and especially of Aristotle (discussed below). More particularly, it came in 1665 from a group of Helmontians, who

---

[7] Culpeper may have been more eclectic in his medical beliefs than at first seems the case. Abdiah Cole in the 1660s was advertising his series of books making up 'The Physicians Library' which included texts by Sennert, Riverius, Plater, Bartholinus, Riolan, Veslingius, Fernel, etc., some of which were claimed to be translated by Culpeper. Culpeper's biographer in the 'Life' at the beginning of N. Culpeper, *Culpeper's School of Physick* (London, 1659), n.p., wrote that a member of the College of Physicians agreed 'That he [Culpeper] was not onely for Gallen and Hypocrates, but he knew how to correct and moderate the tyrannies of Paracelsus.' How far this was put in to make Culpeper acceptable to a wide variety of readers and how far it represented Culpeper's own position is unclear. Thomson wrote that Culpeper was the Galenists' 'trusty servant': *Galeno-pale: Or A Chymical Trial of the Galenists* (London, 1665), p. 9. For an account of Culpeper's writings see Graeme Tobyn, *Culpeper's Medicine. A Practice of Western Holistic Medicine* (Element, Shaftesbury, 1997), pp. 3–37. Also Webster, *Great Instauration*, pp. 267–72.

[8] Nicholas Culpeper, *A Physical Directory or a Translation of the London Dispensary Made by the College of Physicians* (London, 1649), sig. A1ᵛ, not repeated in subsequent editions. The quotation 'all a man [*sic*] hath spent upon Physicians' is from Mark 5.25–7: 'And a certain woman, which had an issue of blood twelve years. And had suffered many things of many physicians, and had spent all she had and was nothing bettered but rather grew worse. When she had heard of Jesus, came in the press behind and touched his garment.' For similar sentiments see: Robert Pemell, ΠΤΩΧΟΦΑΡΜΑΚΟΝ *or Help for the Poor* (London, 1650), sigs. A2ᵛ, A3ʳ; Lancelot Coelson, *The Poormans Physician and Chyrurgian* (London, 1656) sigs. A4ᵛ–A5ʳ; Thomas Cocke, *Kitchin Physick: Or, Advice to the Poor* (London, 1676), pp. 10, 8.

nearly succeeded in gaining royal approval for the establishment of a Society of Chemical Physicians. Historians have explained the Helmontians' rise to prominence in a number of ways, none of which is exclusive of the others.[9] P. M. Rattansi has argued that the apothecaries met the medical needs of the increasing number of tradespeople, middlemen, clerks of merchant companies, etc. who added to London's growing population and were central to its commercial prosperity. They rivalled the physicians, who traditionally tended the nobility and gentry, and sought to obtain formal recognition as medical practitioners. In the dispute between the two groups, the Helmontians for a while became prominent as the allies of the apothecaries, until the inherent competition between the apothecaries and Helmontian physicians, who wanted to make their own remedies, came into the open. Charles Webster has seen the Society of Chemical Physicians as the outcome of the Commonwealth interest in Helmontianism. In his view the Society was anticipated in 1656 by the projected College of Graduate Physicians of William Rand, an unlicensed graduate physician who supported Samuel Hartlib and Robert Boyle in their wish to reform science. Its all-graduate membership would have made it a cohesive and viable alternative to the College of Physicians. The proposed Society of Chemical Physicians contained members of the Hartlib circle and can be partially seen as an outcome of the reforming schemes of the pre-Restoration period. However, Webster believes that it was in a weak position because it was socially and occupationally divided, being composed of a mix of graduate physicians and empirics. This is certainly true. The Helmontians who largely figure in the following pages were very diverse. George Starkey was a New England Puritan educated at Harvard, whilst Thomas O'Dowde was an Irish royalist without a university education. George Thomson had an MD from Leiden as well as being apprenticed to a physician, and Marchamont Nedham took an Oxford degree, was a journalist on the Parliamentary side, changed sides a few times and practised

[9] P. M. Rattansi, 'The Helmontian-Galenist Controversy in Restoration England', *Ambix*, 12, 1964, 1–23; Charles Webster, 'English Medical Reformers of the Puritan Revolution: a Background to the "Society of Chemical Physitians"', *Ambix*, 14, 1967, 16–41; Harold J. Cook, 'The Society of Chemical Physicians, the New Philosophy, and the Restoration Court', *Bulletin of the History of Medicine*, 61, 1987, 61–77. See also the important article by Antonio Clericuzio, 'From van Helmont to Boyle. A Study of the Transmission of Helmontian Chemical and Medical Theories in Seventeenth-Century England', *British Journal for the History of Science*, 26, 1993, 303–34.

medicine from the mid-1640s. William Walwyn, on the other hand, was apprenticed to a silk merchant, became a Leveller with a strong commitment to total freedom in religious belief, and taught himself medicine.[10] In contrast to Webster, Harold Cook has argued that in 1665 the Helmontians for the first time were able to gain patronage at the centre of government, notably from the Duke of Buckingham and the Archbishop of Canterbury, with Thomas O'Dowde, a Helmontian practitioner who was well placed at the royal court as a groom of the bedchamber, actively lobbying members of the court for their support to establish a Society of Chemical Physicians (discussed further in the next chapter). These interpretations indicate that, as with the new society that was founded by the Crown, the Royal Society (1660, chartered in 1662), the formative 1640s and 1650s have to be taken into account as well as events in the 1660s. This is also the case with the 'new science', which in the 1660s was threatening the philosophical foundations of Galenic medicine, and of which Helmontianism seemed at times to be a part.

By the end of the seventeenth century the learned Galenic physicians were no longer the dominant medical elite. They had lost the intellectual and institutional high ground that they had claimed as their own. From the middle of the century the philosophical basis of Galenic medicine was being undermined by a series of new philosophies, whilst the London College of Physicians lost both status and the ability to speak with a single voice. New groups, notably the chemical physicians, made claims to medical authority and expertise, whilst the virtuosi, the gentlemanly members of the Royal Society, who were propagating the new science of 'the moderns' based in varying degrees on experimental, chemical, mathematical and mechanical approaches to nature, were putting into place a new mind set for interpreting nature and

---

[10] Sources: Cook, *Decline*, pp. 42, 146, 148–9; R. S. Wilkinson, 'George Starkey, Physician and Alchemist', *Ambix*, 11, 1963, 121–52; C. Webster, 'The Helmontian George Thomson and William Harvey: the Revival and Application of Splenectomy to Physiological Research', *Medical History*, 15, 1971, 154–67. However, differences can be overemphasised. University men were beginning to work with their hands, and long-established roles were changing and mingling together, though at the same time pride in old social affiliations remained, as, for example, Nedham's letter to Edward Bolnest indicates: '[we] have both been University men . . . but truly I would not willingly have you nor my self, lose one Afternoon's operation in your Laboratory, for all the Honours Academicall': 'Letter to Edward Bolnest' in Edward Bolnest, *Medicina Instaurata. Or, A Brief Account of the True Grounds and Principles of the Art of Physick* (London, 1665), sig. A6ʳ.

the body to replace the Aristotelian–Galenic synthesis of learned medicine. The increase in numbers and commercial success of an old group, the empirics and quacks, provided another context for the medicine of the later seventeenth century: many practitioners attacked them and sought to distance themselves from the label of empiric, and yet in some ways seemed to emulate their methods. At the same time, a demand-driven expansion of the medical marketplace began, which, together with the College of Physicians' increasing inability to regulate London's medical practice, meant that there was room enough for all the different groups of practitioners, and not one of them needed to or was able to establish a monopoly of practice.[11] However, the decline of Galenic medicine did not occur without opposition. The battle between the ancients and the moderns was fought out in the medical arena just as intensely as elsewhere in English culture, indeed perhaps more so given the entrenched institutional, educational and commercial interests of medicine.

Although major changes took place in medicine, it is possible to discern significant continuities. By the end of this book it should be clear why much of medical practice remained the same into the eighteenth century: purging, bleeding and all the other means of expelling disease and putrefaction were carried out as enthusiastically as before, despite the attempt by Helmontian chemical physicians to stop their use. The imaging of the body and disease in certain fundamental senses also remained the same. Moreover, regimen or preventive medicine was unaffected in its structure and in much of its content by the new natural philosophies and medical movements.

---

[11] See, for instance, R. Porter, *Health for Sale: Quackery in England 1660–1850 (Manchester University Press, Manchester, 1989).* The seminal study on ancients and moderns is Richard Jones, *Ancients and Moderns: a Study of the Rise of the Scientific Movement in Seventeenth-Century England,* 2nd edn (St Louis, Gloucester, Mass., 1961). For an influential social science analysis of the new science in England: Steven Shapin and Simon Schaffer, *Leviathan and the Air Pump. Hobbes, Boyle and the Experimental Life* (Princeton University Press, Princeton, 1985). The best account of the effect of the new science on medicine is Cook, *Decline.* Also Cook, 'The New Philosophy and Medicine in Seventeenth-Century England' in David C. Lindberg and Robert S. Westman (eds.), *Reappraisals of the Scientific Revolution* (Cambridge University Press, Cambridge, 1990), pp. 397–436; Andrew Wear, 'Medical Practice in Late Seventeenth and Early Eighteenth-Century England: Continuity and Union' in Roger French and Andrew Wear (eds.), *The Medical Revolution of the Seventeenth Century* (Cambridge University Press, Cambridge, 1989), pp. 294–320.

THE NEW PHILOSOPHIES AND MEDICINE

There was no clear consensus as to what the new science was. There was a series of different mechanical philosophies, for instance Gassendi's, Descartes', Boyle's and Newton's, as well as the Helmontian chemical philosophy; it was not until the end of the seventeenth century in England and well into the eighteenth century in continental Europe that Newton's philosophy was accepted as the true mechanical philosophy, and even then the meaning of what was Newtonianism remained a matter of debate. There was agreement as to what the new science should not be: Aristotelian natural philosophy and the power of past authorities and old books to determine what was knowledge had to be replaced. In England there were some points of agreement as to the direction that the new philosophy should take: it should investigate Nature using observation and experimentation rather than focusing on words. This was very much Francis Bacon's programme for a new beginning for knowledge.[12] In Oxford in the 1650s a group of physiologist-experimenters put into practice the Baconian approach when they developed some of William Harvey's unfinished research topics such as the nature of respiration and of the blood.[13] Some of the group, such as Robert Hooke, Robert Boyle and Richard Lower, then went on to London, where following the Restoration and the triumph of Anglicanism they were prominent members of the newly founded Royal Society, which became the institutional centre for the development of the Baconian programme for science.

Another of the group, Thomas Willis, who in 1660 was appointed professor of natural philosophy at Oxford, and then moved to London in 1667 to continue his medical researches and his lucrative medical practice, compared in 1658 the three natural philosophies of his time.[14] They were the Aristotelian, the 'Epicurean' or mechanical, based on atoms or particles in motion, and the chemical.

---

[12] See Andrew Cunningham on his thesis that in the seventeenth century we should speak of natural philosophy and not science, with the latter only emerging in the nineteenth century: 'Getting the Game Right: Some Plain Words on the Identity and Invention of Science', *Studies in History and Philosophy of Science*, 19, 1988, 365–89; the new programme was set out by Bacon chiefly in *The Advancement of Learning* and *New Atlantis* (London, 1605) and *The Novum Organum* (London, 1620).

[13] See Robert G. Frank, Jr., *Harvey and the Oxford Physiologists: Scientific Ideas and Social Interaction* (University of California Press, Berkeley, 1980).

[14] For an account of Willis' career see Kenneth Dewhurst, *Thomas Willis's Oxford Lectures* (Sandford, Oxford, 1980), pp. 1–27.

The first might help to unfold nature but in a 'dark' manner; it had no 'peculiar respect to the more secret recesses of Nature, it salves the appearances of things, that 'tis almost the same thing, to say an house consists of Wood and Stone as a Body of our Four Elements'. The second:

without running to Occult Qualities, Sympathy, and other refuges of ignorance, doth happily and very ingeniously disintangle some difficult knots of the Sciences . . . but because it rather supposes, than demonstrates its Principles and teaches of what Figure those Elements of Bodies may be, not what they have been, and also induces Notions extremely subtil, and remote from the sense, and which do not suffiently Quadrate with the Phenomena of Nature, when we descend to particulars, it pleases me to give my sentence for the third Opinion beforementioned, which is of the Chymists . . . affirming all Bodies to consist of Spirit, Sulphur, Salt, Water, and Earth.[15]

For Willis the chemists' philosophy was the *via media*, neither too obvious nor too far from observation and the senses, although he conceded that 'the Atomical and our Spagyric [chemical] Principles could merge' if they were derived from 'real conceptions' common to both.[16] As it turned out Boyle was developing such a unified view through his corpuscular philosophy for chemistry, based on the notion that the natures of chemical substances were determined by the arrangement, size, shape and motions of the particles from which they were made. In the *Sceptical Chemist* (1661) he attacked the Paracelsian and Helmontian programmes of deriving all chemical substances, and indeed everything in the world, from a fixed number of basic elements, substituting instead the corpuscular philosophy, although it is clear that, despite his suspicion of Helmontian claims to divine illumination and of their chemical reductionism, he never lost his early interest in Helmontianism and did not repudiate it on a wholesale basis.[17]

Clearly, what was the chemical philosophy was ambiguous and contested; as was typical of the formative period of the new science, a range of opinions was being expressed. Willis, for instance, despite close social and intellectual connections with Boyle's circle, held to a

[15] Thomas Willis, 'Of Fermentation or the Inorganic Motion of Natural Bodies' in *Dr Willis's Practice of Physick, Being the Whole Works*, trans. S. Pordage (London, 1684), p. 2. English translation of *Diatribae Duae Medico-Philosophicae* (London, 1659). Some copies were available in 1658 according to Dewhurst, *Willis's Oxford Lectures*, p. 11.

[16] Willis, 'Fermentation', p. 2.

[17] See Clericuzio, 'From van Helmont to Boyle', esp. 306, 316–19.

five-element theory, though not to the Helmontian single element or
principle of water, yet like the Helmontians and Boyle he believed
that chemical investigations would unlock the workings of the body.
However, unlike the Helmontians, he asserted, as did many Galenists
and virtuosi, that anatomical research was necessary in medicine.
Willis was praised by the Helmontian Marchamont Nedham, who
also approved of Boyle's general approach to the reform of knowledge, whilst George Thomson, who was a more doctrinaire Helmontian and a strong believer in water as the first principle of all
things, acidly wrote, 'Dr Willis his Doctrine taken from . . . Paracelsus and trimly polished for Sale, is to be rejected.'[18] One aspect of
the mechanical philosophy, however, that was quickly accepted was
Descartes' image of the body as a machine, which like a clock
worked or was kept alive by its mechanical parts functioning
properly, rather than being enlivened by the soul. Towards the end
of the century the success of Newtonian physics became apparent
and Newton came to personally dominate the politics and intellectual life of the Royal Society. Willis' second natural philosophy,
the Epicurean or atomic philosophy, now no longer presented as a
classical alternative to Aristotelian natural philosophy, but as a
modern philosophy expressed in the language of mathematics and
mechanics, became the only natural philosophy that ran in England.
And consequently, a number of versions of a Newtonian medicine
were published which overshadowed any remaining Helmontian
influence at the end of the seventeenth century.[19]

For medicine the revolution in natural philosophies would, on the
face of it, appear momentous. One reason for this is that from the
classical period to the present there has been agreement that
medicine is subservient to and dependent upon natural philosophy
or, in today's terminology, the basic sciences. That agreement has
depended in part upon the way natural philosophy and science have
laid claims to be the foundations of knowledge and objectivity, and

---

[18] M[archamont] N[edham], *Medela Medicinae. A plea for the free profession, and a renovation of the art of physick, out of the noblest and most authentick writers* (London, 1665), pp. 237–244; George Thomson, Ορθο-μέθοδος ιατρο-Χυμικὴ *[Orthomethodos Iatro-chimike]: Or the Direct Method of Curing Chymically* (London, 1675), p. 3.

[19] Anita Guerrini, 'Archibald Pitcairne and Newtonian Medicine', *Medical History*, 31, 1987, 70–83, and, 'Isaac Newton, George Cheyne and the "Principia Medicinae"' in French and Wear (eds.), *The Medical Revolution of the Seventeenth Century*, pp. 222–45. Clericuzio, 'From van Helmont to Boyle', 306, 326–34 makes the point that in the late 1660s and 1670s a third generation of Helmontians (Thomas Sherley, Robert Mot, William Simpson, John Webster) assimilated Helmontianism in the corpuscular philosophy.

in part on the place of medical education within the universities, where the students were taught philosophy before they went on to study medicine. Galen's integration of medicine with Aristotelian and to a lesser extent Platonic natural philosophy had allowed him to distinguish his medicine from that of the empiricists, and to bring medicine within the ambit of Aristotelian causality and rationality. This process was reflected in Galen's treatise, *That the Best Physician is also a Philosopher* and by the oft-repeated Galenic saying that 'where the philosopher ends there the physician begins'.[20] The link between medicine and natural philosophy was used to justify the classical knowledge of the university-educated physicians and to help establish them as a medical elite. In the sixteenth and early seventeenth centuries the relationship between medicine and philosophy was, therefore, employed for essentially conservative purposes, as well as, paradoxically to the modern mind, for the reform and improvement of medicine. But the link was later used to justify radical changes in medicine. As long as medicine remained dependent on natural philosophy, then any change in the latter meant that the former also had to follow suit. Only if, as perhaps happened in the case of Thomas Sydenham, the connection between medicine and philosophy was broken might medicine become an independent discipline or craft.

On the whole, Helmontian medical radicals reinforced the dependence of medicine on natural philosophy. Marchamont Nedham began with natural philosophy when he enquired as to 'what old Foundations and Buildings are to be demolished, and what new ones established'.[21] The changes had 'to strike at the very Foundation of our faculty [i.e. medicine]', and he cited Bacon's *Novum Organum* that ''tis in vain to expect any Advancement in Science, "by superinducing or grafting new things upon old; but an Instauration is to be made from the very lowest Foundations"'.[22] And Nedham was able to point to the example of Descartes who had already 'formed unto himself a new Philosophy to lead men to Physick . . . and lay new foundations of Medicine, more consentaneous to the operations

[20] Galen, 'Quod Optimus Medicus sit quoque Philosophus' in C. G. Kühn, *Claudii Galeni Opera Omnia* (20 vols., Leipzig, 1821), vol. I, p. 61. For the Aristotelian origins of this see Charles B. Schmitt, 'Aristotle amongst the Physicians' in A. Wear, R. K. French, and I. M. Lonie (eds.), *The Medical Renaissance of the Sixteenth Century* (Cambridge University Press, Cambridge, 1985), pp. 1–15.

[21] Nedham, *Medela*, p. 232.

[22] Ibid., p. 234, citing F. Bacon, *Novum Organum* (London, 1620), Bk 1, Aphorism 31.

of Nature, than the Book learning that was in fashion before it'.[23] Helmontians believed that the better the philosophy the better the medicine. In 1651 Noah Biggs, a 'chymiatrophilos' or friend of chemical medicine, who remains otherwise anonymous, wrote a vitriolic attack on Galenic medicine and petitioned Parliament for a reformation of medicine. He argued that:

> Natural Philosophy is the Basis or main Fundamental of Medicine: for where Philosophy ends, there Medicine is to be enterprised, whence it's clear, that such as is the insight of a Physician into natural things (namely, whether it be superficial or profound) such also will his perfection be in Medicine. For He who is ignorant of the mystical Arcana's [secrets] of Physicks of neccessity it will follow that the more occult secrets of Medicine shall be hid from his Eyes.[24]

Clearly, Biggs, who was a Helmontian, still wished to share in the philosopher's and, by extension, the learned physician's traditional status of 'one who knows'. Knowledge created its own sense of elitism and exclusivity, and this was especially the case with the Helmontians' (and Paracelsians') belief that they were gifted by God with the chemical skills to search into nature's secrets and principles, and so create a new esoteric natural philosophy. The new medicine, although it might be more charitable and demotic, would not completely repudiate elitism and exclusivity. Moreover, the continued link in the minds of Helmontians of medicine with natural philosophy meant that, when they came to attack the natural philosophical justification for Galenic therapeutics, especially the cure by contrary quality, they had their own natural philosophy to draw upon.

The primacy of natural philosophy over medicine was still being acknowledged at the end of the formative period of the new science. John Quincy, a physician who wanted medicine to be established on a mechanical and mathematical basis (iatromechanism), could look back in 1722 and state that: 'The Study of Medicine has in all Ages been influenced by the Philosophy in vogue, because the Theory thereof is inseparable from a good Competency of knowledge in natural Causes; insomuch that the Terms of Philosophical Writers

---

[23] Nedham, *Medela*, p. 236.

[24] Noah Biggs, *Mataeotechnia Medicinae Praxeos. The Vanity of the Craft of Physick* (London, 1651), title page, p. 16. On Biggs see Webster, *The Great Instauration*, p. 263; Cook, *Decline*, pp. 122–4; Allen Debus, 'Paracelsian Medicine: Noah Biggs and the Problem of Medical Reform', in *Debus* (ed.), *Medicine in Seventeenth Century England: a Symposium Held at UCLA in Honour of C. D. O'Malley* (University of California Press, California, 1974), pp. 33–48.

have been transplanted into the Discourses of Physicians.'[25] Galenists, Helmontians and iatromechanists agreed that the theories and
language of natural philosophy profoundly affected medicine. But it
was not so simple; not only was there a variety of natural philosophies available, but the nature of the relationship between
natural philosophy and a subordinate discipline such as medicine
was changing. Bacon had argued in the *Novum Organum* that natural
philosophy was the foundation of particular sciences and arts such as
astronomy, optics, music, the mechanical arts and medicine;
however, he added not only that it needed to be reformed, but that
there should be a two-way process whereby natural philosophy is
applied to particular sciences, and the findings of particular sciences
and crafts applied back to natural philosophy.[26] His advocacy of
'fructiferous' experiments that would bring forth useful knowledge,
as well as of 'luciferous' ones that threw light on nature, was
designed to undermine Aristotle's definition of the true philosopher
as one who had no practical purpose in mind because that would
limit his enquiries.[27] The examples of Galileo,[28] Harvey, the work of
the Oxford physiologists, the chemical researches of Helmontians
and the experimental corpuscular chemistry of Boyle all combined
to create the view that the new natural philosophy was to be based
on observation and experimentation.[29] The state's encouragement
of useful knowledge also helped to confirm the transformation of
natural philosophy. The Royal Society, and even more so the
Académie Royale des Sciences established in 1666, which, unlike the
Royal Society, was government-funded, embodied the state's commitment to a natural philosophy which could lead to practical
results. Moreover, the interest that the elite sections of society took
in chemical processes, mechanical inventions and searching in a

[25] John Quincy, *Lexicon Physico-Medicum: Or, A New Physical Dictionary*, 2nd edn (London, 1722),
p. ix.
[26] Bacon, *Novum Organum*, Bk 1, Aphorism 80.   [27] See chapter 3 footnote 4.
[28] On Galileo and experiment see Trevor H. Levere and William R. Shea (eds.), *Nature,
Experiment and the Sciences: Essays on Galileo and the History of Science* (Kluwer Academic
Publishers, Dordrecht, 1990); Stillman Drake, *Galileo, Pioneer Scientist* (University of Toronto
Press, Toronto, *c.* 1990); Joseph C. Pitt, *Galileo, Human Knowledge, and the Book of Nature:
Method Replaces Metaphysics* (Kluwer Academic Publishers, Dordrecht, *c.* 1992); Mario
Biagioli, *Galileo, Courtier: the Practice of Science in the Culture of Absolutism* (University of Chicago
Press, Chicago, *c.* 1993); Tamar Szabo Gendler, 'Galileo and the Indispensability of
Scientific Thought Experiment', *British Journal of the Philosophy of Science*, 49, 1998, 397–424.
[29] Though in his own lifetime Harvey did not agree with either the chemical or mechanical
philosophy and was a strong upholder of Aristotle's philosophy.

Baconian manner for nuggets of knowledge from the crafts, continued the process of making the new natural philosophies socially acceptable that had originally begun in the sixteenth and early seventeenth centuries in the royal courts of Europe.[30] The empirical virtuosi gave some respectability to the empirics, who in sixteenth-century England had been compared to vagabonds and criminals without many voices being then raised in contradiction. A leading virtuoso, Robert Boyle, though he did not sell his remedies, certainly published his favourite ones and believed that there was much to learn from the shops of the chemists and from traders.[31]

The language of chemistry also served as a lingua franca for a variety of groups. By the end of the 1660s Galenists were using the language of nitro-aerial particles and of ferments in the blood, and indeed the College of Physicians had shown an interest in chemical experiments from the 1650s.[32] And, of course, Helmontians and corpuscularian chemists and physicians were fluent in the language of chemistry whilst they self-consciously tried to forget the terminology of the old natural philosophy. However, the fact remains that by the end of the seventeenth century Helmontian medicine, which, as we shall see, attempted to revolutionise the practices of medicine, did not form part of the new philosophy and had largely disappeared from view. Its following was never very large: thirty-five chemical physicians signed the 1665 declaration calling for the establishment of a Helmontian chemical society (see below), though small numbers could exert much influence at a time of social and intellectual change as the 'active' membership of the Royal Society demonstrates. In the mid-1660s, the Helmontians were a group who looked as though they were going somewhere. But as we have seen they were a

---

[30] See Victor E. Thoren, *The Lord of Uraniborg: a Biography of Tycho Brahe* (Cambridge University Press, Cambridge, 1990); Bruce T. Moran (ed.); *Patronage and Institutions: Science, Technology, and Medicine at the European Court: 1500–1750* (Boydell, Rochester, 1991), and *The Alchemical World of the German Court: Occult Philosophy and Chemical Medicine in the Circle of Moritz of Hessen (1572–1632)* (Steiner, Stuttgart, 1991).

[31] See R. Boyle, 'Medicinal Experiments: Or, a Collection of Choice and Safe Remedies'; Boyle, 'Of the Reconcileableness of Specific Medicines to the Corpuscular Philosophy'; Boyle, 'The Advantages of the Use of Simple Medicines', in Robert Boyle, *The Works*, ed. Thomas Birch (6 vols., London, 1772), vol. V; and part 2 of 'Some Considerations Touching the Usefulness of Experimental Natural Philosophy' in Boyle, *Works*, vol. II.

[32] See for instance, in chapter 6, Hodges, on plague; George Castle, *The Chymical Galenist: A Treatise Wherein The Practise of the Ancients is Reconcil'd to the New Discoveries in the Theory of Physick* (London, 1667), pp. 40–3; also Cook, *Decline*, pp. 184–5; C. Webster, 'The College of Physicians: "Solomon's House" in Commonwealth England', *Bulletin of the History of Medicine*, 41, 1967, 393–412.

mix of university-educated and apprentice-trained or self-taught and formed an informal, non-elite grouping, unlike the university-educated physicians. Their diverse social backgrounds should not automatically be seen as a reason for their failure. Social diversity was not unusual for radical movements; Paracelsians had ranged from Court physicians to political radicals. But Paracelsianism meant different things to different people, and certainly the English Helmontians held differing views about the nature of Helmontian medicine. What is clear is that, although van Helmont gained a continental European reputation for erecting a rational system of medicine to replace Galenic medicine – despite his distrust of reason[33] – in England his philosophy came to be considered gnomic, esoteric, secretive rather than public. Its principles were viewed as too mystical and too limiting compared with the open-ended public knowledge that was favoured by the virtuosi of the Royal Society, who positioned themselves as the gate-keepers of what was acceptable in the new science. Perhaps also the differences in social status between the gentlemanly ethos of the Royal Society and the Helmontian chemical physicians, whose researches were often linked to their trade as doctors and sellers of drugs, could not in the end be bridged, except on the basis of a patronising interest by the former in the work of the latter.[34] But the Helmontians mounted the most incisive critique of medicine of the second half of the seventeenth century, not only condemning Galenic theory, which was usual across many intellectual groupings, but also, and this was unusual, its practice, seeking to replace it with their own. That they failed in the end to change medicine was partly due to an inability to establish an institutional base and partly – and this is less well recognised – because, as I will argue in the next chapter, Helmontians themselves realised that patients would not discard traditional therapeutic methods. At the same time, this analysis by the admittedly small group of Helmontian medical practitioners of

[33] See Walter Pagel, *The Smiling Spleen. Paracelsianism in Storm and Stress* (S. Karger, Basle, 1984), p. 145. Also Pagel, *Joan Baptista van Helmont: Reformer of Science and Medicine* (Cambridge University Press, Cambridge, 1982).

[34] Though Helmontians did advertise the names of their noble and gentlemanly patrons. Steven Shapin, 'The House of Experiment in Seventeenth-Century England', *Isis*, 79, 1988, 373–404, and ' "A Scholar and a Gentleman": the Problematic Identity of the Scientific Practitioner in Early Modern England', *History of Science*, 29, 1991, 279–327. Lawrence M. Principe, *The Aspiring Adept: Robert Boyle and his Alchemical Quest: Including Boyle's 'lost' Dialogue on the Transmutation of Metals* (Princeton University Press, Princeton, 1998).

their patients' wishes will provide us with valuable insights into medical practice.

HELMONTIAN MEDICAL THEORY: DISEASE AND THERAPEUTICS

A mix of medical, chemical and moral arguments, together with the rational analysis that they professed to despise, shaped the discourse of Helmontian physicians. When they attacked traditional therapeutics, Helmontians rightly pointed out that the cure by contrary quality (see chapters 1 and 2) and the eliminative procedures of bleeding, purging, etc. were central to learned curative medicine. One line of attack was the foundational: change the foundations and all else has to change; this, as we have seen, was well known at this time. If the theoretical basis of medicine was recast, then the therapeutics that was derived from and justified by it also had to change. Take the theory away and, in principle, the practice should also disappear. This move was available to Helmontians as they had created a completely different theory of the world, the body and diseases. Their wish was to bring about a revolution in medicine in which Galenic medicine and its therapeutics would disappear and be forgotten; to use Thomas Kuhn's term, they saw Greek learned medicine as incommensurable with their own, though as we shall see others thought that a conciliation between the two was possible. Helmontians, therefore, viewed Galenic therapeutic methods as irrelevant as well as harmful. One of van Helmont's most fervent English disciples, George Thomson, an enthusiastic polemicist in his concern to establish a new Helmontian practice of medicine and, together with George Starkey, the English writer who best represented van Helmont's medical views, attacked, like his fellow Helmontians, the doctrine of the cure by contrary quality. The Galenists' 'rotten Foundation' of 'Contrarities, Qualities and Complexions' did not justify, he argued, 'their Stately and Pompous Fabrick of Curing'. Moreover:

The Rule of Contraries derived from Imaginary Supposition of the Hostility and Reluctancy of the Four Elements . . . hath been the bane of many Myriads. When they find any notable heat in a Feaver, they presently take Indication to cool the Body, in a degree proportionate to its Antagonist, in hopes thereby to reduce the Body to an *Eucrasie*, but still with unlucky success: For neglecting the Radical Cause, and aiming at the

Abolitions of Accidents, Products or Symptoms, how can it be otherwise, but that they must needs miss the Mark, unless they hit it by casualty? A Faithful Knowing Physitian is unconcern'd and indifferent whether the Patient be Hot, Cold, or Temperate (as to the touch) in a Feaver.[35]

It also made commercial sense for Helmontians, who were often, like Thomson, sellers of their own chemical remedies, to attack the cure by contrary. Galenic theory put limits on the prescription and sale of chemical remedies. These were usually perceived as hot, partly because of their association with the fire of the chemist's furnace, and partly because many spirits and chemicals were hot to the taste and were believed to heat the body. In Galenic medicine such remedies could not be used against hot diseases nor usually against dry ones, though, as we have seen, there was a demand by the public for all types of hot remedies including plant-based ones.[36] Similarly, the attack on bleeding, purging and other procedures, discussed below, that eliminated an excess or putrid humour can be interpreted as designed to make patients rely solely on chemical remedies and so increase their sale. Rather than assign priority to materialistic and commercial motives over ideological commitment, so that the former is seen as shaping the latter, as today the 1970s school of social constructivists would urge us to do, it makes better sense to view the two types of motivation as coterminous and interactive, as part of the package of what it was for medicine to be Helmontian.

Thomson argued that he could cure 'fundamentally'.[37] Like other Helmontians, he believed that he could get at the roots of disease, rather than, as Galenists had done, at its symptoms. Disease became more specific; heat and cold were not the disease. Helmontians, unlike Galenists, drew a sharp distinction between symptoms and diseases. In their eyes a disease had an essential nature, it was a thing in itself. As John Chandler, the English translator of van Helmont's works expressed it, diseases have an 'essential thingliness'

[35] Thomson, *Orthomethodos*, pp. 50–1. See also Biggs, *Mataeotechnia*, p. 12, where he writes of 'the threed-bare and short-coated descriptions and discourses of *Heat* and *Cold*; both in the *Crasis* of things, with the Nature, *Elements*, temperaments, humours, powers; that as out of the monocracy and single-fol'd intemperature of the Liver, they have rendered us perhaps two hundred Diseases; so out of this *Binary* of *Heat* and *Cold*, they have builded their indispensable *Dispensatory*'.

[36] J. Worth Estes, 'The European Reception of the First Drugs from the New World', *Pharmacy in History*, 37, 1995, 3–23.

[37] Thomson, *Orthomethodos*, p. 54.

or 'quiddity'.[38] But this view, which looks so modern, was put into a vitalistic and almost mystical context in the twenty-first-century sense. For, although some diseases could be conveyed externally by contagion through the air, the majority, in van Helmont's view, were recreated internally by the 'archeus', the chemical and spiritual governor of the body. In a process analogous to the hypochondriac imagination of disease, the archeus formed ideas of disease when it was perturbed. These were, as Thomson wrote, 'Dark Images agreeable to the Cause Offensive. According to this Model or Proportion it [the archeus] Acts, never ceasing to follow the Copy or Draught of the Malady by its own Activity.'[39] The 'ideas' of disease had their origin in seeds of disease implanted within the archeus, hence the specificity of Helmontian diseases; and it was the interplay between the power of the imagination and the disturbed archeus that created the reality of illness. A kidney stone, even when surgically removed, could grow again because of the 'Petrifying Imaginary Seed' within the archeus, unless the idea was 'blotted out'.[40] Such a view of disease integrated the physical and the psychological as causes of illness even more than in Galenic medicine, and reversed the arrow of causality from the physical to the psychological. It fitted well with the Helmontian persona of the spiritual adept enlightened by God. Moreover, it retained the Christian origin of disease, for, according to Helmontians, although God did not create diseases, within the fruit that Adam ate lay the power to disorder the soul, to produce lust and then 'Irregular Imagination'.[41]

Also, a new set of 'agents' was now at work within the body, maintaining health or creating disease.[42] For instance, hot fevers and the 'supposed humour called Choller' (Thomson had to use some of the old terminology to make himself understood) were produced, not

[38] J. B. van Helmont, *Oriatrike or Physick Refined*, trans. J[ohn] C[handler], (1st edn, 1662; London, 1664), pp. 484, 485, 489.

[39] Thomson, *Orthomethodos*, pp. 13–14.

[40] Ibid., pp. 17–18. On van Helmont and imagination see Guido Giglioni, 'La Teoria dell' immaginazione nell' "Idealismo" Biologico di Johannes Baptista van Helmont', *Cultura*, 29, 1991, 110–45.

[41] Ibid., pp. 16–17; van Helmont, *Oriatrike*, p. 653, where van Helmont argues that Adam was not cursed by God with death for disobedience, but 'death was placed in the apple', and God merely warned Adam of the danger. For Helmontians this made disease less of a punishment and God less malevolent, which fitted their image of a God of light and enlightenment.

[42] Thomson used the term 'agent' as an external cause of disease: *Orthomethodos*, p. 51.

by hot qualities, but by invisible spirits or a 'Wild Exotick [external] Gas' entering the body and coming into contact with the 'internal spirits of the microcosm' and arousing an unnatural heat inside the body.[43] The heat was merely a symptom and not the disease. The cure involved psychological as well as physical processes. The body's 'enraged vital spirits' needed to be pacified, so they could increase and tame the wild spirit or gas. 'Cooling prescriptions' could never accomplish this; what was needed was to give the archeus a medicine that 'pleases' it, 'indulging it exceedingly'.[44]

Another possibility was that fevers resulted from acid-alkali ferments. In van Helmont's writings ferments were produced by sharpness, sourness, vitriol and alkali-salts, and he believed that they were responsible not only for digestion but for many of the chemical processes in the world and in the body. By the 1660s the language had changed to that of acid-alkali ferments (partly due to the influential writings of Franciscus Sylvius at Leiden), of acid particles and of nitro-aerial particles, and was used alike by 'modern' Galenists such as Hodges, and by virtuosi including Boyle, as well as by chemical physicians.[45] But, again, such ferments for Helmontians not only had physical effects but also produced vital, almost emotional responses, in the body. They created a 'tumult' in the body which had to be quietened. Helmontians argued that the key to curing ferments in the body was to tackle their cause, and it did not matter if the medicine was cold or hot.[46] The rich and complex mix of chemical and psychological effects that made up a Helmontian cure was contrasted with the Galenists' threadbare and simplistic cure by contrary quality. This enabled Helmontians to turn aside the accusation of Galenic physicians that chemical remedies were 'violently Hot, Burning, Drying, Inflaming'.[47] Hot remedies could cure a fever, because what had to be cured was the underlying

---

[43] Ibid., p. 54.

[44] Ibid., p. 54; Thomson in his 'explanation of some terms of art', sig. A8^r, defined Gas as 'a wild invisible Spirit, not to be imprisoned or pent up, without damage of what conteins it, arising from the Fermentation of the Concourse of some Bodies . . .' and, the '*Archaeus* of *Paracel*[sus] and *Enormon* of *Hippo*[crates] is the Seminal Vital Spirit, the Principal Impetuous Agent or Spiritual Contriver and Supporter of every Thing, the Arch Preeminent Author of Health and Sickness'.

[45] Van Helmont, *Oriatrike*, pp. 201–8. See John Mayow, *Tractatus quinque medico-physici. Quorum primus agit de sal-nitro et spiritu nitro-aereo* . . . (Oxford, 1674); Richard Lower, *Tractatus de corde* (London, 1669).

[46] Thomson, *Orthomethodos*, p. 54.   [47] Ibid.

disease and not the heat in the body. Knowledge, practice and commercial interest went hand in hand.

In keeping with the Helmontians' stress on the power of the imagination, they used powerful metaphors to establish the worth of their medicines. The images of light, fire and knowledge which were integral to Helmontianism were contrasted with the 'Dreggy, Drosy, Indigested . . . Unclean, Malignant' medicines of their opponents.[48] They were designed to conjure up the vision of a new enlightened medicine, to blacken the Galenists and to create the impression that their medicines were iatrogenic, or, as Biggs phrased it, they produced 'the foul disease of the medicine'.[49] The language of Helmontian medicine had the capacity both to be the philosophical basis of a new medicine and to serve as a polemical discourse or, more crudely, as knocking copy, in the advertising world of the medical marketplace where claim and counter-claim met.

THE WIDER HELMONTIAN CRITIQUE OF MEDICINE

. . . the whole mode, method and body of Physick, as it is now prescribed and practised . . . groans for a reformation.[50]

Noah Biggs called on Parliament to undertake a general reformation 'of the stupendous body of Universal Learning, Languages, Arts and Sciences especially this of Physick'.[51] Perhaps the most damning indictment of the old medicine was that it was unsuccessful and, what was worse, it killed its patients. Biggs wrote that Parliament could not 'be insensible of the cruelties and unsuccessfulness of the Medical profession', and that even physicians could not avoid acknowledging 'their own unsuccessfulnesse'.[52] George Starkey also stressed the cruelty of Galenic medicine. The 'method' of the Galenists, which in the sixteenth century they had made the distinguishing mark of the 'good' doctor, was 'but bloody cruelty', consisting of 'your martyrdoms and butcheries' and 'tormenting the patient'.[53] The rhetoric echoed the political revolutionary rhetoric

---

[48] Ibid., p. 55.   [49] Biggs, *Mataeotechnia*, p. 7.

[50] Ibid., p. 16.   [51] Ibid., To the Parliament, sig. a3ᵛ.

[52] Ibid., sig. b2, p. 2; at sig. b3ᵛ, he wrote of the 'ocular unsuccessfulness of Physitians', in other words it was obvious to observation, a major criterion of truth for those concerned with destroying the old order.

[53] George Starkey, *Nature's Explication and Helmont's Vindication* (London, 1657), 'To the Reader', sigs., b7ʳ, b6ʳ.

which referred to the oppressions, cruelties and irreligion of the old order, as when Starkey summed up what medicine had come to since its 'original God-given primitive verity and uncorrupted sincerity': '[it] is become the Engine of oppression, cruelty and butchery, the prop of pride, and ambition, covetousness and idleness'.[54]

The accusation that medicine had been cruel and unsuccessful was not new, and had been frequently made by playwrights:

> Trust not the physician;
> His antidotes are poison, and he slays
> More than you rob.'[55]

The frequent association between doctors, death and pain probably found a ready response in audiences that had experienced the pain and discomfort of bleeding and purging. Thomas Dekker played to his audience's distrust of medicine in *The Honest Whore*: 'He might have met with three fencers in this time, and have received less hurt than by meeting one doctor of physic.[56] Many in an audience might also have agreed that doctors were worse than unsuccessful:

> He has no faith in physic: he does think
> Most of your doctors are the greater danger,
> And worse disease to escape.
> . . . he says, they flay a man
> Before they kill him . . .
> And then, they do it by experiment;
> For which the law not only doth absolve 'em,
> But gives them great reward.'[57]

The long-held association of physicians with high fees and lack of care for their patients gave further ammunition to those who called for a new medicine to replace the old:

> Physicians thus,
> With their hands full of money, use to give o'er
> Their patients.''[58]

Biggs could write with some justification that medicine 'is everywhere brought upon the Stage; and made the laughing-stock of the

---

54 Ibid., pp. 14–15.
55 William Shakespeare, *Timon of Athens*, Act IV Scene III, lines 434–5; my thanks to Dr Natsu Hattori for this and the following three literary passages.
56 Thomas Dekker, *The Honest Whore* Part 1, Act IV Scene IV, lines 55–7.
57 Ben Jonson, *Volpone*, Act 1 Scene 4, lines 20–31.
58 John Webster, *The Duchess of Malfi*, Act III Scene V, lines 7–9.

sick-brain'd vulgar'.[59] And Helmontians expounded at length upon what they took to be the self-evident failures and cruelties of Galenic medicine, with 'sad experience' teaching 'that for all this rabble of Physicians, there is not a third part of diseases cured, nor a tenth part by the skill of the Doctor'.[60]

In the manner of the 'moderns' they equated medicine's failure with its lack of progress. The teachings of Hippocrates, whom Helmontians praised and cited to give classical legitimacy to their movement, were based on 'usefull experimental practice', the 'modern' pathway to progress, but they had been corrupted by Galen and his 'vast volumes', resulting in scholastic medicine: concerned with words rather than with the investigation of nature, with books rather than with the book of nature. To this Baconian-style history of medicine, they added that physicians were lazy, they were content with the learning of the past, they were 'ever learning but not the truth'.[61] Only in recent years had there been available a new path for medicine: based on van Helmont's chemistry and leavened by Bacon's stress on experimentation as the key to knowledge.[62] Progress in medicine would come from one's own creative thinking and labour rather than from relying upon that of the past. A new model of research was being constructed for medicine as for the new science. Classical medicine, which in the sixteenth century had been seen as the fountain of knowledge, was viewed now as foreign, atheistic and a barrier to the national self-improvement of

---

[59] Biggs, *Mataeotechnia*, p. 18.   [60] Starkey, *Nature's Explication*, p. 90.

[61] Van Helmont, *Oriatrike* p. 488, referring to Timothy 3.7; 'Ever learning, and not able to come to the knowledge of the truth.'

[62] Biggs, *Mataeotechnia*, sigs. a4ᵛ, b3ᵛ, pp. 2, 5, 13, 23–4; Thomson, *Galeno-pale*, pp. 1–25 and [Orthomethodos] 'To the Reader', sigs. A5ʳ–A7ᵛ; Starkey, *Nature's Explication*, pp. 8, 9–23; Nedham, *Medela*, pp. 2–19, 233–47; Mary Trye, the daughter of Thomas O'Dowde, a member of the proposed Society of Chemical Physicians, wrote in *Medicatrix, Or the Woman-Physician: Vindicating Thomas O'Dowde . . . against . . . Henry Stubbe* (London, 1675), p. 92: 'in so many hundred years the Art of *Learned Physick* is no more improved; Physicians that desire to be *Honoured* with the name of *Learning*, are no more able in their *Science*, than their Masters of Old were near Two Thousand years before them'. On the Hippocratism of the iatromechanists see I. Lonie, 'Hippocrates the Iatromechanist', *Medical History*, 25, 113–50. On the book of nature metaphor see Galileo, *Letter to the Grand Duchess Christina* and also *The Assayer*: 'Philosophy is written in this grand book, the universe, which stands continually open to our gaze.' Galileo added that the language of the book was mathematics: Galileo, *Discoveries and Opinions of Galileo*, trans. with introduction by Stillman Drake (Doubleday, New York, 1957), pp. 177–216 and 237–8. For Paracelsus' use of the book of nature theme see W. Pagel, *Paracelsus* (S. Karger, Basle, 1958), pp. 56–7; Nedham recounted approvingly how Descartes laid aside books and 'betook himself wholly to a contemplation of the Book of the world': *Medela*, p. 235.

medicine. 'As though', as Biggs complained, 'our souls and heads were not our own . . . but we must thus foot it ever to the Times of Trajan and City of Pergamus [Galen's birthplace]', it is a 'terrible thing truely to prefer Aristotle . . . and condemn the truth of God'.[63] Although this had also been the complaint of Paracelsus and Paracelsians, now there was an increasing acceptance of such sentiments by what might be called intellectual society.[64]

More specifically, Helmontians attacked the Galenic physicians' belief that certain diseases were incurable, and condemned them for giving up before they had begun. That some diseases were considered incurable was well known. John Ward wrote that 'The French have a proverb, that the words ending in ique doe mock the physician; as paralytique, hectique, apoplectick, lethargick.'[65] In the list of diseases 'usually accounted *Opprobium Medicorum*, the Physicians shame' were 'the Gout, the kings-evil, inveterate quartein Agues, Fistulas, Cancers and such like chronical Distempers'.[66] Starkey also wrote that Galenic physicians believed that there were no remedies for the gout, strangury, palsy and epilepsy, whilst Biggs had insisted that they 'bring almost all diseases in the *Catalogue* of incurables' in order to excuse themselves.[67] However, Helmontian Christian medicine, infused as its supporters claimed with God's knowledge and with their hard work, could do better. There was no reason, according to Helmontians, why all diseases should not be cured, especially given God's honouring of the physician, his mercy in providing medicine as described in Ecclesiasticus and Christ's curing of 'all manner of sickness and of disease'.[68] God guaranteed that

---

[63] Biggs, *Metaeotechnia*, sig. a4^v, b2^v.

[64] On Paracelsus' attack on Greek medicine see Pagel, *Paracelsus*; one of the first English Paracelsian writers, Richard Bostocke, also prefigured the later rhetoric when he demanded in *The Difference Betwene the Auncient Phisicke, First Taught by the Godly Forefathers* (London, 1585), fol. F III $^{r-v}$ that 'the Chymicall doctrine agreeing with Gods worde, experience and nature may come into the Scholes and Cities in stede of Aristotle, Gallen, and other heathen and their followers. And . . . for every honest student to labour in the Philosophicall searching out of the trueth, by the fire or otherwise . . . eather to adde newe things wel tried to the old that be good, and then to reiect the other bastard, adulterat, sophisticat stuffe, and so ioyne words and deedes together, then should there be no time spent in vayne, and vaineglorious bable and sophisticall disputations, without due triall by labor and worke of fire, and other requisite experiments.' See also Debus, *The English Paracelsians*.

[65] John Ward, *Diary of the Rev. John Ward, A. M., Vicar of Stratford-Upon-Avon . . . 1648–1679*, ed. Charles Severn (London, 1839), p. 119.

[66] Richard Bunworth Ὁμοτροπία *Naturae. A Physical Discourse Exhibiting the Cure of Diseases by Signature* (London, 1656).

[67] Starkey, *Nature's Explication*, p. 151; Biggs, *Mataeotechnia*, p. 13, also p. 23.

[68] Starkey, *Nature's Explication*, pp. 147–52; Matthew 4.23; John Donne citing Matthew 4.23

nothing was impossible in medicine; as Starkey put it, 'it is a good thing that all diseases should be cured, and is any good thing impossible?'[69] But God helps those who help themselves. Helmontians took pride in their hard work. Having received the talent of healing from God, the true chemical physician 'doth not bury it in a napkin, but doth improve it, untill with it he gain two, and with them five, and with them ten talents. He knowes that diseases are all in their kinde curable without exception, death only being out of the power of any man or means.' The 'son of this art' did not become one by reading Galen or Avicenna but by a combination of mental and manual work; 'it requires a mental man, patient, laborious, and one who is not niggardly in expenses, such a man must toyl without wearisomness; and although after several years searching, with the expence of many pounds, he hit not what he aims at, yet must he still patiently proceed'.[70] Moreover, Helmontians argued that, as there were new diseases unknown to the ancients and as old diseases had altered and grown more violent, so new doctrines and rules of healing had to be discovered. The message that consequently hard work was required in 'a Laboratory and a Study' was unwelcome to physicians tied to 'old Methods and Aphorisms'.[71]

At the beginning of the age of progress, a medical system that was validated by the degree to which it conformed to rules set out over a thousand years before began to look ridiculous. To stand immobile in the past now looked like lazy arrogance, and the combination of deadly diseases and a blind adherence to the past led to the seventeenth-century equivalent of 'the patient died but the operation was successful'. As Nedham wrote, when arguing for change and progress in medicine: 'by stiff adherence to them [the ancient precepts of medicine], many a person hath been lost, but the Thing may be justified by Rule and Secundum Artem [according to the art (of medicine)]'. And Nedham retold a story from Boyle about why a doctor would not give a patient stronger remedies: 'He briskly answered "Let him die, if he will, so [long as] he die Secundum Artem"'.[72]

---

added, 'No disease incurable': *Devotions Upon Emergent Occasions*, ed. John Raspa (Oxford University Press, Oxford, 1987), p. 24.

[69] Starkey, *Nature's Explication*, p. 149.   [70] Ibid., pp. 80, 91.

[71] Nedham, *Medela*, pp. 206, 205.

[72] Nedham, *Medela*, p. 206, citing Robert Boyle, *Some Considerations touching the Usefulnesse of Experimentall Naturall Philosophy* (Oxford, 1663), Part 2, Essay 5, p. 118.

Galenic physicians were also depicted as un-Christian and un-charitable. They were hammered as concerned only for the rich and their fees. The example of chemical physicians and dissenting ministers staying on in London during the plague of 1665 and looking after the poor and their congregations gave practical effect to the rhetoric and, in my view, indicates that real idealism lay behind it. And, by the end of the century, partly in response to the heightened awareness about the need to care for the poor created by its rivals and partly because of the competition from the apothecaries, the College of Physicians had set up, after various attempts from 1675 onwards, a dispensary offering charitable advice and low-cost medicine for the poor.[73]

The religious and moral attack on Galenic medicine and physicians was not, as perhaps would be the case today, separated from the medical; the two were intertwined as was usual in polemical writings of the time. For Helmontians this was even more the case, because God and not reason was seen as the origin of both medicine's doctrines and its remedies. He was, according to van Helmont, the God of 'lights', bringing the light of understanding to his chosen adepts, whilst reason had created false knowledge. At a trite but true level, the success and failure of Helmontianism is symbolised by its emblem of light, which was also common to the Enlightenment but which, as it turned out, in the Enlightenment was taken to be the light of reason. Van Helmont saw reason as an enemy rather than an essential part of the soul, bringing with it false knowledge; at the heart of his argument was his belief that 'Reason is accounted to be the life of the Soul, or the life of our life. But, I believe that the Almighty is alone, the way, the truth, the life, the light, of living Creatures, and of all things, but this is not reason.'[74] More specifically, knowledge is gained by the link between the soul and the light of God: '*Solomon* calls the spirit of a man the Lamp or Candle of God. But not that God is in darkness, or that he hath need of the splendor of the spirit of a man. But altogether, because the hidden knowledges of things, are infused by the Father of Lights into us by means of this Candle . . . Whence I concluded with myself, first, that reason doth generate nothing but a dim or dark knowledge'.[75]

[73] G. Clark, *A History of the Royal College of Physicians* (2 vols., Clarendon Press, Oxford, 1964 and 1966), vol. II, pp. 431–47; Cook, *Decline*, pp. 233–5, 238–40.

[74] Van Helmont, *Oriatrike*, pp. 15–18, 15.

[75] Ibid., p. 18. See Walter Pagel, 'The Religious and Philosophical Aspects of van Helmont's

The Helmontian God of enlightenment was very much the Christian God. The chemical physician had to conform in his life and work to Christian values, otherwise he could not receive understanding through the light of God. Moreover, Helmontians emphasised that physicians and medicines were God-given, and so in their eyes medicine was a Christian art, which excluded knowledge that came from non-Christians. A Christian medicine also rejected un-Christian behaviour such as cruelty or a lack of Christian charity and compassion, which in medical practice was exemplified for Helmontians by the bleeding and purging habitually employed by Galenic physicians.

THE HELMONTIAN ATTACK ON BLEEDING AND PURGING

The cure by contrary quality was one lynchpin of Galenic therapeutics, the other was that based on evacuation: bleeding, purging, sweating, etc. which were designed to eliminate an excess of a humour or to get rid of putrefaction or a vitiated humour. Helmontians saw them as crucial targets in their attack on Galenic medicine.[76] Van Helmont, with his usual incisive insight into the structure of Galenic medicine, highlighted 'the universal Succours [therapeutic helps or remedies]: to wit, Bloud-letting and Purging, as the two pillars of Medicine; and the which being dashed to pieces, the whole Edifice falls down of its own accord, as it were into Rubbish: and these Succours being taken away, Physitians may forsake the sick, they not having Remedies besides the Diminishers [bleeding and purging] of the body and strength'.[77] Biggs, who was well acquainted with van Helmont's writing, came to the same conclusion. The superstructure of medicine, 'the studies, books, Orations, Councels, Conversations, Chairs and practices of Physitians', he declared, 'sound of nothing but trifles and anxious disputes'. In reality, 'the whole huge bulke of the art of *healing* seemes now adaies to be moved upon the slender hinges of *purgations, phlebotomy* or *blouding, searing . . . cupping, bath, sweating, fontanels,*

Science and Medicine', *Supplements to the Bulletin of the History of Medicine*, 2, 1944, pp. 1–2, 10–11.

[76] Van Helmont perceptively noted that Galenic physicians had moved from considering degrees of heat when describing the cause of fevers to seeing putrefaction as the cause, for which bleeding and purging were especially recommended; Van Helmont, *Oriatrike*, pp. 939–40.

[77] Ibid., p. 949.

Cauteries, and in short, upon no other than the *diminution* of *strength* and emaciations of the body, and abbreviations of life'.[78] The Helmontians' belief that the 'whole bulk' of medicine was a mere panoply of words underpinned by a few medical procedures expressed their conviction that Galenic theory added little that was worthwhile to practice, and that what there was of Galenic therapeutics was harmful and cruel.

Blood-letting and purging had become habitual practices, so impressed across the population and so essential to learned medical practice that they expressed a point of fusion between popular and learned medicine. Patients demanded them and doctors routinely advised them, as John Ward, a sharp observer of the traditional and of the novel, commented: 'Physicians make blood-letting but as a prologue to the play'; and he placed blood-letting and purging amongst the five arts useful to medicine.[79] Learned Galenic medicine provided reasons for the almost automatic recourse to these procedures: they eliminated disease by evacuating the blood and other humours, whether excess or corrupt, that caused it.[80]

Yet the dangers of the two procedures were well known. Blood-letting could leave an arm sore or gangrenous, or even cause death.[81] The loss of blood, the carrier of life, of the vital spirits and of the soul, was seen as potentially even more dangerous than the localised physical damage made by the lancet. The analogy between

---

[78] Biggs, *Mataeotechnia*, p. 6. Biggs had clearly read van Helmont: compare *Oriatrike*, p. 487, 'nothing more hard, inhumane, and fuller of cruelty, hath been received now for so many Ages, among the Arts of Mortals, than that Art [of medicine], which under a con-centrical subscription, makes fresh experiments by the deaths of men', with *Mataeotechnia*, p. 14, 'there is nothing more hard, more inhumane and full of Cruelty, among all *humane Arts*, through so many ages undertaken and usurp'd, then that *art* which by a concentrick *subscription* doth make new experiments by the deaths of men'.

[79] Ward, *Diary*, pp. 252, 266. The other three arts were those of pharmacy, midwifery and cooking.

[80] Nicholas Gyer, an enlightened 'minister of the word' who wrote a learned treatise on phlebotomy which he saw as being in the tradition of Sir Thomas Elyot's expert lay medical writing, explained that there were two types of excess humour. One was when there was too much of a humour in the body (a 'plethora'), in terms of either its intensity, as too cold, hot, dry or wet, or its amount so that the body's vessels became stretched and close to bursting. The other was when a humour had become vitiated or corrupted. N[icholas] G[yer], *The English Phlebotomy* (London, 1592), Dedication, sig. A7ᵛ, pp. 2–5; Gyer cited Galen, *Methodus Medendi*, Book 13, ch. 6.

[81] For instance, in 1573 Edwarde Saunders, a barber-surgeon, was accused 'that he had let one bloude at Blackwall and that he dyed, his arme fallynge to Gangrena'. The Barber-Surgeons Court also heard in 1624 that 'of late Doctor Grints servingman John Eethell lett a maide blood, her arme mortified and the maid thereupon died'. A. T. Young, *The Annals of the Barber-Surgeons of London* (Blades, East & Blades, London, 1890), pp. 317, 332.

bleeding to death and blood-letting was not far-fetched and helped to frame views about phlebotomy. Ward acidly observed, 'Itt may bee said of some physitians, that they cure their patients as Nero did his senators, but cutting their veins, or rather their throats.'[82] However, medical practitioners had traditionally learnt when blood-letting was contra-indicated or indicated in small amounts. Such knowledge helped to differentiate them from 'the vagabund Horse-leaches and travailing Tinkers who find work in almost every village'. Or, as Simon Harward more kindly put it, in cities, especially in London, there were many 'expert Phisitions and Chirurgians', the one 'to advise', the other 'to lend a helping hand'. 'Yet', he continued:

'in Countrie townes, there are many nowadayes which doe practize the opening of vaynes (almost in every Village one) and most of them neither have any learned counsaile to direct them, neither are of themselves sufficiently instructed in the matter which they take in hand: whereby, though many of them do meane well, and intend all for the best, yet in the event, both to the harme of their patients, and also to their owne griefe, there often issueth more hurt and danger, then ease and succour.[83]

Blood-letting, like the use of herbs, was a popular and universal therapy which was brought within the self-proclaimed safety net of learned medicine. As with herbal medicines, this was part of a process: the interaction between popular and elite medicine that had been taking place in Europe since classical times, and was not specific to England or to the early modern period. The learned physicians both explained why blood-letting worked and provided cautions as to its use. As long as the patient was strong, strong diseases required abundant bleeding, moderate diseases moderate bleeding. The 'phlebotomer' or physician could judge the strength of the patient as the blood was being lost by feeling the pulse, another skill that the learned physician was expected to possess. This was especially necessary if the patient was being bled until *syncope* or fainting. Moreover, further knowledge was necessary for the 'pulse be mightie and full' indicating strength, but the patient could in reality be weak from chronic diseases such as consumption.[84] In other words, the ability to distinguish the different conditions of the

---

82 Ward, *Diary*, pp. 277–8.
83 Gyer, *English Phlebotomy*, sig. A2ʳ; Simon Harward, *Harward's Phlebotomy: Or, a Treatise of Letting of Bloud* (London, 1601), sig. a2ᵛ.
84 Gyer, *English Phlebotomy*, pp. 146–7, 134–5, 140, 141.

patient, and having the education to know what these could be, which were characteristics of learned medicine, were applied to phlebotomy. Phlebotomy was also incorporated into learned medicine, by giving it technical terms such as 'revulsion', moving blood through to another part of the body, or 'evacuation', moving the humours out of the body. The anatomical terminology surrounding which veins to lance, and the debate of the early sixteenth century about which side of the body to bleed from – on the same side or opposite the disease – also 'made' phlebotomy learned. The result was that learned physicians, as well as being concerned in the choice of vein to bleed, in which diseases and how much, were also cautious about whom to bleed. They were especially careful about bleeding in young children, pregnant women and the elderly, as well as those weakened by disease. When to bleed was also linked to the season and the weather, and astrological medicine provided advice on the best and worst times to bleed.[85] Ward summarised his own rules for bleeding:

For phlebotomie, a faire and clear day, not at new moon, nor moon att the full. All such as have weak stomachs, or are wrought upon or opprest by a diarrhoea, or loosenes of the bellie, or who have undergon some indigestion, ought not to bee blooded, nor women with child, especially in the first and last months, and also such as live in a too hot and cold a climate and are of a cold phlegmatic constitution.[86]

Physicians believed that their knowledge was a safeguard for a potentially dangerous procedure. This was part of the rhetoric that saw medical therapies as dangerous unless prescribed by a competent physician; it was probably a sincerely held belief, and it was also a good way of denigrating competitors, something not unknown today.

Purging, the other pillar of learned medicine in Helmontian eyes, was immensely popular. Medicine and purging had become synonymous in English: 'physick', 'working physick' and 'to physick' meant purging as well as medicine. Purging was also integral to the Galenic sense of disease as something that had to be eliminated through the body's channels. As we have seen in chapter 2, purging was considered potentially dangerous, but the expert learned physician who applied the Galenic method of cure correctly to the

[85] Harward, *Phlebotomy*, pp. 72–9; on astrology see pp. 92–9; Gyer, *English Phlebotomy*, pp. 180–4; Nicholas Culpeper, *Culpeper's School of Physick* (London, 1659), pp. 219–21.

[86] Ward, *Diary*, p. 254.

individual circumstances of the patient could eliminate or mitigate the dangers. John Donne, a very learned layman when it came to medicine, reflected the Galenic position: 'The working of *purgative physicke* is violent and contrary to *Nature* . . . To take physicke, and *not* according to the right method is dangerous.'[87] Donne accepted the paradox of purging (and by implication of bleeding): 'O *strange* way of *addition*, to doe it by *subtraction*; of *restoring* Nature to *violate Nature*; of *providing strength*, by *increasing weaknesse*.'[88] Not all agreed that weakening the body strengthened it. Thomas Nashe has Orion, the sun, say in *Summers Last Will and Testament*:

> While dog-days last, the harvest safely thrives
> The sun burns hot, to finish up fruits' growth;
> There is no blood-letting to make men weak.
> Physicians with . . .
> . . . Their gargarisms [gargles], clysters [enemas and/or suppositories]
> . . . Refrain to poison the sick patients,
> And dare not minister till I be out.[89]

Helmontians also believed that bleeding in particular weakened a patient without any healing or strengthening benefit (they were less opposed to purging). In Helmontian theory the effect of blood-letting was that the archeus lost sight of the need to fight a fever, for, though blood-letting seemed initially 'to tame and asswage the intense heat and acutenesse of feavers. Yet it falls out no otherwise then that the Archeus being driven into a horrid extesy by this unexpected unnatural *extravenation*, greatly feares the sudden depletion of the powers . . . and so forgetting the duell or conflict with the disease, neglects to expell the feavorish matter, and exercise its function.'[90] More simply, Helmontians believed blood-letting did not work: it undermined the body and could lead to death. They especially urged that it should not be used in fevers and in diseases such as smallpox. The question of its use formed part of the war of words between Galenists and Helmontians. George Thomson wrote a book-length attack on the use of blood-letting which provoked a vituperative reply by the Warwick and Bath physician and contro-

---

[87] Donne, *Devotions*, p. 108; the editor, p. 182, cites Galen, *De Hippocratis De Acutorum Comment*, XI, Galen, *Opera*, XV, p. 539 and *Hippocratis de Humoribus* in Galen, *Opera*, XII, p. 107 discussing the dangers of medicines.

[88] Donne, *Devotions*, p. 106.

[89] Thomas Nashe, 'Summers Last Will and Testament' in *The Unfortunate Traveller and Other Works*, ed. J. B. Steane (Penguin, Harmondsworth, 1985), p. 169.

[90] Biggs, *Mataeotechnia*, p. 142.

versialist Henry Stubbe.[91] Blood-letting symbolised for Helmontians the intransigent hostility of Galenic medicine to any questioning of its methods and to any innovation. When Mary Trye, the daughter of Thomas O'Dowde, wrote *Medicatrix* (1675) as a vindication of her father against Stubbe, she linked the latter's 'Generous Medicaments; the chief of which, I perceive is his Lancett' with his condemnation of 'all other Societies, Methods and Courses of Ingenuity . . . In fine, he refuses *Chymistry*'. For Trye the use of the lancet stood for past ignorance in contrast to modern enlightenment: 'This Age knows better things.'[92]

GALENIC CRUELTY

Blood-letting also stood for the cold-hearted cruelty of the old medical order. Cutting into the patient's body, seeing the life-blood running out of it, and at the same time coolly calculating the weight of the amount lost, was in Helmontian eyes an un-Christian attack on the patient: 'That the life is in the blood is most certain, and by how much of it is taken away, by so much is the vitall Balsam [of life] wasted . . . the taking of this away doth threaten ruine to the life'.[93] The Bible confirmed the equation of life, the soul, with the blood: 'But flesh with the life [soul] thereof which is the blood thereof, shall ye not eat': Genesis 9.4. The Helmontian emphasis on religion ensured that medicine and religion did not merely co-exist amicably in largely (but not completely) separate spheres as in the traditional Christian accommodation of Galenic medicine. Religious doctrine was positively integrated into medical reasoning. So, the Christian physician, 'bound by the peculiar dictates of conscience and charity to heal the sick', could not abbreviate life, argued Biggs, for according to 'that in the Psalmes, my spirit shall be attenuated, and therefore my daies shortened. And seeing according to Holy Writ for the life lurkes in the bloud, therefore a plentiful profusion of bloud,

---

[91] George Thomson, *ΑΙΜΑΤΙΑΣΙΣ Or, the True Way of Preserving the Bloud* (London, 1670); Henry Stubbe, *An Epistolary Discourse Concerning Phlebotomy. In Opposition to – G. Thomson Pseudo Chemist* (London, 1671), and *The Lord Bacons relation of the sweating-sickness examined, in a reply to George Thomson . . . Together with a defence of phlebotomy in general . . .* (London, 1671); for discussion about Stubbe see Harold Cook, 'Physicians and the New Philosophy: Henry Stubbe and the Virtuosi-physicians', in French and Wear (eds.), *The Medical Revolution of the Seventeenth Century*, pp. 246–71.

[92] Trye, *Medicatrix*, pp. 78, 103–4.

[93] Starkey, *Nature's Explication*, pp. 265, 269.

cannot but be a considerable prejudice to life.'[94] Even if, Biggs
wrote, the incredible happened and 'holy writ which tells us, that
"the life dwells in the bloud" hath not weight sufficient to engage
our credence', at least the danger of blood-letting 'may be made
manifest by the barbarous logick of *Phlebotomy*'. On opening a vein
and 'bleeding largely [profusely] . . . the conclusion and evidence
given in will be "That the strength or powers of the sick are faint
and fall together" '.[95] Bleeding was an attack upon the patient,
which, as Starkey put it, 'is an inhumane barbarous butchery,
because so much bloud as is taken away, so much is cut off from the
thread of life, and so the Doctor becomes Journeyman to *Atropos*
[one of the Greek Fates]; cutting short the life of many by the rules
of his Art, or at least impairing their strength'.[96] Because blood-
letting was familiar to most people, whether in the town or
countryside, it provided pointed realism to the general and apparently hyperbolic condemnations of Galenic medicine such as Biggs'
creation of the ignorant, pig-headed and lazy physician whose
practice led to culpable and cruel murder.[97]

MEDICAL TRIALS AND THE HELMONTIANS

The problem for Helmontians was to convince their readers, the
public, that blood-letting was unsuccessful. Given the way in which
the practice, together with purging, was incorporated into patients'
expectations of medical practice, this was a hard task, as we will see
in the next chapter. There was also little agreement as to how a
medical controversy could be resolved and a consensus reached. In
an age when statistical methods were only just beginning, the
example of an individual patient, especially if of high status, had as
much impact as one drawn from a large number of cases. Trye used
data from the Bills of Mortality, which, since Graunt's work, were
becoming a resource for illustrating or making a point in the course
of a medical controversy: 'If the Lancet be so effectual to the
preservation of the Sick in the common and frequent Disease

---

[94] Biggs, *Mataeotechnia*, p. 151.   [95] Ibid., p. 152.

[96] Starkey, *Nature's Explication*, p. 271. Even Theodore de Mayerne, the Paracelsian royal
physician to James I and Charles I whom Starkey elsewhere praised, was condemned for
letting blood. Bleeding and purging in smallpox being 'desperate dotages, and seldome
expiated with ought but death', Mayerne, wrote Starkey, 'is reported unwittingly to have
kill'd his Son-in-law intended, a just reward for a butcherlike Phlebotomist': pp. 266, 256.

[97] Biggs, *Mataeotechnia*, p. 14.

[smallpox], as he [Henry Stubbe] would have it, how comes the Bills to be so full of Dead Children etc. as sometimes a hundred or more in a week.' She was equally happy to refer to the case of 'a Person of Great Fortune and Quality that fell sick of the *Small Pox* this last Summer in the Pell Mell [Pall Mall], not many days before his intended Nuptials, for although 'tis reported he was blooded in his Sickness [smallpox], *Yet did he dye thereof*'.[98]

It is tempting to use hindsight and say 'if only they had developed medical trials, and knew how to use statistics'. Even today, though, medical journals report the individual case as well as population-wide studies, and for a disease such as smallpox, for which no cure was ever devised and whose natural course varied greatly so that some survived and others died, the success or failure of adjunct treatments would have been very difficult to pinpoint. What can be said from the perspective of the later seventeenth century is that there was a wish to test different medical methods against each other, and to have a listing of effective medicines. However, neither came to anything.

It was a common move amongst Helmontians to challenge their opponents to a trial of their respective medical skills, methods and medical systems. Whoever could cure more patients would be the winner. As far as I know, such trials did not happen, though in the past criminals had been used to try out remedies, and Helmontians were left frustrated in their attempts to prove that they were more successful.[99] But they were useful rhetorical devices, indicating that a practitioner was so confident in his or her methods that they were willing to put them to the test. Trye issued such a challenge, and, unlike in the modern medical trial where the commercial, the competitive and the personal elements associated with a particular remedy or procedure are usually hidden from public view so that it appears completely objective, the personal and the objective were clearly intertwined:

I do hereby take liberty to tell Mr *Henry Stubbe a Physician at Warwick*, That I will Cure the Disease of the *Small Pox* with him without Phlebotomy, or taking one drop of Blood from the Patient: And I will Cure the Patient with that safety and advantage I have before set down; and more, that my Antagonist may have no objection, I will not say Ten; but I will Cure two

---

[98] Trye, *Medicatrix*, p. 104.
[99] Richard Palmer, 'Pharmacy in the Republic of Venice in the Sixteenth Century', in Wear et al. (eds.) *The Medical Renaissance*, pp. 100–17.

for one with him in this Disease; that is I will Cure two Patients of the *Small Pox* by my Method and Medicines, without Phlebotomy, for his one that he shall Cure by Phlebotomy and his Method; and if he desires it, I will give him greater odds yet, rather than decline the Trial.[100]

Clearly the idea of a trial of medicines was taking shape in this period as a means of deciding between conflicting claims, though it was not until the early nineteenth century that the concept of the medical trial emerged. The recognition by medical groups and by natural philosophers of the value of Baconian induction and of experiment meant that medical procedures and medicines became the subjects of new types of scrutiny. George Thomson typically conflated learned and popular medicine when he wrote that the remedies of 'learned authors' had been taken credulously from the mistakes of the common people, 'without Examining them by the Test of Judicious iterated [repeated] Trials'. And, he added perceptively, 'I have thought none more fitting for this Work, than those we call *Virtuosi*.'[101] Certainly, as the correspondence of Henry Oldenburg, the secretary of the Royal Society, shows, there was a tremendous interest amongst the members of the Royal Society in collecting information about efficacious remedies in a Baconian manner from all sources including popular ones. But as late as 1694 Hugh Chamberlen, the royal accoucher, an empiric fined by the College of Physicians and a member of the family famous for its use of the forceps, who perceptively analysed contemporary medicine in his *A Few Queries Relating to the Practice of Physick*, was still hoping in a Baconian manner for 'a true History [listing] of Cures' which would register the outcomes of remedies.[102]

To gain a flavour of how an 'ordinary' Helmontian practitioner

---

[100] Trye, *Medicatrix*, p. 107; for another challenge see Starkey, *Nature's Explication*, sig. b8ʳ⁻ᵛ. Leonardo Fioravanti in the sixteenth century issued a similar challenge: William Eamon, *Science and the Secrets of Nature* (Princeton University Press, Princeton, 1994), p. 179. I am grateful to Professor Nancy Siraisi for this reference.

[101] Thomson, *Galeno-pale*, pp. 126–7. Thomson wanted more than a trial of whether the remedies worked; he hoped to acquire from the virtuosi an account of how they worked in the body. The virtuosi, he declared, should focus on 'the Inspection and Anatomy of Essential Energies of Spirits, lodging in divers Bodies, as they delight, or are displeased when they meet with those of their own Texture, nearly related, or strangers thereto: In that regard exert respectively their Ingenite Faculties producing Characteristicall Effects of Health and Sickness': p. 127.

[102] Hugh Chamberlen, *A Few Queries Relating to the Practice of Physick* (London, 1694), pp. 76–7; on the interest in cures and other medical data such as strange births, etc. see R. Porter, 'The Early Royal Society and the Spread of Medical Knowledge', in French and Wear (eds.), *The Medical Revolution of the Seventeenth Century*, pp. 272–94.

sold his medicine to the public, I now turn to the medical writings of the Leveller, William Walwyn, though we know of so few Helmontians that one has to be cautious about how ordinary Walwyn was in his medical persona. Although we do not possess much evidence of the day-to-day practice of Helmontians, Walwyn helps to bring us down to ground level after the rhetoric and polemics of high-profile Helmontians.

WILLIAM WALWYN'S MEDICINE – A CASE STUDY

A case study of William Walwyn's approach to medicine provides a one-off illustration of how a former political radical combined radicalism in medicine with commercialism. Walwyn, who was considered one of the most astute of the Levellers, was also the 'WW' who advertised his medicines in a series of medical tracts beginning with *Spirits Moderated* (1654). He was clearly influenced by Helmontian ideas, though in his early medical writing he acknowledged the expertise of the learned physicians and of his Leveller son-in-law Dr Humphrey Brooke.[103] Walwyn seldom wrote about Helmontian theory, but when he did so it was with confidence. He presented himself in low-key, humble terms as a self-taught physician whose aim was to improve chemical remedies, especially spirits and cordials.[104] He was not a doctrinaire Helmontian and fiery controversialist, though many of his views were Helmontian, especially those of a Christian slant, and at times he was willing to condemn all theory. His writings demonstrate how the Helmontian message, as well as being a radical call to overturn past practices and to believe in new ones, was put into the commercial marketplace, for, as so

---

[103] W. Walwyn, *Spirits Moderated* (London, 1654), p. 4; reprinted in Jack R. McMichael and Barbara Taft (eds.), *The Writings of William Walwyn* (University of Georgia Press, Athens, Ga., 1989), p. 458: Walwyn wrote that only the learned physician could safely prescribe strong chemical medicines; such deference is absent from his later writings.

[104] In W[illiam] W[alwyn], *Physick for Families* (London, 1669), pp. 101–2, Walwyn used the Helmontian terms 'Alkahest' [the universal solvent that would reduce all substances to their basic matter] and 'Archeus' when arguing that even the 'compleatest Laboratories' fail if the inventor of new chemical remedies does not have a 'natural genius' or aptitude for chemistry, which was a very Helmontian comment. On his view that much of chemistry had failed to fulfil its promise see *Physick for Families*, pp. 102, 113, 116. Spirits and cordials were too strong; they did not comply to 'the golden mean' of moderation and were not appropriate to 'the true humane temperature [temperament]': Walwyn, *Spirits Moderated*, p. 5.

often in early modern medicine, commerce and medical beliefs were intertwined.

Walwyn, like the Helmontians, attacked Galenic medical procedures and, like them, he presented his medicine as essentially Christian. In his later tracts such as *Physick for Families* (1669) he confidently expounded a radical view of medicine. It was Christian and anti-Galenic. Walwyn's true physician was like the good Samaritan,[105] and Christianity was everything that 'the common Road of Physick' was not. It was compassionate, efficacious, certain and true. He rejected ordinary medicine, he declared, because of its 'manifest uncertainty in Principles, Roughness, Harshness and Cruelty in Methods, Impropriety, Impotency, and danger in Medicines'. He withdrew his 'thoughts from out the wilderness of all the uncertain Notions and Guesses of Philosophy, and giving them free liberty in the walks of Scripture', from the Bible, which dealt with ' "the true Original of man", the sole subject of Physick (hid from Phylosophy) being apparent', he was able to deduce the one 'true Humane Temperature [temperament]'.[106] Lacking knowledge of the true human temperament, both the usual 'helps and helpers' of medicine were not 'agreeable to the distinct purity of mans Nature'. What Walwyn offered was knowledge of this temperament and medicines that were suitable to it. The emphasis on the Christian basis of his medicine, and on the cruelty and uncertainty of normal medicine, can be seen both as genuinely held beliefs and as the advertising package designed to elicit favourable responses from Walwyn's readers and persuade them to buy his medicines. The latter should not detract from the former, despite the general Christian wariness of profiting at others' expense. Evangelical Christianity and advertising are not too dissimilar, and the Calvinist doctrine of calling did not exclude making a living by selling goods, especially if, as in Walwyn's case, cheaper medicines were made for those of lesser means.[107]

Like other Helmontian writers, Walwyn demolished Galenic procedures before putting forward his own medicines. His strategy can be interpreted as one of maximising the selling potential of his medicines. Eliminating 'cruelties' such as bleeding, purging, blistering,

---

[105] Walwyn, *Physick for Families*, pp. 1, 3.   [106] Ibid., p. 3.

[107] Walwyn compared his gentler medicine with the 'evangelical doctrine' of the New Testament which triumphed over the harsh 'legal' one, the law, of the Old Testament: ibid., p. 23.

the use of cupping, leeching and 'drawing of Silk through the Neck-skin' (to create a constant 'issue' or drip of fluid), 'all full of pain, hazard and danger', meant that patients had to fall back on medicines. Walwyn also pointed out that the medicines currently in use were dangerous. For instance, opium in its various versions such as laudanum had an 'aptness to miscarry . . . more than enough to make every Dispenser of it to tremble, during the whole time it is in the Patients body . . . instead of rest and sleep, like treacherous flatterers, stroak and stab, and give Death itself in the same instant, to the horror and amazement both of Physitians and bewailing relations'. As Walwyn presented the situation, only his own medical preparations could help the patient. Moreover, having adjusted medical theory by substituting a single human temperament for the traditional humoral constitutions, he ensured that his medicines were suitable for everyone. However, like many others who advertised their medicines, he also gave his customers the reassurance that what they were buying was tailored to some extent to their disease and constitution in the old sense.[108] Each remedy had a very wide range of action; his 'Vis vitae' (power of life), for instance, was advertised as good 'For Dropsy, Scurvy, Spleen, Wind, Gravel, Strangury, Stopage of Water, or of the natural course, or in swellings from thence, or other sweatings; the Dose from two to six Ounces, and at 4 hours may be repeated, and continued, till occassion cease: Also may be similarly taken for prevention of all such Distempers, and for conservation of health and chearfulness, at 3 s[hillings] the pint.'[109]

In the listing of the sixteen remedies in *Physick for Families* 'intended for subduing and extinguishing the most violent, venomous, pestilential, and inveterate Distempers, and securely to be used in all Extremities', none were specific against any one particular disease; instead they were described as good against groups of loosely related conditions. 'Requies Naturae' (Nature's Rest), for instance, was to be used 'In Mother-fits, Vertigoes, Falling sickness, Convulsions, Lightness of the Head, and weakness of the Brain, with, or without Fevers, Agues etc'. On the other hand, Walwyn was not selling a panacea, though some of his medicines such as 'Vindex Naturae' (Nature's Protector) came close to it, covering as it did 'highest Fevers, Pestilence, Tertian and Quartan Agues, with

---

[108] Ibid., pp. 6–18, 19, 30.   [109] Ibid., p. 26.

Vomitings, or Bloody Fluxes, pains in the Head, restlesness Gout, Small Pox, Measels; and where there is often provocation without Evacuation downward; or in any other violent or contagious Distemper; As also for furthering of Childbirth'.[110] We can justifiably interpret Walwyn's limited number of remedies for all diseases, for all constitutions and for all ages as a means of maximising his potential customer base; this was a very common strategy amongst sellers of proprietary or named remedies in the later seventeenth century. That commercial motives as well as reformist sentiments were involved is clear from the simple fact that Walwyn very self-consciously did not list the ingredients in his remedies. Remedy books and plague tracts, by publicising the ingredients of remedies, had facilitated the making of medicines at home, as well as allowing medicines to be charitably produced by lay people for the poor. The commercial manufacturers and sellers of 'secret' remedies advertised their medicines as cheaper than the expensive courses of treatments entailed by the visits of the physicians, and it is true that they created a more affordable medicine based on a named pill or potion. However, by their secrecy they also began the process of closing down and eliminating the common culture of lay and expert medicine, which had provided for the manufacture of remedies by patients or their families.

SECRET REMEDIES

Openness about remedies was seen by some in a positive light. It made knowledge available to all, and was believed to act as a check on malpractice. Books of 'secrets' were published ostensibly for the public good and thus were no longer secret, many named remedies were composed of well-known standard ingredients, and the pharmacopoeias published in European cities had the aim of creating a safe *materia medica* whose details were in the public domain. The learned physicians presented themselves as being open about the medicines that they prescribed. John Donne commented approvingly on how the learned physicians 'prescribe, they write, so there is nothing covertly disguisedly, unavowedly done'. Openness led to patient compliance: 'that the proceedings may be apart, and ingenuous, and candid, and avowable, for that gives satisfaction and

---

[110] Ibid., pp. 30, 32, 31.

acquiescence'.[111] In practice though, the physician's prescription could be as good as a secret, being 'a writ to his Drugger in a strange tongue'.[112]

Walwyn's contemporaries, the virtuosi who supported the new science, also valued publicly available knowledge. Boyle published medical receipts for reasons of charity and because he disliked medicine's closed shop, although, as Michael Hunter has pointed out, he was at the same time wary as a non-medic about writing on medical matters.[113] However, Paracelsians and Helmontians, who saw themselves as belonging to a closed group of adepts, developed a cult of secrecy about remedies, one which they shared with empirics and quacks. Moreover, the commercial imperative to keep one's medicines secret was strong. Walwyn defended the practice, because:

it hath befallen to them [strong distilled 'waters'], as to most other things which come once to be publikely knowen, and to be made the common subject of Trade: That how noble and worthy soever they were in the first inventers, yet Time had infinitely abated their worth: little regard having long time been had in their productions, but how to get Sale; and that not by making so good as they could, but so good onely as they could at the lowe prices they are generally sold for; and that truely is so lamentable.[114]

In other words, the open market, left to its own devices with a product which could be made by anyone, led to each producer striving 'by that which is imperfect, to under-sell one another' so quality suffered.[115] The persona of the Christian 'faithful' physician, on the other hand, was one that guaranteed the quality of a secret remedy, and certainly Walwyn expected others even of higher social status to trust him, and not to ask awkward questions about the ingredients of his remedies: 'it is no absurdity, even for Persons of Honour to put so much trust and confidence in some Students or Arts-men; as to take freely and without scruple those preparations,

[111] Donne, *Devotions*, p. 47; Donne compared medicine and government: openness was necessary to get the obedience of patients and the public respectively.

[112] John Earle, *Micro-cosmographie Faithfully Reprinted from the Edition of 1633* (Methuen, London, 1904), sig. B10^v.

[113] Michael Hunter, 'The Reluctant Philanthropist: Robert Boyle and the "Communication of Secrets and Receits in Physick"' in Ole Peter Grell and Andrew Cunningham (eds.), *Religio Medici: Medicine and Religion in Seventeenth Century England* (Scolar Press, Aldershot, 1996), pp. 247–72. Some of Boyle's motives for publishing receipts noted by Hunter were not only idiosyncratic to Boyle and to his time, but were also part of a long-lived genre justifying the publication of remedies, and also the involvement of laymen in writing about medicine.

[114] Walwyn, *Spirits Moderated*, p. 5.   [115] Ibid., p. 6.

which they judg requisite for their recovery though they knew no part of the Ingredients'.[116] Trust was not only the due of the Christian physician, it was also essential for his livelihood: 'for an Arts-man subsisting by his Art, being owner of it no longer than he keeps it to himself, nothing can be more inproper [sic] or unwelcom than to ask discovering Questions'.[117] Commercial pressures and the esoteric character of Helmontian physicians chosen of God possessed both of arcana, of secrets, and of a Christian trustworthiness combined to justify secret remedies. When the Helmontianism was absent, as it was with many of the sellers of proprietary medicines of the later seventeenth century, then the justification became purely commercial, and the virtues of, for instance, Lockyer's pills were as much to do with brand image and advertising as with their medical virtues.

MEDICINES TO REPLACE MEDICINE

If one takes Walwyn seriously, it is clear that he wished to create a completely new type of medical practice. The physician would no longer focus upon the individual patient; instead, what had to be treated was the disease. His medicines would 'grapple with and subdue the most violent and inveterate diseases whatsoever', and they were very patient-friendly. They could be 'safely and pleasantly to be taken', and 'by all persons in all states of health, or degrees of weakness from the very Cradle to the Oldest Age'.[118] Medicines that could be taken in all seasons as well as by all ages of patient also undercut the principles of Galenic medicine that linked the patient to the environment and the climate, though in practice such fine tuning had often been ignored. Walwyn's medicines, like those of the many empirics in the medical marketplace, were the alternative to learned medicine. They replaced not only Galenic drugs and procedures such as bleeding and purging, but also the traditional relationship between doctor and patient based on a series of visits to the patient, expressive of the individualised attention of Galenic medicine. These visits also involved expense, and possibly the fear and unease that a visit from the doctor can bring, as well as the dangers of such visits which John Earle satirically described: 'If he

---

[116] W[illiam] W[alwyn], *A Touch-Stone for Physick* (London, 1667), pp. 47–8.
[117] Ibid., p. 48.　　[118] Walwyn, *Physick for Families*, pp. 33–4.

see you himselfe, his presence is the worst visitation: for if hee cannot heale your sicknesse, he will bee sure to helpe it. He translates his Apothecaries Shop into your Chamber and the very Windowes and benches must take Physicke.'[119] Some patients, therefore, may have welcomed Walwyn's assurance that his medicines bypassed the normal experiences of being a patient and could be taken 'without any confinement to house or Chamber (except in cases of Extremity), without charge of visits or tedious attendance, and with all possible quickness and hopefulness to the Patient'.[120] In fact, Walwyn rejected not only physicians' visits but the whole panoply of medicine, whether unlearned, learned or chemical; his 'physick', he wrote,

needs feel no Pulses, regards not Urines, Critical Dayes, Climatericall years, state of the Moon, or position of the Stars, sight of the Patient, visits, Diagnosticks, nor Prognostics; That troubles not the head about Circulation, Chilification, or Sanguification, That values not Anatomy, as to the discovery of Diseases, nor the four [Galenic], nor the three [Paracelsian], nor the five [of Willis] Principles, nor the Doctrine of Fermentation, nor the fine spun Thred of Atoms, as any whit advantagious to Cure. That is not beholden to any Book or Books of Philosophy, or Physick for its production . . . That stands not obliged to any Chymical or Laboratory Instructers, nor esteems of their numerous terms of Art . . .[121]

Walwyn was not a complete medical nihilist. His medicines 'Whose Principle is from above' (i.e. from God) would stand in place of medicine. They, or rather it, for he equated 'Physick' with his medicines, was 'powerfully Efficacious for Extirpation and Extinguishing the venomous Courses of Diseases' and was never 'unsafe or unseasonable and keeps good for years in all Climates'. It was advantageous to the sick, and so simplified medicine 'that [it] acquits

---

[119] Earle, *Micro-cosmographie*, 'A meere dull Physician': sig. B10ᵛ–B11ʳ.

[120] Walwyn, *Physick for Families*, pp. 33–4. He was not always so extreme, especially as he, like physicians, gave advice to patients.

[121] Ibid., pp. 116–17. Starkey, *Nature's Explication*, pp. 125–7, had written in a similar but more Helmontian vein that the mark of 'a real and true son of Art, it is his diploma by which he appears to be one created of God, and not by the Schools; for their creatures they adorn with titles, God graceth his with real abilities . . . His cure and care is not consisting only in reiterated Visits, feeling of Pulses, and tossing of Urines, Stirring of Close-stooles, and appointing Purges, Vomits, Bleeding, Fontinels, Blisters, Scarifications, Leeches and such enfeebling Martyrdoms, nor prescribing Syrups . . . and what is more sordid, he doth not oversee the kitchin, to make this Gelly or that Broth, but like a valiant *Achilles* or *Hercules*, he assayles the Disease with powerful and prevailing Medicines . . . He doth not cowardly sum up a Catalogue of incurable diseases . . . a true Son of Art makes it appear that all diseases are in their kinde curable.'

Physitians from *so* many encumbrances and perplexities, both in their studies and practise'.[122] In other words, one tendency in Helmontianism when taken to extremes was to have medicines replace medicine. Other Helmontians, such as George Thomson (see below), who wanted to be physicians as well as sellers of medicines, integrated traditional medical skills such as diagnosis and prognosis with the prescription of Helmontian remedies. Walwyn's position was also one that flowed from commercial logic: sales and prices could be maximised if remedies replaced the visits, etc. of the physician and the medical skills that he offered. The extent of doctors' visits seems to have been idealised by Walwyn, for there was a good deal of medical treatment that did not involve visits from physicians. In the countryside physicians were often not available, and many patients treated themselves or received charitable treatment from lay people. Helmontians were seeking to entice patients away from the learned physicians as well as making medicine available to more of the population.

However, the lack of available physician care was turned against the medicine of the Galenic physicians. Another way of interpreting the wish of Walwyn and of the Helmontians for a new medicine is to see it as part of the general dissatisfaction with the reluctance of physicians to provide medical care for the whole population. Walwyn's medicines, and those sold by Helmontians and by the commercial empirics and apothecaries discussed below, on this reading, became substitutes for the uncharitable reluctance of physicians to visit the poor. It would be an exaggeration to say that the medicines were meant to replace the physicians, for Helmontians often saw themselves as physicians as well as producers of medicines, but it was not too far from the truth; and the message that medicines were more important than physicians would not have been unfamiliar, especially as many people had relied on remedies and managed without physicians.

If physicians and their visits were beyond the reach of the sick poor, then it was a natural reaction to turn against them, to see them as harmful and best done without, especially as a new type of medicine could replace them. What appeared to be a valuable but unobtainable resource could be redefined as worthless and dangerous. Helmontian writers employed this strategy of simultaneously

---

[122] Walwyn, *Physick for Families*, pp. 117–18.

attacking the moral and medical validity of Galenic medicine, and using the former to throw doubt on the latter. Such intermixing of what appear to us today to be separate and distinct categories (the religious/social and the medical/philosophical) was acceptable to many at a time when the boundaries between the two were porous and when religion and its values were seen by some as fundamental to all knowledge, though such a position was becoming less popular in the years after the Restoration.[123]

WALWYN'S MERRY MEDICINES

Whilst physicians, their medicines, procedures and morals came under destructive criticism, the alternatives were presented in glowing terms. The pleasure principle lay at the heart of Walwyn's alternative vision of health and of medicine. His medicines were merry ones: 'The Scripture saith, a merry heart doth good like a Medicine: And if so, in true consequence, ought not the Operations and Effects of kindly and real Medicines, to resemble those of a merry heart? certainly it can be no absurdity to expect it.'[124] Walwyn evoked an association that was well known, merriness and health having been a long-standing part of English medical culture. Being sad or melancholic was seen as a cause of mental and physical ill health, and one remedy was to make the patient merry. Merriness was also a key to a healthy and long life. Regimen or rules of health, such as the Salernitan *Regimen of Health* discussed in chapter 4, prescribed 'Dr. Merry', and merriment was recommended by the Bible (Proverbs 17.22). Moreover, in Helmontian theory merriness was crucial to health: the archeus had to be kept happy, for its rages created the images of disease, and whilst angry it was unable to prevent and to cure disease.

Only those medicines which were pleasant and 'friendly' to the patient were to be used. As we saw in chapter 2, Helmontians were concerned to counter the criticism that their preparations were harsh and dangerous, that they were too powerful, so they described them as friendly, safe, and powerful. Walwyn, who admitted that some of the chemists' medicinal spirits were too harsh, also made the same association between mildness, safety and power.[125] This

---

[123] See Michael Heyd, *Be Sober and Reasonable: the Critique of Enthusiasm in the Seventeenth and Early Eighteenth Centuries* (E. J. Brill, New York, 1995).
[124] Walwyn, *Physick for Families*, sig. A2ᵛ.   [125] Walwyn, *Spirits Moderated*, pp. 5, 18–20.

seemed to fly in the face of the received wisdom that what was powerful was always potentially dangerous, reflected in the traditional view, discussed in chapter 2, that medicines lay half-way between food and poison or that purgatives invariably had deleterious properties. However, Walwyn clearly believed that patients would be attracted to his powerful yet safe remedies, despite possible patient expectation that efficacy required power which implied danger. He wrapped this new set of positive attributes around the medicines that he advertised for sale in his pamphlets. They should 'have friendly and powerful operations, [so] all sadness and sickness, may without pain or trouble be totally Expelled and Extinguished'. They were 'really powerful and benigne', 'kindly and powerful', 'safe and powerful', 'truly good and real', combining 'innocency and efficacy'. Walwyn's spirits were 'friendly and powerful', replacing 'dull putrid helpers'; they were 'called Spirits not for their Heat, but from their sublime Purity and Vivacity, which are more Spiritual Qualities, and through which their Operations are not forcible and violent, but (like Benign Influences) quiet, secret, sure and most effectual'.[126]

Walwyn invited his readers to test for themselves whether a medicine was good or bad. This was a strategy designed to make a fresh start, to challenge the claim of establishment medicine that it alone could assess drugs. It also spoke to the long-established lay practice of assessing remedies. Walwyn advised his readers on what to look for. Purity was joined to the qualities of 'mildness and safety', power and friendliness.[127] Walwyn's clients could well have been attracted to pure medicine, as medicines had been associated not only with poison but also with impurity, despite the idealisation of simples. The traditional *materia medica* included parts of animals, and occasionally of human beings, as well as blood, urine and faeces, whilst merchants and apothecaries were frequently accused of adulterating and counterfeiting their drugs and of using old and rotten ingredients.

The distinguishing 'marks of real medicine' included the fact that it should be liquid to avoid the impurity of solid medicines (significantly, Walwyn sold liquid preparations). The latter, being less pure, were difficult to fully digest; they left 'their remaining earthy parts in

---

[126] Walwyn, *Physick for Families*, sig. A3ʳ, pp. 10, 11, 19; W[illiam] W[alwyn], *Healths New Store House Opened* (London, 1661), sig. A3ʳ, pp. 2, 7.
[127] Walwyn, *Physick for Families*, p. 20.

the coats, films and crevices both of the stomach and bowels', and they would 'clog and tire' the body's expulsive powers, creating a new problem for nature to deal with during illness. The liquid had to be 'transparently, clear and pure' and should not smell bad, as it was 'possible to have liquid things as bright and clear as Chrystal, which yet no carrion ever exceeded in noysomness'.[128] Walwyn applied to medicines the same criteria that were used to assess the purity of water and food, based on the senses of taste, smell and sight (see chapter 4), and, as with water and some foods, another test was that the medicines should 'not be perishable Commodities', although the requirement that they should '(Close stopt) to keep Good for Years (in all Climates) and in full strength and vigour without any the least dimunition much after the similitude of endless life' reflected more the ultimate aim of the perfect medicine, immortality.[129] Like food and water, medicines had to be healthy products; otherwise, and here Walwyn used traditional reasoning on how the body took on the qualities of the food it digested discussed in chapter 4, if the medicines were corrupt, so would the body's blood and spirits likewise become corrupted, and even the strongest would fall ill.[130] Clearly, in Walwyn's eyes it was no longer acceptable for medicines to be impure, or either potentially or actually poisonous, as had traditionally been held to be the case. A further telling test was that the practitioner should take the medicines he prescribed for his patients before they did, and in their sight, the ultimate guarantee against dangerous remedies.[131]

Two other tests suggested by Walwyn were designed to break the old association between power and danger, and reflected the new link that was being made between power and safety or mildness. One test of good medicines was that they could 'tug, grapple with, and subdue the most violent, venemous, pestilential enemies of Mans Health . . . and yet withall so milde, gentle and manageable (like our blessed Lamb and Lion couched together) as children may partake with safety'. Another test was that in health medicines

[128] Walwyn, *Touch-Stone*, pp. 14, 15, 7–8; Walwyn described the characteristics of pure medicines in *A Touch-Stone for Physick*, pp. 7–16, of which an abbreviated version appeared in *Physick for Families*, pp. 21–2.
[129] Walwyn, *Touch-Stone*, pp. 12–13. There may also be an echo of the hermetically sealed, imperishable, medicine.
[130] Ibid., pp. 8–9. For Walwyn's acquaintance with the link between what is eaten and the nature of the body's blood and spirit see *Healths New Store House*, p. 4.
[131] Ibid., p. 10.

'should nourish and strengthen', but that in illness they should act therapeutically: 'the very same Medicines, taken in the same quantity, shall in due time either open or binde, vomit or stop vomiting, sweat or restrain sweating, give sleep or abate excessive sleeping; as the instant neccessity of the body most requireth, or most conduceth to recovery'.[132] In other words, a medicine should be able to distinguish between the healthy and the sick, otherwise the healthy would suffer. This was a new requirement for a medicine, as learned medical theory taught that many established drugs, especially purging and vomiting ones, were dangerous for the healthy.[133]

So long-lasting has been the link between efficacy, power and danger in medicines that we may find it paradoxical even today for medicines to be powerful yet safe and mild. Similarly, it seems strange that a medicine can act like a food in health and switch on different, curative, properties in illness. Our sense of paradox is a sign that the Helmontian revolution in practical medicine failed. Inherently dangerous medicines continued to be prescribed, and the use of purging, bleeding, blistering, vomiting and other unpleasant procedures intensified, so that in the eighteenth century, the so-called 'Age of Agony' in medicine, physicians took pride in applying them heroically.[134]

---

[132] Walwyn, *Touch-Stone*, pp. 10–11.   [133] Ibid., p. 11.
[134] Guy Williams, *The Age of Agony: the Art of Healing, c. 1700–1800* (Constable, London, 1975).

CHAPTER 9

The failure of the Helmontian revolution in practical medicine

INTRODUCTION AND SUMMARY

The question to be asked is, 'Why did the Helmontians fail?' On the face of it, not to have to keep to the stringent diets of Galenic medicine would seem to have been a relief. Pleasant and mild medicines and the elimination of painful procedures should also have been especially attractive to medical consumers. Who would not have wanted to avoid the use of vesicatories 'or Raisers of small and great Blisters, by irksome fretting, if not venomous Plaisters, sometimes flaying off as all the skin from the backs, otherwhiles the shoulders, legs or wrists, the neck, head etc to extream torments, especially when those raw places are rub'd and irritated for diversion of venomous inflammations, hidious Curses and Excrations having been noted the impatient Effects of such cruelties'?[1] Or what patient would welcome the prospect of the 'tearing and rending' of vomiting drugs, or the threat to modesty of clysters or enemas 'by the odd position and Distastful handling of the body'?[2] And yet, the Helmontians' enterprise of a new medicine did fail, and if we believe the comments of Helmontians themselves, this failure was due in large part to patient resistance to their particular brand of medicine.

In this chapter I first consider the Helmontian attack on Galenic regimen which helped to make Galenic medicine distinctive. English Helmontians, unlike van Helmont, did not tackle regimen head on, either because they were more interested in therapeutics or because they sensed the difficulty of uncoupling the association between diet and health, which has continued to the present. The major part of the chapter focuses on the Helmontians' belief that it was patient

[1] W[illiam] W[alwyn], *Physick for Families* (London, 1669) p. 18.
[2] Ibid., pp. 14, 6.

resistance to their therapies that prevented their medicine from gaining ground. In the course of their descriptions of the varied difficulties that they faced in countering the 'prejudices' of patients and bystanders, it becomes clear that the image of disease, the belief in putrefaction as disease and the treatments based on bleeding and purging described in the earlier chapters continued to be attractive to patients. Indeed, Helmontians wrote that Galenic medical practice had permeated through to all levels of the public, whom they saw as being duped rather than actively choosing Galenic therapy for the advantages that they found in it.

The role of patients has been prominent in the recent history of early modern medicine, and Helmontians themselves made patient resistance a key factor in their failure to attract patients, which, at the end of the day, was the key to the success of any medical system or group. This new and major dimension of patient preference has to be added to the well-known failure of the Helmontians to gain institutional recognition, discussed at the end of the chapter, when explaining the overall failure of the Helmontians in England.

DIET AND MEDICINE

In order to be successful in completely revolutionising the practice of medicine, Helmontians would have had to discredit Galenic regimen, which was the preventive counterpart to Galenic therapeutics. But it was difficult for them to eliminate the long-established linkages and boundaries between diet and medicine, between preventive and curative medicine.[3] At first sight, the boundaries between foods and medicines, prevention and treatment, do not seem to have been all that strong in Galenic medicine. Many medicines such as herbs were also used as foods, and advice on food was often part of a cure. Physicians acknowledged that one of their roles was to be, as it were, a cook, and in Hippocratic medicine dietetics had been viewed as the origin of medicine, with medicines being a specialised form of food (see chapter 4). Again, the learned physicians' insistence on rules of regimen often centred on diet, and was a recognition that food could be pathological and that

---

[3] As we saw, Walwyn wished for a medicine that would be a food for the healthy and a remedy for the ill, but Walwyn's views were not in the mainstream of Helmontian opinion as he did not criticise preventive medicine and rules of diet. However, his emphasis on medicines rather than on foods is certainly Helmontian.

preventive and curative medicine were closely linked. Despite such linkages, the learned physicians saw regimen, and especially advice on diet, as a separate and distinct part of medicine. This distinguished them from empirics and other groups who offered to cure patients with medicines but not to prevent disease nor to use diet in combination with medicines to cure it. It also indicated to the world that the learned physicians considered the individual patient rather than, as was the case with empirics, treating the disease and not the patient. Advice on regimen, therefore, was one of the defining skills of the learned physician, and as such could be expected to come under attack from Helmontians.

Helmontians were not as wholeheartedly against regimen or preventive medicine as they were against bleeding or at times purging, but they wished to lessen its importance, believing that much of the advice offered by the learned physicians was unnecessary as well as wrong. Essentially they wanted to emphasise their medicines to the exclusion of all else, but even though, as the learned physicians admitted, few paid much practical attention to medical advice on lifestyle including diet except when ill, to agree that it was unimportant is, I suspect, very counter-intuitive for most people whether living in the seventeenth century or today. And, although some historians might object, using hindsight one can discern from the strength and longevity of the belief in the link between diet and health a long-lasting structure in western medical culture that reflects enduring perceptions of the connection between humans and the world around them. Such a link was designed to give a measure of personal control over one's health, against which Helmontians could have little impact.

Nevertheless, Helmontians played down the significance of regimen and diet, though they acknowledged the scriptural injunctions against gluttony and drunkenness. Van Helmont argued that nature and not the physician was the best guide, hence a natural appetite in fevers should not be reined in, even if it was against the rules of health, yet he also recommended a spare diet, and condemned gluttony which led to bad digestion.[4] Moreover, the archeus, if deprived of its favourite food by the physicians' rules of

---

[4] J. B. van Helmont, *Oriatrike, or Physick Refined*, trans. J[ohn] C[handler] (1st edn, 1662; London 1664), pp. 450–5, 455. Nature showed her hand through the ferments and digestions of the body: 'And so digestions do prescribe rules of Diet' rather than physicians or books.

health, 'doth sumptomatically [*sic*] rage . . . and so in strife, they stir up new strife [illness]'.[5] The rules of health also broke Helmontian Christian social morality. The rules favoured the rich as they reflected the personal preferences of physicians, who often recommended medicines such as gold, powdered pearl, etc., and expensive foods which only the rich could afford. This flew in the face of God's benevolence in making all foods good, so ensuring that the poor would not be disadvantaged. In terms of medical practice, van Helmont saw the rules of diet as attempts by physicians to disguise their lack of effective medicines.[6] He also accused physicians of using patients' disobedience about rules of health and diet to excuse their deaths. Moreover, preventive medicine centred on diet was not effective. Regimen did not avert the entrance of disease, nor could it expel it; therefore, it could not be used to prevent or treat disease as had traditionally been the case.[7]

Van Helmont's contemptuous picture of the medically ineffective 'delicate' cook-physician was the rejoinder of someone who believed that the business of medicine was with curing diseases and not worrying about a patient's lifestyle. In some ways, his critique looks forward to the present day when western scientific medicine robustly focuses upon diseases and their cures, and advice on individual lifestyle is left to the less prestigious speciality of public health medicine, or to 'softer' alternative medicine:

For those Physicians which are somewhat delicate, do study the huckstery of the kitchin, and that they may please the sick, who being destitute of remedies and knowledge, have otherwayes enslaved themselves to a barren profession; for they are those who become teachers of Cooks. How leisurely do they view all things, that they may exercise their commands in kitchins and Parlours; and that they may seem to have foreseen all things diligently, they are ready to exercise their tyranny on the sick. As if meats [foods] and drinks should be the Medicines of the more grievous diseases.[8]

Nevertheless, van Helmont left some space in his medicine for regimen. He stressed the need for patient and physician to pay attention to natural appetite and to the needs of digestion, a central physiological process in Helmontian medicine, and wrote that advice on other aspects of regimen, such as the amount of exercise, rest and sleep and the type of air one breathed, had to take into account the

---

[5] Ibid., pp. 451–2.
[6] Ibid., p. 452. All foods lay 'within the limits of goodnes', so advice on diet was superfluous.
[7] Ibid., pp. 451–2.   [8] Ibid., p. 451.

effect that they had on the various digestions or ferments that controlled the physiological functions of the body.[9] The world outside of the body in the shape of food could not, therefore, be completely ignored, though its significance was played down.

Many of van Helmont's views were repeated by his English followers. Galenic physicians were condemned along Helmontian lines for tyrannising over patients and their natural appetites; this put the archeus into a 'rage' and the vital spirits into such disorder 'that they Coin many foul, Black Images'.[10] Biggs, who copied large chunks of van Helmont on diet, echoed him, writing that dietary advice was haphazard, depending on the personal tastes of individual physicians. They preferred, he added, to rely on diet rather than on their unsuccessful medicines bought from the 'shops', whereas 'Sanation [health] verily is the lovely effects of a *Laboratory* and *medicine*, not of the kitchin.'[11]

English Helmontians were largely silent when it came to giving practical advice about diet. They were focused almost entirely upon therapeutics. The exception was George Thomson. Although a very committed Helmontian, he was also keen to appear expert in the different parts of medicine, and wrote more on diet and regimen than any other English Helmontian. As we saw in chapter 4, Thomson did not reject regimen, and indeed used the categories into which it had been traditionally organised. His discussion of diet illustrates the Helmontian dilemma: were they engaged in a scorched earth revolution that would obliterate all traces of the past, or was theirs a partial revolution after which they would step into the shoes of the learned physicians? Thomson adopted the role of medical

---

[9] Ibid., p. 455. Digestion of food into chyle and the further digestions of chyle were chemical processes, acid 'ferments', that underpinned the nutrition, growth and life of the body and its parts. The stomach together with the spleen ruled the body as the 'Duumvirate' (twin rulers); it was 'this Noble Part', the 'Vital kitchen', the body's central manufacturing plant, that produced blood and spirits, and they in turn nourished the veins, arteries, nerves, bones, etc. of the body. It also helped to control health and illness, for it was responsible for the well-being of the vital spirits that could create the 'hurtful images' which constituted illnesses; Van Helmont, *Oriatrike*, pp. 206–20. On the Duumvirate see ibid., pp. 287, 296–309, 337–41; W. Pagel, *The Smiling Spleen. Paracelsianism in Storm and Stress* (Karger, Basle, 1984), pp. 137–40. Also George Thomson, *Orthomethodos Iatro Chimiche: Or the Direct Method of Curing Chymically* (London, 1675), pp. 22–3, 35.

[10] Thomson, *Orthomethodos*, pp. 24–8; Noah Biggs, *Mataeotechnia Medicinae Praxeos. The Vanity of the Craft of Physic* (London, 1651), pp. 194–5, 199–200.

[11] Biggs, *Mataeotechnia*, pp. 195–6; much of Biggs' attack on Galenic physicians' reliance on diet on pp. 194–211 is based, often verbatim, on van Helmont's '*Victus Ratio*' in Franciscus Mercurius van Helmont (ed.), *Ortus Medicinae* (Amsterdam, 1648), pp. 447–52.

adviser on diet to the sick, though not to the healthy, but he tried to turn the tables on Galenic physicians. He argued that their advice, unlike that of Helmontian physicians, did not take into account the individual idiosyncracies of patients, which was what they had prided themselves on.[12] Moreover, just as with therapeutics, Galenic diet was presented as unpleasant. The Galenic 'Doctrine of Cooling Liquors in Fevers' comprised 'Maukish, Spiritless, Dull, Flat, Posset-drink, Small-beer, Barly-water, loathsome Decoctions of cooling crude Herbs, Pippin Liquors and the like, which starve the Vital Spirit bringing a numness upon it, that it cannot do anything effectually for the expulsion of its Enemy'.[13] Instead, Thomson held out the promise of pleasurable diet based on the patient's appetite. However, as learned physicians and clergymen traditionally had done, he took care to urge 'moderation . . . in all things', and deplored how his advice had been 'abused, witness those to whom I allowed to drink now and then a Glass of Sack in a high Feaver, who unadvisedly forthwith poured down a whole Quart bottle to their Prejudice'.[14]

Galenic dietary advice was also presented by Thomson as wrong-headed in basing itself on the 'Rule of Contraries' and in putting forward affected and 'contrived Cookeries' such as 'Veal, Chicken, Broth, Gellies', rather than the more robust 'Red-herring, Oysters, a Lobster etc.', or plain 'simple Home-bred Food', such as beef and mutton which was 'to be preferred for holsomness, before the fine, pampering, curiously-dressed, far-fetched Dainties'. Patients were urged to trust their natural appetites. Helmontians must have believed that they would have been delighted to read that 'to urge the Sick to eat Sodden when he lusts after Roasted; or Liquid, when he requires Solid, is to cross Nature'. Likewise, a patient might have

---

[12] Thomson, *Orthomethodos* p. 26. Thomson wrote that physicians 'enjoyn *John, Thomas, William*, the same Food, Order, Season and Measure, of taking it alike, without having respect to any Individual or Peculiar Stamp made upon the Spirits in the Womb, whence "Qot [sic] Homines, Tot Diaeta observandae", [as many people, so many diets have to be complied with]. As many Men as there are in the World, so many inseparable Properties are to be indulged as to the election of Eating and Drinking this or that'.

[13] Ibid., p. 28.

[14] Ibid., p. 29. Thomas O'Dowde had no hesitation in advising recourse to the Helmontian pleasure principle in the case of William Miller, a servant, suffering from 'a violent Surfeit, Feaver and Lunacy'. After prescribing a medicine O'Dowde 'desired him to be kind to himself, and (without regard to Dietory Prescriptions) to eat Roast Beef and drink Sack, that night and the next': O'Dowde, *The Poor Man's Physician, Or the True Art of Medicine*, 3rd edn (London, 1665), pp. 22–3.

been expected to respond favourably to Thomson's image of the Galenic physician who used diet to hide his ignorance of medicines: 'That Tyrannical, Severe, Overbusie Precepts the *Galenists* enjoyn their Patients, is to be rejected, for "misere vivit qui medice vivit" [he lives miserably who lives by medicine]. To be rigidly kept from what is Lawful and Useful (for want of fitting Remedies) is little better than *Turkish* Slavery.'[15]

Thomson, as a follower of van Helmont, recognised that most food could be eaten safely, as long as the patient's appetite, digestive power and what he or she was accustomed to was taken into account. But, like the Galenists that he condemned, he recommended particular foods and shared in their moral admonitions. It may be that the desire fully to take the place of the Galenic physician prompted Thomson to take on the persona of the physician as cookery expert, perhaps not as tyrannical as a Galenist, and one whose advice was drawn from the wellsprings of philosophical chemistry rather than from the 'false Suppositions of Heat and Cold'.[16]

Thomson's ambivalence about diet, coming from one of the most fervent of the English Helmontians, may indicate an uncertainty about how far Helmontians secretly wanted to share in the status of the Galenic physicians, a status that they constantly attacked as a sham. In my view, it also indicates that the link between diet and health and illness was very strong, and that it was difficult for Helmontians to ignore or to destroy it. Patients expected to have a special diet when they were ill and the learned physicians had educated them to demand particular diets. As Thomson acknowledged:

the custome and Authority of Malepracticants [Galenists] is so powerful, that the Sick thinks he must be weakned, if he eat not Broth of Flesh, Caudels [hot spiced drinks], Water-gruel etc. which those Diet-mongers have justified . . . will turn into Nourishment: whereas the Stomach hereby becomes more weakened, Excrements engendered abundantly, the rage of the Archeus advanced; hence arise Misty, Gloomy Representations, eclipsing the Sun of Life . . .[17]

PATIENT RESISTANCE TO PLEASANT MEDICINE

The patient resistance that Thomson noted was probably a major factor in the failure of the Helmontian revolution in therapeutics.

[15] Thomson, *Orthomethodos*, pp. 26, 27, 33.
[16] Ibid., pp. 35–6. [17] Ibid., p. 28.

Helmontians attempted to break the belief that serious illnesses require strong, potentially dangerous, medicines. This lies at the heart of the allopathic tradition (i.e. that opposites cure). The dangers inside the body, such as great heat or cold, or putrefaction, that created illness could be countered, it was believed, by medicines posing equal but opposite dangers. Christian sentiment, as we saw in chapter 2, modified this view: simples carried with them an element of innocence since they were gifts from God. Helmontians, nevertheless, emphasised their danger, arguing that they could purify simples further by chemical techniques. However, patients and non-Helmontian physicians either did not wish to or could not break the cognitive link between therapeutic power and potential danger and harm, as the continued popularity of strong purging medicines indicates. Nineteenth-century homeopathic medicine shows it is not impossible for many people to believe in efficacious (though perhaps not powerful) yet mild and harmless medicines. But allopathic ways of thinking have dominated medicine up to the present; the acceptance of some side effects and even of iatrogenic illness is a sign that, although harmful medicines do not go unquestioned, an element of potential harm is still in the twenty-first century a part of what it is to be a medicine.

Patients did sometimes refuse physic, strong medicines, purging and bleeding, but most expected it even if they did not like it. When Queen Elizabeth I was dying she was reported to have 'refused to eate ani thing, to receive any phisike, or admit any rest in bed'. Manningham noted in his diary, 'It seemes she might have lived yf she would have used meanes; but she would not be persuaded, and princes must not be forced.'[18] William Camden commented that Elizabeth had 'enjoyed her sound health, by reason of her abstinence from Wine, and most temperate dyet (which shee often sayd was the noblest part of Physicke)', but when in her last illness, 'as she had done alwayes before in the prime of her age, so now most of all shee refused all helpe of Physicke [that is, therapeutic medicine]'.[19]

Charles II, on the other hand, was more typical in putting up with what seems the whole armamentarium of physic in his last illness, though he was, admittedly, not conscious all the time. He was bled

[18] John Manningham, *Diary of John Manningham*, ed. John Bruce (Camden Society, J. B. Nichols, Westminster, 1868), pp. 207–8.

[19] William Camden, *Annales, Or, the Historie of the Most Renowned and Victorious Princesse Elizabeth* (London, 1635), pp. 584–5.

by 'Dr King, happening to be present', had 'severall hot pans applied to his head, with strong spirits', was given the 'antimoniall cup [a cup made of antimony that communicated its qualities to the ingredients] which had no great effect', and 'strong purgers and glisters', which worked very well, was cupped and had 'put on severall blistering plasters of cantharides [Spanish fly used to raise blisters]'. Sir Charles Lyttelton reported from the court: 'His plasters were taken off this morning, and the blisters run very well; only one is yet on his leg, which is very painfull.' When the king suffered his next convulsion, his physicians were prepared to admit that their blistering plasters had caused it, that they were iatrogenic. The image of the body as composed of a series of channels through which humours and morbific, putrid, ill matter travelled through the body which, as we saw in chapter 3, structured physicians' stories of illness, was in the minds of the king's physicians. Lyttelton wrote, 'The phizitians conclude the sore on his heele was the gowte, and the applying plasters to it repelled the humor to his head.' Their response was to place plasters of cantharides to the head so as to bring the ill humour to the surface of the skin by means of blisters, and then to expel the humour by bursting the blisters so that they 'run'. Such accounts of what was happening inside the body, together with the use of procedures that moved pathological matter through the body, worked together to create strong belief both in the story and in the therapy. More of the side-effects of the king's treatment had to be countered; Lyttelton reported that his 'mouth and tongue and throate are inflamed with the hot medecines, and is the cause he has bine twice let blood since noone; but the 2^d time was because the 1st was unsuccessful; and he bled not above 2 ounces . . . and then he bled 9 ounces'.[20] Clearly, the king's physicians did not subscribe to the Helmontian pleasure principle in medicine, nor to the Helmontians' suspicion of bleeding and the other evacuative procedures.

Such therapies were accepted without quibbling when applied to royalty, and were used on a king who had shown some interest in chemical medicine. The surgeon Edmund King, who was the first medical man on the scene, also practised chemical medicine and was later to be a Fellow of the College of Physicians, and his immediate

---

[20] E. M. Thompson (ed.), *Correspondence of the Family of Hatton. Being Chiefly Letters Addressed to Christopher First Viscount Hatton AD 1601–1704* (2 vols., Camden Society, London 1878), vol. II, pp. 51–2.

reaction was to use his 'lance', to bleed.[21] Nobody blamed him for his action; Lyttelton noted that he acted 'with greate judgement and courage (tho' he be not his sworn phizitian) [and] without other advise, imediately let him blood himself'.[22] King was not in much danger, for onlookers expected bleeding to work, and the familiarity of the procedure made it acceptable. Another reporter of Charles' illness wrote: 'Yesterday, when the king was dressed, hee fell very suddainly down of an apoplecticall fitt or of convulsions (at our end of the towne I have nothing certain) and Dr. King then present and having his lance did presently [immediately] bleed him, which did much good and caused him to recover somewhat of sence.'[23]

The therapeutic power of bleeding and other forms of evacuation had been strongly embedded in the public's consciousness. Lady Anne Clifford noted in her diary in February 1617 that her daughter's 'nose bled which I think was the chief cause she was rid of her ague'.[24] Lower down the social scale, the devout Joseph Lister (1627–1709), who was an apprentice and servant, also equated evacuation with therapy. In his autobiography he wrote how

> I fell into a violent fever, in which, after I had laid some weeks in great extremity, and the doctor ordering me nothing but some easy cordial things, I desired him to give me a bill, for I purposed employing another man, for though I was not against cordials for relieving and strengthening nature, yet I thought it very proper to have some working [purging] physic that might be likely to weaken and remove the distemper.[25]

Lister, who took heed of the advice that the Christian had a duty to take active steps to look after his health, found a practitioner who was both favoured by God and who was also prepared to fall in with Lister's wishes. The new doctor 'was a good man, I believe, and they said a young convert. His name was Doctor Turnstall . . . He first let me blood, and then God so blessed his prescriptions that I did soon recover.'[26]

Patients had been educated to expect evacuating treatments and they continued to believe in them. The association between illness

---

[21] On King see G. Clark, *A History of the Royal College of Physicians* (2 vols., Clarendon Press, Oxford, 1964 and 1666), vol. I, p. 335; Harold J. Cook, *The Decline of the Old Medical Regime in Stuart London* (Cornell University Press, Ithaca, 1986), p. 191.

[22] Thompson (ed.), *Hatton Correspondence*, vol. II, p. 51.

[23] Ibid., vol. II, p. 52 letter of William Longueville.

[24] V. Sackville-West (ed.), *The Diary of the Lady Anne Clifford* (Heinemann, London, 1923), p. 54.

[25] T. Wright (ed.), *The Autobiography of J.L.* (London, 1842), p. 43.

[26] Ibid., p. 43.

and bleeding and purging was partly created by the many practitioners who, as we have seen, automatically made evacuation their first therapeutic response,[27] and the use by practitioners and patients of evacuation procedures at the first onset of illness, repeated across the generations and the centuries from the classical period and the Middle Ages to the sixteenth and seventeenth centuries, produced a mind set that was very difficult for Helmontians to shift. The practice of preventive bleeding in spring also fixed it in the communal culture of the seasons, whilst the numerous phlebotomists, whether travelling tinkers, horse-leechers, barber-surgeons or surgeons, embedded the practice in the economy of the medical marketplace and likewise made it hard to abolish. Purging, which was equally the first recourse of the ill patient, and was also used at any sign of constipation, was likewise integrated into the medical economy, helping, as we saw in chapter 2, to increase the profits of apothecaries and drug importers. The therapeutic expectations of patients and onlookers were also fixed on evacuation because the accounts that physicians gave of illness melded well together with purging and bleeding. The material that was evacuated could also provide its own story. The practitioner declared what the illness was that lay in the blood, faeces or vomit which had just been expelled, and so justified the use of evacuation. Lyttelton, for instance, wrote that his son had been ill with fever, 'so hee was let blood tonight and Dr. [Walter] Needham says, [he] had the most feavorish blood he has seene of so young a child. He is much better after it.'[28] John Evelyn was faced with such diagnostic certainty from his physician about the quality of the blood that had been let out, that no doubt could be brooked about the procedure: '*Monsieur Le Chat* (my physitian) to excuse his letting me bloud, told me it was so burnt & vitious, as it would have prov'd the *Plague* or spoted feavor, had he proceeded by any other method.'[29]

Helmontian practitioners were very conscious that patient expectations and resistance made it difficult to get their new medical practice accepted. They had to compete in the medical marketplace,

---

[27] Nedham also complained that 'letting of Blood is grown so common, that too many by this French Mode of Blooding make it like the *Prologue* to the *Tragedy*, the necessary *Praeludium* of Cure in most Cases that come under their Hands': M[archamont] [N]edham, *Medela Medicinae. A plea for the free profession, and a renovation of the art of physick, out of the noblest and most authentick Writers* (London, 1665), pp. 85–6.

[28] Thompson (ed.), *Hatton Correspondence*, vol. I, p. 221.

[29] John Evelyn, *The Diary of John Evelyn*, ed. E. S. de Beer (6 vols., Clarendon Press, Oxford, 1955), vol. II, p. 522. Evelyn often used bleeding.

and they faced the same barriers to acceptance as those of which the learned physicians had earlier complained: recalcitrant patients, onlookers who undermined their authority and treatments, and other practitioners who were ready to replace them. What was different was that the learned physicians had succeeded in getting their message across to the public, had shaped patient expectations and were expert at satisfying them; at least this was how Helmontians saw the situation. References to patients demanding the old procedures, whether for prevention or treatment, pepper Helmontian treatises. Starkey reported how 'A Gentleman of my acquaintance in London' asked him 'what I would advise him for the purging of his body to prevent diseases (malignant Fevers being then common) I demanded of him what moved him to desire Physick; he told me indeed he found no disorder in his body, but thought it were good to use Physick notwithstanding for prevention sake.'[30] Against such an expectation Starkey, in a typical Helmontian fashion, relied on Christianity to support his scepticism about preventive medicine: 'I told him that Christ's rule therein was not to be contemned, *viz.* That the whole need not a Physician, but such who are sick; and advised him if he were well, to keep himself well.'[31] The acquaintance did not like what he heard, 'but he would needs take the advice of a Doctor'. The story had some of the traditional ingredients: good advice put to one side by dangerous influence upon a patient. The doctor then consulted by the patient was famous, having 'heaped up riches out of the ruines of several persons and families, and for doing it with a grace'. He ordered the patient first a gentle purge, and when that did not work, a stronger one, with the result that the patient first became feverish, which was what he had hoped to avoid by preventive purging, and 'in ten daies' the physician 'rid him both of his Feaver and his life'.[32]

The story was part of Starkey's attack on the learned physicians. Just as previously the latter had deplored the fact that they lost patients to silver-tongued practitioners peddling dangerous medicines, so Helmontians similarly attacked the learned physicians in their turn. But the difference in tone is significant. The learned

---

[30] George Starkey, *Nature's Explication and Helmont's Vindication* (London, 1657), p. 165.
[31] Ibid., p. 164, referring to Matthew 9.12.
[32] Ibid., pp. 165–6; so, 'the Doctor by his Art of preventing diseases, hath not only caused disease, but also promoted it so far, that by it all future maladies had been certainly prevented, and the grave hath covered his error'.

physicians in the sixteenth and early seventeenth centuries saw themselves as medicine's establishment, albeit not secure in its authority, whose medicine had not yet spread out and become dominant through the country. Their opponents were presented as dangerous competitors, but socially and intellectually inferior. Helmontians, on the other hand, accepted that the learned physicians were the medical establishment and that their medicine had become influential. Starkey depicted the learned physician as someone at the top of the medical tree, who worked according to long-established corrupt practices: he took twice as long to cure a fever as was necessary and made the apothecaries' bills costly so that the cure 'is the more esteemed'. Also in Starkey's stories, one can detect deep worry about the fact that patients voted with their feet and went to the traditional learned physicians who were successful, acquired patients and became rich, and did so with 'a grace'. He acknowledged the reality of the social polish that historians have noted was cultivated by physicians and surgeons in this period and in the early eighteenth century in order to obtain the patronage of clients high up on the social ladder.[33] The note of jealous disdain, of contempt and of a half-hidden desire to emulate the social success of the learned physician is easy to discern amongst Helmontians.

The combination of the physicians' persuasive powers, based on acquired or self-projected social status and rhetorical ability, and the patients' fertile and febrile imagination, conspired, Helmontians believed, to deprive chemical medicine of customers and effectiveness. Helmontian theory, which emphasised the imagination and its ability to create states of reality such as an illness, provided a ready explanation of how patients had their imaginations worked upon by physicians. 'Physicians', wrote Thomson in his treatise against blood-letting, 'by reason of their Grandeur, Magnificence, and strong opinion thereby acquired greater Authority over their Patients than verity on their side', and so were able to persuade their patients to believe that they suffered from illnesses of which there was no sign. So by 'frequent, serious, sad, rumination thereon', patients 'have by the power of their Magical Imaginations brought that really to being, which before had no existence, as I could instance in Consumptions etc'. Similarly, physicians were able to make their

---

[33] See, for instance, N. D. Jewson, 'Medical Knowledge and the Patronage System in Eighteenth-Century England', *Sociology*, 8, 369–85. W. F. Bynum and Roy Porter (eds.), *Medical Fringe and Medical Orthodoxy 1750–1850* (Croom Helm, London, 1987).

patients distrust chemical remedies. There were some patients, 'who taking all their Physicians speak for Oracles . . . contentedly acquiescing in their Grave sentences, have slighted all means whatsoever for their recovery: for that they are informed what they labour under is uncurable, according to their Galenical Catalogue [of incurable diseases]'. Such patients, continued Thomson, were strongly resistant to chemical remedies. Their state of mind made them unreceptive and, therefore, physically unresponsive to them:

If it chance any hath so far condescended to the making use of Chymical medicines, it hath been with such regret, and strong thoughts of being . . . past Cure, with such vacillating, anxious conceits, and prejudice infused into them by Mysochemists [haters of chemistry] against this most Effectual, Innocent way of healing, that let the best Artists [chemical physicians] do what they can, contending against the torrent of their perverse conceits, nothing but a Miracle can save them from the pit of destruction.[34]

Thomson added that it was very hard to counteract the power of the patients' imagination. Thirty years later one would say that such patients had become locked into a Lockean association of erroneous ideas:

Some of these I have met with in my time to whom I have engaged a Cure upon condition of a resignation [a giving up] of their vain thoughts, but this Chymophobia . . . hath so rapidly carryd them another way, insomuch as no Hydrophobus bitten by a mad [in modern terms, rabid] dog, hath been more fearful of water than they of those Chymical Remedies, which I can assert by multitude of repeated Experiments to be both safe and sufficient. Such is the force of these prevaricating turbulent passions, that a man is often led Captive by them whether he will or not to his own ruine.[35]

CASE HISTORIES

What Helmontians had to do above all else if they were to change medical practice was to win the war of words around the patient's bedside, to dislodge old ways of thinking about illness and its treatment, and to gain the patient's confidence enough to trust in chemical remedies. Walwyn's 110 anonymous case histories in *Physick for Families* were designed to show that, despite patient resistance and the therapeutic expectations of the onlookers, he was

[34] George Thomson, *ΑΙΜΑΤΙΑΣΙΣ: Or, the True Way of Preserving the Bloud* (London, 1670), p. 68.
[35] Ibid., p. 69.

successful in this. The odd patient might cry out, when first seen by Walwyn, that 'he must either bleed or die', but even those by the end of their case history had become grateful recipients of his medicines, because of the failure of traditional therapeutics and/or because of Walwyn's persuasive powers.[36] Such patients must have existed, for Walwyn publicised his medicines and made a living from them for over twenty-five years; he died prosperous and his medicines continued to be sold after his death.[37] But his accounts of patient expectations indicate a deep-seated resistance to the Helmontian medicine within which his commercially successful remedies were wrapped. Other Helmontians also noted this patient opposition.

Young and old, men, women and children, rich and poor, gentlemen and gentlewomen, as well as a maid, a working man, a sea captain and a merchant all bought Walwyn's medicines; in other words, they were shown to be suited to all types of people as well as all kinds of disease. Word-of-mouth recommendation was shown as spreading the fame of his medicines. Often Walwyn acted as a medical adviser or practitioner in addition to selling his remedies, and by so doing he mitigated the stigma of commercialism and quackery. The remedies were highlighted as bargains; in one case the cure of a man's wife cost twenty-two shillings using Walwyn's remedies, in contrast to the husband's own traditional cure which had resulted in a bill of twenty pounds or more.[38] Walwyn made it clear that the poor could afford some of his medicines, but he also took care to show that the rich were attracted to them: 'An ingenious Gentleman, long time troubled with melancholly, and in hope of recovery, tyred out with [traditional] Physick . . . put himself and his Purse freely into my care.' He also stressed how a whole family would have his medicines 'always at hand'.[39] Within this advertising copy, which may perhaps have been drawn from experience but was certainly selective as failure did not figure in it, there were hints that Walwyn did not always find it easy to get his treatments accepted. Patients and onlookers had their own expectations of medicine. For instance, when treating a child suffering from smallpox he was

---

[36] Walwyn, *Physick for Families*, p. 49.
[37] Jack R. McMichael and Barbara Taft (eds.), *The Writings of William Walwyn* (University of Georgia Press, Athens, Ga., 1989), pp. 46–8.
[38] A twenty-first-century reader might see that as a comment upon the respective value of a husband's and a wife's life.
[39] Walwyn, *Physick for Families*, pp. 40–100, 94, 91, 62, 64, 72.

confronted with strongly held traditional views about illness and treatment which ran counter to his own. The child appeared to have come safely through the different stages of smallpox after taking one of Walwyn's medicines. However, Walwyn was faced with the onlookers' belief that deep in the body there was still something left of the disease:

But Neighbours and Visitants, and kindred were not so satisfied . . . so the Child was purged as they will needs still call it, and very well upon it for a while, but soon after was taken with such strange fits, as he was then thought to be bewitcht, and was very like to have cost him his life: So here the imaginary Dead Dogg [smallpox] was changed for a real tearing Bear [purging], that through its Venemous Nature tortured and troubled the Child even to Death.[40]

Helmontian medicine had to overcome such views if it was to achieve a revolution in therapeutics, but it probably failed to do so; the evidence that patients were not convinced is not direct but rather comes from Helmontians themselves when they alluded to the opposition that they faced. The times were sceptical of old beliefs, but Helmontians found it difficult to harness such scepticism, perhaps because the beliefs they attacked were held in common by both the popular and learned levels of medical culture, for as Walwyn complained:

And yet this [the near death of the child], nor any reason or Argument will prevail, but let one recover either out of Pestilence, Fever, Ague, Small-pox, Meazels or Surfet, the first thing is thought on, oh by all means, the relicks of the Distemper must be cast off by some gentle Purge, or mischief follows, yea if ever the party be ill again, it shall sure be ascribed to the want of Purging after such and such a sickness: In such simple bondage both the weak and wise, remain even in this inquisitive generation.[41]

Belief in bleeding and purging may well have kept patients away from Helmontian cures, but even when they tried out the latter, they were always liable to go back to the old procedures. This was not cultural inertia. The notion of disease as putrefaction, the imaging of disease inside the body and the associated therapies of bleeding and purging remained as attractive to patients as they had been in the sixteenth century. It was a package that provided a bridge between the visible (blood and faeces) and the invisible disease inside the body. The material conditions of life had not changed by the mid-

---

[40] Ibid., pp. 54–5.   [41] Ibid., p. 55.

seventeenth century to affect the package. Putrefaction in the everyday world was still prominent in dunghills, open sewers, etc., and despite the invention of the microscope there was no technology that provided a new observation-based narrative of the working of disease in the body, something which today, in any case, we believe to be impossible as theoretical interpretation permeates observation. Increasing use of chemicals and hydraulic and mechanical machines may have helped to make disease narratives more chemical and mechanical (though this was a two-way process as theoretical interest in chemistry and mechanics also helped to develop the technology), but it did not affect the roles played by putrefaction and evacuation. The visible expulsion of disease in blood, faeces, sweat, etc. seemed to be as attractive as or more so than being told that the disease had been invisibly killed inside the body by chemical remedies.

While complaints were common about patients changing practitioners in the middle of treatment, the Helmontians felt especially vulnerable to such behaviour; they were newcomers whose social status and medicines were in the process of being evaluated by patients and by the bystanders at the bedside. The call of the traditional well-tried procedures could always tug the patient away from the Helmontian practitioner. This happened to Walwyn in the case of a 'Gentleman about 30. Extremely afflicted with a quartane Ague', who 'had run the whole course of [traditional] Physick'. He had then taken Walwyn's medicines. But, when they failed to work immediately, he went back to the usual evacuative stand-bys. Walwyn graphically described the attraction of evacuation, which physically, in the sight of the patient, appeared to carry the disease out of the body:

Our Proceedings ceast for above a week, he hearkening to his former Counsel, being possest that if any thing carried off the Cause of so great disturbance, it must be Purging and Vomiting Physick which rowsing all the parts of the body, and voiding so great a mass of ugly coloured and nasty filth, the Ague or what ever it be must needs out at last: Arguments indeed, with custome of knowing no better, so powerful as deceives both the Learned and unlearned parts of the whole World.[42]

Helmontians did not try to change the social and commercial relationships that surrounded the bedside. They fought for patients within the long-established structure of patient–doctor relationships.

[42] Ibid., pp. 50–1.

Like the learned physicians and all other practitioners, they had to accept dismissal from the bedside, and perhaps being hired back on to the case, at the say-so of the patient or the family. What Helmontians wanted to replace was the traditional establishment physician, who may have sometimes been at the bedside and, if he was not present, then to counter his ideas and methods which they reported were in the minds of those at the bedside. A particular handicap faced by the Helmontians was that in the 1660s Galenic physicians were modernising themselves. Helmontians believed that a number of their opponents had taken on some of their clothes. 'Galeno-chemists' offered the patient an attenuated form of chemical medicine together with traditional medicine. Helmontians, therefore, fulminated against the pomp of the College doctors and against the perversion of the true Helmontian medicine by 'pseudo-chemists' or 'Galeno-chemists'. But the facts as Helmontians presented them were that, at the bedside, Galenic physicians were powerful competitors, with social authority combined with a therapeutic repertoire sanctioned at the popular and learned levels, whilst 'Galeno-chemists' offered a medicine that was also attractive to patients, which combined the reassurance of well-tried procedures and the pull of the new chemical medicine.

Thomson, as we have seen, was openly pessimistic about the Helmontians' ability to convince patients and onlookers that their treatments were best. He illustrated his point with a case history that provides a rare extended account of the bedside clash of competing practitioners and of how tenuous the practitioner's hold on a patient's custom could be. The case was that of Mr Flavell, 'a Canary [wine] Merchant about the age of thirty years lodging in Dukes Place', to whom 'I was sent' on 9 August 1668. The patient did not dumbly acquiesce to whatever treatment was proposed; as in many early modern doctor–patient relationships, a contract was first negotiated between the two parties, in this case an informal one. Thomson had to counter the patient's expectation that he should be bled, 'which course some of his friends advertised him before-hand what Physician soever he made use of would take'. Then the contract was made: in return for being 'ruled by me, I could promise to relieve him in two or three hours' (he was suffering from a fever, difficulty in breathing, a lack of appetite, fainting, etc.).[43] This

---

[43] Thomson, *Preserving the Bloud*, pp. 91–3.

happened as promised, though the cure was to take longer. By the fourth day the patient was 'in a happy condition, being free from any eminent danger of miscarrying as I often intonated in their [the bystanders'] ears'. Practitioners had to convince not only the patient but also friends and relatives gathered around the bedside, who often took it on themselves to give advice on the choice of practitioners and treatments. Their presence ensured that the practitioner was in an isolated and precarious position. In this instance, they held to their own views of what should be done:

Some of the inconstant vulgar about him (prejudiced against this Chymical way that it was too violent and hot) affrighted at every intense motion of the *Archeus* (invigorated by active medicines to profligate [*sic*] whatsoever is hostile) were very busie in prompting to the sick man the worse, representing every thing in the most deformed dress, enough to make him despond at the postergation of the Cure.[44]

Thomson had to agree to share the cure, and to consult with 'another Physician, a kinsman of the Merchants formerly a great Philo-chymist [lover of chemistry] before he entred into the colledge [of physicians]'. Initially there was a period of undeclared war, both sides giving the patient their remedies. Relations began to deteriorate when the College physician complained of not being consulted when Thomson prescribed a vomit; then 'the Galeno-chemist' faced with the patient's heartburn advised the 'non-sensical' use of vesicatories or blistering. Thomson opposed their use, not only because he had 'declaimed against them with my Pen', but also because he believed that the cure was essentially complete.[45] There followed a bout of hurt feelings and a huffy exit, reminding us that competition at the bedside was every bit as human as elsewhere:

Then finding he [the College physician] could not corrupt me with all his glozing Rhetorick and Paralogistical discourse of the rare effects of Cantharides etc., he flung away in discontent, saying, he would now leave the sick man to my Custody, my reply was, and I to yours if the Patient be so pleased, which would by no means be granted by him; being very sensible and thankful that I took a direct means to save his life.[46]

Having kept his place, Thomson tried to secure it by promising the patient 'perfectly to cure him without relapses, and long vexatious Ague . . . This I would make good, or I would have no reward for all my pains and medicine.' The patient agreed on these

[44] Ibid., p. 93.   [45] Ibid., pp. 93, 94.   [46] Ibid., p. 95.

terms, which hint at either Thomson's confidence or possible desperation, 'to resign himself over to my solitary care'.[47] In the meantime, Thomson's bedside enemies were plotting to have him replaced by the College Galeno-chemist. His report of events has the combative ring of someone who knows his medicine is best, but it also has a subservient note, that of a servant who can be hired and fired at will:

> there were not wanting instruments . . . to introduce . . . the said Galeno-chymist who was represented to this convalescent person, as able to do great matters for the removing his Ague by his cooling or more temperate preparations, mine being looked upon (after I had helped him out of the mire) as too strong and burning, now the reason of my dismission, must be coloured over with a fair pretence that the patient would betake himself to kitchin Physick [home remedies]: Through this door was the Galeno-Chymist with his Apothecary entertained once again into the sick mans Chamber to attend him . . .[48]

Mr Flavell's case illustrates how a contract was made between patient and doctor, the former agreeing to therapy, the latter promising a cure.[49] But the contract was liable to be broken at the patient's say-so. Thomson reviewed the case and the mechanics of the breakdown in the relationship between patient and Helmontian doctor. However successful the Helmontian physician might be at curing the patient, the Helmontian physician was undermined at the bedside by the destructive comments of Galenists about his remedies. These were all the more effective for being expressed in the new language of chemical processes and particles which had been incorporated into Galenic medicine. Thomson complained that the opposition made the accusation that 'my Medicines are too hot and violent, where sulphurous particles are advanced and preter-natural [unnatural] fermentation promoted and so the fever encreased . . . How many by this false allegation have been deterred from making use of the right means I am not a little apprehensive.' Such an accusation had its effect at the bedside. Despite giving an accurate prognosis and providing medicines that cured, the Helmontian physician, lamented Thomson, could be dismissed by the inconstancy

---

[47] Ibid., p. 95.

[48] Ibid., p. 96. The chopping and changing among practitioners continued, with three more practitioners being hired and fired, until 'nature' finally cured the patient.

[49] The Galenic physician might have held out the prospect of alleviating rather than curing a disease if it was one of those which Galenic medicine declared to be incurable.

of the patient and the malicious slanders of the onlookers: 'They falsly now upon his Recovery inveigh against me, that I gave him violent hot things: urging withall Vesicatories would have done him most good. He foolishly gives credit to it, whereupon another must be entertained to reap the fruits of my labours, to carry away the credit of the Cure.'[50]

Both socially and medically it appears that Helmontians found it difficult to compete at the bedside. As they admitted, they lacked the authority that the Galenists had acquired; moreover, Galenic accounts of pathological events inside the body and the associated therapeutic procedures were widely accepted, and Helmontian remedies were frequently bad-mouthed. On the last, it may well have been that Helmontian remedies, despite being advertised as pleasant, mild and powerful, were in reality unpleasant, stinking of sulphur and burning, so that the patient was faced with two modes of treatment, both of which in their different ways were unpleasant and feared.

COMPROMISE

To some extent Thomson and his fellow Helmontians mitigated these handicaps. Their revolution was not designed to change utterly the face of medicine. They accepted and worked within the pool of popular and learned knowledge concerned with the identification of disease, Walwyn, for instance, leaning towards a less technical terminology whilst Thomson came closer to the learned language register for diseases.[51] The patient, the Galenist and the Helmontian would generally have agreed on the diagnosis and naming of a disease, if not on its cause. This allowed Thomson to share in the persona of the expert physician whose technical terminology and skill in a diagnostic technique such as judging the pulse allowed him to make a more precise and finer diagnosis than could the lay public. Other Helmontians might reject particular aspects of such expertise

---

[50] Ibid., pp. 100, 102.

[51] This did not mean that they saw diseases as unchanging. When arguing against the blind application of classical medical knowledge to the present, and stressing the need for new knowledge and new remedies, Helmontians pointed out that old diseases such as agues, fevers and scurvy had altered, that the French pox had changed since its first appearances in Europe and that the rickets had only been noted in the seventeenth century: Nedham, *Medela*, pp. 29–46.

as being too closely connected to Galenism; Walwyn, as we saw, included taking the pulse as one skill he could dispense with, and Thomas O'Dowde wrote of the physician's 'Pulse trick' and his 'Glyster-pipe nothing' which went together with his 'pomp, state, greatness'.[52] However, Thomson felt free to show off his diagnostic expertise, so Mr Flavell was described as 'labouring under a malignant feaver, difficulty of breathing a Parapleuritis, i.e. a Bastard Pleurisie, oppression at the stomach, inquietude, Anorexia [lack of appetite] . . . Lypothymia [fainting], a disposition to vomit, ready sometimes to faint with a pulse very high, faster than ordinary, unequal'.[53] Such clinical observation, with its staccato-like precision, could have been seen by Helmontians as Hippocratic in origin and, given their veneration of Hippocrates as the true and uncorrupted father of medicine, a proper part of the chemical physician's bedside skills, despite the fact that the Galenic physicians also exercised such Hippocratic skills. Thomson's stress on prognosis was also Hippocratic.[54]

The ability to diagnose and to give a prognosis were skills that patients expected of physicians. But the pathological stories and therapies of the Helmontians were unfamiliar to patients and could make it difficult for them to accept Helmontian medicine, or rather medicines, for the latter were often what was being offered. One response of Helmontian physicians may have been not to provide their patients with a detailed Helmontian explanation of their diseases. That is certainly the impression given by the case histories set out by Walwyn and O'Dowde, whilst what Thomson said to his patients is unclear, though I suspect he would have found it difficult to refrain from showing off his Helmontian learning. Helmontians, with their sense of constituting a God-selected group of adepts, were generally aware that their knowledge was difficult for their readers to grasp at leisure, and this would be even more the case for sick

---

[52] O'Dowde, *Poor Man's Physician*, p. 91.

[53] Thomson, *Preserving the Bloud*, p. 91.

[54] As was his recognition that: 'A true judicious Prognostication of the progress, state, and termination of a disease, begets in the Patient a strong perswasion of the ability of his Physician, and the sufficiency of his Remedies, this invites him to take liberally of them: this large sumption [consumption] of what is efficacious will in a short time alter the sad scene, suggesting his restauration if he be capable thereof': ibid., p. 101; on Hippocratic prognosis see *On Prognosis*; also Ludwig Edelstein, 'Hippocratic Prognosis' in Owsei Temkin and C. Lilian Temkin (eds.), *Ancient Medicine. Selected Papers of Ludwig Edelstein* (The Johns Hopkins University Press, Baltimore, 1967), pp. 65–85.

patients. The intrinsic difficulty of Helmontian theory was not underestimated by Helmontians. Nedham welcomed the translation of van Helmont's writings into English, but he warned, 'but know 'tis not a slight reading will serve the turn: Ten times over is too little, though a man should have the help of a Tutor to direct him.'[55] It may also be that Helmontian metaphors of what was happening in the body were not as convincing as Galenic or chemical-mechanical ones. Moreover, getting their accounts of disease widely accepted did not square with the esoteric medicine of expert adepts. Like the Galenists before them, they were in a cleft stick: they wanted to keep their knowledge to themselves, but if patients knew about it and believed in it Helmontians were more likely to gain their custom. And, as we shall see, Helmontians complained that the influence of their Galenic opponents upon patients was partly due to their success in getting their knowledge and therapies accepted by the general public. The Helmontian solution to the dilemma was probably to play down theory at the bedside. This made them more open to the charge of being empirics and weakened their group identity, but it was a solution adopted by large parts of commercial medicine in the later seventeenth century. A low level of theory may have appealed to some patients, or may have been a safety-first strategy devised to antagonise as few patients as possible, at a time when there were many theories and approaches to medicine, and 'sound-bites' rather than long-winded theorising were becoming increasingly popular (see next chapter).

Faced with patient resistance it is understandable that Helmontians compromised: they made use of some evacuative procedures and they sometimes referred to putrefaction in the body, though they usually held the line against bleeding. Thomson, in Mr Flavell's case, initially used an 'Emeto-Cathartick' that induced vomiting, which he later acknowledged was a 'Galenical' method.[56] Walwyn acknowledged the public's demand for evacuation, albeit by making it natural, when he took care to point out that the 'good qualities' of his medicines 'were such as to leave nothing behind, but what they put Nature into an ability to Evacuate'.[57] Thomas O'Dowde, in the cases that he detailed in *The Poor Man's Physician, Or the True Art of*

---

[55] Nedham, *Medela*, p. 239.
[56] Thomson, *Preserving the Bloud*, pp. 92, 96.
[57] Walwyn, *Physick for Families*, p. 54, in the case of the gentleman whose illness was extinguished like a candle.

Medicine (1665), boasted as a good Helmontian that he did not bleed. In his comments on the case of John Graunt's son, Thomas, whom he had successfully cured of smallpox, he wrote 'of those Leech-like Physicians of our dayes, who are never satisfied, but in *Blood, Blood* . . . not sparing any from the Prince to the Peasant, and merely, I presume, from the want of *Truly Chymical* and separating Medicines, which my self and others having . . .' However, O'Dowde also took pride in his medicines, which worked by 'stool and vomit', as in the case of Mary Low, the daughter of a baker, and 'brought forth a great quantity of putrified matter, resembling rotten blood commixt with slime'.[58] With O'Dowde it was perhaps not so much a need to compromise his Helmontian beliefs, as a positive and enthusiastic belief in the necessity for purging.

In other cases O'Dowde also used evacuative remedies and clearly believed that the putrefaction was the disease. Mrs Elizabeth Friend 'grew strong, chearful and fat' after twenty-nine days of O'Dowde's medicine, despite having suffered for some years from the falling sickness or epilepsy and being so particular about her medicines that she was 'the most difficult Patient I ever yet, or hope ever shall meet with'. The crux of the cure was the 'at least 200 vomits and the 100 odd stools' produced over the twenty-nine days. In another case, O'Dowde was called to advise on the illness of 'Mr. Gerrard, a French Gentleman, and servant to . . . the Lord Fitzharding', who fell down suddenly with the symptoms of the falling sickness (unconsciousness, brief loss of memory). O'Dowde stressed that it was Charles II himself who, on hearing of the case, recommended O'Dowde's services, and he also underlined how, on taking a mere quarter of a grain of O'Dowde's medicine, the patient

had from its Operation, twenty Chamber-pots full of vomit, being a putrid glutinous matter, and green as glass, and eight stools so great, as to fill a Close-stool-pan twice full, of as ill matter as the vomits. This is his own relation . . . And after this great Operation, he was so very well, that . . . I found him rising to eat his breakfast and resolving to go to Court.

Dowde had no hesitation in advertising the power of his medicine to evacuate upwards and downwards. Despite his contempt for Galenic physicians, and their 'art of the Glyster-pipe', it is clear from these cases and others that O'Dowde, like his opponents, relied on evacuation, and he took pains to illustrate to his readers and possible

---

[58] O'Dowde, *Poor Man's Physician*, pp. 30, 29.

customers how good his medicines were at clearing the body of putrefaction and hence disease.[59] He must have believed that the public remained obsessed with what came out of their bodies, and that they would respond by buying his medicines when they read descriptions that confirmed their views, as, for instance, when he detailed how William Fichet, 'Clark of the kitchin to the Earl of Suffolke', was cured of his falling sickness by going to O'Dowde's 'Laboratory' to take medicine. The selling points of convenience to the patient, the power of the purging medicine and the satisfyingly graphic description of its end product were intertwined into one package:

At last he fell into my hands . . . and first received benefit by two dayes of Medicine; soon after that he took Medicine in my *Laboratory* for five dayes, without intermission, each day coming by six in the morning, and returning to *Whitehall*, the Operation [of purging] ending by ten [in the morning], and the several Operations not only [producing] tartarous [stools], but corrosive, as *Vitriol*, and of the several colours of pure red, green and yellow; after its operation he was at liberty to mind his affairs, and for his dyet he was left to do what he best liked; and from this method he was brought to that happy condition [of being cured].[60]

Commercial pressures as well as personal inclination probably forced a Helmontian such as O'Dowde to water down van Helmont's revolutionary message that purging, as with bleeding, did not cure diseases.[61]

On the question of putrefaction, which linked Galenic theory to therapeutics, being both part of the story of the internal ills of the body and also seen as the disease exiting from the body, Helmontians were at times ambivalent, but on the whole they played down its importance. O'Dowde clearly had no hesitation in highlighting the role of putrefaction in disease. But van Helmont had argued strongly that putrefaction was not in itself a cause of disease as Galenists believed when they wrote that putrefied humours and especially

---

[59] Ibid., pp. 46, 48–9, 28, 79.   [60] Ibid., p. 44.

[61] It could be argued that O'Dowde was not a proper Helmontian, as he did not emphasise Helmontian theory, but his daughter fulsomely praised van Helmont, and in *The Poor Man's Physician* O'Dowde printed the petition for the recognition of a Society of Chemical Physicians with its list of Helmontian physicians that included his own name. One can also note that when O'Dowde lay dying of plague, Edward Bolnest, a Helmontian physician, was called. Mary Trye, *Medicatrix, Or the Woman-Physician: Vindicating Thomas O'Dowde . . . against . . . Henry Stubbe* (London, 1675), pp. 97, 58; O'Dowde, *Poor Man's Physician*, pp. 93–5.

blood caused fever. He also denied that blood could putrefy in the veins, which was a justification for blood-letting.[62] Moreover, van Helmont argued, as did Biggs and Thomson, that the physician could not judge the nature of the disease from the blood taken from a phlebotomised patient, as the blood was not putrefied and not diseased. Therefore, the physician could not show off his expertise and justify blood-letting; rather his performance should be considered similar to the trickery of a uroscopist.[63] Thomson wrote that, rather than using blood-letting, he would cure the ills of the blood whilst it ran in the veins, just as wine that has 'become sick' could be corrected or remedied.[64]

However, this may not have been as satisfying for the patient as seeing the illness being expelled in the blood, or in the faeces or vomit, and having an expert confirm that this was indeed the case. Moreover, by throwing doubt on putrefaction as a primary cause of disease, as well as by their condemnation of evacuative measures, Helmontians were driving out purification and cleansing from medicine. Van Helmont and some of his followers tried to undermine the Galenic link between purgation and purification by arguing that the laxative medicines produced the ill matter seen in

---

[62] Van Helmont did not deny that putrefaction was an important stage in the process of dying, but he lessened its natural philosophical significance when he argued against Aristotle that it was not a necessary stage in the cyclical process of generation and corruption. In medicine, van Helmont saw putrefaction as the product of ferments and of specific diseases, but he did not identify it as the disease, or believe in putrefied humours. He, especially, argued against blood being putrefied. In his view, putrefaction could not be reversed, so blood could not one day be putrefied and the next be healthy; he also used the same argument against the Galenic explanations of intermittent fevers: *Oriatrike*, pp. 149–54, 939–44, 944–8; see also Biggs, *Mataeotechnia*, pp. 161–71.

[63] Van Helmont, *Oriatrike*, p. 942: 'I am wont to compare the Lookers into the blood, unto those who give their judgement concerning Spanish wine, and who give their thoughts in beholding of the urine'; Biggs, *Mataeotechnia*, p. 164; Thomson, *Preserving the Bloud*, p. 84: ''Tis commonly pronounced by the Chirurgeons, and approved by their Masters when the bloud altered by the ambient [air], looks with any deformed aspect, as Green, Yellow, White or Blackish, etc. that 'tis happy this was taken away, supposed to be the only subject matter wherein a Feaver, Scorbute [scurvy] etc. roosted, to which the credulous Patient is forthwith prone to assent, being fully perswaded by his miserable unfaithful auxiliators, that so much of his infirmity is abtruncated or dismembred, as there is bad bloud extramitted. This often lures him to a second and third evacuation. But how inconsiderately this is done, the woful cries of Widows and Orphans do too often proclaim; for this very bloud which they decry, rejecting it as very bad in the Porringer [container for the blood], was running free from corruption, containing parts very useful to nature, which might by the activity of powerful Remedies be . . . easily reduced to its native goodness'. Though Thomson conceded that he or another physician could judge if blood was foul or pure: pp. 83, 121.

[64] Thomson, *Preserving the Bloud*, p. 86; see also footnote 63.

faeces, that it did not exist before the purgative was taken.[65] And, as we have seen, they had many arguments against blood-letting to set against the belief that it purified the body. Instead, Helmontians tried to forge a new association between medicine and purity, based on the purifying power of the chemist's fire and on the purity of their medicines. But they had nothing to take the place of the very obvious cleansing of the patient's body, as the work of their medicines, unless they were purgatives, took place inside the body and was hidden from the patient. Given the deeply held belief in the ideal of cleanliness and purity in religion, politics, in food, drink and the environment that existed even in the midst of ever-present dirt and putrefaction, it would have represented a huge sea change in cultural and medical beliefs to have suddenly got rid of the means of cleansing the body of disease. Such has been the long-lived cultural and perhaps biological necessity for a clean, purified body and environment that hygiene is still today equated with cleanliness, and the language of cleanliness underpins many of the metaphors used to explain the functions of the modern drugs that have now completely replaced the evacuative therapies of the past. It is not surprising, therefore, that Helmontians still employed some of the old evacuative methods, apart from blood-letting, and reverted at times to seeing putrefaction as a cause of disease, rather than its effect.[66] Nevertheless, despite the compromises that they made, it appears from the reports by Helmontians of patient resistance to their medicine, and of patient disappointment at their expectations not being met, that it may well be that the Helmontian promise of pleasant, pain-free, yet powerful remedies could not replace the attraction of the purifying and visible, if unpleasant, procedures of the Galenic physicians.

[65] Van Helmont, *Oriatrike*, pp. 958–9; and on p. 959: 'Therefore they ought to confess, That a Purgation is not a purifying of the Body, but rather a distempering of the Humours left behind, if there were any such.' See also Starkey, *Nature's Explication*, pp. 278–9, who wrote of 'the purging vegetable poysons, commonly known by the name of Purges', which damage and poison the bowels, 'and cast forth in various colours according as the nature of the poyson is'. Starkey took care to point out that what were commonly taken to be the chemists' purges based on mercury cured by their specific virtues; the purging was an accidental by-product: pp. 275–8.

[66] For a strong statement that ill matter is not the cause but the effect of disease, see Thomson, *Preserving the Bloud*, pp. 39–40; for a limited acceptance of evacuation and putrefaction see his *Orthomethodos*, pp. 53, 55, 180; also Nedham, *Medela*, p. 198, on putrefaction in the pox and scurvy.

UNIVERSAL OPPOSITION

The extent of the opposition as presented by Helmontians was great: Galenic medicine was perceived as spread right across society. Old wives, rustics, nurses and others representing popular, unlearned culture were portrayed as well versed in the practices of Galenic medicine. Starkey, for instance, wrote of how the physician 'deviseth a Clyster, which trade almost every old wife hath got from him, who now a daies, can prescribe Clysters as confidently, and as wel as the Doctor'.[67] Galenic medicine, declared Helmontians, because it was in essence very simple could be widely understood; 'what', wrote Starkey, the Galenists' 'Method performes is obvious to, and the by-word of the veriest rusticks in the Nation'.[68] A complex Galenic cure for gout involving fomentations, unguents, plasters, scarifications, blistering, together with sweating and bathing the affected part could be paralleled by a simplified popular cure: 'Oft times a good old woman sweating a party so taken soundly with Cardicus and Camomile-flowers, and bathing the place affected with Brandy Wine warm, hath performed the like.'[69] At other times Galenic physicians were pictured as not putting their knowledge 'to the Test of Solid, Learned, repeated Experiments', but relying instead for their few remedies on 'what Good-wives have Taught them'. The equation of Galenic medicine with 'the Rude contingent Essays of the Plain Candid Immethodical People'[70] meant that the former could be stigmatised with the simple-mindedness associated with the latter, so uniting, in Walwyn's words, 'both the Learned and unlearned parts of the whole World', 'with custome of knowing no better'.[71]

The two-way flow of medical knowledge between the learned and popular traditions is a sign of the partially integrated and widespread medical culture, which Helmontians saw themselves as battling against. It was a culture in which the more lowly providers of medical care were also viewed as Galenists. Thomson wrote that

[67] Starkey, *Nature's Explication*, p. 273.
[68] Ibid., 'Epistle Dedicatory', sig. A6$^{\rm v}$.
[69] Ibid., p. 141; Starkey used this to denigrate Galenic medicine, typically moving from at one moment praising a 'good old woman' to the negative connotations of simple-minded stupidity associated with 'old wives' and attaching them to Galenic medicine: 'This, O this is the Doctors Method, this is the Art they so magnifie, in respect of which a Chymical Physician in contempt is by them termed an Emperick, and a Mountebank, and what not.'
[70] Thomson, *Orthomethodos*, pp. 119–20.
[71] See Walwyn, *Physick for families*, pp. 50–1, quoted on page 415.

those who had opposed him since his 'deserting the Galenical usual manner of prescribing' spanned all the different medical classes: 'I incurred the displeasure, yea, hatred of most Apothecaries, a disrepute amongst Galenical Chirurgions, because I condemn Phlebotomy, and the common way of Healing Wounds, Sores etc. The rash, Incogitant censures, and Raillery of Midwives, Nurses, or such like Creatures, with the Huffings, snibs, repulses of Fortunes Favourites; and the Abuses, Sarcasms, opprobious Language of the ruder sort.'[72]

O'Dowde also presented the opposition to Helmontian medicine as united under the Galenic banner. Admittedly it was a coercive tyranny, in O'Dowde's view, that incorporated a whole range of practitioners into Galenic medicine. But again we are shown that Galenic physicians maybe had succeeded to some extent in their aim, which they had set out in the previous century, of spreading their type of medicine across the country. O'Dowde wrote:

In verity, we could wish the Nation had not just reason to conclude, the *Galenick* Practice of Physick, as 'tis at this day, to be the greatest Cheat of all other; and not likely (if their coercive power over us should be gratified) ever to be other; especially considering that not only Mr. Doctor, but likewise his now numerous Spawn of Chyrurgians, Druggists, Apothecaries, Tooth-drawers and Corn-Cutters, besides old Wives professing *Galenically*, must all have their employements to do mischief.[73]

Helmontians may have wished to exaggerate the strength of the opposition, and it does look odd that they stress this at a time when Galenic medicine was in decline. Clearly such views helped to make the case for a true Helmontian medicine to replace the one that they believed had benighted the whole country. It made sense for Helmontians to adopt the strategy of emphasising the size, influence and limited knowledge of the opposition given their specific aim of getting royal recognition for a Society of Chemical Physicians (Thomson and O'Dowde refer to the large number of different Galenic practitioners precisely in this context as they appeal to Charles II to give the Society his support), and their long-term struggle to create a revolution in medicine. However, such comments can also be seen as actually reflecting the extent of the resistance that they faced when trying to substitute deeply ingrained medical

---

[72] Thomson, *Orthomethodos*, p. 184.
[73] O'Dowde, *Poor Man's Physician*, pp. 90–1.

practices and accounts of illness with new therapeutics and stories of disease.

Up to now the decline of Helmontianism in England has been understood largely in terms of the failure of Helmontians to gain royal recognition for the projected Society of Chemical Physicians. That failure, as Harold Cook has pointed out, was exacerbated by the deaths in the plague of 1665 of at least four (O'Dowde, Starkey, Joseph Day and Robert Turner) of the thirty-five chemical physicians who signed the declaration calling for the creation of the society. The loss of O'Dowde was especially critical as he was the chemical physicians' link to the king and the court. Moreover, after the plague the thirty-eight nobles and gentlemen, with Gilbert Sheldon at their head, who had publicly supported the chemical physicians and their proposed society disappeared from view and were not mobilised again on behalf of the chemical physicians.[74]

There was also failure to gain wider intellectual support. There has been a great deal of excellent historical work tracing how Galenists, Helmontians and Royal Society empiricists all acknowledged in differing degrees the value of chemistry. The shifting influences, allegiances and controversies between these groups have also been ably charted.[75] What emerges is a picture of confused and overlapping identities, and paradoxically of sharp and polemical conflict over apparently well-defined views. In this time of change, although the Helmontians had many views in common with Royal Society physicians, chemists and natural philosophers, such as the need for practical knowledge, the value of experiment and the contempt for old learning (Starkey, for instance, had assisted Boyle), ultimately the core of their medical philosophy was unacceptable to the intellectual elite. Boyle's corpuscular philosophy won out against the chemical philosophies of Paracelsus and van Helmont. Their philosophies came to be seen as part of the old order, in that, like the

---

[74] Cook, *Decline*, pp. 148, 158, 149; Cook numbers thirty-four signatories. The declaration is printed at the end of O'Dowde, *Poor Man's Physician*, as is the statement of support by the nobility.

[75] See, for example, Antonio Clericuzio, 'From van Helmont to Boyle: a Study of the Transmission of Helmontian Chemical and Medical Theories in Seventeenth-Century England', *British Journal for the History of Science*, 26, 1993, 303–34.

philosophy of Aristotle, they explained the world in terms of a limited number of primary elements, whilst Boyle believed that there was a large number of chemical substances which could not be reduced to any set of primary elements. However, Willis' five-element philosophy did not prevent it or himself from being acceptable to the virtuosi, and it was probably because of Willis' network of university acquaintances, his anatomical and experimental researches, his scholarly ability in writing in Latin, and his eclectic and inclusive approach to medical and scientific theories, as well as his belief in the mechanical philosophy, that he, and not the Helmontians, came to occupy the high ground in medicine and the new science. In other words, social as well as intellectual currents flowed against the Helmontians.

It could also be argued that the Helmontians' claim to be gifted by God with knowledge of chemistry was suspect to establishment intellectuals and politicians because it smacked of the 'enthusiasm' of the Civil War sects. Such claims were seen as having fuelled rebellion and disorder, and 'enthusiasm' became a term of abuse in the politics of the Restoration settlement.[76] However, inspired healers such as Valentine Greatrakes, an Irishman who claimed to heal by 'stroking' his patients, or Matthew Coker, who claimed the gift of healing through the laying on of hands, were given a serious hearing.[77] Charles II's court was not hostile to the Helmontians; Charles himself publicly supported chemistry by making Nicholas Le Fèvre, who had taught at the Jardin du Roi and was a signatory of the declaration for the Society of Chemical Physicians, the royal chemist. But royal interest was not translated into royal patronage and recognition of the projected society.

Patient power and expectations were, as social historians of medicine have recently pointed out, significant factors in shaping the

[76] Michael Heyd, *'Be Sober and Reasonable': the Critique of Enthusiasm in the Seventeenth and Early Eighteenth Centuries* (Brill, Leiden, 1995), and 'Medical Discourse in Religious Controversy: the Case of the Critique of "Enthusiasm" on the Eve of the Enlightenment', *Science in Context*, 8, 1995, 133–57.

[77] A. Bryan Laver, 'Miracles No Wonder!: the Mesmeric Phenomena and Organic Cures of Valentine Greatrakes', *Journal of the History of Medicine and Allied Sciences*, 33, 1978, 35–46; Caoimhghin S. Breathnach, 'Robert Boyle's Approach to the Ministrations of Valentine Greatrakes', *History of Psychiatry*, 10, 1999, 87–109; on Coker see Marjorie Hope Nicolson (ed.), *The Conway Letters: the Correspondence of Anne, Viscountess Conway, Henry More and their Friends, 1642–1684*, rev. by Sarah Hutton (Clarendon Press, Oxford, 1992), pp. 100–2; also see in BL.E734, no. 8 (King Pamphlets), *A Short and Plain Narrative of Matthew Coker . . . in Reference to his Gift of Healing* (London, 1654), cited in Nicolson (ed.), *Conway Letters*, p. 100.

medical marketplace and the culture of medicine. Without the support and custom of patients and their relatives, the Helmontians, as they themselves admitted, could not achieve their revolution. Institutional, intellectual and social acceptance at the elite levels of society was important, but so was the brute fact of patient resistance to Helmontian medicine.

In the end, the Helmontians could not control how chemistry was defined. Galenic medicine, in transforming itself into a modernised learned medicine, claimed that it could assimilate the new chemistry without changing its foundations. In his defence of the new learned medicine, Nathaniel Hodges argued that 'the new *Doctrines*, are so far from designing the subvertion of the *ancient foundations*, that they appear considerable *additions*'.[78] He did so by claiming that the substance of medicine remained unchanged whilst its hypotheses, what the Helmontians took to be its foundations, changed; in other words, the practice of medicine remained intact even though expressed in the new language of chemistry:

not a few have misplaced their pains in examining and disputing the *Hypotheses* of *Hippocrates*, *Galen*, and their *Disciples* about the Humors, Qualities, and the like Sentiments . . . if any quarrel with those *notions*, they may take the same liberty of substituting others more agreeable to the *Phaenomena* of *Nature*; but the *substantials* of *Physick* are not altered by the various dresses wherein they appear suitable to every Age.[79]

Such a strategy of assimilation by the learned physicians meant the core of medical practice centred around evacuations did not have to alter, even though theories changed. Moreover, such partial acceptance of the new theories made it difficult for Helmontians to attack either the chemistry or the medical practice of the learned physicians; learned medicine in this period had become a slippery creature.

Allied to this was the Helmontian difficulty in projecting a clear-cut and easily recognisable public identity. They were a motley group, divided not only by education but by religion (see previous chapter). At the intellectual level the tradition, of which Hodges' book was an example, of reconciling Paracelsian chemical medicine

---

[78] Nathaniel Hodges, *Vindiciae Medicinae et Medicorum: Or An Apology for the Profession and Professors of Physick* (London, 1666), p. 6; the book was addressed to Gilbert Sheldon, the Archbishop of Canterbury, and was designed to make him change his mind over supporting the Helmontians.

[79] Ibid., p. 7.

with Galenic humoral medicine, which began with Guinther von Andernacht's *De Medicina Veteri et Nova* (*Concerning the Ancient and New Medicine*, 1571), helped to dilute the impact of chemical medicine. Many chemical remedies were incorporated into Galenic medicine and recognised by official pharmacopoeias. Chemical theories, such as those of ferments and the mechanical and chemical belief in nitro-aerial particles, were also accepted by sections of learned medicine throughout the seventeenth century, so that, except for Helmontians, the title of George Castle's treatise *The Chymical Galenist: A Treatise, Wherein the Practise of the Ancients is Reconcil'd to the New Discoveries in the Theory of Physick* (1667) would not have appeared contradictory.

At the public, commercial level, many who were not true Helmontians sold chemical remedies to the public. Biggs complained of 'a fugitive kind of men from the family of the *Chymists*, who while they brag of select and precious things, sell nothing lesse then poysons, and take all liberty of lying to the deluded ignorants: These fugitives being *apostate* Idiots from the *Chymists* furnaces'.[80] Starkey contrasted the 'true sons of Art' with 'a Renegade Chymist' and with 'Mercenary Chymists' and 'Apostates' employed by Galenic doctors 'foolishly conceiving that every one that was a furnace-monger was straight a Chymist'.[81] The 'Galeno-chemists', whom Helmontians believed had incorporated chemistry into Galenic medicine because it paid to do so, could further confuse an essentially gullible public as to who was and was not a true Helmontian chemist. The 'pseudo-chemist' was, according to Thomson, an empiric, an astrologer or a Galenist or all three combined; he was 'an Upstart thing, as it were a Mushroom, suddenly sprung up' who sowed confusion wherever he went:

He Counterfeits the true Chymist (as the Hyaena a Mans voice) tempting unwary people to come unto him, and then worries them. He, and the Chymical Galenist, like *Davus*, confound the whole World; so that few know how to chuse the Right, and leave the Wrong Way of Curing. He is still sowing his Pseudochymical Tares so thick that Orthochymical [or, legitimate-chemical] Wheat is in danger to be strangled thereby.[82]

---

[80] Biggs, *Mataeotechnia*, p. 27.
[81] Starkey, *Nature's Explication*, p. 105; see also p. 235.
[82] Thomson, *Orthomethodos*, p. 171; see also Thomson, *Galeno-pale: Or a Chymical Trial of the Galenists* (London, 1665), pp. 19, 38–40. Added when in press: for a perceptive analysis of the Helmontian difficulty in retaining their identity, see William R. Newman, *Gehennical*

The danger for Helmontians was that such 'false' heretical Helmontians side-stepped patient resistance by providing popular remedies such as bleeding, together with a mix of chemical and traditional medicines, thus subverting the Helmontian revolution in medical practice.

The creation of the Society of Chemical Physicians might have solved the problem of how the public could recognise who was or was not a true chemical physician. Membership of the society, as with the College of Physicians, would have marked out a practitioner to the public as properly 'belonging' to the chemical physicians. And, indeed, the signatories to the 'engagement' or declaration for the society gave uncertainty over who could rightly claim to be a true chemist as one of the main reasons why it should be founded: 'And whereas some of a different Practice from it [chemical medicine], as well as those many false Pretenders to *Arcanaes . . .* do either maliciously or ignorantly hinder the clear and general understanding of the Vertue and Excellency of such noble Preparations, and by consequence the Publick Good. To the end therefore, that Patients may not spend themselves, their precious time and money in vain; and also that the licentious Abuses of Imposters may be detected . . .' Only such 'Professours [or, practitioners] of Physick' who would improve medicine 'only by Hermetick or Chymical Medicaments' would join the society.[83]

No single reason can account for the failure of the Helmontian revolution in medicine. But the question of identity links the standard account provided by Cook and others, which centres on institutions, groups, controversies and influence, with the issues of patient resistance and acceptance discussed in this chapter. As it turned out, the Helmontians practised a medicine whose popular parts could be imitated, especially by empirics, and the unpopular ones discarded, a process which negated most of its therapeutic radicalism. By the end of the century the English Helmontians, who had never been numerous, had disappeared from view; they left no successors to fight for a new practice of medicine.

It would be a pity to leave the reader with a negative impression of the Helmontians. As well as failures there were positive achievements. They led the way from the mid-seventeenth century in

---

Fire. The Lives of George Starkey, an American Alchemist in the Scientific Revolution (Harvard University Press, Cambridge, Mass., 1994) pp. 201–3.
[83] O'Dowde, *Poor Man's Physician*, pp. 92–3.

producing an incisive critique of all aspects of Galenic medicine, and were not content, as were, for instance, the Oxford group of physiologists, with only changing some of its theories. As we shall see in the next chapter, the Helmontians' distrust of anatomy influenced one of the hero figures of eighteenth-century medicine, Thomas Sydenham. More generally, the Helmontian legacy for eighteenth-century medicine was their contribution towards the emergence of a new view of disease, though it was not identical with theirs, and to the popularisation of chemical remedies across the whole spectrum of doctors and patients. The fire and conviction of Helmontian beliefs should be remembered as well as their whingeing complaints that patients would not listen to them.

CHAPTER 10

Changes and continuities

INTRODUCTION AND SUMMARY

At the close of the seventeenth century much of practical medicine remained unchanged. Disease as putrefaction was still being evacuated from the body, stories of how illness developed in the body were still being narrated, and anatomy still provided the signposting. It appears as if the Helmontian alternative had disappeared without trace. However, this was not altogether the case. Parts of the Helmontian message about disease and its treatment were still in evidence, although one has to be careful about the question of influence: some developments were common both to Helmontian medicine and to other parts of medicine. But, certainly, the Helmontians' view that disease was a 'thing', and their belief that it was medicines above all else that were crucial for medicine, remained very much live issues amongst physicians, empirics and quacks. Other individuals and groups were exerting powerful influences upon the future direction that medicine was to take. Empirics, by their mere presence, which threatened to flood the medical market, gave added importance to medicines and acted as a brake against there being any one dominant theory.

Anatomy, a crucial element in the construction of disease narratives and the progressive ornament of learned medicine, was viewed with increasing scepticism as a factor in the improvement of therapeutics. Helmontians and Thomas Sydenham, probably the most influential seventeenth-century medical writer in the eighteenth century, wanted to have nothing to do with anatomy, but 'modern' learned physicians believed it had the potential to contribute to future developments in therapeutics. Sydenham is discussed at length because he produced a searching critique of practical medicine from diseases to therapeutics, and tried to create new

434

atheoretical conceptions of disease, and also because there was much in his view of medicine, such as the central role of putrefaction in disease and the importance of evacuation, that represents strong continuities with past medical knowledge and practices, which carry over into eighteenth-century medicine. The controversy between physicians and apothecaries as to whether apothecaries could practise medicine is alluded to in order to show how the field of medical education was being contested: on one side the book-based knowledge of the learned physicians, on the other the practical training and modicum of book learning of the apothecary-physicians, with the latter arguing that progress in medicine had been largely due to anatomy and physiology whilst practical therapeutics had been left untouched. Nevertheless, learned medicine did not stand still, as the study of Thomas Willis shows; it modernised itself whilst still keeping to a rational rather than empirical account of diseases and remedies. Willis, like others at this time, helped to move medicine away from Galenic qualitative theory, but he retained the old structure of the disease narrative of hidden events in the body. Into this he incorporated the action of remedies, thus taking them out of empirical medicine and placing them into rational, causal, discourse.

From this melting pot a new, less theoretical, though still rational, medicine was to emerge, one which accepted that the learning of the universities could be combined with practical apprentice-based training, and in which the practical apothecary could take on the role of the physician.

THE MEDICINE OF THE EMPIRICS

The 'swarmes of quackes, mountebacks, chymists, Apothecaries, surgions' whom Thomas Wharton, censor of the College of Physicians, complained 'were ruinous to our old and settled and approved practice of physick', focused, like the Helmontians, on the commercial rewards to be reaped from treatments for diseases.[1] Medicines,

---

[1] Cited in Michael Hunter, *Science and Society in Restoration England* (Cambridge University Press, Cambridge, 1981), p. 138. On empirics and quacks generally see C. J. S. Thompson, *The Quacks of Old London* (Brentano's, London, 1928); S. H. Holbrook, *The Golden Age of Quackery* (Macmillan, New York, 1959); Erik Jameson, *The Natural History of Quackery* (Michael Joseph, London, 1961); W. F. Bynum and R. Porter (eds.), *Medical Fringe and Medical Orthodoxy 1750–1850* (Routledge, London, 1986); R. Porter, 'The Language of Quackery in England 1660–1800' in P. Burke and R. Porter (eds.), *The Social History of Language* (Cambridge University Press, Cambridge, 1987), pp. 73–103; the standard account is now R. Porter,

cordials, pills and powders were advertised as cure-alls. They removed the need for doctors' visits, and lengthy and perhaps costly treatments, and they almost did away with the rhetoric of individualised treatment for the patient.

For instance, Charles Peter, a surgeon, advertised his 'cordial tincture' in a pamphlet which claimed it cured stones in the kidneys, ureters and bladder, diseases of the lungs, scurvy, dropsy, disorders of the spleen, diseases of women, the king's evil, vomiting and 'griping of the guts'.[2] He sold it at half a crown per half-pint bottle, 'To shew the World I am not Covetous'. Such a product no longer had a limited or localised customer base, as was the case with travelling stage mountebanks, or with quacks who sold their remedies from a single outlet, usually their homes. Charles sold his cordial tincture at 'my House in St. Martins-Lane', but for 'Those that live distant from me may send by the *Penny-Post* or otherwise'. And, 'for the Conveniency of Persons more remote', he had arranged for a network of retail agents across the country to sell his product, for example Mr Edward Duck, barber in Marlborough, Mr John Sherfield, shopkeeper in Barnet, Mr Church Simons, bookseller in Newbury, Mr Thomas Biddle, shopkeeper in Reading, Mrs Mary Hebs, draper in Woburn, Mrs Anne Poundall, barber-surgeon in Woodstock and others in Oxford, St Albans, Uxbridge, etc.[3] Such commercial networks were becoming common in the later seventeenth century and were designed to make a remedy nationally available. More famous than Peter's cordial were Lockyer's pills and Daffy's elixir, which were also sold across the country, and George Jones' well-known 'Tincture of the Sun' which, together with his Balsam and Electuary, was sold by his 'trusty Friends' such as 'Mr John Ashtone, postmaster of Warrington, Richard Ballard esq., Mayor of Monmouth, Mr John Russel, postmaster of Arundel, Mr Samuel Brown, apothecary in Leicester', and many more retailers in over fifty places spread widely over the country.[4]

Health for Sale. Quackery in England 1660–1850 (Manchester University Press, Manchester, 1989).

[2] Charles Peter, *The Cordial Tincture, Prepared by Charles Peter, Chyrurgeon at his Bathing-House in St. Martins-Lane near Long Acre* (London, 1686).

[3] Ibid., pp. 15–16.

[4] See broadsheets for 'Lockyer's pill' and for George Jones' 'His Friendly Pills' in the Broadsheet Cabinet of seventeenth-century empirics' broadsheets, Wellcome Institute Library. The Jones advertisement was probably written in 1675. Also Anthony Daffy, *Elixir Salutatis: the Choice Drink of Health* (London, 1675), pp. 7–8, who listed thirty-four retailers throughout London, whilst his widow Elleanor Daffy, who continued to manufacture the

The penetration of such products in the capital and in the rest of the country meant that commerce legitimated the view that a disease rather than the individual patient had to be the focus of the cure. Advertising and availability of remedies helped to create a market for them. But customers must also have been receptive. In some ways, they always had been, as empirics throughout Europe had found ready buyers for their products from the Middle Ages onwards. The attraction of a cure-all was perennial, especially if cheap, though it would often be packaged as coming from exotic parts of the world or as being made from rare and secret knowledge and ingredients. Empiric medicine was also familiar because it was analogous to the centuries-old practice of offering remedies to family and friends; it is worth remembering that family remedies were sometimes equated with empirical medicine and that physicians were seen as attacking both. At the beginning of the eighteenth century a young law student, Dudley Ryder, noted that his cousin:

talked also about empiric medicines, which he said he begun to have a much better opinion of, for he recovered his daughter by some of them given him by a gentlewoman, after all the doctor could prescribe had proved useless and ineffectual. But the doctors had made it their business to decry all this kind of receipts which are in the hands of private persons and thereby made persons of good sense and thought afraid to use them, though no doubt there may be very good receipts lodged in private hands.[5]

The increase in supply of and demand for the empirics' remedies in the later seventeenth century was made possible by increased consumer spending and national prosperity and by the substitution of consumer goods for home-made products, which characterises what historians have called the commercial revolution of the eighteenth century.[6] The new Baconian empirical philosophy and the interest of the virtuosi in remedies, moreover, gave more respectability to the empirics' products and may have attracted some additional customers. And there can be little doubt that empiric medicine benefited from a situation where there was a chaos of medical theories, and the only point of agreement was the necessity for medicines.

---

elixir, had numerous retailers for the counties of England: *Daffy's Original and Famous Elixir Salutatis* (London, 1693), sigs. A3ᵛ–A4.

5 Dudley Ryder, *The Diary of Dudley Ryder, 1715–1716*, ed. William Matthews (Methuen, London, 1939), pp. 176–7.

6 On the increase in consumerism in the eighteenth century see chapter 2 footnote 8.

Identifying who was or was not an empiric was difficult, as everyone wanted to avoid the label; some empirics wrote books, pamphlets and broadsheets by which they attempted to establish their scholarly credentials. They explained their medicines using a little from the old rationalist Galenic medicine and a little from the new experimental and chemical philosophies, thus satisfying customers of all persuasions. For instance, William Salmon, 'the Ring-Leader or king of the Quacks', published books on herbal remedies, on chemistry for medicine and medical case studies, and entered the world of learning, despite beginning as an assistant to a mountebank. He then continued to practise medicine and astrology at the gate of St Bartholomew's hospital, selling 'an antidote against the plague and all pestilential Venom', his 'Family Pills' and an 'Elixir Vitae'.[7] His learning did not prevent him from being attacked in a broadsheet of 1700: 'the Churchyards and Burying places are everywhere ample witnesses of your travels'.[8] Like many other empirics, Salmon combined learning with commerce and used his publications to advertise his wares. His *Medicina Practica: Or the Practical Physitian* (1707) gave his address as the Blue Boar and advertised his 'Balsam de Chili': 'It is an excellent balsam differing from that of Peru . . . but in no way inferior in virtues and excellency as the several experiments late made of it by several learned physicians in curing diseases have given sufficient proof.' He claimed it cured pains, ulcers, bruises, coughs, epilepsy, apoplexy, convulsions and palsies, and that it killed worms, cured ruptures, dissolved soft stones, eased colic and griping, provoked menstruation, and opened obstructions of the liver, etc.[9]

The modern learned physicians' view of an empiric was of someone who

without consideration of any rational Method undertakes to cure Diseases, whose frequent Periclitations [exposing patients to risk or danger] (as he conceits) surpass the notional Theory of Physick, and his proof of Receipts seem to him more satisfactory than the Scholastick odd rules of practice: But what can be expected from such rude Experimentings, not respecting

---

[7] Daniel Turner, *The Modern Quack or, the Physical Imposter Detected* (London, 1718), p. 79; Thompson, *The Quacks of Old London*, pp. 126–31.

[8] Thompson, *The Quacks of Old London*, p. 130. On Salmon I largely follow A. Wear, 'Medical Practice in Late Seventeenth- and Early Eighteenth-Century England: Continuity and Union' in Roger French and Andrew Wear (eds.), *The Medical Revolution of the Seventeenth Century* (Cambridge University Press, Cambridge, 1989), pp. 294–320.

[9] William Salmon, *Medicina Practica: Or the Practical Physitian* (London, 1707), sigs. B1ᵛ–B2ᵛ.

any Indications [from the patient], or other circumstances very considerable in the right effecting of a Cure.[10]

Nevertheless, empirics who published advertisements and books often used the language of causes, constitutions and indications as well as of experience. In his book Salmon comes across as modern, traditionally learned and commercially minded. In cases of hysteria he advised:

To quiet the irregular and turbulent motion of the Spirit and hysteric fumes the following things are fit to be done. First the stomach, and the whole region of the abdomen are to be bathed with *Powers* of *Amber*, or Pennyroyal . . . Secondly, the nostrils are to be often touched with *Postestates Cornu Cervi* . . . Moreover, our *Tinctura Hysterica* should at convenient times be given in a little wine . . . The third intention of cure, is to sweeten the acid salts and juices of the body, for which purpose there is certainly nothing more powerful and admirable than our Spiritus Universalis (which see in our *Phyl Medic Lib.* 2 cap. 2), given twice a day . . . Some possibly may prescribe preparations of Pearls, Corals, Amber, Crabs Eyes etc . . . yet being fixt Alcalies do not immediately enter into the mass of blood . . . The fourth indication is to evacuate the morbific cause, or peccant humor, which you may completely accomplish with my *Pilulae Mirabiles*.[11]

The Latin 'Phyl Medic Lib 2 cap 2' was a nice touch. Clearly, Salmon was imitating the 'modern' learned physician, who knew his Latin and was also familiar with up-to-date reasoning – the acids and alkalis. So here we have an empiric who employed the new philosophy, but who also used the language of traditional Galenic medicine – 'peccant humor', 'intention', 'indication' (though the last two terms were related to the disease rather than to the patient) – and gave a story of what was going on in the body to account for symptoms and to justify the treatment. If profit was really motivating Salmon, then we are being told what, in Salmon's judgement, it was that people wanted to read: a bit of the new (chemistry) and a bit of the old (learned 'rational' medicine). Both theories were mixed at will, and probably did not appear contradictory to most customer-readers. Such mixtures were the accepted norm at this time in many parts of the medical marketplace, and provided good advertising copy. Salmon used them to wrap up his remedies for prospective buyers and to describe how the medicines could intervene in the

10 Nathaniel Hodges, *Vindiciae Medicinae et Medicorum: Or an Apology for the Profession and Professors of Physick* (London, 1666), p. 3.
11 Salmon, *Medicina Practica*, pp. 62–3.

inner happenings of the body. One can also note how Salmon set out an apparently traditional structure of treatment, by dividing it into its different parts to sell a number of his remedies, rather than a single one.

The rhetoric of the empirics at times echoed that of the Helmontians. Not only was there no mention of bleeding, but the images of light, of God and of the practitioner divinely gifted with medicines constantly recurred in empirics' advertising broadsheets. For instance, Lockyer's pill was 'Call'd by the Name of Pilula Radiis Solis Extracta [a pill extracted from the rays of the sun] . . . the only Solar, single and singular Medicine'. It was of 'an All-healing Virtue, the Operator, since it hath pleas'd God to bless his Philosophical Endeavours with the Acquisition and true Perfection thereof'. In their turn, the Helmontians may be said to have echoed empirics such as Lockyer who 'Administred and Experimented the same with Success upon All or Most part of the known Diseases and Distempers of Man (both Internal and External) of all Sorts of Persons, of all Constitutions and Complexions, of all Ages . . .'[12]

Anthony Daffy, 'student in physick', acknowledged the cultural and theoretical signposts of seventeenth-century medicine: God, experience, nature, equilibrium of the temperament, the differences in constitutions and noxious humours. In his advertisement for his 'Elixir Salutatis' he had the best of both worlds: a medicine that he related to all the above beliefs, and yet one that he claimed was a nostrum powerful enough to transcend all the distinctions of learned medicine, and was therefore useful for everyone. Daffy described 'his health-bringing Drink' as:

'A famous CORDIAL DRINK, Found out by the Providence of the Almighty, and (for above Twenty years) Experienced by my self and divers persons (whose names are at most of their Desires here inserted) a most Excellent Preservation of Man-kind

A SECRET

Farr beyond any Medicament yet known, and is found so agreeable to Nature, that it effects all its Operations, as Nature would have it, and as a virtual Expedient proposed by her, for reducing all her Extreams unto an equal Temper; the same being fitted unto all *Ages, Sexes, Complexions,* and Constitutions, and highly fortifying Nature against any Noxious humour, invading or offending the *Noble Parts*.[13]

---

[12] *Lockyer's Pill*, in the Broadsheet Cabinet, Wellcome Institute Library; see also Porter, *Health for Sale*, p. 104 for a slightly different reading of the use of old and new theories by empirics.

[13] Daffy, *Elixir Salutatis*, title page.

Nevertheless, patients may have wanted to preserve some sense of individualised treatments, so empirics gave dosage instructions which took into account age, sex and state of health and strength, whilst still ensuring that no one was precluded from taking the medicine.[14]

The empirics, like the modern learned physicians and probably the rest of the medical world, with the exception of some Helmontians and die-hard Galenists, created an apparently effortless union of the old and the new, a union that in different forms was to persist into the eighteenth century. Part of the mix, perhaps a necessary part, was the reduced role played by theory. The translator of Willis' *The London Practice of Physick* (1685) omitted 'a deal of [Willis'] Theory, consisting of large Anatomical and Physiological Discourses and the like', because he believed that 'There are many Persons to whom the Voluminous Theory of Dr. Willis might prove tedious, who would be desirous of having the Practical part of his Works entire by itself.'[15] Empirics realised that their customers could respond favourably to allusions to different theories, but could also be impatient with too much theorising. What they really wanted to hear was that they could buy medicines that would cure them.[16]

By their increased presence, the empirics changed the shape of the commercial medical marketplace. Their emphasis on medicines would, on the face of it, also seem to subvert theoretical medicine, whether Galenic or modern. However, empirics, by being receptive to scraps of old and new theories, posed no concerted threat to the modernised learned medicine whose rhetoric combined rationality with experimentation. What the medicine of the empirics did was to increase the 'balkanisation' of medical theory, helping to make it less coherent and more piecemeal, whilst at the same time giving added weight to the age-old belief that what mattered in medicine was medicines.

Modernised learned medicine came under stress when the usefulness of anatomy, one of the cornerstones of the old rational/causal

---

[14] See for instance the instructions in William Salmon's broadsheet advertising 'The Vertues and Use of Dr. William Salmon Family Pills' in the Broadsheet Cabinet, the Wellcome Institute Library.

[15] Thomas Willis, *The London Practice of Physick Or The Whole Practical Part of Physick Contained in the Works of Dr. Willis* (London, 1685), Preface, sigs. A3ʳ, A1ʳ.

[16] Robert Boyle, *Occassional Reflections*, section 2, Meditation xv, in Boyle, *The Works* ed. Thomas Birch (6 vols., London, 1772), vol. II, pp. 381–2, provides an example of how an empirical philosopher used both traditional and modern approaches to his own treatment.

accounts of illness and of the newer observational-experimental descriptions of the body, was questioned. It was increasingly seen as contributing little to therapeutics, and for some its role in physiology was also dubious.

THE ATTACK ON ANATOMY

Throughout the sixteenth and seventeenth centuries anatomy had appeared one of the most dynamic parts of medicine. The depiction of the body had exceeded in accuracy the work of the ancients, new structures were observed in the body, and, as English writers did not tire of repeating, the circulation of the blood had been discovered by William Harvey. The triumph of anatomy was celebrated first by the learned physicians and then, in the later seventeenth century, by many supporters of the new science. Anatomy gave the learned physicians kudos amongst the followers of the new science, but it was to be discarded by Thomas Sydenham, the 'English Hippocrates'. It had previously been attacked by Paracelsus and van Helmont for being 'dead' anatomy, for not elucidating how the living body worked,[17] and the English Helmontians were united in their view that anatomy had not contributed to curing disease, though van Helmont had clearly known a great deal of anatomy and had carried out dissections, as also, famously, did Thomson on a plague victim.[18] Biggs called for education in dissection and vivisection, but also asked, 'To what end tends the Anatomy of these two thousand years, with those tedious lectures, if the Sanation [cure] of diseases, be not happier at this day, then of old.'[19] Although Nedham praised the 'incomparable' and 'immortal' William Harvey for his discovery of the circulation of the blood, he wondered 'Whether in the practise of Physick there need be the hundreth part of this ado about Anatomy?', adding that the time was better spent in observing the sick and discovering new medicines.[20] Thomson accepted that

[17] See Walter Pagel, *Paracelsus: an Introduction to Philosophical Medicine in the Era of the Renaissance* (S. Karger, Basle, 1958), pp. 137–9.

[18] O'Dowde also casually commented that he had 'opened' two of his patients, Hannah Burgen and Mary Biggs, and discovered putrefaction: Thomas O'Dowde, *The Poor Man's Physician, Or the True Art of Medicine*, 3rd edn (London, 1665), pp. 86–7.

[19] Noah Biggs, *Mataeotechnia Medicinae Praxeos. The Vanity of the Craft of Physic* (London, 1651), sig. b1^r, p. 9.

[20] M[archamont] [N]edham, *Medela Medicinae. A Plea for the free profession, and a renovation of the art of physick, out of the noblest and most authentick writers* (London, 1665), pp. 17–18, 237.

anatomy was necessary for medicine, but commented that too much time was wasted on it, 'for ostentation, and to get a fame abroad, then for any notable improvement in the Cure of poor miserable Men', making 'a publique Theatrical business of it, for the entertainment of any rude fellows' rather than dissecting in private amongst themselves 'and [to] instruct any ingenious Gentleman, that desires to be informed'. Thomson acknowledged that anatomy interested the 'ingenious', the socially influential gentlemen experimenters of the Royal Society, and, as he pointed out, he himself had carried out an experiment of 'taking out the Spleen of a Dog, without which he lived perfectly well two years and a quarter'. But he added that what mattered to the patient was that the physician was 'master of those Remedies which (proportionate to Diseases) are able to tame and subjugate them to the law of Nature', rather than being told that an experiment had been carried out that was without any practical benefit. Similarly, the 'Invention of the Circulation' was 'highly to be commended', but though it 'gives some satisfaction in the solving certain *Phaenomena* in *Physiologie* and *Aitiologie*; yet we can see the *Therapeutick* part little advanced thereby, so that many stubborn Diseases are equally as hard to conquer (*caeteris paribus*) as they were before its discovery'.[21] Anatomy, in Thomson's view, had a necessary but limited place in medicine. The metaphor of the body as a machine or watch inevitably encouraged a new anatomical vision of it, one that searched out the body's 'mechanical' parts, but even so, for Thomson, the discovery of remedies took precedence:

'Tis certain, every Mechanick ought to have a competent insight of that Machine, as Watch or Clock, etc. which he goeth about to mend; but if he want Instruments and fitting Tools, how is it possible he should rectifie any great *Defect* in it: In like manner it behoves a Physician to be acquainted with the Structure and Conformation of this Θαῦμα Θαυματων [miracle of miracles], *admirable* Engine, Mans Body, so far as is needful and expedient, to instruct him in the *Reparation* and *Restitution* of it, when at any time it is cast off the Hinges of its Sanity [health] . . . But above all it concerns him, to spend the greatest part of his precious time, to bend all his sinews, and to put forth his whole strength, to finde out those powerfull Remedies, which are indeed Θεῶν Χείρες [the hands of God] . . . Desist then ye vain-glorious *Galenists* from spending your dayes about impertinent and superfluous Searches in stinking Carcasses, which are never able to teach you how to destroy the Rampant Diseases daily breaking violently into these living Houses . . .[22]

[21] George Thomson, *Galeno-pale, Or, a Chymical Trial of the Galenists* (London, 1665), pp. 25–7.
[22] Ibid., p. 29.

Anatomy, despite the Helmontians' ambivalence, in the end was seen by them as part and parcel of the failure of medicine to progress; it expressed its ignorance about both disease and treatment. Walwyn, for instance, strongly attacked the belief that anatomy could give an insight into the nature of disease; he recognised how Galenists had intertwined anatomy with their traditional vision of therapy as consisting in the evacuation of putrefaction, and remarked:

who now adays remains in so much ignorance as not to know that Disease is a more lively, active thing, then to reside amongst such muddy matter, as these Purgers can possibly reach, being indeed of a more sprightly and subtile Nature, then to be discovered by the Eye, Hand or knife of the most skilful Anatomists, and only liable to the disquisition of Reason, and an ingenious, intimate conception.[23]

Anatomy, as depicted by Walwyn, was just another futile part of learned medicine. In his analysis of a case report by the French physician Riverius, which Walwyn used to exemplify the cruelty and ineffectiveness of medicine, anatomy has its place in the catalogue of failure by 'this Learned person':

how insensible of the Patients molestations by Glisters, Blisters etc. how regardless of her loss of blood and Spirit . . . of how little use his Learning, and former reading seemed herein, how insignificant all his former opening and Anatomising of Bodies appeared here, where he was afresh fain to open his Patient to learn what her Disease was; And being open'd how meanly he Guesses, taking notice meerly of *apparent* defects of Parts (which are but *Effects*) without any consideration of the cause thereof, which indeed *is the Disease, and indiscernable, but by the Intellectual eye of the understanding*: Also how poorly he was furnished with medicines . . .[24]

In other words, it was not anatomy but only the special God-given understanding with which the true chemist was gifted that discovered the nature of disease, together with, Thomson and others would have added, chemical analysis or 'Pyrotechnical Anatomy'.[25] At first sight, the condemnation of anatomy seems strange. After all, it was based on observation, which was taken to be the basis of knowledge by the English virtuosi followers of Bacon. Yet, it had also been the ornament of learned medicine, rising in status through the sixteenth century as an academic subject from its low position as an

---

[23] W[illiam] W[alwyn], *Physick for Families* (London, 1669), p. 13.
[24] Ibid., p. 112.
[25] Thomson, *Galeno-pale*, p. 29; also on anatomy see Pagel, *Paracelsus*, pp. 108, 137–9.

adjunct of surgery, so that by the end of the century the students at Padua, the premier European university for medicine at this time, were declaring that anatomy rather than natural philosophy was the foundation or basis of medicine.[26] But the observational discoveries of Renaissance anatomists, including those of Harvey, were not intended to challenge learned medical theory on the functioning of the body or in therapeutics.[27] Anatomy, therefore, existed in the old world of learning and the new one of science and appeared progressive in both. Nevertheless, anatomy, despite its association with manual work, did not satisfy another of the demands of the new science: that knowledge should be useful as well as enlightening.

This was not necessarily a fatal impediment. The work of anatomists such as Willis, Glisson and Wharton was certainly acceptable to the virtuosi, especially as anatomical physiology played a significant role in the formative years prior to the foundation of the Royal Society. Anatomy also continued to enjoy its high status within the modernised chemically and mechanically orientated learned medicine. Leiden had replaced Padua as the centre for medicine and anatomy, and Gideon Harvey in 1670 advised the prospective student of medicine that, after having attended Oxford or Cambridge where 'our Student learns to speak like a Scholar and is informed in the principles of Nature', he 'may now pass to Leyden, and enter himself into a *Collegium Anatomicum*, Anatomy being the *basis* and foundation, whereon that weighty structure of Physick is to be raised; and unless he acquires a more than ordinary knowledge and dexterity in this, will certainly be deceived in the expectation, of ever arriving in the honour of being justly termed an *Accomplish'd Physician*'.[28] Harvey went on to recommend, as a logical progression, courses in the practice of medicine.

The problem for some, however, was that the connection between anatomy and the practice of medicine did not seem to exist. Anatomy, despite its gory, stinking and bloody nature, paradoxically created the image of the 'Accomplish'd Physician', but not always of

---

26 See J. Bylebyl, 'The School of Padua: Humanistic Medicine in the Sixteenth Century' in Charles Webster (ed.), *Health, Medicine and Mortality in the Sixteenth Century* (Cambridge University Press, Cambridge, 1979), pp. 335–70, especially p. 364.

27 On this see Andrew Wear, 'Medicine in Early Modern Europe 1500–1700' in L. Conrad, M. Neve, V. Nutton, R. Porter and A. Wear, *The Western Medical Tradition 800 BC to AD 1800* (Cambridge University Press, Cambridge, 1995), pp. 264–92, 325–40; Andrew Cunningham, *The Anatomical Renaissance* (Ashgate, Aldershot, 1997).

28 [Gideon Harvey], *The Accomplisht Physician* (London, 1670), pp. 18–19.

the successful healer. John Evelyn was obviously impressed by anatomical fame, noting in his diary, 'My Indisposition continued: Dr. Joylife that famous Physitian (& Anatomist, first detecter of the lymphatic veins) came to visite me.'[29] Anne Conway, on the other hand, was unimpressed by William Harvey's treatments, and put the care of her chronic ill health into the hands of a variety of notable physicians including van Helmont's son, Franciscus.[30] It is difficult to generalise as to whether fame as an anatomist did or did not make for a successful practical physician in this period. Thomas Willis, who wrote extensively on anatomy and on the practice of medicine, had a lucrative medical practice. As we shall see, he self-consciously tried to integrate anatomy with practice by retelling the pathological stories of disease using the new set of agents provided by the new science, whilst keeping some of the old familiar ones, and most importantly he brought remedies within the accounts of what happened in the body. It is probable that patients were impressed by such abilities; certainly by the early eighteenth century surgeons believed that if they advertised their knowledge of anatomy it would increase their reputation.[31] On the other hand, Willis' immense knowledge of remedies may have been what was most important for patients.

What is clear is that the suspicion that anatomy was a useless part of medicine had become a live issue within elite medicine. George Castle, a Fellow of All Souls College, Oxford, who dedicated *The Chymical Galenist* to Dr Thomas Millington, later President of the College of Physicians, felt the need to defend the practical usefulness of anatomy, but now within the new mechanical framework provided by Descartes:

Anatomy is of no less use in the Curation of diseases, than is the understanding of the springs and Wheels of a Watch, to the man, who

---

[29] John Evelyn, *The Diary of John Evelyn*, ed. E. S. de Beer (6 vols., Clarendon Press, Oxford, 1955), vol. III, p. 186, 18 January 1657.

[30] See Geoffrey Keynes, *The Life of William Harvey* (Clarendon Press, Oxford, 1966), on Harvey's medical practice; for a recent edition of Anne Conway's letters, Marjorie Hope Nicolson (ed.), *The Conway Letters: the Correspondence of Anne, Viscountess Conway, Henry More and their Friends, 1642–1684*, rev. by Sarah Hutton (Clarendon Press, Oxford, 1992), pp. 30–1, 65, 71, 73; also Hutton, 'Of Physic and Philosophy: Anne Conway, F. M. van Helmont and Seventeenth-Century Medicine' in Ole Peter Grell and Andrew Cunningham (eds.), *Religio Medici: Medicine and Religion in Seventeenth-Century England* (Scolar Press, Aldershot, *c.* 1996), pp. 228–46.

[31] Christopher Lawrence, *Medicine in the Making of Modern Britain, 1700–1920* (Routledge, London, 1994), pp. 18–19, gives the example of William Hunter.

undertakes to mend it . . . That the body ought to be Mechanically considered, not onely as to its actions, but also in relation to its Diseases; is, I think the Opinion of every sound *Philosopher*. *Des Cartes*, in his Treatise of the Passions, gives an account of what it is, wherein a dead Man differs from a living . . .[32]

As Thomson pointed out, in practice it was difficult if not impossible to correct an internal mechanical malfunction in the body: 'What would it avail if ye knew the exact site of the smallest *string* or *fibre* in the Microcosme, and yet were not able to reduce it, dislocated, into its right place?'[33]

Christopher Merrett, a Fellow of the College of Physicians and one of its stalwart servants, who was also a Fellow of the Royal Society and an enthusiastic supporter of the experimental philosophy, probably represented the consensus of elite medical opinion when he recognised the need for both anatomy and therapeutics, which he saw as largely but not completely separate.[34] Merrett wrote around 1680 that anatomy and 'the knowledge of Simples' could very aptly be called 'the two legs of Physic'. He added that '*Anatomy* is of greatest fame and repute, tho not of much real use to curing Mankind. The use of Simple doth the most part to the only end of this Art, Man's Health.' However, he believed that human and comparative anatomy were the keys to 'discover the seat of Diseases and Symptoms, their Causes and Effects, Sympathies and Antipathies', and he confirmed anatomy's traditional role in providing the signposting for the narratives of disease inside the body: it discovered, 'which way the matter of Diseases passeth from part to part, and also of all the fluids in our Bodies'.[35] Merrett clearly thought that anatomy could be made more useful to medical practice. As well as noting that knowledge of anatomy already helped in blood-letting and in the placing of cupping glasses,

---

[32] George Castle, *The Chymical Galenist* (London, 1667), pp. 5–7; see also p. 29. Castle quoted Descartes, *On the Passions of the Soul*, part 1, article 6.

[33] Thomson, *Galeno-pale*, p. 28. For Castle, a mechanical explanation of disease, into which he also included Willis' chemical physiology, had the advantage that it was not Helmontian, his book being directed against Nedham's *Medela Medicinae*.

[34] On Merrett see Harold J. Cook, *The Decline of the Old Medical Regime in Stuart London* (Cornell University Press, Ithaca, 1986) for a full account of his role in the medical controversies of the time.

[35] [Christopher Merrett], *The Character of a Compleat Physician or Naturalist* (London [1680?]), pp. 1–2; on the authorship of the pamphlet see *A Catalogue of Printed Books in the Wellcome Historical Medical Library*, compiled by H. J. M. Symons and H. R. Denham, vol. IV, *Books Printed from 1641–1850* (Wellcome Institute for the History of Medicine, London, 1995), pp. 118–19, entry under 'Merrett'.

plasters, fontanels and incisions, he urged that animals should be fed 'with Poisons, Volatil, or Lixivial Salts, or with any of the stronger Simples, and after opening them, to find out the effects upon the Blood, and Humours of the Body'.[36] Anatomy, in other words, would describe the internal effects of remedies and so bring them from empirical medicine into the ambit of observational and rational medicine, into the new learned medicine.

THOMAS SYDENHAM

However, Thomas Sydenham (1624–89), whose influence became generally apparent only in the eighteenth century, held out no hopes for making anatomy more useful. He repudiated both it and the university context in which it and learned medicine in general were taught. John Ward, ever eager for the latest medical gossip, recorded that:

Dr. Sydenham is writing a book which will bring physitians about his ears, to decrie the usefulness of natural philosophie, and to maintaine the necessitie of knowledg in anatomie [to be] in subordination to physick.

Physick, says Sydenham, is not to bee learned by going to universities, but hee is for taking apprentices; and says one had as good send a man to Oxford to learn shoemaking as practising physick.[37]

As Andrew Cunningham has pointed out, the eighteenth century created an eighteenth-century picture of Sydenham as Hippocrates, and in the nineteenth century, when clinical, bedside medicine was fashionable, Sydenham became the Hippocratic clinician.[38] Sydenham as an innovator figures large in such accounts. As a hero figure of eighteenth-century medicine, he symbolised an empirical, almost theory-free medicine, that was a precursor to the eighteenth-century classificatory systems of disease based on the premise that a disease was defined as a collection of symptoms. Sydenham also appeared to anticipate the eighteenth-century Hippocratic concern

---

[36] [Merrett], *Compleat Physician*, p. 2.

[37] John Ward, *The Diary of the Rev. John Ward, A. M., Vicar of Stratford-Upon-Avon . . . 1648 to 1679*, ed. Charles Severn (London, 1839), p. 242, partly cited in Kenneth Dewhurst, *Dr Thomas Sydenham (1624–1689): His Life and Original Writings* (Wellcome Historical Medical Library, London, 1966), p. 17. In the seventeenth century John Locke was very influenced by Sydenham.

[38] Andrew Cunningham, 'Thomas Sydenham: Epidemics, Experiment and the "Good Old Cause'" in Roger French and Andrew Wear (eds.), *The Medical Revolution of the Seventeenth Century* (Cambridge University Press, Cambridge, 1989), pp. 164–90, on pp. 188–90.

with studying disease not only in the individual patient but in groups of patients in society.[39] There is no doubt that Sydenham himself believed he was carving out a new type of medicine. He did so by drawing upon the new philosophies and approaches of the moderns, but, nevertheless, in his medicine there were also some very traditional ways of thinking, especially in therapeutics.

Moreover, anatomy continued to be studied despite Sydenham. Indeed, medicine in the eighteenth century was viewed as having attained the apogee of anatomical knowledge and expertise with, for instance, Giovanni Morgagni making large claims for the usefulness of pathological anatomy.[40] Moreover, the universities, especially Scottish ones, produced a steadily increasing supply of medical manpower, although, and here Sydenham would have approved, the distinction between university and apprenticeship training became blurred as the Scottish universities gave recognition to the latter, and many took degrees in the middle of their practical training with a physician or surgeon.[41]

Sydenham 'belonged' socially and intellectually amongst the virtuosi far more than did the Helmontians. He came from a well-to-do Dorset gentry family, his brothers played prominent roles in the Parliamentary army during the Civil War, and the eldest, William, held high office during the Protectorate. Thomas shared in his family's politics and war service. His studies at Oxford, which he began in 1643, were interrupted when he joined Parliament's forces. He was back at Oxford in 1647, and after another foray into war at the battle of Worcester in 1651, Sydenham spent the following three

---

[39] See Simon-André Tissot, *Avis Au Peuple Sur La Santé* (Lausanne, 1761). Also the inquiry organised by Vicq d'Azyr and the Société Royale de Médecine carried out in the last thirty years of the eighteenth century in France, which related health and disease to topology, climate and people's lifestyles. See also James Riley, *The Eighteenth-Century Campaign to Avoid Disease* (Macmillan, London, 1987).

[40] Albrecht von Haller, *Bibliotheca Anatomica. Qua scripta ad anatomen et physiologiam facientia a rerum initiis recensentur. Tomus I ad annum MDCC. Tomus II ab anno MDCCI ad MDCCLXXVI* (Zurich, 1774–7), 'Anatomes Perfectio', book 9, vol. II. I am grateful to Andrew Cunningham for this reference.

[41] See, for instance, Christopher Lawrence, 'Ornate Physicians and Learned Artisans: Edinburgh Medical Men, 1726–1776' in W. F. Bynum and Roy Porter (eds.), *William Hunter and the Eighteenth-Century Medical World* (Cambridge University Press, Cambridge, 1985), pp. 153–76; and 'Alexander Monro Primus and the Edinburgh Manner of Anatomy', *Bulletin of the History of Medicine*, 62, 1988, 193–214; Lisa Rosner, *Medical Education in the Age of Improvement: Edinburgh Students and Apprentices 1760–1826* (Edinburgh University Press, Edinburgh, 1991). William Cullen, one of the most influential and innovative medical men to hold chairs at Glasgow and Edinburgh in the eighteenth century, was apprenticed to a surgeon-apothecary as well as taking courses at Glasgow and Edinburgh.

years at the university. It was during this time that he met Boyle, who sparked his interest in epidemic diseases and in the experimental approach to knowledge, though, clearly, Bacon was also a major influence.[42] Sydenham was a radical in his politics and in his medicine. After the Restoration, as Cunningham convincingly shows, Sydenham did not follow Boyle in making the new science fit in with the new political ideology. Instead he kept to his political beliefs, and it may have been this, together with a possible inability to attract wealthy patients (though he treated the noble Shaftesbury and Northumberland families and the Earl of Salisbury), that led him to practise amongst the poor, and hence to study disease by observing disease amongst groups of patients, in other words, epidemic diseases.[43] Medical work amongst the poor may not have been only because of necessity caused by adherence to political and religious beliefs. The study of the health of populations had been given a high profile by the work of John Graunt which had been supported by the Royal Society. The poor also provided, as Nedham observed, the opportunity, especially for the gentry, of uniting their traditional Christian service to them with medical research and practice upon them.[44] Significantly Nedham, like Sydenham, fused together medical practice and research, the former providing the

---

[42] Dewhurst, *Sydenham*, provides a good biographical account; Cunningham 'Sydenham and the "Good Old Cause"', pp. 166–174. Also T. R. G. Latham, *The Works of Thomas Sydenham M.D. Translated from the Latin Edition of Dr. Greenhill with a Life of the Author* (2 vols., Sydenham Society, London, 1848–50), vol. I, pp. xi–lxxxix; J. F. Payne, *Thomas Sydenham* (T. F. Unwin, London, 1900).

[43] On Sydenham and Boyle see Cunningham, 'Sydenham and the "Good Old Cause"', pp. 182–4. On Sydenham's medical practice see ibid., p. 175, emphasising his reliance on the poor and exclusion from the wealthy, whilst Dewhurst, *Sydenham*, pp. 49, 170, believed that Sydenham was exaggerating when he wrote to Dr John Maplecroft in a letter for forwarding to John Locke about the case of the Countess of Northumberland, 'Wherefore were she one of those poor people whom my lott engages me to attend (for I cure not the rich till my being in the grave makes me an Authority) I would take the following course . . .' Sydenham's own record in his writings of his patients indicates that many of them, if not rich, were of middling status.

[44] Nedham, *Medela*, pp. 216–17: 'But truly, tis much more honourable to acknowledge, that "the greatest part of what we do know, is the least part of what we doe not know", and thereupon to give all manner of encouragement to searching heads to make further enquiry . . . the Harvest is great, and the Labourers but few; what vast crops are appearing in the spacious Field of Nature, to find work for Ages to fetch them forth! therefore it were well, if all men were invited to the Profession and Practise of Physick and Medicinal Researches, in all Countreys of the world; especially the Nobility and Gentry, who by reason of their Estates and Interests, would be more able, and attain greater opportunities than other men, to enquire, and invent and spend their time in Practise especially among the Poor: which in former time (as we read) hath been the imployment of the greatest Princes.'

opportunity for the latter. As one reads Nedham further, it is clear that he also meant that one learns from the poor as well as practising on them for research. More simply, physicians like O'Dowde saw that the poor provided an opportunity to test out new approaches to medicine.[45] (This can also be read as another example of increasing medicalisation, with the poor starting to come under serious medical scrutiny. The usual interpretation is that this happened at the end of the eighteenth century and especially with 'Paris medicine' at the beginning of the nineteenth century.) The poor also had been identified as a group especially liable to the most dramatic epidemic of all, plague. Sydenham was not alone in focusing upon groups rather than on the individual.

Sydenham's conceptions of disease

Central to Sydenham's medicine was his perception of disease. His aim was to understand disease by observing it. His model was Hippocrates. Like the Helmontians, he saw Hippocrates as the uncorrupted father of medicine, who in a truly Baconian fashion had begun with observations and not with preconceived histories or hypotheses: 'the excellent Hippocrates arriv'd at the top of Physick, who laid the solid Foundation for building the Art of Physick upon, viz. "Nature cures Diseases" [more correctly: "our natures are the physicians of our diseases"]. And he deliver'd plainly the *Phaenomena* of every Disease, without pressing any Hypothesis for his Service, as may be seen in his Books of Diseases, Affections and the like.'[46]

---

[45] O'Dowde, *Poor Man's Physician*, p. 91; also see John Bellers, *An Essay towards the improvement of Physick. In twelve proposals. By which the lives of many thousands of the rich, as well as of the Poor, may be saved yearly. With an essay for imploying the able poor* . . . (London, 1714), reproduced in G. Clarke, *John Bellers, His Life, Times and Writings* (Routledge & Kegan Paul, London, 1987), p. 188: 'The more Visits the Physicians make to the *Poor*, they will have the greater Experience and consequently be the more Capable to help the *Nobility* and *Gentry* when they shall be Sick.'

[46] Thomas Sydenham, *The Whole Works of that Excellent Practical Physician, Dr. Thomas Sydenham* [hereafter *Whole Works*], trans. John Pechey, 10th edn (London, 1734), 'Author's Preface', sig. A5^r; this was the preface of the *Observationem Medicae circa Morborum Acutorum Historiam et Curationem* (1676) which Sydenham published as the third edition of the *Methodus Curandi Febres, Propriis Observationibus Superstructa* (1666). In fact, however, the two often differ; Pechey's translation is freer than that by R. G. Latham in *The Works of Thomas Sydenham M.D.* [hereafter *Works*] but is often closer to Sydenham's contemporary usage of language and influenced the eighteenth-century perception of Sydenham, whilst Latham made Sydenham into a nineteenth-century clinician. The quotation from Hippocrates, *Epidemics*, VI, 5,1, is also given in Latham's rendering: Sydenham, *Works*, vol. I, p. 16.

However, Sydenham differed from the Helmontians in concentrating upon the identification and classification of diseases. Sydenham's intention was to create a new classification of diseases that would replace or be a radical revision of the received catalogue of diseases, knowledge of whose names and symptoms stretched back to the classical world. It had remained largely unaltered, except for a few *ad hoc* additions of new diseases such as syphilis, and some Paracelsian and Helmontian emphases such as that placed on catarrh.

At first sight, it looks as if Sydenham echoed the Helmontian belief that diseases were 'quiddities' or things. Such a view was also in keeping with the new science's relegation of Aristotle's and Galen's primary qualities into secondary ones, formalised by Sydenham's friend, the philosopher John Locke. Hot and cold, etc. were no longer seen as real qualities but as the subjective impressions caused by the motion of particles. This destroyed the reality of subjective sensations and created a subjective–objective divide where before it had not existed. It became difficult to see disease as being caused by an imbalance of the four qualities, as now they were merely subjective, and it was easier to conceive disease as coming from the outside, objective world, or at least from objective material such as putrefaction lodged inside the body.

Sydenham's inspiration for a new description of diseases was Bacon's plea for natural histories devoid of 'fables' and 'needless Controversies'.[47] Diseases, wrote Sydenham, were like plants:

It is necessary that all Diseases should be reduced to certain and definite Species, with the same diligence we see it is done by Botanick Writers in their Herbals. For there are found Diseases that are reduc'd under the same Genus and Name, and, as to some Symptoms, are like one another; yet they are different in their Natures, and require a different way of Cure.[48]

Sydenham focused upon epidemic diseases. He saw them as being caused by the different constitutions of the air that existed in different years because in any one year a particular disease seemed to be the predominant epidemic (though he also discussed epidemic diseases such as scarlet fever, pleurisy and quinsy that could occur in any year and which he termed 'intercurrent fevers').[49] That there were different constitutions of the air also helped to explain why in

[47] Sydenham, *Whole Works*, sig. A3ᵛ.
[48] Ibid., sig. A3ᵛ.   [49] Ibid., pp. 185–8.

one year a medicine worked for a disease and in another it failed to do so. His studies of epidemics were based not on single observations but on a series of observations that produced the natural history of an epidemic.[50] In some ways he had in mind the model of plague when constructing his picture of epidemics. Plague, as we saw in chapter 6, had been seen as a disease of the air, some years being 'plague years'; it varied according to the seasons, and in a 'plague year' plague predominated and other diseases became like it.[51] Epidemics behaved in the same way.

However, Sydenham made a point of emphasising that the causes of epidemics remained 'occult', hidden and unknown, in contrast with the ready confidence with which the causes of plague had been listed by previous writers. According to Sydenham, 'A secret and inexplicable Alteration of the Air, infecting Mens Bodies' caused the acute diseases of epidemics, 'nor', stated Sydenham, 'do they at all depend on a particular Crasis [mixture] of the Blood and Humours, any otherwise than the occult Influence of the Air has imprinted the same upon them'.[52] This echoed Sydenham's refusal to create a classification of disease built around causes. He could not, he wrote, relate specific epidemics to specific alterations of the air, though to those who were used to assign names and causes to fevers by speculating about the changes that occurred to the blood and the humours it would appear very easy.[53] The refusal to assign causes to epidemics, except for the vague 'something in the air', together with the realisation that epidemics changed from year to year or after a number of years and were in any case difficult to describe, meant that Sydenham was unable to define diseases as distinct species. He saw himself, instead, as making a beginning to the very Baconian enterprise of collecting information about epidemics which others could complete. He therefore limited himself to analysing and

[50] Ibid., pp. 4–10.
[51] See for example ibid., p. 8, where Sydenham seems to write with the analogy of plague in mind: 'For it plainly appears, that whatsoever Disease prevails over the rest at that Season, will have the dominion over the rest for the whole Year; to whose Genius all the Epidemics that are Contemporaries with it, accommodate themselves, as far as it consists with their Nature.' To illustrate the change that can occur over time in the symptoms of an epidemic, Sydenham referred to the experience of plague, when initially deaths occurred suddenly before any symptoms had shown themselves, whilst later on plague seemed to weaken and it killed after a few days of illness: ibid., p. 119.
[52] Ibid., p. 3.
[53] Ibid., p. 10, with Latham's translation Sydenham, *Works*, vol. I, p. 40.

synthesising his observations of the epidemics 'that did rage from the Year 1661, to the Year 1676'.[54]

Sydenham focused on what would have normally been called the symptoms of a disease. As a good Baconian empiricist he believed that they gave the best and only knowledge of disease, for only symptoms could be observed, just as observations of plants allowed a botanist to distinguish and describe a particular species of plant. On this reading disease was less of a 'thing' in the Paracelsian and Helmontian sense and more of a collection of symptoms, and this anticipated eighteenth-century views of disease. Sydenham emphasised that unlike 'curious speculators' he was not concerned with remote causes hidden from the senses, as 'the Causes of most Diseases are wholly inscrutable'.[55] He clearly did not share in the Helmontians' confidence that there was an archeus and that they could discover its actions, nor in the Galenists' belief that they had uncovered the physiological powers of the body. Rather, Sydenham termed what he had observed in the patient 'immediate causes',[56] thus conflating symptoms and causes, and avoiding the charge that he was a mere empiricist. He also used terms such as 'method' and 'indications' which had been flourished by Galenists when they wanted to show that their medicine was better than that of the empirics.[57]

---

[54] Sydenham, *Whole Works*, p. 10. On the difficulty of describing and classifying epidemics Sydenham wrote, after stating that 'Fevers, arise from the secret Constitution of Years' and not 'from a morbifick Cause reserv'd in the Body', that, 'In a word, as it is very hard to reduce all the Species of Epidemicks into Classes, according to the variety of their *Phaenomena*, and to decypher the Idiopathyck Characters of each, and to accomodate a Method of Healing particular to every one; so also, because they do not invade in any certain Series of Years (at least not yet known) perhaps the Age of One Physician will not be sufficient to collect an exact *Apparatus* of Observations of them. But tho this Labour be so tedious, we must perform it before we can justly boast of anything we have done, fit to be remembered in explicating the various Series of those Diseases': p. 9; and, 'perhaps I have not so much as repeated all the Families of Epidemicks: Nor can I say that these Diseases, which in years past, whereof I now treat, did mutually succeed one another in that order we shall mention hereafter; will likewise continue to do so for Years to come. All that I pretend to do, is, to declare how this thing has been of late, and to confirm by the Observations of some few Years what relates to these Regions, and this City wherein we live; that I may offer my Mite for the beginning of a Work, which, if I am not mistaken, will be very much to the Advantage of Mankind, when it is perfected by Posterity, who may traverse the whole series of Epidemicks in Years to come': p. 10.

[55] Ibid., sig. A6ᵛ and Sydenham, *Works*, vol. I, p. 20.

[56] Sydenham, *Whole Works*, sig. A6ᵛ, and *Works*, vol. I, p. 20.

[57] See Donald G. Bates, 'Sydenham and the Medical Meaning of "Method"', *Bulletin of the History of Medicine*, 51, 1977, 324–38.

Disease as nature's healing process

Sydenham believed that nature has a curative method, but – and here Sydenham must have had in mind the ancient dual image of medicine as healing and harming – when she applies it the patient can become ill as well as healthy. Disease was brought about by nature's attempt to cure. Disease was nature's response to a disorder, whether coming from the air or, as in chronic diseases, from putrefaction within the body:

Nature provided for her self such a Method and Concatenation of Symptoms, as that she might exclude the peccant matter thereby which would otherwise ruin the whole Fabrick [of the body]; and she would much often than she does, attain Health by these harsh means, if she were not forced out of her Course by the Ignorant. But tho she be left to her self, she destroys the Man, either by doing too much or too little by her self; and so obeys resistless Fate . . .[58]

The methods that nature used to cure a disease showed themselves as the symptoms or immediate causes, making up the description of the disease. Hence a true description of a disease provided clues or indications as to how nature was setting about to cure it, and how the physician could help or restrain nature. In other words, Sydenham's description and classification of disease was integral to his method of healing. The confusion of one disease for another, the lumping of two or more together, and the distortion of accurate descriptions of disease by making them 'serve an Hypothesis', was 'the reason why the *Materia Medica* is so wonderfully increas'd and to so little purpose'.[59] A true, minutely-accurate description of each species of disease not only would aid the physician in its diagnosis but would also indicate how it could be cured:

A Physician may as certainly take the curative Indications from the smallest Circumstances of the Disease, as he does the Diagnostick from them: And therefore I have often thought, if we had an exact History of every Disease, we should never want a Remedy suitable to it, the various *Phaenomena* of it plainly shewing the way we ought to proceed in; which *Phaenomena*, if they were carefully compar'd one with another, would lead us to those obvious Indications, which are taken truly from Nature, and not from the Errors of Fancy.[60]

Sydenham realised that the Galenic method of healing had greatly increased the *materia medica*: because of its focus on the

---

[58] Sydenham, *Whole Works*, p. 2.   [59] Ibid., sig. A4ʳ.   [60] Ibid., sig. A5ʳ.

individual patient the method legitimised one-off remedies. But nature's indications to the physician came from the disease, not from the individual patient as Galenic physicians had believed should be the case. Sydenham argued that repeated 'experiments' from a large number of cases were needed to establish not only a description of a disease but also its treatment; observations of particular cases were not so useful because the remedy used might only be successful in one or two cases and not universally. A consequence of publicising 'that this Disease was once, or oftener cured by this Remedy' was that another 'unknown Medicine is added to the almost infinite heap of celebrated Medicines', and 'what advantage', asked Sydenham, is in that?[61] In treating diseases rather than patients, and with a few rather than many remedies, Sydenham echoed the practice of Helmontians and empirics. Moreover, Sydenham's wish to apply Baconian induction to medicine had the effect of making the individual patient anonymous, hidden as one amongst the many from which knowledge would come, and this is part of the process that took shape in the later seventeenth century, whereby medicine changed from being patient-centred to being disease-centred. The commercialisation of remedies was a major factor in this, and it is significant that Sydenham's argument for a few rather than many medicines fitted, unconsciously, into the economic reasoning that would have a few remedies producing more profit than many diverse products.[62] More specifically, Sydenham helped in the process by giving it respectability, showing that it followed from applying the new philosophy of Bacon and that it also reflected the true, ancient medicine.

Sydenham was anxious to avoid the accusation of being an empiric. He wanted his medicine to be respectable, to have a method, albeit not the Galenic, so he argued that his method of healing was the original method of Hippocrates, founded upon the knowledge of immediate causes.[63] He also emphasised that his book on acute diseases would not provide the reader with 'a great number of remedies'. Instead, he was concerned with indications, the foundation of patient-centred Galenic medicine. Although Sydenham changed the meaning of indications, he still used them, as had

[61] Sydenham, *Whole Works*, sig. A5ᵛ; also *Works*, vol. I, p. 17.
[62] Sydenham advertised 'Dr Goddard's drops' prepared by Dr Goodhall as preferable to all other volatile spirits: *Whole Works*, sig. A7ᵛ, and *Works*, vol. I, 22.
[63] Sydenham, *Whole Works*, sig. A6ʳ, and *Works*, vol. I, p. 18.

Galenic practitioners, to differentiate the true physician from the empiric, 'for', he wrote, 'the Practice of Physick chiefly consists in this, viz, in being able to find the genuine Indications, and not Remedies to answer them: and they that have not observed this, have instructed [or given remedies to] Empiricks to imitate Physicians'.[64]

Sydenham on putrefaction

The true method of cure in acute diseases was to discover how nature set about the process of cure. What was it that nature did? She evacuated morbific putrid matter from the body. In this respect, Sydenham was very traditional. He placed the long-standing view of putrefaction as disease at the centre of his medicine, though he did not define it as disease but as the disorder against which nature acted. Its presence was the reason why nature initiated the process of cure and of disease:

> Reason dictates, if I judge right, that a Disease is nothing else, but Nature's Endeavour to thrust forth with all her might the morbifick Matter for the Health of the Patient, tho the Cause of it be contrary to Nature: For seeing it has pleased GOD, the Governor of all Things, that Human Nature should be fitted to receive the various Impressions that come from abroad, it could not be, but it must be subject also to many Diseases; which partly proceed from Particles of Air, ill agreeing with the Body, which when they have insinuated themselves into it, and are mixed with the Blood, affect the whole with a morbifick Contagion; partly from the various Ferments or Putrefaction of Humours, which are detained in the Body beyond their due time, because it was not able to digest or evacuate them, either upon the account of their Bulk, being too great, or the Incongruity of their Quality.[65]

Sydenham envisaged nature acting as a physician, and, crucially for Sydenham's future reception into the pantheon of eighteenth-century medical heroes, she used the physician's traditional therapeutic procedures of evacuation to get rid of the traditional putrid matter of disease. The philosophy of medicine changed, but much of its practice remained essentially unchanged and Sydenham typified this mix of the new and the old.

To the comment that he had made nature into a human physician, Sydenham would have replied that he had observed nature evacuating disease from the body. Despite his suspicion of causal accounts of disease drawn from speculation rather than from observation, he

---

[64] Sydenham, *Whole Works*, sig. A8ʳ.   [65] Ibid., pp. 1–2.

pictured and interpreted events happening inside and outside the body, and these confirmed that nature cured by evacuation. 'What', he asked, 'is the Plague but a Complication of Symptoms, by which Nature uses to cast out the malignant Particles, by Imposthumes in the Emunctories [glands], or other Eruptions, that were drawn in by the Air?'[66] The events did not have to be obvious extrusions of putrid material, as in the plague buboes; other pathological processes such as the swelling and inflammation of gout and fever were also in Sydenham's view part of nature's evacuative, purifying processes. Disease and therapy were thus integrated with each other:

What is the Gout, but Nature's Contrivance to purify the Blood of old Men, and to purge the deep parts of the Body. . . But Nature performs this Office sometimes quicker, and sometimes slower, according to the different Methods she uses to exclude the morbifick Cause; for when she requires the help of a Fever, whereby she may be able to separate the vitiated Particles from the Blood, and afterwards expel them, either by Sweat, a Looseness, or some Eruptions, or the like Evacuations.[67]

Putrefaction, inner, possibly poisonous, filth as diseased matter, if not the disease itself, therefore figured large in Sydenham's conception of illness and produced a fixed mind set centred around evacuative procedures that would have been recognised by a sixteenth-century physician. For instance, he justified vomiting at the beginning of the epidemic fever of 1661–64, because:

by this means the Sick may be preserved from those dreadful Symptoms that rise from the Filth of such Humours as lurk in the Stomach and neighbouring Parts . . . which either by reason of their Substance past into the innermost Parts of the Body, and are mingled with the Blood, or because they are kept too long in the Body, wax worse, and put on a venemous Quality, which they continually import to the Blood as it passes by their Nest.[68]

Observation of patients suffering from the same disease, that is, being cured of the same disorder by nature, was essential before the physician could treat a patient. How nature cured the patient, how she applied her method of healing, indicated to the physician the kind of disease and how it should be cured. For instance, in the same epidemic fever of 1661–4, Sydenham noted how 'I carefully inquire whether the Sick was inclin'd to Nauseousness or Vomiting at the beginning of the Fever: and if so, I presently [immediately] order a

[66] Ibid., p. 2.   [67] Ibid.   [68] Ibid., p. 18.

Vomit, unless some great Weakness of the Patient, or the tender Age forbid it.' If nature or the physician does not make the patient vomit, then a 'Looseness [diarrhoea] is the chief and most frequent [of the "difficult symptoms"], which commonly follows in the Declination of the Fever, when Vomits were omitted, altho indicated'. Sydenham envisaged nature as a sophisticated, if at times brutal, healer, her indication of a vomit being an attempt to correct the consequences of her therapy: 'for in the Progress of the Disease, when Nature has somewhat quell'd the malignant Humour in the Stomach, and thrust it down to the Guts [the therapy], they are so corroded by a continual Flux of a sharp Humour from this Fountain in the Stomach, that a Looseness must neccessarily follow [the consequences of nature's therapy]'.[69]

By now it should be clear that in some of the essentials of his medicine Sydenham built upon well-established notions. Like other physicians, despite his professed dislike of anatomy and of giving causes that had not been derived from observations, he slid easily into describing the story of what was happening in the body, as with the malignant humour being thrust into the guts and corroding them. Sydenham did not hesitate to narrate the progress of a disease, charted by means of anatomical signposts and enlivened by vivid metaphors, as with the 'scraping' in the passage below, where Sydenham describes the development of the bloody flux or bloody diarrhoea of 'part of the Year 1669, and of the Years 70, 71, 72':

at length the Guts seem to be affected successively downwards, till the Disease is thrust down the right Gut, and ends in a *Tenesmus* [a continual straining to void the contents of the bowels or bladder, but with little or no discharge] . . . the excrementitious Stools cause great pain in the Bowels, the Excrements as they pass through scraping the small Guts, whereas the mucous stools at the same time molest the right Gut wherein alone the Matter is made, and from whence 'tis ejected.[70]

In his conception of disease as nature's healing process, Sydenham was original; in his wish for a natural history of diseases and in his focus on epidemic diseases, he put medicine abreast of the times; in his equation of symptoms or immediate causes with disease as nature's method of healing, he created a bridge of respectability joining empirical medicine with learned medicine. In a period of transition, Sydenham helped to transform and move medicine from

[69] Ibid., p. 16.   [70] Ibid., p. 118.

being patient-centred to disease-centred, a transformation which in terms of its social, economic and scientific ramifications was not completed until the twentieth century.

However, Sydenham was also on the right side, in eighteenth-century terms, in keeping corruption and putrefaction and their evacuation at the centre of his and nature's therapeutics. Unlike the Helmontians, he had no qualms about bleeding, purging, vomiting, etc. Where he disagreed with his fellow physicians was in the details. The physician who was ignorant of nature's indications of cure might apply remedies that would either frustrate nature, or weaken or exacerbate her effects. Some standard practices Sydenham believed were wrong because of such ignorance; so, for instance, he went against orthodoxy by bleeding in cases of plague (see chapter 7) and in replacing the heating treatment used in smallpox for one based on blood-letting and purging. He also retained regimen and the six non-naturals in his practice, as did many eighteenth-century physicians.[71] Sydenham's attack on learned medicine, unlike that of the Helmontians, concentrated less on destroying its structure and its epistemological and social claims to authority, and more on reconstituting some of its parts.

Sydenham and remedies

In one area, Sydenham was *sui generis*. Unlike some of his contemporaries and successors he was cautious about the effectiveness of medicines. Although, like the Helmontians and commercial drug sellers, he argued for a limited number of remedies for diseases, in presenting his medicine to his readers he downplayed their importance. He stressed that doing nothing could often be the best policy; for instance, in a case of 'a virtuous Matron, of good quality' whose periods had stopped, Sydenham 'perceived she would recover, if I did nothing, I committed all to Time by much the best and most successful Physician'.[72] Sydenham noted that when he was unsure

---

[71] Ibid., pp. 5, 14.

[72] Ibid., p. 334; 'Of Hysterick Diseases', translation of the *Dissertatio Epistolaris ... de Observationibus Nuperis Circa Curationem Variolerum Confluentium nec non de Affectione Hysterica* (London, 1682), addressed to Rev. William Cole. Sydenham reported that his policy was resisted: the patient's waiting woman 'whom I had kept hitherto from doing Mischief by her Over-officiousness, persuaded the Husband to have a vein opened instantly in the Wife's foot; which being performed, the Hysterick Fits so far prevailed, that within a few Hours she was seized with Convulsions, and soon after with Death, that ends all our miseries'.

what method of cure to use, and when the patient got no worse from one day to the next, then therapeutic nihilism was the best policy, even if the patient and onlookers did not agree.[73] Moreover, following Hippocrates, Sydenham argued that all that the physician does is to help or restrain nature's attempts to expel disease, and that nature can cure with the help of 'a few simple Forms of Remedies, and sometimes without any'.[74]

He extolled the virtues of a limited range of remedies such as Dr Goddard's pills, the Peruvian bark or cinchona, and opiates,[75] but he believed very few remedies had been discovered that were specific against particular diseases. In chronic diseases where nature did not have a method to cure them, specifics that destroyed 'the Species of the Disease' were especially needed. Using the language of the new philosophy, Sydenham argued that the old cure by contrary quality was useless, for the secondary qualities of heat, cold, etc. could not cure a disease 'whose Essence consists of none of these'. Not only were specifics based on the cure by contrary quality discounted, but so too were remedies that evacuated. For instance, wrote Sydenham, mercury and sarsaparilla were thought to be specifics against syphilis, but if they were true specifics they would act not by evacuation, by salivation or sweating respectively, but by some other property. Such medicines were specific for evacuation rather than for a particular disease; otherwise one would say, wrote Sydenham, that the lancet is specific for pleurisy. In Sydenham's view the only specific that had so far been discovered, despite the belief that many specifics existed, was the Peruvian bark for intermittent fevers, especially quartans.[76]

[73] Ibid., pp. 334–5; Sydenham was aware that patients would contrast his wait-and-see practice unfavourably with that of empirics and physicians. See also p. 184: 'But it is a sad thing, that most of the Sick do not understand, that it is as much the part of a skilful Physician sometimes to do nothing, as at other times to give the most effectual Remedies; and so they will not receive the benefit of a just and fair Proceeding, but count them either the Effects of Negligence or Ignorance: whereas [they think] the most ignorant Quack knows how to add Medicine to Medicine, as well as the most prudent Physician'; not in *Works*, vol. I, p. 237, but is in *Thomae Sydenham . . . Opera Omnia Medica*, 9th edn (Geneva, 1696), p. 293.

[74] Ibid., sig. A5^r; also Sydenham *Works*, vol. I, p. 17.

[75] On the last two see Sydenham, *Whole Works*, sig. A7^r, p. 123, and *Works*, vol. I, pp. 22, 173.

[76] Sydenham, *Whole Works*, sig. A7^{r-v}, *Works*, vol. I, pp. 21–2, and Latham's 'Life of Sydenham', *Works*, I, pp. lxxiv–lxxx. Sydenham noted that, until the advent of the bark, agues and quartans had been 'call'd *Opprobia Medicorum*, and were truly a Reproach to Physicians'. He discussed the initial high hopes for the bark, the sense of let-down when patients died, its subsequent disuse and his belief in its efficacy if taken with methodical care at the right time in the course of the disease: *Whole Works*, pp. 224–9, 'Dr. Sydenham's

Sydenham conceded in a traditional manner that specifics would
be found, for God's bounty and care had provided 'near at hand in
every Country' cures for great diseases. In the persona of a moderate
or modern traditionalist, he wrote that he preferred plant remedies,
adding that he would not condemn the 'excellent Medicines' of
chemistry 'found by the Industry and Labour of Men'.[77] However,
throughout Sydenham's writings there is a constant note of caution
about the usefulness of contemporary remedies. For instance, in
chronic diseases where Sydenham believed that nature alone could
not cure, as she did not have sufficient power to expel the body's ill,
corrupt matter, he argued that specific remedies were needed.[78] But
he rejected what was available. For gout, from which he suffered, the
traditional cooling treatments were, he wrote, dangerous, and he
concluded that, of other 'external remedies to ease the Pain of the
Gout, I hitherto know none, tho' I have tried many in myself and
others . . . And I confidently affirm, that the greatest Part of those
who have in the Gout, have not been so properly killed by the
Disease as by an improper Use of Medicines.'[79] Instead, he advised
patients to improve their lifestyle and to pay attention to regimen,
especially diet and exercise. Though here he fell back on the learned
physician's standby, Sydenham, like the Helmontians and empirics
of his time, and like some practitioners of modern scientific medicine
who believe in therapeutic magic bullets, envisaged a specific curing
a chronic disease without any need for advice on lifestyle. Moreover,
such a specific could be discovered without any prior theory
to explain its action; indeed in Sydenham's view much of the failure
of traditional therapeutics stemmed from physicians' fitting their
practice to their theory. Sydenham could write this because of the

plain Instance whereof we have in the Discovery of the Peruvian Bark, the
best Specifick for Agues. For how many Ages were the Wits of the most
diligent Men exercised in finding out the Cause of Agues, whereby
everyone adopted a Practice best agreeing to the Theory he had framed
. . . in which placing relating the various Species of Intermittents in[to] the
various Humours abounding in the Body, they were wont to direct the

Two Epistles: The First of Epidemical Disease from the Year 1675 to the Year 1680 . . .
The Second, of the History and Cure of the French Pox . . .' first published as the *Epistolae
Responsariae Duae* (London, 1680).
[77] Sydenham, *Whole Works*, sig. A7^v.
[78] Ibid., sig. A7^r.
[79] Ibid., p. 379, *A Treatise of the Gout and Dropsy*, first published as *Tractatus de Podagra et Hydrope*
(London, 1683).

Method of Cure to the Alteration and Evacuation of these Humours. But how unsuccessfully they managed it, the ill Success of their Endeavours, but especially the happier use of the Bark, makes manifest; by the Help whereof now, not regarding these Humours, nor Diet or *Regimen*, by only observing a due Method of giving the Bark, we do the Business effectually.[80]

But the bark was the only specific that had been discovered so far, according to Sydenham. In the meantime, until others were found, he proceeded by a mixture of cautious scepticism, expectant do-nothing treatment, the vigorous use of bleeding and purging, and the use of a few compound remedies that purged or strengthened.[81]

Medicines, Physicians and Apothecaries

Sydenham was a lone voice urging general scepticism about reme-dies. Many in the medical marketplace focused their attention on them and eagerly advertised their virtues. Empirics, as well as Helmontians, feverishly sold the secret preparations that they claimed cured whole classes of diseases. The learned physicians also turned their attention to medicines as never before, partly to rebut the claims of the medical chemists, as in the *Pharmacologia Anti-Empirica or a Rational Discourse of Remedies* (1683) by Walter Harris, one of the royal physicians. Harris' book was a destructive piece of polemic, designed to show the danger and lack of healing power of chemical remedies, the pretentious obscurity of chemical philosophy and the similarity of medical chemists to mountebanks.[82] The question of who could make remedies was also the focus of some physicians, especially those such as Christopher Merrett, Daniel

---

[80] Ibid., p. 383.

[81] Sydenham, unlike many in the medical marketplace, publicised the ingredients of his remedies, so they could be made by patient and practitioner alike. He also preferred compounds to simples, believing that they 'are better . . . to concoct the Humours, than any Simple . . . For tho' when we have Need of the specifick Virtue of any Medicine, that Rule holds good, The simpler it is, the better it is; yet when we design to cure the Sick, by satisfying this or that Indication, every Ingredient contributes somewhat for the Cure of the Disease; and in this Case [internal medicines to concoct and purify the blood in gout], the greater the Number of Simples is, the more powerfully does the Remedy work': ibid., p. 357. It should be noted that Sydenham also used cooling and heating remedies, not so much because of any belief in the cure by contrary, but because they were indicated by nature's actions as in the inflammation of gout which required bleeding, and a cooling medicinal drink: ibid., p. 201.

[82] Walter Harris, *Pharmacologia Anti-Empirica or a Rational Discourse of Remedies* (London, 1683), for instance pp. 38–48, 88–103, at sig. a1^r–a2^r (Preface) Harris gives a succinct if negative account of the claims of the chemists.

Coxe and Jonathan Goddard who inhabited both the new experimental world of the Royal Society and the older one of the learned medicine of the College of Physicians, and who claimed the right to make their own remedies rather than having to rely on the apothecaries. It was ostensibly an attempt to avoid the alleged counterfeiting and adulterating practices of the apothecaries, and to avoid patients having contact with them and being inveigled into longer and more expensive treatments than were necessary. Making their own remedies was also a way for physicians to increase their income, whilst at the same time stopping the apothecaries from practising medicine. This was a war of words which had no immediate results, though the apothecaries at the end of the century gained the legal right to practise medicine. But the controversy illustrates how medicines were on centre stage, as well as showing how it was becoming increasingly feasible that the formal demarcations between physicians and apothecaries could be broken down. The latter can be explained, as Harold Cook has done, by the weakness of the College of Physicians. One can add to that the immense commercial importance of medicines and their increasing status as the major part of medicine, which made it likely that the practice of medicine would be equated by some with medicines and so appear to lie across the boundaries of physic and pharmacy.[83]

Much of the rhetoric in the controversy was traditional, for example, the accusation that apothecaries adulterated their medicines had been repeated across the ages. It was given fresh force by being made at a time when Helmontians had highlighted the purity of medicines and had insisted that the roles of practitioner and pharmacist be combined, the practitioner being the guarantor of his own medicines. Both sides accepted that 'apothecary-physicians' or

---

[83] Cook, *Decline*, pp. 167–78. Harold Cook, 'The Rose Case Reconsidered: Physicians, Apothecaries, and the Law in Augustan England', *Journal of the History of Medicine and Allied Sciences*, 45, 1990, 527–55; Christopher Merrett, *The accomplisht physician, the honest apothecary, and the skilful chyrurgeon, detecting their necessary connection, and dependance on each other. Withall a Discovery of the Frauds of the Quacking Empirick, the Praescribing Surgeon, and the Practicing Apothecary* (London, 1670), and *A Short View of the Frauds, and Abuses committed by Apothecaries; . . . And of the only Remedy thereof by Physicians making their own Medicines* (London, 1669); [Daniel Coxe], *A Discourse, wherein the Interest of the Patient in Reference to Physick and Physicians is Soberly Debated. Many Abuses of the Apothecaries in the Preparing their Medicines are Detected, and Their Unfitness for Practice Discovered, Together with the Reasons and Advantages of Physicians preparing their own Medicines* (London, 1669); Jonathan Goddard, *A Discourse setting forth the unhappy condition of the practice of physick in London, and offering some means to put it into a better; for the interest of patients, no less, or rather much more, then of physicians* (London, 1670).

'practicing-apothecaries' existed (see chapter 1).[84] Their presence breached, nevertheless, the formal barriers erected between physicians and apothecaries. The eruption of the controversy was a sign that medicine was going through a transformation that put under stress not only theoretical but also institutional coherences, however formal and notional. At such times the notional often acquires numinous significance.

The crux of the matter was whether medicine was a simple art, simply learnt by experience and imitation. The apothecaries were reported by Daniel Coxe, 'modern' physician and a chief protagonist in the controversy, as claiming they had the right to 'the liberty of Practicing' because they '. . . understand the Symptoms and Cures of Diseases; if not as well as some Physicians, yet better then many, at least than the young and unexperienced. They have been present at the Death, and Recovery of many Patients; and therefore have had Opportunity to observe the course of the Distempers, and procedures of Physicians: That they have kept exact Diaries of these Transactions, What Medicines the Physician prescribed; especially if they proved successful.'[85] In turn, some of the apothecaries argued that they could tell from previous experience of a physician's prescribing practice what he would order for any particular disease, regardless of the type of patient, that in other words a physician had standard treatments despite the rhetoric of individualised treatment.[86]

The issue between the physicians and apothecaries also concerned how a practitioner should be educated. The apothecaries, Coxe wrote, claimed to be taught medical practice through a form of apprenticeship, learning from 'an Eminent Practioner of Physick, who hath been free in his communications to him; and this is by the Vulgar accounted sufficient to constitute a person, who hath been in

---

[84] Merrett, *A Short View of the Frauds*, pp. 14–15; Anon. *Lex Talionis; Sive Vindiciae Pharmacoporum: Or a Short Reply to Dr. Merrett's Book; and Others, Written against the Apothecaries: Wherein may be Discovered the Frauds and Abuses Committed by Doctors Professing and Practising Pharmacy* (London, 1670), sig. B3^r. The authors of *Lex Talionis* were also sensitive to the fact that chemists, Helmontians and empirics threatened their craft: sigs. D1^v, E3^v. Cook, *Decline*, p. 176 believes that Gideon Harvey was correct in writing that it was written by a 'cabal' of four or five 'Practising Apothecaries', citing the *Accomplisht Physician*, p. 91.

[85] Coxe, *A Discourse*, p. 74.

[86] Ibid., pp. 75–6: 'I have heard several of the Apothecaries confidently (not to say impudently) affirm they were so throughly acquainted with such mens Practice, naming some eminent Physicians, that if they knew the Case, they would lay a Wager they did exactly Predict before they took Pen in Hand what they would Prescribe.'

such circumstances an able Physitian: And the best plea the Apothecaries have, is, that they have collected the Practice of some worthy Physitian for most Diseases'.[87] Physicians, on the other hand, had the benefit of access to the knowledge of physicians across the ages. As we have seen in chapters 2 and 3, medical 'learning' involved the accumulation of theories and observations that went to make up the accounts of diseases, their signs and remedies. In some way the enterprise of learning could be made to appear, with the addition of terms such as experiment, similar to a modern Baconian co-operative research endeavour:

> there is no Physitian but injoys the benefit of the writings of many hundred excellent persons, that were eminent in the same faculty before him: These have faithfully communicated their experiments and observations of the causes and symptoms of diseases, and of their cures; what methods and Medicines they found most beneficial, what things are injurious and to be avoided: And there are others who have left us their writings concerning the virtues of most Simple and Compounded Medicines, in what cases they have been found effectual.

Coxe added that past medical knowledge provided precedents upon which physicians could model their treatments, 'and many (which is perhaps the most profitable way of writing) have left us intire books of Medical Observations, to which Physitians, who have a Scheme of them in their memories have recourse in difficult cases, and by Analogy know how to proceed, as do the Lawyers, on other occasions'.[88] In keeping with the trend of the times, he also tacitly accepted the concept of medical apprenticeship, the physician being apprentice to many past masters. 'Great labour, Industry and Sagacity' were required to gather the 'scattered' knowledge of the past, 'this treasure', which, Coxe believed, was beyond the apothecaries, 'as they do not trouble themselves to search any other Records than they themselves have made of Physicians Prescripts'.

---

[87] Ibid., p. 198.

[88] Ibid., pp. 198–99, see also pp. 79–80 where Coxe asked, 'Now the great question is, how Physicians come by the knowledge of these admirable Properties [of specific remedies]?' He considered but rejected, 'natural Instinct' and 'Divine inspiration'. He showed his awareness of the latest trends by adding, 'I am not ignorant that some talk of a *Medicina Adepta*, but the boldest and most talkative Apothecary I ever yet met with, had not the slightest Pretensions to it; and no wonder for till they leave off their fraudulent unworthy Practices, of all men I know in the world, they have the least Reason to expect revelations in this kind, supposing there were such.' Coxe concluded, 'since there are no other means besides, Physicians must derive this knowledge from Communications, either of living or dead Physicians; or from their own Experience and Observations': ibid., pp. 80–1.

Again, Coxe was aware of contemporary thinking when he conceded, 'let us suppose with some that Physick is altogether Empyrical, being rather a Mass of Experiments then a Science perfectly formed and established on sound unquestionable verities'. But, he argued, the 'studied Physitian' must be judged to be the best; he is the one who 'is furnished with most and best experiments, either from his own observation, or by reading of books which afford him the experiments of all the rest of the world, and can best conclude from the Analogy, Correspondence and Harmony, they have one to another'.[89] In other words, a learned empirical physician was not a contradiction in terms, especially if he possessed what Aristotelian philosophers would have called the 'habitus' or disposition of the mind imparted by education to enable him to order and make sense of the information and then apply it in practice. Such a point of view helped to justify university medical education in the eighteenth century.

The reply of the apothecaries in the anonymous *Lex Talionis; Sive Vindiciae Pharmacoporum* (*The Law of Retribution; Or the Vindication of the Apothecaries*) (1670) was to deny that they based their practice on doctors' prescriptions; rather they claimed that an apothecary, like other practitioners, 'knows it is absolutely necessary to understand the *Diagnostick* and *Prognostick* of Diseases as a Guide to the *Therapeutick*, which the practising Apothecary questionless is not, or should not be ignorant of'.[90] Like the physician, the practising apothecary needed to know the theory of medicine, but there was no need to go to university for this; he could acquire the theory from reading a few books and become 'a rational Learned Apothecary', who by combining his own observations with theory 'may be better fitted for Practice, and I would sooner employ him than many Physicians'.[91]

The changes in natural philosophy and medicine and in the subsequent developments in the theory of medicine were celebrated by both groups as part of the triumphal progress of knowledge. The apothecary-physician could, according to the authors of *Lex Talionis*, learn either from Galenic writers, or from those who wrote after the discovery of the circulation of the blood, especially Willis.[92] But, to the accusation of the physicians that the apothecaries were 'wholly

---

[89] Ibid., pp. 199–200.
[90] [Anon.], *Lex Talionis*, sigs. C3ᵛ, D3ᵛ.   [91] Ibid., sigs. E1ʳ⁻ᵛ.
[92] Ibid., E1ʳ⁻ᵛ; the texts recommended were those of Nicolas de la Framboisière ('Frambesarius'), Riverius and Primrose, as well as Willis.

ignorant of Philosophy, and the very Elements of the Art', the reply was, 'so were they [the physicians] (till of late they were better discovered) and in Anatomy [also]'.[93] The entire medical knowledge of the past did not have to be learnt because:

Physick as to the pathological part, is much bettered and amended of Late by the industrious Labours of some Persons in *Anatomy*, and the *Circulation of the Blood*, first discovered by the Renowned Dr. *Harvey*, which before his time *Physitians* did for the most part practise *more Empericorum* [like empirics], not truly understanding the reason or Causes of Diseases, which since have been admirably demonstrated and made out by that eminent and Learned Gentleman Dr. Willis, and many other Worthy Persons besides.[94]

However, therapeutics remained 'much the same': 'we find the Medicines not much altered, and the same Specificks used in the Cure of Diseases as formerly'.[95] This may at first sound surprising, for the *materia medica* had been transformed by the advent of chemical remedies. A particular sub-text here is that the critics of the apothecaries were pointing out that 'Druggists, Chymists, Sellers of Strong-waters and Oyls have arose distinct from each other', since the original legislation in the early sixteenth century that set out the relationship between the College of Physicians and the apothecaries. Recognition of such rival groups was not in the interests of the apothecaries, hence the claim of no real change in therapeutics.[96] But more fundamental was the increasingly common perception that medical theory and anatomy had progressed, whilst therapeutics was no more successful than it had been. Such a view may have motivated Sydenham, who expected the former to benefit the latter, to decry anatomy and medical theorising. But by and large, if one can generalise about a highly complex and shifting situation, medical theorising and the search for new, more effective drugs continued side by side. The perceived lack of progress in remedies, however, paradoxically served to diminish the significance, status

[93] Ibid., sig. D2^r.

[94] Ibid., C1^v; the circulation of the blood was often (wrongly, if Harvey's intentions are considered) incorporated into the new philosophy, and seen as the dividing point between the old and the new medicine. In *Lex Talionis*, sig. E1^v, it is clear from the discussion of Willis' works 'On Fermentation' and 'On Fevers' that the new philosophy has replaced the old: 'But since the finding out the Circulation of the Blood by the renowned Harvy, get Dr. Willis his Book (viz) his *De fermentatione*, the understanding of it well, will be Philosophy enough . . . and his Book *De Febribus* . . . in which the Causes of Diseases are most learnedly and judiciously discoursed'; there follows a description of the properties of blood according to Willis' mix of chemical-particulate theories.

[95] Ibid., E2^r, C2^r.   [96] Merrett, *A Short View of the Frauds*, p. 22.

and reach of medical theory. Though the apothecaries in *Lex Talionis* cheered the recent progress of medical theory and were not averse to sharing in the status that still surrounded modern learned medicine, they also claimed the territory occupied by remedies as their own, with the implication that medical theorising had not benefited the practice of medicine centred on remedies.

THOMAS WILLIS: OLD STORIES OF DISEASE AND REMEDIES MODERNISED

The links between the old and the new in pathology/aetiology were not completely broken. One could still be a learned rational physician, albeit a modern one, by giving the causes of disease and contructing accounts of the hidden happenings occurring inside the body, using anatomical signposting and the new language of chemistry and mechanics. Such language described the ancient cause of disease, putrefaction and corruption, and was linked to the perennial metaphors of attack upon the body and of its defence. Thomas Willis is perhaps the most significant example of the learned modern medical writer. He not only explained fevers and other ills with a mix of the old and the new in his narratives of disease inside the body, but he also applied the same age-old technique of story-telling in his account of how remedies worked. Willis favoured chemical medicines as well as the traditional plant-based *materia medica*. Though not a Galenist, he still valued the ability of learned medicine to give rational or causal accounts of empirical findings. His *Pharmaceutice Rationalis* (1674–5) was a sustained attempt to do for remedies what Galenic medicine had done for diseases: to give a narrative or causal account of the internal happenings in the body when remedies entered it. His intention, at a time when the country was full of empirical remedies, was to set out rational explanations of 'Medicinal Operations', 'that the Mechanical Means of the Working of Medicines in our Bodies might be laid open'. Up to that time these 'were either neglected or ignored . . . the greatest Impediment that Physick is not come to its perfection, and its whole System rightly framed'. Willis consciously saw himself as describing the hidden effects of medicines in the theatre of the body. He wrote that it had

not yet [been] sufficiently and clearly detected; to wit, what the *Weapons* of those *Champions* are, what Furniture [equipment], what force and Resistance they have, also what Action, Passion, and Reaction may be between the Particles of the Medicine and the Spirits, Humors, and Solid Parts. But since almost the whole business of the *Pharmaceutick Drame* is acted behind the Curtain, therefore the various congressions of *Particles*, 'Fermentation's, *Impulses*, and other diversities of Motions, which performed within, lye hid from the Senses, are to be searched out by a more deep Scrutiny of the Intellect, which if it may be at last performed, there is nothing more will be desired, whereby *Physick* being performed in all its parts, may grow to a true Science and be practised with greater certainty, not inferiour to the Mathematicks.[97]

Willis stressed that anatomy was essential for 'the better laying open of the ways of the whole curing by Medicines', and he provided anatomical descriptions of the parts and connections in the geography of the body at the beginning of the *Pharmaceutice Rationalis*.[98] Then 'Having thus marked out, as it were, the Place of Medicinal action, or at least lightly shadowed forth the first scene thereof', Willis proceeded to narrate the different activities of therapeutic procedures and remedies inside the body. For instance, medicines that produced vomiting had to have particular physical characteristics that would allow them to play their roles in the invisible story that Willis' 'intellect' or imagination brought to light:

All Medicines that you would have to work by Vomit rather than by Stool, ought to consist of such particles, as being irksom, or at least disagreeable to Nature, may likewise be of such quality or quantity, that they cannot be either totally overpowered by the stomach, or so long endured by it, till they may be by degrees wiped off from the fibres or hairy veil thereof, and carried out of the Pylorus [the opening from the stomach to the intestines] with other juices by little and little. Now if those kind of particles do either vellicate or twinge the fibres of the stomach too violently, or stick to it too fast, or disturb or stretch it with their motion, immediately the fleshy fibres are ready for an expulsion, and then by instinct of Nature they are the rather contracted in such a manner, as they may throw off what is offensive with the greater force and the nearest way.[99]

Willis created integrated narratives of the actions of medicines upon diseases as they developed in the body (as in, for example, his

---

[97] Willis, *Practice of Physick, Pharmaceutice Rationalis*, part 1, Preface, sigs. A4ʳ⁻ᵛ. Willis stated that this certainty would allow medicines to be prescribed efficaciously and certainly, in contrast with the dangerous practices of the 'Pseudochymists'.

[98] Ibid., sig. A3ʳ. Willis, on pp. 1–2, set out the general geography in which medicines worked, which was divided into three regions: first, the 'passages' such as the stomach, guts, etc., second the 'Mass of Blood, with all its bloudy appendages, as the *Praecordia*, the Liver, Spleen etc', and third, the 'Brain, and Nerves'; in addition medicines worked on the animal spirits or humours that lodged in the fibres and parts of the body.

[99] Ibid., part 1, p. 20.

account of inflammation of the lungs, with 'morbific matter' and 'effervescency of blood' playing leading roles).[100] By doing so he confirmed and extended the rational nature of medicine, and gave his authority to traditional medical procedures such as bleeding and purging, and conceptions of disease such as putrefaction, whilst he locked medicine into the novel mind set of new science.

Despite the influence of Willis, there was a sense of dissatisfaction with medical theory that continued into the eighteenth century. Practical apprentice-based education for practitioners was increasingly envisaged alongside a university one. Gideon Harvey, a learned if maverick physician, advised the medical student to take lodgings at an apothecary's house to learn about 'Drugs, and of praeparing, dispensing and mixing them into Compositions', to stay a year with an experienced surgeon, 'there by an Ocular inspection and handling of all his Instruments, demanding their names, uses and manner of using . . . to visit his Chyrurgical Patients . . .', and to do the medical hospital rounds in Paris and Padua to get practical experience.[101] Physicians as well as apothecaries and surgeons were being drawn to the view that medicine was a unified craft. John Colbatch, a former apothecary, licentiate of the College of Physicians, army surgeon, advocate of acidic remedies, writer on surgery and nostrums, and knighted in 1716, typified the entry of practically minded 'general' practitioners into medicine.[102] His focus, like that of many practitioners, was on treatments, but he recognised that little progress had been made in the practices of medicine in contrast to anatomy, which, like his contemporaries, he took to include physiology. In an era when progress and practical utility were intertwined in the rhetoric of natural philosophy and medicine, and when a respectable medical career could be made by combining practical manual skills with modern medical learning, it becomes understandable that Colbatch could write:

As for the Improvements made of late, they have principally belong'd to *Anatomy*, and indeed they have bin very considerable; and of all the

[100] Ibid., part 2, pp. 57–61, 61.

[101] [Harvey], *Accomplisht Physician*, pp. 20–6; Harvey, who was implacably hostile to 'the Practising Apothecary' (p. 39), also advised the medical student to study apothecaries' files of prescriptions in order to improve his practical skill: pp. 23, 26.

[102] Cook, *Decline*, pp. 74, 214; G. Clark, *A History of the Royal College of Physicians* (2 vols., Clarendon Press, Oxford, 1964 and 1966, vol. II, p. 471; Harold J. Cook, 'Sir John Colbatch and Augustan Medicine: Experimentalism, Character and Entrepreneurialism', *Annals of Science*, 47, 1990, 475–505.

Physicians of *Europe*, those of own Nation have had the greatest hand in them. But for the Improvements in the practical part of Physic (setting aside the Discovery of the use of the Peruvian Bark in the cure of Agues) they are very inconsiderable: The most that has bin done of that kind, was by the indefatigably industrious Dr. *Sydenham*, and I heartily wish we had more Dr. *Sydenhams* at this day.[103]

CONCLUSION

Theory and learning did not disappear from medicine in the eighteenth century, but medicine became much more flexible, both in relation to the barriers that had separated the different parts of medicine, and in the acceptance of empirical philosophy into medicine. As Boerhaave, the dominant figure of early eighteenth-century medicine, put it:

The art of physic was anciently established (1.) by a faithful collection of facts observed, whose effects were (2.) afterwards explained, and their causes assigned by the assistance of reason; the first carries conviction along with it, and is indisputable; nothing being more certain than demonstration from experience, but the latter is more dubious and uncertain; since every sect may explain the causes of particular effects upon different hypotheses.[104]

The triumph of such a view helped to structure eighteenth-century medicine, with the rise and fall of different systems of classifying diseases, and attempts to describe diseases by their symptoms rather than by their causes. Yet much remained unchanged. Regimen was relatively unaltered. Therapeutics, though enlarged by chemical remedies, was still largely evacuative and was more heroic than ever. Descriptions of disease, even when ostensibly acausal, continued to be put in narrative form, with anatomy and traditional pathological agents such as putrefaction, as well as the newer ones of ferments and of chemicals, acting their roles on the body's stage.[105] Indeed, putrefaction and dirt held centre stage in eighteenth- and nineteenth-century medicine. Diseases such as scurvy and cholera were believed to be caused by them whether internally or externally. The presence of putrefaction motivated nineteenth-century public health measures. The surgical view of the

---

[103] John Colbatch, 'The Doctrin of Acids' in *A Collection of Tracts, Chirurgical and Medical* (London, 1699), p. 474.

[104] Hermann Boerhaave, *Academical Lectures on the Theory of Physic* (6 vols., London, 1742–6), vols. I, p. 42.

[105] On this, see Wear, 'Continuity and Union', pp. 294–320.

body remained essentially the same in respect of operations and their dangers. Lay medical culture continued to play a major role in the medical economy, though its links to learned medicine were being transformed as empirical medicine rose to wield greater influence. As I hope this book has demonstrated, it is as important to focus on continuities and 'placid' history as it is to be aware of controversies if we want to understand early modern medicine and its aftermath.

Index